THE ALHAMBRA

THE ALHAMBRA

A Cycle of Studies
on the
Eleventh Century in Moorish Spain

by

Frederick P. Bargebuhr

Walter de Gruyter & Co.

Berlin 1968

With the support of the Bollingen Foundation and the American Philosophical Society

Satz und Druck: H. Heenemann KG, Berlin

Library of Congress Catalog Card Number: 67—23004

Alhambra, General View (on the right side the Fortress, left side the Palace) with the Sierra Nevada

To

GERTRUD BREYSIG

ACKNOWLEDGMENTS

I wish to express my gratitude for the help received during my research from the following scholars: first, the late Leopoldo Torres Balbás, the former director of the Alhambra and, furthermore from William F. Albright, Jesús Bermúdez Pareja. Franz Dölger, Richard Ettinghausen, Eli Eytan, Oleg Grabar, Hans Güterbock, Don Paolo Künzle, José M. Millás y Vallicrosa, A. Leo Oppenheim, Luis Seco de Lucena, Berta Segall, Anton Spitaler, and Otto Volk.

I received much valuable information from Professor Oleg Grabar's unpublished doctoral dissertation and, for this reason, I was glad to learn that his forthcoming studies of the fourteenth-century Alhambra are based to a large extent upon the findings and conclusions presented in this book. I should also like to say at this point how much I appreciate working in the same field as a scholar of such acumen.

My work received most inspiring furtherance at the Warburg Institute through its director and staff, and in particular from Mr. J. B. Trapp; furthermore, at the Vatican Library, at the American Academy in Rome, and last but not least from the Deans of the Graduate College and the obliging librarians of my own University of Iowa. Many fine suggestions for the wording of this book were contributed by Professor Ralph Freedman. The resourceful help of Mrs. H. Frankfort in obtaining photographic material for this book is sincerely appreciated.

My warmest thanks are extended to Dr. Werner Heider for shaping with me the translation of "The Great Nature Poem" and, in particular, to Professor Ephriam Sando for the collaboration in the English wording of all verse translations in this volume.

Without the generous support of a two-years fellowship from the Bollingen Foundation and various grants-in-aid from the American Philosophical Society and, finally, the assignment of funds for assistants by my own *almissima mater*, the University of Iowa, these studies would not have been possible.

The Warburg Institute of the University of London, July 29, 1965
(Casa Jablonski, Montagnola, Ticino, August 16, 1965)

CHRONOLOGICAL CHART

A few year designations of the historian based on Islamic and Jewish calendars without month and year indications are subject to slight errors when carried over into the Christian calendar system.

Jews	*Muslims*
	710 First Arab invasion of Spain
	711 Mention of Alhambra in connection with the Arab conquest, designated as the year of an Arab victory over a Visigoth king
	756 The Umayyad ʿAbd ar-Raḥmān I established his rule over Islamic Spain
993 Samuel ibn Naghrālla born in Cordova or Merida	
	994 Ibn Ḥazm born in Cordova
	1009 East side of Cordova sacked by Berbers
	1011–12 The suburbs of Cordova destroyed by Berbers
1013 Samuel and the family of Ibn Gabirol left Cordova	1013 Ibn Ḥazm left Cordova and went to Almeria
	1018 Umayyad attempt at restoration
circa 1022 Ibn Gabirol born in Malaga	1025 Zāwī, Berber ruler of the Zīrid dynasty, left Spain. The successor Ḥabbūs built the new capital city in Granada
1027 Samuel was named vizier by Ḥabbūs	circa 1027 Ibn Ḥazm completed his book *Necklace of the Dove*
	1031 Attempt of Umayyad restoration failed
1035 Yehōšeph ibn Naghrālla born	
	1037 Death of Ḥabbūs. Succession of Bādīs as king with Samuel's support

1038 Death of the last Gaon, Rab Hāi. Victory of Granada (with Samuel) over Zuhair, ruler of Almeria, and his vizier Ibn ʿAbbās in a battle near Alfuente

1039 Execution of Yeqūthīel ibn Ḥasan in Saragossa (March—April)

1040 Army of Granada is unsuccessful in struggle against Muḥammad ibn ʿAbbād of Seville

circa
1041 Revolt of Yiddīr. Conquest of Somantin (with Samuel)

1042 Victory of Granada (with Samuel) near Lorca. (Samuel's poetical last will and advice addressed to Yehōseph)

1045 Samuel rescued in battle near Jaën. Ibn Gabirol's ethical work finished in Saragossa

1049 Yehōseph's wedding; Ibn Gabirol present in Granada

1056 Between December 2—11 Samuel died in Granada

1066 Yehōseph murdered

circa
1070 Ibn Gabirol died

1053 Murder of the Berber notables in Seville. Samuel prevented Bādīs from wiping out the Arabs of Granada

1057 Bādīs incorporated Malaga into the kingdom of Granada

1064 Buluqqīn, heir apparent to the throne, was murdered in Granada, allegedly by Yehōseph. Death of Ibn Ḥazm

between
1076—77 Bādīs died

1077 ʿAbd Allāh succeeded to power as the last Zīrid king of Granada

1090 ʿAbd Allāh dethroned and exiled to Africa

"Alhambram, pro! Dii immortales! Qualem regiam! unicam in orbe terrarum crede!"

Exclamation of Peter Martyr on seeing the conquered fortress, January 2, 1492.

Die Poesie leistet mehr für die Erkenntnis des Wesens der Menschheit (als die Geschichte); auch Aristoteles hat schon gesagt: καὶ φιλοσοφώτερον καὶ σπουδαιότερον ποίησις ἱστορίας ἐστὶν. Die Dichtung ist etwas Philosophischeres und Tieferes als die Geschichte, und zwar ist dies deshalb wahr, weil das Vermögen, welches der Poesie zugrunde liegt, an sich ein viel höheres als das des größten Historikers und auch die Wirkung, wozu sie bestimmt ist, eine viel höhere als die der Geschichte ist. Dafür findet die Geschichte in der Poesie eine ihrer allerwichtigsten Quellen und eine ihrer allerreinsten und schönsten.

Jacob Burckhardt, *Weltgeschichtliche Betrachtungen*, Bern, 1947, p. 129.

. . . On y verrait comment, autour d'une pareille découverte, sont venues gronder obscurément des concupiscences et des rivalités d'érudits qui sont loin d'être anodines . . .

J. Doresse, *Les livres secrets des gnostics d'Egypte* Paris (Plon), 1958, p. 142.

CONTENTS

PART III. THE ALHAMBRA PALACE — LITERARY STUDIES

PROLOGUE

The Story of a Discovery and a Reply to Critics

In the major portion of this book my aim is to establish the fact that the old fortification buildings of the Alhambra in Granada were transformed into a palace three centuries before the date commonly accepted. This will involve a fresh examination of Hebrew and Arabic documents, some of them not hitherto considered to relate to the Alhambra, in conjunction with the archaeological evidence. All these sources, as we shall see, combine to show not only that the earliest Alhambra palace was constructed at the date indicated, but also that the patron of the undertaking was Yehōseph ibn Naghrālla, a Jewish vizier who served under the Berber king Bādīs from 1055 to 1065.

Moreover, it can be said with certainty that Yehōseph, a man of vast cultural and political ambition, erected the celebrated Fount of Lions in the Alhambra as a highly symbolic expression of his "Solomonic" aspirations. The Alhambra Palace is revealed by these studies to be the climactic monument of a most complex and deep-rooted development which springs from Islamic, Byzantine, Sāsānian and, last but not least, Hebrew artistic and literary traditions. Subsequent parts of this study will be devoted to the wider literary aspects of this movement.

At the risk of anticipating the content of the second part of this book I offer in this prologue an abrégé of my thesis for those readers who do not intend to follow the proofs for it step by step. For some hasty critics of the first brief publication of my Alhambra studies do not seem to have read further than the first page and have believed themselves able to refute my arguments on that basis alone[1]. I would urge, however, truly interested readers to follow my argument in its full form in Part II. To these readers I also wish to apologize for engaging in polemics, which is certainly not my inclination.

The main sources are the following:

(a) There are various references to Yehōseph in the Arabic memoirs of the last Berber king of Granada, ʿAbd Allāh, the grandson and immediate successor of King Bādīs[2]. This ʿAbd Allāh speaks of Yehōseph, the vizier of his grandfather, with utter hostility, accusing him of the murder of his

Notes 1—2

royal father. Furthermore, he states that Yehōseph had built for himself "the Alhambra fortress," *(al-Ḥiṣn al-Ḥamrā')* [sic], to make this his living quarters once he had usurped power over Granada. He also relates, indirectly within a recounted dialogue between King Bādīs and one of his advisors, that Yehōseph's mansion was more beautiful than the king's own palace. According to the same memoirs as well as other sources, Yehōseph had indeed arrogated to himself the position of a major-domo in the kingdom of Granada and was plotting to dethrone the aging Berber king with the help of the ruler of Almeria.

(b) The primary document, however, which led to my discovery was a Hebrew encomium by Solomon ibn Gabirol. This poem, after a prelude of love poetry based upon the Song of Solomon, describes a palace and is, at the same time, a "descriptive" nature poem and a document of aulic policy designed to further his Maecenas' ambitions[3]. As such it explains the Solomonic symbolism of the building. The poem, which does not name the patron addressed, was re-edited *in toto* only recently (by one of my critics) and describes the magnificent castle erected by this patron, "exalted above all its surrounding" with "its walls fortified with towers" and many gates, with a rotating dome "like the Palanquin of Solomon" above a noble hall, with animal statuary spouting water up to the treetops, and — described in all details and with an interesting clue to its symbolic intent — a fount of lions. This fount, the poet says, was a likeness of the biblical Solomon's Brazen Sea, which was a basin supported by twelve oxen. (Pl. 5) His patron, Ibn Gabirol gives us to understand, chose lions instead of oxen to symbolize the kings whom he kept under control with his guidance as a shepherd keeps his grazing flock. In other words, the basin resting upon the lions symbolizes the patron who has established his rule over kings — symbolized by the royal animals, but by the innuendo of the Solomonic precedent "standing" for oxen. This witty flattery may very well elucidate the patron's true symbolic intent. In further contrast to Solomon's Sea the lions are described by Ibn Gabirol as spouting water.

Was this patron, the addressee of Ibn Gabirol's poem, Yehōseph? Are the fountains described by Ibn Gabirol and the extant Fount of Lions of the Alhambra identical? (Pl. 2) We would first of all have to rely upon ʻAbd Allāh's memoirs in order to relate Ibn Gabirol's praise of an anonymous Maecenas with Yehōseph, as the builder of a magnificent castle. But is there more evidence for this connection? The first question can only be answered by an indirect but conclusive negative demonstration.

Granada had been advanced to the status of a city and of a capital by the eleventh-century usurping Berber kings, the employers of Samuel ibn Naghrālla, Yehōseph's father who, having been trained in all the administrative skills and courtly arts in metropolitan Cordova, could by his own talents and by his ability to attract others confer some splendor on this hitherto provincial town. Yehōseph, and his father, had nourished Solomonic artistic ambitions in poetry and architecture, as will become increasingly evident in the course of this study. The Solomonic implications of the Fount of Lions as it now exists in the Alhambra are not a new discovery: the better guidebooks to Spain contain the observation, made long ago by art historians, that this fount has its unique counterpart and iconographic precedent in Solomon's Brazen Sea. Samuel, who bore the title *han-Nāghīdh*, 'The Leader' (of the Jews), an outstanding Hebrew poet and patron of the arts and letters, the predecessor of Yehōseph, had employed Ibn Gabirol as his house encomiast and, most probably, as Yehōseph's tutor. Ibn Gabirol's relationship to father and son, partly friendly and partly strained, must, according to his extant poems, have overshadowed his entire life. If the patron praised in this poem were not Yehōseph, whose near-contemporary Ibn Gabirol was and with whom he had been associated from their very early years, one would have to look for another Jewish major-domo, a friend of Hebrew poetry, the *de facto* ruler over many kings by the counsel he gave them, a builder of a castle worthy of a king who was emancipated from the injunctions against images and likenesses of Islam and the Second Commandment, a palace filled with works of art of Solomonic symbolism. If such a second person had existed in the eleventh century, in the environment of Ibn Gabirol, the Jewish sources would be full of his praise and accounts of his achievements. I shall explain later why such a poem, in spite of some exaggeration which is easily isolated, cannot be regarded as simply empty flattery: praise of a fervently wooed patron for possessions which are not his, would in the way of a *lucus a non lucendo* be a foolhardy step leading to an immediate rift.

It is, therefore, I feel, incumbent upon my critics to show why King 'Abd Allāh's statement that Yehōseph had built for himself an Alhambra palace, superior to the king's own, should not be accepted as literally true. There is, in addition, another reason why the beautiful eleventh-century parts of the present Alhambra (easily identifiable by their masonry) cannot have been built by these Berber kings themselves, who are frequently described in contemporary sources as utter barbarians and miserable patrons of the arts. Their palace was on the Albaicin Hill opposite the Alhambra Hill (called "The Palace of Bādīs") and there is no reason why nor indication that a Berber king built another palace. 'Abd Allāh, if he had done so himself, would have mentioned such an accomplishment in his memoirs and he, as ruler of Granada, must have known the facts (about Yehōseph) better than anybody else. The remnants of these substantial Alhambra constructions are traceable and are marked in maps showing the growth of the structures in a vague way as "Zīrid" after the family name of this Berber dynasty or as structures antedating certain centuries. Their masonry differs from previous and later structures and consists, as the art historians have pointed out, of square patches of smaller natural stones within frames and belts of brick. We find this "striped" masonry in some of the existing towers of the Alhambra Fortress and also, as I satisfied myself, throughout quite a number of buildings of the present Alhambra Palace, even in the Comares Tower. A number of excavations have been carried out and have revealed more eleventh-century masonry, that of previous structures which connected the now separated Fortress and Palace areas. An attempt to ascribe these extended buildings to ʿAbd Allāh is, to repeat, futile. He mentions in his memoirs, referring to a time after Yehōseph's death, that, while refitting Granada's fortifications, he built a wall to include the Alhambra buildings, in order to prepare the city for a siege which he expected. Evidently now, due to Yehōseph's constructions the Alhambra warranted circumvallation even under pressing circumstances. Had ʿAbd Allāh built more than this on the Alhambra Hill, the passage I cited would be the place to raise such a claim, instead of ascribing the merit to the hated vizier of his grandfather. Conversely, there is no indication of the erection of Alhambra buildings — let alone a palace — before the elevation of Granada to a seat of government by the Berber kings, except older Alhambra fortifications, the foundations of which are still visible as the substructure of Yehōseph's towers. Moreover, the leading Spanish art historian Gómez-Moreno has pointed out that the lions of the existing Fount could not have been executed later than the eleventh century: the Almoravids and Almohades who succeeded the "petty kings" in Moorish Spain were intolerant of three-dimensional plastic art.

This dating is a powerful argument towards settling the second question, referring to the identity of the fount of lions in Ibn Gabirol's poem and that now existing in the Alhambra, in my favor. There are also other, indirect arguments. These all contribute to show the engagement of the Naghrāllas, father and son, in hydraulic projects. First of all, an Arabic poem composed in order to incite the Muslims of Granada against Yehōseph mentions his luxurious mansion to which he had diverted a current of water ("well") which had previously supplied the city[4]. I am convinced that this is a reference to a diversion of water from the River Darro to the Alhambra Hill, without which the hill would have remained waterless. The accusation makes sense only if this refers to quantities which were previously sufficient to supply an entire quarter (most likely highly located) of Granada and then ample enough to supply Yehōseph's watergardens.

Note 4

Again, Ibn Gabirol's description of the fount of lions "like unto Solomon's Sea" and supported by water-spouting lions is extremely specific. I shall show that there is no true counterpart to this traceable in the many descriptions by Arabic poets and historians of eleventh-century fountains and pools decorated with animal statuary. The animals in all other fountains seem to have spouted *into* a basin, whereas, paradoxically enough, the Alhambra lions stand, in imitation of the oxen supporting Solomon's Temple basin, "with their hindparts inward" (I Kings VII. 25) beneath the basin and can, therefore, not spout water into it. They rather direct it away from the basin into channels in the pavement (also mentioned, in another connection, in Ibn Gabirol's poem). On the other hand, the artistic inspiration which underlies the architectural (and poetic) ambitions of Yehōseph is derived, of course, from Moorish courtly ideas. Also, the water-spouting lions themselves (a fashionable contemporary device) were most likely executed by a Muslim artist, presumably the same who fashioned the two carved lions sitting on their haunches and spouting water into the Partal Pond of the Alhambra, which they now decorate.

In two of his poems Samuel ibn Naghrālla describes the elaborate effects he had achieved by the judicious arrangement of water spouts and sources of light. In a third poem — and in the editorial prefatory remarks by Yehōseph who compiled a diwan of his father's poems — Samuel's interest in statuary is apparent: he describes a brazier ornamented with sculptured birds. He also gives a poetical account of a water-garden which Yehōseph, when a mere child, had created as a surprise for his proud father. It therefore cannot astonish us if Yehōseph, on coming to power, carried out such works with even greater ambition and with that very Solomonic symbolism which permeated the thinking of this circle, (as is evident from more than this one poem by Ibn Gabirol).

One document which, at the beginning of my studies, seemed to contradict me was the verse inscription on the basin of the present Fount of Lions, by which the Fount has hitherto been dated. The inscription is ascribed to Ibn Zamrak, the house poet of King Muḥammad V, who ruled from 1354 to 1358 and from 1362 to 1381[5]. But this source itself does not make Muḥammad V the builder of the fountain: the inscription most modestly says: "God gave to him these abodes[6]." Moreover, this apparent obstacle to my argument was removed by the observation, already made by Spanish art historians, that the present basin, oversized as it is, is not that of the original Fount of Lions. The original basin, as one might expect in the "Sleeping Beauty" country of Andalusia, seems to have been preserved and to be identical with that inserted into the floor of the Abencerajes Hall adjacent to the Court of Lions. This, most probably,

Notes 5—6

original dodecagonal basin, if it were re-placed upon the backs of the twelve stone lions of the present fount, would fit with its twelve facets evenly between their necks and fulfil the original intent of the artist. The crowns of the lions' heads would be mirrored and distorted in the undulating surface of the water in the basin (in the fashion of an Achaemenian piece supported by eight lions shown a few years ago in the great exhibition of Persian art and its catalog)[7] (Pl. 5a). My contention that the stone lions themselves belong to a much earlier period than the basin they support at present, has already been accepted by leading Spanish art historians. For example, M. Gómez-Moreno has treated the lions in his standard volume on *El arte español hasta los Almohades* of the monumental *Ars Hispaniae*[8]. I owe my first knowledge of this endorsement of my arguments to my friends among Spanish art historians.

To reiterate: I ask my critics once more to consider my arguments *e positivo:* 'Abd Allāh's clear assertion that Yehōšeph built a superb Alhambra castle; and *e negativo:* the evidence of Ibn Gabirol's poem which describes comprehensively a palace which his patron had erected, which two arguments allow me to challenge them, if they contend that this palace is not the Alhambra palace of the eleventh century, to state reasons why the buildings cannot be identical and to point out where such another building described by Ibn Gabirol could, with some likelihood, have existed, leaving behind, most likely, some traces, material and literary; a palace of that time containing identical motifs, with an identical fount of lions and another Jewish builder among the patrons of Ibn Gabirol who was a promoter of Solomonic architecture, sculptural art, and Hebrew poetry. Given the historical sources and the unique combination of events, in addition to the extant eleventh-century parts of the Alhambra, this would be an absurd and ultimately fruitless undertaking.

The objections leveled against my discovery, which seem to emanate from two sources, reveal a lack of understanding concerning the archaeological problems of the Alhambra, the history of architecture in general, and the documentary value of Ibn Gabirol's "descriptive" poetry, which belongs to a specific Arabic and Hebrew school of "veracity." I also repeat that any poet who writes to satisfy his patron by praise, would certainly not claim in a concise but, at important points, detailed poem, that his patron had constructed a certain palace with specific highlights of decoration when, in fact, he had not done so. Such an act would not only invite dismissal: it could in no way be representative of the philosopher Ibn Gabirol's relationship with a most refined patron of art and poetry.

At the risk of seeming to waste my readers' time, I now specify the two objections raised by my critics. The first consists of the observation that the Arab sources (apparently ʿAbd Allāh's memoirs) speak, in connection with Yehōseph's building, sometimes of a 'mansion' *(dār)*, sometimes of a 'fortress' *(ḥiṣn)*, and, in another case, of a 'castle' or of a 'palace' *(qaṣr)*, and that therefore these sources refer to several separate structures and not to the Alhambra palace.

The castle of Bādīs on the Albaicin Hill (of which only minor remnants are left) was called either *Qaṣr Bādīs* "The Castle of Bādīs" or later on *al-Qaṣaba al-Qadīma* "The Old Capital" or "The Old Capitol" and this at a time when the Alhambra palace, which later became the domicile of the kings of Granada, had become the "New *Qaṣaba*." There can be no doubt that what is now called the Alhambra Fortress contains the oldest parts of the Alhambra buildings (as the brickwork shows) and, as superstructures and additions, the eleventh-century palace of Yehōseph, who added to the fortifications palatial garden courts, described in Ibn Gabirol's poem. For this reason, ʿAbd Allāh's statement that Yehōseph built for himself the Alhambra Fortress *(ḥiṣn)* makes perfect sense and it is no less logical that, when declaring Yehōseph's building more beautiful than the king's own, ʿAbd Allāh uses the word 'palace'. The extant Alhambra, consisting of an Alhambra Fortress and the adjacent Alhambra Palace, best explains the varying usage of terms. Excavations have revealed remnants of original eleventh-century structures which originally linked the two parts more closely. Since ʿAbd Allāh also stresses that Yehōseph built the Alhambra as his living quarters, the use of the word 'mansion' *(dār)* (e. g. in Abū Isḥāq's poem of hatred against Yehōseph) appears no less natural: *dār* applies to both the individual 'house' or 'farm' or, as in *Dār as-Salām* 'Residence of Well-being' (the city of Damascus), to a whole city. Nobody would be astonished to find a writer referring, for example, if only for the sake of variety, to a horse as 'mammal', or 'quadruped', or 'stallion' or 'mare'.

The second objection concerns the year of Ibn Gabirol's death. Moses ibn Ezra speaks of Ibn Gabirol's death as occurring "after he had 'overshot' the thirties" so that one would think in this connection of ca. 1052 or 1053. (The poet's date of birth was most likely 1021—22.)[9] Yehōseph could hardly have built his palace earlier than 1060 when Ibn Gabirol was thirty-eight; consequently, since Ibn Gabirol allegedly died seven or eight years earlier, he could, they aver, not have seen or described Yehōseph's building. But Moses Ibn Ezra was no historian and a notorious muddler of his materials[10]. No more reliable are the Hebrew poet al-Ḥarīzī who in his *Taḥkemōnī* attributes to the poet a life of twenty-nine years, and the Arab historian Abū Qāsim ibn Saʿīd who in his *Ṭabaqāt al-umam (Categories of the Nations)* states, on the one hand, that Ibn Gabirol died "before he was

Notes 9—10

thirty" and, on the other hand, specifies the year of his death as 1057—58 when the poet was thirty-five or thirty-six years old[11]. Abraham Zakkūtō, the learned physician and chronicler of the fifteenth century, indicates in his *Ṡepher hay-Yōḥasīn* the year of Ibn Gabirol's death as 1070[12]. This is in full harmony with an internal evidence: in Ibn Gabirol's hymn *Shoresh Ben-ō Yīshay*, he bewails the termination of the millennium after the Jews' expulsion from their homeland by the Romans, which would indicate the year 1068 (or 1070) when the poet must have been between forty-six and forty-eight years of age. The lines read (in Davidson's translation):[13]

The years are a thousand since broken
and scattered we wander in exile.

Not only the poet but the Jewish community must have placed great messianic expectation in this millennial date. For this reason it would have been ludicrous and even blasphemous to speak of a frustration of these hopes before this deadline had been passed[14]. Furthermore, there are in Ibn Gabirol's great meditation, *The Royal Crown*, in a passage where he speaks of "the remainder of my brief days," words such as one would hardly write before one's advancing thirties; "Is not the bulk of my days passed and vanished " (Davidson's translation)[15].

In a futile attempt to save something of the alleged death "in his thirties," against which there is so much evidence, Professor H. Schirmann decides that the poet died between his thirty-first and thirty-seventh year (1053—58), as if this could be easily reconciled with Ibn Ezra's "overshooting the thirties." He dismisses a similar poem by Ibn Gabirol, *Shenōth-eynū ṡāph-ū*[16] in which the poet speaks of 461 years of servitude under Ishmael. If this is 461 A. H., as is accepted by several scholars, this would refer to 1069. Schirmann disqualifies this hymn as a source for Ibn Gabirol's biography because certain manuscripts give at this place a later, perfectly absurd date. These are evidently retouchings inserted by copyists attempting to bring the poem up-to-date for synagogical use in their day and are immaterial. As long as no manuscript gives a still earlier date, and, most important, as long as the plausible 1069 is supported by the parallel in the above-quoted poem, *Shoresh Ben-ō Yīshay*[17], we are bound to accept it. If forged certificates are occasionally found, this does not mean they take precedence over all others.

Schirmann dismisses this overwhelming internal evidence in favor of the garbled data of Moses ibn Ezra and Ibn Sa'īd's mere chance scraps of characterizations of a few Jewish personalities. He omits the testimony of the later Jewish chronicler but indicates that Ibn Dā'ūd places Ibn Gabirol's death in the year 1070 *(Encyclopaedia Judaica*, article "Gabirol"). Such a reference in Ibn Dā'ūd's "*Sefer ha-Kabbala, Ende*" [sic Schirmann] does not exist. Perhaps Schirmann wished to refer to the author of *Shalsheleth haq-Qabbālāh*, Gedaliah ibn Yaḥyā, or to the *Ŝepher hay-Yōḥasīn* by Abraham Zakkūtō in which the late date of death appears. *¿Quien sabe?*

It is curious to find such an error a hundred years after Geiger wrote: "(Ibn Ezra) is not very exact when he gives thirty years as a figure, because Ibn Gabirol did not pass away before (4829) 1069; moreover, saying that he hardly exceeded the thirties might mean no more than he did not live much beyond forty. For even to such a figure we ought to add something." Geiger offers a psychological motivation for Ibn Ezra's slip, stating: "(Ibn Gabirol) was outstanding when still a youth and Ibn Ezra remembers him among his associates and competitors for the laurel who were much older than he; hence he believed himself justified in stressing his youth which would also offer an excuse for his considerable use of invective. It is a pity, however, that Ibn Ezra's words have been repeated so credulously and caused so much confusion[18]."

Schirmann knows, no doubt, that Geiger is not alone, that other scholars as thorough as Sachs, Munk, Kaempf, Graetz, Dubnow, Dreyer, Baron, and Davidson do not accept Ibn Ezra's statement and attribute to the poet a longer life, mainly on the basis of the testimony of Ibn Gabirol's religious poetry[19]. Yet, referring to the sources, Schirmann speaks of "a clear indication of an earlier death for Ibn Gabirol," i. e., before Yehōŝeph's erection of his Alhambra palace[20].

In order to make Schirmann's bias against my Alhambra discovery comprehensible, I must tell its story and of my experiences with scholars in this field. After offering a lecture on the Alhambra at the Oriental Institute of the University of Chicago, where my thesis was received with active interest and without contradiction, I encountered in Spain a great deal of welcome assistance in my investigations from the lamented Leopoldo Torres Balbás, and was invited to lecture at the University of Madrid. However, shortly before this lecture, I had discussions with Professors García Gómez and Gómez-Moreno and found these scholars bitterly opposed to my thesis. I received the impression that the connection between the Alhambra and the family of the Naghrālla had not been entirely overlooked, but rejected for reasons of bias. At the end of my lecture at the University of Madrid, I found myself publicly contradicted by E. García Gómez — who is in no way an art historian — with statements as sweeping as "every Muslim ruler complains about the extravagance of his prime minister." Terrified by the antagonism of the powerful government speaker the audience had no courage to engage in a free discussion and dissolved hastily. At the same time I had the opportunity to learn, much to my amazement, that even events of the eleventh century were still weighed in Spain for their value in modern politics. Later, a Spanish scholar stated bluntly that the Spanish government would, regardless of the truth, never "accept" my thesis, because it would diminish the Arab contribution to Spain's culture. (I was expected to realize that scholarship was steered by the Government council.) Such an attitude towards my work astounded me, first of all by its absurdity, and secondly, because I had never denied that both the general artistic incentive and the craftsmanship of the Alhambra structures, including those ordered by a Jewish patron, belonged to the Arab artistic domain. It took me some time to understand why eleventh-century history could still be a modern issue. The answers are to be found in present-day ambitions and, e. g., in the Spanish myth of the *sangre nuestra* and in the attitude implied by the adjective "brilliant" which the professor and politician E. García Gómez attributed to the bloodthirsty poem of incitement by Abū Isḥāq from Elvira against both Yehōseph and the Jews of Granada, which contributed to Yehōseph's downfall and to mass assassinations (which poem J. M. Millás rightly calls 'terrible')[21].

My thesis was received with warm enthusiasm at American, German, Dutch, and Israeli universities. However, offering a brief report before the Congress of Orientalists in Cambridge (1954), I was contradicted by an Egyptian spokesman whose field is philosophy, in terms of general disbelief. Also, I found that E. García Gómez was engaging in active propaganda against my thesis. In default of any counterarguments, he labeled it to, among others, French Islamic archaeologists "mysticism" and "fantasies." I was further astonished when the Israeli scholar H. Schirmann, who attended the same congress, expressed to me there and then the same disbelief, without ever previously having seen any publication of my discovery. The contrived nature of Professor Schirmann's argument and this strange alliance of opponents must have specific reasons. Should not any discovery about a building as important as the Alhambra deserve proper consideration and investigation in Israel, Spain and elsewhere? Did not my first scholarly article on the Alhambra, which appeared in the *Journal of the Warburg and Courtauld Institutes*, become, to my satisfaction, the point of departure of Professor Oleg Grabar's lectures and forthcoming publication in this field? Knowledge of architectural history did not come within the scope of my critics. Nevertheless its validity was questioned in a very few lines of superficial observations by Professor Schirmann. I can only suppose that he feels that he has missed an opportunity. It was he who first published in full Ibn Gabirol's Alhambra poem containing all the unique architectural details, and he could have made my discovery himself if he had had any true understanding of the content of the poems he edits and anthologizes. He should have asked himself immediately of what castle and to what patron Ibn Gabirol spoke. In that case ʿAbd Allāh's reference to Yehōseph, which he himself quotes, would have led him to my discovery[22]. This, at least, is the only reason I can see for his antagonism.

His crude obstructionism — if partisan, then more for his own sake than in the service of his party — would be negligible, as lacking all foundation, if he did not own, since the death of the better men in his field, a position of monopoly, being a teacher at the Hebrew University (which lacks a chair of art history). A new edition of Ibn Gabirol's work on the basis of the Schocken MS. 37, which was one of the original tasks of the Schocken Institute, has never been accomplished and very little beside anthologies, based chiefly upon the achievements of the bee-like industry of the late H. Brody (who is rarely quoted) has been undertaken. What should have been done, the elucidation of the content of the Hebrew poet's works by demonstrating their Arabic and other sources, and a true comparative study of imagery and style, let alone personalities, has remained an unfulfilled desire. An outsider is not welcome there, as I have had to experience. As if any living discipline could do without a lively exchange of ideas! Good scholars have always been anxious to see their work utilized and improved by colleagues. (Professor Landsberger, for example, had to realize at an advanced age that many of his conjectured readings of the famous Nabonidus Stela were proved wrong on the basis of the better copy recently brought to light in Harran, and was happy to be confronted with the correction of his errors.) Unfortunately, there seems to be nobody, even in Jerusalem, able to comprehend the documentary content of Hebrew and Arabic poetry after the death of the late L. A. Mayer. This eminent scholar showed an immediate understanding of my thesis, when I outlined it to him at the Cambridge Congress of Orientalists, but nobody else felt competent or willing to deal with my findings, as a letter from Professor Avi-Yonah implied.

The hostility to my findings in Spain did not prevent a Spanish scholar from using some of my specific observations and the illustrations of my article in the *Journal of the Warburg and Courtauld Institutes* in an article of his own, without mentioning their origin or my name. Yet, having known the character of this gentleman, I am very certain that the decisions in this matter were wrested from his hands[23]. Otherwise, the topic of the origin of the Alhambra has not been dealt with in Spain — as if a *cordon sanitaire* were imposed upon this topic since my discovery.

Notes 22—23

From other quarters I have received magnificent support in my work, both intellectual, from, for instance, Professor Leopoldo Torres Balbás, the Warburg Institute in London, and the Oriental Institute in Chicago, and material, from the Bollingen Foundation, enabling me to work in the American Academy and Vatican Library in Rome, from the American Philosophical Society, and the University of Iowa, among many others. I owe lasting gratitude to Professor Américo Castro both as the author of *La España en su Historia* and for his expressions of appreciation of my work.

It is regrettable that, at the present time, studies of this kind are impeded by a dearth of competent scholars and influenced by political propaganda. The great days of objective, critical, and comprehensive scholarship in the field of Arab and Jewish civilisation in Spain are past, as even the briefest mention of names suffices to show.

Scholarly work on the Arabs in Spain found a culmination in R. Dozy's *Histoire des musulmans d'Espagne*, which was later re-edited by E. Lévi-Provençal. The latter most competent historian who also published three volumes of his own *Histoire de l'Espagne musulmane*, was prevented by death from carrying this story beyond 1031, so that he did not deal with our period of the "petty kingdoms." By his labors in the field of Jewish and Arabic philosophy S. Munk, whose work was in many ways linked with Dozy's, reassembled much of the intellectual history of Moorish Spain. The great Jewish historian H. Graetz had a specific interest in this period and its poetry, and S. Dubnow incorporated the bulk of what had been reconstructed at this time in his great *World History of the Jewish People.* Still more up-to-date is S. W. Baron's magnificent *Social and Religious History of the Jews.* But, in contrast to these comprehensive works, the edition and interpretation of individual texts, in particular of the Hebrew poets, has lagged far behind. Since Bialik-Ravnitzki's excellent edition of the poetry of Ibn Gabirol — made with the help of scholars like H. Brody and D. Yellin, and on the basis of the pioneering work of Dukes, Sachs, and Geiger, by now outdated — the field of the textual study of Ibn Gabirol has remained unworked and no major cultural and comparative studies of this school of Hebrew poetry have been made. The later editors of Hebrew poetry have merely decreed what the text should be, without presenting the variant readings and discussing them; and a comparison of their texts with Brody's and Bialik-Ravnitzki's often reveals a backward step in the direction of inferior readings. Also, much of the interpretative work in this field has been impeded by parochial timidity and an apologetic attitude. The awesome figure of a Samuel han-Nāghīdh must not be made to appear heretical or susceptible to ridicule, so that Ibn Gabirol's blatant invective poems against him — insolent acts which were censured by the *graeculus-*

like Moses ibn Ezra — are still interpreted as poems of praise. Ibn Gabirol's arrogant poem, which in fact offers surrender to the patron only on the poet's own terms, is still characterized as a "Poem of Apology," and Ibn Gabirol's many fashionable sacrileges and heresies have not been seen for what they are[24]. It is astonishing to find Israeli scholarship bedeviled by patron worship in this way. How much more independent was the eminent Graetz, for example, and this in his exposed position in the Treitschke era.

For a complete interpretation of the sources which elucidate the origin of the Alhambra I shall have to present a brief characterization of Arab and Jewish intellectual history and of Muslim culture in general and, in particular, of the constituents of the Arab-Hebrew symbiosis in which an emancipation of the Jews became possible. Also, I shall indicate the justification offered by Muslims and Jews for an unheard-of secularism, influenced and shielded by the liberalizing Umayyads. I shall have to discuss the value of aulic poetry as a historical source and I shall present the other Hebrew nature poetry of Solomon ibn Gabirol, with its contemporary Arabic models and counterparts and, in a later volume, his love poetry. I shall elucidate Ibn Gabirol's relationship to the Naghrālla family, the father Samuel and the son Yehōseph, by means of an interpretation of his other poems of praise for them, including his poem of true Renaissance Platonic patronage to a disciple who was most likely Yehōseph. In this fashion the following, somewhat loosely knit studies form, I hope, a ring of the kind of J. G. Frazer's *Golden Bough*, in other words a *cycle of studies* around a central motif. And indeed, the earliest Alhambra palace, as I am essaying to show, is the lofty crowning edifice erected upon an enormously composite or rather exquisitely syncretic substructure to which a Jewish revival, Roman, Byzantine, and Islamic architecture and, in particular, a new Hispano-Hebrew poetry engendered by Hispano-Arab poetry made their contributions. All these elements came together only once: in the circle of Samuel and Yehōseph ibn Naghrālla and of Solomon ibn Gabirol, a round table of émigrés from Cordova to Granada. These studies also constitute an attempt, the first of its kind, at assessing the documentary value of this poetry and, beyond this, at assessing the general merit of these Hebrew poets, pointing out which of the Arabic conceits they took over remained clichés and in what way and how deeply the Hebrew poets transformed and amplified their models. The present book is an attempt at opening free vistas upon the unduly obscured creations of a unique mediaeval renaissance.

This book offers a great many translations and interpretations of poems belonging to a school of Hebrew poetry which, unprecedentedly, originated

Note 24

in Spain in imitation of Arabic poetry. The mastery of the Hebrew poets consists of an adaptation of the biblical Hebrew language to Arabic conceits. Their perfect knowledge of the Bible enables them to use the biblical wording without too much of its context. More of the context, however, remains in the mind of the poet and in that of the trained reader, and tinges the meaning of a passage. In spite of this we should not call the style of an Ibn Gabirol or a Samuel han-Nāghīdh a mosaic style. This may characterize the poetry of an older generation which extracted its wording from Scripture as if it were plants still bearing bulky clods about their roots. The biblical references are listed in the margin of a poem, occasionally in parentheses when an individual word merely, and not the entire motif, is taken over. The reader is thus enabled — particularly in the second section of this book devoted to literary problems — to study the twofold origins of Hispano-Hebrew poetry which are evident in almost every line.

The reader will observe that I have had to sift a vast amount of Hebrew and Arabic material, or rather to discover this, to establish the texts and defend my readings, to translate and to interpret these texts. The Alhambra is only one of the crystallization points around which this material could be arranged. The art of the Arabic and Hebrew metaphor could have been another focus of my book.

The great variety of poetical devices reminding us strikingly of the Elizabethan school of poetry, stems from its origin in western logico-rhetorical skills which the two schools share. The wealth of metaphors, the art of which was very much in the mind of the Arab critics of poetry like al-Jurjānī, received in the hands of the eager Hebrew imitators, with their different personalities and their biblical vocabulary, a new interpretation. In the poetry of this period — as indeed in its architecture — the overriding ideal is that of θαυματοποιικὴ τέχνη, inherited from Byzantium, which aims at the creation of a magical effect. This implies in architecture the use of light effects which dissolve the solid into seeming fluidity and a fantastic surreality, and the use of undulating water surfaces as mirrors to create kaleidoscopic distortions. In poetry, it implies the exploitation of various levels of metaphor. One of these offers a pseudo-causation for the nature it describes. The other animates and attributes human feelings to that nature and the two together, by forming chains of interlocking images, create what almost amounts to a quasi-mythology. Such a technique is not too alien to modern writers. To use the words of Ralph Freedman, "the self of the artist and his object merge together and the new object arises... The self is projected into the world and animates objects... the distortion from animation or such projection is sharpened because of emphasis."

When I was about to return the second galley-proofs of this book, Professor Spuler kindly referred me to a review by Rudolf Sellheim in *Jahrbuch für Ästhetik*, VI, 1961, pp. 209—216. I had heard of Professor Lützeler's intention to commission such a review and Mr. Sellheim had once written to me for the elucidation of a point in my article and been sent an answer (which he seems not to have made use of). Neither he nor the editor of the *Jahrbuch*, however, thought it necessary to send me an offprint of this review. If they had done so, in accordance with what used to be the custom between author, reviewer, and editor, I should have been able to write a full rejoinder at the time, instead of attempting to reply to Mr. Sellheim at this late stage and in conditions which enforce brevity. But to avoid similar misunderstandings — often, in my eyes, the product of vested interest — in the future, I should like to defend myself in as short a compass as may be.

I was shocked by the primitive level of Mr. Sellheim's review, written as it was by a man who has published nothing else in the field of Spanish-Islamic studies, let alone Islamic architecture and Hebrew poetry. He seems to have been prompted by the hope of easy laurels and his methods of argument are strongly reminiscent of those of the "Homeric scholarship," cited below. To quote an example: after admitting that the builder of the earlier parts of the Alhambra is unknown, Mr. Sellheim betrays irritation at being confronted with the clear statements of King ʿAbd Allāh's passage "One": "... by his ⟨Yehōšeph's⟩ building up the Alhambra fortress where he intended to reside .. when Ibn Ṣumādiḥ had entered Granada, under a stabilized situation" (see p. 90 below) and "Two," indicating that Yehō-šeph's castle was "more beautiful than your ⟨the king's⟩ own." Mr. Sell-heim's repeated attacks attempt to obfuscate these clear statements. First he terms them "too vague and too unspecific to be used immediately as a proof." (This 'immediately' is one of Mr. Sellheim's blanket-words of which we shall encounter more.) I can only ask, if we cannot use such proof now, when may we do so?

In particular this statement "Two" comes in for Mr. Sellheim's special treatment. He terms it, in parentheses, 'fictive' *(fiktiv)*, having learned that the great speeches in Thucydides, for example, are not true 'reportage' but free compositions of the historian in the attempt to elucidate a situation and/or personality. Mr. Sellheim fails to take into account the fact that ʿAbd Allāh's book is a collection of personal memoirs and that he reports events in which he has participated and of which eyewitnesses and those who knew of them by word of mouth were alive when the book came abroad. These persons could easily have found out the author in any lies. ʿAbd Allāh, therefore, is much more literally trustworthy than a compiling historian, although, it is true, in certain cases he writes *cum ira et studio,* which he makes no attempt to conceal. This, in fact, is the most particular proof of ʿAbd Allāh's veracity. He has no reason to attribute any merits to Yehōseph in whom he sees the murderer of his father, yet still he credits Yehōseph with having built a superb palace.

This passage "Two" is translated by Lévi-Provençal *"[il] s'est construit un plus beau palais que le tien,"* to which translation Mr. S. finds "in principle" *(an sich)* no objection. This 'in principle' seems to indicate a desire for second — and better — thoughts, which do not, however, materialize. Mr. Sellheim wishes to translate "[he built] something much better than your palace," which, as he hesitantly admits, can actually be "nothing but another palace." Is this not a precious piece of "Homeric scholarship?"

Here Mr. Sellheim's command of language betrays him: *Aḥsan min qaṣrik* does not mean 'something better' (or, as Mr. S. translates, with exaggeration, 'much better') than your palace'. There is no neuter here to indicate 'thing'. By attraction of meaning, the masculine noun *qaṣr*, standing so close to *aḥsan*, determines its gender, so that the only correct translation is 'a better palace than yours'. In order to express the neuter here, the author would have had to use a word like *shay*', 'matter' or 'thing', or else a (possibly paronomastic) *mā—min* construction 'what (he built) of (building)'. Nor is this all. Mr. S. continues: "Whatever this palace construction was, it is not permissible to identify such a palace *mir nichts dir nichts* with the Alhambra." (The German expression used here is the most comic of Mr. S.'s collection of blanket-words, meaning something like 'helter-skelter', but nothing scholarly.) "It is," he continues, "obviously a reference to Yehōseph's city residence which he had, before his death, to exchange, for reasons of security, with the Alcazaba, the royal fortress." I wonder why Mr. S. uses the word 'obviously'. He obviously does so to still his doubts about his own argument. We know nothing of such a city mansion. Yehōseph may have resided on the Alhambra hill even before he transformed the fortress into a palace.

Thus far I have presented a first sample of Mr. S.'s review, trying to render his German into appropriate English (which is, I admit, a problem). I have not begun my reply with the beginning of his review but have chosen his treatment of ʿAbd Allāh's passage on Yehōseph at random, to illustrate his need for an introductory lesson in historical methodology.

It would have been more in accord with the ideals of scholarship if Mr. S. had opened with a consideration of my arguments, but he does not. In fact, his preamble consists of reflections designed to discredit my findings in the eyes of the reader, and he poses the question of why a

Jew should have had the opportunity to become an important builder in the Hispano-Islamic environment.

Then he introduces himself as one of those old-fashioned scholars who do not believe in a possible harmony between rhyme and reason. He attempts to prejudice the uninformed reader by telling him that I had received my first inkling of the origins which I assume for the Alhambra from Ibn Gabirol's poem (which is true). He withholds ʿAbd Allāh's clear statements about Yehōseph, wasting much ink in the attempt to discredit my scholarship because my hypothesis takes a poem for its point of departure. (When at last he does present ʿAbd Allāh's words, as we have seen, he does so inaccurately). To Mr. S. a poem must never be the basis of a discovery, even if it has a counterpart to its content in the prose writings of the contemporary person directly involved. Mr. S. has been taught that poets are lying flatterers who sell their souls for a rhyme. I wonder whether he has ever seen any poem by Ibn Gabirol, whether he is able to read it, whether he realizes that Ibn Gabirol was, beside being an excellent poet, also a neo-Platonic philosopher important enough to become the representative of Platonism when the age-old controversy between Plato and Aristotle broke out again in the Western world (between Franciscans and Dominicans) with the appearance of Thomas Aquinas' writings, such as *De Ente et Essentia*. In other words, Ibn Gabirol's poem describing the palace of his patron is the work of a man who would have made a fool of himself if he had praised his patron for having built an imaginary castle. The very fact that Mr. Sellheim terms the content of Ibn Gabirol's poem "commonplace" *(Allgemeinheiten)* demonstrates that he lacks even a basic insight into Arabic (and Hebrew) descriptive poetry of this type. I challenge Mr. S. to show me any other poem of that time which speaks more specifically e. g. of a rotating dome decorated on its inside with star constellations, where there is reference to a replica of Solomon's Brazen Sea in which the oxen were replaced by lions and a witty iconography or reason stated for such a change. But Mr. S. deems Ibn Gabirol's poem so "indifferent" that no conclusion relative to reality must be drawn from it. He finds fault with the fact that Ibn Gabirol does not mention the name of the patron addressed in his poem nor the name of the castle-palace he describes. If Mr. Sellheim had any knowledge of the customs of that period among Arabic and Hebrew poets, he would know that the best poets were reluctant to attribute a poem to a patron before solid mutual trust and/or a salaried position was assured. Ibn Gabirol names patrons quite rarely and places never. I refer Mr. Sellheim to the passage in Maqqarī, *Dynasties*, I, pp. 35f., where an author refuses to dedicate a book to a patron for very good reasons given. Even major, most likely commissioned, encomia by Ibn Gabirol which are full of references to the character of the addressee may lack the patron's name. But by the choice of specific epithets found also in the encomia of other poets dedicated to the Naghrāllas, by the specific Solomonic symbolism employed by Ibn Gabirol in references to the Naghrāllas, and finally by the uniqueness of these viziers wealthy enough and, with avowed passion, dedicated to the construction of water gardens, the identity of the builder of the Alhambra can be regarded as established, even without the parallel support of 'Abd Allāh's *Memoirs.*

It looks as if Mr. S. had read only a few pages of my Warburg and the German *(Atlantis)* articles when he set out to refute them. He revealingly uses the word "a first glance." He concludes the first part of his review with the haughty words "Let this argument be discontinued with the remark that Bargebuhr's reflections mean nothing." Gradually, however, he seems to have discovered more and more valid proofs (partly misplaced, he regrets, in my footnotes), and he seems to have had second thoughts. He begins a second part, with which he may have hoped to save his soul in the eyes of serious scholars and more careful readers of my articles. Yet he does so without being honest enough to re-write the first part, four full pages of frantic rubbish, interspersed with blanket-words like "immediately" or "*mir nichts dir nichts*" which already betray looming second thoughts. After some seven full pages of misleading the reader by withholding important items of my documentation, such as Abū Isḥāq's invective poem indicating Yehōseph's lavish building activities and the diversion of a water supply, such as the main passages of Ibn Gabirol's poem indicating the size of the palace, its towers and gates, and the Solomonic symbolism of the Naghrāllas, he terms my entire argument, based upon the statements of the most reliable contemporary witnesses one could ever hope to find, "circumstantial evidence, debatable and in one case even refuted." (I wonder in which case?) At the very last he becomes quite meek — perhaps realizing his own inadequacy? — and pleads for a *status quo.* As long as my proofs are not fully solid the matter should rest, in accordance with the old principle *in dubio pro reo.* I wonder who or what the *reus* is? The onus of valid counter-proofs, I think, rests with Mr. S., since information from clear sources must in any case be regarded better than ignorance.

A few more of Mr. S.'s points at random, lest they be repeated *ad nauseam.* The editor of 'Abd Allāh's *Memoirs* does not in the least doubt the veracity of 'Abd Allāh's work. Mr. S., however, tries to misconstrue Lévi-Provençal's footnote to 'Abd Allāh's passage "One" in which that greatest recent historian of Muslim Spain underscores the striking newness of the fact that Yehōšeph built an Alhambra castle. But, Mr. S. seems to ask, why did Lévi-Provençal not consider the conclusions which Bargebuhr draws? Lévi-Provençal did, I am sure, draw the same conclusions as I, but was prevented by his early death from writing the history of this Taifas period, including Yehōšeph's career.

Mr. S. should also have observed that ʿAbd Allāh's *Memoirs* were misquoted by various Arab historians. Western historians have been at some pains to weed out their misinformation. It would have been worth establishing by whom first, and through which developing stemma of false traditions, the wrong data evolved. Such a misquotation, and a very silly one, is cited by Mr. S. It stems from Lévi-Provençal's article "Zīrids" in the *E. I.* of 1934, and is based upon *al-bayān al-mughrib* of Ibn ʿIdhārī (composed in 1306) ed. E. Lévi-Provençal, vol. III. p. 266) quoting the *Memoirs* from memory. According to that tradition the lord of Almeria was supposed to have handed over to Yehōšeph his city of Almeria in exchange for Yehōšeph's delivering Granada into his hand. In fact, the passage in ʿAbd Allāh's *Memoirs* is quite different: there Yehōšeph is blamed for having plotted with the prince of Almeria who was to help Yehōšeph in taking over the rule of Granada. Other terms are not mentioned. Yehōšeph did of course not build the Alhambra to hand it over to anybody else, but, as ʿAbd Allāh clearly states, to reside there after the ruler of Almeria (his ally) would have come. If Mr. S. were a historian and interested in the truth (beyond the present controversy) he would himself have observed the contradiction in the two statements he quotes.

Basing himself upon his claim that Ibn Gabirol's poem contains little more than commonplaces and no evidence, e. g. for the existence of a real walled fortress-palace (which fact is so clearly stated in the first part of Ibn Gabirol's poem, of which Mr. S. only quotes a very few lines), Mr. S. opines that there must have existed many palaces like the unknown one described by Ibn Gabirol. I had presented in my Warburg article all descriptions of fountains I could discover in contemporary sources, mainly descriptions of fountains by the Arabic poets who marveled at these rare instances of short-lived plastic art. But Mr. S. places his trust in the *E. I.*, this time in the 1913 (!) edition, which contained an article "Alhambra" by Schaade and Strzygowski (written at a time before ʿAbd Allāh's *Memoirs* were available to shed light upon the early history of the palace), and cites the existence of many courts like this Court of Lions "everywhere in the Islamic orbit of the Adriatic Sea (sic) and in particular in Sicily." I can only recommend to Mr. S. to read the discussion of this point in my publication. He will find that Sicily, which borrowed heavily from full-fledged Spanish and North-African Islamic art, is mentioned there.

Mr. S. also misses, in the existing Alhambra, the waterspouting hinds mentioned by Ibn Gabirol. Unfortunately, so many old Alhambra parts were destroyed during the many intervening centuries, e. g. by Charles V, that it is a miracle that so much remains. We can only bewail the hinds' *aṭlāl.*

A question of a similar type, raised to undermine my findings, is why the Fount of Lions, if it were an imitation of Solomon's Sea, did not show the typical arrangement in "groups of three" animals, as mentioned in I Kings VII. 23ff. I had tried to make it as clear as possible that Solomon's Sea had in its day, beside the aesthetic, mainly a functional purpose as an ablution basin, whereas that of Yehōseph was entirely representational. I also stated in my article that the Talmud forbids a direct imitation of any element of the Temple in Jerusalem. Out of the spirit of Ibn Gabirol's poem I could deduce other conceivable motives for the avoidance of "groups of three" among the lions. They are represented (according to Ibn Gabirol's poem) as freely "grazing" under the shelter of the protecting basin, representing the ruler of peace; there is no grouping or banding together, for this would indicate a need for protection, a need which no longer existed. But I do not wish to offer interpretations for which I am unable to submit an explicit written document — I leave this to my opponents. I do think that the main reason for the present order of the lions is an aesthetic one, linked with the tradition of sculpturing water-spouting lions at that time. Mr. S. does not seem to have discovered Ibn Gabirol's witty explanation of the builder's intent in the exchange of oxen for lions.

The inscription on the present basin is mentioned by Mr. S. as follows: "Upon it (the present basin) is found 'unfortunately' (this is meant mockingly) an inscription referring to Muḥammad V (1354—1359!)." This inscription, however, proved, as far as my discovery is concerned, to be the most fortunate fact of all. Its wording: "God gave these abodes to ... (Muḥammad)," and not "Muḥammad built these abodes," clearly indicated to me that Muḥammad only added a new basin to an inherited beautiful "bower" and that I had to look for another, original basin. Soon afterwards this basin was pointed out to me, after it had been identified by an intelligent Spanish art historian, as the Abencerages basin. At the same time further proofs of the greater age of the palace were revealed.

On the same basis, and this seems to be indicative of the progress made in acknowledging my findings, Henri Terrasse attributes, in the article "Gharnāṭa" of the newest edition of the *E. I.*, the stone lions, with no doubt, to the eleventh-century Alhambra palace.

The acme of Mr. S.'s "Dear Liza" questions is why Yehōseph's fountain had the function of mirroring objects whereas Solomon's did not. Yehōseph's construction does belong, as I clearly stated, to the contemporary Islamic architectural ambience borrowed, together with its aesthetical urges and, most likely, with the craftsmen, from his environment. Yehōseph was a true son of his time, a true Taifas pretender to a throne, in addition to being, like his father Samuel, a true carrier of Cordovan culture to a hitherto, in many ways, provincial Granada. With the arrival and rise to power of Samuel and the succession of Yehōseph cultural ideas took their seat in Granada which outlived them there both in the continuity of additional Alhambra buildings, stone structures and water gardens, and in many artistic and intellectual activities elsewhere.

Another question raised by my reviewer is why, if Yehōseph's Alhambra existed, the great Arab geographers of the eleventh, twelfth, and thirteenth centuries did not describe it. The best answer to this question seems to be another question, viz.: why did an author as comprehensive as al-Maqqarī, who drew his materials from so many books on Spain and lived around 1600, i. e. at a time when even the latest Muslim parts of the Alhambra existed, not describe the Alhambra? Or earlier geographers who wrote when the Naṣrid buildings of the Alhambra were new and astonishing? The Arab geographers provide useful data with interspersed verses by poets — for the purpose of conveying the spirit and the visual impression — but even the poets are often (and the later the more) abstract and steeped in scholastic intellectualism. I doubt, on giving Mr. S.'s question more thought, whether he has any knowledge of this state of affairs or whether he wishes deliberately to use any, even the most threadbare argument, for his purpose. Other questions should be, to adopt Mr. S.'s interrogative style: could such descriptions have been lost? and, if so, why have they been lost? There are good historical answers to these.

Let us assume — as one tentative answer among many that are conceivable — that, after ʿAbd Allāh had completed the fortification activities in the Alhambra region (mentioned in his *Memoirs*), the palace-fortress was no longer accessible to non-members of the court and of the garrison (like traveling geographers and/or to religiously sensitive mobs, likely to smash sculptured lions in their iconoclastic zeal) until the later kings established their residence there. Maybe the miracle of the preservation of the Fount of Lions should, indeed, be considered together with this seeming black-out in the descriptive records during the subsequent centuries of intolerance to plastic art. Yet, to aver that constructions were, most likely, not existing because they were not described in some books, is another demonstration of lacking historical method. Maybe that there existed, indeed, in books of the eleventh and twelfth centuries which are now lost, whole chapters on the Alhambra. Mr. S. must forgive me if I see in his attempted *refutatio e silentio* and in his motley other asseverations mere φλυαρίαι.

Finally, transgressing all patience and demanding the knowledge of an oracle, Mr. S. asks why ʿAbd Allāh himself did not describe Yehōseph's palace in more detail (if it existed). The answer may be found in the relation of hatred between the two men and in the fact that ʿAbd Allāh shows no artistic interest whatsoever in his *Memoirs*. His own palace, built by his grandfather, remained undescribed as well.

I am reminded by Mr. S.'s review of a remark made in a similar connection by my teacher Gotthelf Bergstraesser: "Otherwise than in the field of science, e. g. in chemistry where a piece of litmus paper demonstrates *ad oculos* whether it has been immersed in alkali or acid, the liberal disciplines depend in their progress upon an individual's insight, upon an act of apprehending the comprehensible, i. e. the ability to follow an argument." Mr. S. may have collected from many sides, as he did from myself, statements of variant views, which, as far as I can see on the basis of my own contribution, he failed to understand and integrate. I should advise him to undertake easier studies. In such as the present, a modicum of insight is required.

A useful article by Hady Roger Idris, "Les Zīrīdes d'Espagne," in *Al-Andalus*, XXIX, 1964 (published 1966), pp.39ff., shows, however, that same uncritical, eclectic attitude to the sources. He reconciles ʿAbd Allāh's passage ONE with Ibn ʿIdhārī's report of Yehōseph's plot (stipulating that the prince of Almeria had to cede to Yehōseph his city against Yehōseph's delivering Granada to him) by translating passage ONE: "*... fit construire (ou fortifier?) la citadelle de l'Alhambra où il comptait se réfugier avec sa famille lors de l'entrée d'al-Muʿtaṣim dans Grenade. On prétend — Ibn Ḥayyān semble-t-il — qu'al-Muʿtaṣim, une fois maître de Grenade, aurait pensé installer le Juif à Alméria dont la population était pourtant essentiellement arabe.*" This passage, with its reference to Granada being a Jewish city and Almeria an Arab city, incorporates a passage in Pérès, *Poésie*, p. 270, where Pérès, to whom the *Memoirs* text was not even available as counterevidence, points out this ethnic division and the absurdity of alleging such a project. If there was any truth to Yehōseph's plotting, then he intended to enlist the help of Almeria for a final take over of the Jewish city where he had — beside all de facto power — provided for himself a regal palace.

Notes to the Prologue

INTRODUCTORY REMARKS

As this book does not address itself to readers who are mainly or exclusively trained linguists, a few devices of customary transliteration are modified to facilitate printing. Arabic words are transliterated, for the most part, according to the system used in the *Encyclopedia of Islam;* but the line employed there to indicate that two Latin characters, e. g. *kh*, stand for one Arabic character has been omitted. Hebrew suffixes and preformatives are, for the sake of easier identification of the verbal themes, set off, in general, by an inserted hyphen.

Words from the Hebrew and Arabic with which the English reader is familiar are quoted in the text, but not in the quotations of the apparatus, in their accepted spelling, e. g. Midrash instead of *midhrash.* So are biblical names and those of biblical books (Jeremiah instead of Yirmeyāhū and Ezra, not 'Ezra). In the translation of poems, however, some biblical names may appear in their King James Version form, whereas they are transliterated in the accompanying notes, in order to demonstrate certain puns. For this reason Samuel and Shemū'el, Ahiah and Aḥīyāh, Jonah and Yōnāh may refer to the same person. Arabic *ibn*, 'son', is reserved, as far as possible, for Arabic names, and Hebrew *ben*, 'son', for Hebrew names. Since, however, some names are mixtures of Hebrew and Arabic elements, the system could not be consistently retained. I follow accepted forms as much as possible.

Since the English reader is accustomed to identify the spirants when adding an *h* to the letters *b*, *g*, *d*, *k*, *p*, *t* — a system devised to transcribe a language like Hebrew — I retain this as the most natural system. In this way the reader may choose if he wishes to pronounce *bh* as *b* or, as in modern Hebrew, as *v*, and *kh* as *k* or *ch* (as in Gaelic or German *loch*, etc.). The Hebrew *ṣādhey* is rendered *ṣ;* *śāmekh* is rendered *ś;* the *shin* in Hebrew and Arabic *sh.*

The Hebrew poets of the Spanish school treat the *ḥāṭeph* vowels and the *shewā mobile* as they fit into the meter. I therefore transliterate texts as they must be scanned metrically, so that the reader may find the same word transliterated differently, e. g., *yaledhūth* or *yaldūth.* Vowels written *plene*, and other long vowels like *qāmeṣ*, are given a length mark. In words of the *fu'l* pattern like *bosheth* and *odhem* an exception is made because of their history in the Hebrew language, and this in spite of their falling into spondaic metrical patterns. The rhyme of a Hebrew poem — mostly a monorhyme, often beginning with a consonant — is indicated above the poem together with the sources, the meter, and a title (of my own coinage). Only in a very few cases, like the "Great Nature Poem," is an imitation of rhyme and meter attempted. The typical conceits taken over by the Hebrew poets from the Arab school of poetry are capitalized in the discussion of the poems.

In points of English editorial usage this book mainly follows the *Style Sheet*, issued by the Modern Language Association of America, in *PMLA*, LXVI, 1951, pp. 3ff. Brackets are used to set off words not directly found in a translated text, inserted when unavoidable in order to adapt the translation to an English mode of expression. Angular parentheses indicate the insertion of titles or fuller forms of names into translated texts and of additions which do not fall within the syntax of the sentence. Suspension points are exclusively used to indicate omissions in a quoted text.

1. F. P. Bargebuhr, "The Alhambra Palace of the Eleventh Century," in *Journal of the Warburg and Courtauld Institutes*, XIX, 1956, pp. 192–258, was reviewed by H. Schirmann in *Qiryath Ṡepher*, XXXIII, 1957–58, p. 256, in a very few lines; also by R. Sellheim in *Jahrbuch für Ästhetik*, VI, 1961, pp. 209-216.
2. See Part II, note 1.
3. See Part II, note 28.
4. See Part II, note 15, dist. 25 of Abū Isḥāq's poem.
5. Cf. E. García Gómez, *Cinco Poetas Musulmanes*, Madrid, 1944, p. 99, note 3 based upon L. Torres Balbás' article "El alminar de la iglesia..." in *Al-Andalus*, VI, 1941, pp. 427 ff. (quoted as García Gómez, *Poetas*).
6. See Part II, D. 6.
7. See Part II, note 116.
8. *Ars Hispaniae*, III, p. 273. For the following see Part II, footnotes 39–42.
9. The poet states his age in various juvenile poems as being sixteen or seventeen years. Since some of these poems were written on the occasion of the death of Hay Gaon in 1038 when the poet was sixteen, and in honor of his Maecenas Yeqūthīel who died in 1039, Ibn Gabirol was (in Davidson's words) "sixteen not earlier than 1038 and seventeen not later than 1039. He must have been born sometime between the end of 1021 and the beginning of 1022." See I. Zangwill and I. Davidson, *Selected Religious Poems of Sol. ibn Gabirol*, 1923, p. 127 (quoted as *Davidson-Z.*).
10. Moses ibn Ezra's Arabic text reads *wa-qad armā ʿalā ʾth-thalāthīn(a)* which means "he overshot the thirties," and which was understood to mean "he reached an age not much higher than thirty." (Al-Ḥarīzī seems to have read *ilā* 'he shot towards' instead of *ʿalā* 'beyond'; and thus M. Steinschneider cites Ibn Ezra's text in his Bodleian Catalogue, col. 2318). Dr. Noah Braun's typewritten text of the poem for a projected edition, which I was allowed to see through the kindness of Dr. N. Golb, reads *ʿalā*. It seems to be useless to conjecture a reading *arbaʿīna* or to realize that 'surpassing the thirties' might mean to reach the age of forty-six, as actually the poet did, and as Professor Roediger suggests, in S. I. Kaempf, *Nichtandalusische Poesie andalusischer Dichter*, Prag, 1858, p. 190 (quoted as *Kaempf*). Characterizing Moses ibn Ezra, Geiger says: "He was more exact as an expert in his art than as a chronicler, for he treats figures very carelessly," in A. Geiger, *Salomo Gabirol und seine Dichtungen*, Leipzig, 1867, p. 111 (quoted as *Geiger*).
11. J. Finkel, "An Eleventh Century Source for the History of Jewish Scientists in Mohammedan Lands (Ibn Saʿīd)," in *Jewish Quarterly Review*, XVIII, 1927–28, p. 5: "... also Sulaimān ibn Yaḥyā called Ibn Jabrival (Jibirwāl) [i. e. Gabirol] a citizen of Saragossa. He was fond of the subject of logic. He had a subtle mind and an attractive way of speculation. He was cut off in the prime of his life, passing away at an age over thirty, shortly before the year 450 A. H." (1058 C. E.). A French translation by R. Blachère is found in *Saʿīd al-Andalusī, K. ṭabaqāt al-umam*, in *Publ. de l'Inst. des H. Etudes Marocains*, XXVIII, 1935, p. 159.
12. S. W. Baron, *A Social and Religious History of the Jews*, New York, 1958–60, VII, p. 291 (quoted as Baron, *History*). Abraham Zakkūtō lists Ibn Gabirol's death in 1070, see Munk, *Mélanges de philosophie juive et arabe*, Paris, 1859, p. 156, n. 1 (quoted as Munk, *Mélanges*).
13. *Davidson-Z.*, p. 71 (166 f.).
14. There is a good discussion of this problem in K. Dreyer, *Die religiöse Gedankenwelt des S. ibn Gabirol*, Leipzig, 1930, p. 59, demonstrating the validity of Ibn Gabirol's millennial hymns as sources for biographical data (quoted as *Dreyer*).

15. *Davidson-Z.*, pp. 120. The death of Ibn Gabirol is discussed by Davidson on p. XXVII and p. 131.
16. H. N. Bialik & Y. H. Ravnitzki, *Shīrey Shelōmōh ben Yehūdhāh ibn Gabirol...*, Tel Aviv, 1925–32, II, pp. 6f. (quoted as *Bialik-R.*); vols. I & II, secular poetry, (quoted as 'vol. I'); vols. III & IV, religious poetry, (quoted as 'vol. II'); vols. V & VI, mixed poetry, (quoted as 'vol. III'); vol. VII, analects, (quoted as 'vol. IV'). H. Schirmann, *Hash-Shīrāh hā-ʿibhrīth bi-Ṡephāradh u-bhe-Provence*, I, Jerusalem, 1959–60, pp. 244f., line 17 (quoted as Schirmann, *Shīrāh*).
17. Discussed in Schirmann, *Shīrāh*, I, p. 245, without a mention of the parallel supports of this date.
18. *Geiger*, p. 111. I think Schirmann would have profited from the idea that Ibn Ezra confused Ibn Gabirol with Ibn at-Tāqāna who, according to Ibn Ezra himself, also died when he was about thirty and whom he mentioned immediately before Ibn Gabirol. He calls Ibn at-Tāqāna "The Twin" without stating whose twin he was. I intend to discuss the exact correspondence of the situation and polemical content between the poem recently identified as the work of Moses ibn at-Tāqāna and of certain poems of invective by Ibn Gabirol who belonged to the same Saragossan circle, in my forthcoming studies.
19. See e. g. Baron, *History*, VII, p. 152; Munk, *Mélanges*, pp. 155ff.; *Geiger*, p. 111; H. Graetz, *Geschichte der Juden*, VI, Leipzig, 1861, p. 61, 388f. (quoted as Graetz, *Geschichte*); English edition: Graetz, *History of the Jews*, Philadelphia, 1956, p. 280 (quoted as Graetz, *History*); *Davidson-Z.*, p. 131; Sachs in *Ham-Maggīdh*, 1874, p. 313; S. Dubnow, *Weltgeschichte des jüdischen Volkes*, IV, Berlin, 1925, p. 236, n. 1 (quoted as *Dubnow*).
20. In his review of my Alhambra in *Qiryath Ṡepher* (see above note 1). Also cf. Schirmann, *Shīrāh*, I, p. 178: "According to Moses ibn Ezra the poet died in Valencia, when he was more than thirty years old. Following the testimony of Ibn Saʿad [sic], an Arabic author of the eleventh century, Ibn Gabirol passed away about 480 A. H. (i. e. 1057–58). From this we may deduce that his death took place between 1053 and 1058." Abraham Zakkūtō, all internal evidence, and the galaxy of distinguished Jewish historians remain unmentioned.
21. See Part II, note 15.
22. In a text beneath a picture of the Alhambra in Schirmann, *Shīrāh*, I, opposite p. 65.
23. I am referring to an article on courtyards with crossing channels by L. Torres Balbás "Patios de Crucero," in *Al-Andalus*, XXIII, 1958, pp. 171ff. Also an article on "Windows above doors" by the same author seems to be provoked by my publication: "Salas con linterna central en la arquitectura Granadina," in *Al-Andalus*, XXIV, 1959, pp. 197ff. with a passage on "Salas con huecos de luz y ventilación sobre las puertas y ventanas."
24. In a passage near the end of this treatise on Hebrew poetry, Ibn Ezra deals a last blow at Ibn Gabirol:

    This poet, with a flimsy side-remark, modulates from the topic of a dark night and a cloud to the criticism of a song:

    its chill is like the snow of Mount Senir or
    the poetry of Samuel, the Kohathite ...

    This is the poem for which he [later had to] apologize and ask for forgiveness in a long poem, because it contained many shortcomings. This Poem of Apology begins as follows:

Arise, o Time, and deck thee with thy charms,

and contains in its context [the line]:

Offer a sacrifice before them . . .

> In truth the wrathful soul does not achieve its aims in the above mentioned distich, for it was to force the nobler soul to write a poem full of submissiveness. He should have humiliated himself before God.

Here Ibn Ezra pretends not to relish even the witty detraction of a mighty man. But questions remain. Why does he quote the distich from Ibn Gabirol? Does he, in fact, secretly relish it? Or does he take a welcome opportunity of preaching the necessity of submission to a man of power and so to God? Is he accurate in asserting that it was this distich which caused the rift between Ibn Gabirol and Samuel? There are much graver attacks on Samuel by Ibn Gabirol, for instance the poem which begins "Samuel was dead, Ibn Labrāṭ" quoted from I Sam. XXV.1 which, only when re-read in a new context, allows the interpretation "Dead was, Samuel!, (Dūnāsh) Ibn Labrāṭ," a shrewd ambiguity of diction which, like more in Ibn Gabirol, reminds one of Catullus (e. g. his ridiculing praise of Cicero as the protector of the oppressed), yet which modern editors, who apparently share the campanilismo of Moses ibn Ezra, still interpret as laudatory. In any case, Ibn Ezra is unreliable as a historian. As to the Poem of Apology mentioned, it is not in the least submissive, as pointed out above. It is almost a challenge, clearly written at a time when Ibn Gabirol knew that Samuel wanted him at almost any price. By employing the word 'Kehathite' (quoted by Ibn Ezra above) he had ridiculed Samuel's claim upon levitic ancestors like Kohath and inherited charisma, made in his ambitious manifesto of victory II, and had wounded Samuel, most likely, at his neuralgic point. The 'wrathful', indeed very angry young poet promises to praise Samuel, but only at the price he names, which is acceptance as an equal. The line 'offer a sacrifice before them', i. e. before the Naghrāllas, irks Ibn Ezra by its sacrilege, as one can feel from other instances. Sacrifices, he feels, belong to God alone. The line speaks of offering before them a scapegoat, which is a loaded *double entendre*. What could he have meant by sacrificing to the Naghrāllas? Most likely this is only lip-service, for there is no word of submission, and it is more likely that Samuel surrendered to the splendor of Ibn Gabirol's poem of reconciliation. The ghetto-soul of Moses ibn Ezra, which is unable to grasp this, is symptomatic of the decline from freedom to servility, from breadth of mind to pedantry, from emancipated wit to protestations of piety and the flattery of patrons: Woe to the respectless, theirs is humiliation, as the good teachers instruct!

As one should deduce from the sources (which are poems) Ibn Gabirol never became a pliable courtier but, admitted to the round table of the prodigiously wise and truly great man of letters and policy and to his, in many ways even more prodigious, son Yehōšeph, he was disarmed and redeemed of his anger by sincere admiration and by sharing the actively redeeming plans of Samuel ibn Naghrālla.

PART I

A Solomonic Renaissance

A. Cordova

As to the word 'renaissance', ever since Charles Homer Haskins' *Renaissance of the Twelfth Century*[1] appeared, the concept of a mediaeval Renaissance has been reserved — together with the Carolingian and Ottonian Renaissances — mainly for the twelfth century, because this was a period of a new ingathering of the neglected possessions of the Western heritage. Although Haskins' book contains a very interesting chapter on translations from the Greek and Arabic, and chapters on the rebirth of science, the beginning of universities, besides the revival of a better Latinity and Roman jurisprudence, and the resurgence of philosophy, insufficient mention is made of the precedent for all these phenomena in the direct interfusion of Christian and Islamic ideas. In particular, the phenomenon of a new canon of secular values, unheard of thitherto in the Middle Ages, is not given the attention due to it. The final evolution of the disciplines and the pitch of achievement reached, seemed to indicate that these developments were exclusively Western, but the derivative character of many of them in the Christian West went unstressed and the question of their origins was not raised. The precedents for the twelfth century Renaissance in south-western Europe have to be sought, of course, in Byzantium, where, for instance, Michael Psellos can be regarded as a hallmark for a Platonic revival in Greek literature, and, to come to my topic, in Arab Spain of the eleventh century — in particular in its capital Cordova under the Umayyad caliphs and, after their downfall, in the new capitals of the Taifas kings. Moreover, the secular values of Western chivalry, developing during and after the Crusades, are unthinkable without intimate contact with the Muslims. Besides chivalry and courtly love, I refer in particular to the poetical production of epics of adventure, to new architectural ideas in the Christian countries, and to the universities established in the twelfth century, with their precedents in the Islamic countries. The influence of Islamic scholasticism and metaphysics upon religious thought in the Christian and Jewish orbits may not have been less than that upon secular developments. I cannot discuss here, however, how far the Arabs merely set an example, their new orientation prompting the other side to reconsider and to compete, and how far there took place a direct or indirect acculturation. In my section on the Jews in this introduction, I shall describe the rise

Note 1

of a new type of a secular Jew who might have played the role of a cultural mediator, even if by merely affecting the Jewry of Christian countries.

The problem of using the term 'renaissance' or 'renascence' for a non-Western development must first be discussed[2]. It is common knowledge that tenth and eleventh-century Cordova looked for a model to the Baghdad of the eighth and ninth century with its revival of ancient studies, the emancipation of courtly women, and the concomitant rise of love poetry, nature poetry, and the various plastic arts. It was these developments that caused Adam Mez to name his book on the culture of Baghdad, *Die Renaissance des Islams*[3]. Eleventh-century Spain, however, adds many 'Western' trends to the Baghdadi achievements which it inherited from the East. Besides a general feeling of a festive life in Cordova and the new capitals of the Taifas period, a Hispano-Arab society breeds and honors virtues which do not belong to the religious scale of values, but which are rooted in an unbroken Arab chivalrous tradition. Parallel to the Arabs' political expansion, following their unification under Islam and their concomitant conquests, we encounter a continuous intellectual expansion. In contrast with the Christians who put an end to the Greek theater, to a Phidian ideal of sculpture, and to free philosophy, the Muslims rather began to discover in the Byzantine countries which they conquered, for the first time, the remnants of the Greek arts and sciences. As late as in the twelfth century Islam established itself more and more firmly with all its inherent ascetic, puritan, and "anti-cultural" tenets. In the light of this continuity I could be wrong in speaking of a 'renaissance' if it were not for the concurrent revival among the Arabs of the Greek and Roman arts and sciences.

Until the tenth century, to repeat, Cordova had looked to 'Abbāsid Baghdad as a superior model; but now with Baghdad's waning, Cordova saw itself as the heir and reviver of that Eastern capital's glories. We encounter there (1) a learned laity, minded to poetry, unknown in the West until much later, congregating in garden symposia and discussing the topic of wordly love as freely as did the Socratic circle in Athens; (2) poets with a deepened feeling for nature and sometimes an almost Western sentimentalized poetry, and artists praising figural plastic art (against all Muslim injunctions); (3) emancipated women, who were addressed in courtly love poems and sometimes able to respond maturely in poetry; (4) a revival of the study of Greek and Roman writings, in particular of Plotinus, Aristotle, and Plato (not clearly discriminated because of the pseudepigraphal transmission); (5) the emancipation of all the senses, in particular the visual, with (6) a consequent creation of a new architecture, including gardens and representational plastic art; and (7) nature poetry

Notes 2—3

which deals as well with buildings and artificial landscapes. This liberal movement, and the Berber menace[4] to such a revival of and freedom for arts and letters contributed to a particular Andalusian nationalism, as we shall see, and to a unique emancipation of the metropolitan Jews who accepted the Arab invitation to love, to love of beauty, to a higher appreciation of nature, to the plastic arts, and to poetry. (Andalusia was the name for all of Moorish Spain.)

Since all these trends most strikingly anticipate later western movements, I find the common denominator of a "Renaissance" quite meaningful, and propose very seriously the term "The Renaissance of the Eleventh Century." I should, however, be willing to replace this word by 'renascence' to comply with Erwin Panofsky's definitions[2]. 'Renascence' is perhaps a better word, for the word 'renaissance' carries with it the idea of the resuscitation of accomplishments which mankind had once possessed and longed to possess again.

This cycle of studies could also have borne the title "Solomon's Ring," and the author was tempted to so inscribe the book. It would remind the reader of the ring which enabled the biblical king to understand the language of trees, beasts, birds, reptiles, and fish (based wrongly upon I Kings IV. 33) and which also gave him command over the jinn, forcing their hosts to build for him miraculous palaces of congealed air and water. But in this case, the word 'ring' would refer to the full cycle of the biblical king's activities and quests, his books and his royal licenses — all of which inspired not only Muslim rulers of various periods and, among the Muslims, a learned laity not yet existent in the Christian West but also, in particular, the lettered Jews of Cordova and Granada, whose monuments and written documents are interpreted in this book, to imitate exactly the biblical king's following of wordly pursuits. Thus (1) King Solomon, the (alleged) author of the Book of Ecclesiastes, became the patron of wisdom literature and philosophical discourse; (2) since the Song of Solomon was in some way also a nature poem, it stimulated the creation of Hebrew nature poetry; (3) as the lover of so many wives and as the (alleged) author of Canticles, he inspired and shielded the composition of hitherto prohibited Hebrew secular love poetry (besides some mystical love poetry), so that the elevation of women as objects of courtly love, developing in the eleventh century, could be called a Solomonic heresy, to modify Father Denomy's term (I shall discuss later a Jewish aspect of the problem of the origin of Western courtly love and love poetry); and, (4) since King Solomon engaged in extensive building activities which included — against the Second Commandment and to the reproach of the Bible itself — plastic art (with the Brazen Sea in the Temple and its "oxen" and the throne

Notes 4 (2)

decorated with statues of lions in his palace), his example encouraged, as the first step in the most ambitious Solomonic program of this period, the Jewish vizier Yehōseph ibn Naghrālla in Granada to build on the Alhambra hill a palace with Solomonic symbolism, a palace of which impressive remnants are still extant.

I discovered this fact owing to a happy coincidence of findings and, since such palace building was the boldest anticipation of the full Solomonic program on the part of these Jewish viziers, I allocate the first place in this book to the study of the palace. The program entailed — as a reliable Arab author tells — even the foundation of a Jewish state in Granada. Hence, this typical renascence was, like other periods thus termed, linked with the idea of a political *renovatio*, as we shall see in more detail.

Some of these glories of old were now felt to be reborn. As almost any great cultural event takes place among men who have previously felt a vacuum and have yearned for that event, both Arabs and Jews in Spain seem to have outdone each other in an insatiable hunger for knowledge and the restoration of more splendid periods of their history. If the Arabs had no glories to look back upon in their own remote national past, the image of King Solomon in the Koran must have instilled a yearning for a renewal of such splendors. Much more than the Arabs, the Jews in Spain, who shared such a longing for Judea's ancient splendors and who lived in anxious expectation of the end of their exile and suspense, were classically predestined by the situation and enabled by the freedom and cultured liberalism of the Umayyads of Cordova to work for a humanistic renaissance — provided they could overcome their "anti-cultural" inhibitions and break the injunctions of this kind imposed upon them for the age before a collective messianic redemption. And in fact the metropolitan intelligentsia of the Jews must have felt able to see in such a freedom-for-culture a revelation of the divine will and had the courage, quite often to the point of heterodoxy, to engage in arts which had hardly been within Jewish scope previously, not even in the Hellenistic age.

As Cordova had long looked to Baghdad for a model, the Christian world soon after the eleventh century had to look, for some time, to Cordova. Western students of the sciences, as is widely known, undertook studies in Cordova and the fact that Thomas Aquinas referred regularly to "The Commentator" (Ibn Rushd—born 1126) and to "Rabbi Moyses" (Maimonides — born 1135), both of them Cordovans, as his interpreters of Aristotle and competent promoters of Aristotelianism, is significant. Modern Spanish scholars, however, were loath to admit the fundamental importance of the Arabs and Jews in the intellectual history of Spain, until Américo Castro devoted a full third of his great book[5] to the Arabs and Jews and

Note 5

attributed to Jewish *lettrés*, among other merits, the earliest formation and fixation of a Spanish literary vernacular. Since the achievements of the Arabs in the fields of science and philosophy are comparatively well known, these will have to be omitted here.

The term "Golden Age of the Arabs and Jews in Spain" is not confined to the eleventh century. It may mean, to conventional historians, the entire seven hundred years' period of the Moorish occupation of Spain. Jewish historians may reserve the term for the time of the most creative contact between Arabs and Jews and may see its termination with the coming of the Almohades; but they also speak of a specific "Golden Age" of Hebrew literature and assign this term to the generation of Jehuda Halevi and Moses ibn Ezra in the twelfth century. These two poets, however, able to draw from several previous generations of founders, were not the truly original re-coiners of poetical Hebrew. Also, their intellectual scope was much more confined, and their art, in spite of a greater musicality, was much more conventional. The twelfth century in general, though it may have contributed much to the spread of both Arab and Jewish culture throughout Spain and thence to Sicily and Southern France, betrays so many components of dilution and conventionality that we may, when comparing it with the fullness, newness, and independence of thought of the eleventh century, regard it as rather epigonic. The birth of an entirely Mediterranean type of the Arab, who reminds us indeed of the Periclean Athenians, is portrayed overwhelmingly in Ibn Ḥazm's *Ṭauq al-ḥamāma*, a book based upon his juvenile poems which are set into a prose (occasionally rhymed prose) text dealing with many phenomena of love. His descriptions of garden parties, more than other contemporary texts, remind one (to repeat) very strongly of individualistic Periclean Athens, with its prose and poetry pervading the general *ambiente* and the whole range of human relationships. If this milieu had not disentegrated, its consequences for the Western world might have been far-reaching; but Ciceronian moments are brief. Ibn Ḥazm describes the setting for a philosophical symposium in the following lines (in A. J. Arberry's translation):[6]

> I was taking a walk in an orchard, the property of a friend of mine, accompanied by a group of comrades, all men of breeding and nobility. We promenaded for an hour, and then sat us down in a most desirable spot. There we stretched ourselves at our ease in spacious gardens; this broad panorama was a joy to the contemplative eye, a rich pasture to the ruminating spirit.

In this setting, which may recall that of Plato's *Charmides* or *Phaedrus*, the young metropolitan *lettrés* began their discussion of philosophical topics

Note 6

such as, for instance, love, with which they were as much concerned as the Athenian group of Plato's *Banquet*. One feels tempted to say that Ibn Ḥazm's *Dove's Necklace* is the most unmediaeval book of the Middle Ages: this in spite of the fact that he had published it, with many apologies, at a time when protestations of asceticism had to supplant his previous Umayyad liberalism, when he had to adjure the reader to believe that he had always been chaste, when he felt compelled to praise the sweet waters of the brooks instead of tasty wine, which he would have been free to praise before 1027. This seems to be a concession to the ostentatious teetotalism of the post-Umayyad period, as this man in his later stages, embittered by his and his group's exile from Cordova, became typical of the narrowing, declining, and hateful tendencies of this time.

B. The Arabs

(1) ARAB INDIVIDUALISM AND HUMANISM

When speaking today of a Renaissance personality we may think of a "man of many parts" combining many and rather disparate talents. Owing to an unbroken tradition of chivalry we encounter among the Arab nobility, together with the universality of skills, a canon of exclusively secular virtues. Such a secular canon appears, as far as I see, for the first time in the Middle Ages, which were dominated so strongly by the clergy and the values of religion, in the *Ḥullat as-siyarā'*, *The Garment of Pure Gold Cloth*, by the Spanish-Arab historian Ibn al-Abbār. Ibn al-Abbār credits the ninth century Spanish poet Sa'īd ibn Jūdī[7] (who flourished around 890) with the following ten gifts of character: (1) generosity, (2) bravery, (3) skill in horsemanship in theory and practice, (4) beauty of the body, (5) poetical talent, (6) eloquence, (7) physical strength, (8) and (9) prowess at spear- and swordsmanship, and (10) skill in archery[8]. These virtues, all of them secular, including the literary abilities of a learned laity, became more specialized in the tenth and eleventh centuries, and a new type of a *poète savant* emerged. These would still claim to be knights of both sword and quill, as the Arabic poet al-Mutanabbī of the tenth century praises himself; but they acquire this typical Renaissance multifariousness until, as it were in spite of their great learning, they surprise us sometimes with their fresh poetical talent and romantic way of life, as does Ibn 'Ammār, the treacherous condottiere (one of those who, like Yehōseph, feel that a kingdom of their own is due to them).

There is in eleventh-century Spain a uniqueness embodied in a few individuals who, for the sake of their own power or that of their Maecenas, could live up to their own most emancipated pursuits and who were conscious of and stressed their new orientation and renaissance-like individualism, together with a new pride for their country and with a marked withdrawal from the previous general admiration for the East, of which I shall speak later. One of the supreme examples of this individualism and Spanish pride is Ibn Ḥazm, from whose *Dove's Necklace* I quoted a passage. The other highlights are the Jewish vizier-warlord-Talmudist-poet, Samuel ibn Naghrālla, with the title han-Nāghīdh, his son Yehōseph han-Nāghīdh,

Notes 7—8

and finally the Jewish poet-philosopher Solomon ibn Gabirol, known chiefly as the composer of most beautiful prayers and hymns for the synagogue. Such types of pioneer artist *cum* scholar *cum* poet *cum* conqueror disappear in the twelfth century under the Almoravid and Almohad holy warriors, who were increasingly opposed to culture. Finally, I feel justified in using the term "humanism" — though not, of course, in the Italian tradition linked with the cultivation of classical Latinity — by the Arabs' (and Jews') rediscovery of the value and dignity of man himself, which gave the word "man" a full new ring, for example, in Ibn Gabirol's poem *Mah l-lākh, yeḥīdhāh*, which I translate in full in my forthcoming German book:[9]

> If you set out to see a man —
> as a man you will be regarded . . .

This consciousness causes such men to feel contempt for people who fall short of their standards and to voice such contempt as does Solomon ibn Gabirol in his "Song of Complaint," where he calls his Saragossan co-religionists "grasshoppers" and men "I would disdain to set with the dogs of my flock" (Job XXX. 1). The keynote is beauty and intelligence.

(2) HISPANO-ARAB PRIDE, NATIONALISM, AND SECULARISM

All renascences seem to be accompanied by a romantic idea of and yearning for a political *renovatio*. We shall look for such traits in Spain and discover specific Spanish-Arab national pride, and this after the lustre of the Eastern models, in particular Baghdad for the Arabs, and the academy cities of Sura and Pumbeditha for the Jews, was declining. The times of Harūn ar-Rashīd and his successors, on the one hand, had become Arabian Nights of unsurpassed fame. On the other hand, Baghdad's glory had been eclipsed by equally fascinating Cordovan sequels. The troubadour ʿAbbās ibn al-Aḥnaf and his beloved "Fauz" of the ʿAbbāsid court had found their successors in the actuality of an Ibn Zaidūn and his *dame fatale* Wallāda[10]. This couple, together with the royal love poet al-Muʿtamid and his Rumaikiyya, became the new models. It is tragic that, while this transcending of the Eastern models was in progress, and while, under the "petty kings" succeeding the dethroned Umayyads, metropolitan Cordovan culture had begun to spread by way of the newly established capitals, the rise of "anti-cultural" Almoravides and Almohades put an early end to these developments. Yet, paradoxically enough, almost simultaneously with the hour of frustration, Arabic poetry reached its high-water mark in

Ibn Khafāja, whose poems show a great thematic unity of observation, description, and sentiment. On the other hand, we find in the twelfth-century Ibn Quzmān, a libertine poet almost totally emancipated from those religious and ethical restraints which might have impeded a falling away from eleventh-century standards, who is able to shock a modern reader as much as a Henry Miller. In Ibn Quzmān's work we can judge, by contrast, the climactic character of the eleventh century[11].

Comparatively little attention has been given to the unique phenomenon of this mediaeval secular movement affecting Muslims and Jews alike. The freedom for, and the immediate inspiration to, such liberal tendencies, as well as craftsmanship in poetry and sculpture, stemmed in particular from the court of the Umayyad caliphs ruling in Cordova and, after their downfall around 1025 A. D., from the dispersion of their ideas throughout Muslim Spain and elsewhere.

The reason why Cordova was destined to become, under the Umayyads, the great intellectual clearing-house of East and West may have to be discovered in the permanent attraction it possessed for men of talent and for ideas. For instance, the philosopher Ibn Sīnā, for good reasons, was read in Cordova earlier and with greater zeal than in his Persian homeland. Whereas Spanish-Arabic poetry was not known in the East in the eleventh century, towards the end of the tenth century Ibn Faraj al-Jayyānī wrote the *Kitāb al-ḥadā'iq*, "Book of Gardens," which, as the surviving extracts prove, was a large anthology of exclusively Hispano-Arabic love poetry, intended to be a counterpart to the the classical book on love and love poetry by Ibn Dā'ūd, the *Kitāb az-zahra*. Half a century later, Abū 'l-Walīd al-Ḥimyarī, a vizier in the kingdom of Seville, wrote a sequence to al-Jayyānī's book under the title of *al-badī' fī waṣf ar-rabī'*, a still extant collection of spring and flower poetry composed by poets from Seville. The introduction to this book contained the following lines:[12]

> The poems of the East which have retained our attention for so long now cease to attract us and to enchant us with their jewels. Furthermore, we can do without them because we no longer need to have recourse to them. For the Andalusians possess astonishing pieces of prose and poems of original beauty ... The easterners, in spite of the care which they bestow upon the composition of verse and historiography, and in spite of the advantage of having spoken Arabic for a longer period, cannot find in their works the metaphors adequate to "description" which I find in the compositions of my compatriots.

The same Hispano-Arab pride in achievement is evident in the great presentation of Spanish culture to the entire Arab world, written at the end of the eleventh century and widely diffused in the Arabian world, Ibn Bassām's *Kitāb adh-dhakhīra fī maḥāsin ahl al-Jazīra*, "The Chest Containing the Beauties of the People of the Peninsula." We shall encounter later, when we come to consider the development of poetry and the arts among the Jews of Andalusia, an analogous process of emancipation from the East, accompanied by a corresponding Hispano-Jewish pride and nationalism.

(3) THE AWAKENING OF THE SENSES

It may be worthwhile to consider within which historical constellations such a secularism could override the overall ascetic and other-worldly orientation both of the Arab begetters of Islam and of the Jews who were held together by their expectation of a divinely implemented messianic redemption, living "in and out of time" (T. S. Eliot).

There is, of course, no "unicausal" explanation for a phenomenon as complex and unique as Moorish Spain. Arabian sensuousness, nurtured by the Spanish environment, was fully developed in the Umayyad climate; it was not a return to pre-Islamic barbarian sensuality, but rather a highly sophisticated and artistic domestication of the original drive of the race. This progress of secularism, sensuality, and literary and artistic sophistication, which, I think, is indicative of a renascence, makes itself felt as an entity pervading many areas of life. For example, under the influence of Greek philosophy, notably the Platonists, the reign of dogmatic thinking dwindled. It was Greek science and philosophy which created and authorized a new sensibility, an awareness of a perceptible world. This awakening of a sense of external form and beauty, of the physical "furniture" of the universe is linked with a secular approach to man. Previously — as in a corresponding Christian era — this sense had been fettered by an ascetic attitude. And yet Arabic secular love poetry of the speculative Middle Ages was also sophisticated, celebrating the physical in a refined and intense perception. The education and emancipation of courtly women allowed more readily for their elevation to objects of veneration by the lover, and a Platonic tendency in poetry assigned to the individual a central place within the order of the universe. And this, in turn, inspired speculation on the nature of love and love poetry.

This secularization of life and of art took place in opposition to many of Islam's prohibitions and inhibitions. It had, of course, precedents in the Baghdad of the ʿAbbāsids with its Sāsānian traditions, and in the Umayyad caliphate of Damascus, and to some extent in Fāṭimid Egypt.

But not all questions of the genesis of this emancipatory trend can be discussed here, and I must content myself merely with enumerating the major elements that made for this secularization on Spanish soil. It should be mentioned, however, that even in this period only a small aristocratic circle had a share in this secularization, and that only for a short time. Only a few examples of plastic art, for instance, were displayed, and these inspired the poets to exclamations of surprised admiration, while scandalizing the "rigorists." Sometimes, rediscovered ancient Roman statues were tolerated in the bath-houses, which were, in many cases, places of reduced religious ostentation. Al-Maqqarī, referring to a period before 1094, mentions three Greek statues of human figures in Spain of which he had knowledge, one in Galicia, another in Tarragona and a third in Cadiz[13]. The few references to animal statues will be discussed in an appendix. It must be stressed that very little three-dimensional figurative art was created in Islamic Spain after the culture of the Umayyad and "successor" kingdoms was obliterated, when liberalism succumbed to the reactionary rule of Almoravides and Almohades.

The philosophy of Ibn Sīnā (Avicenna) (died 1037) which seems to have been popular in Cordova, but which met a great deal of orthodox resistance, reaffirmed the value of external beauty:[14]

> ... the situation in the case of the human faculty of desire. True, this faculty is one of the causes of corruption, but it is necessary in the general desired order which is good, and it is not part of (the) divine wisdom to abandon a great good because of the adverse character of an evil which is small in relation to it.
>
> ... one will never find the wise, ... to be free from having their hearts occupied with a beautiful human form. Therefore, if a man acquires ... the excellence of a harmonious form ... then that man has the strongest claim to receive the very kernel of the fruit of the heart and the very essence of the purest kind of love. Therefore, the Prophet says: Seek ye satisfaction of your needs in those of beautiful countenance ... (Sura V. 87ff.).

A Platonic renascence and a return to the senses belong together. The Christian and Jewish teachers had turned from material reality towards man's inner sphere, as proclaimed by Augustine in his *Noli foras ire in te ipsum redi, in interiore hominis habitat veritas*. This orientation, in which Islam became enmeshed more and more, was consciously renounced in Umayyad Cordova. An anecdote connected with Ibn Ḥazm sheds some light upon this. Ibn Ḥazm belonged to the *ẓāhirī* school of Muslim law. This adhered to the principle of accepting the "apparent" meaning of the Koranic text as the basis for legal decisions and refused to use other methods of exegesis and application, such as typological and anagogical, which the other schools applied. In contrast to these other schools, called *bāṭinī*, to be translated as (the finders of) the "inner" or "essential" (meaning) or simply "essentialist," Ibn Ḥazm — at least on one occasion — makes a play on the word *ẓāhirī* and wittily extends its meaning to signify one who reserves for himself the privilege to be not only one who takes the text of the Koran at "face value" but to be an "evaluator of faces," i. e. one who examines what is visible of things without the application of preconceived and extraneous principles. Thus, in an anecdote relating to his younger years, he is represented as excusing himself for contemplating human beauty with a flaneur's unabashed curiosity. Henri Pérès translates this anecdote from al-Maqqarī as follows:[15]

> Ibn 'Abd al-Barr ... se promenant un jour à Séville dans la rue des marchands de bois avec Ibn Ḥazm le Ẓāhirī, ils rencontrèrent un beau garçon: "Belle image!" dit Ibn Ḥazm. — "Je ne vois que le visage, répondit son compagnon; il se pourrait que le corps qui se cache sous le vêtement ne fût pas aussi beau!" Et Ibn Ḥazm de répliquer par quatre vers dont le dernier était: "Ne vois-tu pas que je suis ẓāhirite et que je me base sur ce que je vois jusqu'à ce qu'une preuve (patente du contraire) sois fournie?"

This anecdote — somewhat reminiscent of Oscar Wilde's dandyism[16], proclaiming that only a fool does not judge on the basis of the outer appearance — shows Ibn Ḥazm in his Cordovan years when he belonged to a well sheltered and wealthy court officialdom which enjoyed full freedom of opinion and expression. Far from being a mystic (as this anecdote may show) but rather a rational and sceptical sensualist, the same man becomes — after being exiled from the ravaged capital — increasingly ashamed of his juvenile love poetry and represents in a negative way the change of climate under the Almoravides. We shall find a corresponding proclamation of the autonomy of the visible by Ibn Gabirol.

Nature poets like Ibn Khafāja are also representatives of such "externalism" among the Muslims. But only for an infinitely short historical "Ciceronian" moment enthusiastic poetical inspiration was solidly based upon this new sensitivity to both nature and modes of expression. The eleventh-century Muslim historian Ibn Bassām criticized the literary life of Moorish Spain, disavowed contemporary literature and, in particular, poetry and prose with their roots in fantasy, and wished to concentrate all concern on reality of life in this verdict: "The realities of perceptible things deserve much more our attention than those unnecessary ones of prose and poetry."

Notes 15—16

(4) ORIGINS

To explain the eleventh-century culmination of Islamic culture, I offer a brief recapitulation of its origin and development. Alexander the Great had dissolved the patterns of Greek life and thought, long established at their various centers, and by disseminating Greek thought and culture in a diluted and adaptable form, eclectic enough in outlook to absorb admixtures from Oriental sources, had thus opened a new "Hellenistic" Western world to ever-increasing Eastern influxes. Such a loosening was, however, counterbalanced, for instance, by the tendencies of the Greek schools of Alexandria to establish canons of texts and taste and later by the unifying political will of the Romans. The main corrective for Hellenistic intellectual looseness lay, of course, in Paul, the Church Fathers, and in the imperial founders of new Christian *ordo* like Justinian, these anti-Alexanders, to use Nietzsche's term[17]. But the price paid for solidification through this stabilization by means of canon and codification, based upon the new religion, was high. Early Christianity, with its strong anti-secular bent, put an end to free metaphysical thought, to the pictorial and sculptural tradition of the artistic imitation of nature, to secular poetry, and to the presentation of the human tragedy in the theater. In becoming the state religion of the Roman Empire, Christianity, however, had to incorporate a minimum of those traditions to satisfy — besides the religious — the most pressing cultural needs of Mediterranean man, and in this way Christianity retained some degree of progressive eclecticism and syncretism.

Islam, in many respects also an ascetic movement, derivative from Judaism and Christianity, originated in the pagan, arid hinterland of Arabia, which had no plastic or dramatic art of its own to be abolished. Islam unified the Arabian tribes and induced them to engage — rather than in centuries-old inter-tribal wars — in the conquest of a vast empire. The Arabic word for 'conquest' is *futūḥ*, which literally means 'opening', and indeed, conquest confronted the Arabs with an overwhelming experience — the culture of the Christian and Persian civilizations. In accordance with both the right and the duty of a conqueror to emulate and to outdo in every respect the conquered, their rulers made bold to resuscitate enough from the remnants of free artistry and thought in the occupied countries to complement their own feeble secular-pagan traditions and produce a high Islamic culture of their own. Very much as had Christianity before it, the new religion tried, concomitantly with the conquest ('opening'), to bind together, to unify the life and ethics of the Muslims. This fusion of civilizations soon led not only to some amalgamation of the conquered nations, but also induced Christians, Jews, Persians, and other peoples living under Arab domination, together with neighboring nations, to

Note 17

imitate the Arab scholars and to surpass them in their artistic pursuits. Muḥammad's ascetic law, proclaimed in the Koran, disavows, besides images and likenesses of the elements of nature and deities, poetry also (Sura XXVI. 224ff.), and even any avoidable discussions with Christians and Jews. It also wished to eradicate the living national and pagan tribal tradition, which satisfied its pride in feats of knightly bravery or in the consciousness of noble descent. In this, however, it was not successful. Now the Arabs became westernized; they were linked with the Judeo-Christian world, not only by Muḥammad's adoption of Abraham as the nation's ancestor, but also because a good proportion of them were thrown physically into the Mediterranean world. As C. H. Becker observed, without the precedent of Alexander there would have been no Islamic idea of world expansion[18] and, one might add, without Solomon and the brilliant picture of him in the Koran and in Muslim legend, drawn from the Bible and Midrash, there would have been no intellectual emancipation and artistic humanism in the courts of the Islamic Middle Ages. But Islam also developed the dynamics to integrate the conquered territories into a unified civilization. Both trends, that of puritanical, rigid religious asceticism and that of liberalizing culture, contributed equally to this unification. The Arabs inherited, for instance in Egypt, the Byzantine traditions of administration. In addition, some of the old Hellenistic schools were still open in Alexandria so that, just as the previous victors over the Greeks, the Romans, had gone to school to Greece, an Arab intelligentsia could, for a whole century, study rhetoric, logic, medicine, mathematics, astronomy, and as much of metaphysics and philosophy as the Christian Byzantine authorities had kept alive there[19]. Also, indigenous Arabic poetry was now clarified and enriched by the application of Hellenistic poetics, rhetoric, and grammar. The Arabs showed themselves to be astonishingly talented absorbers and revivers. With their fresh impulses and the newcomer's naiveté and daring, they soon surpassed the other nations in developments which contrast widely with the original aims of Islam.

The Umayyads, the first Islamic rulers who wished to belong to international royalty, imitated the artistry of Byzantium by borrowing Byzantine artists, and inviting secular scholars and poets from many countries — all this against the tenets of the religion from which they derived their power. Thus Islam did not succeed in suppressing artistic leanings and, particularly under the patronage of their successors in the East, the Fāṭimids, all the liberal and fine arts developed at the centers of Islamic rule in international competition with other kings.

After three hundred years of Islamization, we can still observe in the Arab nations a vigorous struggle between religion and culture. All in

Notes 18—19

all, in particular in the holy wars, we see ascetic doctrines, which were to become more and more predominant in Islam, gaining a slow ascendancy. Yet we also find that the ancient Arabs' pagan and secular traditions of ethnic pride and warrior's chivalry, their prowess in arms, their pride in ancestry (often extolled in poetry), were by now solidly re-established, after receiving a first infusion from surviving Hellenistic and Persian, and later from provincial, traditions, and they constituted more and more that second canon of values vying in importance with the canon of religious values. As such, they were exported to the Christian world and infused the somewhat dormant courtly values there with their energy.

In an attempt to summarize the conditions which fostered the emergence of the culture of Islamic Spain, I introduce the Greek concepts of ἀνάγκη and τύχη and their interplay, under which coordinates history can be interpreted. The ἀνάγκη, the prevalence of the strongest pull in a parallelogram of forces, must in this case be seen in the vigorous conquest of the country by the united Arabs, and in addition, in the rise to power of "culture-minded" rulers, patrons of all the arts and sciences, able and determined to countermand the puritan theologians and militant fanatics who were hostile to kings and royal culture. The τύχη would be seen first in the rise of Muḥammad as a religious founder and charismatic leader, in the escape to liberty in Spain of a single Umayyad, 'Abd ar-Raḥmān I ("The Arriver"), and in his ability to establish himself — with nothing but his pedigree, his talent, and his determination to help him — as a ruler of Muslim Spain and founder of the new Western caliphate of his descendants.

The layer of ascetism imposed by Islam, being comparatively fresh and thin, yielded when a sensibility nurtured on the arid Arabian homeland encountered Iberian lushness and the hardly dreamed-of wonders of rural fertility and urban civilization there. Furthermore when, with the establishment of a new Umayyad empire, a metropolitan life of the highest splendor emerged in the capital, Cordova, this city might justly be called, even by the Christian world, by the only appropriate name — a new Rome. In the words of Hrotswitha, the nun of Gandersheim:[20]

Partibus occiduis fulsit clarum decus orbis,
Urbs Augusta nova, Martis feritate superba, . . .
Corduba famoso locuples de nomine dicta,
Inclyta deliciis, rebus quoque splendida cunctis . . .

Just as their predecessors, the Syrian Umayyads, had, in creating the splendor of Damascus, vied with Byzantium, the Spanish Umayyads built up a

Note 20

highly cultured urban population (including a Jewish intelligentsia which enjoyed great privileges) to challenge comparison with the very liberal or often, even, rather heterodox 'Abbāsid caliphs of the East[21]. The founder of the Western caliphate, 'Abd ar-Raḥmān, was, because of his adventurous escape from being slaughtered with the remainder of his house by the 'Abbāsid rulers of Baghdad and because of his reaching Spanish shores and his establishment of a new Umayyad throne, a highly romantic, though politically ruthless and cruel figure. In the spirit of Damascene romanticism, typical of an Umayyad, he compared himself in one of his poems with a palm tree, an alien in Spain, yearning for his North Arabian homeland[22]. His new line of Spanish Umayyads resumed the tradition of cultural exchanges with Byzantium, importing among other artefacts columns and a precious stone-carved basin embellished with animal figures, as well as bringing artisans able to produce similar works. Such exchanges with Byzantium and imports from other countries as well as the symbiosis of Muslims, Jews, and Christians suffice to settle the question of how Eastern and Western culture could be fused in that context. The feasibility of this could only be doubted by historians who are not well acquainted with the life of Cordova (as described, e. g., in Ibn Ḥazm's book) and who retain the delusion that Moors and Christians met exclusively on the field of battle. Such historians must also have overlooked the fact that royal weddings took place at Christian courts during which Muslim singers and dancers were invited to display their arts. Mozarabic and Mudejar culture was the result of centuries of such Christian and Muslim contacts. In the realm of the Muses there was ample contact between the various sectors of the population. Evidence for this lies in the popular *muwashshaḥ*, which consists mostly of Arabic stanzas each followed by a "belt"-line *(simṭ)* and after the final stanza by a "belt"-line of particular stress *(kharja)*[23] which sometimes employ Old Spanish, or consist of Hebrew stanzas employing an Arab *kharja*, showing that large sectors of the city population were bilingual. Persons like the Jewish Ibn Gabirol and Samuel ibn Naghrālla spoke Arabic in their daily lives just as everybody else in Moorish Spain; but Hebrew poetry, a derivative of the Arabic school, was their means of higher self-expression.

Early in the eleventh century, when the Christian *reconquista* had forced the Umayyad caliphs to take into their service more and more *soldateskas*, mercenaries of Slav or Berber extraction, some of these army chiefs broke their oath of allegiance (most likely harboring resentments from the days of 'Abd ar-Raḥmān I, who allegedly killed more than 30,000 Berbers) and turned against their Umayyad employers. Their sack of Cordova and repeated revolts led to the downfall of the dynasty and to the establishment of small *diadochi* kingdoms, resulting, with the weakening of the Arab cause, in a short-lived dissemination of metropolitan artistic refinement to and from new capitals where the model of Cordova was supreme. I am dealing exclusively with this period, the eleventh century, which may have been the climax of "this-worldliness" in the Middle Ages. Almost every aspect of life was celebrated in secular poetry. First — and there was a precedent in Baghdad — wine, though forbidden in Islam, was consumed, in particular during festivals in the vineyards and in boats on the cool rivers, and became more and more a source of joy and the theme of unabashed songs[24]. (But the same century also saw a pietistic reaction to this.) Second, one of the century's most original contributions to the mediaeval world was (to repeat) the idolization of a woman, which often reached the level of a cult of love as such. Whereas pining away in chaste love had been regarded previously in Islam as a martyrdom for the sake of heaven, ensuring an after-life in Paradise, it now, with a certain renewal of the sense of the tragic, became a secular courtly attitude, by which the community and nobility of true lovers, and the unity of all these lovers—prince and common man—was proclaimed.

The influence of Islamic scholasticism and metaphysics upon religious thought in the Christian and Jewish orbits may not have been less than upon secular developments. I cannot discuss here, however, how far the Arabs merely set an example, and how far a new type of secular Jew might have played the role of a cultural mediator, even if by merely affecting the Jewry of Christian countries. This book, if focused upon architecture and poetry, concerns itself marginally with religious and social observations. I omit the sciences and theology. Yet, before I turn to the Jews in Moorish Spain and their parallel pursuits, I insert a brief characterization of Arabic poetry and the social status of the Arabic poets.

(5) ARABIC POETRY

Arabic poetry is ruled by rigid poetics, akin to those of the Hellenistic tradition, with quantitative metrics. If its natural flow is perhaps restricted thereby, nevertheless this poetry must be termed — according to its most striking qualities — playful, almost whimsical, and ornamental, and for this reason its thematic continuity is much weaker than in typical western poetry. We very rarely observe in Arabic poetry one permeating mood and progression of thought carrying the reader towards its consummation. The individual couplets form in themselves well established units, but their integration into the structure of the poem as a whole is not a primary

Note 24

intent of the poet. The main unifying element, even in long poems, is the maintained monorhyme (strangely enough, the rhyming syllable usually begins with the same consonant). The Arabs' own metaphor for such monorhyme poetry is a string of pearls, in which the rhyme serves as the connecting thread. As an additional link there may appear within the couplets (and occasionally extending into following couplets) word plays, assonances, anaphora, and the like. It is hard for us to determine whether these *jeux d'esprit*, so precious to the poets, are to be regarded as superficial ornamentation, mere tinsel, or as underlying structural elements. Another main intent of this poetry is to flatter the listener by confirming his self-esteem as a connoisseur. To this end the poet uses his witty inventions in ever renewed twists of well-known metaphors. In other words, Arabic poetry is intellectual and conceptual, and its imagery, although not too limited, is rather stereotyped, and the art of the poet is demonstrated by his ability to move within a given territory. The poetical ideal which still reigns is that of Horace's line:[25]

Dixeris egregie notum si callida verbum
reddiderit iunctura novum

(You will have expressed yourself admirably
if a clever setting gives a spice of *novelty* to a familiar word).

We find in this line the conception of 'novel' which — in Arabic *badī'*, also 'creative', 'stylish' — signifies poetic inventiveness. Since each poet worked with the conceits of his predecessors, everybody was in some way plagiarizing, in the same way as the poets of Elizabethan times took over entire lines from Italian models, or as a rug-weaver constructs infinite variations of the same motifs. The Arabic poets had at least to introduce changes in order to avoid being accused of direct plagiarism, but even so, some of the poets complained, like the Hebrew Ibn Gabirol, of having lost their novel inventions to thieves. (His complaints become more significant when it is realized that he, even more than any of his fellow poets, prided himself above all on his unique individual and pioneer position. And yet the most moving parts of Ibn Gabirol's *The Kingdom's Crown* are a magnificent adaptation of motifs from penitential prayers by Sa'adya Gaon.) The poets engaged in a cult of the Arabic word; the pun and other forms of word play have a legitimate place. Sometimes a certain *chiaroscuro* is intended by using an ambiguous word in such a way that only the progress of the poem clarifies the intended meaning completely and delimits its range of allusion. The great compendium of such devices (be they truly

Note 25

artistic or merely devious according to our taste) is the famous *Maqāmāt* of al-Ḥarīrī (the devices in which were imitated almost to the last detail in Rückert's ingenious German translation). There exists a large bulk of critical literature dealing with Arabic poetics:[26] *The Mysteries of Eloquence* by the eleventh-century Persian al-Jurjānī and the tenth-century *I'jāz al-Qur'ān* by al-Bāqillānī, for example, are easily accessible to the reader in translation[27]. Many individual aspects of Arabic poetics will appear during the interpretations of the large number of poems offered in this book.

These observations, in general, apply as well to Hispano-Hebrew poetry, which was created by subjecting the Hebrew language to Arabic metrics, and its rules of quantity. Such transposition from one language to another involved, of course, mutations; for instance, particular meters might prove more adequate in one language than in another.

A brief anecdote might illustrate the place of the poet within eleventh-century society in which he held a semi-public, though temporary, office established by a prince or nobleman at his court.

The King of Seville allocated a house to the poets, according to al-Maqqarī, and reserved one day of the week for the poets' performance. Ibn Jākh, already famous, arrived in Seville and upon declaring himself a poet was admitted to this house. He did not, however, reveal his identity[28]. Asked by the other residents to recite one of his compositions, he did so, but with such ineptitude that he was mocked and regarded as a poetaster. When the day of the formal introduction arrived, Ibn Jākh, still unrecognized, was introduced to the prince at the head of the group of poets. To the astonishment and chagrin of his fellow poets he addressed the prince, in exquisite style, as follows:

Day of severance by distance, how you rent my heart
    and denied my eyes their comfort, the ease of sleep ...

O king, support of hope, who, by his ancient lineage,
    towers above all kings, raised aloft by his nobility.

Poetry is lowly held in our province, but here it finds
    good market and offer, far from all debasement.

"You are Ibn Jākh!" the prince exclaimed. When the poet admitted his identity, he was appointed chief poet and received the concomitant robe of honor and stipend, and no other poet was permitted to recite that day.

This story also illustrates the fact that the poets had to wander from court to court. Some even had to laud petty village nobles and were often miserably remunerated. For, as Henri Pérès points out, certain patrons soon grew tired of a poet who could not offer ever fresh topics. At a great court, however, the eminent poets were highly coveted, lavishly received, and were occasionally the objects of contention between princes. The ideal patron, on the other hand, did not regard the poet merely as a prize, but — in the Graeco-Roman tradition — as a peer, and accorded to him an almost princely position. As a result, a humanist platform was established on which political power and intellectual merits met on equal footing.

The life of the Hebrew poet and scholar Ibn Gabirol was conditioned by this social order. The scanty biographical data available to us contain evidence of his migration from at least one patron to another. Various names, some of the most outstanding of his time, appear as his, most likely occasional, patrons in his odes of praise or reproach. In a few poems a patron is addressed, but his name withheld (although in many cases the connection can be reconstructed). In a third group we discover a dedication, but instead of an addressee a word like 'the noble XY'. These could be poems kept on hand for future dedication or may be explained as withdrawn dedications. Samuel han-Nāghīdh was an exceptional case, inasmuch as his position as a statesman provided him with ample support and with the means of patronizing other poets, both Hebrew and Arab, and even academies in other countries.

Some of the models for the Arab and Hebrew poets of the eleventh century were bards who had lived in the East, like al-Mutanabbī, whose poems were political to such a degree that his Maecenates depended upon his favor for their fame, whereas in some instances his disfavor made a former patron infamous. In addition to those models already mentioned, al-Maʿarrī whose pessimism, partly motivated by his blindness, as well as his pride and independence greatly influenced Ibn Gabirol.

The Cordovan poet Ibn Jūdī, of the ninth century, fell in love with the voice of a woman whom he celebrated in poems without ever having seen her. Another troubadour of the eleventh century, Ibn Zaidūn (mentioned before) became famous for his tragic love of a princess. Abū ʿĀmir ibn Shuhaid, of the early tenth century, acclaimed vizier and epicurean at the court of the famous al-Manṣūr, sang a famous dirge to the sacked city of Cordova. Ibn ʿAmmār, a contemporary of Ibn Gabirol and Samuel han-Nāghīdh, enjoyed the love and confidence of a noble prince, the troubadour king Al-Muʿtamid, the lover of the famed Rumaikīyya, and broke his faith repeatedly in attempts to carve out for himself a Taifas kingdom as ill-gotten as the others[29]. Another younger contemporary was Ibn as-Sīd from Badajoz, poet and philosophical encyclopaedist. These examples reveal the various careers and roles open to the court poet — *mutatis multis mutandis* also to the Hebrew bard — of that day.

Note 29

C. The Jews

When given the freedom to develop, Jews have a tendency to go a step beyond their foreign models in cultural or social activities. In many cultures, however, the products of their activity can be regarded as indicators of an entelechy, which is otherwise still hidden; they are like a barometer of the cultural weather. The Jews in southern Spain, having been settlers there much longer than the Arabs, accepted the challenge of Arabic culture in a number of fields; and, in this respect similar to the Jews of the Hellenistic period, they had to compete in order to preserve their self-respect, to maintain their older prerogatives and to promote their hopes of a final spiritual predominance among the nations. On the other hand, unlike the Hellenistic Jews, who wrote in Greek, they imitated the Arabs' profound devotion to their language in reviving classical Hebrew, and the most striking proof for the 'Renaissance' character of this time, discussed before, may well be this unique linguistic revival. To parallel my brief outline of Arabic intellectual history, I insert a passage on the Hebrew constituents of Umayyad and post-caliphal Spanish civilization.

The Spanish epoch of the Jews owes its character and importance to the flourishing of a Mediterranean Arab culture. Muḥammad had established a link between Islam and Judaism rather than between Islam and Christianity: he had claimed a pedigree for Islam back to the Patriarch Abraham who was held to be the father of the Arabs' ancestor Ishmael, his firstborn, with whom he had built the Kaaba in Mecca. Moreover, in the Koran, Muḥammad appeared as the apostle of the last divine revelation, which was to supersede Old and New Testaments, the Koran being claimed to be the dispensation of the original book of which the two Testaments had merely been preliminary excerpts and copies. With such an affiliation one would have expected Islam to crave a brotherly link with its two predecessors; but the old antagonism between the two earlier groups, the prevailing black-white demarcations, and the bracketing of religion with aspirations of political power were too deeply rooted among Christians and Jews to condition Islam for ecumenical thought, so that it could become a connecting third element. Finally, as to dynamics, the missionary vigor of Islam was not sufficiently lasting and cogent to accomplish, after such a precedent, this mission (if it had felt it). Yet there existed, particularly in Spain, but also under the liberal Fāṭimid caliphs in Baghdad, under Sultan Saladin in Egypt, and elsewhere, a deep mutual understanding between Arabs and Jews, both in their daily confrontations and in intellectual intercourse and productions. The dignity of man, which has always blossomed in the Mediterranean countries, as long as tyrants or religious fanatics did not suppress it, ensured such encounters. Like the Hellenistic Jew, the Ṡephāradī is an entirely new type, created by Spanish-Arab acculturation. Though still smarting from the wounds of wanton oppression by ferociously intolerant Visigoth rulers, the Jews of Spain, who had welcomed the Arab conquerors enthusiastically and supported them actively, had recovered rapidly. While the following generations of Arabs awoke more and more – in and out of contact with the Christians — to secular endeavors in the arts and sciences, they aroused among the Jews many dormant secular and — because of the complexity of the nation's character — religious activities.

The dynamics of Jewish history, so different from those of other nations by being anchored in the non-physical, deserve fuller discussion. One may differentiate in the history of the Jewish people, with its progress *de longue haleine* through the millennia, periods of systole and diastole. To use Bergson's terms, there was a shift from periods of a *durée réelle* to periods of a teleological orientation, periods extending towards a point in future time which, by being the exclusive aim and "assignment," degraded all intermediate time to the status of a mere obstacle.

To change the metaphor, from its well-springs in Babylonia and Egypt, Jewish history proceeds like a river, developing from time to time into, as it were, a lake. This happens for the first time during the conquest of Canaan when the river expands, when there is added to the longitudinal dimension the other dimension of expansion over the homeland-to-be. With the Babylonian Exile, the nation (having lost its state), again contracted between narrow banks and was able, so to speak, to recede into that first coordinate, time, and lived on merely by prophetic promises and hopes of a new period of settlement. The post-exilic period could be symbolized by a second transformation of river into lake. After such a resurgence, the Jews did not see in their second exile by the Romans a termination of their national and/or religious mission; they had the vision and strength to accept this renewed exile rather as a return from normal national existence to the previous riverbed of time. There was even a precedent for this. The community of the Dead Sea had returned previously and voluntarily to the wilderness, to initiate theurgically a renewal of the primordial periods of the exodus and wilderness (romanticized by Hosea and Deuteronomy as a period of blissful holy matrimony or a father-child relationship between God and Israel) and to "pave the way in the desert" for a new ideal Davidic and Levitic state. This, more than anything, demonstrates the certitude of the Jewish conception of recurring redemption.

The spiritual expansion of Judaism and the absorption of foreign ideas in its home country and diaspora during its Hellenistic period follow different patterns. Judaism could compromise with Aryan lore, adopting its dualism (in conceptions like "children of light" and "children of darkness") or its re-incarnationism (appearing for instance in Matthew XVI. 12ff.). As long as they could strengthen Jewish ethical and ascetic ideals these Aryan notions were welcomed as an ally against pagan this-worldliness, against supranational amalgamation and the integration of the nation into the new syncretistic *ecumene*. The statement that three nations — Romans, Jews, and Japanese — were the most ingenious absorbers is corroborated for the Jews by their Hellenistic (and Moorish) periods. The ability to absorb is, of course, a demonstration of strength. Thus, on the one hand, Judaism at this time showed the greatest elasticity in cult and culture, and although Jewish historians, in particular those of religious history, are loath to admit this, Judaism — and not only its Christian development — had been transformed by contact with the world of the Greeks and other highly literate nations to a point beyond return and recognition, and the Jews themselves underwent a consummate acculturation by Hellenistic thought and rites. The very spirit of the Septuagint translation and the allegoric and apologetic writings of Philo demonstrate that Judaism at the time came close to a Hellenistic mystery cult, so that there is little continuity between a Saul and a Philo, not even between a Solomon and the Essenes of Qumran. On the other hand, this continuity can be seen, most strikingly, in the overriding w i l l to continuity. Submitting to acculturation, the Hellenistic Jews, in this respect differing from the later Jews of Muslim Spain, did try (as was re-emphasized recently by Goodenough)[30] to win the Greeks over to their ideas and thereby to transform their neighbor's thought (from which effort Christianity benefited). And indeed, when the Jews of the Hellenistic period yielded to the appeal of the Greek Muses of poetry, philosophy, and other disciplines, they created works in Greek, fashioned to interpret their own heritage.

As to the results, Hellenistic Judaism did not survive the second Christian century[31]. What remained for instance of the destroyed Jewish communities in Egypt was ideologically re-absorbed in the ideas of normative Judaism. Yet it can be said that the Jewish spirit, which thenceforth retained a considerable Hellenistic admixture, had also subjugated decadent Hellenism. It was Roman Christianity with its forces of con-

Notes 30—31

centration, order, and sacramental persuasiveness that accomplished this victory.

The Spanish period, to resume our metaphor, was only a small widening of the river-bed, but the dynamics of the historical development are demonstrated by it. By this untimely damming-up, imperiling its rectilinear flow towards feebly-banked downstream river-beds, the enlarged shores of an incomparably fertile foreign province were indeed watered for a while. Yet the mediaeval Jew did not lose, even in Spain, his awareness of being a part of the prolonged development which I have termed a "river" or, in another image, a "chain." Each link in this chain, even if it was a period of utter suffering, was fervently clutched and held as the divine pledge, safeguarding progress towards the messianic end. Moreover, their *heilsgeschichte* was the axis of world history. This was the guiding idea for all decisions and all activities. Now among the Arabs, who became members of the family of Mediterranean peoples, the Jews, culturally so much older members of this community than these new neighbors, could become the guides in many secular, and, of course, in some theological fields. There arose for the Jews, with the relative freedom given to them to live up to their aspirations, which were in many ways more parallel than opposed to Islam, no immediate danger of being absorbed *in toto*. By now the line of demarcation was clear — here Muḥammad and there Moses, as the two national leaders of monotheistic nations against the pagan environment of their time. Nevertheless, Jewish groups and a number of outstanding individuals, admitted to the Arab cultural forum, were converted to Islam. (This happened at least with much less coercion than Jewish conversions to Christianity at a later time.)

(1) ACCULTURATION AND CONTEST

A famous writer once differentiated between the daily insignificant transactions and understandings among the burghers and "those symbolic higher misunderstandings" and exalted clashes beyond compromise "for which the Greeks reserved the tragic stage." The interest of the intellectual historian lies less in the episodic encounters between the two nations, since these could never bring them permanently together, than in the contacts between men of creative genius. By these contacts something of the Arab achievement in secular and, especially, artistic pursuits engenders in certain choice spirits among the Jews a counterpart which must be regarded as abnormal, or even heretical, according to mediaeval Jewish standards. Heresies, however, often illustrate *e contrario*, better than normative doctrines, the true nature of a religion. I shall deal first (as in the bulk of this book) with individual secular activities, and then with the collective aspects and the religious justification of Jewish secularism in Moorish Spain.

One might think that, proceeding from dark shade into the dazzling cultural light of the Arabs, the Jews of this period must have at least been confused in their feelings. Living by the doctrine of an interim period of exile as a preparation for the *eschaton* to come, when their nation would initiate the redemption of the world, they refrained from active participation in the making of history and this-worldly expansion like a seed or bulb in the desert waiting for the spring rain; or — if I may use New Testament imagery to explain the passionate yearning of the nation — they wished to preserve in chastity the oil for the lamp to illuminate the bridal night. And now they awoke to a cousin's wedding feast where their own lamp, if lit, though adding some brightness, could not be a prime source of light, at least for a while. As citizens of the Mediterranean world they could not repudiate an invitation to the new beauty and ennoblement of life in secular culture after so radical a change of environment and after so miraculous a retribution had been meted out to their previous oppressors. Only a barbarian or a person grown too bitter and obtuse by past tribulation would not have responded to a new neighbor's friendliness, thereby violating the golden rule or the admonitions of Jeremiah to the Babylonian Jews (Jer. XXIX. 26ff.).

The responsible leaders must have seen the danger loom that larger segments of Spanish Jewry might surrender to the Moors' happy worldliness, if they did not lend their imagination to producing a collective Jewish counterpart to the general musicality (that danger which caused Shakespeare's Shylock, "the man without music," to lose his daughter, Jessica, to the enticements of the Venetian festival of life). In particular, an aristocratic sector of the metropolitan Jewries would have drifted away, had their leaders not fostered and directed the growth of an autonomous Jewish culture. The self-respect and ancient prerogatives of the Hebrews were at stake when the upstart cousin seemed about to place the older nation in a position of doom-laden stagnation. In the longer view, however, the gain in self-respect which accompanied cultural competition might not have outweighed the loss of unequivocal religious determination to outlive the exile, the loss of that general Jewish resistance based upon self-denial.

A perceptive Jewish avantgarde has always been sensitive, as a barometer registers any fluctuations of atmosphere and predicts good and bad weather, to forthcoming neighborliness and opportunities for fruitful participation in their environment. Jewish orthodoxy very often functioned, so to speak, as a blocking mechanism. It would first register even delicate secular contacts with a warning signal of the danger of absorption, and would then automatically switch off these contacts and tighten the isolating capsule. In so doing, orthodoxy deserves both justification and reproach: justification because the mediaeval Jews whose exilic slumber was light (if their yearning pernoctation can be thus termed) had to deafen their ears in various instances to the enticing tidings of a false dawn. All participation in secular culture entailed a debilitating loss of the dammed-up energies required for the realization of the one aim of the nation: to survive in order to fulfil its final mission. But it also deserves reproach, because, once the nation had thus withdrawn into a brittle capsule, it would be in danger of missing the *kairos* and even of demobilizing its active forces for fending off, in time, attacks upon its physical and intellectual existence.

Now, under Islam, a Jewish intelligentsia (which also regarded itself as orthodox) observed the national barometer pointing to "very fair weather." Its members were attracted, to the same degree as their ancestors were to Hellenism, by the new Arab culture which was in many ways its heir. It was, however, less their aim to win their Arab neighbors into their fold by their cultural contributions than it had been the aim of the Hellenistic Jews. They were bent more upon a healthy competition as a means, in itself, of national self-satisfaction and Hebrew-centered self-expression — which cannot arbitrarily be termed assimilation[32].

One might think that the Persians, who were humiliated similarly in their national pride by being subdued not only culturally, but also religiously by the upstart Arabs, and who obstructed with their Shīʿite sectarianism Islam's effort to mould a monolithic empire, may very well have been the precedent and model for the Jews' emancipation of their national spirit in producing intellectual and artistic counterparts.

The most cultured group among the Jews, although they were not forced like the Persians to embrace Islam, became equally emancipated from certain old and new restraints as they were captivated and absorbed by Arab culture and had to "react creatively"[33] (very much as the Persians), to reaffirm the purpose and dignity of a nation which had existed for so long, and to avoid becoming driftwood on the river of time. In this way these Jews paradoxically and heterodoxically revived the Hebrew language, hitherto reserved for divine services and theological writings, in order to give voice to secular poetry of nature and love, *encomia*, and drinking songs in Arabic meters. To repeat: much like the Persians, the Jews had to face a dire challenge to their national pride and a threat to their prerogatives. If they wished to prevent the cultural vacuum on their side from being filled by Arab abundance, they had to dedicate themselves similarly to the arts and sciences, and in order to maintain their national identity, they had to recognize, with the aid of the highly polished mirror of Hispano-Arab civilization, their own characteristics and make themselves look — even in the becoming contemporary guise — dignified and more than fashionable. But, as a result, members of a first generation of full-fledged acculturation in Cordova felt, as I shall show, deep compunction. Another generation of Jews had to justify actively their straying from the sacred norm on messianic grounds in order to integrate this self-redemption with past and future hopes and tasks. No plausible rationale for such an enforced Jewish secularism and self-redemption had ever been voiced. The offer of participation in a new cultural life had to be interpreted, like everything else in Jewish history, as a revelation of the divine will, and with this alternative we are in the religious sphere and on a tragic level. The enlightened of this first generation knew in their innermost conscience that such a time had not legitimately come. A subsequent generation, like that of Samuel han-Nāghīdh, may have been more diverted from such qualms by being born into a tradition of emancipation and carried away by dazzling successes; and a third generation, that of Ibn Gabirol, even further secularized and to the same degree individualized, also initiated or symbolized late in their lives a return to the religious norm. One might parallel these generations with those of the Florentine Renaissance: a first renewing the beauties of Ciceronian Latin and repenting of such vanities towards the end of their lives; a second enchanted by the visual splendor of Donatello's art; and a third, that of Michelangelo, returning late to mysticism and ascetism[34]. The violent death of Yehōseph han-Nāghīdh might have had an effect upon the Jewish developments similar to that of the preaching of Savonarola and the upheaval which surrounded his life and death upon Florence.

To illustrate the compunction felt by a spokesman of the first acculturated generation of Cordovan Jews, I present a precious document stemming from the poet Dūnāsh ibn Labrāṭ. It shows how in the general festival of life the intellectual Jew of high spirituality could not feel unalloyed happiness; he had to feel consciously or semi-consciously guilty for crossing the barrier of the sacred prohibitions.

In a muwashshaḥa (a poem of rhymed stanzas with "belt" lines rhyming with each other), the poet rejects the invitation of a (most likely fictitious) friend to a drinking festival. With its turn from the singular in the initial address by this friend to the final protestation in the poet's reply — the poet, who acts as a judge interfering in a discussion, will occur again in Ibn Gabirol's Alhambra poem — with its collective "we," standing for the whole nation, the poem reads (in an abbreviated form):

Note 34

Frivolous Feasting — a muwashshaḥa

Dūnāsh ibn Labrāṭ: *We-ōmer al tīyshan* — *Bialik-R.*, I, p. 149 (erroneously attributed to Ibn Gabirol)

◡ - - - - - *(Muḍāriʿ)* — Schirmann, *Shīrāh* I, p. 34f.

Simṭ ("belt" line) rhyme: *-līm*

Rhyme Scheme b b b a
c c c a
d d d a etc.

WHEN ONE SPEAKS: "do not sleep,
Drink old wine —
There is camphor blossom and roses
Cant. IV. 14 — And myrrh and aloes ...

Let us drink in the bowers
Fenced about with roses
Let us put to flight sorrows
With songs of joy —

II Kings XX. 13 — We anoint us with goodly oil,
We fumigate with moist wood;
Is. XXVIII. 2 — Before doom's day comes upon us
Let us enjoy fullness,"

THEN I REBUKE HIM: "hush, hush!
That far — how can you go,
While the Holy House, the Footstool
Of God, belongs to the heathen?

In foolishness you spoke
And sluggishness you chose,
In vanity you spoke
Like fool and froward.

You left meditation on
The Law of God, the Highest.
You rejoice while in Zion
The jackals roam.

How may we drink wine?
May we raise our eye?
We, to nothing reduced —
Rejected and abhorred!"

The puzzling question must have been: if freedom for rejuvenation and power for action were granted, what did God will the Jews to do, now and ultimately? Could this be a snare or a delusion, an illicit maturation of the promised fruit, an undue anticipation and indulgence? A sacrifice to an idol, likely to jeopardize the one final salvation? Or was it a divine foreboding of the ripening fruit of the *eschaton?* I will ask again whether the eclipse of the Jewish hopes in Granada, of which more later, justifies the orthodox in their insistence upon passive perseverance. Or does any beautiful attempt, even if it is doomed to an early failure, justify such a sacrifice, for the mere fact that what once existed, even if it bloomed prematurely, proves at least an ever-latent potential to eyes which may have begun to doubt? Do not the glories of fulfillment, even if tragically illtimed, illustrate a potential and create new horizons by their example[34a]? But this, indeed, touches upon the final question of the messianic expectation, and more specifically upon the Jewish mission in time and eternity.

The Jews participated in the philosophical discussions of the times to which the Persians had contributed so much, and although Persia was distant from Spain, Persian refinement may very well have inspired the Jews in particular, who by their expectations from the future had to be *novarum rerum cupidissimi.* Jews, like Persians, became astronomers, mathematicians, chemists, and physicians in studying Galen and Hippocrates and composed Arabic books, shaped in the terminology of their canons.

With all their intellectualism and spirituality the Jews had to bear the pressure lying upon the minorities, which (as the Muslims said without qualm) mellowed them, but which also overshadowed their *naiveté* and joy of life, attributing in particular to the exiled of dispersed Israel that *judenschmerz,* that minor key of their souls. Moreover, the pressure of the religious warfare between Muslims and Christians and, following the downfall of the caliphate, the vicissitudes of the successor kingdoms weighed upon all of Spain and soon there set in an ascetic reaction which strove to replace the free arts and sciences — if at all — by scholastic doctrine.

It may be appropriate to remark that even if metropolitan Jewries could bask for a while in the splendor of the great courts and live in considerable affluence, the social situation of the Jews as a whole was not too favorable,

Note 34a

but the participation of the Jews in secular cultural activities must have been substantial, when compared with that of other groups.

(2) HEBREW ACTIVISM

Politics and administration became another secular activity of the Jews as another aspect of their fresh engagement in history. The first outstanding figure remained Ḥaṡdāy ibn Shaprūṭ. Arab historians report two specific masterpieces of his *savoir faire*, also praised by the Hebrew poet Dūnāsh ibn Labrāṭ. The young and sickly King Sancho of Leon was dethroned by a vassal, a Christian like himself, whereupon he turned for help, together with his grandmother, Queen Tota of Navarra, to his previous foe, ʿAbd ar-Raḥmān III. Ḥaṡdāy ibn Shaprūṭ, the Jewish physician and also an important statesman at the Umayyad court, acted as the caliph's emissary and brought the two, Sancho and Tota, to Cordova where they were subjected to a dramatic but not unfriendly ceremony of surrender to vassalage after the Byzantine style. Moreover, in exchange for the cession of fortresses, Sancho was reinstated, the usurper punished and, grace upon grace, he himself, after treatment by Ḥaṡdāy, was returned to his throne in a condition more fit for rule than ever before[35]. In the case of John of Goricia, an emissary of Otto the Great, who seems to have craved the death of a missionary martyr, Ḥaṡdāy, who again represented the caliph, was able with the greatest tact and diplomacy to reach a level of *realpolitik*. The one, man of the world, and the other, a mind of a heavenly orientation, represent the chasm between the secular spirit of Cordova and the ecclesiarchic Ottonian empire. Ḥaṡdāy ibn Shaprūṭ had found, at the Umayyad court, the freedom to develop into the prototype of the Jewish individualist and man of action, to such an extent that he had invited comparison among the Jews with the great figures of their past.

The conversion to Judaism of the Khazar empire or czardom in Southern Russia in the eighth century had aroused great hopes among the Jews. Now when the tenth-century Ḥaṡdāy ibn Shaprūṭ conceived of the possibility of an alliance against Byzantium between the Cordovan caliphate and the Khazar empire[36], this opened political vistas in which, no doubt, Ḥaṡdāy intended to play an active role. The details are obscure, but it can at least be said that the Jews of Cordova celebrated a Khazar victory over Byzantium as the first-fruits of such a policy.

These successes, then, pointed to more than ephemeral possibilities and must have aroused high-flown hopes. Moreover, because of the nature of mediaeval Judaism, eschatological overtones vibrated in the manifestoes and encomia of the Jewish poets. It may be dangerous to overrate such orientation on the part of an ambitious *realpolitiker* such as Ḥaśdāy. Yet the praise for these men is so hyperbolic that the borderline between secular encomium and messianic proclamation is quite often blurred, as it is in some biblical psalms which flatter a ruler, like Psalm CX, which so manifestly gave rise to Jewish messianic ideas. If these activists had a conception of a collaboration of heaven and earth, they proffered a vigorous initiative on the part of man.

A Hebrew encomium of the victory of the Khazars over Byzantium, commissioned by Ḥaśdāy and composed by Menahem ibn Śārūq, is a representative document of the re-awakened Jewish international diplomacy. This poem, by the way, does not follow the Arab metrical and distich scheme, but has the monorhyme. It adheres to biblical parallelism, and is, with its choice of contrived and rare words, rather bombastic but in parts also truly majestic[37].

Menahem ibn Śārūq: *Letter of fraternal congratulation of Ḥaśdāy ibn Shaprūṭ and the Jewry of Cordova on the occasion of the Khazars' victory over Byzantium addressed to the Jewish King Joseph of the Khazars between 956 and 961*[38].

Aphuddath nezer Schirmann: *Shīrāh*, I, 6

Free rhythm. Rhyme: *-'āh*

A crowning fillet for the Tribe of Rulers, the remote Kingdom! Ex. XXVIII. 8; (Ju. XVII. 5; Mi. IV. 7); Is. XIV. 5
God's grace upon it and peace upon all its governors and its vast army! Ju. V. 9
Salvation, as a raiment, upon its Shrine and Chamber and Convocation! Is LIX. 17; IV. 5 Lev. XXIII. 4
The forces of its host and the shields of its knights — may they be strengthened by the Hand Mysterious!
The horses of its chariots and its charioteers — may they never turn back with faltering spirit! Prvbs. XV. 13
The banners of its Paladins and the crossbows of its fighters — may they be arrayed in glory of glories! Ex. XV. 1 (Ps. LXX. 13)
May the arrows of its archers arrive and its flashing spears with crushing weight! Josh. XV. 13; Is. XXX. 27
May they split the heart of the enemies of my lord, the king, to multiply havoc!
May the prows of the chariots harbor strength, vehemence and terror! Job XLI. 14
May its charioteers be redeemed to return in safety from dreaded earth!
Thus my soul bursts forth: happy is the eye that sees
The king march out on a day of battle, like the sun radiant and wonderful!

Notes 37-38

Nah. II. 5; Deut. XXXII. 30; Ju. XX. 10 — His soldiers dart like lightning flashes; two match a myriad and one a hundred!

Amos II. 13 — Their foes are pressed as a full cart pressed down.

I Sam. II. 8; Is. LXVI. 8 — Perceive then, Pillars of the Earth! Who has heard or seen the like:

Ezek. XXIX. 15; Judges V. 13; Amos VI. 8 — The subduing of the Mighty by a Remnant? They flee and surrender city and folk!

Is. XXII. 2; Job XXXVI. 29; Ps. LXXXVIII. 5; CXVIII. 21 — The strength of the Arm of the Most High is their energy, nay their salvation manifest in uproar!

Ps. CIX. 20 — These are the wages of the ALMIGHTY-Shadday and a portion of His retribution for the sinful kingdom,

I Ki. XI. 36 Is. XLVI. 3 — To increase the glory and majesty of the Lamp of the Nation, exalted from the womb!

Ps. LXXVII. 12 — I shall proclaim the portents of old, and the great outrage and venom I had to swallow;

(Ps. XXXVI. 9); Zeph. I. 12 — When [the Nation of Israel] couched upon her paradise [pastures] and settled upon her lees

Cant. V. 10 — Only she was celebrated — and now she is scattered to all winds and regions;

Cant. I. 6; Ps. CXXI. 6 — The sun has tanned her and even smitten her: she has found no rest;
She was not ransomed and the time of freedom failed to come;

Ex. XXI. 6 — She was pierced as with the earmark [of slavery] and to liberty never went forth;

Is. LI. 21; Nah. I. 10; I Sam. I. 15 — Thus she remained afflicted and heavy-headed but not inebriated from drink.
Those ravaging her caught her and from the Sacred Sanctuary she was ousted.
The times dragged on and the days lasted long and no sign was seen;
Vision and prophet were sealed up; no spirit penetrated nor any apparition;

I Sam. III. 1; Dan. IX. 24 — The visions of [Daniel,] the Greatly Beloved are not uncovered nor any prophecy left.

Ps. XXII. 20; (XLIV. 21) — Yet, from God is my fortitude: I spread out my palms with thirsty soul [praying],

Job XXX. 3 — That He may gather from waste land those dispersed to the extremities and dispelled to peripheries.

Zeph. III. 18 — Those sorrowful for the Solemn Assembly will then profess to God: Behold the time we had hoped for has come!

Lev. XVIII. 28 — The Tabernacle of David, the town of the Mighty King, will spew them out as it has spewed out before!

Is. XXXVIII. 4 — The eyes of the remnant left will see the loftiness of the Citadel;
And the kingdom of Jesse's Son prophesied through the mystery of vision:

Mi. IV. 13 — "I shall make thine horn iron," from that day on for evermore.

It may be difficult to decide for what reasons the language of this letter-poem is so highly 'coded'. Some aspects of its indirectness belong of course to its inner form; the acrostic is a usage mainly reserved for religious poetry (the acrostic which pervades the entire poem reads: "*Anī Ḥasdāy bar Yiṣḥāq bar Ezra bar Shaprūṭ Menaḥem ben Śārūq*": 'I am Ḥasdāy' etc.; the repeated *bar* may stand for *ben rabbi* and not for the Aramaic *bar* meaning 'son'). The veiled nature of the language could be explained by the fact that this letter was addressed to an almost unknown receiver, for reports about the Khazars had been scanty and contradictory. Furthermore, there was the danger of an interception of this letter, so that for political reasons no direct mention is made of kings, Byzantium, Cordova, and detailed political proposals.

Against the background of the sad status of the Jewish nation bright hopes in further military victories of the Khazars and a final redemption of the nation are clearly voiced. Ḥasdāy's other messages contain a description of his personal power at the caliphal court and pleas addressed to Byzantium for better treatment of the Jews.

(3) HEBREW HUMANISM, LIBERALISM, AND HERESY

For the first time in the Middle Ages Jewish leaders emancipated themselves from social and religio-intellectual shackles, loosening many rabbinic restrictions. Samuel ibn Naghrālla's ambition of establishing in Granada a Jewish kingdom of wisdom, beauty, and power surpassed everything the Italian Renaissance suggested to the Jews and anticipated much later developments.

A Samuel han-Nāghīdh is, of course, forced to break the Jewish sabbath and dietary laws while engaged in warfare, but when he stresses in a poetical doxology—which is the end of a thanksgiving poem for being rescued from an encounter with a white whale—that there is nothing heterodox in him, he fails to convince us entirely, for we hear the sound of a *qui s'excuse s'accuse*. But Samuel is subjectively an orthodox Jew and, as a very competent Talmudist and qualified by the power and position of the nāghīdh, the leader of the Jews recognized by the Muslim authorities, he is and remains an eminent law-giver.

As for the rabbis of his environment, there is a shocking document demonstrating the grim contempt which Samuel feels toward those unable to combine beauty and orthodoxy. I quote from this invective, which I entitle "Graceless Performance," against a rabbi who was not a Reform rabbi:[39]

Note 39

... Here was the rabbi, and the students wagging
their heads like one 'destitute in the desert';

In their talk they reviled Hillel and Shammay
and smote Rabbi Akiba upon the cheek,

While the rabbi indulged in long-winded notes
and snatched jot and tittle from their tongues.

I sat down, my face anguished by
what I saw, and my soul was sad in me.

I saluted the rabbi with a polite "How fare ye?"
but he answered like a man of strife and hostility.

Then he began to chant the Hundred Blessings
with a voice as raucous as that of mobs and throngs;

But when he blessed God for having created him a man
and not a woman, then I plied him with a reply:

"Do you put yourself among the males?
God wot, you belong to the feeble gender."

Samuel used his position magnificently for the reform and renewal of Jewish community legislation with an authority which, regrettably, only a very few Jews after him were able to exert. The healthy Arabic mundaneness and possibly a specifically *ẓāhirī* world view of Cordova under the last Umayyads had initiated such an emancipation and secular orientation. The biblical heroes are no longer the devitalized and demythologized stereotypes of the Halakhic canons of behavior, current in both learned rabbinical academies and the higher and lower lay schools with their *Bible moralisée*, but are resurrected as romantic figures whose stories can be felt to be re-enacted in the lives of the poets. Ibn Gabirol, his younger contemporary, for example, sees himself in one instance as Isaac, the victim bound upon the altar, and in another as Jacob, limping at Peniel. The life of this period was so rich that it could be felt to mirror itself in the glorious biblical past or that it seemed reborn. We find in Samuel's poems lines like these (addressed to God):[40]

Do you not fulfill each year such deeds the like of which
You fulfilled for the fathers and for the glorious rulers?!

Note 40

The general enlightenment and spread of culture attributed a unique importance to the individual. Samuel likened himself or was likened to the biblical Samuel, to David, or King Solomon; the two poets mentioned sometimes felt that their relationship re-enacted that of Elisha to Elijah, of Isaac to Abraham, of David to Saul.

The exilic Jew had built such a barrier between himself and the great biblical personalities — even their foibles and virtues had received a theological superstructure — that a re-enactment of their deeds and words in such contexts may well have actually and literally appeared to such a man as a parallel to the heresy of the Karaites, who renounced the rabbinical writings and acknowledged only the Bible and for whom the rabbinic use of the biblical word was a rape. But the fact is that Samuel han-Nāghīdh and Ibn Gabirol did what they did in the midst of the orthodox camp. The two men not only lacked any leanings towards the Karaites, but Samuel persecuted them cruelly. Also Samuel and the Granadine Talmudic school of Lucena under Samuel's jurisdiction did outstanding Talmudic work. Ibn Gabirol who, no doubt, had an excellent Talmudic training (his poetry contains innumerable allusions to the Talmud) belongs to the same camp, but he emancipated himself gradually from the Talmudic spirit, as can also be observed in his poetry and in his philosophical works. It may be partially correct to excuse Ibn Gabirol and Samuel for their cultivation of this literal attitude to biblical figures by remarking that this took place merely or mainly in their most private sphere of communication. This would nevertheless be far from the whole truth. In the first place Ibn Gabirol's poems circulated in countries as distant as Egypt and Iraq (as he says in those poems) and Samuel's victory poems were destined for the Jewish leaders all over the world. Moreover, their position in the Jewish community was such that even their unofficial actions must have had an official character.

In contrast to the Jews, the Muslims, with their imaginative relation to stories, including those in the Koran, maintained a rather undogmatic and creative rapport with the Koranic figures. The difference between the Jewish and the Arab spirit can be illustrated by the freedom exercised by the Arab poets in composing their many versions of the romantic Joseph story. This would have been impossible for a Jew. Nor would the Jew have felt himself licensed to employ such daring formulae as "If I had been Adam ..." which the Arab poet uses without a qualm. (This particular example occurs in my section on the Berbers.)

Ibn Gabirol, as I think, mainly in his twenties and mainly in Granada, developed occasionally a light-heartedness which we cannot expect to find in Samuel, the vizier to a Berber ruler. His famous "Water-Song" shows this levity with regard to the divine miracles in Egypt (which he mentions simply as the deeds of Moses). In the poem he mocks a host named Moses whose supply of wine ran out before the feast was over, most likely for the above mentioned lightheartedness. The name of that Moses, the biblical leader who struck water from the rock, appears here as the name of an apostle of prohibition. Its use has, possibly, an added force in that, literally translated, the name means 'one drawing (from water)' rather than, as it is rendered in Exodus II. 10, 'I drew him from the water'. (This song has regained quite a popularity at Israeli banquets.)

Moses, the Water-Host

Ki-khlōth yeyn-ī — *Bialik-R.*, I, p. 156
---- ---- *(Pāshūṭ)* — *Barukh, Mibhḥar*, I, p. 30
(Two groups of four long syllables) — *Kaempf*, p. 183f.
Geiger, p. 84
Millás, p. 36f.

Rhyme: aaa, bbb, etc. and refrain *(mayim)*

As the wine runs out, let my eye flow forth
Ps. I. 3 runnels of water, runnels of water.

The "seventy" [wine] are the heroes,
the ruling "ninety" [water] annihilated them,
the songs are silenced, for the mouth of the singers
is full of water, full of water.

Bread, how could it be tasty to the eater,
or how could food please the palate
when to the people in cups
they offer water, offer water?

Ex. XIV. 21 The son of Amram dried up the Red Sea
Ex. VIII. 10 and caused the rivers of Egypt to stink.
Ex. XVII. 6 Alas, following him, this second Moses
pours water, pours water.

Behold, I became the frog's companion,
I croak with him and cry for help
since, like him, my mouth knows
a song of water, a song of water.

May he become a Nazir before his death,
may his lot be like that of Rechabites, Jer. XXXV. 6
may his sons and sons of sons be Josh. IX. 21
drawers of water, drawers of water.

'The seventy' in the first stanza is the "cabbalistic" numerical value of the Hebrew letters of 'wine', 'the ninety' that for 'water'; these arcana appear here and hereafter so widely divulged that they became, as we see, goliardic slang words.

These documents must never induce us to forget that Samuel and Ibn Gabirol were people who bore the entire responsibility for their nation, the one before men and God, the other before God and men of letters and devotion. Samuel's theopolitics are astounding: it was he, as mentioned above, who actively planned a transfer of the power previously exerted by Exilarch and Gaon of the eastern academies to Spain by setting up a Talmudic academy in Granada and by the marriage of his son Yehōseph to the daughter of the principal disciple of the great Gaon of Pumbeditha. After Samuel had ascended to the vizierate of Granada and led the Granadine armies to a victorious battle against the prince of Almeria, he began to send out poetical manifestoes. Swelled by an individualist's feeling of having re-wrought biblical events, he invites the Jewries of other countries to celebrate his victory as a new annual national festival:[41]

... establish a second Purim for God who rose
and lopped Amalek, flower and bough.

Make it heard in Africa and Egypt
and make it known to the sons of the chosen Sanctuary,

Let it be announced to the Elders of Pumbeditha
and to the peers, the sons of Bey Rab in Sura,

And call its name "a sister to the event
of Ahasuerus and Esther, the Princess!"

And write it up in your books, that it be
for ever, from generation to generation, a memorial!

Note 41

The same Samuel han-Nāghīdh speaks of a childhood vision in which divine protection was promised to him against all vicissitudes[42]. In one case he calls himself the "David of his generation[43]."

Spain seemed to restore to both the Hebrew nation and the individual the dignity of a new and decisive confrontation with God. Though Ibn Gabirol had belonged to a camp opposed to Samuel, only in Granada could he find the freedom needed for his very free and universal philosophical opinions[44]. It is most likely that he composed his *Fons Vitae* in Granada — this book which is no less unmediaeval than Ibn Ḥazm's book on love, for it does not contain a single reference to the Bible. Ibn Gabirol's so-called "Poem of Apology", (or better "of Reconciliation") to Samuel han-Nāghīdh is, under closer scrutiny, not an apology at all but a document of Spanish pride. I quote a few lines from this poem of very conditional surrender which may well have preceded the eventful wedding of Samuel's son Yehōseph:[45]

Arise, o Time, deck thee with thy charms
and don thy sun headgear adorned with moons.

An introductory line which, if translated into Latin with "Surge, Fortuna, et indue delicata tua" (using Steinschneider's version), sounds shockingly pagan. Within such associations one is tempted to compare Ibn Gabirol's relationship to Samuel with that of Catullus to Julius Caesar in his *Nil nimium studeo, Caesar, tibi velle placere Catullus! (Carmen XLIII)*[45a]. Samuel remained in Ibn Gabirol's eyes, for a long time, the upstart and he received a full blast of the youth's vilifying talent in poems which must have entailed the danger of widely spread ridicule. Thus it was upon Samuel to woo him and salary him for aulic services at his court. While in full vizier's power he had to put up, most likely in an aulic performance, with the lines of Ibn Gabirol's Poem of Reconciliation (dist. 17ff.):

Is. XIII. 4; against I Sam. VII. 10; II Ki. XVII. 9
You thunder with a tumultuous noise which you rose up
unfairly as the trampling boots of your troopers.

Is. IX. 4f.; ISam. III. 11; Ps. LXXIV. 23
Do not think my ears rang on that day
Is. XXXVII. 29; II Ki. XIX. 28
when you raised your presumption against them.

I Chron. XIX. 6
If my soul wished to reel like an earthquake
Job XIV. 19
then my waters would corrode your stones...

Notes 42—45a

Nevertheless Ibn Gabirol praises Samuel in this poem as the great Levitic singer of his day and, making Samuel's cause the cause of Spanish Jewry, nay of all Spain, he proclaims that the messianic rose or lily (from Solomon's Song) now sprout on Spanish soil (dist. 51-54):

> ... With you the horn of Spain rises, from the day
> that you hast been until thine old age!
>
> With you Spain opens her mouth wide over the children of Shinar ⟨Babel⟩
> who draw from thy well-springs.
>
> Why dost thou gloat, Babel, and why dost thou boast
> over Shinar with the strongholds of thy majesties ⟨Geonim⟩?
>
> Know, in our country is a rose, the like is
> not found on the lees of thy Sharons [meadows]

The renaissance of the Hebrew language in scholarship and poetry had thus filled Spanish Jewry with a sense of superiority to the Jews of Babylonia with their old academies and exilarchs whose power was only now beginning to wane.

Ibn Gabirol who had no position of secular power was, under the protection of Samuel, even more emancipated than his master. Besides being a devout synagogue poet, he is, in his secular Hebrew poetry, an eminent representative of contemporary Arab trends. He is greatly influenced by the pessimistic and in some ways gnostic Abū 'l-ʿAlā' al-Maʿarrī. Blending various heresies, he advocates childlessness as an ideal, which reminds us of Abū 'l-ʿAlāʿ al-Maʿarrī's lines (in R. A. Nicholson's translation):[46]

> I see but a single part of sweet in the many parts sour
> and wisdom that cries: beget no children, if thou art wise.

Ibn Gabirol's denunciation of the world and of offspring is steeped in fear of hell-fire to such a degree that it may be regarded as an Islamic poem in the Hebrew language:

Im te'ehabh	*Bialik-R.*, I, p. 145
- - ᴗ - - - ᴗ - - ᴗ - *(Sarīʿ)*	Schirmann, *Shīrāh*, I, p. 234
	Schirmann, *Nibhḥ.*, p. 75
	Baron, *History*, VII, p. 158
	Rhyme: *-ledh*

Note 46

If you desire to live on with men of eternity,
Nah. II. 4 if your soul trembles before the Underworld's flame,

Make light of the world's values, and let beguile you
neither riches, nor honor, nor even offspring.

Find poverty precious and debasement,
I Chr. II. 30 and die as Seled did, without child.

Mind your soul well, for it alone
Job XIX. 26; XVI. 15) outlives both flesh and skin.

That such a heresy, eschewing offspring, paired with a praise of poverty and self-imposed debasement and complete contempt for the world, is found in the person of this poet of courtly love is astonishing and deserves further consideration. Arabic ʿUdhrī love poetry has, as far as I know, never been branded as a heresy, since it is based upon a *ḥadīth* in which the pure lover who dies of unfulfilled love is promised Paradise. But Ibn Gabirol is no Muslim nor an ʿUdhrī lover or make-believe ʿUdhrī crooner; he does not speak of heavenly reward. The poem sounds like the sincere expression of, at least, a momentary mood. This phenomenon, however, of multiple heresy or the prevalence of the two types of heresies, that of courtly love (branded a heresy by Christianity) and that of renunciation of progeny, has been observed at the identical cultural centers of Provence, those of the Albigenses, by the historians of Christian courtly love. Ibn Gabirol's denunciation of the world must not be interpreted as an abdication from love. There is, of course, the possibility that the period of his life in which he wrote love poetry did not coincide with that of his abdication. But, inasmuch as Ibn Gabirol had been characterized, on the ground of his many poems of scorn for the skittish Dame World[47], as averse to women, the discovery of his love poems came as a surprise and their correct interpretation has still to be made. The keynote in Ibn Gabirol's work is freedom and the awakening of an unmediaeval immediacy of reaction to human beauty which may indeed be the key to his extreme leanings. He may owe some inspiration for the proclamation, with such freedom of his appreciation of human beauty, to Ibn Sīnā, who was read in Cordova earlier than in his Persian homeland, and, quite likely, to Ibn Ḥazm, whose dandyism has been mentioned. All this will be discussed on the basis of poems to be presented later, according to their genres.

There is a short poem by Ibn Gabirol which, though it looks like no more than an *aperçu*, could be regarded as a manifesto of a new combination of secular and religious love of beauty:

Note 47

The Beauty of a Child, God's Masterwork — is this Vanitas?

Imr-ū le-mī — *'Aph'appey ṣebhī*, No. 6

– – ◡ – – – ◡ – – – ◡ – — *Leqeṭ shīr-īm*, p. 21

– – ◡ – – – ◡ – – – – (*Rajaz*) — Rhyme: *-qer*

Tell ye! Whose hair has embraced his own cheek?
How would moon embrace the morning?

Would one not deem Ecclesiastes in sin,
for calling beauty vanity and grace a lie!

What remains: your cheeks witness the truth
that there is no fathoming the works of God.

Here we have the great Jewish affirmation of external beauty. That this is a new orientation is implicit in the shockingly heretical chiding of Solomon's teaching concerning vanity. The divine is declared immanent, and human nature here is much more than (as the stock phrase is) "a book of parables for the greatness of the Creator[48]." The adored person is, almost after the fashion of the Greeks, a manifestation of the divine.

There is also a sequence of some six love poems. They are the poet's address to a girl named Abigail and to a girl called Tamar "by her neighbor women" (the two are most likely the same girl). Some of the poems are seemingly conventional, but the fact of their being written in Hebrew and of their using Biblical figures as illustrations for courtly attitudes makes their heretical character appear flagrant:

Tamar-Abigail II — Dame sans merci

Ke-thāmār att — Schirmann, *Shīrāh*, I, 213

◡ – – – ◡ – – – (*Hazaj*) — *Millás*, p. 31

Rhyme: *-āth-ekh*

You are like a palm in loftiness,
you are like the sun in comeliness. Ps. XCII. 13

I thought you were a gracious lady,
Abigail, for your gracefulness, Jud. V. 11

Note 48

Till I found you would slay me
I Ki. XVI. 31ff. like Jezebel, in your wickedness. —

Lam. II. 15 Consummate glory, noblest shape,
I am wretched for you with lovesickness.

Conjure up my soul from the Pit,
I Sam. XXVIII. 11 lest I die before you [sorceress].

The motif of the Witch of Endor, conjuring up the spirit of Samuel from the grave, is playfully yet passionately used in supplicating the beloved sorceress to bring up his soul from the "threshold of the Pit." The same theme of sorcery appears more conventionally in another poem to Abigail, the first lines of which read:

What art has Abigail that she seized
my soul by her eyes, there to be kept?

The end of the poem reads all the more shockingly:

Though there is — while exile lasts — to God no sacrifice,
to her I will proffer sacrifices and offering.

Foreswearing one's life and religion is an Arabic trick of style. Here, however, juxtaposed as it is with the exile of the Jews and the destruction of the Temple, the poet's declaration that he wishes to replace the sacrifice in the holiest shrine of Jerusalem by a sacrifice on the altar of the beloved, is quite striking and typical of an eleventh-century Renaissance personality. The Hebrew poet Moses ibn Ezra, who lived a short generation later than Ibn Gabirol and, having grown up in the shadow of the Naghrāllas, remained the eternal underling, ostensibly attacks Ibn Gabirol chiefly for being the daring coiner of non-biblical Hebrew wording. One feels, however, that in all instances, it is not as much the daring neologism and free grammatical usage (to be traced in Samuel's poetry as well) as it is the heterodox or otherwise disrespectful content which induces him to cluck his tongue in discomposure.

Two poems offer us insight into the complicated character of Ibn Gabirol. He compares his love to that of the unfortunate son of David,

Amnon, to his half-sister, Tamar, a love which was, as is known, violent and fleeting. Yet he beseeches his friends to bring Tamar to him in the finery of a bride. The comparison with Amnon evokes the question whether the poet expects his love to survive. His other love poems exhibit many typical Arabic motifs, but they take a larger step further in both their realism and their symbolism. A poem which recalls by its descriptive art and its primary motifs the influence of Ibn al-Muʿtazz, reveals in a coded but interpretable way the unhappy lover's frustration. But its astonishing symbolism almost reminds one of French symbolism of the last century or perhaps invites, or rather demands, a Freudian interpretation.

Imitating lines attributed to Ibn al-Muʿtazz in which a girl, emancipated enough to visit her friend freely and to reprimand him for his melancholy[49], Ibn Gabirol introduces an unnamed girl who also chides the poet for his tears, aiming at extorting a declaration of love from him. It contains the unabashed distich:

The harvest — they harvest with a scythe
putting in a sickle, the blade to the crop.

Since none of these poems have ever been understood by editors, let alone translated into English, I shall give here in full one last poem which, in the poet's confession of his lucklessness as a lover, uses a similar sexual symbolism:

Tamar I

We-raʿyāth-ī mehullālāh — *ʿAphʿappey ṣebhī*, No. 10
◡ - - - ◡ - - - ◡ - - *(Wāfir)* — Schirmann, *Shīrāh*, I, p. 214
Haaretz, April 1, 1938

Rhyme: *-n-ōth*

My love, renowned among the maidens,
a queen — as the sun in heavenly dwellings.-

Sister of the Sun, and Mother of the Moon,
or Palm, as called by the women, her neighbors,

Her name moves forth, glowing with her grace,
her mention is good and fair among the counties.

Note 49

She contends with me when I flow with tears
and send forth waters down my cheeks.

I answered her, "How shall I delight, exult?
How can I lift my heart to joyful shouts,

When there is no wine, no must in the vats,
no grain, no wheat in the storing bins?"

The poet's confession that "there is no wine, no must in the vats, no grain, no wheat in the storing bins," which a modern editor interpreted as a confession of material poverty, should not, since we have the guidance of the previous poem, be misunderstood. It is the confession of being in love without being a lover. No social gain is to be foreseen from such a confession, and no heavenly reward, as expected by the 'Udhrī poets, is mentioned. Such an idea of being a 'martyr of love' invaded Judaism, as can be shown, in the twelfth century *Book of the Pious*, *Śepher ha-Ḥasīdhīm*[50]. But Ibn Gabirol allows the sphere of love in his life to occupy an entirely separate secular realm. One might say that he attributed to this sphere, which is in some ways playfully handled and borrowed entirely from Arab courtly practices and values, no more than a secondary importance; but this would not do. There is an observable cleavage right through his personality. In some way one might compare him with a Cicero who confesses to being Greek in culture besides being the great Roman patriot. These Jewish savants are indeed in some ways Jewish and in others Arab or citizens of the newly felt *ecumene*.

Is he aware of the sacrilege when calling his patron "Lord of my soul" *(adhōn naphsh-ī)* and when, in an address to his disciple, using the most sacred words of the Hebrew creed (beginning "Hear, o Israel!"): "with all my heart, with all my soul, and with all my might?"[51]

After these examples, it can no longer astonish us when we find, in Ibn Gabirol's philosophical poem, an entirely neo-Platonic godhead which he describes first as that transcendent Universe "in Whose hand rests the universe" and second as a power immanent in the yearning of "not-yet-formed matter" towards God's forming nearness in which yearning this deity reflects its own glory. Such a conception is hard for us to reconcile with the active and personal God as he appears in Ibn Gabirol's religious hymns. But we find in his great meditation, *The Royal Crown*[52], the mystic's answer to this paradox. The godhead is there called the one great mystery behind all formulations, transcending all attributes. With this we are also very close to the heretical "double truth" of a Siger of Brabant.

Notes 50—52

(4) THE BEGINNING OF HISPANO-HEBREW POETRY

There was always a trickle of Hebrew verse-making in the early Middle-Ages. A marked revival of religious poetry, in some instances of a beautiful simplicity, is represented by Saadya (died ca. 942). But a new beginning, much more pivotal, came when a first generation of Hebrew secular poets began, at the time of Ḥaśdāy ibn Shaprūṭ, to "twitter" (as the expression of Abraham ibn Dā'ūd in his Ṡepher haq-Qabbālāh has it) and to open the way for later generations to acquire the means of melody and a free and full prosody[53]. According to some historians, the golden age of Hispano-Hebrew poetry begins either with Samuel han-Nāghīdh and Ibn Gabirol or with a following generation, that of Yehuda Halevi and Moses ibn Ezra. The first attempt at Hebrew metrical poetry had been made in the East, where the last representative Gaon of Babylonia, Rab Hay, (died ca. 1038) composed, among other verses, a religio-didactic poem "in the fashion of Phocylides" (Graetz). The new secular Hebrew poetry could almost be termed Arabic poetry in the Hebrew language, but the Hebrew spirit and biblical overtones color the adapted Arabic imagery and add depth, bestowing upon it a more "western" character. As a matter of fact the tnew religious poetry of the Jews in Spain also was indebted to Arabic poenry which permeated the entire life of southern Iberia, rather for its inceftive and its formal and metrical model than for its wealth of specific motis (but even these must not be underrated).

In the realm of letters the Arabs were more highly sophisticated than the Jews: they had refined their language by the application of grammar and by the study of comparative linguistics (in a rudimentary fashion) and they possessed a fully developed system of poetics. Thus the Jews were forced, like Saadya in Babylonia before, to spend much toil and sweat on the Hebrew language, its grammar, lexicography, and semantics. The discovery that their holy language was in many ways less flexible and less vivid than that of their brother in Shem was a shock to be recovered from. But the conception of a pure biblical Hebrew to be resuscitated and cultivated as "classical" was derived from the Arabs' idea of classical Koranic Arabic[54]. Once this task was done, an even more arduous task was undertaken — that of creating a new Hebrew poetry set to Arabic meters and with Arabic stylistic means, like metaphors. Not all Jewish groups — even in Spain — participated in such employment of the Hebrew language for secular poetry. Its spread remained confined to the metropolitan centers, where the Muslim courts had established these courtly arts. The cry "sacrilege" was here and there heard among the provincial mob guarded by the orthodox taboo-police, the upholders of the ethos of the exilic interim. (We find in Ibn Gabirol's *Shīr Telūnāh*, "Song of Complaint," a denunciation of Hebrew poetry attributed to the people of Saragossa[55].)

The Hebrew language, as mentioned before, had, in keeping with the exilic lot of the nation, mainly been reserved for sacred use. It had slept a sabbatical slumber within standardized prayers and biblical commentaries, like the nation itself awaiting its redemption by a messianic prince. Now the protective capsule was forcibly broken open and — horror and sacrilege! — under the spell of Arabic music the drowsy body of the Hebrew language began to move. Its first steps, as it were, when aroused to unfamiliar dances, seemed gauche before the awakening to an authentic and individual expression. Nevertheless, the revival of Hebrew must, in itself, have been an enormous triumph and, in retrospect, must have appeared a deed of Solomonic magic or even of pre-messianic redemption, to be greeted by some as a manifestation of God's approving will and by others as a sacrilegious "forcing of the end." The orthodox attitude was that only God announces when it is time to awake, and only He and His Anointed can redeem His Hebrew nation and tongue. An emancipation by means of the arts and within a wave of inspired life like that of Cordova remained without parallel in Jewish history (unless we see one in the Haskalah movement of the nineteenth century, which also produced the revival of contemporary Hebrew poetry). In reality, the resurrection of the language came rather by strenuous synthetic and analytical work. The entire bulk of classical Hebrew was examined as to its linguistic material and its grammatical structure, and the scholars compiled the equivalent of rhyming dictionaries, which included ἅπαξ λεγόμενα, rare word forms, and words of problematic origin and of varying interpretation, to be put to use. Also, the earliest poems impress one rather like mosaics, patched together from small fragments of biblical material with heavy mortar lines and clumsy cement fillings in between. If Arthur Koestler feels, with regard to today's modern Hebrew, that "a ram's horn be not the instrument for a scherzo," we may state that the Hebrew of the Spanish period and of today uses, besides the ram's horn, more and more the other instruments of the Temple orchestra: harp, lyre, flute, cymbal, and kettle-drum.

The sweat of such ardent toil, the titanic effort of smelting the language ore, stains even Ibn Gabirol's brilliant verse. Although he had inherited the accomplishments of a full century of new Hebrew poetry with its successful borrowing of Arabic meters and previous coinage of many Hebrew parallels to the rich Arabic imagery, only a genius of his rank could transcend the shortcomings of this school and attain both the directness and command of nuance which we find in his most inspired creations. While endeavoring to express himself as naturally as the Psalms, Job, and

Note 55

the prophets, he had to carry the burden under which even the rich new Hebrew language sometimes quailed, burdens of meter and heaped rhymes, very much like those which the Provençal language soon afterwards imposed upon itself. Stylistic means, like anaphora, antithesis, which the Arabs had adopted from Hellenistic traditions, were no less "late" and smelling of the lamp, cold and turgid. But they did, it is true, help to overcome the last remnants of the by now antiquated biblical parallelism with its standard similes. It is these remnants that make the style of poems by Samuel han-Nāghīdh, a generation earlier than Ibn Gabirol, which describe a battle or an encounter with a sea monster, remind one of Tacitus' involved antitheses.

The poets craved pure biblical Hebrew; the vocabulary of the Talmud and references to its content were comparatively rare. A command of the entire Hebrew vocabulary as such was no innovation of Moorish Spain. Anyone who had attended the rabbinic schools or, as in rare cases, the Karaite schools (which most likely specialized even more exclusively in biblical studies but cannot be called rabbinic) knew the Bible more or less by heart[56]. Moreover, the rabbinic method used biblical statements entirely out of context and often eisegeted entirely heterogeneous nuances of meaning in order to support an opinion within the discussion of ritual and legal questions. The revival of Hebrew poetry demonstrates a drastic turn away from such rabbinic rape towards the original connotation of the words. The most arduous task, rarely accomplished, was the composition of poems with a simple message that moved the reader's sentiment. The poets are *poetae docti*, but their learnedness was to be subservient to the *gaya scienza* of a full life. Ibn Gabirol shows a vastly different, but equally immense erudition in his religious poems and in particular in his riddles, the Hebrew diction of which is difficult to interpret and impossible to imitate. He cannot even avoid learned allusions in his goliardic drinking songs, but in his circle of learned baccalaureates this must have been a recommendation.

The Hebrew poets were all trained in Arabic poetry and could have made a contribution to the art of their neighbors and teachers, and some of them, indeed, did so. For not only was Arabic their mother tongue, some like Samuel han-Nāghīdh, were excellent Arabic stylists. Samuel was highly praised by Arab historians as the state epistolarian of Granada[57]. Their themes and their imagery remained Arabic, so that their Hebrew imitation in a certain sense was their main accomplishment. On the other hand, the choicest elements of Hebrew were newly uncovered with so much enthusiasm that the rendition of Arabic images in Hebrew became most effective and added a new dimension of depth. As an intellectual delight the expert was able to deduce from such detail an inspired interpretation of a biblical passage or ἅπαξ λεγόμενον. The biblical vocabulary is small compared with the vast Arabic vocabulary. The Book of Job, however, in particular enlarges the stock of poetical Hebrew. Without its plethora of unusual word images and display of poetical *hypsos* in general, no Hebrew competition with the Arabic language of poetry would have been successful.

A parallel to such creation of a new poetry may be seen in that of the Latin poets — Virgil, Catullus, Horace, and Ovid — in imitating Homer, Anacreon, Sappho, and Theocritos. Another precedent and parallel, that of the Persians, previously mentioned, seems to have escaped the historians. The Persian renewal of their language and imitation of Arabic imagery was so powerful and successful that some Arabic writers complained bitterly about such pillage[58]. Also the ability of many Persian poets to write very good Arabic accomplished almost a re-acculturation of the Arabs and contributed substantially to a first flourishing of Islamic culture. The Jews, who in their vast majority were not converted to Islam, remained more isolated, and that not only in their Hebrew poetry, than the Islamized Persians. There were indeed converts to Islam, even among outstanding Hebrew poets. Abū Isḥāq Ibrāhīm ibn Sahl al-Isrā'īlī from Seville (died 1251), began as a Hebrew poet and became a well-known Arabic poet, retaining the cognomen "Israelite" even after his conversion[59]. So did the son of the Hebrew poet Abraham ibn Ezra who also composed a poetical affirmation of his conversion[60].

What has just been said about the language awakening from long slumber could be stated with equal truth about the emancipated Jewish avant-garde of Cordova. Only a small group and a few isolated individuals freed themselves slowly from the current exclusively scholastic other-worldly orientation and were able to break out of the frame of the rabbinic and casuistical cast of mind with its "as-if" reality and to look up from the looking glass of "speculation" into reality. These intellectuals pay dearly for knowing the Bible by heart and their intellectualism stands in the way of their feeling. Ibn Gabirol, even though he is able in his poetry occasionally to allow his senses to be his guide rather than his intellect, so that a genuine nature romanticism takes over — as in his "Great Nature Poem," discussed in Part III — still struggles against these intellectual shackles. A deliberate and revolutionary breaking out of these traditional shackles in another direction is apparent in his philosophical work in prose, the *Fons Vitae*. Here he seems to be building a new neo-Platonic cosmos of his own, in which scriptural quotations have no place, not least because the work is written in Arabic and addressed to the entire *ecumene* of pure thought.

Notes 58—60

I must underscore once more the fact that the Cordovan humanism which an exiled metropolitan intelligentsia exported all over Moorish Spain and North Africa cannot be regarded as a movement among the larger masses of the population. It was in no way a lasting orientation toward the secular, either in Spanish Islam or Jewry, and, since it drew to an early close at its birthplace, it was mainly important because of its radiation. The Jewish *hommes de lettres* of Cordova, from whose second and third generations hailed Samuel ibn Naghrālla and Solomon ibn Gabirol, were no more than a small but leading group set off from the bulk of the Jewry of Arab Spain, and even these reserved some of their secular activities for *intra muros*, whereas *extra muros* they imposed upon themselves considerable moderation. After the downfall of the caliphate and the succeeding petty kingdoms, intellectual Islam, as well as Jewry, dissociated itself, under the pressure of Almoravid clerical reaction, more and more from secularization, the Arabs returning to normative Islam accentuated by the exigencies of holy war. Similarly, the Jews returned to the typically mediaeval withdrawal from an active participation in history into the taut tent of the Law, in passive expectation of the Messianic end. The Cordovan Aristotelian Maimonides of the twelfth century was forced to apostasize to Islam and to flee from Spain and — which, in fact, may betoken the change — only at the court of Sultan Saladin of Egypt did he find the freedom for a return to Judaism and his immense literary and scholarly production as an Aristotelian and as a Talmudist.

Jewish historical sources for the eleventh century are scanty, but it is possible to demonstrate how Jewish literary critics and, somewhat later, poets viewed the rebirth of Hebrew poetry in Spain. I quote passages from two *makamas* of al-Ḥarīzī's *Taḥkemōnī* (ca. 1220)[61] which, in the manner of a catalog, enumerate and evaluate the Hebrew poets. This work of rhymed prose was designed to be a Hebrew counterpart to the famous *Maqām-āt* of al-Ḥarīzī and its two main characters, Hemān hā-Ezrāḥī (Ps. LXXXVIII. 1) and Ḥebher haq-Qenī (Judges IV. 11), match those of the Arabic model. In its eighteenth *makama*, which gives a verdict on each poet, al-Ḥarīzī says:

It happened to pass in 4700[62], counted from the Creation,
That there rushed upon the sons of Spain in the seventh century a spirit of counsel and might Is. XI. 2
And of sifted language.
Then the Hebrews began
To take their tongues for walks on the ways of songs. (Hos. XI. 3)

Notes 61—62

Now the pyres of eloquence began to inflame their hearts,
Jdgs. XX. 38 And a smoke cloud began to arise from the city[63],
But their eloquence at that time was faulty
And their tongue limping on the path of song,
Until the eighth century approached;
Then they bestirred themselves to play the eight-stringed harp
And prepared the house of poetry after the proper fashion and pattern
And they measured out the scheme.
In those days there arose in Spain a sun of psalm-singing
And the sky of greatness;
This was the great Nāsī, Rabbi Isaac the Spaniard, ben Ḥasdāy[64].
May he rest in the shade of Shadday . . .
Then the Nāsī died with all his brothers and all of that generation
And the ninth century came in which R. Isaac ben Khalphōn was born[65]
Who filled with his songs the rim of the west and the north . . .
In his days there was the great Nāghīdh, R. Samuel hal-Lewī, of blessed
Is. III. 10 memory, who bared in the craft of poetry an uplifted arm
And brought forth the hidden to light[66].
At the end of his days R. Solomon the Small[67] was born who swung
(Alludes to Ibn G.'s *Nibar*, dist. 32.) the incense burners of poetry, incense the like of which came
no more[68].
And nobody his equal arose after him
Because all the poets coming after him,
Though they wished to learn from his song,
Did not even attain the dust of his feet
Owing to the power of his parables
And the strength of his words.
Had he lengthened his days
He would have composed mighty wonders from the mysteries of songs.
However his wreath, still green, was plucked off
(Alludes to Ibn G.'s *Meliṣāth-ī*, dist. 2.) And the fresh sap of boyhood was wrenched away from him[69]
And as a son of twenty-nine his light gave out,
And thirty he did not reach . . .

That the Jews of Spain were aware of having cradled a new Hebrew poetry, which spread to other countries, is seen from another poets' catalog in al-Ḥarīzī's third *maqāma*[70].

He answered and said:
Be it known to you that the loftiest poetry
Bedecked with pearls

And not outweighed by the gold of Ophir Job XXVIII. 16 (Alluding to Ibn G.'s *Yeshūre-nī*)
Betook itself from Spain
And spread over all the ends of the earth.
For the poems of the sons of Spain are strong and sweet
As if carved from a flame of fire; Ps. XXIX. 7 (Kingdom's Crown)
And compared with its masculine poets
The poets of the world are female-frail [71].
In days of yore there were many poets among them,
They grew like willow trees, Is. XLIV. 4
But their lines were obstructed
By words they could not carve out, Is. LVII. 14; Nu. I. 17
Like Menahem ben Śārūq and Dūnāsh ben Labrāṭ and Samuel ben Abhūn,
And many others besides, whose poems are no longer remembered
For the weakness of their contents.
Then came the great Nāghīdh ['ruler'], Samuel han-Lewī, of blessed memory,
Whose poems were ruling and towering Prvbs. VIII. 6
With contents strong and new;
But most of his poems, being profound and hard,
Will require commentaries.
There was in his generation Rabbi Isaac ben Ḥalphōn of whose poems some are strong
And some are brittle and thin
Because they wasted the vast growing vines. Hosea X. 1; (Isa. XXIV. 1); Nahum II. 3
Rabbi Joseph ben Ḥasdāy is the Father of the "Orphan Song" [72]
Which begins "Does the gracious gazelle have determined strength and bravery?"
(She is the Orphan) who is her mother's only daughter
With no second daughter among her nation's children.
The songs of Rabbi Moses ben Tāqāna bear the token of the mind's refinement [73], Eccl. XII. 9
They are plants of a pleasant plantation. Ps. CXLIV. 12; Is. XVII. 1
But there are the songs of Rabbi Solomon the Small [74]
Before whom everyone great becomes small;
Like him none had arisen since the days of Eber, the father of Joktan [the dwarf]; Gen. X. 25ff.
In comparison with him all the poetry of his generation became nonsense and sham. Prvbs. XV. 4
"The small one shall be captain;" Is. LX. 22
He alone scaled the highest heights of poetry;

Notes 71—74

Gen. L. 23; XXX. 3 Eloquence bore him on the knees of the Muse
Gen. XXXVIII. 28 ff. And bound on his hand a scarlet thread, saying, "This came out first,"
For all poets who preceded him —
Their poems are like a wind and a jumble compared with his,
And none his equal arose after him.
All those who did come after him learned from his skill
And received the spirit of poetry from him.
God anointed him king over all the songs of his people:[75]
Cant. I. 1 The song of songs — by Solomon!
Even the strong poets must struggle
To comprehend his profound poems,
For his rhetoric is too lofty for all of us to understand:
Deut. XXX. 12 "Who will go up for us to heaven and bring it down for us?"
Even in the ritual for the Fasts
He proved himself tremendous and formidable,
As he did in his Day of Atonement liturgy.
Cant. V. 14 All his contents are like nard with camphor
And overlaid with sapphires,
Lordly songs,
Bases for buttresses of thought.

I hope that this introduction which describes the cultural ambiente of Moorish Spain during the eleventh century will have prepared the reader for the discussion of the origins of the first Alhambra Palace which follows. The Berbers who ruled Granada at the time when the events described in the second part of this book took place receive a treatment of their own, along with the Arabs and Jews, which will be found in an excursus to part D. But I may stress that the Zīrid dynasty which ruled Granada and which did not excel in the human and humane sphere is matched by other highly cultured Berber dynasties like those of Toledo and Bougie.

Note 75

Notes to Part I

1. Reprinted, New York, Meridian Books, 1958.
2. The discussions aiming at a definition of the concept "renaissance" which took place between E. Gilson, E. Cassirer, P. O. Kristeller and H. Baron are well described in Herschel Baker, *The Image of Man*, New York, 1961, pp. 220ff.; cf. E. Panofsky, *Renaissance and Renascences in Western Art* (*Figura*, vol. X), Stockholm, 1960, pp. 42ff.
3. A. Mez, *Die Renaissance des Islams*, Heidelberg, 1922.
4. For Berbers cf. Henri Pérès, *La poésie andalouse en arabe classique au XI*[e] *siècle*, Paris, 1937, pp. 258ff.; 283 (quoted as Pérès, *Poésie*).
5. Américo Castro, *La España en su Historia*, Buenos Aires, 1948.
6. Translated by A. J. Arberry, *The Ring of the Dove*, London, 1953, p. 191 (quoted as Ibn Ḥazm, *Ring*); translated by A. R. Nykl, *The Dove's Neck-Ring*, Paris, 1931, p. 143 (quoted as Ibn Ḥazm, *Neck-Ring*).
7. Pérès, *Poésie*, pp. 432f. (XXIV).
8. The German historian, Konrad Burdach, referred to Ibn Jūdī as a representative of early love poetry in the West; cf. J. Hell, "Al-ʿAbbās ibn al-Aḥnaf," in *Islamica*, II, 1926, pp. 271ff.
9. Definitions of humanism: in H. A. K. Hunt, *The Humanism of Cicero*, Melbourne, 1954, p. 190: "Rostovtzeff says that Jambulos (of the third century B. C.) was not actually Stoic. His account does reveal that contemporary impulse to reconcile social organization for a common end with individual freedom and regard for the equality of man." Ib., p. 200: Cicero's humanism is defined as: "... the belief that reason is shared by all mankind and the gods." (*Leg.* I. 23). Reason is found both in man and in god ... [they] also have the right reason in common ... those who share these must be considered members of the same commonwealth's partnership in justice (*Rep.* III. 45) ... if they obey the same authorities and powers and 'respect both the individual and the common weal' (*Rep.* III. 47)." J. Maritain, *True Humanism*, London, 1938, pp. XIIff.: "Humanism essentially tends to render man more truly human and to make his original greatness manifest by causing him to participate in all that can enrich him in nature and in history." Friedrich Gundolf, *Rede zu Goethes Hundertstem Todestage*, Berlin, 1932, p. 70: "Humanismus, das heißt das Vertrauen in die Gnade und in das Verdienst des Menschen als des Mittlers, Trägers und Sehers der Welt, mag man diese anbeten in Person, Gesetz, Zahl oder Wunder." Ibid., p. 23: "Der Humanismus der Renaissance hatte die Freiheit des selbstbewußten und eigenwilligen Ich von allen Gemeinschafts-Bindungen und Autoritäten beansprucht, Freiheit des Denkens, des Tuns, des Genießens." For the Arab tradition see A. Badawi, "L'humanisme dans la pensée arabe," in *Studia Islamica*, Paris, 1956, pp. 67ff.; see also Louis Gardet, *La cité musulmane*, Paris, 1961, pp. 273ff. The line by Ibn Gabirol is found in *Bialik-R.*, I, p. 14, dist. 21.
10. See above note 8.
11. See A. R. Nykl, *El Cancionero*, Madrid, 1933.
12. Pérès, *Poésie*, p. 52f. We shall find praise of Spain voiced in the Arabic nature poems in Part III. For the emancipation of Cordova from Bagdad see Pérès, *Poésie*, pp. 392 f. The influential Cordovan poet and courtier Ibn Shuhaid

(992-1035), the author of the *Risālat at-tawābi' wa-z-zawabi'* strove to create a new, Andalusian poetry of its own, sparing with rhetorical means i. e., returning to simplicity and naturalness. See James Dickie, Ibn Šuhayd, in *Al-Andalus*, XXIX, 1964, pp. (243 ff.) 279, 299 ff, (quoted as Dickie, *Shuhayd*).

13. See Part II, note 34.
14. Ibn Sīnā was born in 980 near Bukhāra; (*G. A. L.*, I, pp. 452; S. I, p. 812). "A Treatise on Love by Ibn Sīnā," translated by Emil L. Fackenheim, in *Mediaeval Studies*, Toronto, 1945, VII, p. 221. Cf. E. Lévi-Provençal, *La civilisation arabe en Espagne*, Paris, 1948, p. 25; also Renan, *Averroës et Averroisme* (*Oeuvres complètes*, III), p. 24: "*Les livres composés en Perse et en Syrie étaient souvent connus en Espagne avant de l'être en Orient ...*" etc.
15. Pérès, *Poésie*, p. 406.
16. For Ibn Ḥazm's dandyism, see Pérès, *Poésie*, p. 406; also Emilio García Gómez, *Poesía Arabigoandaluza*, Madrid, 1952, p. 68. This license of the *ẓāhirī* school, which had resulted in a tragic end for a *faqīh* in Bagdad about a hundred years before Ibn Ḥazm, is discussed in Hellmut Ritter, *Das Meer der Seele*, Leyden, 1955, pp. 383f. His growing bigotry may be illustrated by his attack upon Samuel quoted below in Part II; see there n. 14.
17. Compare F. Nietzsche's *Unzeitgemässe Betrachtungen* (Fourth): "Richard Wagner in Bayreuth," *Werke*, II, Leipzig, 1906, p. 424, where he predicts such anti-Alexanders, "Welche die mächtige Kraft haben, zusammenzuziehen und zu binden, die entfesselten Fäden heranzulangen und das Gewebe vor dem Zerblasenwerden zu bewahren."
18. C. H. Becker, *Islamstudien*, Leipzig, 1924, p. 34.
19. M. Meyerhof, "Von Alexandria nach Bagdad," in *Sitzungsber. d. Preuss. Akademie d. W., Phil.-hist. Kl.*, Berlin, 1930, pp. 392ff.; F. Rosenthal, *Das Fortleben der Antike im Islam*, Zurich, 1965, p. 75.
20. From *Passio S. Pelagii*, in *Die Werke der Hrotsvitha*, ed. K. A. Barack, Nuremberg, 1858, p. 65, lines 12ff., quoted after Dreyer, *Die religiöse Gedankenwelt des Salomo ibn Gabirol*, Leipzig, 1930, p. 14.
21. R. Dozy, *Histoire des musulmans d'Espagne*, ed. E. Lévi-Provençal, I, Leiden, 1932, pp. 188ff. (quoted as Provençal, *Histoire*); E. Lévi-Provençal, *Histoire de l'Espagne musulmane*, Leiden, 1950—53, pp. 95ff. (quoted as Provençal, *Espagne*).
22. Quoted in R. A. Nicholson, *A Literary History of the Arabs*, Cambridge, 1941, p. 418 (quoted as Nicholson, *History*) and in my German book.
23. Klaus Heger, *Die bisher veröffentlichten Ḫarǧas und ihre Deutungen*, Tübingen, 1960, pp. 87, 93ff. (quoted as Heger, *Ḫarǧas*), with bibliography, entailing the leading monographs by M. Hartmann, S. M. Stern, G. S. Colin, and E. García Gómez.
24. Pérès, *Poésie*, p. 208 and *passim*.
25. *Ars Poetica*, I, lines 47f.; in *The Complete Works of Horace*, ed. C. T. Kraemer, jr., New York, 1936, p. 398.
26. ʿAbd al-Qāhir al-Jurjānī, *The Mysteries of Eloquence*, ed. by H. Ritter, Istanbul, 1954; also (in German) *Die Geheimnisse der Wortkunst*, ed. by H. Ritter, Wiesbaden, 1959 (quoted as Ritter, *Wortkunst*).
27. *Al-Bāqillānī, A Tenth-Century Document of Arabic Literary Theory and Criticism*, transl. by G. E. von Grunebaum, Chicago, 1960 (quoted as *Bāqillānī*).
28. Pérès, *Poésie*, pp. 74f.
29. A portrait of these poets can be found in A. R. Nykl, *Hispano-Arabic Poetry*, Baltimore, 1946 (quoted as Nykl, *H[isp].-A. Poetry*).
30. E. R. Goodenough, *Jewish Symbols in the Greco-Roman Period*, VIII, New York, 1958, pp. 224ff.

31. See V. A. Tcherikover, "The Decline of the Jewish Diaspora in Egypt in the Roman Period," in *The Journal of Jewish Studies*, XIV, 1963, pp. 1ff.
32. The terms "assimilation" and "competition" appear in Ahad Ha-ʿam's famous article under this title.
33. This expression occurs in Goethe's *West-Östlicher Divan*, in which Goethe vies with Hafis.
34. Michelangelo's envy for Fra Angelico's art of the heart, his surrender to God's grace, his turning from mortal love and human beauty as "distractions from higher duty" are reflected in his sonnets, ed. Frey, Nos. CXLVII and CXXIII, written between 1547 and 1554. Quoted in Sir Anthony Blunt, *Artistic Theory in Italy*, 1450–1600, Oxford, 1964, p. 78ff.

34a. This view was, as I am happy to find, beautifully expounded by a Ḥasidic rabbi. See M. Buber, *Tales of the Hasidim*, *The Early Masters*, New York, 1947, p. 229.

35. H. Graetz, *History of the Jews*, III, Philadelphia, 1957, pp. 155ff.; S. W. Baron, *A Social and Religious History of the Jews*, III, Philadelphia, 1957, pp. 155ff.; IV, p.29; S. Dubnow, *Die Geschichte des jüdischen Volkes in Europa*, IV, Berlin, 1926, pp. 196ff.; Provençal, *Espagne*, II, pp. 69ff., with references, p. 69, n. 2. The *vita* of John of Goricia by John of St. Arnulf (in *Mon. Germ. Hist.* Script. IV, pp. 335-77, ed. G. H. Pertz, Hanover 1841 and Leipzig, 1925) elucidates the gaping contrast of the Cordovan and the Ottonian courts. (In particular pp. 370-372).
36. *Dubnow*, IV, pp. 195ff., 202ff.; D. M. Dunlop, *The History of the Jewish Khazars*, Princeton, 1954, pp. 120, 125ff., 156ff., and passim (quoted as Dunlap, *Khazars*); Graetz, *History*, III, pp. 219ff.
37. For literature see: Provençal, *Espagne*, I, pp. 326ff.; Dunlop, *Khazars*, pp. 133, 134 (where lines 15–18 are translated), 165, 169; quoting J. Starr "The Jews in the Byzantine Empire (641–1204)," in *Texte und Forschungen zur byz.-neugriech. Philologie*, XXX, Athens, 1939; Baron, *History*, III, pp. 156–8.
38. Notes to the Text *of Menahem ibn Śārūq*

Line 18: The term *gemūl*, standing parallel to *peʿullāh*, shows that the latter word here means 'wages for work' as in Ps. CIX. 20 and Lev. XIX. 13 (not only 'work'). Standing in contrast to 'glorious kingdom' in line 1, the 'sinful kingdom' is, of course, Byzantium, intolerant of Judaism, which had been recently defeated by the Khazars. See Dunlop, *Khazars*, p. 136.

Line 19: "The Lamp of the Nation" seems to be a reference to the Son of Jesse, the Davidic Deliverer, referred to in line 36; the wording stems from the promise given in I Kings XI. 36 to the House of David to rule Judah forever: "David, my servant, may have a light (lamp) always before me in Jerusalem," and from Is. XLVI. 3: "... all the remnant of the House of Israel which are borne by me from the belly, which are carried from the womb," a prophecy referring to the entire nation of Israel. The poem speaks in line 1 of the Khazar empire as the 'remote kingdom' *mamlākhāh nahalāʾāh*, a feminine noun; in line 19 appears *leʾōm* 'people' referring to all of Israel including the Khazars ('the Nation exalted from the womb'), normally masculine but, identified with *ummāh* (Ps. CVIII. 1) and *mamlākhāh*, the feminine gender remains prevailing, so to speak κατά γύνεσιν, but also because of the poet's need for rhyme.

Line 21: 'Paradise (pastures)'; the Hebrew *ʿadhān-īm* has to be understood as both the plural of 'garden of Eden' and of *ʿedhen* in its literal meaning of 'pleasure', 'delight'.

Line 26: The one 'heavy-headed, but not inebriated' is Hannah (I Sam. I. 15) with whom Israel is identified here for a moment. Similarly, in the previous line, Israel was the Beloved of Solomon's Song who says, "I am black because the sun has tanned me."

39. A. M. Habermann, *Kol shīrey R. Shemū'el han-Nāghīdh, Dīwān*, Tel Aviv, 1947, I, 3, p. 19 (quoted as Habermann, *Diwan*). Ibn Shuhaid reports, in an interesting parallel, a celestial journey where he encountered a pedantic teacher who boastfully declared himself the father of eloquence, whereupon he answered, "No, by God: you are like a mediocre singer who isn't good enough to afford us pleasure and yet isn't bad enough to allow us to forget him." (After Dickie, *Shuhayd*, p. 301)
40. Schirmann, *Shīrāh*, I, p. 94, dist. 1. Habermann, *Diwan*, I, 1, p. 16, dist. 1.
41. Habermann, *Diwan*, I, 1, pp. 3ff., dist. 145ff.
42. Habermann, *Diwan*, I, 1, pp. 151ff.
43. Habermann, *Diwan*, I, 1, pp. 34ff., dist. 38.
44. I shall discuss the most likely logical and chronological sequence of poems and relational steps between the two in a forthcoming book.
45. *Bialik-R.*, I, pp. 66ff.

45a. This parallelism and the true Renaissance pride of the poet struck me when reading the article by A. D. Leeman, "Catullus, 'Angry Young Man'," in *Castrum Peregrini*, LXX, 1965, pp. 5ff. This poem is, by the way, one of the comparatively few in which the poet addresses the patron by name. In many other instances the identity of the person praised (or attacked) can only be deduced from hints or situations. Names of places of residence are never mentioned. This fact escaped the reviewer of my first Alhambra article who tried to derive conclusions from the absence of names in the poem which I am calling "The Alhambra Poem."

46. *Nicholson*, p. 90: al-Ma'arrī's own epitaph shows that he practiced his teaching:

> This wrong was by my father done
> to me, but never by me to one.

A hellenistic precedent to this was Dionysos of Tarsos who said in his epitaph:

> I never married and I wish my father never had;

quoted after S. K. Eddy, *The King is Dead*, Lincoln, Nebraska, 1961, p. 155. (For the opposite attitude in gnosticism see H. Jonas, *Gnostic Religion*, Boston 1958, p. 231.) Ibn Gabirol's "Great Nature Poem" shows that his denial of the world does not have its roots in material woes; his pains are the philosopher's neurosis and not linked with being a social misfit. Also his expression would shun banalities like those of the later Abraham ibn Ezra who bewailing his fate states that if he were a dealer of candles the sun would not cease to shine. Ibn Gabirol is far from commerce.

47. *Bialik-R.*, I, p. 14, dist. 10; p. 137, dist. 1ff. etc.
48. See E. R. Curtius: *Europäische Literatur und lateinisches Mittelalter*, Bern, 1948, pp. 322ff.
49. Lines attributed to Ibn al-Mu'tazz but not found in the printed parts of his diwan:

> She came to me and scolded me for my weeping.
> But she was welcome with her scolding.

See Ritter, *Wortkunst*, p. 325.

50. M. Harris, "The Concept of Love in *Sepher Hassidim*," in *JQR*, L, 1959, pp. 13ff.
51. Cf. F. P. Bargebuhr, "Ibn Gabirol's Poem Beginning 'Ahavtikha' ...," in

The Review of Religion, 1950, pp. 5ff.; the poem is found in *Bialik-R.*, I, p. 112; it contains the formula of the not-yet-formed matter mentioned below. As to *adhōn naphsh-ī*, also Joseph ibn Ḥaśdāy uses this as an apostrophe in his "Orphan Song" (dist. 25).

52. *Davidson-Z.*, pp. 83ff.
53. See the passage from al-Ḥarīzī at the end of this part. Cf. the excellent chapter on Belles Lettres in Baron, *History*, VII.
54. S. D. Goitein, in his *Jews and Arabs*, New York, 1964, pp. 138ff., pointed this out most lucidly for tenth and eleventh-century pure biblical Hebrew, conditioned by the Arabs' devotion to their Koranic language. He also demonstrated that, in contrast, the Jews have always been willing to use foreign languages and had become instrumental in elevating vernaculars to literary languages by engaging in the literary fixation of their own spoken dialects.
55. *Bialik-R.*, I, pp. 4ff., dist. 26f.
56. A good description of Jewish education in the Middle Ages is found in J. R. Marcus, *The Jew in the Medieval World*, Philadelphia, 1960, pp. 373ff.
57. See the passage from Ibn Ḥayyān, cited in Part II, n. 22.
58. U. M. Daudpota, *The Influence of Arabic Poetry on the Development of Persian Poetry*, Bombay, 1934, p. 155 (quoted as *Daudpota*).
59. Pérès, *Poésie*, p. 141.
60. Schirmann, *Shīrāh*, I (II), p. 287. Also Abū 'l-Faḍl ibn Ḥaśdāy, whose description of a royal river party will be discussed in Part III, belongs to the Jewish literati who adopted Islam.
61. I use two editions; that of Y. Toporobhski, *Taḥkemōnī*, Tel Aviv, 1952, pp. 183f. (quoted as *Toporobhski*); and that of Paul de Lagarde, *Iudae Harizii Macamae*, Hannover, 1924, pp. 88f. (quoted as *Lagarde*). For bibliography see Schirmann, *Shīrāh*, II, pp. 689f.
62. This is 940 of the Christian Era.
63. The city, is, of course, Cordova.
64. I abbreviate Rabbi in future as 'R.' Ḥaśdāy ibn Shaprūṭ (Shaphrūṭ) lived from 915—970.
65. Isaac ibn Khalphōn [also, later on, Ḥalphōn, '(money)changer'], who died after 1020, was an older friend of Samuel han-Nāghīdh who died in 1056; see Sachs, *Synagog. Poesie*, pp. 216, 289.
66. This refers, of course, to Samuel han-Nāghīdh.
67. Solomon ibn Gabirol, as he refers to himself in the acrostics of poems.
68.—69. These allusions to poems by Ibn Gabirol, as well as a subsequent allusion to his *Kingdom's Crown*, were most likely relished by the contemporary reader with immediate understanding.
70. *Lagarde*, p. 21; *Toporobhski*, pp. 43f.
71. The criterion of 'masculine' and 'feminine' for 'strong' and 'weak', as in Arabic, is found at the end of Samuel's mocking poem against the rabbi, "Graceless Performance", from which I quoted a few lines above.
72. The famous "Orphan Song" or "Unmatched Song" by Joseph ibn Ḥaśdāy was an encomium of Samuel han-Nāghīdh. It was thus called because, as the poet boastfully said, it was solitary in its kind with no equal kin to it. Arabic (book) titles which included the word *yatīma* 'orphan girl', or 'pearl' supplied the title of this poem.
73. 'Tāqāna' and 'token' is an attempt at imitating a similar Hebrew pun between 'Tāqāna' and 'refined' (cf. Arabic *mutqan*).
74. See above n. 67.
75. Lagarde reads *beney* 'sons' instead of Toporobhski's *shīrey* 'poems'.

PART II

The Alhambra Palace — Art History

Grenade à l'Alhambra

L'Alhambra! L'Alhambra! Palais que les Génies
Ont doré comme un rève et rempli d'harmonies;
Forteresse aux crénaux, festonnés et croulants,
Où l'on entend la nuit de magiques syllabes,
Quand la lune, à travers les milles arceaux arabes
Sème les mures de trèfles blancs!

Victor Hugo, *Les Orientales*

A. Dramatis Personae (In Full)

In his personal memoirs, written in exile in Morocco, the last Berber king of Granada, ʿAbd Allāh (1073—1090), grandson and successor to King Bādīs ibn Ḥabbūs (1038—1073), makes such lengthy references to Ismāʿīl and Yūsuf ibn Naghrālla, the two Jewish chancellors, that we cannot fail to realize their importance[1]. ʿAbd Allāh speaks of the chancellor father, Ismāʿīl abū Ibrāhīm ibn Naghrālla [best known by his Hebrew name Shemūʿel (Samuel) han-Nāghīdh], describing him as the adviser to his royal family, the Granadine Zīrids[2]. Of Samuel's son, Yūsuf ibn Naghrālla [Yehōseph han-Nāghīdh], his successor in the chancellorship, he speaks with violent resentment[3]. I shall refer to these two men as Samuel and Yehōseph ibn Naghrālla. ʿAbd Allāh declares Yehōseph to have poisoned King Bādīs' heir to the throne, ʿAbd Allāh's own father, and to have usurped practically all power in the kingdom[4]. Yehōseph is also accused of having plotted against the aging King Bādīs by allying himself with the neighboring Tujībid king of Almeria[5]. ʿAbd Allāh describes Yehōseph as having "made himself into a Barmecide" (i. e., having played the great patron of the arts, like the famous viziers of the ʿAbbāsids), and as "being able to command and forbid at will[6]." Considerable sections of this royal chronicle deal with Yehōseph's activities. The situation of this young chancellor, born to a brilliant father, under a senile monarch who had taken to heavy drinking (as the royal grandson expressly states), was characterized by E. García Gómez as *(un) secuestro en que tenia la voluntad del anciano y alcoholizado Bādīs*[7].

Under these circumstances Yehōseph found ample opportunity to increase the power of his office, for Bādīs accorded him the same unlimited confidence bestowed upon his father Samuel, as he himself became less and less willing to bear state burdens. The chancellor's power, however, seems to have been as precarious as it was absolute. Many political factions and individuals reacted strongly against Yehōseph, and when the king failed to show sufficient concern in protecting both his state and his chancellor, events may have forced Yehōseph into a desperate plot; he allegedly invited the Taifas ruler of Almeria, "al-Muʿtaṣim" Muḥammad ibn Maʿn ibn Ṣumādiḥ (1051—1091), a member of a noble dynasty of pure Arab stock, to occupy Granada and take over the Granadine fortified towns[8]. The situation during

Notes 1—8

the imputed plot, this last stage of Yehōseph's career, is described by 'Abd Allāh:

> In the meantime, the gap between the Jew and the population [of Granada] widened, and the trouble increased. The Jew, afraid of the population, changed his habitation, moving [temporarily] into the Alqazaba, until his hopes should materialize. By this he alienated the residents [of Granada] as well as by his building up the Alhambra Fortress *(al-Ḥiṣn al-Ḥamrā')* [sic], where he intended to reside with his family when Ibn Ṣumādiḥ had entered Granada, under a stabilized situation[9].

We need not doubt, then, that Yehōseph's power permitted him to erect a fortified mansion for himself on the Alhambra Hill. That this edifice — though, most likely, not even completed in all its ambitious details — was of a monumental character may be deduced from another passage of the royal chronicle, where a member of the royal council, offering an address designed to influence the king against his Jewish chancellor, describes Yehōseph's building to the king as "better than your own castle[10]." The royal castle referred to is *Al-Qaṣaba (al-)Qadīma* (now almost destroyed) which was situated on the Albaicin Hill opposite the Alhambra Hill.

We have no reason to question the correctness of King 'Abd Allāh's reference to the Alhambra construction, since these events must have been common knowledge at the time. 'Abd Allāh's memoirs are regarded as one of the most reliable sources of Zīrid history, and are corroborated in many points by other independent historians of his time. Furthermore, there is no reason to doubt that the name "Alhambra" has always referred to the same hill, for the name appears in Arab sources as early as the end of the ninth century[11], just as the Albaicin Hill and Castle of the Zīrid kings remained "the Palace of Bādīs." Considering what is known of the cultural importance of the Banū Naghrālla, it will be our task to examine the assumption that the present Alhambra buildings, including their present and future excavations, preserve traces of Yehōseph's Alhambra and to look for the existence of further references in the contemporary literature which might amplify 'Abd Allāh's information.

Unlike Samuel han-Nāghīdh, his father, Yehōseph was unable, as we gather from 'Abd Allāh, to ingratiate himself lastingly with the various groups of Granada's inhabitants. As a result, his policy seems to betray a strange blend of *hybris* and despair, the first symbolized by his building, the latter by his intrigues and his flight into the royal palace, both of which trends invited his own downfall (in 1066) after about ten years of rule[12].

Other reasons for Yehōseph's downfall have to be sought in the change of the intellectual and emotional climate in Muslim Spain which took place after the downfall of the Umayyads and the rise of the shortlived successor princelings *(Reyes de Taifas)*, soon to be replaced by the fanatic Almoravid conquerors whom some of the petty kings themselves had invited from Africa to fight the Christians. In an almost pathetic fashion, some of these princelings mustered the urge and ability to establish in their new capitals a "court" with poets, musicians, builders, gardeners, and the other paraphernalia of the caliphal tradition, and were thus instrumental once more in disseminating Cordovan culture over what had hitherto been hinterland. Yet the general development, conditioned by the instability of rule after the demise of the caliphs and subsequent eclipse of petty royalty, led to a nervous rallying of the masses towards resistance prompted by the machinations of an emboldened clergy, and this, in turn, led to austerity, bigotry, and hostility to artistic pursuits. Finally, the return to centralization effected by an absolute and unenlightened power destroyed then, as often in the history of Spain, the continuity of regional cultures.

The bigotry characteristic of this time infected even a mind as educated as Ibn Ḥazm's and we find this man not only involved in heinous religious propaganda against Judaism and Christianity but also in a personal literary attack upon Samuel. Ibn Ḥazm and, in his wake, Abū Isḥāq, "the *faqīh* from Elvira," seem to have created an animosity against the Naghrāllas that influenced wide circles in Islamic Spain against them[13]. In both cases the reasons were also personal. Ibn Ḥazm, the Muslim, born into the most influential circles of caliphal Cordova, educated in almost all the liberal arts of his time, had to live in an environment unsympathetic to his metropolitan pride. On the other hand, thanks to the triumph of the treacherous Berber upstarts over the caliphate, and their need for a man trained in the Cordovan administration and independent of the various opposing factions, Samuel, the Jew, had risen to a major-domo-like position in Granada, a town previously belonging to the caliphate. The accumulated bitterness of his exile and the angry comparison of his lot with that of Samuel han-Nāghīdh (provoked by a book written by the latter, which seems to have contained refutations of Islamic teachings), stung Ibn Ḥazm into a frantic anti-Jewish literary attack upon Samuel in particular, and the Jews in general. Such an intertwining of personal and group hatred, of general bigotry, and wounded aristocratic pride appears strikingly in a passage of attack upon Samuel in Ibn Ḥazm's work of learned calumny, which reads:[14]

> ... A man who was filled with hatred towards the Apostle (Muḥammad) — a man who is, in secret, a materialist, a free-thinker, a Jew — of that most contemptible of religions, the most vile of faiths ... loosened his tongue ... and became conceited in his vile soul, as a result of his wealth. His riches, his gold and his silver robbed him of his wretched senses; so he compiled a book in which he set out to demonstrate the alleged contradictions in the Word of God, the Koran ... When I came to know of the affair, of the work of that accursed creature, I did not cease searching for that filthy book, so that, with the gift bestowed upon me by Allāh, I might be of service by helping His faith with words and insight, and in defending His community with eloquence and knowledge. I was fortunate, and obtained a manuscript containing a refutation written by a Muslim. So I copied out the passages the polemicist had reproduced from the work of that contemptible ignoramus. I proceeded at once, with God's help, to refute his evil thoughts. By God, his argumentation proves how poor is his knowledge, how narrow his mind, about which I already knew something. For I used to know him when he was naked, except for charlatanry, serene, except for anxiety, void except of lies.

The parties vying for power had been wisely balanced by Samuel. Yehōšeph, however, appointed a large number of Jews to government office and exerted a less cautious control over the factions. As a result the discontent seething among the Berber pretorians grew into a violent rebellion against the Jewish usurper and the dominant part played in the affairs of the kingdom of Granada by his community rather than the king[15].

Poems, publicly recited, served in those days as the medium of propaganda, and the venomous quill of the aforementioned Abū Isḥāq Ibrāhīm of Elvira seems to have been most instrumental in arousing animosities. According to the historian Ibn al-Khaṭīb, Abū Isḥāq, who was a fanatic Muslim *faqīh*, had earlier been banished from Granada by Yehōšeph, and the vengeful poem had been sent to Granada to be used by Abū Isḥāq's partisans and agents against Yehōšeph. In his libellous poem he addressed himself to King Bādīs and to the other Berbers and Muslims, whose support had aided the Zīrid kings in their rise to power. The poet appeals to their pride and religious prejudice by demanding that they revolt against the government of an infidel and kill him. He ignores the known facts of the virtues of these Jewish chancellors and their contributions to the well-being

Note 15

and growth of the kingdom from its bare beginnings. Speaking of King Bādīs, he says, in the relevant passages: [16]

... Your lord has sadly erred
and his foes are rejoicing

He has selected an infidel to be his chancellor,
one who, had he wished, could have been one of the Faithful.

Giving an alarming description of the arrogance of Granada's Jews, he continues:

The earth cries out at their immorality ...

and:

They divided up Granada, capital and provinces,
and everywhere there is one of those accursed ones;

They seized her (Granada's) revenues ...

and, speaking of Yehōṡeph ibn Naghrālla himself, he says:

That ape of theirs has his mansion lined with stones[17]
and makes the purest spring flow thither[18].

Our needs are in his charge
and we must wait at his gate ...

in these lines Abū Isḥāq clearly refers to Yehōṡeph's building activities. On the one hand the poem gives the reader a sense of the major-domo's immense power over Granada, its provinces, and its Muslim population and officialdom; on the other it identifies him definitely as the builder of a lavish mansion. The poet cites as examples of Yehōṡeph's extravagance his use of precious materials, and, worse, the abuse of his power in diverting "the best well into his mansion." The poet's anger at Yehōṡeph's diversion of the best of Granada's springs indicates, in all likelihood, that this supply served not only the household but also irrigated gardens, and was possibly used for wasteful display, in the fashion of contemporary Moorish castles.

Abū Isḥāq does not specifically mention the Alhambra by name, so that in themselves these details might apply to another mansion located in Granada, though these polemic remarks, together with ʿAbd Allāh's memoirs, seem to be provoked by both the construction of the Alhambra and its Jewish builder. However bilious and blood-thirsty the poem may be, it would not have served its purpose if its statements had been obvious lies. Some exaggeration may be involved, but an accusation of having diverted a source of water and having created a provokingly extravagant mansion is too cunningly employed here to be a false allegation. The stone facing *(rajjam)* might refer either to floors or walls.

The memoirs and the poem support each other, and there is no reason to doubt the fact that Yehōšeph ibn Naghrālla carried out lavish constructions on the Alhambra hill.

Ibn Ḥazm's and Abū Isḥāq's invectives appear to have served their purpose, for in 1066 a fanatic mob stormed Yehōšeph's temporary domicile in the King's *alcazaba* of the Albaicin, and Yehōšeph and a large number of Granadine Jews perished in the ensuing slaughter[19].

The story of the house of the Jewish major-domos is mentioned in both monographs written on Abū Isḥāq, and in various other studies. Samuel ibn Naghrālla belonged from early youth to the highly emancipated and refined circle of Cordovan Jews who were later forced to flee to Malaga after the sack of the city by the Berbers in 1013[20]. This man, Ibn Naghrālla, owed his career both to the fact of this exile and to the fund of Cordovan culture he had brought with him. As a result, Samuel ibn Naghrālla was employed as chancellor of the Ṣinhāja Berber dynasty of the Zīrid kings who ruled at Granada.

The precedent for having a Jew in so paramount a position may be found in the case of Ḥašdāy ibn Shaprūṭ who had been chancellor (though not vizier) at the court of the Umayyad caliph ʿAbd ar-Raḥmān III in Cordova (891—961)[21]. As chancellor to the court of the newly established capital, Samuel was instrumental in raising it to a level of great splendor. At the same time he expanded his own power. The colorful family of chancellors aroused the admiration both of Arabic and Jewish contemporary writers, and of subsequent ones as well. The judgment passed on him after his death by the contemporary Arab historian Ibn Ḥayyān may certainly be regarded as objective, since the latter was in no way a mercenary court flatterer. He writes (typically enough for the postcaliphal period and its rising prejudice):[22]

> This accursed Jew was in himself one of the most perfect men, although God had denied him His guidance. He excelled in learning, endurance, intelligence and wit, charm of character, perseverance,

astuteness, cunning, self-control and natural courtesy. He knew how to act according to the requirements of the moment, how to flatter his enemies and remove suspicion from their hearts by his fine manners. What an uncommon man! He wrote with two pens [i. e. Arabic and Hebrew] and cultivated two fields of learning [i. e. the Arabic and the Jewish]. He was passionately interested in the Arabic language, explored it, studied its literature, and investigated its roots. His hand and his tongue mastered it quite freely and he used to write in Arabic in his own name and on behalf of his king, applying if necessary Muslim invocations to God and his Prophet. He extolled Islam and enlarged on its advantages, so that his letters sounded like propaganda for that faith. He was also proficient in the learning of the ancients [i. e. the Greeks], in the various branches of mathematics, and his lore of astronomy surpassed that of the astronomers. He also knew all about geometry and logic. His consummate debating crushed his opponents. As he was wise, he spoke little, but he thought much. He collected a splendid library. He died between the 11th and 20th of Muḥarram of the year 459. The Jews carried his bier on their shoulders and bore him to the cemetery; stricken with great grief they bewailed his end, voicing long-drawn-out laments. Samuel had induced his son Yehōseph, surnamed Abū Ḥusain, to devote himself to books; he assembled for him teachers and *literati* from all countries and had recommended him to devote himself above all to the art of letter writing. As soon as the young man was educated, his father obtained for him employment as secretary with the son of his master, Buluqqīn the heir to the throne, and Yehōseph contrived the disastrous death of the latter. On Samuel's death [at the time indicated above], Bādīs accorded his confidence to Yehōseph; he enjoyed his company and regarded the son as the successor to his father.

That Samuel led the military forces of Granada as a war lord or "army chancellor" during ten years of generally victorious warfare is documented in poems and Arabic prefatory notes recently found in Hebrew manuscripts. He established an academy of Jewish scholars, and his school chiefly raised Hebrew secular poetry to a classical standard. His Hebrew kasidas, describing his battles, combine Cordovan artistry and a *condottiere's* individualism with a belief in a personal, almost messianic, mission. In some of these poems he speaks of his inner voice and of the divine protecting power, which will lead him unharmed through all the dangers of battles and seafaring, and possibly regards himself as the Shiloh, mentioned in

Genesis XLIX. 10, who will bring about the messianic deliverance[23]. He seems to have felt equally safe upon the murderously slippery floors of the audience hall of an Oriental potentate. *Nāghīdh*, "Leader" or "Prince," is the title for the highest secular office, used for Saul (I Sam. IX. 15) and for Solomon (I Kings I. 35). In Daniel IX. 25 in the form of *māshīaḥ nāghīdh* the title received a messianic connotation. Its adoption for the heads of the Jewish community at this time must be understood in the light of the Jewish tradition and situation[24]. Living under the rule of Muslim princes, the Jews could of course not have independent kings; yet the title *nāghīdh*, conferred upon the Naghrāllas by the Jews, was confirmed by the Muslim authorities. (A "king" under a foreign rule might have invited a comparison with Jesus, mockingly referred to as 'king of the Jews' by the Roman authorities.) Samuel han-Nāghīdh was talented in intrigue, using this talent on behalf of his king, and was instrumental in choosing the royal successor[25]. The son of Samuel, Yehōseph ibn Naghrālla, inherited his father's refinement, his intellectual interests, his far-reaching ambitions, but not his political genius. Born into a world of splendor, educated by a father who idolized him and instilled into him dreams of a romantic revival of a Solomonic kingdom, Yehōseph, who had not the "humility" of the *dhimmī*, strained his potential power to the utmost[26]. The account of these developments given by 'Abd Allāh (who saw in Yehōseph the murderer of his royal father and his own mortal enemy) may very well be somewhat biased; however, if he did so at all, it would seem that Yehōseph began to plot against the Zīrid dynasty only as a measure of precaution against the event of the wavering or the death of his only real supporter, old King Bādīs himself. What would seem to indicate that Yehōseph was innocent of plotting against his king is the fact that Bādīs nourished bitter feelings against Yehōseph's murderers[27].

Since we know from Jewish sources that Yehōseph, like his father, surrounded himself with a circle of scholars and poets to glorify his court, might we not expect to find references to the erection of that castle in their writings also? We do, indeed, find an additional source of corroborative evidence in a panegyric poem of the famous Hebrew poet and philosopher, Solomon ibn Gabirol. This poet maintained very close ties with father and son Ibn Naghrālla and was a distinguished member of their circle. A good many poems, chiefly panegyric but also aggressive, addressed to them by Ibn Gabirol, have been preserved. I deal briefly with the relationship among the three men in a succeeding chapter.

Notes 23—27

B. Ibn Gabirol's Testimony: A Nature Poem and Encomium to a Maecenas and his Castle

Ibn Gabirol's family, like that of Samuel han-Nāghīdh, belonged to the group of Jewish refugees from Cordova that escaped to Malaga. Although born in Malaga and laureled early in the Tujībid capital of Saragossa, this Hispano-Hebrew poet, one of the most emancipated of minds, had a typical Cordovan orientation, so that Moses ibn Ezra, when speaking of Ibn Gabirol, called him a Cordovan. He is famous for both his poetical work and his Neoplatonic philosophy. In the latter connection his *Fons Vitae* had gained such prominence in the Christian West that it became the main target for St. Thomas Aquinas' attack in his *De Ente et Essentia*. Ibn Gabirol shared with Samuel the prevailing bent towards a secular sensibility and realism, and evolved a dream kingdom of his own, in the tradition of his Biblical namesake Solomon. Such secularism and what we shall call, later on, "Solomonic heresy," in no way conflicted with an ardent religiosity which prevailed in both Samuel han-Nāghīdh and Solomon ibn Gabirol. We find in Ibn Gabirol's secular *dīwān* poems of love and friendship, poems of literary strife, aulic praise of his Maecenates, and also the typically Arabic self-praise poems. There are also dirges and elegies and, most indicative of his urbane awareness of external beauty, descriptive poems. In one of these poems[28] we find, in addition to the topics of "Praise of a Maecenas" and "Announcement of Spring," a vivid description of a castle and the figurative art of its interior. A preoccupation with such art would have been taboo to earlier and later generations within both Islam and Judaism. The building described is singularly reminiscent of the Alhambra in Granada:

Le khā re'ī — Schirmann, *Shīrāh* I, p. 223 ff.

◡ - - - ◡ - - - ◡ - - *(Wāfir)* — *Qobheṣ hōṣā'ath Schocken le-dhibhrey siphrūth*, Tel Aviv, 1941, pp. 146 ff.

Rhyme: *r-īm*

Go forth my friend and friend of the heavenly luminaries,
go forth with me and let us lodge in the villages. Cant. VII. 12

Cant. II. 11f. (Jer. VIII. 7) Behold, winter is past and we hear
in our land the stirring voices of swallows and turtledoves.

Let us lodge in the shadow of the pomegranates and the palm tree
(Lev. XXIII. 40) and the apple and all the splendid citrus plants.

Let us walk in the shade of the vines
let us long to see faces resplendent with grace

In the palace exalted above all its surroundings
and erected with precious stones,

(I Sam. XXVI. 4; Ps. XI. 3; LXXV. 4) Gauged uprightly from its foundations,
and its walls are fortified with towers.

(I Ki. VI. 5) And a leveled gallery surrounds it —
(Cant. II. 1) roses of Sharon adorn allco the urtyards.

Neh, VII. 4 I Ki VI. 4; Mid. to Lev. XXXI. 7 The buildings are built and decorated
with openwork, intaglios and filigrees,

Esth. I. 6 Paved with marble slabs and alabaster —
I cannot count its many gates.

Ps. XLV. 9 I Ki. X. 12; XXII. 39 (II Chr. II. 7) The doors are like those of the ivory mansions
reddened by palatial algum woods.

And there are windows, transparent above them,
I Ki. VI. 4 skylights where dwell the luminous planets.

Cant. III. 9 The dome is like the Palanquin of Solomon
(Isa. II. 16); Job XXXVIII. 12 hung above the glories of the chambers,

That rotates in its gyre, shining like
opals and sapphire and pearls;

Thus it is in the daytime, while at dusk it looks
like the sky whose stars form constellations;

The heart of the poor and burdened delights in this,
the perishing forget their poverty and bitterness. Prov. XXXI. 6f.

I saw this and forgot my burden
and my heart was relieved from sorrows;

Yea, my body all but soared in my joy
as upon wings of eagles.

And there is a full sea, like unto Solomon's Sea, I Ki. VII. 23ff.
though not on oxen it stands,

But there are lions, in phalanx by its rim,
as though roaring for prey — these whelps Ps. CIV. 21

Whose bellies are wellsprings that spout forth
through their mouths floods like streams.

And there are hinds embedded in the channels,
hollowed out as water spouts Talm. B. Nid. 71

To douse the plants in the beds,
and upon the lawns to shed clear waters (Hos. XIII. 15; Ezek. XLVI. 14; Gen. XXIV. 20)

Wherewith to freshen the myrtle garden —
they are like clouds sprinkling the treetops

Whose scent is like balsam scent,
as if they were fumed with myrrh-incense. Cant. III. 6, IV. 14

And birds give sound among the branches Ps. CIV. 12
and look down upon the fronds of the date palms. (Lev. XXIII. 40)

Flowers for luxuriant bowers-to-enchant,
like roses, nards, and camphor blossoms, Cant. I. 12ff.

They vaunt themselves, one above the other (Judges VII. 2)
(they are all choice, however, in our eyes).

The camphor blossoms speak: "Lo, white as we are
we are sovereign over the luminaries."

Nah. II. 7; Is. LIX. 11 And the doves, moaning in their musing,
say, "We rank above the turtledoves.

These wherewith we spellbind the heart
are, more than opals, precious."

(Cant. II. 7) And the 'gazelles' arise against the maidens
and shroud with charms their charms

And also vaunt together above them,
for they are like young hinds.

Yet when the sun lifted herself above them —
I answered her: "Be still! Try not to slip through loopholes!

Confess to the prince that he eclipses you
with a lucent light excelling the luminaries

Before whose face all royal splendor droops
and every ruler's excellence fades;

(Neh. V. 7) By whose advice kings become kings
and with whom regent and duke consult.

They raised him as their king, that he became
(Dan. IV. 25; Is. XI. 7) a lion-whelp among them and oxen all their hosts;

II Sam. XIV. 17 He being among them like the messenger of God,
I Sam. III. 1 when from a god they found out no words.

Is. XL. 11; Cant. II. 16; Ez. XXXIV. 23 Shepherd leading his sheep upon still pastures:
Ps. XXIII. 2; Is. XL. 26 nought was ever missing from the flocks!

Precious-souled, heaven's adornment, generous-hearted:
(Ps. XXII.25) without vowing he keeps the vows!

Deut. XXXIV. 7 Whose eye has never dimmed while he pours out gifts,
Prov. XVI. 15 as his cloud has never withheld its rains;

Whose words are fastened to his deeds,
even as crowns are fastened to heads.

All regents — to him they repair, II Chr. IX. 22
as unto the sea are drawn the rivers. Eccl. I. 7

In truth, he is like a 'head' above the earth, (Hosea II. 2; *K. J. V.* I. 11)
he, the one, set off from all creatures!"

The literary genre of this poem is the Arabic "description" *(waṣf)*. The majority of the images, the syntax, tenses, cognate meaning, etc., are inspired by Arabic models. To what degree Ibn Gabirol's poem remains in the orbit of the two Arabic themes *waṣf* and *madīḥ* (aulic encomium) and how far his Hebrew symbolism transcends these (and contributes in this case a specific ideology) will be apparent to the reader, but I shall discuss it on the basis of the analysis of other poems by our poet.

The "contractility" or compactness of this poem betrays the latest style of the poet. Several questions suggest themselves. (1) What induced Ibn Gabirol, whose authorship of this poem is beyond question, to render so striking an image of the castle? (2) For whom and under what conditions was it written? (3) Finally, is the castle described here indeed the Alhambra? If so, could the fount of lions described in this poem of the eleventh century be identical with the present Fount of Lions in the Alhambra (Pl. 2), hitherto ascribed to the fourteenth century?

From internal evidence it would seem that the poem, first of all, must have been directed at a person able to read Hebrew, no doubt a Jew, and most likely a learned Jew, who would understand the Biblical allusions and be interested in this highly secular Hebrew *dolce stil nuovo*, a man subject neither to the prejudices of Islam nor the strictures of the Second Commandment on plastic art, and the builder of a castle where such art was monumentally displayed[29]. Among Muslims, representational sculpture was tolerated within the courtly circles of some ʿAbbāsid, Fāṭimid, and Ṭūlūnid rulers and, as we shall see, of a few other later Muslim courts. However, plastic art found its most established place under the two Umayyad caliphates at the courts and castles in Syria and of those of Cordova. After the downfall of the Spanish Umayyads, plastic art lived on for a while under the "successor kings" *(mulūk aṭ-ṭawā'if)*.

In the case of Hebrew poetry no other document like this is known; only in the sphere of Cordovan emancipation did such freedom from inhibitions have its short-lived bloom. Ibn Gabirol's lack of prejudice against "graven images" is indeed indicative of his membership in the Cordovan intellectual elite. In the history of the Jews in Spain of this period only father and son Ibn Naghrālla fit completely the requirements set up by our poem for the builders of such a castle and the addressees

Note 29; Plate 2

of such a poem. Moreover, we know from King ʿAbd Allāh's aforementioned memoirs that Yehōseph ibn Naghrālla built the "Alhambra castle" for himself[30]. Even if the poem had been a gross exaggeration of reality, it would, nevertheless, remain a source of factual evidence. I shall discuss this in detail after an analysis of the poem itself.

Our secular poem, in a manner typical of Ibn Gabirol, includes many themes. The introduction is an "invitation to a journey," very boldly paraphrasing the Song of Solomon and, also in parallel with this Biblical book, an "announcement of spring":[31]

> Go forth my friend and friend of the heavenly luminaries,
> go forth with me and let us lodge in the villages.
>
> Behold, winter is past and we hear
> in our land the stirring voices of swallows and turtledoves.

The first part of the poem, in the style of the Arabic love phantasy, *nasib* or *taghazzul*, is addressed to the Maecenas. The language, although borrowed from the Song of Solomon (VII. 12), is here made to serve a secular purpose with the insertion of the hyperbolic address to the "Friend of the Luminaries" *(reʿa ham-meʾōr-īm)*. This expression belongs, strangely, to the gnostic vocabulary. In the system of Mani, the "Friend of the Luminaries," Narisaf or Narishank, is the "First Man's" first helper, created during a "Second Creation[32]." Such grandiloquence of address by Ibn Gabirol is not unique, it is of course no more than hyperbolic speech for 'over-man'.

The Song of Songs owes its preservation in the Bible itself, and its esteem during the ascetic Middle Ages, solely to the fact that it was given a mystical interpretation, symbolizing the love between God, the Messiah, and Israel, or Jesus and the Church, or God and the individual soul of the mystic. But when, during the eleventh-century renascence in Spain under the impact of Arabic poetry, still relatively close to its pagan roots, Hebrew poets again began to write secular lyrics, Solomon's Song was heard again, for the first time in its original secular tonality.

In the light of the discussion below, we cannot but assume that the Solomonic "announcement of spring" in our poem may well have messianic overtones. The poet, daring to use, in relation to Yehōseph, the invocation from Solomon's Song, so often used as an invitation to the Messiah (and similarly in Ibn Gabirol's own religious poems), may do so with various implications: (a) he may do so as an acme of flattery, attributing, semi-sacrilegiously, messianic traits to his Maecenas; (b) he may sincerely wish with his Solomonic address to initiate Yehōseph, temptingly, into the messianic rôle expected from him; (c) he may wish to show himself initiated into the secret pretensions of the Naghrāllas and their esoteric language, A poet in his quasi-ecstatic suspense, in listening to his own inner voices. may have been able to combine all these attitudes. But, as we shall see, messianism itself, in Cordova and Granada to some degree self-messianism, was, paradoxically enough, secularized; and when given a Solomonic liberal and artistic orientation it was reduced occasionally to court flattery, an element inherent in it from its beginning but forgotten[33] in the circles of purely rabbinical orientation.

The love-phantasy introduction ends in an *invitation au voyage*, *à la* Baudelaire, but we are surprised to discover that the journey is into the gardens of a castle. The castle is then described at some length in purely physical terms; towards the end, as an act of bravura, the typically Arabic motif of contest for supremacy *(munāẓara)* is introduced, an argument imaginatively enacted by the objects in the castle, such as trees and statues, and its inhabitants — boys, girls, the prince, etc.[34] In much the same way as in Homer's description of the shaping of Achilles' shield (a method extolled in Lessing's *Laocoon*), one part of the castle after the other moves of itself to the fore, vying, with self-praise, for pre-eminence[35].

Dist. 33: With distich 33 the poet interrupts the contest[36] to exclaim, in courtly flattery, that this contest is futile, since there is, of course, nothing in the castle more splendid than its master, who, in his viceregal power, is praised in superlatives, and with the employ of authenticating biblical parallelism (which the Arabic taste of our poet repudiates more and more), and is described as a major-domo and adviser of kings.

ist. 5 f.: The castle itself is described as being situated upon a hill, "high above all its surroundings," "fortified with towers," and large ("I cannot count its many gates"). It has extensive gardens and a court of myrtles. The
st. 18 ff.: highest praise is accorded its fountains, among them a fount of lions, which has a phalanx of lions circling its base supporting a "sea" reminiscent of Solomon's "Brazen Sea." These lions are hollow, and spout water from their mouths. There are water channels, and there are also hinds spouting water as high as the tops of the trees. The owner and builder of this castle
t. 35 ff.: is a man of royal splendor, "before whose face all royal splendor droops and every ruler's excellence fades; by whose advice kings become kings and with whom regent and duke consult" who "raised him as their king, that he became a lion-whelp among them and oxen all their hosts."

In asserting the documentary value of such panegyrics I base myself, as I have said before, on the common-sense assumption that to praise someone as the owner of something he does not own would be a grave

Notes 33—36

insult. Indeed, the Arab attitude towards poets who praised a Maecenas for things he did not own is demonstrated by Abū Shirwān, who said: "He who praises you for a merit that is not yours might also blame you for a fault that you did not commit[37]." Whenever poets do, on occasion, misrepresent or exaggerate facts, common-sense analysis, again, will expose the reason for the poetic licence. What must also be considered in this case is the position and dignity of Ibn Gabirol, the philosopher, the author of an ethical treatise and of religious poetry, whose work is pervaded by his philosophical integrity and his very specific, rather Spanish pride in his Solomonic heritage of wisdom, which he himself extols in many poems of *fakhr* in the Arab taste. Such a man would have been loth to make a fool of himself and to alienate a Maecenas by an off-key panegyric poem. In his invective poetry, indeed, Ibn Gabirol betrays an aggressive temper, and we know that he alienated the objects of his attacks. However, it is absurd to imagine that he was so poor a poet and son of his time, that he did not know whether or not one of his panegyrics fell into the pleasing or offensive pattern of taste. It has been correctly observed that the Cordovan poets of the generation of Ibn Ḥazm (and Ibn Gabirol) made a point of veracity and condemned previous mendacious poets. When Ibn Ḥazm (like the contemporary al-Maʿarrī) complained that poets were liars, he, the Cordovan, distinguished himself from them, and frowned at such licence[38]. The same Ibn Ḥazm has been characterized above as the re-instater of the value of direct sensuous perception. Ibn Gabirol was carried along by this wave of sensitivity, which Cordova experienced on the threshold of the eleventh century. In his 'descriptions' of nature and, as here, of buildings, he speaks with the fidelity of immediacy; his veracity is one aspect of the contemporaneity of passionate enchantment. This distinguishes him and his generation from the artificial and affected earlier and later Arabic and Hebrew poets. I shall treat this subject more extensively, in connection with Ibn Gabirol's great nature poem, in Part III.

Notes 37—38

C. Location of Yehōseph ibn Naghrālla's Alhambra Palace

Ibn Gabirol's poem describes in detail a fortified palace. The poem also mentions the most precious materials employed in the construction of this fortified castle, and specifically, a dome construction as well as a fount of lions which aroused the poet's admiration. Where among the remnants of the present Alhambra are we likely to find the vestiges of such a construction[39]? The foundations and lower parts of almost the entire present "Alcazaba" of the Alhambra show typical eleventh-century masonry: horizontal lines of bricks inserted between oblong patches of rather small, usually round, flattened stones (Pl. 8) — the masonry of the Zīrid period well known from the oldest parts of the fortress of Malaga (Pl. 4)[40]. We know more facts about the Alhambra of the period from the memoirs of King ʿAbd Allāh, the last Zīrid king, who re-fortified Granada. However, there is not the least indication in the sources to justify the assumption made by L. Torres Balbás that ʿAbd Allāh had to complete the Alhambra palace on this occasion. Consequently, since we do not know of other builders at work on the Alhambra during this period, it would be difficult to deny the likelihood that the Zīrid elements of the Alhambra, both of the Alcazaba and of other parts, belong to Yehōseph ibn Naghrālla's construction[41]. Outside the precincts of the present Alcazaba (of the Alhambra), Zīrid masonry appears, in the present "Alhambra Palace" area, in the Puerta de Vino (Pl. 3), as part of a wall, recently unearthed, which connected this gate with the Torre do Machuca area[42], and also, as I have satisfied myself, in the sub-structures of various other towers, such as the Torre de los Picos, and the Torre de Comares. These data together seem to indicate what must have been the area covered by Yehōseph's constructions.

Notes 39—42; Plates 3—4, 8

D. The Court of Lions

(1) MODERN DESCRIPTIONS

I invite the reader to follow me now into the core of my investigation, devoted to that unique monument of Muslim plastic art, found on innumerable posters advertising southern Spain and in books on the history of Spanish art — the only remnant of its kind and the true heart of the Alhambra castle. No modern visitor to southern Spain could easily forego exposing at least his camera to it. As long as the origin of the Fount of Lions was veiled, the travel handbooks of the last century tried to give some answer to the riddle of its genesis, but, though they discerned its Solomonic typology, they were far from realizing its Jewish origin.

The days are past when poetical travelers wrote cicerones to accompany other tourists, and when their sentimental journeys were allowed to set the tone for other, less original souls thirsty for enchantment. I quote descriptions of the Court of Lions, one French, one English, one Italian, one German, and one of my own.

(a) A. Germond de Lavigne, *Itinéraire de l'Espagne et du Portugal*, Paris, 1883, pp. 338f. (other edition, Paris, n. d., pp. 613ff.):

Nous avons dit que la célèbre Cour des Lions (Patio de los Leones) communique avec la cour des Arrayanes.

La cour des Lions a 32 mèt. (120 pieds) de long, 20 de large (73 pieds); les galéries qui l'entourent mesurent 6 mèt. ($22^1/_2$ pieds) de haut. Elles sont formées par 128 colonnes de marbre blanc, appareillées dans un désordre symétrique de 4 en 4 et de 3 en 3. Ces colonnes, dont les chapiteaux très ouvragés conservent des traces d'or et de couleur, supportent des arcs d'une élégance extrême et d'une coupe toute particulière. Au milieu de deux des côtés, s'avancent sur la cour deux élégants portiques de 8 mèt. (29 pieds) de haut, soutenus par un même système de colonnes, mais écrasés sous de lourdes toitures en tuiles rondes remplaçant les jolies terrasses aériennes qui couronnaient l'édifice. Ces portiques et les galéries qui enveloppent la cour forment intérieurement un ravissant ensemble d'arcs pendants, de petites voûtes, de niches et de colonnettes, soutenant une coupole de bois ouvragé et assemblé comme une précieuse marqueterie. Le sol est dallé en marbre blanc, et au milieu [de chaque portique s'élève, au niveau du sol] (une vasque) un bassin de 1 mèt. (4 pieds) de diamètre avec un jet d'eau. Au centre du patio, qui jusqu'en ces derniers temps était planté (d'orangers, de rosiers, de jasmins, de camellias et d'autres fleurs choisies), d'arbustes et de fleurs choisies se trouve une fontaine ornée dans le style de tout ce qui l'entoure. La vasque qui forme un polygone à douze côtés, de 3 mèt. (10$^1/_2$ pieds) de diamètre et 60 cent. (2 pieds) de profondeur, est soutenue par douze lions grossièrement sculptés. "Les pattes, dit Théophile Gautier, sont de simples piquants pareils à ces morceaux de bois à peine dégrossis qu'on enfonce dans le ventre des chiens de carton pour les faire tenir en équilibre; les mufles, rayés de barres transversales, sans doute pour figurer les moustaches, ressemblent parfaitement à des museaux d'hippopotame; les yeux sont d'un dessin par trop primitif qui rappelle les informes essais des enfants. Cependant ces douze monstres, en les acceptant, non pas comme lions, mais comme chimères, comme caprices d'ornement, font avec la vasque qu'ils supportent un effet pittoresque et plein d'élégance, qui aide à comprendre leur réputation. *La taza de los leones* jouit dans les poésies arabes d'une réputation merveilleuse, il n'est pas d'éloges dont on ne comble ces superbes animaux." Du centre de la vasque, nommée el mar, s'élève une base qui supporte une autre vasque plus petite de 1 mèt. $^1/_2$ (4 pieds) de diamètre et de 40 cent. (18 pouces) de profondeur [c'est celle-ci qu'on nomme *la taza*]; un jet d'eau en jaillit à une assez grande hauteur; d'autres s'élancent de la grande vasque, et les lions eux-mêmes versent par la gueule des torrents sur le marbre de la cour. Cette cour est le plus précieux des monuments arabes que possède l'Espagne, mais elle est malheureusement mal conservée; la toiture dont nous avons parlé est d'un aspect ignoble, et sous prétexte de restauration on a gratté les colonnes et la fontaine d'une façon grossière, et on a impitoyablement détruit et effacé les sculptures, les arabesques et les inscriptions qui les ornaient.

(b) *Murray's Hand-Book of Spain*, John Murray, London, 1847, pp. 139f., reprinted as Richard Ford, *Granada, escritos con Dibujos Ineditos del Autor*, Granada, 1955, pp. 209f.

Retracing our steps through the *Patio de la Alberca*, we pass by an anteroom, much altered by Ferdinand and Isabella, into the Court of Lions, a Moorish *cloister*, but one never framed for ascetics. Here bad taste and vandalism have done their worst. The vile tiled roof, fitter for a barn than a palace, was clapped on by the Irishman Wall in 1770 — a round hat on a gorgeous Mameluke. The cockney garden was the work of the French; that, thank God! had been done away with recently. The repair and white-washings are Spanish. *Ay! de mi Alhambra!*

The patio is an hypethral quadrilateral oblong of some 120 feet by 60: more than 100 pillars of white marble support a peristyle or portico on each side; at each end elegant pavilions project into the court. The columns are placed sometimes singly, sometimes grouped; although they are so slender that they scarcely seem able to support the arches, five centuries of neglect have not yet destroyed this slight fairy thing of filigree, which has not even the appearance of durability; wherever the destroyer has mutilated the fragile ornaments, the temple-loving martlet, guest of summer, builds his nest, and careers in the delicate air, breaking with his twitter the silence of these sunny, now deserted courts, once made for Oriental enjoyment, and even now just the place to read the *Arabian Nights* in, or spend a honeymoon.

The *fuente* in the centre is a dodecagon basin of alabaster, resting on the backs of twelve lions: they are rudely carved, and closely resemble those of Apulia and Calabria, by which tombs and pulpits of Norman-Saracenic mosaic work are supported. These Arabian sculptures make up for want of reality by a sort of quaint heraldic antiquity; such were those described by Arnobius (*Adv. Gen.* VI), *Inter Deos videmus leonis torvissimam faciem.* Their faces are barbecued, and their manes cut like scales of a griffin, and the legs like bedposts; a water-pipe stuck in their mouths does not add to their dignity. Lions, from remote antiquity, have been used as supporters; the Oriental type will be found in the throne of Solomon (I Kings VII. 29; X. 20). In fact, the whole Alhambra must have been like the ancient and Byzantine palaces. The Hypodromus, the 'portico with a hundred pillars', the *azulejo* pavement, the cypresses, the net-work of fountains, the sound of falling waters, are all detailed by Martial (XII. 50) and Pliny, jun. (Ep. V. 6)[43], and such was the palace of Justinian described by Gibbon.

Since the damages done by Sebastiani, the fountains of the amphibious Moor, which played here in all directions, are ruined and dry. That of the Lions alone is restored, and occasionally is set in action. Some of the most beautiful chambers of the Alhambra open into this court: beginning to the r. is the *Sala de los Abencerrages*; the exquisite door was sawn into pieces in 1837 by the barbarian governor; observe the honeycomb stalactite roof; the slender pillar of the alcove explains how Samson pulled down the support of the house of Dagon. The roof and *Azulejos* were repaired by Charles V.; the guide points out some dingy stains near the fountain as the blood-marks of the Abencerrages, massacred here by Boabdil; alas, that boudoirs made for life and love should witness scenes of hatred and death! And oh, dearest reader! believe this and every tale of the Alhambra, a sacred spot far beyond the jurisdiction of matter-of-fact and prosaic history; do not disenchant the romance of poetry, the *genius loci;* where fairies have danced their mystic rings, flowers may spring, but mere grass will never grow: above all, eschew geology; deem not these spots ferruginous, for nothing is more certain than that heroic blood never can be effaced, still less if shed in foul murder. Nor, according to Lady Macbeth, will all the perfumes of Arabia mask the smell. This blood is quite as genuine to all intents of romance as is that of Becket at Canterbury. Beware, says Voltaire, 'des gens durs qui se disent solides, des esprits sombres qui prétendent au jugement parce-qu'ils sont dépourvus d'imagination, qui veulent proscrire la belle antiquité de la fable — gardez-vous bien de les croire'.

(c) Andrea Navagiero, *Il Viaggio fatto in Spagna et in Francia*, Venice, 1563, pp. 23f.[44]

... Detta Alhambra ha le sue muraglie a torno: et è com' uno castello separato dal resto della città: alla qual predomina quasi tutta. vi è dentro bon numero di case: ma il più però del spatio è occupato da un bel palazzo, que era de Re Mori: que in vero è molto bello, et fabricato sontuosissamente, si de i marmori fini, como di ogn' altra cosa: i qual marmori però non sono ne i muri, ma ne i suoli in terra: vi è un gran corte, ò spatio, al modo Spagnolo, molto bella, et grande, circondata da fabrica intorno, ma da una parte, ha una torre singular et bellissima, che chiamano la Tor de Comarez [sic] nella qual vi sono alcune sale, et camere molto bone, con le fenestre fatte molto gentil et commodamente, con lavori moreschi assai eccelenti, si nelli muri, come nel cielo de gl'allogiamenti: i lavori parte son di giesso con oro assai: et parte di Avorio, et oro accompagnato: in vero tutti bellissimi: et massime il cielo della sala da basso, et tutti i muri, la corte è tutta saleggiata di finissimi et bianchissimi marmi, delli quali vi sono pezzi grandissimi per mezzo vi è come un canale pieno di acqua viva, d'una fontana che intra in detto palazzo, et se vi conduce per ogni parte fina nelle camere. da un canto a l'altro di detto canale vi e una spallera di mirto bellissima, et alquanti pè di naranci. di questa corte si intra in un' altra minore, ma saleggiata di bellissimi marmi anchor lei, et cinta di fabrica da ogni canto, et un portico: ha anchor questa alcune sale belle, et ben lavorate, et fresche per la estate, ma non però si belle come la torre di sopra detta, in mezzo il spatio vi è una bellissima fonte che per esser atta di alquanti leoni che gettano l'aqua per la bocca, da nome alla corte, che si chiama il spatio [sic] de los Leones. questi Leoni sostengono un vaso della fonte, et son fatti di tal maniera, che quando non vi vien acqua, se un' huomo dice alcuna parola alla bocca d'un di questi Leoni, dicala quanto bassa si vuole, se si pone alla bocca di tutti gl'altri la orecchia, in ogni parte risponde si la voce che s'intende tutto quel che dice. vi son tra l'altre cose in questo palazzo alcuni bellissimi bagni sotto terra, tutti saleggiati di marmi finissimi, et con i suoi luochi da lavar pur di marmoro tutti: et hanno il lume dal tetto, con molti vedri posti come occhi in ogni parte. di questo palazzo si esce per una porta secreta di dietro ... et si intra in un bellissimo giardino d'un palazzo ... detto Gniahalariffe [sic].

(d) From Clemens Brentano's Alhambra poem.

(40) Von mir gefühlt, von mir gesponnen,
Gewebt, erlebt! — du Zauberlust,
Die hier umschirmt den Löwenbronnen,
Lagst wie ein Kind an meiner Brust!

(41) Berauscht vom Duft der Rosenhecken,
Wo kühn die Lust dem Dorn entschlüpft,
Trägt Löwen-Grossmut Marmorbecken,
Vom Demanttropfen kühl durchhüpft.

(42) O Halle der Abenceragen!
Die Blutspur klaget laut genug,
Die Wunden, die mir sind geschlagen,
Die Wunden, die ich andern schlug.

(43) Dies Seufzen, Stöhnen, Flehen, Schwirren,
Die Geisterklage, die hier tönt,
Sie fleht zu mir — dies bange Girren!
Es fleht aus mir, ach seid versöhnt!

(44) Ach fortgehn, fortgehn! Bitte, bitte!
Ins Gärtchen dort ich gehen will,
Dort blüht's in des Palastes Mitte,
In sich gehüllt geheim und still.

(45) Kleinod der süssen Lindachara,
Du der Alhambra Blumenstrauss,
Lieb sprichst du süss, wie Dulcamara,
Mit Leid in einem Namen aus.

(46) Beschlossnes Gärtchen aller Wonne,
Wo keusch der Mond im Brunnen spielt
Und sich der Strahl der Mittagssonne
Im Schoss der vollen Rose kühlt.

— After Wilhelm Fraenger: "Clemens Brentanos Alhambra," in *Castrum Peregrini*, 1964.

(e) A First Visit to the Alhambra (by the author, in *Atlantis*, XXXI, 1959, pp. 241 ff.).

Although the solid walls, towers, and gardens of the Alhambra stand out and are accentuated toward the steep western precipice, forming a strong fortress, the general impression of the Alhambra is one of integration with its environment. Absurd as it may sound, the enclosed castle dissolves into the landscape. Seen from a distance, the Alhambra is not isolated upon its hill, for a few other strongholds with their surrounding parks further uphill adjoin its walls, and all these form an interconnected network of water-gardens. The water brings a green ambiente indoors, a lush natural growth inside the cloisters. (I am not confusing in my memory the greenness of El Greco's Toledo picture with the evergreen Granadine fortress and palace.)

The visitor coming from the center of Granada leaves the city by the Puerta de las Granadas. As soon as the city discharges him he is enchanted by the murmuring of the runnels hidden in the shades of the Alhambra copses, re-entering Paradise from the Land of Nod, as it were, to use Calvin Kentfield's words. Two paths, one steep, one comfortably level, invite him into the woods; but the rich undergrowth still hides the Alhambra above. Upon reaching the castle he finds his path blocked by a fountain of Charles V outside the walls, but is also directed by it through what is now the main entrance gateway. Once within the ring of walls he is drawn forward by the varied sights. On entering the first tower edifice he is guided toward a magnificent window, which gives a view of the city deep down to the foot of the steep cliffs. But the series of courtyards draws him on until he reaches the Court of Lions and it enfolds him in an almost overwhelming tranquility. This square court — even though familiar to the visitor from pictures — comes a surprise. It surrounds the Fountain like the setting of a jewel, and, compact as it is, it accommodates the visitor well. How could something so clear, so perfectly formulated, offer us so much mystery and charm and enmesh us in its fairy-tale web? Is it light, water, or sound which enshrines its secret?

Even the stone, with its unchanging gesture, enthralls us with so much persuasion.

A Gothic building overwhelms us, dwarfs us, until it draws us upward; an Indian temple absorbs us by its jungle-like maze, introduces us to the mystery of the authentic behind all dazzling multiplicity, nay dissolves us with a foretaste of Nirvana. The Greek temple is not a receptacle for us. Its dimensions are to invite the Olympian gods, it embodies the Idea, it reminds us of the Transcendental Form, which has its dwelling above the heavens. The courtyards of the Alhambra, however, in harmony with themselves and with us, fill our spirit, are both frame and content, are background and foreground, are a triumphant this-worldly manifestation of a Beyond. There is further enchantment in the other courts of the palace. There is the Court of Myrtles with its pool, so large that it almost completely occupies the court, the roofed halls with their stalactite domes and the smaller towers, the pavilions and also, following the crest of the hill, the gardens of the Generalife.

One might wish, as Washington Irving did, to live here for a long time and share his discovery with others. But the Western mind may also yearn to perpetuate itself in *mnemosyne* and to secure its property in the storehouse of reason and understanding. It may wish to give intellectual thanks, and inquire who are the authors of such magnificence to whom this tribute is owed. Thus the first enthralling experience suggests a host of questions about the origin of the Alhambra structure, its ideas, its symbolism and its builders.

The following questions may come foremost: which imaginative generation lifted itself to fashioning such spellbinding beauty? Was it the spirit of the oriental fairy tales of Baghdad or that of the hanging gardens of old? Did these ideas stem from the realm of the desert mirage, or was it imperial Rome, or Byzantium? Was the strong desire for formation, ornamentation, and dynamic fluctuation, paired with a propensity towards dissolving solid matter into frail filigree, towards mirroring and distorting of solids by light and water undulation, a tendency to produce the illusion of magic? Since we know of the Islamic anathema against figure images, we realize that these restrictions seem to have provoked an overwhelming flourish of ornamentation in its place. But in two instances the urge must have been too strong and created the lion statues. These are our questions, and let us anticipate the answer. Indeed, all this is alive here in addition to the heritage of the Old Testament, for the Moorish period was the most ingenious assimilator in Western history. When discovering ribbons of letters inserted into the tapestry-like ornamentation of the wall, the building begins to interpret itself to the Arabic-reading visitor. A poet's enchantment, akin to that of the architect, tells us in many stanzas what the building itself wished to say to its contemporaries and what the spirit of the period was. These ribbons speak of windows in which star constellations "lodged"; of water which cascaded from basins upon mirroring floors and upon sculpture in a way which did not allow to discern which of these phenomena were solid and what was fluid. Thus we understand that the famous stalactite surfaces of the Alhambra domes produce an illusion: the vaults resemble dripping waters made solid by an everlasting spell. But not all questions are answered by the inscriptions.

The Alhambra has its origin in the blend of Oriental and Occidental themes, techniques, and temperaments, in this old tradition for which one might mention as specimens Hadrian's villa in Tivoli or possibly Nero's Golden House in Rome, creations of similar syntheses and creativeness, or else Byzantine art as such. For this reason it has rightly been observed that the only extant typical late Roman and Byzantine gardens were those of the Alhambra. But the Alhambra buildings owe their main ideas to the eclectic genius of the very first Islamic century which fully established a Moorish style, and furthermore to a new blend of Byzantine and Moorish ideas accomplished by the Umayyad dynasty of Cordova. And still there is no other monument in this prolonged tradition paralleling the romantic constellation and the unique interfusion of incongruous factors and ambitions which constitute the Alhambra. As the nearest counterparts to such migration of ideas we could mention the romantic flight and restitution of the last Umayyad survivor of Damascus, who was able to visualize and establish the Cordovan caliphate of the West.

The art historians and the travel guidebooks, depending upon the information supplied by those, did not give this building proper attention; on the basis of the names of various rulers of the fourteenth century who immortalized themselves in the inscriptions of the walls, they dated the origin of this building — as if such plaster decorations could not have been superimposed upon earlier ones. Parts of the building are much older, as was commonly known, and the actual mystery of its origin remained unsolved and hardly even mentioned. How much more meaningful than these mere dates is what the poets had to say. Muslims and Christians sang praise to its splendors, and in the nineteenth century Washington Irving collected and retold its sagas, which he still found orally transmitted among the people of Granada. In his book (ca. 1830) *The Alhambra*, he endeavored by depicting "its mixture of the heroic, the poetic, and the grotesque; to revive the traces of grace and beauty, fast fading from its walls; to record the legends and chivalrous traditions concerning those who once trod its courts, and the whimsical and superstitious legends of the motley race now burrowing among its ruins," and at another place: "to the traveler embued with the feeling for the historical and poetical, so inseparably intertwined in the annals of romantic Spain, the Alhambra is as much an object of devotion as is the Caaba to all true Muslims. How many legends and traditions, true and fabulous, — how many songs and ballads, Arabian and Spanish, of love and war and chivalry, are associated with this Oriental pyre!"

(2) THE FOUNT OF LIONS

Ibn Gabirol's Description and Interpretation (a)

My claim here, to repeat, is that the Fount of Lions stems from the eleventh century. The present beautiful courtyard was built around it at a later period.

Ibn Gabirol mentions a relationship between the fountain of his Maecenas and Solomon's "Brazen Sea" (Pl. 5). The basin of Ibn Naghrālla's fountain stood upon lions which spouted water and which looked as if they were roaring for prey (Pl. 6); otherwise it resembles Solomon's Temple basin of brass. To refer to the text once more (dists. 18—20):

Dist. 18 ff.:

And there is a full sea, like unto Solomon's Sea,
    though not on oxen it stands,

But there are lions, in phalanx by its rim,
    as though roaring for prey — these whelps

Whose bellies are wellsprings that spout forth
    through their mouths floods like streams.

In the end the poet seems to return once more to the fountain and the symbolism of lions and oxen, interpreting this with a courtier's flattery. Speaking of Yehōšeph ibn Naghrālla, who reduced the kings to puppets and forced them to consult him as their superior, the poet continues thus, in explanation of the use of lions instead of oxen (dist. 37):

Dist. 37:

They raised him as their king, that he became
    a lion-whelp among them and oxen all their hosts.

Plates 5—6

Excursus: Lions and Oxen

We are surprised, incidentally, at Ibn Gabirol's disrespect for oxen, in spite of their place in Solomonic symbolism, although the use of the word "oxen" for bulls in the Book of Kings itself might have its origin in the Biblical writer's opposition to Solomon's dubious animal symbolism, and no less contemptuous sounds Ps. CVI. 29: "They made a calf at Mount Horeb... and converted their honor into the likeness of an ox eating grass." There are various disrespectful allusions to oxen in Ibn Gabirol's poetry, representing of course mainly the courtly Arab attitude toward the agricultural beast of burden; as, e. g., Ibn Ḥazm calls the author of the Pentateuch 'less intelligent than an ox'[45]. Ibn Gabirol laments, in his poem *Yeghōn ḥesheq*, apparently addressed to Samuel (or Yeqūthīel):

Yeghōn ḥesheq — *Bialik-R.*, I, p. 127 ff.

◡ - - - ◡ - - - ◡ - - *(Wāfir)* — Rhyme: *-r-īm*

Grief of longing passion and boyhood love
abandoned me disheartened, in anxiety.

My eyes kept open, not finding sleep,
for the gates of love which were barred,

While God placed his stars in my care, as if
I were the shepherd and they the flocks,

And He tested me like Abraham, the Tested, Gen. XV. 5; XXII. 17
by saying, "Arise and count the countless."

The sight of these and those, my friend,
will bring me to a grave in misery. Gen. XXXVII. 35

Griefs pressed and constrained me,
yea, put me sevenfold to a smelting test in crucibles ...

Towards the end of this poem, when speaking of the inferior poets of his time, he continues (dist. 34):

In their night sleep they deem themselves lions,
but it dawns on them early that they are oxen.

At the conclusion of the same poem he says while speaking of his maturing poems:

Note 45

They will place me in the eyes of the men of my time
like a lion in the eyes of oxen.

In his passionate song of youthful despair, beginning *Mah-llāh yeḥīdhāh* ("What ails you, my soul?"), he speaks with scorn of his contemporaries, describing his own predicament:[46]

Behold, imprisoned among oxen,
alas, what has befallen me!

A witty epigrammatic poem of three distichs — although belonging to the Arabic genus *qiṭʿa*, literally 'fragment' or better 'tidbit' or 'aperçu poem' and, as the double rhyme in the first distich proves, an entity in itself — refers to oxen and also, to the horror of the later Hebrew poet and critic Moses ibn Ezra, disrespectfully to King Solomon:[47]

The Singer of Canticles Rebuked

We-shinney haṣ-ṣebhī — *Bialik-R.*, I, p. 165

⏑- - - ⏑- - - ⏑- - *(Wāfir)* — Rhyme: *-r-īm*

The teeth of the 'gazelle' are sharp and cold,
appearing like pure bands of pearls;

I marvel at Solomon who compares,
Cant. VI. 6 although so wise, such pearls with flocks,

As if he had turned livestock-minded
and lost his heart to oxen.

The topic "oxen" is found in the "Matchless Song" *(Shīrāh Yethōmāh)* by Joseph ibn Ḥasdāy, an ode of praise for Samuel han-Nāghīdh[48]. In this poem, which may have set the tone for some lines of Ibn Gabirol's Alhambra poem, we find:

Ps. LXXX. 16 And every king walks in the light of his countenance,
and every countenance is covered by confusion;

Dan. IV. 25ff. All princes before his countenance are like oxen
Is. LIII. 7 and every counselor is like a sheep that is dumb.

Notes 46—48

Lord of my soul in whose love my soul is settled . . .

In a poem by Moses ibn at-Tāqāna, Ibn Gabirol's contemporary and companion during his youthful Saragossa days[49], we read:

Must I muzzle myself like one mute and be mum Deut. XXV. 4
as if the wells of my songs were stopped? Ps. LXIII. 12

Nay, I must compose pure song all my days
yet I need not teach the oxen.

Ibn Gabirol does not seem to be concerned with the fact that the wild ox has sometimes served as a symbol for the Messiah. According to the Talmud[50], the ox, appearing in the blessing of Moses for Joseph, was interpreted as a reference to the Messiah, son of Joseph. The passage in Deut. XXXIII. 17 reads: "His glory is like the firstling of his bullock, his horns like the horns of the white ox; with them shall he push the people together to the end of the earth."

The connection of "kings" with "oxen" may also have reminded the reader of the story (told in Dan. IV. 25ff.) of Nebuchadnezzar who, as punishment for his sinfulness, was transformed by an illness into a beast "and ate grass like an ox." This story, as we are only now learning from both a Dead Sea scroll fragment and a cuneiform stela unearthed in Ḥarrān, referred originally to King Nabunaid[51].

Ibn Gabirol's Description and Interpretation (b)

If we may go so far in interpreting this symbolism, Solomon, the Biblical king, had glorified himself and God in erecting a Temple basin supported by oxen, lowly-born beasts of burden. Yehōšeph, however, who imitated this monument freely (and for different purposes), achieved, with the changes he introduced, a different self-symbolic expression. By replacing Solomon's oxen with lions, he made it clear that he had inverted previous hierarchies (by making himself, the royal servant, the actual ruler). What further makes these lions symbols of sovereigns is their snarling:

. . . seeming to roar for prey — these whelps (dist. 19).

The Alhambra lions are indeed represented as snarling, with wrinkles of anger, and with teeth threateningly bared (Pl. 6). Also, they are standing, not crouching in submission, which fact may be explained, at least partially, by the need for their horizontal backs to carry the basin. (The lion lifting himself up appears, incidentally, as a symbol for Israel in Num. XXIII. 24.) The lions, although subdued as carrier figures (yet not entirely; originally, most likely with their necks protruding above the basin's rim) they (see Plate 9) symbolize with their vigor and ferocity proud princes, according to the accepted symbolism of the time. However, what is implicit in Ibn Gabirol's poem, and what, so to speak, the princes must not realize themselves, is that they are actually oxen by typology, by the inherent Solomonic order of the Temple fountain in which they stand. They are congregated below the basin as if they were grazing; the basin, "standing for" the major-domo, shelters them: the major-domo described as the Davidic

Dist. 39: Shepherd leading his sheep upon still pastures (dist. 39).

This line has also a Solomonic (Canticles) and messianic note. Rabbinic tradition (also found in Philo and the Pseudepigrapha) has it that the animals which once lived in blissful accord with man in Paradise, either shied away from him after the Fall or were submissive to him only through terror. Yet they returned to man's domination under Solomon. He was the King of Paradise to fulfill such prophecies as those in Leviticus XXVI. 6 and to be the warrant of those heralded by Ezekiel XXXIV. 23 for a time when (Isaiah XL. 7) "the lion shall eat straw like the ox[52]."

This interpretation of the basin as symbolizing the patron cannot be too far-fetched, since a third and last allusion to the symbolism of "rivers" and "princes," (which is abruptly inserted in dist. 43—44 and can only be understood in its true *double entendre*), proves that the poet is still concerned with the symbols of the fountain. The overflow of the abundant fountain now becomes the symbol for the generous munificence of the Maecenas:

Dist. 43 f.:

Dist. 41: Whose eye has never dimmed while he pours out gifts,
as his cloud has never withheld its rains (dist. 41).

The Hebrew word *'ayin* meaning both 'eye' and 'well' (cf. Spanish *ojo de agua*) appears together with the word I translate 'dimmed'. Thus the formula shifts back and forth, referring to the generous eye of the Maecenas as an inexhaustible well, allowing in the same breath for two interpretations: (a) (alluding to a current Arabic expression) "his EYE does not become glazed (or dull) while giving," losing its shine because of ill-suppressed greed; just as (b) "the WELL does not become (so to speak) dry-eyed and opaque from its lack of water." If anyone should still doubt all this *double entendre* (the allusion to the Maecenas referring also to the Fount and *vice versa*, the basin standing all the time for the Maecenas) then dist. 41,

Note 52; Plate 9

which speaks of a cloud not withholding its rain, leads us even more directly to the symbolism of the fountain, although ostensibly referring to the "prince." The overflow of the basin finds its typical simile in a rain-giving cloud (so, for instance, in the Arabic inscription of the present lion fountain basin, which will be discussed later). In the same way dist. 43 may now be interpreted:

All regents — to him they repair,
as unto the sea are drawn the rivers.

By this the poet refers, consciously or not, to the fountain, with its various "rivers" and one "Sea." (In the poem, the jets spouted by the lions were called "rivers;" and the channels, as found in the present Court of Lions, were also expressly described):

In truth, he is like a 'head' above the earth,
he, the one, set off from all creatures![53] (dist. 44)

The ruler is the "one head" above the earth. At the first glance we may assume that the *double entendre* is interrupted here, as a reference to the fountain is not immediately obvious. However, for the Hebrew reader, a familiar connection between "head" and "river" exists, stemming from Genesis II. 10, which reads in literal translation: "A river flowed out of Eden to water the garden, and there it divided and became four 'heads'." In an accepted allegorical interpretation, yet typical of Ibn Gabirol, found in his *Kingdom's Crown*, he makes the river and the 'four heads' of Paradise allusions to Primordial Matter and the four elements deriving from this[54]. We shall show, later on (at the conclusion of the discussion of the various ancestries of the Fount of Lions) that the 'Four Rivers', found in many oriental gardens and rugs made in imitation of gardens, and in our Court of Lions, were often a conscious reference to the biblical Paradise. The Hebrew *rō'sh* means chiefly 'head', 'summit', 'chieftain', and also '(fountain) head'. The basin, therefore, is as much the 'one head' above the earth as is the Maecenas, and this because of the allusion in the messianic context of Hos. II. 2 (I. 11): "Then the children of Judah and the children of Israel shall be gathered together and appoint themselves one head." The continuity of the poem is preserved only when one regards all references to 'the one' and 'the many' — the one sea and the many rivers; the one 'head upon earth' and the many oxen and princes — as two-fold allusions to both major-domo and fountain. As the one elevated basin overshadows, shelters, unites or feeds the various 'creatures', 'lions' and 'rivers', so

Notes 53—54

Yehōseph, the unique, stands as the one head above all his charges. I shall return to this topic in the section on symbolism and messianism.

The fountain, in other words, represents the messianic world order: beasts of dormant violence ('creatures'), symbolizing the world's potentates, are assembled in a harmonious circle below a basin which sheds Paradisial abundance and, finally, symbolizes the Davidic ruler. This "Family of Kings," like grazing lions, is lined up and sheltered under the fountainhead which feeds the rivers of Paradise. For the idea of taking shelter in the shadow of a ruler cf. Judges IX. 15. The ruler also appears in our poem as the type of a Byzantine πρωτοσύμβουλος. The last line of the poem contains a play upon the word *nāghīdh*, actually interpreting its meaning in visual terms ('over against'). In place of my translation:

> he, the one, set off from all creatures

one might read "the ruler stands alone in his rank and transcends thus the animals standing opposite." *Nāghīdh* gains by this a connotation of "otherness," "beyondness," and of the superhuman. I translated this line into German as:

> Geschöpf steht hüben, er — in andern Sichten[55].

The question of whether or not these last stanzas of our poem contain a reference to the Fount of Lions (as the previous part of the poem did) does not affect the documentary value of the poem as a whole in relation to the history of the Alhambra.

So much detail in describing the physical form of the fountain and so much stress upon the interpretation of its symbolism, with the fountain made the monument of his Maecenas' power, indicates clearly, of course, that the poet cannot be speaking of a figment of his phantasy.

(3) ICONOGRAPHY AND IDENTITY

Solomon and Solomonism (a): The Brazen Sea and the Alhambra Fount

The "Brazen Sea" which adorned Solomon's Temple consisted of a large basin supported by twelve oxen. Its description, found in I Kings VII. 23 and 25 reads:[56]

> He made the molten sea; it was round, ten cubits from brim to brim, and five cubits high, and a line of thirty cubits measured its circum-

> ference. ... It stood upon twelve oxen, three facing north, three facing west, three facing south, and three facing east; the sea was set upon them, and all their hinder parts were inward.

As early as 1831, Richard Ford (in the text quoted above from *Murray's Handbook*) had observed that the next-of-kin to the Alhambra Fount of Lions was "Solomon's Throne," which must be an erroneous reference to Solomon's Brazen Sea. Similar statements were later made by historians, among them Valladar, A. Almagro Cárdenas, and Ernst Diez[57]. The latter, a very competent historian of Islamic art, maintains the thesis of a typological kinship of the two structures, because of the fact that there were no precedents for this type of animal-supported fountain within the Islamic orbit. However, without a knowledge of Ibn Gabirol's poem (which was first published only a few years ago) it could not have occurred to these historians that the Fount of Lions was designed by a Jewish builder and indeed intended to be a replica of Solomon's Temple fountain, with modifications in its zoological detail.

Solomon's basin had twelve supporting oxen, the "hindmost parts inwards"; the Alhambra fountain has its twelve lions, in the same position. There were, of course, Byzantine and Islamic basins or pools which received water, spouted from animals placed *upon* them, as for instance, the two lions of the Partal basin of the Alhambra. (The extant descriptions of such basins are discussed in a chapter of this book.) Whereas the animal-borne basin seems to have been an alien element in the Muslim art of this period, in this case, to repeat, the basin is borne by the animals as was Solomon's, and the lions spout into channels in the floor *beneath* the fountain.

The major part of this book is a positive argument in favor of the identity of the two fountains, that described in Ibn Gabirol's poem, and that extant today in the Court of Lions of the Alhambra. The argument is based on various literary documents, all, I think, supporting each other most logically. Yet to repeat again, I also advance an argument *e contrario* suggesting that no other animal fountains of the type and with the detail described in the poem existed; in other words, that the Alhambra fountain, the twelve animals of which support, as caryatids, a water basin, and spout water, not into this but in the opposite direction, had no counterpart or precedent. To advance such a negative argument I have investigated the Arabic literary sources in which contemporary animal fountains are described. These show that animal-shaped fountains were indeed most fashionable, and that these furnished the inspiration for the hydraulic design of the Alhambra lions. The fact that the lions of the fountain spout

Note 57

water is, indeed, the main deviation from Solomonic typology (together with the replacement of lions by oxen, which our poem explains). It is, however, the adherence to the Solomonic order which forced upon the lions of the fountain the strange paradox of 'hind-parts inward', and of water-spouts outward so that the water has no communication with the basin. The historical Solomonic archetype was only a storage basin.

Investigation of contemporary Arabic fountains revealed that tree- and animal-shaped fountains were mostly designed to spout water. Some of the elements found in the descriptions of these are stunningly similar to Granadine ideas and are reminiscent of Byzantine water *automata* as well. But nowhere is there a direct return to the Solomonic works mentioned in the Bible. A certain spark was necessary to make the transition from playful, imitative artfulness into a direct re-infusion of Biblical art. And I feel that this spark could have been generated solely in this circle of Cordovan emigrés to Granada, the "City of the Jews," where an unheard-of Biblical humanism (in a Ciceronic sense) was promoted, and enacted in autonomous political enterprise.

It may not be entirely superfluous, however, to stress once more that if the fountain described in Ibn Gabirol's poem were not the Alhambra Fount, we would have to look first for a no longer extant second fountain of lions (which spouted water), second, for a castle with an unknown Jewish vice-regal builder, and this among the friends of Ibn Gabirol, who promoted plastic art which employed Hebrew symbolism of the Alhambra type and of daring heterodoxy. In other words, one would have to look for an exact counterpart to something as unique as the Alhambra fountain itself. But the constituents necessary to produce, once only, this climactic Jewish vizierdom of the Naghrāllas and a Hebrew renascence of art are so enormously specialized and individual that such an attempt is absurd. Certain negative arguments occasionally leveled against investigations like this remind one of the statement of the Homeric scholar: "Even if the man whom the Greeks credited with the composition of *Odyssey* and *Iliad* did exist and, as cannot with certainty be excluded, bore the name Homer, this person would of course not be identical with the fictitious Homer of the Greeks[57a]." The fact is that the present Alhambra fountain is identical in the main details of iconography with the fountain of the poem, with one physical exception: the basin now borne by the lions is obviously a later replacement.

The well-known Spanish historian of the fine arts, Manuel Gómez-Moreno, found it necessary to make a place for the lions of the Alhambra in the third volume of *Ars Hispaniae*, in which he deals with the period *hasta los Almohades*[58]. There he states:

Notes 57a—58

Having studied this [the twelve lions of the Alhambra fount, the two lions in the *Barrio de los Axares*, the *pila* in the Alhambra showing lions slaying horned animals, and an inscription bearing the name Bādīs ibn Ḥabbūs] it appears difficult to admit that works which betray so many characteristics attributable to the tenth and eleventh centuries, could have been created under the Naṣrids, who did not leave behind any known sculpture, sculpture being incompatible with their pietism.

This is to say that, for purely art-historical reasons alone, the lions of the Alhambra have already been ascribed to our period, although the basin bears an inscription referring to Muḥammad V (1354—1359 and 1362—1391). Yet the same art historian offers a highly plausible solution of this problem. In the lines immediately preceding the above passage, Gómez-Moreno says: "There are the twelve lions of white marble placed around the famous fount in the *Casa Real*, to which the basin in the hall of the *Abencerajes*, of a dodecagonal shape, with its outer entirely flat surface, could be related."

In other words the basin, the object of such sad legends, now set into the floor of the Abencerajes Hall, was most likely the original basin supported by the twelve lions, and belongs to the same early period (Pl. 7). I also share the opinion of the art historians who hold that the stilts now supporting the basin do not belong to the original fountain. If this low dodecagonal basin were placed directly upon the lions' bodies, it would permit the backs of the lions' heads to protrude slightly above the low rim of the basin and be mirrored by the water in it (Pl. 9). I myself measured the Abencerajes basin and ascertained that it fits exactly between the necks of the lions as they now stand in relation to one another.

Dist. 18 f.: Thus we understand the poet's likening the patron's fountain to Solomon's Sea with only the oxen replaced by lions (dist. 18) standing beneath the basin and, furthermore (dist. 19), his speaking of a phalanx of lions arrayed by, or on, the rim of the fountain. This rim is by no means the basin only, but Solomon's "Brazen Sea" is a term which includes its unique pedestal. The poet is following the diction of I Kings VII. 23 f., but the primary meaning of *'al sephath hay-yām* is 'by the sea shore', standing for the dry land of the sea shore rather than for a place above the sea itself. For this reason I had to translate 'by its rim'.

The daughter of Professor Gómez-Moreno is more outspoken when she writes:[59]

La tosca escultura de los leones resultaría disonante con la delicadeza del patio, si su misma infantil estilización no sirviese de contraste.

> Su estilo es tan semejante a otras interpretaciones árabes de animales del siglo X, que asalta la sospecha de si pertenecerían a una fuente antigua y fueron utilizados aquí[60]. Aun parece confirmar tal suposición el hecho de existir en la sala de los Abencerajes otra pila, a ras del suelo, lisa, pero casi exactamente igual en forma y tamaño a la de la fuente, y que pudo ocupar, con sus leones en ruedo, el centro del jardín primitivo, sobre el que fué organizado, según consta, este palacio.

Albert Champdor quotes a statement by Miss Gómez-Moreno:[61]

> Récemment M. E. Gómez-Moreno dans *Mil Joyas* ... a prétendu que les lions de l'Alhambra sont de quatre siècles plus anciens que la vasque et qu'ils ont dû soutenir dans ce même patio, qui n'était alors qu'un jardin, la fontaine que l'on peut aujourd'hui voir dans la salle des Abencérages ...

Miss Gómez-Moreno, as we see, shares these views with her father and, indeed, professes them in writing and orally.

The obvious dependence of our fountain on Solomon's "Brazen Sea" was obscured, however, when it suffered deformation: in accordance with the doctrine that what is already beautiful may be enhanced by addition, both a smaller basin and a vertical spout were set on the top of the present basin. These "embellishments" have only recently been removed (Pl. 23). It is well known that such *albercas* were employed in Islamic architecture mainly for their mirroring effect (as in the Tāj Maḥall). A slight undulation of the water surface for the purpose of continually varied distortions and a rippling of the mirrored picture caused by rising bubbles, was a coveted effect. However, forceful jets liable to stir up the surface to the point of destroying the mirroring effect would hardly have been used.

The replacement, in the Alhambra fountain, of Solomon's oxen by lions, was, as we observed, an occasion for some witty flattery of the Maecenas by the courtly Ibn Gabirol. The actual illustrative intent, however, was probably very close to the poet's version, for lions are of course more symbolic of royal splendor and force than oxen, and that not only in Ibn Gabirol's poetry[62].

Excursus: The Talismanic or Aesthetic Value of the Lions

The mediaeval spirit attaches symbolic value to any representational art. In this case, however, we may assume that such symbolism was employed somewhat playfully. I refer to the Naghrāllas' other architectural devices, discussed below as they are described, together with their symbolism, in Samuel han-Nāghīdh's poetry and the prefatory remarks found in his *dīwān*. As, for instance, Ibn Gabirol's epigrammatic quatrain accusing Solomon of being "livestock-minded" illustrates, the symbolic value of bulls (let alone oxen) was nil in the Islamic courtly orbit; their odor of labor and peasantry ran counter to knightly qualities. The regular symbolism of lions is, of course, *fuerza dominadora*, to quote Gómez-Moreno[63], and may be exemplified by the reference to lions in contemporary descriptive poetry and also by another inscription in the Alhambra praising two water-spouting lions of the *baño:*[64]

> O admirable object of both new and old [times]:
> a lair of [crouching] lions in a house of delight.
>
> One lion faced by his equal; ⟨the couple⟩
> they placed themselves by the lord in the place of a servant.
>
> They distribute among themselves the two characteristics ⟨virtues⟩ of his nobility:
> he possesses ardent energy and universal generosity ⟨raining⟩.

This inscription in the Alhambra bath seems to indicate, as Professor Nykl interpreted it, that the two lions were used to spout hot and cold water. It seems possible that the fragment of a lion in the Alhambra Museum belonged to one of them.

It must not be forgotten in this connexion that the Fount of Lions is primarily a work of secular decorative art. True, it had inherited forms of art which originally served magical purposes, but the enlightened late mediaeval centuries, within the Islamic sphere, were able to make free use of such pseudo-magical material.

Metaphors in this type of Muslim poetry, as Hellmut Ritter pointed out, betray an innocent and playful return to a make-believe dynamism, merely pretending that the lifeless is animated, and that the *similia* really "stand for" the compared object, and that certain dream or imaginary causalities were the real *causantes*[65].

There is an excellent account of the various symbolic meanings of a lion when employed in connexion with, or as a representation of, a king, by Jeannine Auboyer[66], who deals with lion thrones of many countries and periods:

> … le symbolisme le moins difficile à définir: le lion étant considéré comme le roi des animaux par sa force, sa noblesse, sa légendaire invincibilité, il était tout naturel de lui associer le roi des hommes. Doué d'une voix puissante qui fait fuir et trembler ceux qui l'attaquent, il est normal qu'on veuille lui assimiler, par une sorte de magie imitative, le roi belliqueux et conquérant, type parfait du monarque universel. Enfin, son pelage roux, sa crinière rayonnante, l'ont souvent fait comparer au soleil; doué de ce symbolisme solaire, il est tout indiqué pour être l'image du roi qui, en bien des contrées, est le substitut humain de la divinité du soleil. Il représenterait dans l'esprit de ceux qui l'ont figuré sur les sièges, soit un des symboles, ou bien la totalité d'entre eux. Le lion était donc l'animal royal et divin par excellence.

The image of a lion for a king is current in the extremely popular *Kalīla wa-Dimna*, which is an Arabic adaptation of the Indian *Pañcatantra*[67]. In this the bull is occasionally the king's minister[68].

In the light of the Arabic texts on animal sculptures quoted in this book and of Ibn Gabirol's and Samuel's references to their own artistic intentions with statuary, Professor Gómez-Moreno is evidently mistaken in ascribing talismanic value to the Cordovan animal statuary. In the same way it would be absurd to ascribe talismanic intentions to a Byzantine emperor who aimed at cowing "barbarian" envoys with his lion-throne, his automata, and his other awe-inspiring displays. The difference between a magical attitude to talismans and a caliph's enlightened aestheticism, most likely paired with an urge to ostentation aimed at gaining prestige, is clearly shown in Yāqūt's story of the talismanic lion of the city gate of Hamadhān and the collector's interest of a caliph in it:[69]

> It is reported that among the memorabilia *(ʿajāʾib)* of Hamadhān there is the representation *(ṣūra)* of a lion in stone upon a city gate, the character of which lion was interpreted to be a talisman against the cold. It was designed by Balīnās (Apollonius), master of talismans, when Qubādh [sic] approached him for a device to ward off afflictions from his territory. At Hamadhān the snowfall and cold could allegedly be so severe that a horseman would drown with his horse in the snow. After he [Balīnās], however, had designed for Hamadhān this lion-shaped talisman the snowfall diminished and the situation was remedied. The same man also fashioned a talisman against snakes on the right side of the lion, and a third against scorpions …

Notes 67—69

> The ['Abbāsid] Caliph al-Muktafī who saw the lion and was impressed by its beauty *(istaḥsan)* had the intention of moving it from the gate of Hamadhān to Baghdad, and he issued, in a letter to the regional governor *('āmil)*, an order to this effect. Hereupon the notables of the district assembled and declared: "This is a talisman for our region for the aversion of many grievances; its removal cannot be tolerated lest the region perish." The governor, therefore, wrote [back] to this effect. Since, however, the transportation offered difficulties on those rough lands, mountains and mud stretches, [the caliph] had [already] given an order to transport it on an elephant's back for the sake of expediency. When he now received this information his determination cooled off so that it [the lion] has retained its place until today[70].

The story gives us the rare instance of an ancient statue of a lion being found upon the city gate of a Muslim city during the early 'Abbāsid period. It owed its preservation to its reputation of being a talisman, fashioned by the legend-shrouded Apollonius of Tyana, surnamed "Alexicacos" (rather than possibly Apollonius of Pergamon or, as A. V. Williams Jackson suggests, Pliny)[71].

The different grounds on which such a sculpture was valued are clearly contrasted: we find on the part of the Hamadhānīs provincial belief in the talismanic magic or apotropaic charm of an image against the cold. Lions have been, of course, throughout history, often set up for talismanic purposes, to mention only the Lion Gate of Mycenae, as well as the later gate of Jerusalem. As to the gate of Hamadhān, A. V. Williams Jackson asserts clearly that at a time when the sculptured lion was sitting on the ground and in reach of the people, it became the object of quasi-cultic attention:[72]

> Dozens of superstitions are attached to it. Mothers hold up their babies to pat the huge beast or kiss its face, barren women touch its brow to remove the curse of sterility, and pilgrims lay offerings of stones, some of them carved, upon its head as a coronet or on the block below its mouth.

The caliph's reaction is aesthetic: he admires the lion as a work of art and his collector's covetousness is aroused. He is barely prevented from confiscating the statue for his palace in Baghdad by diplomatic deference to the convictions of his subjects, which he did not easily realize. He is in no way prejudiced against representational art by Islam's prohibitions[73].

In the light of this story and of the Arabic fountain poems quoted, it appears impossible that the Alhambra lions have any talismanic significance, as M. Gómez-Moreno suggests. They belong entirely to the sphere of courtly artistic display. The Arabic poets quoted in my passage on lion founts are the natural spokesmen for the royal art patron's intentions. Their exclamations of fear or confusion are an affectation attributing life and feeling to the animals, such as I shall discuss in connexion with Ibn Gabirol's nature poetry. If we insist, however, upon an analysis of the effect of such ostentatious display, then we may assume that these symbols of a ruler's and his architect's cunning may have evoked, indeed, some awe in the naive visitor to the place, yet could never have had the terrifying effect desired from the Byzantine lion automata upon delegations of "barbarians." More important, the absence of any belief on the part of the employer in the magic character of the statues forbids, of course, their classification as talismans. In the same way, even if we were to assume that Yehōseph's Solomonic symbolism which underlies the fountain stemmed from a desire to invite theurgically, with such splendors, the return of a Solomonic age (somehow comparable with Lady Hester Stanhope's maintaining her prodigious horse for the arrival of the Anointed) the term talisman (implying that the intention was to avert evil) is entirely out of place.

Solomon and Solomonism (b): Solomon's Throne in the Jewish Legend

By the insertion of the twelve lions into his fountain Yehōseph ibn Naghrālla achieved a unification of the royal Solomonic throne insignia, as described in I Kings, X. 20 ("Twelve lions stood there, one on each end of the six steps; the like of it was never made in any kingdom"), with the Brazen Sea of the Solomonic Temple. Moreover, the combination of oxen and lions had a precedent in Solomon's Temple itself: the 'stands' described in I Kings VII. 29:

> ... and on the borders that were between the ledges were lions, oxen, and cherubim: and upon the ledge there was a base above: and beneath the lions and oxen were certain additions made of thin work ...

That such symbolism was alive during the entire Middle Ages in the Christian and Muslim world, as well as among the Jews, can easily be demonstrated. The Byzantine emperor claimed that his throne was identical with Solomon's. The symbolism of Solomon's throne was also in evidence in 'Abbāsid Baghdad.

The urge to imitate Solomon's Temple is documented as early as Justinian's erection of Hagia Sophia and as late as Vienna's Karlskirche with Fischer von Erlach's twin columns like Solomon's Boaz and Jachin. The universal fame of the throne of Solomon is illustrated by its representation in the frescoes of Dura Europos. Furthermore, the emperor Theophilos (829—842) possessed a golden tree fashioned in imitation of that of the Solomonic throne and its mechanical wonders[74]. A similar tree is documented as having existed in the Fāṭimid Palace of Egypt. According to Alföldi, Theodoric the Great, the king of the Goths, expressed in 507 A. D. the wish to present such Italian-made automata to neighboring kings. In the same way, whenever fantastic architecture is discussed, Muslim and Jewish literature abound in Solomic allusions[75]. The extent to which the consciousness of Solomon reverberated in Jewish folk-lore, perhaps in part owing to a wish to outdo, at least in imagination, the Byzantine achievement, is evident in the following extract from Louis Ginzberg, *The Legends of the Jews:*

> None before him and none after him could produce a like work of art, and when the kings, his vassals, saw the magnificence of the throne they fell down and praised God. The throne was covered with fine gold from Ophir, studded with beryls, inlaid with marble, and jewelled with emeralds, rubies and pearls, and all manner of gems. On each of its six steps there were two golden lions and two golden eagles, a lion and an eagle to the left, and a lion and an eagle to the right, the pairs standing face to face, so that the right paw of the lion was opposite the left wing of the eagle, and his left paw opposite the right wing of the eagle. The royal seat was at the top, which was round.
>
> On the first step leading to the seat crouched an ox, and opposite to him a lion; on the second, a wolf and a lamb; on the third, a leopard and a goat; on the fourth perched an eagle and a peacock; on the fifth a falcon and a cock; and on the sixth a hawk and a sparrow; all made of gold. At the very top rested a dove, her claws set upon a hawk, to betoken that the time would come when all peoples and nations shall be delivered into the hands of Israel. Over the seat hung a golden candlestick, with golden lamps, pomegranates, snuff dishes, censers, chains, and lilies. Seven branches extended from each side. On the arms to the right were the images of the seven patriarchs of the world, Adam, Noah, Shem, Job, Abraham, Isaac and Jacob; and, on the arms to the left, the images of the seven pious men of the

Notes 74—75

world, Kohath, Amram, Moses, Aaron, Eldad, Medad, and the prophet Hur.

On the upper part of the throne stood seventy golden chairs for the members of the Sanhedrin, and two more for the high priest and his vicar. When the high priest came to do homage to the king, the members of the Sanhedrin also appeared, to judge the people, and they took their seats to the right and to the left of the king. At the approach of the witnesses, the machinery of the throne rumbled — the wheels turned, the ox lowed, the lion roared, the wolf howled, the lamb bleated, the leopard growled, the goat cried, the falcon screamed, the peacock gobbled, the cock crowed, the hawk screeched, the sparrow chirped — all to terrify the witnesses and keep them from giving false testimony.

When Solomon set foot upon the first step to ascend to his seat, its machinery was put into motion. The golden ox arose and led him to the second step, and there passed him over to the care of the beasts guarding it, and so he was conducted from step to step up to the sixth, where the eagles received him and placed him upon his seat. As soon as he was seated, a great eagle set the royal crown upon his head. Thereupon a huge snake rolled itself up against the machinery, forcing the lions and eagles upward until they encircled the head of the king. A golden dove flew down from a pillar, took the sacred scroll out of a casket, and gave it to the king, so that he might obey the injunction of the Scriptures, to have the Law with him and read therein all the days of his life. Above the throne twenty-four vines interlaced, forming a shady arbor over the head of the king, and sweet aromatic perfumes exhaled from two golden lions, while Solomon made the ascent to his seat upon the throne.

It was the task of seven heralds to keep Solomon reminded of his duties as king and judge . . .

The mediaeval reader of the account in the *Targum Shenī* must have been awestruck at the mirabilia of Solomon. If he was a Jew, he must also have felt pride at the supernatural achievement of his great ancestral ruler, but he would never have nerved himself to an attempt at emulation of the wonders wrought by the divinely inspired cunning of the King. An emperor or a prince of the church may have felt that his position was closely enough akin to that of Solomon to challenge comparison with him. Such potentates are so rare, that the only two of whom we have any such record arc Justinian and, as it seems, Khosro.

For a Jew, there were other obstacles. He would be fully aware that he was attempting to emulate, not the ruler of a rival nation, but the sacrosanct person of the Jewish king κατ᾽ ἐξοχήν. Moreover, he would be violating both the Second Commandment and the specific Talmudic injunction quoted below. Such a practical violation of the Law on the part of otherwise orthodox Jews is only conceivable in terms of a theurgic anticipation of the Messianic age: it is one of the "strange acts" of the Messiah, in whose time the Law will cease to be binding. No mere feeling of injured pride, or of the exigencies of prestige, such as may have given rise to the legendary accounts of Solomon's deeds, can account for the unmistakable imitation of the Brazen Sea represented by the Fount of Lions. The instigator of such a project must have been in deadly earnest, however playful the execution of it may have appeared to the outsider. We shall not, I think, be exaggerating if we term the messianism of the Naghrāllas secularized, courtly, and arrogant to the highest degree.

If this source, the *Targum Shenī to the Book of Esther*, was at this point nurtured by the Jews' feeling of injured national pride, then there is a possibility that the Persians invented a similar Throne of Khosro out of similar feelings of injured pride, even if at a somewhat later period.

Solomon and Secular Solomonism (c): The Image of King Solomon in the Naghrālla circle

The specific climate for something like a secular messianism among the Jews of this period was generated by the re-establishment in Spain of the Umayyad caliphate, under which they enjoyed tolerance and encouragement of their own religious and cultural aims [76]. We have seen, as one example among many, the way in which secular Hebrew poetry, the very achievement of the cultured liberalism of the Hebrew élite of Umayyad Cordova, had here in Andalusia restored to the Song of Solomon some of its original application.

To illustrate my point by another example: Ibn Gabirol refers, in an earlier poem of dejection, to Solomon as his "ancestor."

> I shall seek as long as I am, and scrutinize the
> commandments of Solomon, my ancestor.
>
> Maybe the Unveiler of the depths will
> unveil wisdom to my eye.
>
> Since this is my share alone
> from all my toil and my fortune [77].

Notes 76—77

Ibn Gabirol marked many of his poems acrostically with his *nom de plume*, "Solomon Minor," Solomon Major being, of course, King Solomon[78].

Samuel han-Nāghīdh may have dreamed of an imminent re-establishment of a Solomonic kingdom of art, wisdom, and power in Granada either by himself or by his son, Yehōseph, to whom he had passed on these dreams and the education to fulfil them. Samuel's poems express his romantic hopes, which were a more-than-quixotic vision. We may see an expression of this Solomonic renascence, of which the Naghrāllas were the Medici, in the fact that Samuel entitled his three collections of Hebrew poems, in imitation of works ascribed to Solomon and David, *Ben Qōheleth* ("The Modern Ecclesiastes"), *Ben Tehillīm* ("The Modern Psalms"), and *Ben Mishley* ("The Modern Proverbs")[79]. Samuel's son, Yehōseph, as I am convinced, clearly continued in every way in his father's tradition. Ibn Gabirol most likely contributed to Yehōseph's education, and there must have been hours when Ibn Gabirol saw in the son, even more than in the father, a fulfilment of his own highest hopes. (Unfortunately only one of Yehōseph's own poems has survived.)[80] At this point I interpret the Solomonic allusions contained in a poem of Platonic patronage by Ibn Gabirol, in which the poet seemingly addresses Yehōseph. Samuel, at times estranged from Ibn Gabirol (as many poems show), is indirectly addressed as well:[81]

The Solomonic Father

Yedhīdh-ī maʿaseh — *Bialik-R.*, I, p. 113f.

⏑ - - - ⏑ - - - ⏑ - - *(Wāfir)* — *Geiger*, p. 72

Rhyme: *-m-īm*

My friend, Hiram's work is what your countenance resembles,
  roses are aglow in your face.

Your father, when he sent to Tyre,
(I Ki. VII. 13ff.) whence came to him the father of all inventors

And wrought all the work of the House of God
  and also an altar on which to atone for transgressions —

There, one might think, God shaped you, and Hiram
  decked you there by his art with adornments,

Notes 78—81

And, while he shaped, upon a column, the lip of the Sea (*ibid.* VII. 26)
he shaped your lips in comeliness.

The poem alludes to the Biblical passage quoted above, found in I Kings VII. 23ff.: "Then he made the molten sea ... its brim was made like the brim of a cup, like the flower of a rose ..." (also translated 'lily').

The intention of this poem is visibly a *rapprochement* with Samuel han-Nāghīdh, most probably written at a time not immediately following a rift. Although the son is addressed, the father, Samuel, is also wooed. He is praised for having, among his Solomonic treasures, a son and "an altar on which to atone for transgressions." With this line the note of atonement for transgression of his "Poem of Apology" (distichs 13 and 14 are the most memorable in this connection) is modulated to a different key:

... thou hast a strife with the sons of Levi, thy precious ones;

Sacrifice before them a goat as sin offering:
perhaps thy guilt may be offset by this.

I am sure that the Solomonic father, flatteringly mentioned in this poem as having ordered a Hiram from Tyre to execute Solomonic designs, is Samuel. However, the Solomonic child, the work shaped in the Solomonic workshop (together with the altar upon which Ibn Gabirol wished to atone for his sins — those against Samuel, no doubt), can be none other than Yehōšeph. The Temple fountain and Yehōšeph are mentioned together. Although this poem, of course, was written before the erection of the Alhambra Fount by Yehōšeph, at a time when Samuel was still alive and Yehōšeph a child, these Solomonic symbols belong to a stage already set for the Fount. It is unlikely that Samuel, as A. Geiger believed, was the direct addressee. It is true that the conventional Arabic style of "love poetry addressed to a Maecenas" was employed (in Hebrew) by Ibn Gabirol in poems to Samuel; but the loving tone of this poem is that of an older person to a younger, whom he observes growing up. Samuel han-Nāghīdh was twenty-eight years his elder, and Yehōšeph, born 1035, thirteen years his junior. Ibn Gabirol's poems of this courtly kind addressed to Samuel have a ring of distance and awe, reminiscent rather of, and often directly alluding to, the relationship between David and Saul than that between David and Jonathan.

It need not surprise us, therefore, that the same emphasis upon the original Hebrew motif and upon the urge to restore and to re-enact, which we find in literary effort, was also extended to the plastic arts. Only in an atmosphere as pregnant with song as Arab Andalusia could such a rebirth have come about. In the same way as Solomon ibn Gabirol's Hebrew poetry belongs to two literary traditions, the ancestry of our Fount of Lions is twofold: however typical of a centerpiece of a Moorish (or Byzantine) palace its function, position, and craftsmanship may be, its symbolism is Hebraic. And yet it could only have been created by a member of the emancipated Jewish circle of Cordovan liberalism, indulging in its elegant Solomonic heresy. Both orthodox Jew and Muslim should have been shocked by three-dimensional plastic art: Ibn Gabirol in his poem was jubilant.

Dist. 39: Since, as we have seen, one of the messianic prototypes is the "King of Paradise," as visualized in Is. XL. 11, and Ez. XXXIV. 23, identified as Solomon and alluded to in our poem (dist. 39), it cannot be overlooked that, in this circle and especially in this case, gardening belongs, together with poetry, plastic art, and wisdom, to a fulfillment pattern as conceived by Ibn Gabirol and the Naghrāllas. Adorned with 'roses of Sharon' the Dist. 7: landscaped courtyards of the palace are Solomonic (dist. 7).

Ibn Gabirol's Alhambra Poem is by far too enlightened and emancipated from "normative" Jewish restrictions to represent a message fit to fire the imagination of the Jewish diasporas with a heroic account of the new Jewish ruler in his splendor who will soon liberate the nation. Had this been his object, he must have written an entirely different message. The poem as it is, if used as a widely-broadcast manifesto, could only have failed, because of its private character. The opening lines, with their personal invitation to a stroll in a garden and the search for "beautiful faces," are in the mode of an 'Abbāsid court poet, such as Abū Nuwās. The "miracles" of the place are described in a realistic way, as art to be enjoyed. The poet's exclamation of being 'lifted up ... as upon eagles' Dist. 17: pinions' (distich 17) by the spectacle of the domed hall is so lyrical and subjective that it could never meet the requirements of a messianic *kerygma*. The witticism of making the dependent kings into oxen does the rest. The poem remains urbane and secular. Although the facts related are fabulous enough, there is nothing legendary, no overtones of a *gralserzählung*, not even a Prester John quality. It is fanciful, in the sharp key of the triumphal assertion of an accomplishment. The praise of representational art is not of a nature to provoke in the reader the awe of a holy *scandalon*. Neither could one imagine a reader in the camp of rigid exilic norms who would even enjoy this. He would possibly receive an unholy shock and would reject the libertinism of Jews involving themselves in heathen *divertimenti* like plastic arts. Though no less extravagant, the religious poems by Ibn Gabirol which are devoted to the quasi-messianic hopes linked with

Samuel han-Nāghīdh are entirely different in character. But we may ask: why is this poem so un-messianic in spite of all its messianic motifs? Did Yehōseph and/or Ibn Gabirol become quite sober in their relation to power? Or did Ibn Gabirol at this time have reservations as to the qualifications of Yehōseph, to his motives and his mission? The general tone of the poem is most cordial.

The Naghrāllas' own messianic ideas, and Ibn Gabirol's in their wake, are discussed in the excursus which follows.

Excursus: The Messianic Conceptions of Ibn Gabirol and the Naghrāllas

The question whether the quasi-messianic claims made by Samuel for himself are to be taken with the full weight of their wording as a "program", or rather as the hyperbolic speech of an exalted moment, will be discussed elsewhere. I am inclined to assume the former on this basis of Samuel's infringement of the Second Commandment and of his literary licences, which may invite interpretation as the "strange acts" of the Messiah, such as performed by earlier "messiahs" like Zonarias and Isaac-Obadia ("Abū 'Īsā")[82].

Further arguments which corroborate my observation that the Naghrāllas laid claim to a near-messianic status are the following: (1) Samuel calls himself, in one of his victory poems, the David of his generation, thus asserting his vocation as a psalmist. (2) Being a Levite by descent, he quotes the great names of the earlier Levitic Psalmists of the Bible and claims to have inherited their charisma. (3) He interprets his own name and that of Yehōseph as tokens of a heritage to be lived up to. (4) He may have invoked the "reserved name" of God, the tetragrammaton, to be pronounced only by the High Priest, as he intimates in his battle poem "Do you not fulfill . . ." (dist. 58f.) which line I quoted above[40].

Samuel's messianic orientation is partly Davidic, although he was a Levite. The same, of course, applies to Yehōseph. The synagogue hymn, composed by Ibn Gabirol for Yehōseph's pre-wedding service, abounds with Davidic-messianic allusions. Other synagogue hymns by Ibn Gabirol also express messianic hopes connected with the Naghrālla family. If the observation is correct that Samuel claimed in his youth to be the Shiloh predicted in Gen. XLIX. 10[83], he may have identified this Shiloh, as did many, with King Solomon, yet also with himself as being the new "Son of David." This, then, may be another aspect of his Solomonism.

David and Solomon belong together in the sense that each is thought of as a righteous ruler. David, especially in his character of the Psalmist, lived on in the image of *rex et propheta*, of the harper shepherd-king and the knightly redeemer of his people, while Solomon, the builder of the

Temple, established an eternal paradigm of royalty: wise, priestly, magnificent in all his dealings, the epitome of the cultured lover and the privileged and enlightened patron of the arts. In the "advanced" environment of Arab Spain the secular aspects of these great Jewish prototypes must have fired the imagination of both Jews and Arabs. The ideal of the nobleman, excellent in arts and arms, was long established among the Arab bards. The Arab rulers, in turn, shaped themselves according to this image. It follows that any latter-day re-embodiment of David or Solomon, at Cordova or Granada, must have been influenced by such Arab courtly models. Moreover, since the cousin-nations of Jews and Arabs both held to the ancient tradition of a poetical charisma, a messianic ruler who was not a poet himself and a patron of poets was unthinkable in that time and that place.

The Umayyads, whose throne ideology — as far as this can be reconstructed from the sources — will be discussed later, are most likely more Solomonic than Davidic. As Muhammad's kindred by blood, they regard themselves born to the purple as Solomon was; but in addition to prerogatives of inheritance and the actual possession of power they individually justify their claim upon the throne as inspired legislators, preachers, poets, patrons of art, and occasionally by an adopted royal international ancestry. This being the case, there must have been to Samuel's and Yehōšeph's poetry, and possibly to their garden architecture and even to their campaigns, a Davidic and Solomonic flavor. As far as garden architecture is concerned, David, in his embodiment as King of Paradise[84], and Solomon, as the maker of pools and the layer-out of gardens, as he appears in Ecclesiastes, are the protectors of the Naghrāllas. But another messianic archetype, continually present in Judaism, is the Messiah of the House of Levi, the new Aaron and/or Moses whose example is alive in the references to the Naghrāllas' teaching and writing (law-giving) and in Samuel's singing of "Psalms" like his levitic forebears. As had happened before in Jewish history, the synthetic figure of two Messiahs in one person is now apparently alive, for Samuel's proclamation of his pretensions to this re-embodiment (or office or status) — a blend of Davidic and Levitic aspirations — is made in one of his poems, *She'ey minn-ī*[85], lines 36—40, and must have deeply shocked his contemporaries:

If someone said to me: "Are you one to compose psalms?"
I would answer him: "I am the David of my generation."

(I Sam. XIX. 24; X. 11 f.) And if he mocked: "Is Saul then among the prophets?"
I would retort: "A heritage is it from Merari

Notes 84—85

And also from Asir, Elkana, and Asaph
and Mishael and Alzaphan and Sitri." (Ex. VI. 22, 24)

This claim upon being the New David and, as such, the author of songs equal in rank to the Psalms is shocking, since the Psaltery is regarded by orthodox Judaism a book of a very specific inspiration. What may have given rise to such a statement and thus mitigate the arrogance of these lines is the existence of a Muslim counterpart in the lines of the caliph Yazīd III, which I shall quote later in connection with the topic of the "Family of Kings," where the caliph lays claim to the heritage of all great kings of the world. The caliph is merely boasting about his ancestors, genuine and fictitious — in a way similar to that in which Ibn Gabirol calls Solomon, arrogantly enough it is true, *his* ancestor — but Samuel is doing much more. Provoked by the taunt of an adversary that he was arrogating to himself a position which was pitifully beyond his grasp, he retorts by taking the bold step of setting himself up as the re-embodiment of his forebears. He seems to be proclaiming himself, on the strength both of his office and of his poetical calling, a new David — more than a mere "captain" like Saul, (whose affiliation with the 'fatherless prophets' was felt to be out of place even by his own biblical contemporaries and countrymen) — as well as asserting his status as a Levite, a descendant of all the families of the messianic tribe of Levi, the priestly Temple singers[86]. A Davidic messiah, the reader will remember e. g. from Matthew I. 1ff., was expected to emerge from the direct lineage of the biblical king, the root of Jesse. Nevertheless, the overriding model for the secular, and especially the artistic, ambitions of this circle remained Solomon, as he appears not only in the Bible but in the Muslim and also Jewish legends. It may, therefore, be worthwhile to enlarge somewhat on the topic of Solomon, the builder, in Islam.

Excursus: Solomon in the Koran and Islamic Legend

The name Sulaimān, which is derived from the same root, meaning peace and fullness, as the word Islam, must have lent its bearer great authority and splendor in the eyes of the Muslims, who were fundamentally opposed to the idea of kingship. He appears in the Koran as one of the ancestors of Islam, and it is his illustrious example that allows the Umayyads to set themselves up as kings in the teeth of the opposition which censured them for having introduced *mulk*, 'kingship', a word of opprobrium, into egalitarian Islam.

I interpose at this place some of the Koranic passages referring to Solomon, together with aṭ-Ṭabarī's commentary:[87]

Sūra XXI. 82: Some of the satans dived for him and wrought work for him while we guarded them.

A similar passage is found in Sūra XXXVIII. 37:

. . . the satans, every builder and diver, and others fettered in chains. This is our gift. Therefore give freely or withhold without reckoning.

Sūra XXXIV. 12: To Solomon [we subjected] the wind, whose morning [journey] was that of a month and whose evening [journey] was that of a month, and we caused a fountain of molten brass to flow for him and certain *jinn* worked under his sway by the command of his Lord, and whoever among them turned aside from our command, we gave him a taste of the punishment of flame. 13: They fashioned for him whatever he wanted: halls, images, bowls like water troughs, and fixed pots.

Sūra XXVII. 17: And there were gathered unto Solomon his armies of the jinn and humankind, and of the birds, so that they were set in array.

As a commentary to Sūra XXXVII. 16, aṭ-Ṭabarī adds[88], possibly using Sūra XXXVIII. 18 for his commentary, "we made the mountains subject to him (David)": These are the temples which the *divs* have built and the images which they made since the days of Solomon, colored likenesses. The first thing, the representation of quadrupeds, was on the throne of rubies. Below the throne, two vultures were represented who sheltered Solomon with their shade. The 'bowls like watering troughs' *(plats comme des bassins)* were large reservoirs, basins, and solid kettles like the mountains. It was from the time of Solomon that people began to dive to the bottom of the sea to look for pearls. For this he employed *divs*. When he was angry at a *div*, he gave the order to blind him and to put him in the middle of a great stone and to saw him apart together with the stone. And God had given him a fountain of copper and bronze, as it is reported in the Koran (Sūra XXXIV. 11).

At another passage in aṭ-Ṭabarī[89] we find more comment concerning this passage, using all the possible etymological connections of *jawāb*, such as 'crushing stones',

'Kettles like the mountain' (Sūra XXXIV. 13: *wa-jifānin ka-l-jawābi wa-qudūri(n):* 'kettles like water troughs and fixed pots'). The *divs* had cut a piece of a mountain and formed from it a kettle and made underneath immovable hearths. There they cooked the food. As to the images mentioned in the Koran, those were permitted which

Notes 88—89

represent Jesus, the son of Mary, the spirit of God, and were formed according to an order of God.

Qaṭar, 'liquid metal' in the Koran, refers to liquid copper; no one before him had anything similar. In this fountain he had them crushed and then threw them into the sea (see above Sūra XXXVIII. 37).

As to the fast-driving wind, Solomon had a carpet five hundred parasangs long. When unrolled, three hundred thrones of gold and silver were placed upon it, and Solomon ordered birds to join wings to shade him and his retinue from the sun. One also relates that there were a thousand very beautiful crystal houses in which he placed his wives. Then he ordered the wind to propel the carpet with everything found on it, as in Sūra XXXIV. 12 above *(il soufflait un mois le matin et un mois le soir)*.

Another reference to Solomon's building device is in the well-known story of Solomon and the Queen of Sheba where, in a manner similar to that of the previous stories, Jewish legends are interwoven. Sura XXVII. 44 reads:[90]

One said to her, "Enter the palace." And then when she saw it she deemed it a lake and she bared her shanks. He spoke, "Behold it is a palace panelled with glass."

The commentary to the last passage by aṭ-Ṭabarī reads:

The *divs* tried to divert Bilqīs from Solomon; she was all-beautiful, but had goat hair on her legs. To see her legs Solomon built a castle and in front of it a crystal pavement, a hundred ells long by as many wide ... to pour water upon the crystal and then to place his own throne upon this crystal. She [the queen] pulled up her trousers and uncovered her legs.

To summarize, the standard aspects of Solomonic fantasies are the *jinn*, castles and their furniture, bronze castings of fountains and images, basins, and glass and water architecture with *trompe l'oeil*. I shall return to Islamic descriptions of Solomonic palace constructions in connection with the rotating dome appearing in Ibn Gabirol's poem.

I mentioned that the Umayyad palace in Madīnat az-Zahrā' near Cordova had a glass floor in one of its halls. Discovering thus that the Arabs employed the descriptions of architecture in the Koran as suggestions for their own fantastic projects, we cannot be astonished to discover that the

Note 90

Jews, in the wake of such precedents — and being at home with Solomonic motives in the biblical sphere — would employ the Solomonic motives found in the Bible.

It was left to Arabic poets to interpret the patrons' constructions on Solomonic grounds and, whether deservedly or not, to use the language of the Koranic passages referring to Solomon for such an interpretation and for praise. To quote one example of such poetical references to Solomonic buildings, I give three lines by Ibn Ḥamdīs, the Sicilian, from a poem in which the poet praises the palace of al-Muʿtamid (1088—91) in Seville[91]. Although this poem must have been written twenty-five years after Ibn Gabirol's Alhambra poem and could therefore not have been the model, the similarities of tone and style are striking. In a fashion reminiscent of distichs 10ff. of Ibn Gabirol's Alhambra poem, the poet exclaims:

42 I forgot the Iwan of Khosro over this, which shows
that it had a matchless master,

43 As if it had been Solomon, David's son, whose fear
allowed not the jinn to slacken in raising it.

44 It is as if its look-outs were eyes of charm above any
beholder, capping, nay, nonplussing him.

The notion of a *jinn* assisting Solomon in his building of the Temple is repugnant to the enlightened Jewish poet. The sphere of the Haggadah is unfit for his secular metaphors.

(4) FURTHER DOCUMENTATION: THE NAGHRĀLLAS' OTHER FANTASTIC ARCHITECTURE

A final documentary support of the thesis that the Naghrāllas promoted such a symbolic architecture, and that Yehōseph particularly, from his youth, designed artistic water-gardens, is found in poems of Samuel ibn Naghrālla's *diwan*. Yehōseph himself collected his father's poems and edited them in the order of the *diwan* in which they are preserved, adding many prefatory remarks in Arabic[92]. One poem is introduced as follows: "I [Yehōseph] planted a round patch of lawn and surrounded it with a circular water channel. After this I suggested to him ⟨Samuel⟩ that he take a walk to the place and rest there. He did so, liked it, and improvised:

Notes 91—92

The Young Yehōseph's Garden Construction — A Surprise for his Father

Yehōseph yaṭ — Schirmann, *Shīrāh*, I, pp. 160f.

⏑ - - - ⏑ - - - ⏑ - - *(Wāfir)* — Habermann, *Diwan*, I, 2, pp. 83f.

Sassoon, pp. 92f.

Rhyme: *-lāh (lā')*

Yehōseph bends the heart of his father with one word
to grant a request, be it grave or slight.

Once he said: "Let us go to the garden, since
it is filled with buds and flowers;

And there is a circle which I planted as my resting-place,
and shaped it uniquely for my refreshment;

It is surrounded by a channel that is curved
as the sky is curved about the earth."

Then we went forth into a garden of beds,
laid out like the columns of a scroll,

In whose hearts there are highways for all who are noble,
and towards whose entrance there is a highway for everyone who asks[93].

We settled down in the shade of pomegranate and plantain (Hos. IV. 13)
like unto a palace, not in the shade of pine and oak.

Beneath us grasses served as pillows, (Job XXXVII. 9)
while the leaves above our heads formed a sheet.

The cup-bearer fills the goblet with purple
and places upon the vessel spotted papyrus,

And sends it, like a bride under a canopy, by the water[94] (Is. XVIII. 2)
to the drinker, [as unto] a bridegroom.

He empties it and sends it to rejoin his goblets:
it returns as before to the cup-bearer,

Notes 93—94

Who will not tire, stretching out his hand to the drinker,
saying to him, "Drink it!" — There is no noise.

Yes, it is a marvel, great to behold;
he who has not seen its like has never beheld greatness.

And to what the brethren do,
drinking by the stream, there is no equal[95].

The poem supports my thesis by demonstrating that even in Yehōseph's childhood the idolized son had developed an inclination for landscape architecture, and was free to follow it. The father, coming home, probably from warfare or a diplomatic mission, is surprised with a new *buen retiro* designed by the child. The opening words of the poem seem to refer to a young child captivating an enchanted father who idolized his son. (The boy was not much more than six and a half years old when he began to collect the poems his father sent to him in 1044[96].) The circular lawn surrounded by a water channel answers metaphorically to the earth surrounded by the sky. If this is indeed cosmic symbolism, then it is akin in spirit to that of the rotating dome, the sky-like 'canopy' of Ibn Gabirol's poem and the imitated Temple "Sea". These verses lead us into the innermost sanctum of the Jewish chancellor family, where father and son were in lonely accord in the pursuit of courtly Cordovan artistry at home, a pursuit in which Granadine royalty certainly had no share.

Yehōseph, of course, was no more than the heir to his father's Cordovan predilection for fairy-tale architecture. Samuel han-Nāghīdh attests his own experiments in water and light effects, achieved by the artefacts of the period, in his Hebrew verse descriptions. One such poem is prefaced by the following editorial remarks, written by Yehōseph. "This poem describes a fountain which was in his house; from its head, water poured forth and fell in the form of a dome upon a floor of alabaster and marble; lights were set inside this 'dome' and were thus covered by it; there was also a wax light on top." The poem runs:

A Water and Light Construction[97]

Emōr lī māh	Habermann, *Diwan*, I, 3, p. 41
⏑ - - - ⏑ - - - ⏑ - - *(Wāfir)*	*Sassoon*, p. 89, No. 113
	Rhyme: *-laḥ*

Tell me what is the torch upon the lamp
that spouts its crystals onto a crystal base?

Notes 95—97

A stream that will not kill fire in its midst,
its waters standing like a wall and missiles?

A sky encrusted with an onyx skin
stretched over a ground of opal?

Another fountain poem is prefaced as follows: "He also composed a description of a sprinkling vessel in his house shedding forth water; out of this vessel pipes protruded, flinging water in all possible directions": [98]

A Flower-shaped Fountain of many Branches

Ḥabhaṣṣeleth — Habermann, *Diwan*, I, 3, p. 42

⏑ - - - ⏑ - - - ⏑ - - *(Wāfir)* — *Sassoon*, p. 89, No. 114

Rhyme: *-ph-īm*

There is a lily in the earth, although she is not planted there,
most beautiful; and most beautiful are her children!

She bears upon her head a sprig like onyx,
and silvery branches surround her.

A third piece dealing with plastic art is introduced thus: [99] "This is his description of a 'brazier, before him, burning on winter days' (Jer. XXXVI. 22), around which statues of birds were placed" (Pl. 25):

The Brazier Decorated with Metal Birds

Emōr mah ṣ-ṣippor-īm — Habermann, *Diwan*, I, 3, p. 43

⏑ - - - ⏑ - - - ⏑ - - *(Wāfir)* — *Sassoon*, p. 89, No. 115

Rhyme: *-lām*

Say, what are the birds in whom there is no soul,
placed upon a pyre of light forever,

Who do not fly off in the heat of the light
into the distance, and whom the light does not devour?

Such experimental *montages* of water and light, akin to Byzantine constructions, belong to the trend of court architecture of those decades. I shall discuss their Byzantine counterparts later, but now insert a description of a glass, water, and light pavilion contemporary with Samuel's water and light experiments. Yaḥyā ibn Ismā'īl al-Ma'mūn, King of Toledo (1043—1075), erected his glass pavilion towards the end of his life, as al-Maqqarī reports (therefore his pavilion can hardly have been the model for the work of Samuel, who died in 1056)[100]:

> This [the afore-mentioned *majlis* of Madīnat az-Zahrā', built by 'Abd ar-Raḥmān an-Nāṣir] reminds me of what someone else reported about the mighty castle which al-Ma'mūn ["al-Manṣūr;" in full *Yaḥyā ibn Ismā'īl al-Ma'mūn ibn Dhī 'n-Nūn*], King of Toledo, elevated in this town, and about its highest perfection on which he spent lavish sums. He constructed in the middle (of his palace area) a lake, in the centre of which lake he built a pavilion *(qubba)* of stained glass, and encrusted with gold. The water was caused to rise to the top of the pavilion by an artful device invented by his engineers, so that the water would descend from the summit of the pavilion, encompassing it, the various streams uniting themselves with one another. In this fashion the glass pavilion was within a sheet of water which was shed across the glass, and which was flowing incessantly while al-Ma'mūn sat within the pavilion without being in the least touched by the water; and even torches could be lighted in it, producing, thereby, an astonishing and marvellous spectacle. And once, being in this pavilion with his slave girls for a night, it happened that he heard a songster sing ...

The verses that follow contain the prediction of the king's early end as a punishment for such extravagances. They read:

> Should you have built an eternal monument
> when your life — if only you knew it! — must be short?
>
> The shade of the *arāk* tree is sufficient for one who
> is every day the transient in continual travel ...

The superstitious king saw in these lines a warning and avoided the pavilion henceforth. As the last lines imply, it is in the name of an ascetic norm that the extravagant ruler was rebuked. He, as a "successor king," was disturbed by the censure. There had also been criticism of the Umayyad an-Nāṣir's construction of his Madīnat az-Zahrā', but the records do not indicate that the Umayyad was in any way affected by such pious vituperation[101].

Notes 100—101

It thus appears that the villa of Samuel han-Nāghīdh, which was probably
located in the Mauror quarter of the Jews, displayed water and light effects
in its garden and court which in some way anticipated those of Yehōśeph's
Alhambra. These animal statuettes and illuminated fountains are, of course,
in no way comparable to the elaborate dome construction, the Fount of
Lions, and the statuaried courts of the Alhambra palace, but the germinal
idea is authenticated here.

One earlier Jewish precedent for this penchant towards animal fountains
can be cited: the poet Dūnāsh ibn Labrāṭ praises the water-spouting hinds
of his patron, the Umayyads' physician and politician Ḥaśdāy ibn Shaprūṭ.
The analogy between Ibn Gabirol's following of Dūnāsh and Samuel's
following of Ḥaśdāy is striking: [102]

> ... There are brimming bowls   Josh. XV. 19;
>   ponds and channels   Cant. IV. 12
> and there are hinds
>   like the hinds of the forests,
>
> Panting at all seasons   Ps. XLIII. 2
>   without slacking   Lam. III. 49;
> to water the beds   Gen. XLV. 26
>   with gushing waters ...   Micah I. 4

This poem is evidence of the transplantation of metropolitan artistic
interests among the Jews from Cordova to the provinces. It should be
observed, however, that the poem has no Solomonic overtones, and makes
no attempt at representing a renewal of Jewish art.

At the conclusion of this section, which offers the chief documentation
of the Naghrāllas' responsibility for the earliest Alhambra palace, I add
some further material concerning Yehōśeph ibn Naghrālla's person and
about alleged living descendants of this remarkable family [103].

Excursus: Yehōśeph, Life and Aftermath

Ibn al-Khaṭīb and Ibn ʿIdhārī accused Yehōśeph of wishing to erect a
Jewish commonwealth in Granada. The same Ibn ʿIdhārī judges Yehōśeph's
person, as it appears, most fairly:

> Yehōśeph, who had not known the humble situation of the *dhimmī*
> or the filth of Jewishness *(qui n'avait pas connu les juifs méprisés, et qui*
> *ignorait à quelles conditions les dhimmīs jouissent de la protection d'un gouverne-*
> *ment musulman)* had a handsome face; he lived in strict abstinence;
> he conducted the affairs of the kingdom with energy, assembled funds,

Notes 102—103

saw to it that the taxes were paid with punctuality and entrusted Jews with public affairs. Bādīs treated him with increasing distinction. However, Yehōseph maintained spies in the royal palace. They were women and servants whom he remunerated.

There are Arabic verses referring to Yehōseph by Ibn al-Farrā' al-Akhfash ("The Day blind") ibn Maimūn which read, together with their introductory lines (in my translation)[104]:

> Having acquired literary training *(ta'addab)* in Cordova, he returned to the court of Granada and there became involved in eulogizing the Jewish vizier; which encomia entailed the following:
>
> Seek his well-being and you will encounter hope and bounty,
> will behold in his hall the beauty of the sun in the sign of the Ram.
>
> A friend has never encountered in him a frailty;
> he was unturned — whatever turn changeable Time took.

We can see in this poem, beside praise of Yehōseph's person, some note of admiration for his mansion, but the poem is too vague to allow a conclusion as to whether or not it refers to his Alhambra palace. That a Cordovan-trained *littérateur* who comes to the court of Granada should find employment under Yehōseph and, apparently, not under Bādīs, is significant, for whatever and whoever was metropolitan in Granada was introduced by the Naghrāllas and remained associated with them. (The image of the "Sun in the sign of the Ram" is, of course, known in European literature to stand for mild springlike warmth offered by the ascending luminary[105].)

That this praise was sincere and so interpreted, is proven by the following text[106] from the same source, which tells that (apparently after Yehōseph's demise):

> ... the poet Ibn al-Farrā' arrived in Almeria and composed there an encomium for Rafīʿ ad-Daula ibn Muʿtaṣim, the son of Ṣumādiḥ; then somebody who wished to cause him harm told (the prince): "My Lord, do not receive this accursed one, since he has said, in speaking of the Jew:
>
> As for me: loyalty is my religious code *(sharīʿa)*,
> wherewith I offended Islam which deplores non-belief."

Notes 104—106

> But Rafī' ad-Daula answered: "This is, by God, a noble man upon whom one must bestow kindness. If he had not had warmth, he would not have wept for an infidel after his death, for we have found among our own people some who have not paid attention to a Muslim, even when he was alive ..."

The prince seems to interpret Ibn al-Farrā's lines of praise as a eulogy for Yehōseph. This, however, is not in the text. To allow for such an interpretation of the distich, Munk interpreted it more freely:

> Mais pour moi la fidélité est une réligion,
> en vertu de laquelle j'ai cru permi de pleurer le mécréant.

It is comforting to realize that Yehōseph had at least been surrounded by noble-minded and sincerely admiring Muslim friends, partakers with him in a spirit which lingered, even if only sporadically and faintly, in southern Spain until the last decades of the eleventh century. These lines are important, far beyond the history of the Granada circle, as a portrayal of the society of literati of this time. Between the learned clergy and the princes, an aristocracy, hailing from all classes, is established, supported by a new canon of values — that of the nobility of heart and mind. The princes in an environment not exclusively devoted to *realpolitik*, with a clergy not entirely steeped in the transcendental and possibly not as well educated as the literati, depend for their prestige upon these *hommes de lettres* poets enjoying often a greater prestige of their own, and must yield to their influence. If the clergy's power had been greater at this time, expressions like 'loyalty is my religious code' and the profession of loyalty to a non-believer would have been persecuted. E. Wechssler points out that it took Europe infinitely longer (with repeated efforts) to establish such a scale of humanistic values and a Rousseau had to write his *Julie* and a Goethe his *Werther* to promote this ideal. Within the Islamic world, with its higher degree of democracy, it came to a much earlier bloom, although it also began to fade soon after the Crusades. (Under Saladin a very similar liberal orientation could be proved, for instance, by verses of praise, similar to those of Ibn al-Farrā', written for a Christian official in Egypt, Abū 'l-Maliḥ, the Coptic grandfather of Ibn Mammātī — in the middle of the Crusades.) Yehōseph's hopes of establishing a Jewish rule *(li-'l-yahūd daula)* in the state of Granada might have found some justification in the fact that there existed, within the kingdom, the town of Lucena, a Jewish self-governing commonwealth. This state of affairs in Lucena (responsible only to, and taxable directly by the king) and, no doubt, other positions of power reserved in the kingdom for certain Jews, continued even after the downfall of the Naghrãllas. Others seem to have returned to this town later and resumed positions of influence. Azariah, a son of Yehōšeph, of tender age, was saved from the Granadine carnage by the poet and Talmudist Isaac ibn Giyyāt who reared him in Lucena, the Jewish city, with all affection, to be a poet, Talmudist, and head of the community; yet he was to die there when twenty years old[107].

I was assured by Professors Seco de Luceno and Gómez-Moreno, both of them particularly interested in mediaeval Granada and themselves Granadines, that the families bearing the name Agrela, now living in Granada, are regarded (as De los Rios also points out)[108] as the descendants of the Naghrãllas of the eleventh century (the N of Naghrãlla having been dropped together with the n in *Ibn*). Such preservation of family history is most typical of stolid Spain and finds its explanation in her Sleeping Beauty situation. The daughter of a Granadine, Señor Agrela, who was financially influential and who was knighted of late, became, by marriage to a duke, the Duchess Rosario Agrela de Lécera. The lady presently divides her residence between Madrid and a *carmen* on the Alhambra hill slope previously belonging to the composer De Falla. In one of her *fincas*, three stone lions were found, two of which she donated to the Museum of Granada, where I was able to see them. The duchess most graciously sent me photos showing the three lions which, though badly weathered, clearly betray Iberian extraction. There is, of course, no connection between the Alhambra lions and these.

I do not know whether the possibility of having an illustrious but Jewish ancestry is a *partie honteuse* for a duchess who herself, as I am told by Granadines, traces her background (in contradiction to the local tradition) vaguely to Portugal. The lady would share a Jewish ancestry with many illustrious and powerful Spaniards, and in her case ancestry might connect her with the patron of the Fount of Lions, which ranks among the foremost art monuments of Spain! Hence, I could not interpret with certainty the refusal on the part of the lady to discuss her extraction either in letters or in person. I was informed, however, by the daughter of a distinguished Spanish scholar that there existed, in Spanish fascist circles, a blood myth, a counterpart to Hitler's doctrine of the German-Aryan master race, according to which the Arabs belong to the desirable *sangre nuestra*, whereas the Jews do not. If such Manichean dualism should indeed be adhered to, then I would understand more clearly why my discovery of a Jewish ancestry of the Alhambra, by rather connecting this with the Bible than with the Koran, has seemed to embarrass some Spanish scholars. One is, of course, baffled to think that Spaniards should distinguish between the letter and the spirit of the Old Testament and the blood of its begetters when it comes to their own ancestry. Would that this spirit be soon overcome by its own absurdity, now that political hopes involving Arabs and Berbers have not matured in spite of wooing! Should historical truth be disavowed in Spain in deference to a fictitious blood myth? Such a question causes one to ponder whether it is indeed more than an antiquarian neurosis that induces the historian to re-assemble the *disjecta membra* of a defunct organism and to restore to the misidentified its true rights, even if, hereby, a greater dignity is secured for such remnants. When the so-called Abencerages basin was first pointed out to me as, most likely, the original basin of the Lion Fount, I was struck by the similarity of the fates of the lady and the basin. The legend-adorned trough is taken off its heroic pedestal and inserted into the floor of the beautiful hall. Spain strangely preserves memorable objects, yet often commits their origins to the underground. There, with their identities disguised, they are safe. *Jam seges crescit ubi Troia fuit.*

(5) SUMMARY

Typology and Iconography of the Fount of Lions:
(a) The Hebrew Iconography

The typological ancestry of our Fount of Lions may be described as follows:

(1) functionally: it is the monumental central fountain of a palace court, for cooling as well as decorative purposes, like those of Madīnat az-Zahrā' or the Umayyad "Hall of the Caliphs" in Cordova. Such basins, however, were not supported by, but "decorated" by human and animal figures spouting water.

Although the symbolism of the Fount of Lions is Solomonic, the function of the fountain of the Alhambra is indeed quite different from that of Solomon's Temple fountain. It was created at a different time and for different practical and more decorative exigencies. The restrictions of the Talmud would, in any case, have prohibited an exact replica of any of the elements of the Temple. The relevant passage reads:

> A man may not make a house in the form of the Temple, or an exedra in the form of the Temple hall, or a court corresponding to the Temple court, or a table corresponding to the Table [in the Temple], or a candlestick corresponding to the Candlestick [in the Temple], but he may make one with five or six or eight lamps, but one with seven he should not make, even of other metals [than gold] ... or even of wood[109].

Note 109

Solomon's fountain is said to have stored water for ablutions; the Alhambra fountain served as a cooling device in the Arab manner, and as an artistic exhibition of playing water.

(2) decoratively: it belongs to the Oriental traditions of basins and statues supported by carved lions (or bulls), transmitted through Umayyad or Byzantine channels. In our case such a tradition was no doubt uniquely revived by the Biblical description of Solomon's "Brazen Sea," his throne, and the "stands" decorated with the royal lion symbol. In detail: spouting lions are well documented in Islamic Spain — for instance, the lion that decorated 'Abd ar-Raḥmān III's aqueduct of Cordova. This lion, however, was certainly a crouching one. The legs of a standing lion would hardly have allowed a very large quantity of water to enter the body.

We must not forget that any work of art belongs both to an iconographic lineage (or often, to various stemmata), and, to no less a degree, to the imaginative urge of the individual who has occasioned it. The ancestry of the Fount, as we have indicated, is twofold. It was the Cordovan spirit that caused this circle of emigrants to divert a rivulet of the contemporary Arab renaissance in poetry and the plastic arts into a Hebrew channel.

The "Sea" of Solomon's Temple, and similar temple basins found in Greece, seem to belong to an old Mesopotamian type of ablution fountain[110].

In Ibn Gabirol's interpretation (and he may be the legitimate spokesman for the Naghrāllas' intentions) the Fount represents, as previously mentioned, "the Family of Kings" symbolized by lions, which are gathered together and sheltered "to graze" like a "flock." An immediate Islamic (Umayyad) precedent for the representation of a very similar conception is traceable and, before that, a Sāsānian and Byzantine ancestry: the gathering of the "Family of Kings of the World." I devote an excursus to this topic at the end of this chapter.

The word "sea" in the Bible appears to be a translation of Akkadian *apsū*, a word etymologically akin to the word "abyss," and such temple water-containers are mostly interpreted as having symbolized the celestial or subterranean waters[111]. The Solomonic bulls (oxen) are by common tradition "a symbol of fecundity" (Albright); "associated with the raingiver Hadad (Baal) ... in connexion with the life-giving water of rivers and the underworld" ... They also represent in their specific "arrangement in groups of three ... the four seasons of the year." Yet if one remembers the mosaic representations of the Zodiac and other groupings of twelve figures in a circle, one is reminded of the related astronomical symbolism[112].

Notes 110—112

Bulls such as those of Solomon's sea forming a pedestal are recorded in the animal-throne tradition of many Near Eastern gods and goddesses. Certain deities like Ishtar and Belit or the Syrian Kadesh (Qadesh) were in many regions of the Middle East represented as standing on animals[113]. Various Hittite monuments, for example, also show statues of gods upon lion and other pedestals (Pl. 9a). Those recently unearthed in Carchemish are supported by two lions or two bulls.

One pedestal from Carchemish, decorated with bulls, its surface scooped out in the form of a trough, bears no statue but seems to have been intended to serve as a basin rather than as a support[114]. If the archaeologists are correct in their assumption that this was a temple fount we have in this a functional, if not a direct typological, prototype of our Fount of Lions (Pl. 10). Later examples of animal-borne basins are abundant.

Some Greek basins (one from Corinth and one from Olympia) show three lions bearing on their backs human figures, which in their turn support a basin (Pl. 10a)[115]. In the Temple in Jerusalem the bulls appear to have served to a certain degree a decorative purpose. However, since we know the extent to which Solomon's Temple followed the tradition of Canaanitic shrines, and that the "Brazen Sea" itself was of Phoenician design, W. F. Albright is willing to regard it as a specimen of the current "syncretistic" Phoenician symbolism. So much for the most ancient ancestry of the Fount of Lions.

(b) The Iranian Heritage

The ancient Near Eastern art from which the Phoenician art of Solomon's Sea descended, sent forth other branches as well. The "Solomonic" order of caryatid lions below a basin is represented in that small Achaemenian limestone basin which recently came to light from a private collection in New York. If not fullfledged lions, at least protomes of such, eight in number, are carved from one block with the small basin which they support. They lift their heads, which protrude as if growing through the basin, so that their necks could be reflected in its water. This piece, displayed at the Iranian Exhibition in Paris, 1961—1962, measures no more than 26 5/8 inches and is dated "6th to 5th century[116]." (Pl. 5a) Yet there is a great stylistic difference between the Alhambra lions and these protomes. Iranian art was very inventive in modulating the theme of animal supports. As another example, three free-standing lions, forming a "bronze support," in the Teheran Museum (6th and 5th century)[117], are, since they are quite naturalistic, ascribed to an Ionian artist. There was a shaft for a basin, no longer extant, between the lions, as in the Alhambra fount.

The origins of Achaemenian art, of which a letter by Prince Arsames, Satrap of Egypt, gives us an impression, remind us, through the fact that it was controled "by an imperial organization," how this eclectic art, or, actually, any other imperial art, must have been developed, and how also the workshop in Cordova must have functioned. The Alhambra lions, at least, show an overwhelmingly Near Eastern style, akin to some Iranian sculpture which, of course, inherited the art of the ancient Near East and absorbed, in addition, some Indian and Far Eastern influences.

On the carved capital from Mathura, in northern India, of the 1st century A. D., now in the British Museum, which is akin to Persian art, we find wrinkles around the mouths of the two animals which recall those of the Alhambra lions[118].

According to Ibn Gabirol's interpretation, the Fount also belongs to another iconographic stemma. It symbolizes a "gathering of the kings" and has a counterpart in the painting of the Umayyad "desert bath" of Quṣair 'Amra. Ibn Gabirol's iconographic commentary to the Fount of Lions is entirely different from known interpretations of Solomon's Brazen Sea. He could have cited from Arabic fountain poetry much more current interpretations, and on the basis of biblical imagery he could have spoken of the patron's position being made unassailable by guardian lions of Judah who guard him as the cherubim guard the Tree of Life. He could have interpreted the lions as symbols of Yehōseph's own virtues as a warrior, since he was as brave as twelve lions; but he remained within Davidic-Solomonic symbolism with its messianic overtones, which, as I am sure, was the Naghrālla circle's own: In *Targum Shenī* to Esther I. 3 Solomon wrote to the Queen of Sheba .. "all kings from .. come to greet me" (see I Kings X. 24).

To complete the main discussion of the iconography of this fount I insert an excursus on adopted ancestry and the "Family of Kings," which leads us to Islamic motifs.

Excursus: Adopted Ancestry and the "Family of Kings"

An Arab claim to noble ancestry or kinship is found in the lines written by the Umayyad Caliph Yazīd III, ibn al-Walīd (ruled in 744 only). These lines must have been widely known in the orbit of the Spanish Umayyads:

> i am the son of Kisrā and my father is Marwān and
> Qayṣar is my grandfather and my [other] grandfather
> is Khāqān[119].

This distich is a claim upon the heritage of Khosro of Iran, upon that of Muḥammad and his tribe, upon that of Caesar of West and East Rome, and upon that of the Khāqān of China. (Similarly, Byzantine emperors and Sāsānian princes, in their turn, boasted a fictitious universal legitimacy and descent.) Dr. Oleg Grabar interprets the above lines as follows:

> This verse implies a new concept: Yazīd asserts his right to the throne through an imagined ancestry. The Umayyad caliph — the verse may have been written before Yazīd became caliph, but he had always been ambitious ... — is the descendant and the heir of kings who, at one time or another, had been defeated by the Arabs. They are his ancestors.

Yet, as Grabar mentions, Yazīd is also the heir of the Sāsānians, by his Sāsānian mother.

> The concept of a "Family of Kings" was not an original one with the Umayyads. Studies by Ostrogorsky, Holtzmann, Dölger, and others have shown the intricacies of the "spiritual" (πνευματικός) family relationships between the rulers of the world (τέκνα) and the common father of all, the *basileus* of Constantinople. ... [In] the Persian tradition, as it is embodied in such writers as Qazwīnī, Mas'ūdī Ferdawsī, and Tha'ālibī, we find, first of all, a greater degree of universality than in Byzantium. While the Byzantine hierarchy of states comprised essentially the successors of the Roman Empire, Christian states, and immediately neighboring states, the Persian tradition stresses the relationship of rulers from China to Byzantium[120].

An assembly of six kings, as Grabar (re-interpreting Herzfeld) has demonstrated anew, is the topic of a painting in the Umayyad desert bath of Quṣair 'Amra[121]. Ibn Gabirol, in his interpretation, links the Fount with this theme. The kings, symbolized by lions, are assembled under the Hebrew overlord, and the lions support him[122].

(c) The Islamic Ancestry of the Fount of Lions

In the erection of this central fountain, which he intended to be a monument of his vice-regal splendor, Yehōseph ibn Naghrālla adopted an Umayyad building element, an artistic device imported to Cordova from Byzantium. A precedent for his fountain was the fountain of 'Abd ar-Raḥmān III (912—961), decorated with sculpture and erected (ca. 950) in Madīnat az-Zahrā', the Versailles of Cordova and a daring architectural wonder soon doomed to perish. We know of a few other pieces of sculpture in Muslim Spain of this time, for the most part from contemporary poetry and descriptions, together with the few pieces that survived the invasions of iconoclastic Almoravides and Almohades. Those specimens permit us to guess at the character of the sculptural efforts of this period. However, only two examples of caliphal representational fountain sculpture in the round seem to have remained intact and in use: the lions of our fountain, which correspond to the exact description in Ibn Gabirol's poem, and the two lions of the Partal pool of the Alhambra, originally a decoration of the Māristān (Pl. 13).

The predilection of the early Umayyads for representational art is shown in the human figures found in the recently excavated luxurious bath palace at Khirbat al-Mafjar[123] and other Umayyad castles like Qaṣr al-Ḥair al-Gharbī. In addition to ten, or possibly twelve, statues of young men and women in a row, alternating with each other around the tympanum of the dome of the palace, there were two figures set into the porch façade. One of these, in so far as it can be identified, appears to be the image of Caliph Hishām himself, wearing a long red robe and grasping the hilt of his sword (Pl. 12). The figure stands on a pedestal decorated by two squatting lions in very high relief, proof that the tradition of resting statues on lion-bases was revived in Islamic art under the Umayyads.

In these early Muslim secular buildings Byzantine motifs, themselves greatly influenced by the architecture of the Near East, exist side by side with Arabian and Persian elements[124]. The Eastern Umayyad caliphs carried on a building contest with the Byzantine emperors, and these in turn competed with the 'Abbāsids, as for instance Hārūn ar-Rashīd who had revived the splendor of the Sāsānian kingdom. It is not astonishing, therefore, to learn that the Spanish Umayyad caliphate, in its political and particularly in its cultural alliance with Byzantium, carried on and intensified this eclectic and eager building tradition. The exchange of manuscripts, treasures, learned people, and craftsmen between Cordova and Byzantium began in 820 and reached its peak in 936 under 'Abd ar-Raḥmān III, when his great palace in the center of Madīnat az-Zahrā' was built. (The Byzantine tradition traceable in the Court of Lions of the Alhambra will be discussed later on.) Some details of this palace are described in the *Kitāb al-muktabas* [or *muktabis*] *fī ta'rīkh al-Andalus* by Abū Marwān ibn Ḥayyān, quoted by al-Maqqarī as follows:[125]

> The number of columns imported from Africa was 1013; those from the country of the Franks, 19; the king of Rūm [Byzantium] made 'Abd ar-Raḥmān an-Nāṣir a gift of 140 columns. The rest came from Spanish quarries, from Tarragona and elsewhere. The province of Reiyo [Malaga] furnished columns of veined onyx; white ones were collected from other places; reddish and green ones from a church of Sfax in Africa. That stone-carved and gilded basin, so admirably shaped and costly, was brought from Constantinople to him [the

> caliph] by Aḥmad the Greek (al-Yūnānī) and the Bishop Rabīʿ, when Aḥmad returned from Jerusalem. The small green basin decorated with carvings of human figures was brought by Aḥmad from Syria [or Damascus] or, as others say, from Constantinople, also by the Bishop Rabīʿ ... [The Caliph] an-Nāṣir placed this in the sleeping quarters of his eastern mansion [*majlis*], known as al-Mūnis [or better, al-Mu'nis]. He placed upon it twelve red-gold statues, encrusted with precious pearls, coming from among those statues manufactured in the [royal] workshop [*dār aṣ-ṣināʿa*] in Cordova. [Among these 12 statues were found]: a lion, flanked on his right by a gazelle, on his left by a crocodile; on the opposite side was [a group consisting of] a dragon, an eagle and an elephant. On the remaining two sides were first a dove together with a falcon and a peacock, and [second] a hen with a cock and a vulture. All these statues consisted of gold encrusted with precious jewels, and water poured from their mouths.

Unlike many Byzantine basin decorations, the animal statues mentioned here and produced in Cordova were probably non-automata.

How significant and unusual these basins were can be deduced from the fact that a historian, in a passing [historical] reference to Madīnat az-Zahrā', characterized the amenity of this palace-town by mentioning one of these basins. The passage from the *kitāb ar-rauḍ al-miʿṭār* by Abū ʿAbd Allāh ibn ʿAbd al-Munʿim al-Ḥimyarī quoted by al-Maqqarī, reads:[126]

> ... in Madīnat az-Zahrā', a city west of Cordova, ordered to be built by an-Nāṣir li-dīn Allāh, who expended great effort in its construction and ingenuity in its ornamentation, who brought there colored alabaster and clear marble, and the famous basin from [distant] lands and regions ...

The sentence which follows, to the effect that the basin was placed "upon a column," does not seem to be established well enough in its text to allow conclusions. If one accepts it, however, I would assume that it refers to the stone-carved and gilded basin, whereas the green one of the dormitory and all other basins bearing spouting statues were set into the ground. My assumption is that a basin on a column would have exposed to view (from below) the lead pipes carrying the water to the various spouting animal statues on its rim. Such plumbing is under cover in the case of animals upon pools or basins which are in or on the ground, like the plumbing of the Partal lions of the Alhambra (Pl. 13). In the case of the sarcophagus-like type of Islamic fountains, like the *Pila* of Ḥabbūs, the plumbing was inserted into a stone post standing by the small side of the *pila*, as in the Corral de Carbon fountain in Granada. A way of reaching the center of an elevated basin was a supporting middle column, as can be observed in the present Alhambra basin (between the lions). Yet we may be sure that the plumbing was always covered. Yehōšeph's basin was filled from below through the center. It was perforated in the center for a spout (as older photographs show). Therefore the above-mentioned stone-carved and gilded marble basin in Cordova, which presumably had its human-shaped decorations on its rim (which may not have been spouting and may not even have been sculptured in the round but mere relief decorations) might have been placed upon the ground.

A single colossal water-spouting lion, this one adorning the end of ʿAbd ar-Raḥmān III's aqueduct in Cordova, is described as follows[127]:

> In the beginning of this year (329 a. H., i. e., 941 A. D.) the construction of the western aqueduct was completed for [the caliph] an-Nāṣir, a structure through which good water ran from the mountains of Cordova to the Qaṣr an-Nāʿūra [the Water-Wheel Tower or Wheel Watercastle; the word *nāʿūra* was adopted into the Spanish language as *noria*] in the west of Cordova, by means of well-engineered pipes, and across linked arches. Its waters ran, according to an admirable plan and ingenious workmanship, into a vast basin; upon this basin was a lion of huge size and excellent workmanship, so awe-inspiring that none more beautiful is attested among all the plastic arts of the kings of bygone days. It was covered with purest gold, and its eyes were two jewels flashing powerfully. The water entered through the hindquarters of this lion (as in the Partal lions of the Alhambra) (Pl. 13), and he spouted it into that basin from out his mouth, and the onlooker is fascinated by its beauty and the awesome appearance and the abundance of its flow ... and this aqueduct, its pool, and the statue which spouted into it, are among the greatest monuments of the kings of the past.

This Cordovan giant sculptured lion spouting water, was, of course, an imitation of its famous counterpart in Byzantium. The water entering through the hind parts may be studied in a fragment of a squatting lion (showing the inner water channel bared by the break), which was found in the former monastery — now "Parador" — of San Francisco in Granada, and which is at present in the Museum of the Alhambra. In the case of the (standing) lions of the Court of Lions the water enters through the animals' right fore-leg.

The well-known *Pila* of Ḥabbūs, preserved in the Alhambra, bears an inscription indicating that Bādīs ibn Ḥabbūs "collected all marbles"

(Pl. 14)[128]. In agreement with Professor Nykl (and in opposition to Professor Lévi-Provençal) I am inclined to believe that this *pila* was acquired from Madīnat az-Zahrā'. When in Granada, I observed that its carved lions attacking horned animals, represented in relief on the two sides, are not entirely identical; holes, presumably intended to hold jewels, have been drilled into the eyes of the lions on the front only. The insertion of jewels for eyes is a typically caliphal Cordovan device, and is known to us from the above-quoted text by al-Maqqarī. The use of precious stones for other decorative purposes is evident from the wall stuccoes (showing similar holes) found in Madīnat az-Zahrā', and in the ceiling mentioned in Ibn Gabirol's poem[129].

It seems quite possible that all of these representational works of art were ordered or "collected" from Cordova at the instigation of Samuel han-Nāghīdh, in the name of Ḥabbūs, just as the "Ḥabbūs *Pila*" was "collected" in his name. It appears most unlikely that the idea of collecting art was a spontaneous notion of the *nouveau riche* Berber kings of Granada, hardly true lovers of the arts. Perhaps for reasons of state, Ḥabbūs received the credit in the *pila* inscription. The presence of various animal figures on the Alhambra hill may point to the fact that the actual collectors were the Naghrāllas. (In Cordova Caliph al-Ḥakam II seems to have for that time established the tradition of a royal collector of plastic art.)

It is significant that all this representational sculpture has little precedent or sequel in Islamic art in Spain, but flourished for only a short period under certain Umayyad caliphs. The custom of collecting statuary (or of commissioning sculptors) was apparently introduced to Granada at a time when Cordova, ruled by the Almoravides, no longer exhibited or purchased such works because of rigorously enforced religious restrictions. For the several following decades, however, the ruins of Madīnat az-Zahrā' and other caliphal buildings were plundered. This could account for the fact that identical column capitals have been found in both the Alhambra and the Mosque of Tlemcen, though the possibility that artisans (and settlers) invited from Cordova or Granada to North Africa produced plastic art has also been confirmed. (The existence of water-spouting lions at other Islamic Mediterranean courts during these decades may find its explanation in these circumstances.) The connection of such sculptures with Cordova and Madīnat az-Zahrā' is stressed by Professor Gómez-Moreno. In other words, the lions of the Alhambra fountain belong in one sense at least to the caliphal tradition, ending with the eleventh century, whereas the present basin supported by them is dated by a late inscription and replaces the original.

Excursus: The Berber Rulers of Granada and Culture

The question whether the four generations of the Zīrids who ruled Granada developed "culture" for themselves and their kingdom seems to entail some value judgments. I find the facts concerning the Berbers, the Jews, and the Arabs of that century excellently elucidated in the few pages devoted to this question by Pérès[130]. In Spain it was common Muslim opinion that the Berbers had destroyed not only the caliphate but, in subsequent times, also the country in general and had "made it a roaming place for wolves." The period of the "petty kings" and the permanent warfare between these, entailing a weakening of the Muslim power of resistance against the Christians is, no doubt, in general the result of the mutinies of the Berber and other mercenary soldiers. The merit of these pages by Pérès is the collection in them of the most relevant materials. As a king, ʿAbd Allāh represents the fourth (or fifth) generation of a dynasty in power and a Berber family whose background was certainly unenlightened. ʿAbd Allāh, its last ruling member, most likely had more culture than his grandfather, Bādīs, and his great-grandfather, Ḥabbūs. However, compared with the other Berber dynasty of the Banū Dhī 'n-Nūn of Toledo, even ʿAbd Allāh is not outstanding. The old Berber Samāja aṣ-Ṣinhājī had served as the young ʿAbd Allāh's instructor, a man marked by his *nomen gentile* as a member of the Berber population. If this man, described as a ruthless pillar of orderliness, gave the prince skill, as one might suppose, mainly in arms, there is room for the hope that the prince received supplementary erudition in other fields. The educator, apparently employed at other times as a police official, is characterized thus: "A man found drunk would not escape death, unless he could pay a very high fine [to him][131]."

Two contradictory portraits of ʿAbd Allāh are found in the Arab historians of that period, a favorable one drawn by Muḥammad ʿAbd al-Wāḥid al-Ghāfiqī, known as "al-Mallāḥī" (born 1154)[132], and an unflattering one by both Ibn al-Khaṭīb (who, however, also incorporated al-Mallāḥī's characterization) and by Abū Bakr ibn aṣ-Ṣairafī. This ambiguity is discussed by Lévi-Provençal, who decided to save ʿAbd Allāh's character, calling him "cultured" and "lettered[133]." I see no sense in passing further value judgments. However, I am puzzled as to why Lévi-Provençal, who had to wrestle with ʿAbd Allāh's imperfect Arabic and the often rather ignoble and garbled content of the *Mémoires*, which contain hardly a single exact date, or reference to poetry or to a higher ethical maxim, comes to this decision. Other kings of this period would certainly have been better writers; there were well-known poets among them. Or, at least, a more cultured person might have found ways, in the leisure of an exile, to order and polish his writings. Even if ʿAbd Allāh is reputed to have written some poems and to have copied the Koran in his own handwriting, and even if the mere attempt at writing memoirs may betray literary ambitions (although they might merely have been dictated to a man of some literacy), the typical ideals of a Muslim prince, as embodied by some of his contemporaries and described in the extensive Arabic *fürstenspiegel (adab as-sulṭān)* literature, finds no example or echo in his comments. As for the discipline of his mind, ʿAbd Allāh does not always care to distinguish clearly between the two Ibn Naghrāllas, father and son, (for which reason other historians seem also to have confused them). He refers to Samuel mostly as the "(Shaikh) Abū Ibrāhīm," but when he uses the expression "the Jew" or, derogatorily, "the swine," the two seem to be one and the same. Similarly, he speaks of the two kings of Almeria indiscriminately as "Ibn Ṣumādiḥ," as a generic term, ignoring the fact that the one who allegedly conspired with Yehōšeph ibn Naghrālla was no longer the first Taifas ruler of the Banū Ṣumādiḥ house, but was rather Muḥammad ibn Maʿn, commonly known as al-Muʿtaṣim. I translate the following passage from Dozy's "Essai sur l'histoire des *Todjibides*", based upon as-Suyūṭī[134]:

> ... The *hommes des lettres* had even more reason for complaints than the rest of the population, since, in the eyes of the ferocious tyrants of Granada, human intelligence was a dangerous enemy which one had to eradicate at any price. Having seen the sword always hanging above their heads, the representatives of the mind emigrated in great numbers but at different periods. The greater part went to Almeria with the certainty of being accepted by the generous sovereign who ruled there, and who, himself being a true Arab, hated the Berbers as much as they hated him. A nephew of Ghānim al-Makhzūmī of whom we have spoken, was one of these refugees[135]. His uncle, the great philologist, with whom he had stayed, induced him to leave the states of Bādīs. "This tyrant," he said to him, "is attempting to take the life of all *hommes de lettres*. I myself do not care for my life any more. I am old and I shall become an owl ⟨I shall die⟩ today or tomorrow, since Bādīs, the prince of Granada, is bloodthirsty, but I care for my works and I would not wish them to perish. Here they are, take them, you who are young, and establish yourself in Almeria. The tyrant may then kill me, but I shall at least take down to my grave the consoling idea that my works will survive me.

Notes 134—135

Even if as-Suyūṭī, or his sources, merely voice Arab resentment, and even if we refrain from comparing, unfairly, a warrior like Bādīs with a refined ruler (and poet) like al-Muʿtaṣim[136], we are able to ascertain that ʿAbd Allāh, the grandson of Bādīs, born in the purple, in no way met the standards of the cultured prince of his day. The following text after Ibn al-Khaṭīb bears this out:[137]

> Another of these refugees was as-Sumaisir, from Elvira, one of the most ingenious poets of this period, proscribed for satires which he had written against the Berbers in general and particularly against their king ʿAbd Allāh ibn Buluqqīn. He had already arrived on the territory of Almeria, where he believed himself to be safe, when he was arrested upon the order of al-Muʿtaṣim, who had been persuaded that he had also composed satires against him. Brought before the prince, and ordered to read the satires, he said, "I swear by the one who has delivered me into your hands that I did not say anything improper about you. This is what I composed[138]:
>
> I saw Adam in my sleep and said to him:
> 'Father of mankind, there are people who say
>
> That Berbers are descended from you,' and he
> quoth: 'Eve is divorced, if that be true!'
>
> The prince ʿAbd Allāh proscribed me for these verses; fortunately, I was able to escape by placing a frontier between me and him. Then he conceived the idea of bribing a man to report to you verses which I have never written. He hoped that you would kill me ..."

We must, of course, consider that even in this late writer, drawing solely from Arabic sources, considerable racial bias may have tinged these reports. The unbridled Berber warriors were, even in the rôle of protectors of Moorish Spain, the natural enemies of the literati.

Excursus: Literary References to Animal Fountains in the Caliphal and Taifas Periods

Poetical praise for princes who constructed water gardens goes back to Baghdad and Damascus; al-Buḥturī's poem on the ponds of the Caliph al-Mutawakkil is found in almost every Arabic anthology of poetry. However, the progress of "holy wars" and the growth of fanaticism, fostered by non-Arab tribes, put an early end to courtly poetry and garden statuary in most parts of Muslim Spain.

Notes 136–138

I have found no mention of basins supported by animals in any of the literary documents accessible to me which describe Muslim basins decorated with animal statues. All these descriptions tend to create the impression that the statues were on top of the pools or basins, and this impression is often confirmed by the particular indication that these figures spouted water into the basins.

Henri Pérès lists in his book, *La poésie andalouse .. en arabe classique*, the references both to the few human statues found in Islamic Spain of the eleventh century and to the representations of animals mentioned in documents of the period[139]. Having listed above the references in al-Maqqarī to the two famous basins in Madīnat az-Zahrā' and the colossal lion at the end of the Cordovan aqueduct constructed by 'Abd ar-Raḥmān III, an-Nāṣir li-dīn Allāh, I shall present below al-Maqqarī's further references to decorated basins and pools built by later Muslim rulers in the Cordovan (Byzantine) tradition. The degree of fascination exerted by such arts may be measured by a typical passage referring to Madīnat az-Zahrā':[140] "There was a large basin of craftsmanlike construction and pools and statues *(tamāthīl)* of marvellous character which imagination cannot find adequate ways to express ..."

The employment of sculpture by the Umayyad caliphs of Cordova as decoration of ponds and basins served of course as the precedent for all the later Moorish counterparts of this kind, so greatly cherished by the various *Reyes de Taifas*. A significant passage consisting of prose and poetry in al-Maqqarī reads:[141] "The kings of Andalusia developed the utmost perfection in council halls and palaces. In a description of the council hall *[majlis]* of al-Manṣūr ibn abī 'Āmir by the vizier al-Jazīrī, we find a testimony for such a basin in the following:

> Silver forms its midst; in its cavity is
> the daughter of tortoises who does not cease gurgling *(naqnaq);*
>
> She would strive to move away from the [two] jaws of a lion if he were brave of heart;
> yet behold, his mouth is stupefied.
>
> They shaped him after a model, and the purest pearl formed
> the two sides of his neck which is garlanded.

Apparently a basin was decorated with statues of a tortoise and a lion on the attack; the poet feels that if the lion were alive the tortoise would try

Notes 139–141

to flee. We have no reason to assume that both tortoise and lion were used as caryatid animals of a basin; instead, they rather evoke the impression of inhibited movement on the rim.

A third passage referring to animal-statues, contemporary with the Alhambra fountain, contains the following:[142]

> Abū Muḥammad ʿAbd Allāh ibn as-Sīd al-Baṭalyausī ... informed me that, together with al-Maʾmūn ibn Dhī ʾn-Nūn[143], he visited the [famous] Majlis an-Nāʿūra ⟨'Council-Hall of the Wheel'⟩ in the Munya [quarter] of Toledo [a most famous and splendid palace containing large gardens] and there was a garden which dew sprayed, and there were lions who opened their mouths and spouted their waters ... He described them thus:
>
> O sight! when I beheld its pleasantness it reminded me
> of the beauty of the Immortal Garden ⟨Paradise⟩.
>
> Soil of musk and air of amber and a cloud of aloe
> and a gentle rain of rose water!
>
> And the water is like lapis lazuli into which
> the mouths of the lions string pearls.
>
> And it is as if the bubbles bustling about in the water
> played backgammon on its left and right[144].

The poem above speaks of water, blue as lapis lazuli, in which the jets from the lions' mouths form strings of white foam pearls. The same poet described, in a rhymed prose passage, the same *majlis*, which he visited together with al-Qādir bi-llāh ibn Dhī ʾn-Nūn, which passage is also quoted by al-Maqqarī (after Ibn Ẓāfir):[145]

> The water — its black and white checkered serpents are running between the herbs, and then there is a filled pool / as if it were a tin-plated mirror / on the shores of which the lions of gold ⟨or copper⟩ take hold of a thicket / and they jet into it as saliva a palatable type of water / and it is as if they were real lions which stick out tongues of silver / neither ceasing to throw out water nor tiring.

Here also we gain the impression that the lions stood on the shores of the pool and did not form a pedestal.

Another passage in al-Maqqarī contains a quotation from the poet ʿAbd al-Jabbār ibn Ḥamdīs from Sicily in which he describes a palace built by

Notes 142—145

the Ḥammādid al-Manṣūr ibn Nāṣir ibn Aʿlā 'n-nās (1088 — 1104) in Bougie[146]. The poet glorifies crouching lions and other animals placed "upon the edges" of a pool, spouting water into it. The following is my translation of this poem together with al-Maqqarī's introductory remarks:[147]

> He mentions in this [palace] a pool above which [stood] trees of gold and silver, the branches of which threw jets of water. Then, digressing, he glorifies lions which, [placed] upon its edges, also spewed water. This is his poem:[148]

As to the lions that inhabited a jungle lair of rulership,
they abandoned their roaring for the murmuring of water in it ⟨the palace?⟩

It is as if gold enveloped their bodies
and liquefied the crystal in their mouths.

Lions who, in rest, seem to be moving in their souls,
as if they found there someone who stirred [them] up;

As they think of their acts of violence, they seem to
be leaning upon their hind parts in order to attack.

You might imagine, as the sun brings out their color,
that they are fire and their licking tongues light;

And it is as if they drew swords of streams which
melted without fire and turned into a pool.

The same castle is praised in another poem by Ibn Ḥamdīs, introduced by al-Maqqarī as follows:[149]

> From this [poem] is taken his description of a basin into which the water flows out of jets *(shādhrawān)* from the mouths of birds, giraffes, lions and all the like, in the palace which he ⟨Ibn Ḥamdīs⟩ describes profusely in a long kasida:

[A giraffe] is in the pool on the edges of which stand
lions humbling themselves before the majesty of the Sultan.

Their souls are on the way towards the oppression of souls
and therefore they have left their bodies.

Notes 146—149

It is as if the cold of the water [coming] from them
extinguished a fire incensed by hatred,

And as if serpents [proceeding] from their mouths
flung themselves into the ponds,

And it is as if the fish did not fear them,
having received from al-Manṣūr a warrant of protection.

Whereas the giraffe seems to be standing within the pool itself, the lions, "lifeless," are clearly assigned to the edges, and spout serpent-like jets of water, very much in the way of the Partal lions in the Alhambra.

The quotation that follows the previous one in al-Maqqarī, taken from the poet Abū 'ṣ-Ṣalt Umayya ibn 'Abd al-'Azīz, the Andalusian[150], describes a castle in Cairo, called Manzil al-'Izz, erected by Ḥasan ibn 'Alī ibn Tamīm ibn al-Mu'izz al-'Ubaidī[151]. The poem mentions representations of battle scenes, packs of wild animals, and birds flying in the air; in his urge to surrealize the poet attributes to the static scenes the impression of movement. The poet fails to mention the media and technique employed for these representations, but these were, of course, pictorial or mosaic, and not three-dimensional.

Verses by the poet 'Abd al-Jalīl ibn Wahbūn of Murcia are quoted by al-Maqqarī after Ibn Ẓāfir (who, in turn, cited them from Ibn Bassām)[152]. They contain a description of an elephant-fountain decorating the pool of a palace belonging to the 'Abbāsid al-Mu'tamid in Seville (1069—1091):[153]

> Ibn Bassām says: There was in the palace of al-Mu'tamid a silver elephant on the rim of a pool, jetting forth water, and 'Abd al-Jalīl ibn Wahbūn says this about it in a certain kasida:

He vomits water into it like a sword-blade,
a paragon of elephants who does not complain of nausea.

He has grazed on grasses of silver which have become solid
so that you can see how little he fears emaciation.

The animal stands again on, not below, the rim and 'vomits' the water into the basin. One has the impression that the poet is slightly embarrassed at the degradation of a beast as noble as an elephant into a mere faucet. To conceal his embarassment and because he lacks the power to surrealize the animal he takes refuge in a witty turn — a medical prognosis which asserts the good health of the elephant in spite of his apparent suffering from nausea.

Two verses written by the famous Blind (al-Aʿmā) of Tudela (d. 1126), describing a lion, are also found in al-Maqqarī:[154]

> The Blind One of Tudela said in a description of a marble lion which spouted water upon (the surface of) a small lake:
>
> A lion, yet if I made the account meticulously,
> I should say: a rock,
>
> Likened unto the lion of the sky,
> spouting from his mouth the Milky Way.

We find no indication either that this solitary lion spouting water which, leaving in the air (or in the sky-like waterpond) a trace like the Milky Way, served as a support of a basin.

A last reference to three-dimensional representations of lions spouting water may be found in the *Arabian Nights*. In the tale of *The Fisherman and the Jinni* of the Seventh Night a king finds a miraculous palace in the wilderness close to his town[155]. The text reads, in my translation:

> He ⟨the king⟩ entered from the vestibule into the heart of the castle and found nobody in it. Yet it was furnished and in its centre was a basin upon which there were four red-golden lions flinging water from their mouths like pearls and jewels.

The passage indicates clearly that the four lions were, in the customary way, set upon the basin and spouted water into it. This passage is quoted by A. von Kremer in his *Culturgeschichte des Orients unter den Chalifen*. Von Kremer's conclusion that such fountains were part of the ordinary equipment of the wealthy household in caliphal Baghdad seems to be entirely wrong. It is much more likely that this was a fairy-tale motif, in keeping with the spirit of the book, an echo of fabulous rumors of distant lands and bygone days. Although the existence of the kernel of the *Arabian Nights* is attested to by as early a writer as Masʿūdī of Baghdad (died in 956) and although Baghdad under the ʿAbbāsids is the setting of many of the stories, the Arabic book was not completed until the Mameluke period, so that any conclusions which have been drawn about the origin and currency of sculptured fountain animals would seem to be far-fetched.

Moreover, Islamic metalcraft employs representations of lions on the top rather than at the foot of a vessel. Bronze pitchers are decorated with

Notes 154—155

small non-caryatid lions, either fully round and freestanding towards the top of the vessel, or in relief[156].

On the basis of all these quotations we may safely conclude that no Islamic precedent for the supporting arrangement of the Alhambra Fountain exists. All the fountain lions spouted water into the basin they decorated, and were rather placed upon the rim, like the crocodile in the Villa Hadriana (Pl. 15) underneath like the Alhambra lions which spout water away from the basin into channels beneath it. Therefore, it would seem that the arrangement of the Alhambra basin is directly derived from the arrangement of Solomon's basin as described in the Bible.

Ibn Gabirol's references to the lions of the Fount are in many ways different from the Arabic poems on animal fountains that have been quoted. The Arabic poet wishes, for instance, to give witty reasons for the transitory postures of the fountain animals made static, that fact which could be bewildering to a naive onlooker. He can either declare, as we saw, that these animals are stunned in awe before the majesty of the prince (who commissioned them) or he pictures the animals' minds as far away on predatory raids — being wide awake in their imagination though seemingly in a stupor of dreams and owning a "real" jungle ferocity and watchfulness. He also manufactures, with greater or lesser inventiveness, a rationale for the lions' being reduced to a technical device. Ibn Gabirol accepts the lions as they are, in their static character, and makes them symbols of the intended iconography to represent tamed princes assembled in the paradisical world order of peace under the protection of a messianic shepherd. Such different orientation cannot be accidental, for Ibn Gabirol is familiar, as his Spring poems and flower portraits show, with all the fashionable devices of quasi-causation. For Ibn Gabirol the fountain stands for his patron's real ambitions and his mind is intent upon the Solomonic iconography of the fountain, which invites biblical associations and belongs in quite a degree to the religious foundation upon which the hopes of his nation are established. Therefore, there is no room in this poem for playful and fanciful "as-if" talk. The poet's relationship to the carrier and promotor of a Jewish rule of peace, Yehōšeph, is the sincerest stratum of his endeavors. The veracity of this poem is — since it is a courtly encomium as well in the spirit of its time — the highest degree of a patron's flattery. Nevertheless, the poem is not absolutely free from the hyperbole inherent in its genre and the prerogative of any poet. To this sphere
Dist. 9: obviously belongs the statement, in distich 9, that the poet "cannot count the many gates" of the palace and the comparison of the trickle of water
Dist. 20: from the mouths of the lions with "floods like streams" in distich 20, (as, above, Germond de Lavigne did) but such a mere *façon de parler* belongs

legitimately to the realm of contemporary poetry and does not in the least minimize the documentary value.

It is, therefore, not acceptable to differentiate between the true Alhambra palace which Ibn Gabirol saw and an ideal palace of his imagination. The contemporary hearer of poetry must have known full well, e. g. in the case of the Arabic poems on fountains, where he had to differentiate between the fictitious and the real. Although containing elements of free play and appeals to the imagination — of which no creation of art is devoid — Ibn Gabirol's interpretation of the iconographic intent of the Fount of Lions is related to the very absolutes of his faith and hopes. With anything less this philosopher and religious poet of international fame would have shattered his standing.

(d) The Byzantine Ancestry of the Fount of Lions

It seems unnecessary to devote a substantial section of this volume to the Byzantine heritage in the Alhambra Palace of the eleventh century and, in particular, in the Fount of Lions, for the following reasons: (a) some general descriptions of Byzantine palaces and of the exchange between East and West have been recorded above, and (b) such exchanges occurred only through the mediation of Cordova and not directly with Granada.

I have quoted, for example, the description of a basin decorated with twelve animal statues imported to Cordova from Byzantium. Strangely, such a basin also may belong to a Solomonic tradition, Byzantium being the link between the Biblical king Solomon and Arab Cordova. Thus the imitation of Solomon's artistry in itself seems to belong to a representative Byzantine pattern going back, at least, to Justinian, the emperor who in his Hagia Sophia set out deliberately to outdo Solomon. Justinian's imitation of Solomon's temple basin in the portico of this church, employing, in addition to twelve lions, six other groups of twelve animals each, is described by the historians. Texts, approximately identical, discussing the Hagia Sophia fountain, read:[157]

> Justinian, however, began at his own expense and completed the church [Hagia Sophia], without anyone's contributing or giving support to the building. What was a miracle to behold were the beauty and freshness of the colors, and the waters of the ever-streaming rivers, for he named the four corners of the nave "the streams coming from Paradise" ...[158] He also made in the main basin (φιάλη) twelve fountain niches in a circle and lions to spout the water for the ablutions of the common people. On the right side

> of the Gynaikitis he made a "sea" (ϑάλασσα) for the water to rise up to one span in depth and a stairway (κλίμακα) above this sea so that the priests could pass over it. He also placed opposite the basin cisterns for rain water, and he formed twelve lions, twelve panthers, twelve deer, eagles, hares, calves, and crows, all in twelves, so that water spouted from their mouths for the ablutions of the priests alone. He also named the place Leontarion (place of lions), and Metatorion the beautiful gilded sleeping room which he erected so that he might be able to sleep when going to the temple.

To complete and perpetuate his triumph, the emperor Justinian had placed in front of Hagia Sophia a statue of the biblical king shown in a pensive and admiring posture. Justinian's exclamation, "I have defeated you, Solomon!" was thus illustrated[159]. The employment of the word "sea" in the above description is also indicative of the Solomonic tradition. Here we have a fountain functionally equal to Solomon's temple fount, although much more ornate. However, other artistic fountains still more playful in design and employing the pseudo-magical automata (which also have a flavor of Solomonic cunning) were used for secular purposes.

Byzantium had been the heiress of the architectural traditions of the entire *orbis terrarum*. The Byzantine garden court combined western and eastern architecture: on the one hand, the Greek *peristyle* and Roman *atrium*, and their statuary ornamentations of pathways and of basins (the *putealia sigillata* which Cicero collected), including orientalized late Roman imperial palaces together with, on the other hand, eastern *mirabilia*, such as ancient, jewelled artificial trees (as the Gilgamesh Epic describes in the Hades episode), Sāsānian magical thrones and rotating domes, and the fairy-tale gardens of Baghdad. We may not be wrong to claim a western parentage for their symmetry and mathematical layout, and an eastern one for their exuberance, labyrinthine and phantasmagorical. It must be remembered, nevertheless, that eastern and western elements had been thoroughly amalgamated long before Byzantine days, for instance in Nero's Roman edifices.

It may, however, be worthwhile to demonstrate the parallelism of artistic intention between the courtly circles of Christian Byzantium, Muslim Cordova, and Hebrew Granada by comparing some Greek descriptions of Byzantine gardens with their contemporary Islamic and Hebrew counterparts found in al-Maqqarī and in Ibn Gabirol's and Samuel han-Nāghīdh's poetry. I quote a description of a palace garden with the typical quadrangular central basin from the anonymous Byzantine national verse epic, named after its hero, the Basileios Digenis Akrites. Such Byzantine descriptions of gardens descend from the account of the palace of Alcinoos in Homer's *Odyssey* and, to give another instance, of the palace of Electra in the *Dionysiaca* by Nonnos[160]. The garden description in *Digenis Akrites* reads, in its Trapezuntian version:[161]

> Cold water sprang up in the middle of the garden, and everywhere in that palace the water was running. However, there existed channels in that well that took off the water.

This is based upon a prose novel by Achilles Tatius, which is also preserved. The plagiarized passage, somewhat more elaborate, permits an even more definite conclusion about the aesthetic tendencies of its time[162]. It reads, in my translation:

> In the middle of the flowers a well sprang up and a handmade quadrangular channel was dug all around for the overflow. The water itself offered a reflection for the flowers so that the garden appeared to be double, one real, the other its reflection.

The element of the illusory, to which these channels contribute, is thus coveted to the same degree by the Byzantine and Cordovan garden architects[163]. It is in this connection that the mirroring channels in the floor of the Court of Lions will be discussed.

The applied θαυματοποιική τέχνη of the Byzantine artist is very often concentrated upon fountains, and the playful automata are worked into these, although the Alhambra fountain does not fall into the category of the automata — but rather that of Yehōseph's rotating dome, which I shall discuss. I insert for the sake of a contrast the description of a fountain with automatic devices which appears in Eustathius Macrembolites' tale *Hysminia and Hysmine* of the eleventh century. Marie Luise Gothein retells the main content of this passage, which reads, in a more literal translation, as follows:[164]

> The well reached to four cubits in depth. The form of the well was sling-shaped. A round column stood in the centre of the well; this, too, was stone: a hundred-colored Thessalian marble. A cup placed upon its top was of the same material. And upon that basin was a gilded eagle receiving the water. The eagle stretched forth his wings as if he desired to be let loose. A newly born goat, kneeling on her forelegs, drinks the water; and the goatherd, sitting by the goat, strokes her udder; the goat drinks water and he milks white milk: as long as she keeps drinking the goatherd keeps on milking. The

> herdsman's pail, beneath the goat, however, is not water-tight, so that the water runs out through holes and fails to retain the outflow from the goat. A hare, sitting together with the others on the circumference, to the right of the goat's forefeet, digs out a spring of water in proportion to his body, and wets his entire face. There also sits on the edge a swallow, and a peacock, and a dove, and a cock, all of which Hephaestus made and the hand of Daedalus fashioned. From their lips runs forth water, and the outflow of this water endows the birds with voices ...[165]

The more clearly one sees that an orientalizing, rather stylized representative art became a more adequate expression at this Christian court than Greek and Hellenistic naturalism, the more difficult it is to understand how the naturalistic animal automata could not remain confined to garden architecture, but "encroach even on the setting of the solemn receptions of the emperor." According to the report of the North Italian Bishop Liutprand, the emissary of Otto I, "two lions of enormous proportions guarded the throne ... they were covered with gold and beat the ground with their tails at a given moment, and they gave forth roars with open throat and moving tongue[166]." The Byzantine artist found an outlet — and final satisfaction — in the fantastic pseudo-magical art, which was able to make the seemingly illusory a reality. Oriental art came as a most welcome support for the need for abstraction, Moorish tapestries were imitated in Byzantine stone reliefs and Byzantium absorbed Hittite and Sāsānian styles. The inroads on Byzantine art made by Oriental art, for the most part under the Macedonian emperors, have recently been discussed by A. Grabar[167].

(6) THE INSCRIPTION ON THE PRESENT BASIN

A last link in the chain of argument that Yehōseph ibn Naghrālla erected the Fount of Lions is still to be inserted.

The present basin of the Fount bears verses which are part of an ode to the Naṣrid Muḥammad V (of the second part of the fourteenth century), attributed to Abū ʿAbd Allāh Muḥammad ibn Zamrak, who was the house poet of the Alhambra and who claimed to be the author of all the inscriptions on the Alhambra stucco wall decorations. The courts of the Alhambra underwent various redecorations on special occasions by the application to the walls of new stucco slabs containing calligraphically-inscribed poems [168]. They are not reliable evidence for dating the building itself, since the structures they conceal may be much older than this decoration. Inscriptions like these afford us no more than a knowledge of the way in which the Muslims at certain times viewed this building. Nevertheless, for lack of a better source of information than one of these poetical inscriptions, the Fount of Lions has been in its entirety ascribed to Muḥammad V. This poem, on the present marble basin, merely praises God for having *given* to Muḥammad the beautiful quarters of the Alhambra, and nowhere suggests that Muḥammad built them. The inscription reads:[169]

Blessed be He who gave to the Imām Muḥammad abodes
which grace by their perfection all abodes.

Or does not this bower contain wonders like unto which
God did not allow Beauty to find an equal!

I am thinking of a carved monument whose veil of splendor consists of pearl
and which adorns the environs with the diffusion of gems.

[You see] silver melting which flows between jewels, one
like the other in beauty, white in purity.

A running stream evokes the illusion of being a solid substance
for the eyes, so that we wonder which one is in truth fluid.

But of course, it is the water that is running over the rim of the fountain —
the monument offering long channels for the water —

Like one in love whose lids overflow with tears and
who curbs the tears for fear of a slanderer.

What else is it in truth but a mist which sheds forth
from the fountain drenchings toward the lions.

It ⟨the fountain⟩ resembles in this the hand of the caliph when it happens
to shed forth subsidies to the lions of the Holy War.

O thou who beholdest the lions whilst they are crouching —
timidity preventing them from becoming hostile —

O thou [direct] heir of the *anṣār*[170] ⟨Helpers of Muḥammad⟩ and thus not through distant kith:

Notes 169—170

an heritage of glory enables thee to raise even the well-rooted [mountains]!

God's blessing upon thee, and mayest thou be blessed eternally
to reiterate celebrations and to wear down thine enemies!

This poem does not betray any insight into the iconography underlying the Fount. The 'diffusion of gems' and the 'veil of splendor (which) consists of pearl' is a hyperbole for the spraying water. The comparison of a larger body of water (in the basin) with silver was found in lines by the vizier al-Jazīrī quoted in the Excursus on Literary References to Animal Fountains.

(7) THE QUESTION OF THE ORIGINAL LOCATION AND FORM OF THE FOUNTAIN

Among other questions concerning the Fount of Lions, the following arise: is the present site of the Naghrāllas' fountain identical with the original site? Did the lions originally stand in this order? Did the Fountain undergo major changes?

It will have become apparent that it is my belief, indeed, that the present site of the fountain is the original one, although I am unable to prove this by external evidence. That the fountain was surrounded by gardens is evidenced by Ibn Gabirol's poem and also by much later documents — a conclusion at which, without any knowledge of Ibn Gabirol's description, Miss M. E. Gómez-Moreno arrived. The fact that the old dodecagonal basin is found so close by, and that the topography favorable to the present water supply could hardly have been changed, also corroborate my belief.

Another question, as to the authenticity of the supports which raise the basin above the lions' backs, is equally difficult to answer and remains a matter of dispute among Spanish scholars. Emilio Lafuente y Alcántara asserts: "According to experts in the field of Arabic architecture, the basin originally rested ... directly upon the lions[171]." Professor Gómez-Moreno discovered, rather ingeniously, that certain bronze parts from Elvira, at present at the provincial museum of Granada, belong to this typology[172]. They consist of a large lion's paw connected by a non-zoomorphic link with a lion's head, although the artist wished to invoke the impression of an open, spouting mouth. (Similar supports have been found in Bougie, North Africa[173].) Both head and paw point in the same direction; the link between them is bent outward, apparently to allow for the setting of a vessel between them. An *aleta* is attached to the back of the heads, the function of which remains unaccounted for. In such an arrangement the lion-heads merely imitate decoratively the well-known motif of lions spouting water into a basin, although these strange bronze pieces actually have a functional value only as supports. Vessels displaying paw-like supports existed, of course, as early as the Bronze Age. Lion heads, used as water spouts, were also ubiquitous in ancient Greece. Lions were represented in numerous Islamic basins of all sizes, bearing animal figures, like the famous green basin in Cordova mentioned above. The caryatid Alhambra lions, to reiterate, do not spout water into the basin they support, but in the opposite direction into a channel in the court pavement. What seems alone to distinguish the Alhambra lions from other water-spouting lions is their standing position. We may deduce from this that they were intended from the beginning to support a basin rather than be borne by it. The lions spouting water *into* the Partal Basin are seated, and do not have flat backs of a design capable of supporting a basin.

(8) THE MANUFACTURE OF THE LIONS

Since there are hardly any extant counterparts to the Alhambra lions nor much literary evidence for the origin of such lions, it may seem futile to discuss their manufacture. It may, all the same, be worthwhile to summarize the suggested possibilities and the rather vague statements made by art historians so far. Two alternatives seem to arise: either the lions were fashioned in Granada itself, or they were imported. For the first assumption speaks the presence of the two related lions still existing by the Partal Basin and the half lion in the Alhambra museum in Granada, in addition to the twelve of the Court of Lions and to the other animal sculptures mentioned in Ibn Gabirol's and Samuel's poems. The lions of the Court themselves support this thesis. Their somewhat crude and conventional style might suggest a provincial craftsman. But a Cordovan craftsman is also credible, because of the conventional treatment of the lions' manes, tails, and tongues, which betray an old convention. Since the workshop in Cordova was, around 1065, most likely no longer in existence, because of the new anti-artistic rulers, and the royal textile workshop of Cordova had been transferred to Almería[174], it might very well be assumed that a Cordovan sculptor found temporary employment at Yehōseph's court, just as metropolitan poets found shelter there.

But since there is no evidence that Granada became the seat of a permanent sculptural studio fashioning statuary for water gardens, it appears more likely that a Cordovan studio, the existence of which is certain, or

Note 174

an artist trained there, produced such fashionable *objects d'art*. Under the Naghrāllas and the inartistic Zīrids, such sculptors could hardly have found regular employment. I do not think it likely that an ordinary artisan employed in the construction of buildings in Granada also occasionally embarked on these artistic productions, since so many fountain animals are accounted for in the above-quoted poems, indicating a certain market for them. An argument in favor of the lions' extra-Cordovan origin is their material, allegedly marble from Almeria, a city rather distant from Cordova, but close to Granada[175]. Should we conclude, therefore, that an emigré Cordovan artist supplied such art from a new Andalusian capital (employing marble from Almería), since the demand for such sculpture seems to have been greater in the new provincial capitals than in the fallen metropolis? The spouting stone elephant on the aqueduct near Madīnat az-Zahrā'[176] (Pl. 11) is stylistically akin to the lions, yet the lions look rather superior in artistic quality to this. The possibility cannot be excluded, of course, that Yehōseph merely procured the lions second-hand in the same way as the *Pila* of Ḥabbūs was "collected," according to its inscription[177]. Although the ruins of Madīnat az-Zahrā' and possibly the many ravaged palace gardens of the Cordovan nobility seem to have become the art dealers' Dorado, could they have been the source of so many pieces? The authors quoted by al-Maqqarī mention, with so much admiration, only a few such works of art in Madīnat az-Zahrā', though these may have been merely the choicest examples. So large a reserve for art-hunting at that one place seems hardly credible. If, however, the courtiers like Ḥaśdāy ibn Shaprūṭ and the princes mentioned in the Arabic poems quoted in the excursus also owned sculptural art, whether it came from the caliphal art studio in Cordova or not, this would prove that not only the caliph but also others were able, by donation or purchase, to acquire such objects. In this case, the various pieces owned by Samuel and Yehōseph could, in part or in bulk, have come from Cordova. Considering the Naghrāllas' interest in typically Cordovan sculpture and the fact that the *Pila* of Ḥabbūs was in Granada, we may not be wrong in assuming that collecting went along with this interest. This is also considered a possibility by Professor Gómez-Moreno, who incorporates the lions in his *Arte árabe español hasta los Almohades*, and considers that they might have come, like the *Pila* of Ḥabbūs, from an originally eleventh-century location. His very vague statement on the relocation of the *Pila* reads:[178]

> ... el traslado de esta pila y su adopción por el sultán nazarí Mohámed III en 1305, abre sospechas respecto a otras piezas que pudieron haberse traido a la Alhambra de igual modo. Son los doce leones de

mármol blancc puestos alrededor de la famosa fuente, en la Casa Real, a la que pudo corresponder en su origen la pila de la sala de los Abencerrajes ... En la misma Alhambra, procedentes de la Casa de locos magnífica, erigida por Mohámed V en el barrio de los Axares, se ostenta otra pareja de leones, más corpulentes y sentados sobre sus cuartos traseros, pero de arte igual; aun apareció ahora allí mismo parte de otra figura pequeña, semejante a estas últimas y de más arcaico aspecto. Estudiado ello, parece difícil admitir que obras tan bien caracterizadas como atribuibles a los siglos X y XI, se hayan podido inventar bajo los nazaríes, cuando nada de escultura conocida dejaron ni se consentiría su pietismo.

(9) THE STYLE OF THE ALHAMBRA LIONS

After the re-establishment of the Umayyad caliphate in Spain, Islamic architectonic traditions found a continuation. Yet, as I have demonstrated, a new influx of Near Eastern and Byzantine art, invited by the Cordovan caliphs, contributed to the creation of a new branch of Islamic architecture, which then, in turn, radiated influences upon Christian and Muslim art. Granada, as there is ample literary and architectural evidence besides the Alhambra to testify, became a centre of Cordovan art in the broadest sense. Further new foreign influences may have intervened, perhaps via the port of Almería, which is near Granada and had more direct contacts with the East than Cordova. Almería may thus have been the intermediary diffusing the art of such centers as Bougie which, as the capital of another Berber kingdom, related to that of Granada, had established a short-lived similar artistic tradition. But such an intervention could only have been subsidiary, and there can be no doubt that the major, and direct, influence on the civilization of Granada came from Cordova.

The Near Eastern style of the Alhambra lions has long been observed. It is more marked than in the few extant remnants of Muslim sculpture in Spain. This could be explained by the presence of Near Eastern artists in the Cordovan studio, as attested by al-Maqqarī. Yet there are no counterparts to so marked a Near Eastern quality as that of the Alhambra lions. These oriental traits are reminiscent of Mesopotamian and, as Torres Balbás states, specifically Hittite sculpture, of the lions of Tell Ḥalāf, formerly in the von Oppenheim collection in Charlottenburg (burned during the last war)[179]. This scholar, as well as Georges Marçais, do not seem to think that the lions were made in the caliphal workshop in Cordova.

Marçais is inclined to think that the lions might not belong to the Cordovan tradition, for, I assume, the reason that no three-dimensional stylistic counterparts to the Alhambra lions which are of Cordovan or other Hispano-Islamic origin are preserved. We must consider, however, that the lions mentioned in the poems of my excursus, which might have belonged to the type of the Alhambra lions, and might have originated in the same workshop, have perished. The relevant passage in Marçais' book reads:[180]

> On connait les lions du Moristan (hôpital) qui se trouvent maintenant au Partal de l'Alhambra, et ceux de la Cour des Lions, dont la raideur archaique fait un contraste si éloquent avec l'élégance savante des arabesques voisines. Ces sculptures semblent bien d'imagination persane, mais les documents nous manquent pour affirmer qu'elles sont complètement indépendantes de la tradition omeiyade.

Torres Balbás seems to have a similar orientation, but does not speak of the manufacture of the lions[181]. He seemingly contradicts Gómez-Moreno:

> These lion sculptures belong ... to an extraordinarily archaizing current of Oriental art, with roots in remote times. Confronted with the Hittite lions of Tell Ḥalāf of the second millennium B. C. in the Museum of Charlottenburg, and with others in Constantinople, they would be ascribed to the same artistic cycle.

Unfortunately this discussion is doomed to remain vague because of the multiplicity of unknown factors.

It is impossible to ascribe the origin of the lions conclusively either to an Asiatic or to a Byzantine (or even Iberian) tradition, because of the scarcity of comparative artistic material, and because Hispano-Islamic art was basically influenced by imported Byzantine art, and, moreover, contemporary Byzantine art itself was "orientalized." Where these influences were amalgamated is not possible to reconstruct. In particular, we are unable to assess with certainty how much work of a similar nature may have perished in the post-Umayyad period, and in what style it was fashioned. One can analyze the individual features of the lions and elucidate their stylistic sources to a considerable degree. I reserve a full discussion of the Alhambra lions and their style for a later publication where the subject can be treated at length with the maximum of illustration. This will discuss the few extant specimens of Iberian lions in the Museums of Cordova and Granada which do not seem to have influenced the style of the Alhambra lions. The evidence of coins, of textiles, and of the pedestal lions in al-Mafjar, with the small lion sculpture inserted into an archway in the Qalʿa of the Banū Ḥammād, the kinsmen of the Zīrids in Bougie, which is in no way akin to the Alhambra lions, will also be considered. The lions of the *Pila* of Ḥabbūs (in high relief) and the other lions in the Alhambra are loosely related.

Meanwhile, it will be sufficient to point out that the Alhambra lions are, like the whole of Umayyad art, inconceivable without the free use and adaptation of the Sāsānian heritage. It can be proven quite clearly that the "oriental" traits in the lions were not taken over directly from ancient Near Eastern art by an Islamic workshop, but were received through the medium of Sāsānian art which absorbed these traits before. The Alhambra lions can very well be understood as the result of a specific interfusion of styles. Such an eclectic process can be observed in the royal art studios of various dynasties: Achaemenid, Sāsānian, and Umayyad art have a very similar phylogenesis, and ancient Near Eastern art contributed to all three. But Sāsānian art, in particular, radiated subsequently in many directions, for instance into Armenia. The material I have collected contains sufficient specimens of lion sculptures found in countries other than Spain, in which Sāsānian art had contributed to a new eclectic style.

The assumption that a Christian craftsman might have executed the lions, as Washington Irving thought, is not at all convincing. If such a Christian artist had hailed from Byzantium we should expect to find in the Alhambra lions a greater evidence of surviving Greco-Roman stylistic elements. Alternatively, if we should wish to ascribe them to an artist of the Romanesque school, we should be mistaking the direction of the migrations of artistic ideas, in which the West was the recipient and not the giver[182].

There are indeed many western aquamanilia and other representations of lions which are almost contemporary with the lions of the Alhambra, but none of these examples antedates the production of counterparts coming from the Umayyad (and Fāṭimid) workshops. In fact the influence of Hispano-Arabic art upon both Muslim and Christian art was very marked. As has been generally accepted, the caliphal art of Cordova constituted so new a departure that the countries on the opposite coast of the Mediterranean remained merely recipients of, and not contributors to, the art of the eleventh century. However, the full stylistic analysis has, to repeat, to be deferred until a later time.

(10) THE COURT OF LIONS AND ITS WATER CHANNELS — DATING THE "ZĪRID" STRUCTURES

The idea of transforming the top of the Alhambra hill into watered gardens is typical of the early Taifas period, with its Cordovan tradition. Water had to be diverted from the River Darro, from a place where its bed is higher than the crest of the Alhambra, and forced into this stra-

Note 182

tegically safe and climatically healthy but naturally arid area. There is evidence, I have been assured, that water wheels also existed, during the Arab period, on the Mauror side of the Alhambra hill supplying the Alhambra estates. It is thus not impossible that Yehōseph's "diversion of the well," for which he is blamed in Abū Isḥāq's incendiary poem, was accomplished in this fashion. A general idea of the appearance of such water wheels can be gained from a leaf of a manuscript of the period of Akbar (1556—1605) in India (the sixteenth century miniature of MS. 8788 of the Metropolitan Museum of Art, New York (Pl. 16). Many such water wheels are still in use in contemporary Spain. The Ḥammādid tyrants of North African Bougie had undertaken an even greater task in attempting to transform a rugged and arid valley enclosed by mountains into a paradise. Their water-spouting lions were described in my passage on Islamic animal fountains. Ponds and one multilobed basin have been unearthed at the Ḥammādid residence al-Qal'a[183].

I am unable to establish whether the present plan of the Court of Lions differs basically from that of the original garden court built by Yehōseph. The architecture of the surrounding arcades belongs, no doubt, to a period at least three hundred years later than that of the Naghrāllas. However, the plan of such a court, containing at least one water channel, and ending at the two extremities with protruding pavilions or platforms, follows a strikingly eastern tradition, which is traceable (as an import, however, to the West) in ancient Pompeii (as Prof. Erwin Palm pointed out to me)[184]. In the case of the Alhambra it may have been imported from Byzantium.

The water channels intersecting the Court of Lions are an inversion of an old tradition, established when, and at places where, in the absence of water pipes, open channels served the purpose of supplying or draining a basin (Pl. 17, 18). Usually two sections of one channel, forming a straight line, conveyed the fresh water to, and drained the overflow from, a basin set between them. Lashkarī Bāzār, the great fortress built in the early eleventh century by Maḥmūd of Ghazna (990—1030), which was discovered and excavated by Professor D. Schlumberger, contained such open channels and a central basin. Professor Schlumberger has kindly sent me a photograph showing such channels and a description of one of these basins, which was the center-piece of the audience hall (Pl. 17a)[185]. A longitudinal channel interrupted by a central fountain adorns the courtyard of the Mosque al-Qarawiyyīn of 1135 in Fez[186]; and here we find two protruding pavilions almost identical with those of the Court of Lions in the Alhambra. We thus observe that this motif already was current about sixty years after Yehōseph's Alhambra construction.

Notes 183—186; Plates 16, 17, 17a, 18

The same arrangement of channels crossing a courtyard had already appeared in the court of the ninth-century Mosque of Sāmarrā and in the gardens of the Balkuwārā palace in Mesopotamia[187]. In the Alhambra the channels served for draining and cooling purposes, since the fresh water was actually conveyed to the central fountain through pipes. Of course the Alhambra channels, following also the tradition of garden irrigation ditches in Byzantine and Persian garden-halls, were kept permanently filled to allow for an additional slight mirroring effect. There is so perfect an early Iranian counterpart for a middle fountain symbolizing "Paradise" and the "Four Rivers thereof" that the symbolism seems to be well established. This was also a commonplace on garden rugs (Pl. 19). The description of Paradise in the Koran also points in this direction (Sūra LXVI. 8): "... And bring you into gardens underneath which rivers flow[188]." The Court of Lions was, doubtless, from the beginning a formal garden court in the Mediterranean tradition, whether it was surrounded by hedges, by walls, or porticoes. (To reintroduce the original garden character, a few shy orange trees have been recently planted in the patio.)

A rather hybrid development of the idea of an ornamental channel is represented in the base of the ʻAbbāsid fount, from Sāmarrā (ninth century), which is now exhibited in the ʻAbbāsid Palace in Baghdad. Here the water is carried in and out and around the base of the reddish granite fountain in a small stonecarved groove; this groove reaches and leaves the fountain on the same side of the Court, and forms a meandering line in the part that encircles the fountain's base (Pl. 20)[189].

A quotation from a Byzantine poet, praising a garden for the mirroring effect of its channels, has been inserted above in the section on the Byzantine ancestry of the Fount of Lions.

I assume that in Yehōseph's original Court of Lions the channel in the longitudinal direction carried the main water supply-line of the castle gardens, and that this filled the basins of some adjacent court. I imagine that another supply of water, larger than that flowing now, was carried under pressure through the twelve lions. I understand that the quantity was reduced and the metal mouth-pieces adapted to this smaller flow by the French engineers who refitted the plumbing in the early years of the nineteenth century[190]. The width of the inner channel of the carved lion fragment in the Alhambra Museum supports my view, but I have unfortunately not found any scholarly discussion of these questions in the publications of modern experts on the Alhambra. I have been assured by Professor Gómez-Moreno, whose father carried out excavations in his son's presence, that at least one additional early basin existed in the adjacent area now covered by the Palace of Charles V. Thus the disposition of an

Notes 187–190; Plates 19, 20

"L" of the Courts of Lions and of Myrtles, which has aroused the speculation of art historians, may find its most logical explanation in the assumption that they were built around the earlier basins, which in turn were kept in the vicinity of the main longitudinal water-supply following the line of highest altitude along the Alhambra hillridge[191]. I hope my conjecture will at least provoke a fuller discussion of these questions.

It has been impossible, as yet, to ascertain the exact area that was covered by Yehōseph ibn Naghrālla's fortified Alhambra palace. Future excavations may shed more light upon this problem. As to the literary evidence, there is a note in the work of the Arabic historian Idrīsī to the effect that the Zīrid King Ḥabbūs fortified Granada with both a wall and a fortress, which fortifications were completed by his son Bādīs. Professor Torres Balbás was able to demonstrate, in his article "La Alhambra de Granada antes del Siglo XIII," that these fortifications are traceable in some still extant city walls, in the Torres Bermejas and on the Albaicin Hill[192], yet he found no indications of such early traces in the Alhambra region. This hill apparently did not belong to the fortified area before ʿAbd Allāh.

If the subsequent Zīrid ruler erected any structures on the Alhambra Hill, these would be purely fortifications but not habitations, for the Zīrids had their residence on the Albaicin Hill, called al-Qaṣaba al-Qadīma. And, indeed, such fortifying activities are accounted for in the *Mémoires* by King ʿAbd Allāh, the immediate successor to King Bādīs. He clearly mentions having built a wall — but no place of habitation — and this as part of his preparations for a siege of Granada, preparations which consisted of strengthening and refitting the city walls. The passage in ʿAbd Allāh's *Mémoires* reads in Lévi-Provençal's translation[192a]:

> ..."je donnai l'ordre de construire le rempart contigu à l'Alhambra, à la suite de la décision que j'avais prise en vue des événements qui sont trop connus pour que je les commente ..."

The words translated by Lévi-Provençal *le rempart contigu à l'Alhambra (as-sūr al-muttaṣṣil bi-l-Ḥamrā')* stand no doubt for a wall which surrounded the built-up Alhambra area and, most likely, connected the Alhambra area with the general fortification of the city. It stands in no way for the construction of a palace.

A second passage in ʿAbd Allāh's *Mémoires*, which shows the exact circumstances within which he carried out this additional fortification work, reads[192b]:

> Aussi mis-je tous mes soins à relever les châteaux-forts, à les restaurer, à les mettre en état de soutenir un siège éventuel. Je pris toutes décisions nécessaires et les fis exécuter: établissement de citernes et de

Notes 191, 192, 192a, 192b

> moulins, dépôts de boucliers, de fléches, de machines à lancer des projectiles et de vivres de toutes sortes, toutes choses que je retirai des bourgades . . . pour plus d'un an. Surtout mon activité se porta sur ma capitale; les préparatifs que j'y fis sont assez connus . . .

The statement provokes, most logically, the questions: why had it not been worthwhile before under Ḥabbūs and Bādīs to include the Alhambra in the city fortification? Something must have enhanced its value and importance, something that did not exist at the time when Ḥabbūs and Bādīs built the circumvallation of Granada? Because of what changes in itself had the Alhambra area become valuable enough to warrant fortification now under ʿAbd Allāh and this under pressing circumstances?

To these activities of ʿAbd Allāh Professor Torres Balbás wrongly ascribes the large sections of Alhambra masonry belonging to the Zīrid period. However, such masonry appears mainly in the lower parts of many inner Alhambra walls. Common sense indicates that "repair work" and fortification does not consist of extended substructures to entire palace areas. The vague fashion, however, in which Torres Balbás deals with this question seems to betray indecision. He ascribes the Zīrid elements of the present Alhambra to "certain projects which ʿAbd Allāh ordered to be built in Granada and in the Alhambra."

The physical evidence proves that the man responsible for the "Zīrid type" masonry in the Alhambra Palace was a builder and not a re-builder and mere fortifier, and ʿAbd Allāh himself, as we read in his *Mémoires*, is willing to credit, specifically, his own adversary with the merit of having built up for himself "the Alhambra fortress." Professor Torres Balbás also places the Alhambra construction of the "Zīrid period" in the years 1052—56, under the mistaken impression that the reference to the Naghrāllas' Alhambra in the *Mémoires* refers, not to Yehōšeph, but to the last stage of the life of Samuel Naghrālla who died in 1056. Subsequent structures are attested only for later rulers: al-Mustanṣir ibn Hūd Saif ad-daula (after 1145), and Ibn al-Aḥmar, the founder of the Naṣrid dynasty, in 1237 or 1238.

Other scholars working in the wake of Torres Balbás are altogether silent on this problem of Zīrid masonry in the Alhambra area. Yet, as mentioned before, the extant Alhambra contains a considerable volume of masonry of the Zīrid period, and the possibility cannot be excluded either, that more Naghrālla masonry exists beneath and hidden within some other parts of the present Alhambra buildings, such as the vaulted tunnel between the Patio de la Reja and the Baño area. The foundations of many parts are inaccessible. The surface architecture of many walls of the present Alhambra indicates the imposition of masonry and decoration of later periods.

Since the masonry of the Zīrid period is clearly identifiable (as discussed before), the masonry of older periods, not to be ascribed to Yehōseph, can also be identified. With the exception of Torres Balbás' unsatisfactory article on "The Alhambra before the Thirteenth Century," art historians have hardly mentioned that the question of the origins of the earlier Alhambra is still open. With reference to the Naṣrid ruler, Yūsuf I (1314—1325), who redecorated Alhambra buildings, Georges Marçais at least admits: "Il n'est pas possible que Yousof I ait fait travailler à cette partie apparemment ancienne de l'Alhambra"; and he reproduces a map showing clearly the parts "older than Yūsuf I[193]."

It has often been regretted that the founder of a building as outstanding as the original Alhambra Palace is unknown. Now, after a most authoritative testimony has come to light which credits Yehōseph with such a deed — a man who represents the very spirit of Cordovan artistic traditions which are alive in the oldest Alhambra parts — should not the discovery of such evidence be a step forward?

Note 193

E. Other Constructions and Works of Art Found in the Present Alhambra which may have been Yehōseph ibn Naghrālla's

There are also, however, the following individual structural elements within the present Alhambra which are recognized as being two or three centuries older than the later constructions of the fourteenth and fifteenth centuries. Two identical column capitals in the entrance to the *Cuarto Dorado* in the old *Casa Real* are described by Torres Balbás as being in the Almohade tradition[194]. A companion to these capitals exists in the *miḥrab* of the Almoravid Mosque of Tlemcen (dated 1135). Similarly, two black marble capitals of the earlier period were set into the fourteenth-century structure of the Court of the "Harén[195]." Other capitals of the so-called "wasp's nest" type which are preserved in the museum of the Alhambra, are commonly offered as proof of the migration and collection of sculptured elements[196]. Mrs. Mildred Byne's idea that such capitals suggest "a late return to the wasp's nest type" in the fourteenth century lacks any corroboration. This wasp's nest style, of Byzantine conception, flourished in Cordova under ʿAbd ar-Raḥmān II (833—848). Examples of capitals of an "unadorned type," like the black marble capitals mentioned above, are also found in earlier buildings elsewhere in Spain, for which reason Mrs. Byne has made her assumption that they "probably stem from an earlier building." There is no doubt, as I have shown, that in the eleventh century there existed a flourishing trade in separate sculptural elements in and around the Iberian peninsula. The ruins of Madīnat az-Zahrā' and Elvira were, as aforementioned, depleted by traders and collectors. Sculptors, no longer employed in Cordova after the downfall of the caliphate, seem to have helped disseminate caliphal art in North Africa and elsewhere where the newly established kings attempted to recreate a Cordova of their own. Some wooden corbels from the Torre de las Damas of the Alhambra, preserved in the Alhambra Museum, which were formerly assigned, for stylistic reasons, to the twelfth century (since the same style occurs in the Mosque of Tlemcen), are stylistically older[197]. The motif of these corbels probably made its way to this mosque via the Andalusian craftsmen who are known to have been invited to work in Africa, e. g., in Tlemcen and Tinmel. This ascription, however, does not

Notes 194—197

necessarily indicate that these corbels belong to a time much earlier than 1135[198]. Professor Torres Balbás (in conversation) pointed out that the nature of craftsmanship in wood, which is notoriously conservative, might explain the retention of stylistically earlier characteristics.

The *pila* of Bādīs ibn Ḥabbūs must be mentioned again in this connexion. This water trough, *pila*, belonging to the sarcophagus type, is richly decorated along its sides with high relief figures of four long-horned animals, each attacked by a lion. The *pila* bears an inscription visibly superimposed upon an older one, and itself partly superimposed upon by a later one. The first part of the inscription reads:

> Bādīs ibn Ḥabbūs aṣ-Ṣinhājī [had] all pieces of marble (?) [transported] to the castle of his capital (?) Granada, may God protect it.

The rest of the inscription refers to the later ruler, the Naṣrid Muḥammad III, and bears a date equivalent to May 25, 1305. The archaeologists who have studied this *pila* agree upon its Umayyad or ʿĀmirid origin. Professor Lévi-Provençal is convinced that the basin came from Elvira[199], whereas Professor Nykl, with much more justification it seems to me, believes that it originated in Madīnat az-Zahrā' (Cordova). R. Castejón points out that Hispano-Islamic zoomorphic art flourished almost exclusively in caliphal Cordova and in a few other towns in the caliphal period and he discusses the few extant specimens of such art[200].

F. Again Ibn Gabirol's Poem: The other References to the Palace

Ibn Gabirol's poem mentions architectural elements apart from the Fount of Lions, which prove, first, that architectural ideas which are found preserved only in much later buildings were already in existence in this poet's time; and second, it is indicated by such lines from Ibn Gabirol's Alhambra poem that the constructions of the Banū Naghrālla set the tone for future buildings:

Dist. 11: And there are windows, transparent above them ⟨the doors⟩,
skylights where dwell the luminous planets

and of the dome:

The dome is like the Palanquin of Solomon
hung above the glories of the chambers,

That rotates in its gyre, shining like
opals and sapphire and pearls;

Dist. 12–14: Thus it is in the daytime, while at dusk it looks
like the sky whose stars form constellations;

These few lines are a rare expression of the pseudo-magical tendency in Granada, established previously in Cordova, inherited from the θαυματοποιικὴ τέχνη art of Byzantium. These tendencies did not remain confined to Granada, but found their way into the West[201].

The notion of buildings covered by a rotating dome is ancient:[202] Babylonian kings erected a counterpart to Marduk's heavenly throne hall to symbolize their being the counterpart of Marduk on earth, and to manipulate the universe by sympathetic magic[203]. Ernst Herzfeld, Karl Lehmann, and H. P. L'Orange may be credited with having traced the transmission of this idea from the Near East to Rome, where Nero's Domus Aurea seems to have had an actually rotating hall. During a students' visit to the ruins of the Domus Aurea under the guidance of Axel Boëthius a student pointed out the way in which the impression of the rotation of the hall could easily have been given by means of a rotation of its floor. The main octagonal hall has a water chute placed so that the water from it would have flooded the hall. If, therefore, a large platform were raised above the main floor on a central hub and the water were made to describe a circle below this platform, the attachment of a few rudders to the lower side of the platform would make it revolve. A similar construction linking a ceiling with swimming floats could, of course, have been constructed as well in the Alhambra and elsewhere. The existence of such a rotating dome in Byzantium is discounted by Paul Frankl, despite the legendary accounts of it that exist.

The other most important embodiment of this conception was the "throne" of the Sāsānian King Khosro II (590—628 A. D.)[204]. From this construction, the destruction of which by the Emperor Heraclius is often pictorially represented, the motif pervaded with renewed radiation the imagination of Eastern and Western architects and poets. Frankl gives an admirable account of architectural fantasies as they appear in Western mediaeval epics[205]. Among his specimens of these is the epic *Eracle* of 1164, in which the throne of Khosro is described in some detail. (Accounts of the Temple of the Grail reveal similar fantastic ideas.) H. P. L'Orange, who also pointed out Nero's shortlived Domus Aurea as an example of this Babylonian tradition, also referred to Khosro's throne, to which the heavens, with sun, moon and stars, form the roof, as described by Kedrenos, a Greek author of the eleventh century. L'Orange also quotes the description of the same throne in Firdausī's *Shāhnāmēh*. The jewels of this throne baldachin formed the twelve signs of the zodiac, the seven planets, and the moon, all circling in their orbits, and showed the moon running through its phases according to the actual calendar and the exact hour of the day or night[206]. (In Quṣair 'Amra, a rectangular room was decorated with the signs of the zodiac.)

The immediate model for Yehōseph's rotating dome, or possibly a dome made to appear to be rotating, was apparently the famous "Hall of the Caliphs" in 'Abd ar-Raḥmān III's palace Majlis al-Mu'nis in Madīnat az-Zahrā', described in the *kitāb al-muqtabis fī ta'rīkh al-Andalus* by Abū Marwān ibn Ḥayyān, and quoted by al-Maqqarī, thus:[207]

> ... and (there was) the carved, gilded basin from Syria (or Damascus), or, as others say, from Constantinople, upon which were carvings and representations of human beings, which was priceless. When Aḥmad, the philosopher (others say, another man), brought it, an-Nāṣir ordered it to be placed in the center of the east *majlis*, known as al-Mu'nis; and he placed upon it twelve statues. He also built in this palace

Notes 204—207

> *(qaṣr)* the majlis named "The Hall of the Caliphs" *(Qaṣr al-Khulafā')*. The ceiling, which was made of gold and dull alabaster, was within the hall's bright-colored body of various colors. The walls of this *majlis* were like this [hall]. In its center the pearl was placed which the "king of Constantinople," Leo, had presented to an-Nāṣir. The roof tiles (visible from within the hall), of this palace were of gold and silver. In the middle of this *majlis* was a huge cistern filled with quicksilver. On each side of this *majlis* were eight doors joined to [vaulting] arches of ivory and ebony, encrusted with gold and various kinds of jewels, and resting upon columns of colored alabaster and clear beryl. Whenever the sun entered these doors, and whenever its rays struck the ceiling and the walls of the *majlis*, then a light would be created which would suspend eyesight. Whenever an-Nāṣir wished to awe a man present in his *majlis* crowd, he would signal one of his Slavic servants to put in motion that quicksilver, thereby light would be produced like lightning flashes which would arrest the hearts of those assembled, until it appeared to all in the *majlis*, as long as the quicksilver was in motion, that the place was rotating about them. It was said that this *majlis* circled and oriented itself toward the sun; and it was also said that it was resting upon the rim of the cistern.

The possibility, therefore, arises that the rotation of which Ibn Gabirol speaks in his poem was, in effect, produced by lights, though probably in a way different from that employed in the Hall of Caliphs in Madīnat az-Zahrā'. However, in view of all we have heard of these and the Naghrālla's light-experiments and the trends of this time, there is good reason to take Ibn Gabirol's description as based upon fact and observation.

I have referred above to the Hebrew and Muslim wonder-fables of the magical palaces built by Solomon, which filled the fairy-tale-minded world of those days, and set the tone for Cordova, Seville and Granada[208]. The "fairy-tale" color of the architectural ideal invades Ibn Gabirol's poem. The rotating dome, apparently the most imaginative innovation of the entire castle, moved Ibn Gabirol to exultation; he compares it with the "Palanquin of Solomon," and after the verses quoted above, he expresses
Dist. 15 ff.: his excitement (distich 15ff.). Together with the doors "like those of the ivory mansions, reddened by palatial algum woods", with a leveled gallery
Dist. 7; 11; 8: (dist. 7), with the skylights (dist. 11), 'openwork' (dist. 8), borrowed from I Ki. VI. 4ff., the main "program" of Solomonic building motifs mentioned in the Bible is thus re-fulfilled.

It need not be emphasized that the architectural spirit of the Alhambra domes, of the *celosía*, lace-work type, and those of the stalactite type, and

Note 208

that of Ibn Gabirol's description belong to the same mentality. These domes were designed to produce the impression of being rotating cosmic spheres and, since they were built of a material of crystalline or foam-like appearance (or studded with gems), they reminded one of the heavens and/or dripping water congealing under a magic spell.

The present domes in the Alhambra are false ones; they are not the actual roof constructions, which consisted of vaults of brick or other material or, in the case of later ones, of timber and tile, but are suspended below them. Unfortunately, the "Alberca" dome, one of the most precious Alhambra treasures, was destroyed by fire during the last century. Windows, or rather lunettes, many or few, were inserted into these shells, recessed, and they formerly had shutters of wooden lacework which filtered the light of the turning day. Unfortunately, such filtering shutters no longer exist in the Alhambra halls. These effects may be studied in the modern "Alhambra Room" in the palace of Aranjues. Others, again, like the restored dome of the Comares Hall, have a lacework ceiling inlaid with white fillings which appear to be sources of light but which actually only reflect it (Pl. 21). The dome in the poem is described as receiving the light from windows set in above doors, and possibly in the dome itself, a variegated Hagia Sophia motif also preserved in the *Sala de Comares (Embajadores)* and the *Sala de las Dos Hermanas* (Pl. 22). The result is that the stars seem to "lodge" in these windows at night, an effect which is the object of all such dome and window constructions. Thus we observe that the precedent for these lighting effects in the Alhambra was set in the eleventh century. This illusion may be illustrated by a verse from another Alhambra inscription:[209]

Et combien d'arcs s'élèvent dans la voûte sur des
colonnes qui paraissent ornées par la lumière!

Tu dirais: ce sont des corps célestes; leurs sphères tournent,
les premiers rayons du matin naissant les éclairent.

It was the tendency of both the early and late Alhambra architects to enact some of those architectural fables or, as might also be said, to dematerialize structure into a fairy-tale web. A line of a fourteenth-century Alhambra inscription betrays the underlying illusionistic trend:[210]

Behold, that palace of glass, whoever sees it thinks
it is a body of water ...

Notes 209–210; Plates 21–22

The reference is, of course, again to Solomon's water palace described in the Koran and the legends. The constant aim of this architecture (as well as that of the Fountain) is dematerialization and illusion; the later stalactite domes look, indeed, like water and dripping foam (Pl. 22). The verbal expression of these architectural tendencies is preserved in Ibn Zamrak's poem describing the Alhambra Fount of Lions as he saw it three hundred years later than Ibn Gabirol:

> You see silver melting which flows between jewels, one
> like the other in beauty, white in purity.
>
> A running stream evokes the illusion of a solid substance
> for the eyes, so that we wonder which one is fluid (dist. 4-5).

Ibn Gabirol's reference in distich 12 to Solomon's Palanquin, alluding to the Song of Solomon III. 6, has cosmic overtones, familiar from Jewish legends. The motif of the "Palanquin" made of precious stones and pearls, giving out the four streams of wine, milk, honey, and balsam of the Heavenly Garden of Eden, and the motif of lions spouting streams of perfumes (with an interpretation of the twelve Solomonic oxen as the twelve "officers" of the king) are found in the *Second Targum of the Book of Esther*[211]. Our poet expresses most clearly his unprejudiced pleasure-to-the-point-of-ecstasy caused by the artifice when he exclaims (again in biblical parallelism):

Dist. 14–17:

> Thus it is in the daytime, while at dusk it looks
> like the sky whose stars form constellations;
>
> The heart of the poor and burdened delights in this,
> the perishing forget their poverty and bitterness.
>
> I saw this and forgot my burden
> and my heart was relieved from sorrows;
>
> Yea, my body all but soared in my joy
> as upon wings of eagles.

The healing effect of beauty upon the sick is an Arab conception found, for instance, in the *Arabian Nights*[212]; yet the poet, in alluding to his 'burden', evokes the figure of Job (Job XXXVII. 12), the language of which book he had employed in the previous lines; the wording 'that rotates in its gyre' (literally: 'that rotates and turns around') is borrowed from Job XXXVII. 12: "He loads the thick cloud with moisture; the clouds scatter His lightning. They turn round and round by His guidance, to accomplish all that He commands them on the face of the habitable world." Thus the rotating dome linked with the motif of divine wonders — at least for the reader familiar with the biblical context — receives praise borrowed indirectly and heretically from the biblical passage.

As to the cosmic ideas embodied in the later Alhambra, the present restored ceiling of the Comares Hall represents, in its solid lacework — consisting of six tiers of rosettes and one rosette at the highest point — the six heavens and the empyrean (Pl. 21). Such cosmic ideas, intended to be incorporated in Yehōseph ibn Naghrālla's building, as well as in the later domes of the Alhambra, are expressed in various extant inscriptions. The exact Islamic counterpart to Ibn Gabirol's reference to Job is found in an Alhambra inscription which appears below the dome of the Comares Tower — the name "Comares" refers to its stained glass effects (*qamriyya* i. e., "lunettes"). Its symbolism is based upon Sura 67 of the Koran, which according to A. R. Nykl, indicates the intentions of the architects[213]:

> Blessed is He ... who created the seven heavens ... you see no incongruity in the creation of the Beneficent God; then look again, can you see any disorder?

Another great inscription found below the group of three northern windows of the "Hall of the Ambassadors," or "Throne Hall" (in Professor Nykl's words, "decidedly the most majestic of all halls of the palace"), consists of verses expressing the architect's ideas, which apparently remained unchanged from the days of the Naghrāllas and Ibn Gabirol. These distichs, in the first person, varying between singular and plural, are meant to be the self-praise of the trio of windows:[214]

> "Long may you live!" Thus when you enter in mornings and evenings,
> the mouths of boon, bliss, felicity, and charm greet you in my name.
>
> She is the high-domed hall and we are her daughters;
> however, mine is the pre-eminence and the honor in rank.
>
> We are members among which I am the heart, unchallenged;
> for the power of spirit and soul originates in the heart.
>
> And if my symbols represent the constellations of her heaven,
> then in me, and not among them, is the grandeur of the sun.

My master Yūsuf has decked me (may God support him!)
in garments of pride and flawless artistry.

He made me the seat of the kingdom, and thus she ⟨the hall⟩ has strengthened his rank
with the true light, with the seat and the throne.

These inscriptions, though they refer to the ruler Yūsuf of the later Naṣrid dynasty, are nevertheless relevant in that they bear witness to the continuance, indeed the universality, of cosmic dome symbolism. A domed hall representing the sky and decorated with celestial symbols remained the focal point both of a patron's architectural ambition and a poet's praise.

An important ingredient, of course, is the light of the clear sun, compared in its brilliance with the whiteness of teeth, and that of the moon of the southern latitudes itself. The architect knows that only domes, tent-like forms and gently profiled surfaces with soft transitions, provide the shadings of light-value which will allow the eye, in that harsh southern light, to interpret all the lines of a building and receive aesthetic satisfaction from them. Or, to state the same once more *e negativo*, disturbing as the excessive light in these regions can be, its intensity is enjoyable when it is thus orchestrated and controled. Whereas sharp breaks in the surfaces, or, for instance, a widely-protruding roof-line, and large glass panes, create a harsh shadow and interrupt for the eye the flow of lines, such a control and continuity is achieved by the evocation of delicate shadings[215]. It was such an aesthetic intuition which induced the Alhambra architects to invent stlyes consisting almost wholly of mild transitions of shades, styles in which angles were avoided as much as possible. Together with their *horror vacui* or, expressed more positively, with that tendency towards an all pervading tapestry-like ornamentation (inducing them to cover entire surfaces with ornaments), they seemed to feel a *horror anguli*, which led them to reconcile the dimensions and to blend abutting ceilings and walls with each other, to introduce stalactite vaults, serrated arches, and very delicately profiled or honey-combed stucco reliefs. Since such an absorption of light and guidance of the eye by the light itself is an aesthetic aim of Muslim architecture, the windows consist of, or are covered with, stone or wooden lattice-screens filtering and dimming the light inside; but also, and with no lesser importance, these screens prevent the interruption of the surfaces, in fact carry the flow of light throughout the edifice.

What, in Ibn Gabirol's poem, is imagination and what is reality has been discussed above. The poet does not indulge in architectural fantasies, but describes fantastic architecture, and happily abandons himself, as might any other spectator, for instance, to the enchantment of rotation.

Note 215

Domes, illuminated only through windows or transoms which also made visible the movement of the heavens, may have occasionally created the illusion that the dome itself rotated with the stars. It is, as mentioned above, conceivable that the poet — as a courtier — had to muster enough sophistication to take the intent for reality. That is, he had to play the game and profess to see rotation where such an impression was achieved, for instance, only by a trick of illumination. However, the hyperbole expressing the poet's happiness and "levitation" at this point in the poem is more than a *façon de parler* and bespeaks, as I believe, with its enthusiasm the sight of actual rotation. We can be equally assured that a large part of the Palace and Fortress, including the Fount of Lions, as described by Ibn Gabirol, actually existed during his life. Any doubt could spring only from unfamiliarity with this type of panegyric poetry and with its accepted documentary value — or from a prejudice which has its origin in political fears and interests, and which will imperil true historical investigation, even after nine hundred years.

We are unable to trace descriptions of castles in the Arabic world all the way back to its origin. Some of the oldest go back to the time of the origin of Islam and describe the famous castles of Yemen. They are easily found in al-Hamdānī's book on the antiquities of Yemen, entitled *al-Iklīl* ("The Crown"), the eighth book of which contains these poetical documents hailing from the days of the Ḥimyarite dynasty[216]. The spirit of these poems, which contain many dry historical facts, enumerated to commemorate the merits of the dynasty, and some detailed description, is rather alien to our documents and without relevance here. The history of the Arabic descriptive poetical art remains to be written.

Instead, I turn to Ibn Gabirol's other descriptive poetry in order to enable the reader to evaluate by comparison the poet's sense of reality as shown in his Alhambra poem. Since the Alhambra poem is a spring poem I begin with his other verse composed on this topic.

Note 216

Notes to Part II

1. E. Lévi-Provençal, "Les 'mémoires' de 'Abd Allāh, dernier roi Zīride de Granade," in *Al-Andalus*, III, 1935, pp. 232—344; IV, 1936—39, pp. 29—145; VI, 1941, pp. 1—63 (quoted as *Mémoires*). Published as a book: *k. at-tibyān 'an al-ḥadītha al-kā'ina bi-daulat Banī Zīrī fī Gharnāṭa*, Cairo, 1955.
2. The following literature on Samuel han-Nāghīdh ibn Naghrālla (also spelled Naghrīla) exists. The pioneer in the rediscovery of the then forgotten Ibn Naghrālla family was the distinguished S. Munk, with his article, "Notice sur Abou'l-Walid Merwan ibn Djana'h ...," part II, *Journal Asiatique*, XVI, 1850 (quoted as Munk, *Notice*), pp. 201 ff. with translations from Abraham ibn Dā'ūd's *Śepher haq-qabbālāh*, Amsterdam, 1711, pp. 43 ff.; R. Dozy, *Histoire des musulmans d'Espagne*, edited by E. Lévi-Provençal, Leyden, 1932, III, pp. 18 ff.; particularly pp. 70 ff. (quoted as D.-Provençal, *Histoire*); for some additional details M. Perlmann, "Eleventh-Century Authors on the Jews of Granada," in *Proceedings of the American Academy for Jewish Research*, XVIII, 1949, pp. 269 ff. (quoted as Perlmann, *Eleventh Century*); J. Schirmann, "Le diwan de Šemū'el Hannāgīd considéré comme source pour l'histoire espagnole," in *Hespéris*, XXXV, Rabat, 1948, pp. 163—188 (quoted as Schirmann, *Diwan*); idem, "Samuel Hannagid, the Man, the Soldier, the Politician," in *Jewish Social Studies*, IV, 1951, pp. 99—126 (quoted as Schirmann, *Samuel*); R. Dozy, *Spanish Islam*, London, 1913, pp. 607 ff., 616, 643 f., 650 (quoted as Dozy, *Islam*); S. M. Stern, "Zōṭ-ōth le-thōledh-ōth R. Shemū'el han-Nāghīdh," in *Zion (Ṣīyōn)*, IV, 1950, pp. 135—145. A bibliography on Samuel by Schirmann is found in *Qiryath Śepher*, XIII, 1936, pp. 373—382. Schirmann's studies on Samuel han-Nāghīdh, like Schirmann, *Dīwān* and Schirmann, *Samuel* (see list of abbreviations) are doomed to be one-sided and fragmentary, as long as he neglects materials as valuable as the passage on al-Munfatil in the *kitāb adh-dhakhīra* by Ibn Bassām. Mr. Dov Yarden's excellent edition of Samuel's *Dīwān* with a complete bibliography came too late to be used.
3. Yehōšeph is treated in the same literature as mentioned above, note 2; in particular *Mémoires*, in *Al-Andalus*, III, pp. 244 ff.; VI, pp. 38 ff.; and, further, H. Schirmann, "Yehōšeph han-Nāghīdh," in *Me'oznayim*, VIII, 1938, pp. 49—58 (quoted as Schirmann, *Yehōšeph*); J. Schirmann, "Jehosef, fils du Nagid," in *Hespéris*, XXXV, pp. 164 ff. quoted as Schirmann, *Fils*). These articles, though quite readable, have an irritating "creative" and subjective tinge and lack scholarly documentation throughout. If the accusation that Yehōšeph had poisoned the heir to the throne is true, then Yehōšeph might either have done so in self-defense or even in defense of the throne of Bādīs and with the consent of the king. The fact that Buluqqīn once intended to murder Yehōšeph is admitted by his son, 'Abd Allāh, in his *Mémoires*, p. 283). The latter possibility could be suggested by the fact that he did not fall from the grace of the king after the event. At the court of Granada there was incessant plotting by the ladies of the harem, each for the succession of her own son to the throne. Bādīs, himself, tried to poison his rival, Muḥammad ibn Idrīs, with an *'irāqī* cup; see Ibn 'Idhārī, *Bayān*, cited in Pérès, *Poésie*, p. 370.

4. A powerful and cultured vizier added to the glamor of a Muslim ruler. The ʿĀmirid major-domos in Cordova, usurping at times all power, like Almansor, continued the tradition established by the Barmecides in Baghdad. A position similar to that of Samuel ibn Naghrālla was held by his mortal enemy Ibn ʿAbbās under Zuhair, Slav ruler of Almeria. Cf. Schirmann, *Samuel*, pp. 119ff.; also Dickie, *Shuhayd*, pp. 284 f.
5. Provençal, *Espagne*, III, pp. 467ff.
6. These facts are confirmed by Ibn al-Khaṭīb, *Iḥāṭa*, Cairo, 1901, I, pp. 272ff., and by Ibn ʿIdhārī, *Bayān*, Paris, 1930, III, pp. 264ff., quoted after Perlmann, *Eleventh Century*, p. 288, nn. 57 and 58, where the main references in *Mémoires* to Yehōšeph's (and Samuel's) position are listed. For "playing the Barmecide," being a generous supporter of the arts, *Mémoires*, III, p. 285, n. 3.
7. García Gómez, *Poetas*, p. 108.
8. For Yehōšeph's plot with Abū 'l-Aḥwaṣ Maʿn ibn Ṣumādiḥ, commonly called "al-Muʿtaṣim," cf. *Mémoires*, III, pp. 253, 287 n. 5, 296ff.; for Almería see L. Torres Balbás, "Almería Islamica," in *Al-Andalus*, XXII, 1957, pp. 411ff., 443.
9. *Mémoires*, II, p. 273, pp. 299 bottom, and 300: *maʿa bunyāni-hi li-Ḥiṣni 'l-Ḥamrā'*.
10. Yehōšeph "built a palace better than your own," "*banā khairan min qaṣr-ik*." King Bādīs is addressed: *Mémoires*, III, p. 292 (Arabic text p. 269).
11. For the origin of the name "Alhambra" see Georges Marçais, *Manuel d'art musulman*, Paris, 1926, I, pp. 257ff.; for its first appearance in the ninth century: II, p. 536. He refers to H. de Castries, "Du nom d'Alhambra ...," in *Journal Asiatique*, XI series, vol. XVII, 1921, pp. 133—138, in which the author points out that this adjective *al-ḥamrā'* became, quite early, *un véritable substantive*. For the Albaicin and Alhambra hills, cf. R. Dozy, *Recherches sur l'histoire et la littérature de l'Espagne*, Paris/Leyden, 1881, p. 384 (quoted as Dozy, *Recherches*). The Albaicin — *rabaḍ al-bayyāzīn* i. e. "Suburb of the Falconers" — is described by M. Gómez-Moreno in *Ars Hispaniae*, III, Madrid, 1951, pp. 254ff. The Albaicin Castle continued to be named "The Castle of Bādīs ibn Ḥabbūs" after its builder; thus it is named by a later historian ("El Anonimo de Madrid y Copenhague") in connection with the conquest of Granada by Abū ʿAbd Allāh ibn al-Aḥmar (1239—40), ed. and transl. by A. Huici in *Anales del Instituto General y Técnico de Valencia*, Valencia, 1917, p. 168; similarly Ibn Khaldūn, "Histoire des Banou l'Aḥmar, rois de Grenade," tr. by M. Gaudefroy-Demombynes in *Journal Asiatique*, IXme série, XII, Paris, 1898, pp. 319, 322f., 337. The same author mentions the Alhambra in the same connections on p. 323 (cf. p. 337, n. 47).
12. Cf. Schirmann, *Fils*, pp. 164ff.; *Jewish Encyclopedia*, IX, p. 142. Munk, *Notice*, pp. 210—211, translates from Abraham ibn Dā'ūd's *Šepher haq-Qabbālāh*, Amsterdam, 5471/1711 as follows: "... De toutes les bonnes qualités de son père, il ne lui manquait aucune; seulement il n'était pas modeste comme son père, parce qu'il avait grandi dans la richesse, et qu'il n'avait pas porté de joug dans sa jeunesse. Son coeur s'enorgueillit jusqu'à mal faire, et ayant excité la jalousie des chefs berbers, il fut massacré le jour de sabbat, 9 tebeth de l'an 4827 (30 décembre 1066), lui et la communauté juive de Grenade, et tous ceux qui étaient venus de pays lointains pour être témoins de son instruction et de sa grandeur. On prit le deuil pour lui dans chaque pays et dans chaque ville ... Après sa mort, ses livres et autres choses précieuses furent dispersés et se répandirent partout; et les élèves qu'il avait formés devinrent les rabbins d'Espagne et les guides du siècle." The text continues: "Now the people understood why the ancient savants, the authors of the *Scroll of Fasts*, had stipulated (so long ago) that

the ninth of Ṭebheth should be a day of fast." The Hebrew text is accessible in Ad. Neubauer, *Mediaeval Jewish Chronicles*, London, 1887, p. 73.

The Naghrāllas' tombs, consisting of rough field stones, located outside the Elvira Gate, were known to Jews even centuries later (Pl. 24). Yehōseph's body was nailed against this gate.

13. Perlmann, *Eleventh Century*, p. 291; E. García Gómez, "Polémica religiosa entre Ibn Ḥazm e Ibn al-Nagrīla," in *Al-Andalus*, IV, 1936, pp. 1—28; García Gómez, *Poetas*, p. 133. Ibn Ḥazm's attack and "refutation" is found in his *Fiṣal*, begun between the years 1027 and 1030, cf. Miguel Asín Palacios, *Abenhazam de Córdoba y su "Historia crítica de las religiones,"* Madrid, 1927—1932, II, pp. 291 ff. For the influence of Ibn Ḥazm upon Abū Isḥāq cf. Dozy, *Recherches*, I, p. 290. Passages of personal incitement against Samuel and other Jews in the service of Muslims are quoted in Schirmann, *Samuel*, pp. 111 ff.
14. This passage is quoted from Perlmann, *Eleventh Century*, p. 282.
15. For the rôle of Jews and Berbers in establishing Granada as a center of government and of cultural life, cf. E. Lévi-Provençal, *La péninsule ibérique au moyen-âge*, Leyden, 1938, p. 30, quoting the *kitāb ar-rauḍ al-miʿṭar*:

> Ce fut Ḥabbūs le Ṣinhāgien qui donna à Grenade son aspect urbain, le dota d'une enceinte fortifiée et construisit sa citadelle. Sous le règne de son fils et successeur Bādīs b. Ḥabbūs la construction de la ville s'acheva et Grenade ne cessa plus ...

The fact that this new town was called by the Arabs "the town of the Jews" together with a description of the position of its Jews as it appears in the poem by Abū Isḥāq al-Ilbīrī are discussed in García Gómez, *Poetas*, p. 97 (107 ff.):

> ... The Zīrid rulers of Granada, unable to protect themselves against both the rude and ignorant Berbers of their own tribe and againas Arabs and Andalusians, because of the mistrust which the latter had for them, fell into the hands of the Jews. A famous Hebrew family of the Banū Naghrālla obtained thus, to the unspeakable scandal of the proud Arab aristocracy and Moslem orthodoxy, an almost sovereign position in an Islamic court, unique in the history of Andalusia and, I am sure, in the entire Middle Ages ...

The phrase "fell into the hands of the Jews" is misleading and confirms our previous impression of the author's showing rancor and flippancy at least against the Jews of the Eleventh Century. In actuality the two Jewish viziers cannot be called "the Jews," and Samuel, by securing the throne of Granada for Bādīs, forced an influential group among "the Jews" (which had sided with another pretender) to flee from there. The Zīrids derived the greatest advantage from their Jewish viziers, more so the city of Granada and most so the Granadine Arab community which Bādīs intended to exterminate and which Samuel saved by countering the Berber king's commands. See note 25 below. As to the "unspeakable scandal": among the many prominent "court Jews" at Islamic courts, Ḥaśdāy ibn Shaprūṭ, under the powerful caliph ʿAbd ar-Raḥmān III, was the most influential minister. (Cf. D.-Provençal, *Histoire*, II, pp. 164, 169—171; Dozy, *Islam*, pp. 437, 440—443; Provençal, *Espagne*, II, pp. 69 ff., 151.) Another powerful figure was Abū 'l-Faḍl ibn Ḥaśdāy in Saragossa, whose poetry we shall encounter in Part III. Jewish politicians, financial administrators, and ambassadors belonged to the tradition of many Muslim (and Christian) courts in Spain. The "scandal," typical for the post-Umayyad period, was, however, voiced by the poet Ibn ʿAmmār and the historian Ibn Bassām. Cf. Pérès, *Poésie*, pp. 268 ff. If the man from dethroned Elvira voices his

Plate 24

feelings of scandal for the "Jewish rule" in Granada, he is careful not to mention that Granada had been the "City of the Jews" before it had ever been a Muslim town and before any Berbers had settled there. The aggressive bigotry of this time led to the revolt against Jewish government officials. Pérès, *Poésie*, p. 265 quotes Ibn Ḥayyān's account of an attack of Muslims upon Jews at this time in Seville. The basely anti-Semitic character of Abū Isḥāq's "brilliant" (G. Gómez, *l. c.*) poem may be brought out by a translation of a few lines of this poem into German, preserving the meter and rhyme scheme (couplets 3—5; 35; 39):

ʿAlā qulli Ṣinhājati (n)
⏑-- ⏑-- ⏑-- ⏑- *(Mutaqārib)*

2 Vertan hat sich, sattsam vertan euer Herr
erbaut dieserhalb ist der Schadfrohen Sinn:

3 Bevorzugt als Kanzler den Kāfir, obwohl
er fänd seinen Mann unter uns Muslimin.

4 Der Juden verächtliches Volk macht er dreist,
in feist-frecher Freude sie recken ihr Kinn ...

35 Geziert hat ihr Affe mit Steinwerk sein Haus,
dort wagt er den lautersten Quell hinzuziehn ...

39 Ermannt euch! Den Mastwidder, fett wie er ist,
als Schlachtopfer, auf! Greifet ihn! Macht ihn hin!

This part and others of the poem, found in Aḥmad ibn Muḥammad al-Maqqarī of Tlemcen (died 1632), *Nafḥ aṭ-ṭib min ghuṣn al-Andalus ar-raṭīb wa-dhikr wazīri-hā Lisān ad-dīn ibn al-Khaṭīb*, Book VII, appear in passages omitted in an abridged translation in P. de Gayangos, *The History of the Mohammedan Dynasties in Spain*, London, 1840—43 (quoted as Maqqarī, *Dynasties*), and were first cited by S. Munk in his *Notice*, prior to the editorial work by R. Dozy *et al.*, *Analectes sur l'histoire de la littérature* des Arabes d'Espagne, Leyden, 1855—61, II, pp. 652ff. (quoted as Maqqarī, *Analectes*); also Dozy, *Recherches*, I, pp. 285ff. Professor J. M. Millás, in his review, in *Sefarad*, 1958, pp. 158ff., of my Alhambra study, in *Atlantis*, XXXI, 1959, calls this poem "*la terrible invectiva.*" Two excellent analyses of this poem and the contemporary political situation are found in Pérès, *Poésie*, pp. 268ff. and pp. 270ff. and Perlmann, *Eleventh Century*, pp. 285ff.

16. The most important references to this poem are given in Perlmann, *Eleventh Century*, p. 284 n. 46; García Gómez, *Poetas*, pp. 107, 131ff.; Dozy, *Recherches*, I, pp. 286ff. and LXIff.; D.-Provençal, *Histoire*, III, pp. 71ff.

17. *Rajjama dārahu*, cf. note 15 verse 35a is supported by dist. 9 of the "Alhambra Poem." It may refer rather to paved courts which are now found in the Alhambra than to stone-faced walls not now apparent there. The Cordovan garden of Abū Marwān as-Zajjālī, mentioned in a poem by Ibn Shuhaid (beginning "Arise, my friend...") and described by Ibn Khāqān, contained, as a luxury of this kind, a courtyard "of pure white marble." Cf. Dickie, *Shuhayd*, pp. 296 f. For "ape" and "Jew" see Pérès, *Poésie*, pp. 240ff. n. 6.

18. *Namīra 'l-ʿuyūn*, in Dozy, *Recherches*, I, p. LXVI, v. 35b.

19. Cf. D.-Provençal, *Histoire*, III, p. 73; García Gómez, *Poetas*, p. 119; Dozy, *Recherches*, X. For Abū Isḥāq's banishment from Granada cf. Dozy, *Recherches*, I, p. 293. The pogrom is described in *Mémoires*, III, pp. 300ff.; D.-Provençal,

Histoire, III, p. 73; cf. *ibid.* note for sources. Dozy's studies in the field of the house of the Naghrāllas (incomplete because the *Mémoires* were unknown to him) are collected in R. Dozy, *Ibn-Adhari de Maroc: Al-Bayano 'l-Mogrib*, Leyden, 1848–51, pp. 78 ff. (quoted as Dozy, *Ibn ʿIdhārī*). The reasons for the pogrom and the question of Yehōseph's plot are discussed ibid., pp. 98 ff., 102 f. The results of the pogrom are described by Ibn al-Khaṭīb in Dozy, *Recherches*, I, p. 285; cf. also E. Lévi-Provençal's edition of Ibn al-Khaṭīb, *k. aʿmāl al-aʿlām*, Rabat, 1935, pp. 265–267. Schirmann's description of these events in his *Yehōseph* seems to be quite distorted.

20. For the sack of Cordova by the Berbers after the downfall of the ʿĀmirids, cf. Dozy, *Islam*, pp. 556 ff.; Provençal, *Espagne*, II, p. 320. The city fell after a siege of twenty eight months, ending with the killing of more than twenty thousand inhabitants.
21. See note 15 above. Chancellor stands for the Arabic *kātib*. It is difficult to define the exact rank of *kātib* (as the Naghrāllas are most often designated by the Arab historians), or his varying assignments. *Cf.* al-Maqqarī's remark, translated in Munk, *Notice*, p. 220 (204): "*C'est l'usage des gens d'Espagne que le vézir est en même temps le cātib (secrétaire).*"
22. A French translation of this passage is found in Dozy, *Ibn ʿIdhārī*, pp. 96 ff.
23. Schirmann, *Samuel*, pp. 100 ff., 102, 106 ff., 109 ff. For Samuel's literary activities, ibid., p. 115. Yehōseph's introductory remarks to his father's poems are accessible in full only in a MS in which they appear in an early, but often faulty, Hebrew translation. Some of the original Arabic remarks have been discovered in fragments from the Genizah in Cairo now in Oxford, but they have not been catalogued or edited. Information about this point, which I have received from Dr. S. M. Stern in Oxford, is gratefully acknowledged.
24. For the title *nāghīdh* cf. Schirmann, *Samuel*, pp. 113 ff.; R. de Vaux, *Ancient Israel*, New York, 1961, p. 94. The term *nāghīdh māshīaḥ*, found in Dan. IX. 25, added great prestige to this office. Originally, in its reference to Saul, the choice of the title *nāghīdh* in the Bible may have reflected upon the Hebrew's aversion to kings; *cf.* Erwin I. J. Rosenthal, "Some Aspects of the Hebrew Monarchy," in *The Journal of Jewish Studies*, 1957, pp. 8 ff. For the office of the *nāghīdh* see S. D. Goitein, *Jews and Arabs*, New York, 1964, p. 123.
25. Samuel had been instrumental in securing for Bādīs the succession to the throne, cf. Schirmann, *Samuel*, p. 106. He had saved his life, ibid., according to *Mémoires*, VI, p. 29 (241) and actively prevented him from destroying the Arab population of Granada, cf. *Mémoires*, III, p. 248. (Dozy, *Ibn ʿIdhārī*, pp. 94 ff.)
26. About "submissiveness" or "humility" *(dhull)* see Perlmann, *Eleventh Century*, p. 289, n. 64 a, referring to Ibn Dā'ūd's passage, translated by Munk and quoted above, note 12.
27. Cf. above, note 8; Dozy, *Ibn ʿIdhārī*, p. 102, *Mémoires*, III, pp. 299 f.
28. The full text of this poem was first published by Schirmann in *Qobheṣ Hōṣāʿath Schocken le-dhibhrey ṣiphrūth*, Tel Aviv, 1941, pp. 146 ff. Later in Schirmann, *Shīrāh*, I, pp. 223 ff. An earlier fragmentary publication is found in Bialik-R., III (V), pp. 17 ff. and notes pp. 17 f. Cf. also J. M. Millás y Vallicrosa, *Šelomó ibn Gabirol como poeta y filósofo*, Madrid, 1945, pp. 28 f. Distich 18 of this poem was quoted by Moses ibn Ezra; cf. A. M. Habermann, in *Tarbīṣ*, 1948, p. 189. I now give, as I shall later do for the "Great Nature Poem," the full Hebrew text:

לְכָה רֵעִי וְרֵעַ הַמְּאוֹרִים / לְכָה עִמִּי וְנָלִין בַּכְּפָרִים
וְהִנֵּה הַסְּתָיו עָבַר וְנִשְׁמַע / בְּאַרְצֵנוּ הֲמוֹן סִיסִים וְתֹרִים

וְנִתְלוֹנֵן בְּצֵל רִמּוֹן וְתָמָר / וְתַפּוּחַ וְכָל־צִמְחֵי הֲדָרִים
וְנִתְהַלֵּךְ בְּצִלֵּי הַגְּפָנִים / וְנִשְׁתּוֹקֵק רְאוֹת פָּנִים הֲדוּרִים
בְּאַרְמוֹן נַעֲלֶה מִכָּל־סְבִיבָיו / וְנִבְנֶה בַּאֲבָנִים הַיְקָרִים
אֲשֶׁר תָּכַן עֲלֵי נָכוֹן שְׁתוֹתָיו / וְקִירוֹתָיו בְּמִגְדָּלִים בְּצוּרִים
וְיָצִיעַ מְיֻשָּׁר, מִסְּבִיבָיו / שְׁרוֹנִים פֵּאֲרוּ כָל־הַחֲצֵרִים
וְהַבָּתִּים בְּנוּיִם וַעֲדוּיִם / בְּפִתּוּחִים פְּתוּחִים וַאֲטוּרִים
מְרֻצָּפִים בְּאַבְנֵי שֵׁשׁ וּבַהַט / וְלֹא אוּכַל סְפֹר כַּמָּה שְׁעָרִים
וְדַלְתוֹתָם כְּדַלְתֵי הֵיכְלֵי־שֵׁן / מְאָדָּמִים בְּאַלְגּוּמֵּי דְבִירִים
וְחַלּוֹנִים שְׁקוּפִים מֵעֲלֵיהֶם / שְׁמָשׁוֹת שָׁכְנוּ בָהֶן מְאוֹרִים
וְהַקֻּבָּה כְּאַפִּרְיוֹן שְׁלֹמֹה / תְּלוּיָה מִשְּׂכִיּוֹת הַחֲדָרִים
אֲשֶׁר תִּסֹּב וְתִתְהַפֵּךְ בְּעֵינֵי / בְּדֻלָחִים וְסַפִּירִים וְדָרִים
וְזֶה בַּיּוֹם וּבָעֶרֶב דְּמוּתָהּ / כְּשַׁחַק כּוֹכָבָיו בַּלֵּיל סְדוּרִים
וּבָהּ יִיטַב לְבַב כָּל־רָשׁ וְעָמֵל / וְיִנְשׁוּ אוֹבְדִים רִישָׁם וּמָרִים
רְאִיתִיהָ וְשָׁכַחְתִּי עֲמָלִי / וְהִתְנַחֵם לְבָבִי מִמְּצָרִים
וְכִמְעַט קָט גְּוִיָּתִי תְעוֹפֵף / בְּשִׂמְחָתִי כְּעַל־כַּנְפֵי נְשָׁרִים
וְיָם מָלֵא וְיִדְמֶה יָם שְׁלֹמֹה / אֲבָל לֹא יַעֲמֹד עַל־הַבְּקָרִים
וּמַצַּב הָאֲרָיוֹת עַל־שְׂפָתוֹ / כְּאִלּוּ שָׁאֲגוּ טֶרֶף כְּפִירִים
אֲשֶׁר קִרְבָּם כְּמַעְיָנִים יְפוּצוּן / עֲלֵי פִיהֶם זְרָמִים כַּנְּהָרִים
וְאַיָּלוֹת שְׁתוּלוֹת בַּתְּעָלוֹת / נְבוּבוֹת לִהְיוֹת מַיִם מְעָרִים
וְלָרֹס הַצְּמָחִים בַּעֲרֻגוֹת / וּבְאָחִים זְרֹק מַיִם טְהֹרִים
וְגַנַּת הַהֲדַס בָּהֶם לְהַשְׁקוֹת / אֲמִירִים כַּעֲנָנִים הֵם וְזוֹרִים
אֲשֶׁר רֵיחָם כְּרֵיחַ הַבְּשָׂמִים / כְּאִלּוּ הֵם מְקֻטָּרִים בְּמֹרִים
וְעוֹפוֹת יִתְּנוּ קוֹל בַּעֲפָאִים / וְנִשְׁקָפוֹת עֲלֵי כַפּוֹת תְּמָרִים
וְצִצִּים רַעֲנַנִּים נַעֲמָנִים / כְּשׁוֹשַׁנִּים נְרָדִים עִם־כְּפָרִים
אֲשֶׁר מִתְפָּאֲרִים הֵם זֶה עֲלֵי־זֶה / וְהֵם כֻּלָּם בְּעֵינֵינוּ בְרוּרִים
וְאוֹמְרִים הַכְּפָרִים כִּי אֲנַחְנוּ / לְבָנִים מוֹשְׁלִים עַל־הַמְּאוֹרִים
וְהַיּוֹנִים מְנַהֲגוֹת בַּהֲגוּתָן / וְאוֹמְרוֹת נַחְנוּ שָׂרוֹת לְתֹרִים
וְאֵלֶּה בָם נְכַשֵּׁף הַלְּבָבוֹת / לְמַעַל מִבְּדֻלָחִים יְקָרִים
וְקָמוּ הַצְּבָאִים בַּבְּתוּלוֹת / וְכִסּוּ אֶת־הֲדָרָן בַּהֲדָרִים
וְגַם הִתְפָּאֲרוּ יַחַד עֲלֵיהֶן / לְמַעַן הֵם כְּאַיָּלִים צְעִירִים
וְעֵת כִּי נַעֲלָה שֶׁמֶשׁ עֲלֵיהֶן / עֲנִיתִיו דֹּם וְאַל־תַּעְבֹר מְצָרִים
וְהוֹדֵה לַגְּבִיר כִּי הֶחֱשִׁיכָךְ / בְּאוֹרָה הַמְּעֻלָּה בַּמְּאוֹרִים
אֲשֶׁר שַׁח כָּל־הֲדַר־מֶלֶךְ לְפָנָיו / וְהָיוּ מַעֲלוֹת כָּל־שַׂר חֲסֵרִים
אֲשֶׁר בּוֹ יִמְלְכוּ כָל־הַמְּלָכִים / וּבוֹ מִתְיָעֲצִים רוֹזְנִים וְשָׂרִים
הֱקִימוּהוּ כְמוֹ מַלְכָּם וְהָיָה / כְּפִיר בָּהֶם וְכֻלָּם הַשְּׁוָרִים

וְהוּא בָהֶם כְּמַלְאַךְ הָאֱלֹהִים / בְּעֵת לֹא מָצְאוּ מֵאֵל דְּבָרִים
מְנַהֵל צֹאן עֲלֵי מִרְעֵה מְנוּחוֹת / וְלֹא נֶעְדָּר מְאוּמָה מֵעֲדָרִים
יְקַר־נֶפֶשׁ עֲדֵי־שַׁחַק נְדִיב־לֵב / בְּלִי יִדֹּר יְשַׁלֵּם הַנְּדָרִים
אֲשֶׁר לֹא־כָהֲתָה עֵינוֹ בְּמַתָּן / וְלֹא עָצַר עֲנָנוֹ הַמְּטָרִים
אֲשֶׁר מִלָּיו בְּמִפְעָלָיו קְשׁוּרִים / כְּרָאשִׁים נִקְשְׁרוּ בָהֶם כְּתָרִים
וְכָל־הָרוֹזְנִים אֵלָיו יְסוּרוּן / וְכַיָּם נִמְשְׁכוּ אֵלָיו נְהָרִים
וְאָמְנָם הוּא כְּרֹאשׁ עַל־הָאֲדָמָה / וְהוּא אֶחָד כְּנֶגֶד הַיְּצוּרִים·

Variant readings to this poem:

Dist. 6b: I read *be-mighdāl-īm* 'with towers' instead of Schirmann's *ke-mighdāl-īm* 'like towers'.

Dist. 7: *Yaṣīʿa*, cf. Arabic root *waḍaʿa*, 'to place', 'to spread': 'leveled gallery', also translated 'chamber', 'floor', 'story'. *Sherōn-īm* stands for *ḥabhaṣṣal-ōth hash-Shārōn* from Cant. II. 1 'roses of Sharon', most likely, on the Arabic level, "the poet's narcissus" (Arabic *bahār*), praised by the Hispano-Arabic poets. See Pérès, *Poésie*, pp. 170 ff.

Dist. 18: A. M. Habermann, "*Tashlūmey shīr-īm uphīyyuṭ-īm*," in *Tarbīṣ*, XIX, 1948, p. 189, lists a *varia lectio* of this verse as quoted by Moses ibn Ezra: *we-yām gādhōl yeḥushshābh yam Shelōmōh*, i. e., "there is a great sea which might be thought to be Solomon's Sea."

Dist. 21: Cf. *mey maʿārāh* in *Talmud Yerūsh*: *Berākhōth* 7.4.

Dist. 28: For the whiteness of camphor cf. Pérès, *Poésie*, p. 186.

Dist. 30: I read *we-eleh bām (nekhashsheph hal-lebhābh-ōth) le-maʿal* ... 'and these wherewith we bewitch the hearts, are above ...'; *le-maʿal*, 'above', acceptable to Bialik-R., is preferable to Schirmann's *le-maʿan*, 'because', which seems to be a dittograph of the same word in dist. 32.

Dist. 31: Bialik-R. read, preferably to Schirmann's *kab-bethūl-ōth*, 'like the virgins', *bab-bethūl-ōth*, 'against the virgins'; *ba-hadhār-īm*, translated 'with charms' could, with less likelihood, stand for 'among the citrus trees'; the male gazelles symbolize young men, as in Arabic poetry.

Dist. 33: Instead of Bialik's (III, p. 17) *naʿalāh*, 'lifted herself', Schirmann's *naʿaleh*, 'lifted himself', is better, because *shemesh*, 'sun' appears throughout this line in the masculine gender.

Dist. 41: I read with Habermann (l. c.) *ʿanān-ō*, 'his cloud' instead of Bialik-R.'s *ke-mattan*, 'like the gift'. The cloud, used metaphorically for a king's generosity, is not only an Arabic conceit, but is found in Prov. XVI. 15.

Dist. 42: For the phrase "attach a crown to," i. e., 'to praise', cf. Y. Grazovski's Hebrew Dictionary under *kether*, 'crown'. The same phrase is used in reference to the angels' praise of God and to the calligraphical adornment of certain letters with 'crowns'. See Shabbath 89 a *(tagg-īn)*.

Dist. 43: For the wording of "rivers 'drawn' to the sea" cf. *Tośephta Baba Qamma*, 6.2, quoted after Grazovski, (l. c.) article *māshakh*, 'to draw'. See below footnote 54.

Dist. 44: See below, footnote 53.

29. I have stressed before that Ibn Gabirol rarely addresses recipients of poems by their name. (The same refers to other contemporary poets). The fact that Ibn Gabirol's poem is indeed addressed to Yehōseph ibn Naghrālla is further suggested by the specific similarities in an encomium of Yehōseph by another poet (giving the impression that he was trying to imitate Ibn Gabirol's tone and form) as well as by Joseph ibn Ḥasdāy who, by his

"Matchless Song," addressed to Samuel han-Nāghīdh may, in turn, have influenced our Alhambra poem.

I insert here the anonymous and poor poem of *laudes* for Yehōseph on the occasion of his return to Granada after a victorious campaign. It abounds in flattering terms and depicts well the quasi-messianic hopes fastened upon him. Its meter and its rhyme-scheme are, strangely enough, identical with the great poem of praise sung by Ibn Gabirol to Samuel, beginning *Tehillath ha-ḥokhmāh* (*Bialik-R.*, I, pp. 70ff.). However much this fragment may imitate Ibn Gabirol's "tone," it is infinitely weaker. The poem was brought to light by J. Schirmann and appeared in the Hebrew daily *Haaretz*. The most striking difference in meter and rhyme between this poem and Ibn Gabirol's model (?) for it, is that in Ibn Gabirol's the first syllable of the scheme ⌣- - - would always be short, whereas here this syllable is *anceps* and additional short syllables appear irregularly.

Anonymous Praise of The Victorious Yehōseph

We-gham hirb-ū — *Haaretz*, Sept. 29, 1939.

Six long and irregular short syllables. — Refrain rhyme (a): *-rīm (-r-īm)*;
stanza rhymes: b b b (a);
c c c (a); etc.

Increase now joy,
put to flight sighing,
since the Pasha is coming:
(Ps. LXXXIII. 12) my prince for generations!

Gen. XLIX. 22 Blessed be Ben Porath ⟨Joseph, 'The Fruitful Bough'⟩
like a vine by the Euphrates!
he who went forth to meet
Ps. LXXXIII. 7 the king of the Hagarites.

Then supported him
the One with no other beside Him;
He girded Himself with strength
Hab. III. 8; Ps. XCIII. 3 and raged against the rivers.

And He fought his battle
as He did with the sons of Ham
and He overturned with no mercy
towns and cities.

Ex. XV. 9 And He fulfilled His desire
against the idol worshippers;
their becoming a shame
caused His countenance no blame.

He lifted the face of my lord;
Is. XLI. 4 for him he "performed and acted"
and He raised his throne
above all sovereigns.

And He brought my prince
to the city of his rest
to become the height of joy Ps. CXXXVII. 6
at evenings and morns.

When I see his countenance
I become satisfied with his dainties
and the grace of his meditations,
with the depth of his sayings. (Is. LI. 10)

All the people exulted
when they saw the king;
"this nation" composed well (Ex. XV. 16)
praises and songs.

They all faint, yearning
before his face, shining II Sam. XIV. 17
like an angel of God
and the two luminaries.

God has sent him as a sustenance
for the nation storm-tossed, afflicted Is. LIV. 11
in the land of Ispamiah,
in burning compassion.

May He remember His steadfast love
to Israel, His servant,
by lifting His hand
to gather the scattered.

In stanza 2 the wording 'Blessed Ben Porath' ('the Fruitful Bough') stems from Jacob's blessing for Joseph in Gen. XLIX. 22 and refers here to Yehōseph. The Ishmaelites, here termed sons of Hagar, the Hagarites, are of course Arabs, most likely a petty king and his troops whom Yehōseph 'faced' in battle. In a seemingly synonymous way the expression 'sons of Ham', actually the Canaanites of biblical days, appears in stanza 4. The flattering expression 'king' in stanza 9 could, as in the Talmud, refer to a Talmudic scholar; 'king' could also refer to a prophet or angel (cf., e. g., Leo Baeck, *Aus Drei Jahrtausenden*, Tübingen, 1958, p. 313). Yet following after stanza 6 "his throne / above all sovereigns," and with the preceding address of 'prince' in stanza 7, it is most likely meant literally. The title of Yehōseph, *nāghīdh* is, as in the case of Solomon, tantamount to *melekh*, 'king', and, as often, e. g. in I Sam. II. 10 *melekh* is "the anointed" par excellence.

This poem may serve to confirm that Ibn Gabirol's praise for Yehōseph was in no way unique, but had parallels in tone and diction. It also employs Ibn Gabirol's exact phrase 'angel of God', for the Maecenas. One would think that this poem was written after the victory of the forces of Granada over the troops of Seville in Malaga in 1064. Cf. e. g. A. R. Nykl, ed., *Selections from Hispano-Arabic Poetry*, Beirut, 1949, p. 137.

30. 'Abd Allāh relates Yehōseph's Alhambra construction to the last period of Yehōseph's life, which ended in 1066. Therefore, this year, with a short preceding period, might be the approximate date for the Naghrālla Alhambra and Ibn Gabirol's poem.

31. For "Frühlingsverkündung" cf. A. Mez, *Die Renaissance des Islams*, Heidelberg, 1932, pp. 249ff., 252. For the topic of "Description of Spring" as an introduction (*maṭlaʿ*) of panegyrics, see Pérès, *Poésie*, pp. 185ff.
32. For 'Friend of the Luminaries' see A. Christensen, *L'Iran sous les Sassanides*, Copenhague, 1944, pp. 185, 189, 399. For "*First Man*," ibid. pp. 42, 188, 218ff.; also for these two conceptions, see H. Jonas, *The Gnostic Religion*, Boston, 1958, p. 217, 221, 290, quoting W. Henning, "Geburt und Entstehung des manichäischen Urmenschen," in *Nachr. Gött. Ges. Wiss., Phil.-hist. Klasse*, 1932, Göttingen, 1933, pp. 217ff. The expression, "First Man," *Ādhām Qadhmōn* standing for the "Unfallen Adam," mentioned in Gen. I. 26ff. (and identified with the content of Job. XV. 7) is found in Hispano-Hebrew poetry, e. g. in the first line of the plea for clemency addressed by the unhappy Menaḥem ibn Ṡārūq to the Jewish statesman Ḥaṡdāy ibn Shaprūṭ whose prisoner he was. This is found in Schirmann, *Shīrāh*, I, p. 8.
33. The return to such roots had precedents at the court of the Umayyads, the first Islamic dynasty of rulers, which, against all reproach on the part of the traditional Muslims, introduced kingship *(mulk)* into Islam, and infringed many Muslim prohibitions. Whence they took the inspiration and authorization is still an open question. Professor Hitti, and following him Oleg Grabar, cite the cultic necessity to live up to the Byzantine and Persian tradition of imperial life and art. The root of messianism in court flattery appears in Ps. XIV. 6; see Hugo Gressmann, *Der Messias*, Göttingen, 1929, p. 29. It may not be superfluous, however, to stress that the aristocratic group of Cordovan Jews, which imitated the Umayyad court in "courts" of their own, did not shed all their inhibitions in favor of the courtly fashions, and probably even less so in their daily life than in its poetical expression. There is no reference to hunting, a Muslim courtly sport, to slave girls and slave boys, etc., and not even very much to instrumental music, which was on the index of influential Muslim groups. See H. G. Farmer, *A History of Arabian Music to the XIII Century*, London, 1929, p. 20 and passim. One would have to speak of liberalism in contrast to libertinism!
34. Pérès, *Poésie*, pp. 330ff., in particular, p. 331, n. 1, after Maqqarī, *Analectes*, I, pp. 82, 84. A good many representative statues must have perished, however, during the Almoravid and Almohade periods. Statues of Umayyad rulers (or, as in Madīnat az-Zahrā', allegedly of a concubine) decorated the exterior walls of castles or town gates.
35. The tendency of Arabic nature poetry to "animate" nature is observed by Pérès, *Poésie*, p. 187. For "debates about supremacy" cf. Pérès, *Poésie*, pp. 183ff. Cf. also G. E. von Grunebaum, "The Response to Nature in Arabic Poetry," in *JNES*, IV, 1945, p. 147, n. 89, and Helmut Ritter in *Der Islam*, XIV, 1925, pp. 397—401. Also H. Walther, *Das Streitgedicht in der lateinischen Literatur des Mittelalters*, Munich, 1920, e. g. pp. 14ff. The diatribe of the type as in Judges IX. 8 seems to have existed in many literatures. For *munāẓara*, cf. Moritz Steinschneider, "Rangstreitliteratur," in *Sitzungsberichte der A. W. Wien, Phil.-Hist. Kl.*, CLV, 1908; also G. E. von Grunebaum, *op. cit.*, under "Description of Buildings," p. 146. For poetical descriptions of gardens, a literary genre termed *rauḍiyya*, as an introductory part of the Arabic poem, and for further literature, cf. Pérès, *Poésie*, p. 183, n. 5. The models for Arabic descriptive poetry are Abū 'l-ʿAbbās ʿAlī ibn al-Muʿtazz (died 908 in Baghdad); al-Buḥturī, al-Walīd ibn ʿUbaid Allāh (born 821); Abū Bakr M. ibn A. aṣ-Ṣanaubarī (lived in Aleppo, died 945). A poem by al-Buḥturī about the Vaulted Hall erected by Khosro (who will be mentioned later), and a similar poem by Ibn al-Muʿtazz, is discussed by G. E. von Grunebaum in *Al-Andalus*, XX, 1955, pp. 268ff.

36. The topos of the INTERFERENCE OF THE POET IN A CONTEST FOR SUPREMACY is discussed by Grunebaum, *Kritik und Dichtkunst*, p. 61: "Der Dichter Abū Ḥumrān stand auf ..." The poet frequently stops discussions in this fashion. See the poem by Dūnāsh ibn Labrāṭ in Part I.
37. This is quoted by Gaudefroy Demombynes in his notes to Ibn Qutaiba, *kitāb ash-shi'r wa-sh-shu'arā'*, part II, p. 57 (note 53). A Jew would have quoted Prvbs. XXVII. 14.
38. The commonplaces of Arabic criticism: "The best poetry is the most mendacious," and an opposite statement "the best poetry is the most veracious" are discussed at length by the eleventh-century Persian 'Abd al-Qāhir al-Jurjānī in his Arabic *Mysteries of Eloquence* (in H. Ritter's edition: *Asrār al-balāgha*, Istambul, 1954, pp. 249ff.), and in Ritter, *Wortkunst*, pp. 292ff., 296.

Ibn Gabirol's secular poetry is greatly influenced by Abu 'l-'Alā' al-Ma'arrī (born 973 A. D. near Aleppo), and it could be justly said that Ibn Gabirol belonged to his school. This poet stressed particularly the veracity of his poetry. Al-Ma'arrī's main statement to this effect has been translated by R. A. Nicholson in his *Studies in Islamic Poetry*, Cambridge, 1921, p. 50, n. 2. "My aim is to speak the truth. Now the proper end of poetry is not truth, but falsehood ... therefore I must crave the indulgence of my readers ..." The traditional Muslim attitude to fictitious poetry is found in a statement by as-Suyūṭī quoted in the same footnote: "... grave poetry is fiction: therefore the poet has no choice but to tell lies or to make people laugh ..." The identical attitude is reflected in Moses ibn Ezra's repetition of the judgment that "the best of a poem is its lie." *Cf.* I. Goldziher, "Bemerkungen zur Neuhebräischen Poesie," in *JQR*, XIV, 1901–1902, pp. 719ff., 731 n. 2 as well as the same author's *Abhandlungen zur arabischen Philologie*, I, 23, Anm. (quoting Steinschneider, *ZDMG*, XXIX, p. 559 n. 20). The claim of veracity is made in particular by the Hebrew poet Moses ibn at-Tāqāna in his poem *Ha-Dhūnāsh qām*, Schirmann, *Shīrāh*, I, pp. 287ff., dist. 13:

> Alone his [the poet's own] mastersongs — integrities,
> but ours, nay every other singer's — lies.

I have dealt with Ibn Ḥazm's dandyism in Part I, B, 3, "The Awakening of the Senses."
39. Among the rich literature on the Alhambra should be mentioned in particular L. Torres Balbás, *La Alhambra y el Generalife*, Madrid, no date; idem, *Ars Hispaniae*, IV, *Arte almohade, arte nazarí, arte mudéjar*, Madrid, 1949 (quoted as *Ars Hispaniae*, IV), pp. 83–132; idem, "La Alhambra de Granada antes del siglo XIII," in "Cronica Arqueologica de la España Musulmana," VI, in *Al-Andalus*, V, 1940, pp. 159ff. (quoted as Torres Balbás, *Alhambra antes*); A. F. Calvert, *The Alhambra*, London, 1907; Owen Jones, *Plans, Elevations and Sections of the Alhambra*, London, 1842–48; Georges Marçais, *L'architecture musulmane d'occident*, Paris, 1954, pp. 302ff. (quoted as Marçais, *Architecture*); cf. José and Manuel Oliver Hurtado, *Granada y sus monumentos arabes*, Malaga, 1875. E. Lambert, "L'Alhambra de Grenade", in *Revue de l'art ancien et moderne*, LXIII, 1933, pp. 145–164 etc. A comprehensive Alhambra bibliography appeared in G. E. C. Creswell, *A Bibliography of the Architecture and Crafts of Islam*, London, 1961, pp. 352 ff.
40. For the Alcazaba of Malaga, cf. *Mémoires*, III, pp. 20ff.: Torres Balbás, *Ars Hispaniae*, IV, pp. 162ff.; M. Gómez-Moreno, *Ars Hispaniae*, III, *La arte español hasta los Almohades ...*, Madrid, 1951, pp. 224ff. A description of Zīrid masonry is found in L. Torres Balbás' article "Nuevas perspectivas sobre el arte de al-Andalus bajo el dominio almorávide," in *Al-Andalus*,

XVII, p. 420 (and the picture of the Puerta Monaita in Granada, Plate 28) (quoted as Torres Balbás, *Almorávides*): *Lajas tendidas separan algunas hiladas, mientras otras están formadas por sillares todos a tizón. Estos aparejos son característicos de la época de Almanzor, es decir, de los últimos años del siglo X y de los primeros del XI.* The author refers to *Ars Hispaniae*, III, pp. 173–174, 255–256. This mixed masonry seems to have outlived the middle of the eleventh century, at least in Granada and in the Zīrid buildings in Malaga and Niebla. A masonry mixed from bricks and fieldstones belongs to an old Roman building tradition found in Italy and the Byzantine Empire. Whenever used materials of previous buildings are re-used, such a system offers itself most naturally. For this reason, it is not confined exclusively to specific districts and towns. Professor Krautheimer regards the re-occurrence of this structural method in Italy as an Eastern influence in his "San Nicola in Bari und die apulischen Architekten des 12. Jhdts.," *Wiener Jahrbuch für Kunstgeschichte*, IX, 1934, p. 11.

41. Although the passage referring to Yehōseph's Alhambra construction in the royal *Mémoires* seems to have prompted Torres Balbás to write his *Alhambra antes* (the only reference to this passage I have found in any Alhambra literature), this scholar was, at that time, not willing to credit Yehōseph with any major contribution to the Alhambra. Cf. *ibid.*, pp. 159ff., 169. Cf. Torres Balbás, "El Alminar de la Iglesia de San José," in *Al-Andalus*, VI, 1941, p. 440, n. 3. ʿAbd Allāh's passage appears in *Mémoires*, IV, pp. 101 f. For al-Mustanṣir ibn Hūd cf. Torres Balbás, *Almorávides*, p. 424, note 3; for Ibn al-Aḥmar, the founder of the Naṣrid dynasty in 1237 or 1238 cf. Dozy, *Recherches*, I, pp. 384 ff.; Ibn Khaldūn; see above note 11, (Torres Balbás, *Alhambra antes*, p. 170). For the fortification of Granada (yet not the Alhambra) ascribed by al-Idrīsī to Ḥabbūs and Bādīs cf. Torres Balbás, *Almorávides*, pp. 419ff. The mistaken identification of the man (Yehōseph) credited by ʿAbd Allāh with "building the Alhambra Fortress for himself" with his father Samuel; cf. Torres Balbás, *Alhambra antes*, p 159.

42. For the wall between the Puerta de Vino and the Torre de Machuca, cf. J. Bermúdez Pareja, "Exploraciones arqueológicas en la Alhambra," in *Miscelanea de Estudios Arabes y Hebráicos*, Granada, 1953, pp. 54ff.

43. Penguin edition, 1963, pp. 139ff.

44. The author undertook his voyage in 1523–28 as the Venetian ambassador to the court of Charles V. Cf. Gerda Gollwitzer (editor), *Gartenlust*, Munich, 1956.

45. In M. Asín Palacios, *Abenházam de Córdoba*, I, Madrid, 1927, p. 193: *el buey es mas discreto y el burro mas avisado que él.* Ibn Gabirol's *Yeghōn ḥesheq* is found in *Bialik-R.*, I, pp. 127ff.

46. *Bialik-R.*, I, p. 15, dist. 43.

47. *Bialik-R.*, I, p. 165; also cf. *Geiger*, p. 83 and n. 87.

(1) Davidson reads *ṣaḥ-īm* 'shining ones', instead of *Bialik-R.'s* conjectured *ḥadd-īm* 'sharp ones'. See *Bialik-R.'s* notes to this poem.

(2) The poet alludes, in distich 2, to Solomon's Song, VI. 6: "Thy teeth are as a flock of sheep . . ."

48. Schirmann, *Shīrāh*, I, pp. 172ff.

49. *Ibid.*, pp. 286ff., dist. 49ff.

50. *Baba Qamma*, p. 76 (note 2); cf. Sigmund Mowinckel, *He That Cometh*, Nashville, n. d., p. 290f. (note 3); also Joseph Klausner, *The Messianic Idea in Israel*, New York, 1955, p. 487.

51. Millar Burrows, *More Light on the Dead Sea Scrolls*, New York, 1958, p. 400.

52. See L. Ginzberg, *The Legends of the Jews*, Philadelphia, 1947, V, p. 120. Cf. Percy E. Schramm, "Das Herrscherbild in der Kunst des frühen Mittelalters," in *Vorträge der Bibliothek Warburg*, 1922–23, p. 107.
53. The idea of having the ruler on one side, facing all the inimical world opposite, is found in Ibn ʿAmmār in his encomium of al-Muʿtaḍid on his victory over the Berbers quoted by Pérès:

   God is with you when the enemies are yonder,
   so that when you leave them united opposite you, you are the only one,

   also, that of the ruler as embodiment of all men expressed by Abū Nuwās:

   It may not be deemed strange on the part of God
   if He unite all mankind in a single individual.

   Daudpota, p. 85, with additional specimens.
54. *Bialik-R.*, II, p. 65, line 74. For "head of well," see above. For the conceit of the ALL RIVERS DRAWN TO THE ONE SEA, see Ibn Gabirol's poem *She'el-tem ʿal lebhābh-ī*, (*Bialik-R.*, I, pp. 81 f.), dist. 4.
55. In "Das 'Rote' Schloss der Gärten und sein Geheimnis," in *Atlantis* (1959), p. 241. For the idea of confronting one king with 'all kings' in Arabic poetry see Ibn Zaidūn (born in Cordova, 1003), who praises Abū 'l-Walīd ibn Jahwar and his family for their victory:

   These are kings! Whereas the other kings of the earth are beneath them,
   like the clouds illuminated by the full moon surpass those feebly lighted.

   (Pérès, *Poésie*, p. 89).
56. Cf. also II Chronicles IV. 2–6, 14.
57. Ernst Diez, *Die Kunst der islamischen Völker*, Berlin-Neubabelsberg, 1917, p. 177. Cf. Albert Champdor, *L'Alhambra de Grenade*, Paris, 1953, p. 96. See my passage on animal fountains. The "sketches by Richard Ford" advertised as forthcoming by Jesús Bermúdez Pareja together with an English text for the Patronate of the Alhambra in *Al-Andalus*, XX, 1955, p. 443, n. 11, appeared subsequently under the title *Granada: Escritos con dibujos ineditos del autor*, Granada, 1955. The typological relationship between the Fount and Solomon's Brazen Sea is mentioned in K. Baedeker, *Spain and Portugal*, 1913, p. 349.
58. *Ars Hispaniae*, III, p. 271; figures on p. 273. Torres Balbás devoted an article to the Alhambra lions: "Figures de leones en decoraciones arquitectónicas mudéjares," in "Crónica Arqueológica VI," in *Al-Andalus*, V, 1940, pp. 188 ff. As to the upper *taza*, the stilts, and the *surtidor* of the fountain, cf. Glück-Diez, *Arte del Islam* (in *Historia del Arte Labor*), V, Barcelona, 1932, p. 704, notes to pp. 427 ff. (quoted as Glück-Diez, *Islam*); Marino Antequera, *L'Alhambra et le Generalife*, Granada, without date, p. 40.
59. Maria E. Gómez-Moreno, *Mil joyas del arte Español*, Barcelona, no date, pp. 236 f. (quoted as M. E. Gómez-Moreno, *Mil Joyas*).
60. Whether the lions were made to order for the specific place within this Alhambra Fount or re-utilized is also discussed by Glück-Diez, *Islam*, p. 107. There was, somewhat later, a trade in carved lions between Christian Sicily and Spain. Similar lions, found as supports for sarcophagi in both Sicily and Spain, seem to bear out this observation; none of them, however, is designed to spout water.
61. Albert Champdor, *L'Alhambra de Grenade*, Paris, 1953 p. 96.

62. See *supra*. The vulgar Ibn al-Ḥajjāj, on the Arab side, uses 'oxen' as the customary word of vilification. See Mez, *Renaissance*, p. 238.
63. Gómez-Moreno, *A. Hispaniae*, p. 191.
64. A. R. Nykl, "Inscripciones árabes de la Alhambra y del Generalife," in *Al-Andalus*, IV, 1936—39, p. 183 (quoted as Nykl, *Inscripciones*).
65. Hellmut Ritter, *Über die Bildersprache Niẓāmīs*, Berlin, 1927, particularly pp. 6ff. (quoted as [Ritter], *Niẓāmī*).
66. Jeannine Auboyer, *Le trône et son symbolisme dans l'Inde ancienne*, Paris, 1949, p. 108, n. 1.
67. See, e. g., W. Berges, *Der Fürstenspiegel des hohen und späten Mittelalters*, Leipzig, 1938.
68. *G. A. L.*, I, p. 234ff., etc.; *E. I.*, II, 744ff.
69. *Yāqūt*, *Muʿjam al-buldān*, Cairo, 1906, VIII, p. 478.
70. Cf. article "Hamadhān" in the *E. I.* and discussion in G. E. von Grunebaum, "Aspects of Arabic Urban Literature," in *Al-Andalus*, XX, 1955, pp. 265f. note 22.
71. See A. V. Williams Jackson, *Persia, Past and Present*, New York, 1906, p. 160, n. 3; *Ibid.*, pp. 159ff., where this squatting lion is described and a photo attached. Jackson assumes, on the basis of Masʿūdī, *Les prairies d'or*, ed. Barbier de Meynard, Paris, 1877, IX, 21—22 (*G. A. L.*, I, 144; Suppl. I, 220), that this lion stood, not *upon*, but "by the Lion Gate." Jackson also quotes Horn, "Geschichte Irans in Islamischer Zeit" in *Grundriss d. Iran. Philologie*, II, 564, and (p. 161, note 1) other western authors who described the lion of Hamadhān. Cf. also Lord Curzon, *Persia and the Persians*, London, 1892. *Vide E. I.* under Balīnās; also Pauly-Wissowa, *Real-Encyclopaedie* ..., Stuttgart, 1895, III, p. 146; Hastings, *Encyclopaedia of Religion and Ethics*, 1910, I, pp. 609ff. For Apollonius of Tyana, the contemporary of Jesus, see Franz Rosenthal, *Das Fortleben der Antike im Islam*, Zurich, 1965, p. 332, with a passage from the *sirr al-khalīqa*, ascribed to Appollonius: "At my home town there was a stone sculpture standing upon a wooden columm, on the front of which was inscribed: "I am Hermes, the thrice wise. I erected this monument publicly, but veiled it in my wisdom, so that only someone as wise as I can get to it." This 'hermetic' wise, Apollonius, is made in Yāqūt's account a contemporary of the no less legendary Sāsānian King Qavādh I, 488—531 A. D. (or Qavādh II, 628 A. D.). The ʿAbbāsid caliph al-Muktafī, who desired to "collect" the lion, ruled from 902 to 908. Von Grunebaum, loc. cit., quotes for such city talismans in western cities L. Olschki, "Storia letteraria delle scoperte geografiche," in *Studie Ricerche*, Florence, 1937, pp. 126ff. He also mentions a poem on this talismanic lion by Ibn al-Ḥājib.

    Professor Hans Güterbock refers me to lions at gates or upon walls of cities. He writes in a letter: "... comparable to the re-employed lion of Hamadan ... are the 'late Hittite' lions at the gate of Marʿash. Both are now in the Museum of Istanbul; one with a hieroglyphic inscription, the other uninscribed. Regarding the inscribed one I find the following: L. Messerschmidt, 'Corpus Inscriptionum Hettiticarum, I: Beschreibung,' in *Mitteil. d. Vorderasiat. Ges.*, V, 1900, 4, pp. 17f., Pl. XXI:

    > Als Humann [und] P[uchstein] 1883 nach Marʿasch kamen, fanden sie den Löwen auf der (S. 18) Mauer der Citadelle von Marʿasch neben einem Thor, einem anderen, inschriftlosen Löwen gegenüber aufgestellt vor ..."

    Humann and Puchstein, *Reisen in Kleinasien und Nordsyrien*, Berlin (Reimer), 1890 mention the two lions on pp. 390f., with reference to the plate in their volume of plates, Pl. XLVIII, 1 and 2. There is a picture of the uninscribed lion, when it still sat high above the gate, in Perrot-Chipiez, *Histoire de l'art dans l'antiquité* (first French ed., Paris, 1887), IV, p. 529, Pl. 268. The entire castle is mediaeval; the lions, therefore, obviously borrowed. However, their placement high overhead, as seen in the plate in Perrot-Chipiez, is reminiscent of what you describe."

72. A. V. Williams Jackson, op. cit., p. 160.

73. As regards the representation of lions under the Umayyads, the two lions in Khirbat al-Mafjar, supporting the hitherto unidentified statue of a caliph (shown in our (Pl. 12)) must be mentioned (see R. W. Hamilton, *Khirbat al-Mafjar*, Oxford, 1959, Pl. LIV, 1), as must the lion attacking a gazelle in the mosaic of Khirbat al-Mafjar, loc. cit., frontispiece and Pl. XXXIX, bottom. Representations of lions are discussed in his text, pp. 52, 102, 313, 331, 338, and esp. 229. Finally, there is an Umayyad coin, showing two lions, in the Archaeological Museum in Istanbul, see the *Fourth Report*, 1950, pp. 20ff. (cited in O. Grabar's unpublished thesis, referring to *Encycl. Photogr. des Arts*, I, 1936, no. 3135, Pl. CCV).

The discussion of this topic (and many others of this kind) with my resourceful research assistant in London, Miss Coralie Noltenius, contributed greatly to the clarification of this point and is herewith warmly acknowledged.

74. For the throne in the Magnaura and the "House of the Tree" in Baghdad cf. Lars-Ivar Ringbom, *Graltempel und Paradies*, Stockholm, 1951, pp. 61, 64 (quoted as Ringbom, *Graltempel;* Professor W. F. Albright's kindness in calling my attention to this work is gratefully acknowledged); A. Alföldi, "Der Throntabernakel," in *La Nouvelle Clio*, 1952—1953, p. 76. For the Byzantine throne (and trees) see Gerard Brett, "The Automata in the Byzantine Throne of Solomon," in *Speculum*, XXIX, 1954, pp. 477—487, where the possibility of ʿAbbāsid influence upon the Byzantine throne is discussed. Artificial trees are discussed in Marie Luise Gothein, *Geschichte der Gartenkunst*, Jena, 1926 (quoted as Gothein, *Gartenkunst*), I, p. 147 and note 14; also p. 201, quoting Qazwīnī, *Kosmographie*, Göttingen, 1848, II, p. 210. The fountain tree fashioned by G. De Boucher in the thirteenth century for the Khan of the Tartars was discussed by Leonardo Olschki, *Guillaume Boucher, a French Artist of the Court of the Khans*, Baltimore, 1946. For the "Tree of Paradise" see Gressman, op. cit., pp. 266ff.

For the "Throne of Khosro" compare, specifically, Ernst Herzfeld, "Der Thron des Khosro," in *Jahrbuch der Preussischen Kunstsammlungen*, XLI, 1920, pp. 145ff. Professor Oleg Grabar reminds me that the discussion about Khosro's throne, i. e. whether it actually existed or was invented for the purpose of establishing a counterpart to the Byzantine Solomonic throne, is still open. Another counterpart to this allegedly original Solomonic throne in Byzantium is a fanciful description of the original throne of Solomon in Jewish sources. Cf. Wünsche, *Salomos Thron und Hippodrom*, Leipzig, 1906 (quoted as Wünsche), based mainly upon the *Second Targum.* I intend to deal with the topic "Solomon in the Middle Ages" in detail. Cf. *Targum Scheni zum Buch Esther*, ed. L. Munk, Berlin, 1876, pp. 5ff., 19f., and same, ed. S. Gelbhaus, Frankfurt, 1893.

The following excerpts inserted into the discussion are from Ginzberg, *The Legends of the Jews*, IV, pp. 157—159, taken mainly from the *Targum Shenī*, which dates back to Byzantine days.

75. I have discussed in Part I the topic of Solomon as the patron of secularization, who, setting the precedent, shielded, in particular, (courtly) love and plastic arts. The "Solomonic" books of the Bible and widely-spread legends inspired, as aforementioned, fantastic architecture in the Byzantine and

Muslim world, and as we see here, also among the Hebrews. A later section of this book summarizes the main Byzantine parallels and precedents to the activities of the Naghrāllas. For Fischer von Erlach see Georg Kunoth, *Die Historische Architektur Fischers von Erlach*, Düsseldorf, 1956, p. 212; and H. Sedlmayr, *J. B. Fischer von Erlach*, Vienna and Munich, 1956, with references to Solomonic architecture on pp. 125, 129ff. My unforgotten teacher Ernst Kantorowicz called my attention to the epistolarian Guido Faba (1190-1243) who, in a way parallel to the Granada circle, made King Solomon the patron of a literary enlightenment. See E. H. Kantorowicz, *Selected Studies*, Locust Valley, 1956, p. 200 n. 25.

Further Solomonic architectural tendencies originated in the Christian orbit under Charlemain and in particular under Henry the Lion. See H. Swarzenski, "Aus dem Kunstkreis Heinrichs des Löwen," in *Städel-Jahrbuch* VII—VIII, 1932, pp. 241ff., and Peter Bloch, "Siebenarmige Leuchter in Christlichen Kirchen," in *Wallraf-Richartz-Jahrbuch*, XXIII, 1961, pp. 55ff.

About an application of the term "Solomonic art" see J. M. Millás y Vallicrosa, "Sobre la terminología artistica de ›Salomò‹," in *Sefarad*, XVII, 1957, pp. 357ff.

76. Such expectations may have been based upon Obadiah, v. 20. (His prophecy for the Jews of Ṣephāradh seems to have referred originally to those of Sardes.) The precedent for a delivery by and rulership for Levites (as the Naghrāllas were), was established by the priestly Maccabees. See J. Klausner, *The Messianic Idea in Israel*, New York, 1955, pp. 304ff. (quoted as *Klausner*).

77. *Bialik-R.*, I, p. 6, v. 52ff. Similarly, in a very early poem, Solomon ibn Gabirol describes himself as the ruler of the kingdom of poetry, in a way different from the customary self-praise of the period and quite unique in Hebrew poetry. It reads (*Bialik-R.*, I, p. 183, notes p. 137):

> Patesi am I, potentate of Poesy,
> I, the harp for all poets and minstrels.
>
> My song is the crown for kings
> and mitre on the heads of viceroys.
>
> My body walks upon the earth
> yet my spirit ascends the clouds.
>
> Behold, with my sixteen years —
> like the heart of a man of eighty, my heart is wise.

Ibn Gabirol's titanism will be discussed in Part III.

78. Precedents for such naming of oneself "minor" are discussed by N. Avigad. "Excavations at Beth Sheʿarim," in *Israel Exploration Journal*, V, 1955, p. 223, In the light of Ibn Gabirol's Solomonism as it appears in his verse, I see in this adopted diminutive name no expression of modesty.

79. Editions of Samuel's poetry: D. S. Sassoon, *The Diwan of Shemuel Hannaghid*, London, 1934 (quoted as *Sassoon*); Sh. Abramson, *Shemūʾel han-Nāghīdh, Ben Mishley*, Tel Aviv, 1948 (quoted as *Abramson*); and Habermann, *Diwan*.

80. Yehōṣeph incorporated his poem in his father's *diwan*, which he edited. The prefatory remarks read: "He took me with him when he went to invade and to battle at a nearby place in the month of *Nīšān* of the year 1045 (or 1044). My soul yearned for my home and my relatives, and I composed these four couplets. He [my father], may God love him, helped me with them, for which reason it was easy for me to invent them, as follows":

Be-ṭerem neśī'āh Schirmann, *Shīrāh*, I, p. 293
⏑ - - ⏑ - - - ⏑ - - ⏑ - - - (*Ṭawīl*) Habermann, *Dīwān*, I. 1, p. 58
Sassoon, p. 62

Rhyme: *-bheth*

Before the journey my request was for going;
at the time of separation my desire was to stay a little.

One that, nine years old, could endure parting
would have a heart like iron or like chiseled stone.

I wish well to those [women] weeping at my taking leave! Do they know that
I am well, and esteemed like the one "in the second chariot?" Gen. XLI.43

And yet I wish: may God destroy Separation,
and may she no longer rise upon heart and mind.

The one "in the second chariot" is of course the Biblical Joseph in his exaltation by Pharaoh in Egypt. Separation personified is an Arabic commonplace, appearing in many poems by Ibn Gabirol, (to be discussed later).

81. *Bialik-R.*, I, pp. 113f.; notes pp. 95f.; *Geiger*, p. 72. Abraham Geiger, with remarkable insight, had ascribed this poem to Ibn Gabirol's relationship to Samuel han-Nāghīdh, as subsequently did Bialik and Ravnitzki. Bialik made Samuel the addressee because of the latter's Solomonic book titles like "Modern Ecclesiastes," by which he styled himself a modern Solomon, as mentioned above. To do Geiger and Bialik justice, we have to realize how little material referring to Yehōseph was then available to them. These Solomonic claims and hopes with their messianic echoes were not limited to the communications between the Naghrāllas and Ibn Gabirol. A poem of cringing flattery of the Naghrāllas by an unknown author, expelled, as was Ibn Gabirol, from the Naghrāllas' "court," was recently published by S. M. Stern (among others) in his article, "*Zōṭ-ōth le-thōledh-ōth R. Shemū'el han-Nāghīdh*," in *Zion (Ṣiyōn)*, XV, 1950, p. 144. This poem contains very similar Solomonic addresses. A translation and detailed interpretation of it, and of a similar poem, appear in my forthcoming study on the relationship between Ibn Gabirol and Samuel han-Nāghīdh.
82. See Simon Dubnow, *Weltgeschichte des Jüdischen Volkes*, Berlin, 1926, III, p. 421; for later messiahs, see G. Scholem, *Major Trends in Jewish Mysticism*, Jerusalem, 1941, pp. 308ff., and the same author's *Shabbethay Ṣebhī*, Tel Aviv, 1957, *passim;* see Index under *ma'as-īm zār-īm.*
83. Cf. Schirmann, *Samuel*, pp. 102ff. For 'Shiloh' see *Klausner*, p. 30; for 'Messiah ben Joseph', *ibid.*, pp. 463, 501, 521; cf. *Sanhedrin* 98b, also Gressman, *op. cit.*, pp. 461f. Asín Palacio's interpretation of Ibn Ḥazm's passages has, however, been doubted. Cf. Asín P., *Abenházam*, II, pp. 45, 267, 291; Ibn Ḥazm, *K. (al-fiṣal fī) al-milal (wa-l-ahwā) wa-n-niḥal (Book of Religions and Sects)*, Cairo, 1321, *A. H.*, I, p. 152.
84. See *Gressmann*, *op. cit.*, pp. 278ff.
85. Habermann, *Diwan*, section I, pp. 34ff.; also Schirmann, *Shīrāh*, pp. 76, 109ff.
86. For the idea of the reborn David, Messiah ben David, see Gressmann, op. cit., pp. 277, 278f., 327, 355ff., 347, 349; Habermann, *Diwan*, pp. 27ff., 327, 335ff., 347, 349, 388, etc.; Sigmund Mowinckel, *He That Cometh*, tr.

G. W. Anderson, New York, N. Y., pp. 155f., 159ff., 286ff., 289ff., 295, 306f., 318, 324f. (quoted as *Mowinckel*); *Klausner*, op. cit., *passim*. For the Messiah ben Levi, see *Gressmann*, pp. 268, 329, 391; *Mowinckel*, pp. 287ff., 318, 322f., 382, 395ff.; *Klausner*, pp. 304f., 311ff., 326, 409, 454. For the fusion of the two messiahs into one, see *Mowinckel*, p. 287, n. 1.

87. Quoted after M. H. Zotenberg, *Chronique de ... Tabari ...*, Paris, 1867, I, pp. 433ff., and 436ff. Cf. also H. Speyer, *Die Biblischen Erzählungen im Qoran*, Hildesheim, 1961, pp. 383ff.; also D. Sidersky, *Les origines des légendes musulmanes*, Paris, 1933, p. 124.
88. Zotenberg, op. cit., I, pp. 433ff.
89. Op. cit., pp. 488ff.
90. Op. cit., p. 442. For a "sea of glass" cf. Apocal. XV. 2. A floor of crystal (literally 'salt'), most likely a related idea, appears in Samuel's poem, beginning "Tell me, what is the torch ...," where he speaks of "crystals onto a crystal base." See above. O. Grabar called my attention to a "glass floor" recently unearthed in Raqqa, showing the spread of "Solomonic" ideas; published in *Annales Archéologiques de Syrie*, I, 1951, p. 115 *et seq.*
91. Pérès, *Poésie*, p. 139; *Mélanges Basset*, pp. 238ff.

The Young Yehōseph's Garden Construction

92. Unfortunately, the Arabic prefatory remarks to this poem are accessible only in Hebrew translation.

Dist. 6: 93. The poet seems to allow the reader two possibilities of connection; it is either the garden beds which offer highways for the noble or, somewhat more likely, it is the companions to whose hearts there is an access.

Dist. 10: 94. For the comparison of a goblet to a bride see Pérès, *Poésie*, p. 165: *La coupe de cristal conduisait (vers le domicile de l'époux) le vin comme une fiancée qu'on expose avec tous ses atours alors que les fleurs des branches s'éparpillaient à profusion.* Cf. Ibn al-Muʿtazz, in O. Loth, *Über Leben und Werke des ʿAbdallah ibn al Muʿtazz* Leipzig, 1882, p. 57:

... a warrior
who harbors murder, though lacking arms;

The cup in his hand is, as it were, a bride
who wears a sash of fresh pearls.

Dist. 12: Praise of a banquet for the absence of noise is found in Abū Nuwās.

Dist. 14: The employment of the ἅπαξ λεγόμενον *yūbhal* ('stream'), from Jeremiah XVII. 8 ("He is like a tree planted by water that sends out its roots by the stream"), recalling Jacob's blessing of Joseph in Genesis XLIX. 22 ("Joseph is a fruitful bough, a fruitful bough by a spring"), may bear out Samuel's spirit of devotion to his prodigy of a son and his devout mental associations. Yehōseph, of course, knew how happy he made his father by demonstrating that he shared his father's penchant for art.

Note to the Text

Dist. 12: I read *yīghaʿ* 'he will (not) tire' instead of *yiggaʿ* 'he will (not) reach out', as is self-explanatory.

95. This improvisation in a Cordovan spirit may have been inspired by the chapter on "Contentment" in Ibn Ḥazm's *The Dove's Neck-Ring* (from which I quoted the relevant passage in my Prologue) which also contains the following lines in Professor Arberry's translation (Ibn Ḥazm, *Ring*, p. 193):

And waters all among the trees
Ran as they listed; sweet delight
Awaited the appraising sight,
And joy was there for hand to seize;

And all the spirit could desire
Was given to companion us —
Friends highly born and chivalrous,
Artificers of glory's spire; ...

This book, written approximately in 1022, must have been in wide circulation by this time.

96. Cf. Schirmann, *Yehōseph*, p. 50.

97. Note to the Text:

A Water and Light Construction

Dist. 1: Literally: "upon the surface of salt something like salt ..."

98. Habermann, *Diwan*, section 3, p. 42. Cf. al-Maqqarī's quotation of a poetical description by Ibn Ḥamdīs of a fountain in the form of a tree, upon which birds perch, from which poem I have quoted some lines in my passage on Islamic animal fountains. Al-Maqqarī also quotes a poem describing a fountain between two torches.

99. Ibid., section 3, p. 43.

100. The following description of this Solomonic glass building is quoted by al-Maqqarī from the *kitāb al-muqtabis fī ta'rīkh (rijāl) al-Andalus* by Abū Marwān ibn Ḥayyān (died 1075 — see *G. A. L.*, I, p. 338; S. I, p. 578); this is found in *Analectes*, I, 348 with an inferior parallel text in I, page 239. — The fulfillment of this prophecy is attested by al-Maqqarī (though hardly based upon the testimony of Ibn Ḥayyān who died in the same year as the king, but upon that of Ibn al-Khaṭīb who lived two hundred years later). The strange family name of the Banū Dhī 'n-Nūn (in the singular: "Ibn Dhī 'n-Nūn," i. e., "the son of Dhū 'n-Nūn") is a significant Arabization of the Berber name of an assimilated family, which became proverbial for its lavishness. "Like a Dhū 'n-Nūnid banquet" remained a standing comparison (see Dozy, *Histoire des musulmans d'Espagne*, II, p. 255). For their court of Muses, see Nykl, *Hisp.-A. Poetry*, pp. 201 ff. The ideas underlying such glass and water palaces must be sought in the legends describing Solomon's (and Khosro's) miraculous edifices. A few additional verses found in al-Maqqarī, I, p. 348, mentioning al-Ma'mūn, also refer, most likely, to this fabulous spectacle. Pérès, *Poésie*, pp. 150 f.

101. See Pérès, *Poésie*, pp. 120 ff.; Lévi-Provençal, *Espagne*, p. 229.

102. The lines of Dūnāsh's encomium are found in Schirmann, *Shīrāh*, I, pp. 36 f., lines 19 ff.

103. Ibn al-Khaṭīb in his *Iḥāṭā fī akhbār Gharnāṭa*, Cairo, 1901, pp. 266, and Ibn ʿIdhārī, *al-bayān al-mughrib fī akhbār al-Maghrib*, Paris, 1930, III, pp. 264ff., accuse Yehōseph of "seeking that he might establish for the Jews a state," (after Dozy, *Ibn ʿIdhārī*, p. 99); cf. also Munk, *Notice*, pp. 21 ff.

104. Cf. Maqqarī, *Dynasties*, I, p. 319, n. 30; Ibn al-Farrā' from Ḥuṣn al-Fīdāq (a fortress in the province of Granada) belonging to the branches of the Qalʿat Banī Saʿīd (cf. Maqqarī, *Dynasties*, II, p. 27); these verses are quoted by Abū Muḥammad ʿAbd Allāh ibn Ibrahīm al-Ḥijārī in his *K. al-mushib fī faḍā'il ahl al-Maghrib*, preserved by al-Maqqarī, which I quote from Munk, *Notice*, pp. 220—221.

105. Cf. Chaucer's description of April in the "Prologue" to *The Canterbury Tales* "... the yonge sonne Hath in the Ram his halfe cors y'ronne,"; in the Persian tradition the sun's entering the constellation of Aries was marked by the New Year's festival, *Naurūz*.
106. Cf. Munk, *Notice*, loc. cit.
107. Cf. *Encyclopaedia Judaica*, under "Gajjat," etc. The same Isaac ibn Giyyāt composed dirges upon Yehōseph's death (published in H. Schirmann, *Shīr-īm ḥadhāsh-īm min hag-Genīzāh* ..., Jerusalem, 1965, pp. 190).
108. J. Amador de los Rios, *Historia Social, Politica y Religiosa de los Judios de España* ..., Madrid, 1875f., p. 210, n. 2.
109. Babylonian Talmud, *Rōsh hash-shānāh* 24 a., London, 1938, XIII, pp. 105ff. (and *'Abhōdhāh Zārāh* 43 a; *Menāḥōth*, London, 1948, II, p. 184).
110. Cf. W. F. Albright, *Archaeology and the Religion of Israel*, Baltimore, 1953, pp. 148f. and id. in *JAOS*, XL, 316f. I mentioned that the scandal of the erection of representational art by Solomon seems to have been felt only much later. The bulls were removed by King Ahaz, possibly not as an act of piety but owing to financial pressure (II Kings XVI. 15). Cf. R. de Vaux, *Ancient Israel*, New York, etc., 1961, pp. 319; 321–322.
111. In the above-quoted "Itinerary" by Germond de Lavigne (in 1883) we were told that the Lions' basin was still called 'Sea'.
112. Wünsche, *Thron*, pp. 32 and 40 refers to the zodiac in this connection, see below.
113. For such gods and the "Woman on the beast" (as in Revelation XVII. 7) compare H. P. L'Orange, *Studies on the Iconography of Cosmic Kingship*, p. 54 (51ff.), showing the Assyrian Maltaya rock relief, after H. Gressmann, *Texte und Bilder zum A. T.*, p. 335, and quoting "Kadesh" after Gressmann, l. c., pp. 270ff.; 276 (307) (Plate 9a). Also Sir Leonard Woolley, *Carchemish*, II, 1921, Plates B. 25, B. 26; III, 1952, B. 53, B. 54. Like the Alhambra lions, the Carchemish lions show their teeth, although they open their mouths more widely. Both have "abstract" ornament-like semicircular ears, and their beards are suggested by horizontal linear incisions. I am greatly indebted for the references to the Carchemish lions to Professors Hans Güterbock and Leo Oppenheim, of the Oriental Institute of the University of Chicago, and to Dr. Bertha Segal, Johns Hopkins University. Cf. also *Mittheilungen der Orientalischen Sammlung*, Heft XIII: *Sendschirli*, Berlin, 1902, pp. 365, 380; plates LVII, LXIV, LXV. To illustrate the continuity of such motifs in Islamic architecture note that a base of a column decorated with four lions in relief used as a water basin is found in the "Garden of the Forty Columns" in Isfahan (of the seventeenth century). Cf. R. Bernheimer, *Romanische Tierplastik*, Munich, 1931, Pl. XXVII.
114. Sir Leonard Woolley, *Dead Towns and Living Men*, London/New York, 1920, p. 93; Woolley, *Carchemish*, Part III, Pl. B. 47, upper picture. Dr. Güterbock informs me that Sir Leonard Woolley in his latest Carchemish volume specifically refers, in connection with this pedestal presumably used as a font, to its kinship with Solomon's temple basin. Dr. Güterbock also sent me a picture of a late Hittite stone trough with the following description:

> Granite trough, found on the surface of a mound near the village of *Dokuz* on the middle Kizilirmak (Halys River), reported as seen there by Gerhart Bartsch, *Archiv für Orientforschung*, IX, 1933–34, pp. 50–52. Now (summer of 1959) it is set up in the area of the Hirfanli Dam of the same river; the village and mound of Dokuz are now flooded. It may or may not have been taken to the Ankara Museum. Will be published by Prof. Ekrem Akurgal of Ankara Univ.

Plate 9 a

Date: *certainly* Hittite, *before* 1200 B. C.;
possibly Old Hittite, before 1400 B. C.

This is an unusually large, otherwise sarcophagus-like trough. On the shorter side, two full round bull heads protrude, each with a hole in the middle of its mouth as a water spout. The width of the trough allows, as it were, for two imaginary bull bodies, in proportion with the heads contained in the volume of the trough.

115. Two Greek tripods with human figures inserted between lions and basin, made to serve as holy water fountains, one from Corinth and one at Olympia, are published in Percy Gardner, "A Stone Tripod at Oxford," in *Journal of Hellenic Studies*, XVI, 1896, pp. 275 ff., Dr. Gardner's description of the Oxford tripod reads:

> On a round pedestal... recline three lions, on each of which stands a female figure clad in a long chiton ... Each grasps in one hand the tail of the lion whereon she stands ... On the heads of the three women rests a basis, supported also by a central column, in the form of an hour glass, with torus in the midst. The basis has in the midst a hole ... It seems evident that into this hole fitted the stem of a large circular basin. The basin was in fact turned round in the hole until part of the upper surface of the support was worn smooth; it was then fitted in its place by lead.

The other tripod, as it could be reconstructed from scanty fragments, is very similar. The female statues are freestanding. The crouching lions hold their heads erect like watchdogs. Dr. Gardner adds:

> ... I am disposed to think that serious mythological meaning has passed from these figures standing on lions, and that they have become merely architectonic in character (ibid., p. 279).

A tripod similar to the fragmentary ones was recently found in Corinth. I owe this information to Dr. E. Cahn in Basel and to Dr. W. L. Brown of the Ashmolean Museum, Oxford. A specimen of the same motif, in lead, has been found in Sparta. (Cf. Frederik Poulsen, *Der Orient und die frühgriechische Kunst*, Berlin, 1912, p. 139.) A small Etruscan ivory basin supported by four caryatid figures is found in the Villa Giulia Museum in Rome. This type of basin, supported by four human figures seated upon lions, lived on in Romanesque baptismal fonts. English baptismal fonts upheld by, or decorated around their bases with lions, are discussed in E. Tyrell-Green, *Baptismal Fonts*, London, 1928, pp. 62 ff., which shows specimens, e. g. p. 63. For Danish lion fonts see M. Mackeprang, *Danmarks Middelalderlige Døbefonte*, Copenhagen, 1941, pp. 288 ff. There are, of course, also modern replicas of Solomon's fount as, for instance, the baptismal font of the great Mormon Temple in Salt Lake City.

116. In A. Malraux and G. Salles, *The Art of Ancient Iran*, Plate 303. The practice of preserving an older basin together with a new one appears in the Madrasat al-ʿAṭṭārīn in Fez.

117. Op. cit., Plate 291.

118. Op. cit., Plate 461, termed "Indian Art."

119. Found in al-Masʿūdī, *murūj adh-dhahab*, ed. and tr. Barbier de Meynard and A. Pavet de Courteille, Paris, 1861 ff., VI, p. 32; also in Tabarī, *Annales*, ed. N. de Goeje, Leiden, 1885, II, p. 1874. I am greatly obliged to Dr. Oleg Grabar for sending me offprints of his articles which appeared in *Archaeology* and *Ars Orientalis*. The distich quoted above and its interpretation with its literary references cited below are from his article "The Painting of the Six Kings at Quṣair ʿAmra," in *Ars Orientalis*, I, 1954, pp. 185—186:

The contention that the Moslems did not represent living things in the decoration of their edifices is slowly disappearing. In some Umayyad palaces of Syria, sculptures in high relief representing human figures have been encountered in recent excavations; and the use of animals in sculptural decoration becomes more frequent in Islamic Spain, particularly during the period of Almansor (the last years of the tenth and first of the eleventh centuries when some of the best known examples were made). Their importance is great even with regard to the history of the origin of Romanesque sculpture, some of which strangely resembles its Islamic prototypes.

Islamic opposition to (and fear of) any representation of the living is borne out in the well-known *ḥadīth*, according to which Muḥammad said:

The masters *aṣḥāb* of these pictures *ṣuwar* will be punished on the Day of Resurrection and it will be said to them: "Bring to life what you created." And he [the Prophet] said: "The house in which there are pictures will not be entered by angels."

All the more striking are the new discoveries illustrating the license of the Umayyads and other dynasties in this respect. Cf. O. Grabar's unpublished thesis, *Ceremonial and Art at the Umayyad Court*, Princeton, 1955. R. W. Hamilton, *Khirbat al-Mafjar*, treats this point very tactfully, see specifically pp. 231 ff.; 343 ff. For Qaṣr al-Ḥair al-Gharbī cf. Daniel Schlumberger, "Les fouilles de Qaṣr el-Ḥeir el-Gharbī (1936–1938)," in *Syria*, XX, 1939, pp. 195 ff., 324 ff. About the origin of Umayyad art cf. Herzfeld, "Die Genesis der islamischen Kunst und das Mschatta-Problem," in *Der Islam*, I, esp. p. 32, cited by Schlumberger, op. cit., p. 357; *Selections from the Ṣaḥiḥ of al-Bukhārī;* edited by Charles C. Torrey, Leyden, 1906, p. 16, lines 6 ff. Cf. K. A. C. Creswell, "The Lawfulness of Painting in Early Islam," in *Ars Islamica*, XI and XII, 1946, pp. 159–166; O. Grabar, "The Umayyad Dome of the Rock," in *Ars Orientalis*, III, 1959, p. 56, n. 22; Bishr Farès, *Essai sur l'esprit de la decoration islamique*, Cairo, 1952. Excavations of the Umayyad constructions of Khirbat Minyah (seventh century) have been undertaken by the University of Michigan under O. Grabar. The results, of which the principal is a mosaic, have not yet been published, see note in *IEJ*, 1959, p. 276.

For the attitude of the Jews toward the Mosaic injunctions against images, see E. E. Urbach, "The Rabbinical Law of Idolatry in the Second and Third Centuries in the Light of Archaeological and Historical Facts," in *IEJ*, 1959, pp. 149 ff.; 229 ff.

120. For related literature, cited in Grabar, op. cit., see also E. Herzfeld, "Die Könige der Erde," in *Islam*, XXI, 1933, pp. 233 ff.; F. Dölger, "Die 'Familie der Könige' im Mittelalter," in *Historisches Jahrbuch*, LX, 1940, pp. 397 ff.; G. Ostrogorsky, "Die byzantinische Staatenhierarchie," in *Seminarium Kondakovianum*, VIII, 1936, pp. 41 ff.; K. Holtzmann, "Der Weltherrschaftsgedanke des mittelalterlichen Kaisertums ...," in *Historische Zeitschrift*, CLIX, 1939, pp. 251 ff.; A. Christensen, *L'Iran sous les Sassanides*, 2nd ed., Copenhagen, 1944, pp. 411 ff. For Quṣair ʿAmra see G. L. Harding, *The Antiquities of Jordan*, London, 1960, p. 156, where these figures are interpreted as the enemies of Islam.

121. A Sāsānian precedent to this, which existed near Kermanshah, is described in Yāqūt, *muʿjam al-buldān*, ed. F. Wüstenfeld, IV, Leipzig, 1866–73, p. 70 (quoted Yāqūt, *Buldān*); the passage is cited in Grabar, op. cit. p. 185.

122. Cf. the many mediaeval thrones supported by carved lions.

123. Cf. the *Illustrated London News* of Saturday, May 28, 1949, pp. 726 ff.; R. W. Hamilton, *Khirbat al-Mafjar*, Oxford, 1959, pp. 231 f., Pl. LV, 1. In Spain

plastic representations were produced mainly during the period of the caliphate. Cf. L. Torres Balbás, *Ars Islamica*, XV and XVI, pp. 180–181.

124. For Byzantine gardens, animal statues, cf. Ch. Diehl, *Manuel d'art byzantin*, Paris, 1925, I, pp. 414ff. For the famous throne of the Emperor with its mechanical devices of sound and movement (and its two lions), cf. ibid., p. 421. Charles Rufus Morey in *Medieval Art*, New York, 1942, p. 101, describes, following the *Book of Ceremonies* of Constantine Porphyrogenitus:

> The influence of the east ... in the descriptions ... of the palace which the emperor Theophilus built in Constantinople in which one can divine an imitation of Arab palace planning ... Beyond this (semicircular) terrace was a colonnaded court descending to the open area of the Phiale whose central feature was a bronze fountain ... with a waterspout in the form of a golden pine cone. Around this central portion extended collateral rooms whose names connote the luxury of their decorations – the Hall of Love, the Triclinium of the Pearl – and pavilions in the midst of gardens, incrusted with marble, and with ceilings of gold mosaic, adorned with a subtile elegance that suggests names such as those of Musikos and Harmonia, given to the sleeping chamber of the empress. The oriental luxury of such installations was supplemented by ingenious displays of mechanism; in the hall of the Magnaura the imperial throne was shaded by a golden plane tree with its foliage interspersed with birds; the throne was flanked by golden lions and griffins, and faced organs ornamented with enamels and jewels. On the occasion of receptions of state, the moment of obeisance to the emperor was marked by operation of the mechanisms; music came from the organs, the birds raised their wings and sang, the griffins rose, the lions lashed with their tails and roared.

Cf. Louis Hautecoeur, *Mystique et architecture*, Paris, 1954, p. 170.

125. Found in Provençal, *Espagne*, II, p. 149, also, in part, in Maqqarī, *Dynasties*, I, pp. 234ff., also similarly in Girault de Prangey, *Essai sur l'architecture des arabes ... en Espagne*, Paris, 1841, pp. 50ff.; its Arabic text in Maqqarī, *Analectes*, I, pp. 373f. (Cf. Nicholson, *History*, p. 413, n. 1.) This work contains in its introduction to the biography of Ibn al-Khaṭīb, "the famous vizier of Granada," the most important information on Islamic Spain. Cf. also the introduction to James C. Murphy, "Arabian Antiquities of Spain," in John Shakespear and Thomas Horne, *The History of the Mohamedan Empire in Spain*, London, 1816, pp. 167ff.

126. Maqqarī, *Analectes*, II, p. 676; Maqqarī, *Dynasties*, II, p. 271.

127. Maqqarī, *Analectes*, I, p. 371; Maqqarī, *Dynasties*, I, p. 241. Lions attached to water spouts existed in Egyptian temples of all periods; cf. Jean Sainte Fare Garnot, "Le lion dans l'art égyptien" in *Bulletin de l'Institut français d'Archéologie Orientale*, XXXVII, Cairo, 1937, pp. 75ff. The lion's solar head as the source of a solar divine fluid, and the Nile as the seminal flow of Osiris, appearing in Egyptian symbols of mythological conceptions, live on in purely artistic lion fountainheads, see E. R. Goodenough, *Jewish Symbols*, New York, 1956, V, p. 181f. For the old tradition of using the mouths of lions as water spouts, I quote E. Curtius, "Die Plastik der Hellenen an Quellen und Brunnen," in *Phil. Hist. Abh. d. Kgl. Akad. d. Wiss. zu Berlin*, 1876, pp. 139–140, 143:

> ... die Energie des felsspaltenden Wasserstrahls [wird] mit der unwiderstehlichen Kraft reissender und stossender Tiere (Löwe, Wolf, Eber, Widder, Stier) verglichen, und die Reihe plastischer Symbole, wie das Stirnhorn der Flüsse, wurzelt in dieser Anschauung.

[Für die] bei den Völkern des Altertums weit verbreitete, den Griechen und Italikern gemeinsame und auch im Neugriechischen durch alte Tradition erhaltene Anschauung, dass man die Quelle das "Haupt des Wassers" nannte. [Cf. "Haupt" in *Index Lect. Berol.*, 1869—70, under κρουνοὶ λεοντοπρόσωποι] ...

Im Peloponnes ... wo der bis dahin unterirdische Alpheios aus dem Boden hervorbricht und neben ihm die Quelle des Eurotas, lagen einst als Denkmäler des seltenen Wassersegens zwei Marmorlöwen vor dem Tempel der Göttermutter ..., welche ... jene Zwillingsquellen hervorgerufen hatte. Deshalb sind die Löwen hier ohne Zweifel nicht als Werke decorativer Kunst anzusehen, sondern als Symbole der Gottheit und ihrer ... Kraft.

On page 147, *op. cit.*, Curtius mentions a representation of two lions, rising against each other, which are watching a well in a rock. He speaks also of animal masks as the regular form of water spouts of fountains and gargoyles in Pompeii.

I should mention, in this connection, the famous sarcophagi with their Dionysian symbolism which combine the idea of the winepress with that of the sarcophagus. A faint survival of Dionysian burial ideas is found in the Islamic period in some Persian and Arabic poems and also, through them, in Ibn Gabirol; see my discussion of his poem *Bārāq asher ʿeyn-ō*, distich 11. in my German book on Ibn Gabirol.

128. Cf. Rafael Castejón, "La Nueva Pila de Alamiria," in *Boletin de la Real Academia de Ciencias, Bellas Letras y Nobles Artes de Cordova*, Cordova, 1946, pp. 197ff. (picture on p. 198); Gómez-Moreno, *Ars Hispaniae*, III, pp. 187ff. For the inscription cf. Nykl, *Inscripciones*, p. 185; E. Lévi-Provençal, *Inscriptions arabes d'Espagne*, Leyden/Paris, 1931, pp. 195ff.

The claim that one of the Berber kings collected sculpture is most surprising. Lévi-Provençal's opinion that this *pila* came from Elvira is based mainly upon the fact that King Bādīs had plundered the town of Elvira and embellished Granada. (See below.) However, R. Castejón, like other archaeologists in this field, points out that Hispano-Islamic zoomorphic art flourished almost exclusively in Cordova and the residential towns during the period of the Umayyads and the ʿĀmirids. He also illustrates his article with the most outstanding specimens of zoomorphic art preserved from that period. There are a marble elephant in the round, found near Madīnat az-Zahrā' (Pl. 11) and metal aquamanilia in the shape of an animal (following a practice not typical of Spain alone). The representation of gazelles or antelopes attacked by lions is an ancient Eastern (Sumerian) motif reappearing also, for example, in the al-Mafjar mosaics. (A tiger attacking a calf is shown in a mosaic in the Palazzo dei Conservatori.) A lion attacking a deer is also a symbol for death and violence in general. See below note 178.

129. See Nykl, *Inscripciones*, p. 185, n. 50. Holes that remain from the insertion of stones into eyes can be observed in the stone reliefs of the caliphal period, illustrated in Gómez-Moreno, *Ars Hispaniae*, III, p. 187, fig. 247c from Cordova, and p. 186, fig. 246b and 246c from Seville, Marrakesh, and the Alhambra. A few human representations belonging to the eleventh century are preserved on the *pila* from Játiva; see Gómez-Moreno, *Ars Hispaniae*, III, pp. 275—276.

130. Pérès, *Poésie*, pp. 59f., 251—287, p. 14f.

131. The reference to the prince's educator ibid. pp. 60 and 366, after *Histoire de l'Espagne musulmane extraite du k. Aʿmāl al-aʿlām* (by Ibn al-Khaṭīb) par E. Lévi-Provençal, in *Coll. de textes ar. publ. par l'Inst. des H. Études marocaines*, III, Rabat, 1934.

132. Cf. *Mémoires*, III, pp. 259f. (n. 59).
133. Ibid.
134. Dozy, *Recherches*, I, pp. 259f., taken from *Bughyat al-wuʿāt fī tabaqāt al-lughawiyyīn wa-'n-nuḥāt* by the Arabic historian as Suyūṭī, Cairo, a. H. 1326, p. 47, also found in Dozy, *Histoire des Todjibides*, pp. 211ff.; also 93f.
135. Cf. Pérès, *Poésie*, pp. 59. Cf. Nykl, *H.-A. Poetry*, p. 303 (also p. 188f.).
136. For al-Muʿtaṣim, Prince of Almeria, cf. Pérès, *Poésie*, pp. 391, 388, etc., verses by him, ibid. pp. 244, 276, 294, 314, 351, 464, 488.
137. Translated from Dozy, *Recherches*, I, pp. 259f. after Ibn al-Khaṭīb (after Maqqarī, *Analectes*, II, p. 280); García Gómez, *Poetas*, p. 100. Other references to the subsequent verses ibidem.
138. For the subsequent verses, found in Maqqarī, *Analectes*, II, p. 280, see Nykl, *H.-Arab. Poetry*, p. 191; García Gómez, *Poetas*, p. 100; Pérès, *Poésie*, p. 260. The topic of the Berbers in Spain see Pérès, op. cit., p. 14f. Georges Marçais gives an *abrégé* of the history of the Zīrids, beginning from their employment by, and alienation from, the Fāṭimids, and arrives at the conclusion that at least one branch of this house acquired culture, or, as I think, more convincingly, well-administered riches. These were the rulers of Bougie. Cf. Marçais, *Architecture*, pp. 64ff.; L. Golvin, *Le Magrib central a l'époque des Zīrides*, Paris, 1957.
139. Pérès, *Poésie*, p. 334; Provençal, *Espagne*, II, pp. 1ff. (also p. 131, another reference to water jets).
140. Maqqarī, *Analectes*, I, p. 372.
141. Maqqarī, *Analectes*, I, p. 348, line 6; Abū 'l-Ḥasan ʿAlī ibn Ḥafṣ al-Jazīrī, cadi of Algeciras, flourished ca. 1100; cf. Nykl, *H.-A. Poetry*, pp. 263f.; the famous "Almansor," the first ʿĀmirid regent in Cordova (981—1002); cf. Provençal, *Espagne*, II, pp. 196ff.; 222ff.
142. Maqqarī, *Analectes*, I, pp. 425f.; this passage is also found in Ibn Ẓāfir, *Badā'iʿ al-badā'ih*, Bulāq, 1278, p. 169 (quoted as Ibn Ẓāfir, *Badā'iʿ*); cf. Pérès, *Poésie*, p. 152; p. 334, n. 2.
143. Ruled in Toledo from 1043—1075, cf. L.-Provençal, *Islam d'Occident*, Paris, 1948, p. 119; Pérès, *Poésie*, p. 294; D.-Provençal, *Histoire*, II, p. 56; III, p. 239. This ruler and his palace are mentioned in my discussion of Samuel han-Nāghīdh's water and light experiments.
144. The wording "on the left and right" (literally: "on its two sides") suggests that there were two lions spouting water into a pool, hereby producing bubbles.
145. Maqqarī, *Analectes*, I, p. 426; Ibn Ẓāfir, *ibid.;* For al-Qādir of Toledo, cf. Pérès, *Poésie*, pp. 192; 223; 263.
146. Maqqarī, *Analectes*, I, p. 322; this passage is translated by Henri Massé in *Mélanges René Basset*, Paris, 1923, I, pp. 239ff.; Pérès, *Poésie*, p. 334, n. 2. Ibn Ḥamdīs lived from 1055—1132; cf. Nykl, *H.-A. Poetry*, pp. 168ff.; Henri Massé, loc. cit., p. 239, n. 5. The many forms of the name Ibn Aʿlā 'n-nās, are discussed in Ibn Khaldūn (de Slane's translation: *Ibn Khaldoun, Histoire des Berbères*, II, pp. 51ff.).
147. Maqqarī, *Analectes*, I, p. 322, line 8 from bottom.
148. Translated also in Henri Massé, *loc. cit.*, p. 241.
149. Maqqarī, *Analectes*, I, p. 324, line 3 from bottom; Henri Massé, loc. cit., pp. 244f.
150. For Abū 'ṣ-Ṣalt Umayya, cf. Nykl, *H.-A. Poetry*, pp. 238ff.
151. Maqqarī, *Analectes*, I, p. 325; Abū 'ṣ-Ṣalt Umayya (1068—1134) cf. Nykl, *H.-A. Poetry*, p. 238. This passage is also translated by Henri Massé, loc. cit., pp. 246f.; for the castle and its builder, see ibid., n. 2.

152. Maqqari, *Analectes*, II, p. 612 Ibn Ẓāfir, *Badā'i'*, p. 212; Pérès, *Poésie*, p. 334, n. 5 'Abd al-Jalil ibn Wahbūn died 1087 or 1090; cf. Nykl, *H.-A. Poetry*, pp. 165ff.: L. Ecker, *Arabischer, provençalischer ... Minnesang*, Diss. Bern, 1934. p. 111, Abū 'l-Ḥasan ibn Bassām from Santarem (born ca. 1069), cf. Nykl. *H.-A. Poetry*, pp. 219ff. For 'Abd al-Jalīl, cf. Pérès, *Poésie*, pp. 36; 101f., et al.; Nykl, *H.-A. Poetry*, pp. 165ff.
153. For al-Mu'tamid, cf. D.-Provençal, *Histoire*, III, p. 83; Nykl, *H.-A. Poetry*, pp. 134ff.
154. Abū 'l-'Abbās ibn Huraira, known as "al-A'mā at-Tuṭīlī," i. e. "The Blind One of Tudela," died 1126; cf. Nykl, *H.-A. Poetry*, pp. 254ff.; Pérès, *Poésie*, p. 334 and *ibid.*, n. 7, 339, 415, 426. Maqqarī, *Analectes*, II, p. 275, also II, p. 336 (here the lion is described as a brass statue). Translated also in A. J. Arberry, *Moorish Poetry*, Cambridge, 1953, p. 152:

    A lion? No: if I
    More closely pry
    Methinks that I must own
    'Tis but a stone.
    Old Leo yonder sits,
    So I should say,
    And from his mouth he spits
    The Milky Way.

155. Arabic text, Miṣr, 1325, I, p. 32; R. F. Burton's translation, I, p. 67. Dr. Richard Ettinghausen's kindness in calling my attention to this passage and its quotation in von Kremer, *Culturgeschichte*, Vienna, 1875ff., II, p. 194, is gratefully acknowledged.
156. Found in F. Sarre, *Erzeugnisse Islamischer Kunst*, Berlin, 1906, pp. 10, 11; Pl. V. For the sake of completeness only, I refer to the pre-Islamic head of an army standard in the Assyrian tradition, which shows two flat lion-like supporting figures, op. cit., p. 4; Pl. I. Yemenite pre-Islamic bronze lions, producing a sound, are mentioned in al-Hamdānī, *Iklīl (Antiquities of Yemen)*, tr. N. A. Faris, Princeton, 1938, VIII, pp. 25f. These are ascribed to King Lisharḥ ibn Yaḥṣub of Saba in the first Christian century; see Detlef Nielsen, *Handbuch der Altorientalischen Altertumskunde*, Copenhagen, 1927, I, pp. 89ff., cf. Yāqūt, *Buldān*, III, p. 811.
157. Georgios Kedrenos (ca. 1100), translated from J. P. Richter, *Quellen der Byzantinischen Kunstgeschichte*, Vienna, 1897, pp. 47f. after F. Combefis, *Originum rerumque Constantinopolitanarum variis auctoribus manipulus*, Paris, 1664, and Anselmo Banduri, *Imperium Orientale sive Antiquitates Constantinopolitanae*, Paris, 1711.
158. Water emanates from beneath a sanctuary in the apocalyptic context of Ezekiel XLVII. 1ff. The arrangement of four fountains at the four corners of a building or a courtyard was an idea executed repeatedly after its reintroduction during the Italian Renaissance.
159. This statue showed Solomon holding his chin in his hand as if he were contemplating the beauty of the church and, mournfully, his own defeat by a builder of even greater ostentation. It was melted down by "Basil, the Macedonian" (the First or Second?). The sources are quoted by R. Janin, *Constantinople byzantine*, Paris, 1950, p. 157 (and 202), after Th. Preger, *Scriptores Originum Constantinopolitanarum*, Leipzig, 1901—1907, I, pp. 39ff.; II, pp. 171f. Cf. also Richter, op. cit., pp. 358; 407, from Socrates, *History of the Church*, III, XX. 11. The description of another fountain decorated with brazen cocks, he-goats, and rams is found in Richter, op. cit., p. 355, translated from Constantine Porphyrogenitus, *Basilicas*, 1833—70, p. 55; and Theophanes Continuatus, V, p. 83.

160. Odyssey, VII, 112ff.; Nonnus, *Dionysiaca*, III, vv. 140ff. Cf. E. Rohde, *Der Griechische Roman und seine Vorläufer*, Leipzig, 1914, p. 545 (515).
161. My translation from the Greek, quoted from Otmar Schissel, "Der Byzantinische Garten," in *Sitzungsberichte der Akademie der Wissenschaften in Wien, Philosophisch-historische Klasse*, vol. 221, article 2, Vienna, 1942, p. 16 (quoted as Schissel, *Garten*). Text from the Trapezuntian Digenis version, lines 1889ff.
162. Achilles Tatius, XXI, 31ff.
163. A typical simile for the flashing and mirroring illusions afforded by running water is "blades of swords," appearing, for instance, in Ibn Ḥazm's *Ring of the Dove*, Arabic ed., Damascus, 1349, p. 97; cf. also "silver ewers," in Arberry's translation, p. 191.
164. Eustathius Macrembolites, Καθ' Ὑσμινίαν καὶ Ὑσμίνην Δράμα Leipzig, 1792, pp. 10ff. Gothein, *Gartenkunst*, Jena, 1926, I, p. 146. Suggestions for this translation, kindly supplied by my colleague James Frank Gilliam, are gratefully acknowledged.
165. A rare illustration of Byzantine fountains is offered by one of the mosaics of the monastery of Daphni near Athens. It shows a fountain consisting of a "hundred-coloured marble" and an elaborate system of spouts, originating, in part, from a pinecone-shaped fountain top, as illustrated in Gothein, *Gartenkunst*, l. c.
166. Gothein, *Gartenkunst*, l. c.
167. A. Grabar, "Le succès des arts orientaux à la cour byzantine sous les Macédoniens," in *Münchener Jahrbuch der bildenden Kunst*, 3. Folge, II, 1951, pp. 32—60; also G. C. Miles, "Byzantium and the Arabs ...," in *Dumbarton Oaks Papers*, XVIII, 1964.
168. Stucco parts have been transplanted within the Alhambra halls. Inscriptions are in the process of vanishing, owing to whitewashing. According to Lafuente two lines of an inscription, which were still legible to Shakespear (see above), could no longer be read by Lafuente. Cf. Emilio Lafuente y Alcántara, *Inscripciones Árabes de Granada*, Madrid, 1859, pp. 113ff., inscription no. 77 (quoted as Lafuente, *Inscripciones*); cf. also J. Derenbourg's edition and translation of the Alhambra inscriptions in the Appendix to Girault de Prangey, *Essai*, quoted above (quoted as Derenbourg, *Appendix*).
169. The inscription doubtless has Ibn Zamrak for its author. Cf. García Gómez, *Poetas*, p. 257. The text of this inscription is found in Derenbourg, *Appendix*, pp. XVIff.; Lafuente, *Inscripciones*, pp. 120ff.; Nykl, *Inscripciones*, p. 182. Professor Anton Spitaler, in Munich, contributed various valuable textual emendations to this interpretation which are hereby gratefully acknowledged. In line 3: *shaffu;* line 4: *ʿadā*, not *ghadā*, as Nykl suggests, also *maddat*, and not *baddat* or similarly with Nykl; line 3: *murfaḍḍi 'l-jumān*. Cf. García Gómez, *Poetas*, p. 257.
170. The need for an ancestry as a support of power in Islam appears quite clearly here in the stress upon the Naṣrid ruler's being a direct descendant of the *anṣār*. With this fact, the ancestor has, so to speak, a low membership-card number of the Muslim party. There may, most likely, have been an emphasis on merit surpassing the mere fact of kinship which afforded the main authorization to the Umayyads.
171. Lafuente, *Inscripciones*, p. 120, note (a).
172. Gómez-Moreno, *Ars Hispaniae*, III, p. 328, fig. 391; discussion of the Alhambra fountain pp. 326ff.
173. Cf. Louis de Beylié, *La Kalaa des Beni-Ḥammād, une capitale berbère de l'Afrique du Nord au XIe siècle*, Paris, 1909, Pl. XXVIII. L. Golvin, *Le Magrib central*, quoted above in note 138. Very similar pieces from Persia are shown in

the Catalogue of the Exhibition of Iranian Art in Rome, 1956. Such parts often belonged to incense burners. Lions, both caryatid and water-spouting, could not be traced in any written account of this time.

174. See L. Torres Balbás, "Almería Islamica," in *Al-Andalus*, XXII, 1957, p. 432, n. 3.

175. The finds in Almeria, from the country estate of the famous ʿĀmirid majordomo, Al-Manṣūr (Almansor), include some representative plastic art, but it is in relief only and not extensive enough to allow any conclusions on a specific animal style developed in Almeria or the Cordovan workshop. See Rafael Castejón, *Alamiría*, Cordova (Tipografia Artística), n. d.

176. I have been informed that the elephant was partially hollow and spouted water out of the two tusks, but most likely not, as has been assumed, from a clearly visible hole in its forehead. Cf. *JWCI*, XIX, 1956, Pl. 44b. Pl. XXIV.

177. See discussion above, note 128 and the discussion on pp. 173ff.

178. Cf. Gómez-Moreno, *Ars Hispaniae*, III, p. 271. As to caliphal art in general, Gómez-Moreno feels they are to be credited with a "talismanic value and Oriental extraction," which I have good reason to doubt, as pointed out before. He continues (op. cit., pp. 188, 191) in connection with reliefs on parts of fountain troughs found on the grounds of the Alhambra (Fig. 246a, b. c.):

> In early Chaldean art one finds the eagle resting upon two deer, in Mycenaean art, the lion who overthrows an animal chewing the cud and bites it; these and other analogous representations appear in Hittite, Achaemenid, Ionian, and Phoenician art; finally to Byzantine art belong the eagle, lions and panthers devouring deer and hares, as well as borders with birds caught in nets. According to the mediaeval bestiary the eagle symbolizes pride, and the lion domineering force. It is therefore likely that these images were based upon an Oriental model, and conceived ... with the intent to secure for oneself victory over an enemy, the latter being symbolized by cowardly animals.

A lion attacking and overthrowing a mammal is, of course, in no way exclusively a motif of Mycenaean art, not even in origin. It is also inappropriate to contrast with each other two periods of art as far apart in time as Mycenae and Byzantium, the latter, in particular, is atypical because it had absorbed artistic motifs from the entire *orbis terrarum*. To illustrate this point, a monument, in Byzantium, of a lion overthrowing a bull was so well known that it gave the region its name, Boukoleōn. Cf. R. Janin, *Constantinople byzantine*, p. 120. For the same motif, in Byzantium, cf. also Ch. Bayet, *L'art byzantin*, Paris, 1883, p. 318, fig. 105. There are two lions like this in the Byzantine Museum in Athens, see *Guide du Musée Byzantin d'Athènes*, p. 36, fig. 8; also D. Talbot Rice, "Iranian Elements in Byzantine Art," in *IIIe Congrès International d'Art et Archéologie iraniens. Mémoires*, Leningrad, 1935, p. 205, Pl. XCI and XCIIIc, showing this and a similar carved lion in the Ottoman Museum in Istanbul.

179. L. Torres Balbás discusses the fourteen Alhambra lions and the fragment in *Ars Hispaniae*, IV, p. 193.

180. Marçais, *Architecture*, p. 351.

181. See note 178 above.

182. Torres Balbás admitted in his "Bibliography of Spanish Muslim Art," 1939–1946, in *Ars Islamica*, XV–XVI, 1951, pp. 180ff.:

> The Muslim art of Spain originated in the Orient but upon reaching the Iberian Peninsula it developed distinguishing characteristics when it came into intimate contact with Western Christian art on the same

soil. While Christian art had very little influence on the art of Islam, the inverse influence of the latter was extraordinarily fecund, manifesting itself in a new mixed art which is characteristic of Spain. From the twelfth century to the seventeenth, influences and repercussions of Muslim culture were to be encountered all over the peninsula, touching every field of artistic production.

Cf. Gómez-Moreno, *Ars Hispaniae*, III, pp. 192ff. (the chapter "Repercusiones andaluzes en oriente"). For Islamic influence upon Cistercian architecture (yet not vice versa) see Torres Balbás, *Ars Hispaniae*, IV, p. 249. (The author seems to have given up the idea of a reverse influence expressed in his "El Patio de los Leones de la Alhambra de Granada ...," in *Al-Andalus*, III, 1935, pp. 175ff.) For the after-life of Granadine art in Africa see Henri Terrasse, "Le rôle du Maghrib dans l'évolution de l'art hispano-mauresque," in *Al-Andalus*, XXIII, 1958, pp. 138ff.

183. Cf. *Beylié*, e. g. p. 110 Fig. 10.

184. See *Berühmte Kunststätten*, vol. 68 (Pompeii), pp. 113, 149, illus. 106.

185. The passage in Professor D. Schlumberger's accompanying letter reads:

> "... le bassin central de la salle d'audience (cf. *Syria*, XXIX, 1952, p. 260: "Report préliminaire" fig. 4); vous y voyez le canal d'arrivée (au premier plan), le canal de départ (au fond), et les niches semi-circulaires de la partie ouest du bassin."

Professor Schlumberger also referred me to a description of another garden basin discussed in *CRAI*, 1951, p. 11. Cf. also *The Illustrated London News*, March 25, 1951 and June 1951, p. 973.

186. For the Mosque al-Qarawiyyīn see Marçais, *Architecture*, pp. 197ff. A counterpart to the present Alhambra court is the so-called "Castillejo" of Monteagudo (Murcia). (Cf. Gómez-Moreno, *Ars Hispaniae*, III, pp. 279ff.; Marçais, *Architecture*, p. 214.) The specific tradition of a porticoed courtyard decorated with pavilions in the corners and/or with projecting pavilions in front of the central doors (covering there an ablution basin) may have had an intermediary precedent in the Mosque of the Umayyads in Damascus and possibly in the Hagia Sophia. Cf. L. de Beylié, *L'habitation byzantine*, Paris, 1902, pp. 59, 61. In Quṣair ʿAmra a basin was filled by four channels forming a cross. Cf. Ringbom, *Graltempel*, p. 67, after Ernst Diez, *Die Elemente der persischen Landschaftsmalerei und ihre Gestaltung*. Cf. Gómez-Moreno, *Ars Hispaniae*, III, pp. 279ff., in accord with L. Torres Balbás, "El Patio de los Leones ...," quoted above, l. c. Also Gómez-Moreno in Diez-Glück, *Islam*, p. 704. The channel cross of the Alhambra Court of Lions is described (together with some counterparts) in Torres Balbás, *Ars Hispaniae*, IV, p. 113. Its Iranian origin is pointed out. Two years after the first publication of my Alhambra studies, Professor Torres Balbás published a discussion of "Patios de Crucero," in *Al-Andalus*, XXIII, 1958, pp. 171ff., based in many respects upon details of my Alhambra article in the *Warburg Journal* but without referring to this (as mentioned before). The Talmud, *Berākhōth*, 50b; *Pešiqta R.*, section 37 predicts that in the messianic age God will erect seven baldaquins of gems and pearls for His Messiah. From each of these will proceed four rivers, of wine, milk, honey, and pure balsam. These four rivers of Paradise have their counterpart in the Milky Way, which divides itself into four parts; see Wünsche, *Thron*, p. 40.

187. Ernst Herzfeld, *Sāmarrā*, Berlin, 1907, p. 23. The court of the Mosque of Sāmarrā has a central rectangular water basin. Two water channels crossing each other rectangularly lead the water to and from the basin. "Groups" of debris found within this basin seem to indicate that a fountain construction *(Brunnenanlage)* rose in the basin. It may be worthwhile to mention that the

Muslim countries carry on the tradition of water fountains decorated with sculptured representations. For instance, the wealthy citizen of modern Baghdad, al-Khudaira, became famous through his *shādhrawān* in the gardens of his villa.

188. That the Naghrāllas interpreted their buildings and gardens symbolically is corroborated by Samuel han-Nāghīdh's poem on Yehōseph's juvenile landscaping: the curved water channel, encompassing the lawn island, was compared with a sky covering the earth. The combination of a garden and a fountain shaped the conception of "Paradise." For the architecture of "mystical" Founts of Life cf. Ringbom, *Graltempel*, pp. 426ff. (Cf. Song of Solomon IV. 5, comparing the beloved with a well: "A fountain of gardens, a well of living waters ..."). The introduction to Rome of the oriental idea of the "paradise" is attested by Pierre Grimal, *Les jardins romains à la fin de la République et aux deux premiers siècles de l'Empire*, Paris, 1943, pp. 86ff. Rivers in these gardens were given symbolical names by the owners in this Roman spirit "qui voulait voir dans ces jardins le symbole d'autre chose qu'eux-mêmes. L'eau était mise au service d'un exotisme un peu naïf qui s'exprime dans ces noms évocateurs: l'Euripe, le Nil ..." The Christian iconography of the four Paradise rivers is discussed by Karl Lehmann in "The Dome of Heaven," in *Art Bulletin*, XXVII, 1945, pp. 1ff. Among the pictorial materials appears an early mosaic showing Christ with the names and symbols of the four rivers, which cross each other diagonally, fig. 22. The names of the four Paradise rivers appear in a Christian sanctuary as early as that of Ostia.
189. Dr. Richard Ettinghausen of the Freer Art Gallery referred me to the stone water-basin recently excavated in the ʿAbbāsid castle of Baghdad, which has been made into an archaeological museum. Thanks to the kindness of its administration, I have been able to obtain a photo and literature concerning this basin. A description of a quadrangular pond in al-Mafjar is found in D. C. Baramki, "Excavations at Khirbet el Mefjer, IV," *Quarterly of Department of Antiquities of Palestine*, X, no. 4, 1942.
190. See *supra* in my section "*Modern Descriptions.*"
191. A topographical map like that in Torres Balbás, *Ars Hispaniae*, IV, p. 84, supports this. Cf. footnotes 39; 40; 41 *supra*. This mixed masonry, consisting of small fieldstones and surrounding layers of brick, belongs to a late Roman tradition, but it reappears in various parts of the Roman Empire, cf. R. Krautheimer, "San Nicola in Bari und die apulischen Architekten des zwölften Jahrhunderts," in *Wiener Jahrbuch für Kunstgeschichte*, IX, 1934, p. 11: "Der Wechsel von Haustein und Backsteinschichten zeigt nach dem Osten."

 The late Miss Marion E. Blake who was an expert in Roman architecture, wrote to me about this *opus mixtum:*

> It was used extensively in Pompeii and the other regions devastated by the earthquake of A. D. 62; it is found sporadically in the region about Rome during the first, second, and third centuries of the Christian era, was popularized by Maxentius, and became the common method of building during the fourth century.

192. Cf. Torres Balbás, *Alhambra antes*, p. 166.
192a. *Mémoires*, IV, p. 113 (93) .
192b. *Mémoires*, IV, pp. 101 f. (88).
193. Marçais, *Architecture*, pp. 304f. Marçais is, for a moment, quite close to ascribing the Patios de los Leones and de las Arrayanes to the earlier parts of the Palace, i. e. to the eleventh century; he writes: "*On est tenté de l'imaginer pour les deux parties du Dār al-Baḥr de la Qalʿa des Beni Ḥammād, organisées autour de deux grandes cours* ...," built, as we know by the other Zīrid dynasty

of this century. But he adds: "*Mais cela n'est rien moins que sûr*," and his map does not ascribe these two courts to the period "*antérieur à Yoûsof*."

194. Torres Balbás, *Ars Hispaniae*, IV, pp. 98 and 94 (fig. 82); and p. 52, fig. 45 on p. 49. Torres Balbás, *La Alhambra y el Generalife*, p. 56. Gómez-Moreno, *Ars Hispaniae*, p. 287; Marçais, *Architecture*, p. 235.

195. Cf. H. Terrasse, *L'art hispano-mauresque des origines au XIIIe siècle*, Paris, 1932, p. 57 (quoted as Terrasse, *L'art*); also Mrs. M. S. Byne, *The Sculptured Capital in Spain*, New York, no date, text below Plate 37. Mrs. Byne categorizes this type of capital (showing the capital standing on its head) as a "severe type introduced into Andalusia by the reforming Almohades." The truth seems, rather, to be that this strongly orientalized type was developed in Umayyad Spain with other imported elements. On the same page of Mrs. Byne's book is shown a "black marble capital of unadorned type in the Harem (of the Alhambra) which is probably from an earlier building." This motif, somewhat akin to Visigothic art *de palmes à bandeau* appears also on the capitals in the Alhambra courts of the Alberca and of the Lions. Cf. Terrasse, *L'art*, p. 57. Cf. A. F. Calvert, *The Alhambra*, Plates XXII and XXIII, and Byne, l. c., plate 36 (the same flat lotus-leaf-like ribbon motif which is actually a rudimentary form of a Corinthian capital without the acanthus detail and as such quite common in the Christian orbit as well, appears in capitals of the Mosque of Ceuta, completed 1346–47, and in Sicily). Cf. Torres Balbás, *Ars Hispaniae*, IV, pp. 143, 49, 138; Marçais, *Architecture*, p. 235.

196. One capital of a column in the Alhambra Museum of the 'wasp's nest' type is described as follows in Mrs. Byne's book, *The Sculptured Capital in Spain* (her texts below the two pictures have to be interchanged): "XIV century, Mohammedan, Museum of the Alhambra Palace, Granada. Capital suggesting a late return to the 'wasp's nest' type." The excavations of Madīnat az-Zahrā' unearthed various capitals of this type belonging to the tenth century. Cf. Ricardo V. Bosco, *Medina Azzahra y Alamiriya*, Madrid, 1912, Plate XXVf.; M. E. Gómez-Moreno, *Mil Joyas*, p. 95. There is, of course, no necessity for the assumption that there was a late return to this style; however, the continuation of a rather undiluted Byzantine style in works of the tenth and eleventh centuries appears here. A comparison of this Alhambra capital (assuming that this capital was found on the grounds of the Alhambra) with those of SS. Sergius and Bacchus in Constantinople or St. Demetrius in Salonica might demonstrate the above dependence. Cf., for instance, Charles Diehl, *Manuel d'art byzantin*, I, pp. 144, 191. Other capitals of the "wasp nest" type preserved in the museum of the Alhambra were published in *Al-Andalus*, IV, 1936–39, p. 176 and VI, Plate 3a after page 424. Here the capitals are said to have come from the bath of Bādīs's Palace on the Albaicin Hill and to date from the tenth century. Cf. Terrasse, *L'art*, plate XXVIII, after page 156.

197. Cf. Terrasse, *L'art*, p. 366 and plate LXIII.

198. L. Torres Balbás, "Aleros Nazaries," in *Al-Andalus*, XVI, 1951, pp. 174ff. For the conservatism of the style of wooden architecture compare German Renaissance frame buildings, which still show Gothic wood decoration. There are in the Alhambra, however, corbels decorated in a naturalistic style and ascribed by Gómez-Moreno to the twelfth century, for which there is a counterpart in the mosque of Tlemcen, built in 1135 and with slight later variations, in fact, all over North Africa. An example appears in Torres Balbás, l. c., p. 169.

199. L.-Provençal's assumption seems to be based upon al-Idrīsī's report of the despoliation of Elvira by Ḥabbūs in favor of his new capital Granada. Cf.

Description de l'Afrique et de l'Espagne par Edrisi, ed. Dozy et de Goeje, Leyden, 1866, pp. 203, 250.

200. See above, note 128.

201. The specific tendencies of this architecture could be summarized as a tendency toward the illusory *(trompe l'oeil)* including an attempt at interchanging the appearances of the solid and the fluid, and also at mirroring, and at the iridescent, the latter being accomplished by the insertion of precious stones into surfaces with light playing on them. For this ideal the dove's necklace remained the current symbol. It was chosen as the name for Ibn Ḥazm's book and referred to in our Alhambra poem, in distich 30, and elsewhere in Ibn Gabirol. For the θαυματοποιικὴ τέχνη in Byzantium compare Gervase Mathew, *Byzantine Aesthetics*, London, 1963, p. 113.

To give an impression of a contemporary's reaction to the pseudo-magic of Byzantine architecture I quote from Procopius:

> ... And upon this circle rests the huge spherical dome which makes this structure exceptionally beautiful. Yet it seems not to rest upon solid masonry, but to cover the space with its golden dome suspended from Heaven. All these details, fitted together with incredible skill in mid-air and floating off from each other and resting only on the parts next to them, produce a single and most extraordinary harmony on the work, and yet do not permit the spectator to linger much over the study of any of them, but each detail attracts the eye and draws it irresistably to itself ... the beholder is utterly unable to select which particular detail he should admire more than all the others ... observers are still unable to understand the skilful craftsmanship, but they always depart from there overwhelmed by the bewildering sight.
>
> Procopius, *Buildings*, *Opera*, VII (Loeb), pp. 21 ff.

Another testimony is Eusebius' panegyric on the building of churches addressed to Paulinus, bishop of the Tyrians, in which he uses expressions like "The dazzling appearance of the workmanship ... the loftiness that reacheth heaven ..." And he draws a parallel between the actual building and the cosmic house of God, the Church which was itself "the edifice the Son of God created in His own edifice ..."

Eusebius, *Historia Ecclesiastica*, X, (Loeb, II), IV, 2 ff., quoted after Baldwin Smith, *The Dome*, Princeton, N. J., 1950, p. 92.

202. The Hebrew word *qubbāh* meaning "dome" or "vaulted hall" often used to mean "mausoleum" ('alcove') has the same meaning (and equivalent phoneme) in Arabic. This word, with its occurrence in Numbers XXV. 8, interpreted, by some, to mean "the Tent of Meeting," has, with this, other overtones.

203. Cf. Ringbom, *Graltempel*, p. 69, note 28. As in so many instances, there was the precedent of an ancient Roman interfusion between the ancient East, Rome and/or Byzantium. Axel Boëthius quotes the "Phengitis temple of Fortuna of the Domus Aurea" described by Pliny XXXVI, 163. Boëthius, *The Golden House of Nero*, Ann Arbor, 1960, p. 121, n. 39.

204. For this topic: Ernst Herzfeld, "Der Thron des Khosro," in *Jahrbuch der Preussischen Kunstsammlungen*, XLI, 1920, p. 145; also F. Saxl, "Frühes Christentum und spätes Heidentum in ihren künstlerischen Ausdrucksformen," in *Wiener Jahrbuch für Kunstgeschichte*, II (XVI), 1923, p. 63 (esp. pp. 102 ff.). Cf. Ringbom, *Graltempel*, pp. 71 f. (58–64); H. P. L'Orange, *Cosmic Kingship*, pp. 18 ff.; 28 ff.

205. P. Frankl, *The Gothic: Literary Sources and Interpretations through Eight Centuries*, Princeton, 1960, pp. 161 ff. I am much indebted to the late Professor Frankl for having let me use his book while it was still in manuscript. The great

modern architect, Frank Lloyd Wright, could not possibly overlook this architects' boon. Near Eastern influence embodied in the spiral of Hadrian's Roman mausoleum and that in the minaret of Sāmarrā re-appears in his Guggenheim Museum, New York; however, the modern architect has to mask his fantasy with functionalism. The same refers to the Arizona desert villa.

206. H. P. L'Orange, "Domus Aurea" in *Serta Eitremiana*, Oslo, 1942, pp. 68ff.; for Nero *ibid.*, p. 72; p. 78.

207. Maqqarī, *Analectes*, I, p. 346; Maqqarī, *Dynasties*, I, pp. 231f.

208. The sources of the "fairy-tale" tradition contributing to the architects' design of imaginative domes are connected with mediaeval legends concerning Solomon, and mainly centering upon a submarine dome and an aerial city. The following Islamic account is found in Abū Manṣūr ʿAbd al-Malik ath-Thaʿālibī, *K. qiṣaṣ al-anbiyā'*, Cairo, A. H. 1324, p. 190 (born 961 in Nīsābūr, *G. A. L.*, I, p. 284), quoted after M. Asín Palacios, *Islam and the Divine Comedy*, London, 1926, p. 211.

> Solomon sees rising from the bottom of the sea a pavilion, tent, tabernacle, or tower, vaulted like a dome, which is made of crystal and is beaten by the waves ... The aerial city is erected by the genii at the order of Solomon, who bids them build him a city or palace of crystal a hundred thousand fathoms in extent and a thousand storeys high, of solid foundations but with a dome airy and lighter than water; the whole to be transparent so that the light of the sun and the moon may penetrate its walls; a white cupola, surmounting the highest storey and crowned by a brilliant banner, with a resplendent light lit up the route of Solomon's army during the night, when the king floating through space in his aerial castle ...

For Jewish sources on Solomon's glass palace see Ginzberg, *Legends*, IV, p. 145; VI, p. 289. For Solomon's dominion over spirits, ibid., VI, p. 291. For the same motif in Iraq as a precedent for Spain, see Al-Buḥturī's ode to Yūnis ibn Baghā (*Diwan*, Istanbul, 1300, vv. 14—16; "... palace covered with crystal glasses — the jinns of Sulaimān would fall down" before it).

209. Found in Derenbourg, *Appendix*, p. XXII, no. 11—12.

210. In this way inscription No. 13, Derenbourg (*Appendix*, p. XXIV), of the fourth hall in the south, a poem above the two false windows looking towards the gardens, verse 6, speaks of a palace of crystal, beginning *dhāka ṣarḥ az-zajjāj*. The openings above doors, like those now extant at the Alhambra, which afford an artistically desirable chiaroscuro, may be explained, in part, by functional needs: (1) to keep people, chiefly women, hidden but still able to watch proceedings from their upper floor, and (2) to provide a source of light and ventilation when the massive doors were closed. See Torres Balbás, "Salas con Linterna Central en la Arquitectura Granadina," in *Al-Andalus*, XXIV, 1959, pp. 198ff. Albert J. Gayet, *L'art arabe*, Paris, 1893, p. 179, interprets the role played by glass in Arab architecture as follows:

> ... par la nature du vitrail, les pleins l'emportent de beaucoup sur les vides, et sous la lumière translucide du ciel pale de l'Orient, les rayons filtrés à travers le rouge des tulipes, le violet des jacinthes ... tombent dans la nef en poudroiement d'opale, d'or, de pourpre, de saphir, et d'émeraude, et c'est un jour si assourdi et si mélancolique! ... il semble venir de si loin! ...

211. See Wünsche, *Thron*, pp. 32 and 40.

212. *The Arabian Nights* (German Insel edition), Wiesbaden, 1953, V, p. 88.

213. Nykl, *Inscripciones*, p. 181. Professor Nykl does not seem to be aware that this ceiling is not the original one. For such Solomonic throne and heaven symbolism as in the two following Alhambra inscriptions compare *Midrash Rabbā* to Exodus XV. 26, London, 1939, p. 196:

> God made six heavens and resides in the seventh, and of Solomon we read there were six steps to the Throne (1 Kings V. 18) while he himself sat on the seventh.

Ginzberg, *Legends*, IV, pp. 157 ff.

214. Lafuente, *Inscripciones*, pp. 113 ff., Inscription No. 77; Derenbourg, *Appendix*, pp. XV ff., no. 9.

215. Théophile Gautier in his *Affinitées secrètes*, dedicated to the Alhambra, seems to express a related phenomenon:

> Marbre, perle, rose, colombe,
> Tout se dissout, tout se détruit;
> La perle fond, le marbre tombe,
> La fleur se fane et l'oiseau fuit.

216. Professor Oleg Grabar has referred me to roaring lions in mediaeval accounts of the pre-Islamic architecture of Yemen in al-Hamdānī, *Antiquities of Yemen*. These are partly edited by D. H. Müller, *Südarabische Alterthümer im Kunsthistorischen Hofmuseum*, Vienna, 1899, in an appendix; and in a complete Arabic edition of the *Iklīl* made by N. A. Faris, Princeton, N. J., 1940, vol. VIII, pp. 25 f. These are, of course, related to the ancient oriental lions, but they are interesting in indicating yet another way in which the idea penetrated into Islam.

PART III

The Alhambra Palace – Literary Studies

Wer das Dichten will verstehen,
Muss ins Land der Dichtung gehen;
Wer den Dichter will verstehen,
Muss in Dichters Lande gehen.

Motto to Goethe's Notes to his *West-Eastern Diwan.*

The interrelating of logic and rhetoric as sister-disciplines is especially clear at this point, and their combined influence upon the neighboring art of poetry can be seen in the form of organization of the short poems, and of the long images in longer poems, which have come down to us from this period.

Rosemond Tuve, *Elizabethan & Metaphysical Imagery,*
Chicago, 1963, p. 300

A. Introduction

Nature Poetry of the Eleventh Century

Ibn Gabirol's poem, in which he describes the Alhambra Palace of Yehōšeph ibn Naghrālla, a palace, so highly 'literary' (to quote Oleg Grabar), belongs as much to the contemporary genre of "love poems in homage to a patron" as to the genre of description of gardens and buildings, and moreover the poem conveys the general spirit of the patron's architecture in buildings and gardens. For the purpose of determining the documentary value of this Hebrew poem I pause to investigate contemporary Arabic poetry and to discover in it the poet's models and masters. Confronted with these, the specific intent and talent of Ibn Gabirol may appear more clearly, and, by contrast, general differences between Hebrew and Arab poetry may be observed. Finally, a comparison between, and an assessment of the quality of these works will elucidate the literary and philosophical tendencies of the Jewish minority and also those of the Arab majority. Thus we shall discover certain ideas not fully developed in the Arabic literature of Andalusia or at least not documented among the Arabs anywhere. These ideas may very well represent the Jewish transformation of Arabic concepts. Often in their history the Jews have proved themselves able to adopt, more rapidly, activities which developed at a slower but steady pace among the more settled population of their neighbor nation; or, to change the metaphor, they sometimes produced a rather shrill descant to the more sonorous alto and bass harmonies of their contemporaries.

If we compare Ibn Gabirol's work with contemporary Arabic garden poetry, based upon ever-repeated standard metaphors, and the similar descriptions of castles, which are lacking in poetical mood, we discover that Ibn Gabirol strives for a *melos* and fills his poems with the pathos of his quasi-religious plight. He does not succeed everywhere in transcending the limits of the craftsman and the craftman's aggregation of topics. But the very recasting of what is in Arabic hackneyed and derivative may add in newly re-coined Hebrew a great deal of musicality. Something of the unique breath of a Job or a Second Isaiah, with their passionate religious intensity (by which the Arabic writers are untouched), permeates so much of Ibn Gabirol's personality that, even where he wishes to be an Arabic poet in the Hebrew language, the Old Testament, so to speak, takes over. If this sounds like an exaggeration, then I should modify the statement and say that, in this poetry, generated by a late Hebrew tradition, in a new contact with the Semitic sources, some parts of the Old Testament assumed once more for this generation their pristine resonance. The Hispano-Hebrew poets must have felt the kinship of their own Song of Deborah with old Arabian battle poetry, of *Canticles* with Arab love poetry, and many lines of *Job*, *Proverbs*, and *Psalms* in their relation to the wealth of gnomic poetry and even the Koran of the Arabs.

In many cases we shall observe what of Arabic descriptive poetry is not employed by Ibn Gabirol and from this draw conclusions about his reservations in the use of his models, his natural remoteness from the forms of contemporary taste and tradition.

(1) A BEE AND A PALM POEM

I compare, as a marginal illustration, Ibn Gabirol's Bee Poem, in itself a nature poem, with the earlier Palm-Tree Poem of the Umayyad ʿAbd ar-Raḥmān I,

The Bee

Le-iṭṭ-ekh dabberī Schirmann: *Shīrāh* I, 220

⏑ - - - ⏑ - - - ⏑ - - *(Wāfir)* Rhyme: *-ōrāh (-ōrā)*

Ju. V. 12 Softly sound forth your hosanna, oh Bee,
that "Hear, oh Israel," hummed on in your fashion,

Talm. Ber. LX. 72 Professing God as "One," drawing out its n-n,
Talm. Ber. II. 4 rapt in your praying to the Awesome and High,

Him Who placed honey beneath your tongue
Deut. VI. 19 and, to repel your foes, also bitter gall.

Though small in your own eye, distinguished
are you, a firstborn's right is yours:

Dan. X. 11 You, purified by charms, are set apart,
Numbers XI. 20 no longer swarming insect: nay purest lord of wings.

The Palm Tree

'Abd ar-Raḥmān I: *Yā nakhlu*

--⏑- ⏑⏑-⏑- -- *(Kāmil)*

Maqqarī: *Analectes* II, p. 41

Maqqarī: *Dynasties* II, pp. 419; 422f.

Dozy: *Notices*, p. 34 from Ibn al-Abbār: *al-Ḥulla as-siyarā'*

Nykl: *Poetry*, p. 18

Rhyme: *-li (lī)*

A poem is addressed to a "date palm he had planted in the garden of his country seat called ar-Ruṣāfa, a replica of his uncle's country seat near Damascus" (between Palmyra and the Euphrates):

O palm tree that I behold in ar-Ruṣāfa,
far in the West, far from the palm tree land:

I said: You, like myself, are far away, in a strange land;
how long have I been far away from my people!

You grew up in a land where you are a stranger,
and, like myself, are living in the farthest corner of the earth:

May the morning clouds refresh you at this distance,
and may abundant rains comfort you forever!

We discover that, in either poem, the author identifies himself with a certain natural being. The *tertia comparationis* in Ibn Gabirol's poem between himself, the poet, and the bee, are a) his small size and insignificant position according to the clumsy face-value judgment of his fellow 'beings', b) the devotion to a task of gathering, c) the pious sound of prayer, incessantly uttered by the two as in a mystic rapture, d) the harboring of sweetness and the ability to sting, e) an intensity and almost tragic and heroic quality, by virtue of which the poet's given standing in this world is transcended in the direction of a true reality. Similarly, the *tertia comparationis* between the Umayyad poet-ruler and the palm tree are a) the climatic and general environmental displacement from the East. The other *tertia*, which appear in the subjunctive mood, make it clear that, b) the palm-tree would, very much like the poet, weep for their true company in the East in which they would live "naturally," c) both seem to be forgetful of these friends. The beauty of this latter poem may be found in its greater playfulness, its freer flow, its lesser condensation, and the absence of a learned quality. Whereas the Arabic poem is a mood, the Hebrew poem is "existence." The blessing at the end of ʿAbd ar-Raḥmān's poem, an address *(iltifāt)* to a loved Thou, and more than a make-believe Thou to the poet, is powerful. For such benedictions of a place or other natural feature, compare the Arabic model quoted by al-Bāqillānī, "May you be given water by abundant rain, oh ye tents," or "May you always be at the watercourse and in the green woods (oh doves)[1]!"

If we compare these two poems with the famous cicada poem by Anacreon in which the Greek poet in his old age saw himself as a dispassionate, unconcerned being, by now a sapless creature of the earth, carrying on his 'song' without any disturbance by passion from without or within himself, Ibn Gabirol's poem is in its Hebrew imagery, despite its learned Jewish allusions, quite alien to the feeling of normative Judaism. The poem is as individualized as its Arabic and Greek models.

Ibn Gabirol's poem shows the typical syncretism of his school. According to the pagan ideal, the bee symbolizes the knightly Arab bard, who is gall to his enemies and honey to his friends. Ibn Gabirol, by making the bee into a mystic also and a pious Hebrew adorant, is not able to avoid a discrepancy and may thus allow us to observe that his personality is split between two opposed cultural ideals. This need not, it is true, be a specifically Hebrew predicament: an Arab, or even a Renaissance writer such as Boccaccio — or, as Nietzsche thinks, Spinoza — may be subject to a similar cleavage. But the imagery in which Ibn Gabirol's poem is couched, involving Rabbi Akiba, is thoroughly Hebrew. Neither of the two poems can be regarded as conventional nature poems. Both the bee and the palm are images for the poet's other self, not objects for description: they are more felt than seen and, in many ways, reduced to a *tertium comparationis*.

I insert a brief characterization of the Arabic nature poetry and, in particular, of the descriptive Arabic poetry roughly contemporary with Solomon ibn Gabirol. I do so as an attempt to understand the Arab reaction to nature as apparent in nature poetry and garden architecture in their literary and historical development. The sources of inspiration for garden architecture were Hellenistic, found by the conquering Arabs in countries like Syria and Egypt during the "conquest of the countries." Byzantine artists carried out mosaics and frescoes for the early Umayyad buildings sacred and as "profane" as that of Quṣair ʿAmra. Among the mosaics of the Umayyad mosque of Damascus we find medallions portraying ideal

Note 1

Hellenistic buildings surrounded by gardens. This should put the survival of Greco-Roman motifs in Arab artistry beyond question. The Arabs also found in countries like Syria enough living Hellenistic poetry and teachers of stylistics to derive from them a vivid inspiration for creating new types of poetry in their own language. "Rūmī" female slave singers were imported into the Arabian home country and, gaining there a new position in society, helped to deepen the appreciation and production of art. With the Arabs, however, rests the merit of having been enthusiastic and able enough to transform a primitive eclecticism into a mature syncretism.

(2) ARABIC NATURE POETRY — ITS DEVELOPMENT

The main counterparts to Ibn Gabirol's nature poem which are also, in part, his models are the great Arab nature poems composed in Iraq, Syria, and Spain. Such poems are mostly inspired by the gardens of the poets' patrons. Notwithstanding the fact that such poems were written to order, the inspiring effect of gardens is truly apparent in them. Not infrequently, also, natural scenery not shaped by the human hand is the subject. The great names of the Arabic nature poets in Spain are Ibn Khafāja, Ibn as-Sīd al-Baṭalyausī, Ibn ʿAmmār, ʿAbd al-Jalīl ibn Wahbūn, Ibn Ḥamdīs (from Sicily). Among these, Ibn Khafāja, in particular, was called the Garden Poet. Their models in turn were the Irāqī poets of the ninth and tenth centuries, and chiefly those of the ʿAbbāsid court, such as al-Buḥturī (d. 897), Ibn al-Muʿtazz (d. 908), and aṣ-Ṣanaubarī (d. 945)[2].

The earliest Arabic poetry preserved, belonging to the time shortly before and contemporary with the rise of Islam, excels less in thematic composition than in the art of description. It impresses us by its naive realism or naturalism, which goes along with very elaborate formal rules of meter and monorhyme. The models remain at all times the famous Muʿallaqāt and the large bulk of tribal poetry like that of the Hudhaylites. The urbanized poetry of the Umayyad and ʿAbbāsid caliphates, however, becomes more and more conceptual and limits and slants its scope of visual and experiential reality remarkably in favor of an artistic variation of certain themes: the previously autonomous love and nature poetry was replaced by poetry in which an autonomous artistry seems to override the naive interest in the *sujet*. This development was never really reversed, at least in the Middle Ages, not even by that popular branch of poetry which deviated from the old literary standards, developing the popular genres of *zajal* and *muwashshaḥ*. Instead of the old naively descriptive poetry, however, new genres are developed, in addition to conceptual poetry, which incorporate abstract philosophical and religious ideas. As a first document I cite the description of Paradise in the Koran:[3]

Notes 2—3

> The stars and the trees adore. And the sky He hath uplifted; and He hath set the measure, That ye exceed not the measure, But observe the measure strictly, nor fall short thereof. And the earth hath He appointed for [His] creatures, Wherein are fruit and sheathed palm-trees, Husked grain and scented herb.

Or another:[4]

> But for him who feareth the standing before his Lord there are two gardens. ... Of spreading branches. ... Wherein are two fountains flowing. ... Wherein is every kind of fruit in pairs. ... Reclining upon couches lined with silk brocade, the fruit of both gardens near to hand. ... Therein are those of modest gaze, whom neither man nor jinni will have touched before them, ... [In beauty] like the jacynth and the coral-stone. ... Is the reward of goodness aught save goodness? ... And beside them are two other gardens, ... Dark green with foliage. ... Wherein are two abundant springs. ... Wherein is fruit, the date-palm and pomegranate. ... Wherein [are found] the good and beautiful ... Fair ones, close-guarded in pavilions ... Whom neither man nor jinni will have touched before them ... Reclining on green cushions and fair carpets.

Or a third passage:[5]

> Oh ye who believe! Turn unto Allah in sincere repentance! It may be that your Lord will remit from you your evil deeds and bring you into Gardens underneath which rivers flow, on the day when Allah will not abase the Prophet and those who believe with him. Their light will run before them and on their right hands: they will say: Our Lord! Perfect our light for us, and forgive us! Lo! Thou art able to do all things.

A last passage:[6]

> And the foremost in the race, the foremost in the race: those are they who will be brought nigh in gardens of delight; a multitude of those of old and a few of those of later time, on lined couches, reclining therein face to face. There wait on them immortal youths with bowls and ewers and a cup from a pure spring wherefrom they get no aching of the head nor any madness, and fruit that they prefer and flesh of fowls that they desire. And [there are] fair ones with wide, lovely eyes, like unto hidden pearls, reward for what they used to do. There hear they no vain speaking nor recrimination [naught] but the saying: Peace, [and again] Peace. And those on the right hand; what of those

on the right hand? Among the thornless lote trees and clustered plantains, and spreading shade, and water gushing, and fruit in plenty neither out of reach nor yet forbidden, and raised couches; Lo! We have created them a [new] creation and made them virgins, lovers, friends, for those on the right hand . . .

For the son of the arid peninsula the Iberian gardens, richly irrigated, offering shade, beautiful colors and aromas — there is strangely no reference to scents in the Koranic passages — were in themselves Paradise, even if they did not contain houris. His hopes for the future Beyond were nourished by impressions and memories of rich gardens in more highly favored places even than those of "Arabia Felix." Literary sources describing Paradise were known to Muḥammad from the Bible and Jewish and Christian oral tradition, where they in turn were nourished by sources as old as the Gilgamesh epic. The Arab's anticipation was thus "no more desert," which means no more thirst and no more deprivation, but eternal oases with sweet and abundant water from wells which exhale freshness, with cooling noises and, in addition, fruits which can be plucked while lying — all this besides other comforts. No doubt tapestries, carried on desert journeys, also inspired fancies of gardens and kept up the yearning for Paradise (with, possibly, an inherent admonition to virtue).

Secular Arabic nature poetry seems to begin around 600. Stereotyped as this oldest school was in its main motifs and in its "flat key," it describes the *aṭlāl*, the places where the beloved once camped with her tribe in the sands and where now the sands begin to cover the last traces of happy hours in an even more deserted desert. The sleepless poet, "pasturing the stars," may describe the night sky beneath which he voices his complaints. What else does he have to describe here but the desert, the beloved, and his own feelings! Besides these, the occasional oases are, of course, as mentioned, the blessed abodes, inviting description as well. Their and her image or mirage may transport the poet from the hardship of his desert faring, and make him willing to pay the price of being doubly miserable when re-awaking to reality. Natural events of the desert, such as thunderstorms and inundations, brought about by the swelling wadis, are also depicted. Although, with growing urbanization, the cities, with all their fairy-tale splendor, became objects of poetization, the "call of the desert" was not lost upon the city dweller for a long time, and poetry kept this alive in the ever-repeated classic topic of the *aṭlāl*.

The excitement evoked by the abundance of nature can be felt, for instance, in the *Arabian Nights* and also among the historians, where rhymed prose passages and metrical poetry as an expression of *hypsos* are inserted. During the ʿAbbāsid period the garden became the preferred object of the poets; Abū Nuwās, one of the ʿAbbāsid's house poets, numbers a garden among the four desirable things of life, together with "water, wine and a beautiful face[7]." As to the natural scenery, the ideal is, according to von Grunebaum, a bright and friendly landscape, a well-watered plain, perhaps surrounded by mountains. Spring is the season the poet loves best, and joy and gracefulness are the ambients which he hopes to find and to establish. The courtly climate demands the pleasant. "Elegance," in von Grunebaum's words, "replaces grandeur," just as "playful wit" replaces the "exertion and danger" of previous periods. Even "if a catastrophe is chosen as the subject the poet offers a lively, precise, but still smiling vignette. The power of rendering the forceful and indomitable aspect of nature is lost"[8] and Abū Nuwās, for example, dares to admit that he loathes leaving comfortable Baghdad in order to undertake the strenuous pilgrimage to Mecca[9]. Scenes depicting both untamed nature and royal palaces, along with, preferably, ruins, appear in the poems of the ʿAbbāsid school.

The Syrian poets a century later, aṣ-Ṣanaubarī and Sarī ar-Raffāʾ, show a marked skill in describing the cities of Aleppo and Mosul. Although Ibn Qutaiba (d. 889)[10] attempted, as a conservative stylistic arbiter, to restrict the poets in their customary description of flowers (mainly employed in their *munāẓaras*, 'tensons') to those of the desert instead of the domesticated rose and narcissus, the city-dwelling poets of the following centuries developed a particular mastery in portraying the fruits and flowers of the garden. During the Umayyad period, which ended around 750 in the east, with the rise of the ʿAbbāsids[11], a certain quasi-sentimental transposition of a natural event into the sphere of metaphors connected with the human body and human emotions, which can be traced faintly in the old Arabian poetry, had been resumed and developed further. The house poets of this dynasty, however, discarded "the romantic attitude" and tended more to a sober realism and precision of high artistry than to personification and animation. They aimed rather at description than at sentimental interpretation. This is the time when the most daring comparisons develop, so to speak, a life of their own, and when occasionally two or more metaphors form almost a second level of a fantastic causation in the sphere of an as-if-reality. In this the poet, to use Hellmut Ritter's language[12], makes the *juxta id* the *propter id*.

Von Grunebaum, following Ritter, quotes as an example that line by Ibn Muʿtazz used by me above to illustrate distich 21 of Ibn Gabirol's "Great Nature Poem":

Notes 7—12

As if, when the light of the morn urged darkness to hurry away,
we would stir up a raven with white wing tips ...

He also quotes in this connection al-Buḥturī's line:

You see him in the darkness fight and you imagine him
to be a Moon[13] attacking the enemy with a star ...

which I employed to interpret the first battle poem by Samuel han-Nāghīdh (dist. 64, in my German book on Ibn Gabirol). The metaphor of the moon with the star as its missile belongs to a fantastic level of reality, in which the events described are no longer related to the soul of the poet. The celestial bodies are here elevated into animated acting and feeling beings, which interpret in some way the poet's fanciful mood (which was the Umayyad poets' technique).

There would be, therefore, a certain justification in the detection of a predominantly ʿAbbāsid heritage in Samuel han-Nāghīdh's battle descriptions and a typical Umayyad tradition in Ibn Gabirol's nature poems, particularly in his Rose Poem, which I interpret later on.

What seems to a Western observer to be the weakness of Arabic poetry is that, even if it is able to bring into being this fantastic level above reality and thus create many poems of "conspicuous beauty ...," its manner of perception contributes "... to removing Arabic poetry from life, from reality, and to freezing it, as it were, at a stage where the decorative had become the leading viewpoint, and where variety could only be maintained by ever-growing affectation, and the admission into description of *recherché* witticism[14]." That poem of Ibn Gabirol's in which he describes his skin disease, would be an acme of such ʿAbbāsid recherché witticism. On the other hand, such a poem, although it is so blatant an aberration of taste, accomplishes its purpose to horrify a reader into sympathy. Under the Umayyad caliphs of Spain, and in the poems of the first ʿAbd ar-Raḥmān, sentimental animation and personification reappear, as for instance in this Umayyad's palm poem, and reach their zenith in Ibn Khafāja. Ritter's observation, in his book on Niẓāmī, that Arabic and Persian poetry does not possess a mood pervasive and powerful enough to enmesh the hearer in its dynamics, applies in particular to nature poetry; but the aesthetic effect exerted, especially upon the susceptible connoisseur, must not be underrated. I have mentioned that the Arabic kasida is in many ways a rather loose sequence of units perfect in themselves, linked only by the monorhyme. The comparison with a string of pearls, within which the individual gem may gain as much as it loses, is thus the appropriate one. The order intended by the poet for these kasidas was frequently not entirely clear, and one sometimes even receives the impression that the poet has deliberately upset their logical order. (I shall discuss this phenomenon in Samuel's first battle poem, which was modeled after early Arabic battle poems, in a subsequent study.) Long-lived oral tradition and the habit of quoting individual distichs may have added to the confusion. Ibn Gabirol's Bee Poem and his philosophical poem show a definite logical process, but the sentimental is chastely hidden. It is to modern European poets like Ezra Pound, with an intellectual orientation, that one must turn for help in leading us to a greater appreciation of this Arabic and Hebrew poetry where, in particular, the avoidance of nineteenth-century Victorian sentimentality makes itself blissfully felt.

(3) POETICAL DESCRIPTIONS OF EDIFICES IN SPAIN

Owing to the salaried position of the poets, descriptions of the princes' gardens and cities are prevalent, but we also find descriptions of untouched scenery. Thus the nature which the poet was employed to praise was mostly, so to speak, courtly, a landscape with buildings commissioned by a sovereign for his residence. This recurrence of ancient tradition in Arab Spain anticipates the Italian Renaissance, and is yet one further justification for speaking of the arts of that time and place in terms of a renascence. It may be noted that the financial ledger of the wealthy Chigi family recorded as the fee for a laureate poet like Egidio Gallo, hired to praise the creation of the Farnesina, "10 ducats for the poet XY[15]." But we must beware of terming the feeling for nature of the Arab patrons and nature poets superficial and mercenary. The fact that a poet praises a landscape or garden created by or for his patron does not exclude his enchantment by untouched nature. The German poet Jean Paul, for example, was inspired to write his glorious landscape descriptions both by contrived French gardens and "natural" English parks. A current of water, whether natural or artificial, and shrubs, either allowed to grow naturally or trimmed in hedges, can be equally appealing under the glow of sunset. It is true that preferences vary with times and persons, but the possibilities of admiration remain constant.

Turning now to descriptions of buildings, I quote first the praise by Ibn Ḥamdīs (born 1055) from Sicily of a palace in Seville built by al-Mu'tamid 'Alā 'llāh (ruled 1088—1091), of which we shall hear more (although this poet belonged to a generation later than Ibn Gabirol):[16]

Notes 15—16

35 Superb habitation like this for which God decided
that all power be ever renewed there, never to perish.

A hallowed habitation! If Moses, God's spokesman, had traced his steps
over its ground, he would have doffed his sandal.

Nothing else it is but the prince's abode
before whom everyone hopefully deposits his burdens.

When its portals fling open you might think they exclaimed
with grace to the one passing through them, "Welcome!"

[The builders] implanted the prince's traits in the building,
and they accomplished this transformation:

40 They created, at the royal bidding, a great hall
and little lacks that it rise to the clouds[17].

In truth they took its breadth from his breast, from the complexion of his face its brilliance,
from his renown the decoration and from his largesse its firm distribution.

His rank among the kings was taken as a model that proportioned the elevation of its audience hall,
and, owing to this, it rises beyond the constellation of Arcturus and the Virgin's Spica[18].

It made me forget the palace of the Khosros
for it shows me that its master is in merits incomparable.

44 As if Solomon, the son of David, whose terror
did not allow respite to the jinn in its construction ...

48 You see there the sun like unto a wool-padded inkwell
out of which hands draw their designs by which they reproduce those of the sun.

49 These designs are moving, although they are immovable
and the hand does not follow the foot when these shapes move about ...

56 When we are blinded by the brilliance of the sunlight
we use the splendor of the hall as a salve for our eyes.

Notes 17—18

Distich 40 in this poem is vaguely reminiscent of distich 6 in Ibn Gabirol's Alhambra poem and distich 41 of Ibn Gabirol's distich 36. We encounter very little direct observation but most abstract and far-fetched plays upon words, recherché metaphors, and allegory at its worst. The same poet praises a palace built in Bougie by al-Manṣūr Aʿlā n'-nās who ruled 1088–1104:[19]

Its constructions would have embarrassed the ancient Persians
who erected the buildings and laid out well the plans;

The centuries passed in review for the Romans, but they built
for their emperors nothing similar nor comparable.

You remind us of Paradise when you show us the high chambers
and palaces whose structure you caused to rise.

Virtuous people, when seeing it, increase their good works
Sura XXXV. 30; LVI. 12 — and hope for such a Paradise and silken garments.

Sura II. 136 etc. — Whereas the sinners turn towards the bridge Ṣirāṭ,
so that their good works blot out in full their faults.

This is a heaven betwixt heavens, and
disregarding even full moons, he makes al-Manṣūr shine forth.

I looked at him, and what I saw was the most admirable sight;
Sura LXVII. 4 — then I turned away, my eye being wearied,

And I believed myself to dream when I saw the prince,
so great in this palace.

And when the young servants open its gates,
they do so whispering "Welcome!" to the guests.

Lions bite the rings of the doors,
and their jaws are opened to show their fangs;

It seems as though these lions were placed upon the doors,
prone to rend asunder whoever enters unauthorized.

Note 19

The thoughts leap high in this palace like horses loosely bridled,
and then they stumble, unable to reach the goal.

Seeing its marble court, you would deem it carpeted
with crystal and cushioned with a cover of camphor.

When seeing it strewn with pebbles like pearls, you would deem
its floor to be musk, exhaling its perfume or other aromas.

The dawn ranks lower; for this appears
like the morning resplendent upon the black of darkness.

There follows in this poem a description of "lions, inhabiting the jungle" which I quoted among the texts relating to animal fountains comparable to the Fount of Lions. The reader will have been reminded of the poems by Ibn Zamrak from the basin of the Alhambra fount and from the walls of the Alhambra, quoted in Part II, which belong more closely to this Arabic tradition.

Whereas the first poem by Ibn Ḥamdīs referred to a hall with large dimensions and to the prince, the second poem evidences closer observation on the part of the poet; the marble floor and the lions biting the door-rings and the young servants opening the doors are of course no figment of imagination. In the same poem, the poet goes on to describe a pond on the rim of which there are golden and silver trees, the branches of which jet water[20] and where he sees statues of crouching lions which spout water as well. The height and extent of the building are praised in hyperboles. The greatest building-patrons of history are allegedly eclipsed by it. The gardens remind one of paradise and thus multiply virtue (is this a courtier's justification for near-sacrilegious lavishness?). We see the prince integrated harmoniously into this artful landscape, receiving guests, and are reminded of a Persian miniature. Certain ideas are elevated from make-believe to reality. The door lions protect the building against intruders, but little talismanic value such as must have been inherent in the famous ancient gates of lions like that of Mycenae is involved in these courtly times. The author of this poem returns, without the desire to convince, to pseudo-magic, a more literary device. The pretense of Ibn Gabirol's Alhambra poem, on the other hand, is not linked with talismanic ideas at all, most likely because this would have been felt to be foolish and conflicting with both the enlightened monotheism of this circle, and, possibly with the metaphysics and theurgic aims of the Naghrāllas.

Note 20

If these poems about castles seem rather derivative and, as it were, stuck in the literary medium, then we should consider that the prince himself wished from the beginning that his constructions should be "conversation pieces," and that the very ideas embodied in his constructions were to a great degree of literary-symbolic origin. The merit of creating truly visual beauty remains the architect's secret. Very much as the poets, the princes worked with given motifs and conceits and strove to outdo each other in ever-bolder versions. The aesthetic is in many ways subordinated to the intellectual. In certain cases the prince himself praises his constructions.

The famous ʿAbbādid ruler Muʿtamid described, from memory and in longing during his captivity in Aghmāt, his various palaces in Seville[21]. These were — in addition to the one called az-Zāhir, 'The Blossoming', erected by his royal father Muʿtaḍid — first, al-Mubārak, 'The Blessed' (most likely superseded by the present Alcazar); another, ath-Thurayya, 'The Pleiades' (named, of course, after the palace built by the ʿAbbāsid caliph Muʿtaḍid, and praised by Ibn al-Muʿtazz in lines quoted above), most likely a part of al-Mubārak; also al-Waḥīd, 'The Unique' and the smaller az-Zāhī, 'The Splendid', with its domed hall standing above the Guadalquivir, and Saʿd as-Suʿūd, 'Felicity of Felicities', another astral name of the twenty-fourth moon mansion.

Could I know whether I would once more spend a night
with a bower before and behind me and a pond

Upon a ground which makes the olive trees sprout and which bestows nobility,
where the doves coo and the birds twitter,

In az-Zāhir, found there with high towers, watered generously by the rain;
when it seems as if ath-Thurayyā gave us a signal or we gave one to it,

When az-Zāhī with its Saʿd as-Suʿūd [Hall] looks at us like two jealous ones,
(someone obsessed with love is very jealous!) . . .

In these lines we encounter, instead of observations of natural or artificial landscape and flattering praise, memories from afar, filtered through a veil of grief, and besides, a high degree of artistry aiming at concentration and surprising in the extent of its variation.

Note 21

Three palaces, the Ruṣāfa near Valencia, the Munya erected by Ibn 'Abd al-'Azīz, and the palace of al-Ma'mūn in Toledo, aroused the particular imagination of the poets. "On the day when the Ruṣāfa was dedicated, the 'Āmirid Manṣūr, who reigned in Valencia from 1021 to 1061, and who erected this palace, was host to a festival which gathered the flower of the kingdom. A hundred pages, from ten to fourteen years of age, served as waiters and butlers. The prince distributed that day twenty thousand gifts, and gave away property as important as fiefs [22]." All princes reigning in Valencia resided in that Munya, according to Pérès, and the Cid himself expressly demanded occupation rights from Ibn Jaḥḥāf. A lesser-known poet, 'Alī ibn Aḥmad, describes its assembly hall at a time when the Munya had apparently become a public park: [23]

> Arise! Pour out drinks for me after the Garden has donned
> a brocade of flowers woven by the Rain
>
> In the hall which resembles the sky
> wherein appears the full moon of the face of the one whom I love;
>
> The Sun has tainted its tunic with 'uṣfur-red,
> and the earth shows pearls of dew upon its verdant garments.
>
> The water channel is like a Milky Way
> which the commensals line like glittering stars.

The address to the cup-bearer is taken over from wine-poetry. The rest is truly descriptive, dealing more with the garden in its Spring splendor than with building, although the standard simile of the moon for a face appearing in a building or rather garden court is employed. What follow are the other standard metaphors and *similia* which we find in Ibn Gabirol's spring poems: that of the personified Rain (in other poems, clouds) that weaves a garment for the Garden, a figure derived from natural science rather than observation. Later the Earth, wearing green vestments, is personified, as well as the Sun, which also has a garment. The address to a wine-pouring companion reminds one of the enlivening element in the beginning of Ibn Gabirol's Alhambra poem, in which the Maecenas is invited to join the poet for an outing in the vernal gardens: "Go forth, my friend ... Let us lodge ... Let us walk." I list the conceits for comparison with Ibn Gabirol:

a. The green of the gardens — a garment woven by the dew or rain.
b. The face of the Maecenas and/or friend — a moon.

Notes 22—23

c. The clouds or mists — the garments of the sun.
d. A rivulet or channel — the Milky Way, and, linking two metaphors,
e. The guests — stars.

The comparison of a water channel with the Milky Way would be entirely trite, were it not linked with a new simile, that of the stars, standing for the guests, in glittering flattery indeed.

For the sake of comprehensiveness, I also cite the description of a ruined princely residence, in which the old Arabian *aṭlāl* poetry lives on, as it does in the famous descriptions of the decaying Sāsānian palaces by the ʿAbbāsid poets, which I quote elsewhere. Al-Fatḥ ibn Khāqān mourned the palace of the dethroned ʿAbbādids in poetical prose:[24] "The branches sway in their baskets; the flowers with their intoxicating perfumes lift up again him who had died from suffering. The birds of the garden bowers wailed over these (the ʿAbbādids) like the mothers deprived of their children who sigh over their fall and the vanishing of their joy. The lizard plays in their palace and over all habitations croaks a raven." The idea that beauty or an appeal to a human sense other than the eye resuscitates someone stricken down by pain appears similarly in Ibn Gabirol's Alhambra poem. The transformation of 'places of pleasure' into 'haunts of horror', wept for in the tradition of the Biblical *Lamentations*, lives on in these descriptions of ruins[25]. A great masterpiece is Ibn Ḥazm's description in 'rhymed prose' of the same ruins of Cordova, and in particular those of his family mansion in Balāṭ Mughīth[26]. The capital, despoiled and deprived of the caliphal court, found in Ibn Shuhaid's lament an expression, which is outstanding for immediacy and a certain simplicity:[27]

> No friend has remained among the ruins to guide me;
> whom then could I ask to learn what has become of Cordova?
>
> Ask no one but Separation: only she will tell you
> whether your friends have gone to the highlands or the plain.
>
> Time has shown itself tyrannical towards them;
> they are dispersed in every direction, but most of them have perished.
>
> The disastrous Events have punished their abodes
> and them as well, afflicting these and those differently.
>
> I wish Fortune would produce a light in their courts
> which might allow their hearts to brighten.

Notes 24—27

For a city like Cordova there are not tears enough
which the eyes with continual flow are shedding.

O Abode! May God forgive the faults of its residents
who have now been Berberized, Occidentalized, and Egyptianized[28]!

In all directions groups have been dispersed,
restless at having abandoned her.

When I knew her, all her residents were united
and life was beautiful . . . (four distichs omitted)

14 The palace belonging to the Umayyads was filled with everything,
and the caliphate was the greatest thing.

15 The Zāhiriyya was resplendent with royal cortèges
and al-ʿĀmiriyya was thronged by an affluence of stars.

The highest Mosque overflowed with all sorts of people who chanted the Koran,
listened to the discourses they desired, and were attentive.

The ways which led to the market place evidenced that the summoning to the Last Judgment
would not be extended to all the people walking on these ways.

O Paradise! Against which the wind of hostility has blown as a tempest
to destroy it, as it blew upon the inhabitants to wipe them out . . .

Comparison of these lines with Ibn Gabirol's Alhambra poem will make it plain to the reader that Ibn Gabirol used much less Arabic imagery than in other instances, but drew authoritatively and with great poetical precision from that very Hebrew imagery of architecture and Solomonic reminiscence which the patron himself, to whom the poem is addressed, must have cherished most.

There are, however, many common Arabic conceits in Ibn Gabirol's other nature poems, which are presented later on, and for this reason I first introduce Arabic descriptions of natural landscapes and seasons. Though the Arab poets' experience of nature has had from the beginning its legitimate place in Arabic poetry, the Spanish Arab bard described his specific Iberian experience. Spain had been a Roman province long enough

Note 28

to have benefited from Roman techniques of irrigation, of viticulture and horticulture, and also from the elaborate Roman architecture of villas and their pictorial representations. Spain must have appeared to the conquering Arab, coming from arid Africa and Arabia, like a giant oasis or the terrestrial paradise. The perennial streams in particular and, compared with Arabia, the inversion of the relationship between verdure and aridity must have appeared miraculous. Spain's praise wells up time and again for centuries. An anonymous poet composed the lines:[29]

> What admirable land is this Andalusia,
> granting me all joy incessantly;
>
> Twittering birds, fresh and thick shades,
> rushing waters and palaces!

The great spokesman for the Spanish landscape is Ibn Khafāja:[30]

> O residents of Spain! What fortune is it for you
> to have waters, shades, rivers, and trees!
>
> The Garden of eternal felicity is nowhere if not in your territory;
> if the choice were given to me, I should choose the latter.
>
> Do not believe that you may enter Inferno tomorrow;
> nobody enters Gehenna by way of Paradise.

This type of courtly sacrilege, based upon the old stylistic device of foreswearing religious creeds to emphasize temporal truth, here, in a witty fashion, belongs to the skepticism typical of the eleventh century. We encountered this element in Ibn Gabirol's love poems in our Prologue and in certain lines in which he almost critically dismisses biblical figures in order to flatter a patron like Samuel or himself. (Ibn Khafāja was, however, a generation younger than Ibn Gabirol and, although the similarity between the two in their nature poems is sometimes striking, Ibn Gabirol could hardly have been fundamentally influenced by him.) Ibn Khafāja seems to be more assured of Spain's beauty than of the reality of Paradise; but through the reality of Spain, this natural paragon of Paradise, Hell becomes unreal and the poet loses all paradigms for such an unreality. The poet's enchantment, however, comes from the *paradis artificiels*, the parks of the princes.

Notes 29–30

A natural river landscape is described in a poem by Ibn al-Labbāna, in which he deplores the death of al-Muʿtamid (1069—1091) in his exile in Aghmāt:[31]

There was a land which seemed to be covered by torches
which the plants, elevated in spirit, had lit.

On the banks of its river there were gardens of hills
with copses of elms shading them.

One might say that this river was the necklace around her neck:
(Is not the greatest beauty found in necklaces and necks?)

Often I betook myself to the bay encountered there;
in this bay there were moments of joyous quiet for people loving the wine.

And in the plantations — may they never be parched! —
there were Plantations of Felicity ready to be plucked ...

The comparison of a flower to a star is related to our simile of torches for plants. The spirit attributed to the plants which causes them to rise is, of course, an aspect of anthropomorphic animation. The image of a necklace for a river is almost as common as that of a sword as in the previous poem. One of its variations is the "dove's necklace." The reader may have observed the sparse indications of color in comparison with the rich descriptions of light and form, with movements which are mostly pretended and taken from fictitious and merely metaphoric emotions. But human groups are harmoniously imbedded into the natural beauty of the described scenery. One feels that urbanization led the Arab aristocracy of this time to a romantic desire for rural experiences, often more feigned, unlike, yet still related to, their ancestors' true Bedouin form of life.

To amplify the account of natural landscape poetry, I quote the poem by Abū 'l-Qāsim ibn al-ʿAṭṭār, in which he praises the River Guadalquivir in Seville, the name *(al-Wādī 'l-Kabīr)* of which means "the large river;" but since *al-Kabīr*, "the Great One," is a typical epithet for God in Islam, the name also has a more metaphysical sound:[32]

We embarked upon that byword of God which had become river,
to be called also a serpent with bubble-spangled attire on its belly,

Or rather a sword whose gleaming blade was whirled around
to occupy with an extended shade a splendid sheath.

The lines show in their beginning a remarkable dearth of visual imagery and, instead, learned and far-fetched metaphors of mere wit. The 'byword of God that became river' is of course a take-off of John, chapter I. 1. The comparison of the river with the serpent is trite, as well as that of the bubbles with pearls; yet the transposition of this metaphor, most likely employed to raise the level of originality by a show of greater wit, is the 'attire of bubbles' around the serpent's belly. Such contrived imagery, with its lack of proportion, is the acme of the non-visual. Another simile for the river, a sword swung violently back and forth, is no less commonplace. But this seems to be used with more than usual success when, as here, the visible part of the river seems to be equated with the whirling blade, whereas the other parts of the river, less sparkling, seem to be like the handle or the hilt of the sword, quietly embedded in the shady landscape, which is compared with a sheath.

To complete the répertoire of Hispano-Arabic descriptions of rivers and to introduce another Jewish courtier who could improvise Arabic poetry when the situation called for it, I quote lines by Abū 'l-Faḍl ibn Ḥasdāy, recited during a fishing festival to which his prince, al-Musta'īn bi-llāh, invited his intimates. The source is the Arabic historian al-Fatḥ ibn Khāqān, who lived in the Almoravid period, and who died in 1134—35 (or 1140). The prince belonged to the Banū Hūd and ruled from 1085 to 1110 in Saragossa on the River Ebro. The hot summer days lured the court and the wealthy to outings on the cool waterway. The Arab historian describes the occasion on which the improvisation originated, which was a fishing party during a time when the Ebro teemed with fish and also with vessels surrounding the prince's barge. "The tunes of the strings arrested chant; with artful devices the fish were brought forth and the fishing appliances plunged down to them to display them to the eyes like branches of pearls and ingots of gold." On this occasion Ibn Ḥasdāy exclaimed:[33]

O admirable Day! How his face was sparkling
and what silvery and golden hues he took on in dusk and dawn!

One might say that Time, after afflicting us with much evil before,
wished on this day to restore its grace and to show us greatest indulgence.

We floated in our skiff which the barges surrounded on all sides,
some in perfect order, some scattered ...

Note 33

The rest of the poem contains a metaphor for the skiff and some *bons mots* for the river, the fish, and the drinking company around the sovereign. The personification of the day appears in Ibn Gabirol's spring poems, to be discussed later on. The references to the sparkling of the noon and the silver and gold of morning and evening betray a poetical sensitivity to color, but they also abandon the personification, which is replaced in the following distich by the personified Time (or Fate). The poem, by translating the happy experience into the medium of the word, is an attempt at enhancing the mood of the party assembled for a banquet. This is the courtier's task: he accentuates and memorializes the event by contributing a felicitous 'water music'.

We fail to discover in Ibn Gabirol's poetry descriptions of idyllic scenery. He rather describes nature during the passage of the seasons and garden landscapes. Neither do we find more than a very occasional description of drinking bouts, which some Arabic poetry describes in such a way as to reduce nature to a mere background for these. Also, Ibn Gabirol's Alhambra poem proves, by comparison, to be more than a paradigm of contemporary school poetry. It is not as playful as Arabic poems are, in which the details are not truly integrated, and where individual observations make the distichs turgid with intellectual invention. No hybrid pseudo-causality is ascribed, e. g., to the lions and gazelles of the Alhambra fountains. The element of a contest for supremacy is no more than the Homeric device in describing the progress of the work on the shield of Achilles, viz. to dramatize instead of enumerate, to integrate detail into a developing action instead of merely enumerating it in a sort of catalogue.

Ibn Gabirol's Alhambra poem which begins with a prelude of love and spring motifs is a spring poem deriving its inspiration from Hebrew and Arabic sources. I therefore introduce Arabic Spring poems, both earlier, from the Arabian homeland and later ones from Spain.

(4) HISPANO-ARABIC SPRING AND GARDEN POETRY

As a specimen of these Spring poems, showing what the Spanish Arab poets inherited from the East, I quote some lines by aṣ-Ṣanaubarī (died 945 in Syria), the first great master of nature poetry:[34]

Rise, gazelle, and look! the beds revealed their miracles,
their beautiful faces were covered, now spring has removed the veil;

There are roses like cheeks and narcissus
like eyes that see the beloved;

Note 34

Anemones like red silk-cloaks with black inscriptions;
cyprus trees like singing girls with garment trussed up to the knee.

One of them looks like a slender girl in the
breeze playing at midnight with her playmates.

Soft winds drove forth the leaves
into the brook, causing it to tremble.

If I had the power to keep the gardens,
no common man should step on their soil.

A comparison of flowers with young girls will be found in Ibn Gabirol's poem "The Present of Roses" (Part III E). Many poets concentrate upon detail, be it a tree or a flower. Even the most advanced nature poet in Arab Spain, Ibn Khafāja, excels mainly in depicting trees or flowers. Pérès praises Khafāja for having a sense for the landscape as a whole, but this seems to be only relatively correct. This is the description of another landscape during a rain-shower:[35]

How many flower chalices, before which the morning dropped
the veil and revealed, by this, cheeks covered with dew,

As in a vale where the mouths of the daisies sucked
at the breasts of each cloud shedding forth generously!

The hand of the south-east wind strewed across the lap
of the Earth pearls of dew and ducats of flowers.

The branch of the sandy region draped himself in his cloak
and the [channel-] necks adorned themselves with water bubbles
these gems.

I settled down there where the water is like the cheek of a laughing
and merry person,
there where the river reminds one of a minion who first appears.

The breeze from the early morning shakes the hair of the hills
and the drizzle moistens the face of the trees.

I divided my attention between the beauties of a hill's summit
and the waistline of a low ground,

Note 35

And also an arāk tree, which for the ringdove, singing in the branches
at the moment when the dawn uncovers the forehead of the day,

Stirs his resilient boughs, and often the bird dons
the cloak which the flowers gave to him.

To list the conceits:

a. The flowers are living beings, possessing cheeks (later on also the water current is compared with a human cheek).
b. The daisies have mouths.
c. The personified clouds have nursing breasts.
d. The south-east wind possesses a hand lavishly strewing pearls of dew and gold pieces, which are flowers. Should the poet's mouth be speaking *ex abundantia cordis?*
e. A branch has a green mantle.
f. Rivulets are necks adorned with water bubbles.
g. Water bubbles are compared with jewels.
h. The water is a cheek stirred as if by human emotions.
i. The river is compared with a minion, the *tertium comparationis* seeming to be the appearance of a shy youth.
j. The hills are [heads] covered with hair.
k. The trees have a face.
l. The breeze and the drizzle are introduced as active, but they are not necessarily personified.
m. The *arāk* tree (which Pérès fails to identify with any Iberian tree or bush, as I am unable to identify some birds and flowers mentioned by Ibn Gabirol) is credited with human emotions; it is agitated by joy over the cooing of the ringdove[36].
n. The forehead of the day is uncovered by the dawn.
o. The bird decks itself in the cloak of flowers.

The anthropomorphism, as a method, becomes somewhat stereotyped, or rather it would, were it not for the self-introduction of the poet who shares the excitement and the predominantly happy emotions of the refreshed "furniture" in this garden-picture with his words (in the first person) "I divided my attention ..."

Another description of a garden by Ibn Khafāja contains the lines:[37]

Could he be dew-slaked on the day when I stopped by the foot
of a great tree with luxuriant vegetation, whom the north wind
teased, offering himself for play!

Inebriated from hearing the chant of the dove, he bent himself down
with joy and when the cloud served him a potion, he drank it.

Happy day that revelled: the banner of youth
unfolded itself there and the star of pure wine ascended.

The garden was a face of sparkling whiteness, the shade
was black hair curls and the water a mouth with beautiful teeth.

There the dove cheered us one evening,
letting us hear her sweet tune.

The trunk of a branch was agitated for the joy which he experienced for us,
and the sunset smiled, uncovering the mouth of the crescent moon,

This crescent to which beauty is tightly linked —
did it not resemble a gold necklace upon the mantle of the cloud?

The hidden subject in the first line — hidden for the purpose of emphasis — is of course the garden, or the landscape.

a. The north wind is introduced as the playmate of a tree.
b. The tree, personified exactly as in the previous poem, stirs again with joy for the song of the dove.
c. And the clouds with slight variations are not nurses but, in general, offerers of drinks.
d. The next distich, again introducing the topic of the banquet, compares youth with a banner.
e. Pure wine, in a far-fetched comparison, is like a star (in other instances like the sun).
f. A metaphor for the garden is a white human face and, in a sophisticated chain of metaphors, its shade is hair (as in the previous poem).
g. The water, possibly a pond or a *seguia*, is compared with a row of teeth.

With a turn toward the sentimental, a faint relation to the poet's feeling, the song of the dove "one evening" is mentioned and, a second time, a branch agitated by joy, this time for its human company, appears.

h. A sunset is compared with a smile.
i. This smile uncovers the crescent, which is compared or equated with a mouth.

j. The crescent is also said to resemble a gold necklace upon the clouds.
k. The cloud is, in turn, compared to a mantle.

As a further example by Ibn Khafāja, which again features a *genre* picture of a thunderstorm together with its standard simile, the banquet of the garden:[38]

Drink from small cups the wine when the breeze is sweet,
when the shade is fresh like a trembling pavilion,

When the flower is an eye which awakes in tears,
when the water, with glittering teeth, is a smiling mouth that seduces.

Out of lightning from every cloud arose
through the atmosphere a flag and an army squadron,

Until the moment when each fresh branch of the well-watered grove
swayed softly and when vales and river-beds overflowed with water.

Out of gratitude for this lightning the *arāk* tree bowed down and then stooped with joy,
and the stock-dove sounded forth its cooing in the branches.

The garden waves its cloaks in delight like a drunken man
who, bent by the wind, would be drooping.

This beautiful garden — dew has silvered it and then taken leave,
and afterwards evening came to gild its cheeks.

This variation seems to be slight. The address to the garden in the first distich (again a hidden subject) vitalizes an otherwise merely descriptive enumeration of elements, "decorated" with standard similes. The "little cups" may be those of flowers, and the joys of a banquet are, with this, aroused in the reader. The poem shows an astonishing thematic unity.

a. The comparison of the shade with a trembling pavilion reminds one of a simile used by Samuel han-Nāghīdh in the description of Yehōseph's new garden construction, beginning "Yehōseph bends the heart ...," in which he says:[39]

We settled down in the shade of pomegranate and plane trees
like unto a palace, not in the shade of pomegranate and oak trees.

b. The flower is an eye, filled with tears of dew.
c. The body of water is compared with teeth shown by a smiling mouth.
d. The lightning and clouds are compared with the flag within a dark array of soldiers, in a way closely akin to Ibn Gabirol's line 18 in his Great Nature Poem, in which the clouds are compared with the throngs of wailing people. I discuss this image in my treatment of that poem below.
e. The tree and the branches, again showing human emotions, sway in delight and react to the voice of a bird.
f. The garden itself shakes its foliage like a cloak.
g. In another comparison the garden is like a drunk man, stooping, unable to steady himself in the wind (whereby the wind is a strange alien body coming from the sphere of real causation).
h. The dew appearing upon the garden is metaphorically termed silver.
i. The garden has a face, the cheeks of which are gilded by the evening light.

The most permeating, although in no way supporting, image is the inebriation of the garden within its banquet.

Two final examples might best elucidate how repetitive this imagery is:[40]

Often an *arāk* tree shaped a canopy moistened by dew above us;
and then when the starry firmaments of cups performed their revolution,

The base of its trunk was surrounded by the Milky Way of a water runnel
above which the white flowers strewed their stars.

The tree with its rivulets was like a belle,
her waistline held by a girdle.

The crystal cup conveyed the wine looking like a bride presented in all her attire,
now that the blossoms of the branches are strewn in abundance

In a garden where the shade has the density of darknesses
and where the flowers condensed themselves into light.

Luxuriant garden, where the merchant spread out for me his striped tissues
and where the perfume dealer crushed his musk!

Note 40

The twittering arose then when the dew had moistened
the face of the Earth and when the flowers were awakened.

The water, adorned with the jewels of the dew, resembled a neck
around which the trees had buttoned their shirt collars.

This piece, most sophisticated and at the same time most descriptive, seems to be inspired by the sight of the tree within a *seguia*.

a. For this tree in the water, the poet has coined *ad hoc* (in distich three) a fresh, unhackneyed simile of a woman with a girdle.
b. The favorite *arāk* tree forms, with its foliage, a roof, which is compared to a canopy (similarly to the previous poem). The image appears in Samuel's description of Yehōseph's new garden quoted above, which was also a banquet poem[41].
c. Far-fetched, almost anticipating Gongorism, is the comparison of the cups to rotating stars, forming firmaments.
d. The crystal cup is seen as a bride in her wedding accoutrements, almost exactly as we find it, again, in Samuel's garden poem: "... like a bride under a canopy." Here the adornments are the blossoms of the trees, whereas in Samuel's poem the cups were covered with papyrus lids[42].

There are more comparisons similar to the previous ones:

e. For the shade we have darknesses.
f. For the flowers we have, in beautiful antithesis to the shade, a body of light.
g. The garden is compared with a textile merchant and his merchandise, completing a market scene with a perfume dealer spreading an aroma of musk.
h. The Earth is personified to a certain extent — she has a face — and so are the flowers, which seem to be aroused from slumber.
i. The dew strewn upon the banks of the river is compared to jewels, as often before. Against this cliché we have the surprising comparison of the rivulet to a neck around which the trees form a high-buttoned collar, an inversion of the simile in distich 8. This may be a variation of a well-known metaphor which we also find in one of Ibn Gabirol's spring poems, that of a garden "donning shirts," or rather "chemises," (which word is derived from the Arabic word, meaning 'undergarment').

Notes 41–42

It is difficult to assay the strength and type of poetical emotion which underlies these poems. The playfulness may be reflected by the reference to the lower and lighter aspects of human life in the chosen metaphors, like drinking, being drunk, and, as in some following poems, like games of chance. One feels that the poet's bravado is his ability of μετάβασις εἰς ἄλλο γένος, an artistry invented to stun the hearer with its wit. If we are unable to draw conclusions from this upon the degree of the poet's enchantment by nature, we may at least see in his poetry a means to evoke an equal degree of enchantment in his hearers by his artistry. We observe beyond the artistic practice of the poetical school, an, as it were, professional enthusiasm among the manifestations of his vast training. He shows in this the typical romanticism of the city-dweller, which is conditioned by the rarity of his exposure to nature. The listener, even if he could not share at all an enchantment by nature, would feel satisfied by his own connoisseurship in a merely literary medium. The poet himself seems to experience his deepest satisfaction when a new rare comparison and a felicitous choice of words become in themselves an equivalent for the observation of something rare in his environment, which is, at least most likely, not fictitious. Verdure seems never to have lost its emotional grip for the Arab, even if his family had for many generations been resident in Spain. Water, in particular, is surpreme bliss. A comparison of the Spaniard Ibn Khafāja with the Sicilian Ibn Ḥamdīs shows a different degree of observation and expression: through all these hackneyed clichés we feel a deeper link with nature, and though much of this verbosity leaves us unimpressed, we cannot overlook the genuine feeling.

I quote a few additional pieces; the first by Abū 'l-Ḥasan ibn Ḥafs, from Algeciras, though he belongs to the twelfth century:[43]

How many times did I walk in the morning hours in the gardens
where the branches reminded me of the lovers' gestures!

How beautiful they were when the wind entangled them
one with another, like [human] necks.

The roses are cheeks; the daisies smiling mouths,
with the jonquils supplanting the eyes.

A very strained human image is thus constructed from branches which are necks seen in their spirited interaction and from flowers providing cheeks (no longer are the cheeks roses but vice-versa), eyes and mouths, faintly reminding us of a composition by Arcimboldo. The comparison of entangled branches to lovers or drunkards is found but once in Ibn Gabirol (in his sixth Spring Poem, last distich), but his anthropomorphism of flowers is carried very far.

Notes to Part III A

A. INTRODUCTION

1. G. E. von Grunebaum, *A Tenth-century Document of Arabic Literary Theory and Criticism . . . al-Bāqillānī's I'jāz al-Qur'ān*, Chicago, 1960 (quoted as Grunebaum, *al-Bāqillānī*), pp. 40f. A similar turn to a blessing for the addressee is found in Ibn Gabirol's Rose Poem at the end of this chapter. For the two Ruṣāfas cf. Pérès, *Poésie*, pp. 191, n. 3; (132).
2. R. A. Nicholson, *History*, p. 418.
3. Sura LV, 6—12 after *The Meaning of the Glorious Koran*, trans. Mohammed M[armaduke] Pickthall, 1959, p. 382.
4. Sura LV, 46—76 (abbreviated), op. cit., p. 383.
5. Sura LXVI, v. 8, op. cit., p. 407.
6. Sura LVI, 10—38, op. cit., p. 384f.
7. G. E. von Grunebaum, "The Response to Nature in Arabic Poetry," in *Journal of Near Eastern Studies*, IV, 1945, pp. 137—151 (quoted as (von) Grunebaum, *Response*), p. 145.
8. von Grunebaum, *Response*, p. 146.
9. von Grunebaum, *Response*, p. 146.
10. Op. cit., p. 43.
11. Op. cit., p. 147.
12. Ritter, *Niẓāmī*, p. 7.
13. In spite of some misgivings, mainly the fear of over-emphasis, I have chosen to capitalize those nouns which, as the context shows, are quasi-personified in the Arabic and Hebrew poems cited.
14. von Grunebaum, *Response*, p. 150.
15. C. L. Frommel, *Die Farnesina . . .*, Berlin, 1961, pp. 39ff.
16. Pérès, *Poésie*, p. 139; *Mélanges R. Basset*, 1923, pp. 238f.; C. Schiaparelli, *Il Canzoniere del Poeta . . . Ibn Ḥamdīs, il Siciliano*, Roma 1897, p. 332, distich 35—43, 48—49, 56 (quoted as Schiaparelli); after al-Maqqarī, *Analectes*, I, 321.
17. Distich 39 is missing in Pérès, *Poésie*.
18. Distich 41 is missing in *Mélanges Basset*. For the 'ear' in Virgin in antiquity see E. Simon, "Zum Fries der Mysterienvilla bei Pompeji," in *Jahrb. d. D. Archäol. Inst.*, LXXVI, 1961, pp. 137 f. (Quoted as Simon, *Mysterienvilla*).
19. Found in *Mélanges Basset*, pp. 240f.; *Schiaparelli*, p. 483, dist. 6—20. See above footnotes 146f. of Part II.
20. These lines are found in al-Maqqarī, *Analectes*, I, p. 322. I quoted these lines in the excursus on Islamic descriptions of animal fountains.
21. Pérès, *Poésie*, pp. 136ff.; al-Maqqarī, *Anal.*, II, p. 620.
22. Al-Maqqarī, *Anal.*, I, pp. 436f.
23. Pérès, *Poésie*, p. 154.
24. Basset, *Mélanges*, p. 251.
25. For instance in the line of Ibn Gabirol's *Meliṣey ahabhāh* (dist. 11) which will be discussed in my section on love poetry:

    Lo, Separation united with their foes
    and rendered Union's habitations desolations.
26. Arberry, *Ring of the Dove*, p. 180.

27. The poet Abū ʿĀmir ibn Shuhaid, born 992 in Cordova; (cf. Nykl, *H.-A. Poetry*, pp. 103ff.) cited after Pérès, *Poésie*, p. 122.
28. The coining of denominative verb forms in which, following this tradition, Ibn Gabirol engages in his *Mī z-zōth* was criticized by Moses ibn Ezra — in his role as guardian of the grail.
29. Pérès, *Poésie*, p. 116.
30. *Ibid.*
31. Pérès, *Poésie*, p. 208.
32. Pérès, *Poésie*, pp. 208ff.
33. Pérès, *Poésie*, p. 210 *et al.* Cf. Schirmann, *Shīr-īm ḥadhāsh-īm min hag-genīzāh*, Jerusalem, 1965–66, pp. 200ff. with references to Ibn Bassām and Ibn Ṣaʿīd (which he cites as Ibn Ṣāʿad, see note 11 to the Prologue above) and inserting a poetical fragment dedicated to Abū 'l-Faḍl in which the anonymous poet speaks of comfort for a bereavement, reminiscent of this poet's reference to grief. See Baron, *History*, VII, p. 304, n. 56, where Baron avers that Abū 'l-Faḍl was the son of Joseph ibn Ḥaśdāy, the author of the "Orphan Song" or "Matchless Song," the encomium of Samuel to which I refer several times. Would not the fact that this courtier received Hebrew poems prove that he had not broken with his Jewish co-religionists?
34. A. Schimmel, in *Lyrik des Ostens*, Munich, 1958, p. 54.
35. Pérès, *Poésie*, p. 164; *Anal.*, I, p. 452; II, p. 136. It may be worthwhile to mention that the Hellenistic tradition of ἔκφρασις ἔαρος known in particular from Libanius lived on in Byzantium; cf. E. Rohde, *Der Griechische Roman*, Darmstadt, 1960, pp. 508f. (541); pp. 512 (545); 355 (360)ff.
36. A counterpart to such "fallacious" causation, like joy or animated conversation given for the agitation of the branches, is found in Ibn Gabirol's "The sky's Clouds lowed" where the thunder is "explained" as horn signals given by sailors located on the masts, the sails of which had appeared as a mere simile the lines before.
37. Pérès, *Poésie*, p. 164; Ibn Khafāja, *Diwan*, p. 32.
38. Pérès, *Poésie*, p. 165; *Anal.*, II, p. 136.
39. Habermann, *Diwan*, I, 2, p. 83, dist. 7.
40. Pérès, *Poésie*, p. 165; *Anal.*, I, p. 455.
41. Habermann, *Diwan*, I, 2, p. 83, dist. 9.
42. *Op. cit.*, dist. 8f.
43. Pérès, *Poésie*, p. 163; after *Anal.*, II, p. 466; Nykl, *H.-A. Poetry*, pp. 263f.

B. Ibn Gabirol's Great Nature Poem

Late, late yestreen I saw the new Moon,
With the old Moon in her arm;
And I fear, I fear, my Master dear!
We shall have a deadly storm.

Scottish Ballad of Sir Patrick Spence
Epigraph to Coleridge's "Dejection, An Ode"[1]

(1) IBN GABIROL AND NATURE

Certain movements of thought which represented departures from the ideas prevailing during the Middle Ages and changed mediaeval man himself, such as a newly felt immediacy of relation to Nature concomitant with the re-discovery of the visual and objective as a whole, the re-institution of the sacredness of human love and passion as taught by Plato (and forgotten), of "pure" reason (independent of Biblical authority), all these appear prodigiously represented at a surprisingly early time in the unique person of Solomon ibn Gabirol. Ibn Gabirol, whose importance is still far from being evaluated, anticipated in Islamic Spain developments which can be observed only centuries later in the Christian West, mainly in Italy, where they appear, in strikingly similar embodiments, in the works of, for instance, Petrarch, Dante, or Giordano Bruno. Ibn Gabirol's writings are among those valves (of which only a few are traceable) through which pulsed the new enlightenment into the West[2].

Ibn Gabirol's philosophical *magnum opus: The Source of Life (Fons Vitae)*, written in Arabic, became in its Latin translation a textbook of Neoplatonic thinking. It did not free itself from the meshes of extreme philosophical realism and was therefore (and for other reasons) attacked by Thomas Aquinas in his *De Ente et Essentia*[3]. Yet even if its philosophical realism could not continue to be valid in its argument, its "pure reason," its *raisonnement*, independent of revelation, its modern feeling for an all-pervading cosmic power, moving all matter (the spheres, the angels, and human souls) towards a divinely dispensed form; its attempt at harmonizing Plotinus (often pseudepigraphically transmitted as Aristotle) with Hebrew

Notes 1—3

monotheism of a pantheistic kind, helped to break the fetters of "impure" dogmatic thought, and helped, during almost two centuries, to keep open the theological questions that the *Fons Vitae* itself raised with astonishing independence and consistency.

Moreover, Ibn Gabirol introduced neo-Platonic cosmology into his poetical Hebrew prayers and hymns. From there some of his conceptions, adopted to form a philosophical reconciliation of reason and faith, were later paradoxically absorbed into the neo-gnostic speculation of the Kabbalists. Among these Ibn Gabirol's terms like Matter and Form, used in the Plotinian tradition, became, together with genuine mystical elements found in his work, divine hypostases, theosophical conceptions of the channels or "spheres" of the divine emanation. The Platonic spark seems to have been transmitted, in a curiously authentic form, to this Granadine Jew, the singer of the synagogue and the heir of Arab knightly and mystical ideas. In so far as the direct lineage of his strangely genuine Platonic influence is traceable, his heirs are the thinkers like Jehuda Abravanel (Leone Ebreo), who carry his teaching into the Renaissance until it eventually influences Spinoza[4]. Had it not been for this premature flowering of a short-lived Jewish Platonism in Moorish Granada, the Jewish contribution to Renaissance thought would have been minimal.

Finally, Ibn Gabirol's secular poetry, which is his most intimate surviving medium of expression, reveals this "modern" person and, thereby, his time, more clearly. The man, who was a theologian, grammarian, allegorical interpreter of the Bible, philosopher, and poet, appears here as reflected in his most private motivations and moments. Here he speaks only in his own name and feels himself understood only by a very few. (His occasional failure to give these secular poems their final lustre may betray their private character.) However, in his individualism and isolation, he is one of the few in whom an independent and rich "I" is reborn, master of and subject to his own direct intellectual experience and visual or visionary encounters[5]. His secular personality, his unparochial, comprehensive and truly Platonic mind made him an alien among his people, so that he seems to be caught and conspicuous among them like an insect in amber. Always in advance of his own time, he is a major contributor to a premature "waning of the Middle Ages" in Spain, four centuries before the rest of Europe. As to Judaism itself, there was for centuries no after-life for Ibn Gabirol's Platonism. His *Fons Vitae* was abrogated in Ibn Dā'ūd's *Exalted Faith*, which remained the final verdict of normative Judaism[6]. Nevertheless, the Synagogue, static and ecstatic as it is at the same time, found in him a learned and loyal contributor of religious poetry and as such he became, as I think, to a varying degree, the voice of the whole nation.

Notes 4—6

The profound and daring contents of Ibn Gabirol's work are the expression of a "new soul." It is not his veiled and also bold language, censured vicariously by the conservative Abraham ibn Dā'ūd and Moses ibn Ezra, but his emancipated feeling and thinking as a whole which trespassed beyond the limits of container and content of the new Hebrew literary creativity with its tendency, visible in Ibn Ezra, to rapid degeneration into a pleasant and hackneyed eloquence[7]. He remained an outsider, and yet he was the pilot and pioneer of the new school of Hebrew, was plagiarized, used as a specimen, and often reprimanded. Ibn Gabirol, and in another way Samuel han-Nāghīdh, were intrinsically filled with the spirit of old and new Arabic poetry, and, carried by their own Hebrew Muse, played the instrument — all their own — with absolute mastery.

The standard conceits of the Arabic and Hebrew poetical schools assume in Ibn Gabirol's poetry reality and meaning. He, even where he is the imitator, means more literally what he says and re-coins it in sincerity more than do his Arabic models; he fills with genuinely felt content some of their fanciful and fashionable pseudo-pagan imagery[8]. The blind Arabic poet, Abū 'l-ʿAlā' al-Maʿarrī, is the great champion of a new veracity[9]. His manifesto, quoted above, reads: "My aim is to speak the truth. Now the proper end of poetry is not truth, but falsehood ... therefore I must crave the indulgence of my readers ..." The traditional Muslim attitude to poets, as voiced by as-Suyūṭī, a later poet, reads: "... grave poetry is fiction: therefore the poet has no choice but to tell lies or to make people laugh ..."[10] The new veracity was one aspect of the re-instatement of the value of the visible and this, in turn, stemmed from the rebirth of the "outer eye." (The customary cynical approach to the truth is found in the aforequoted Arabic formula cited by Ibn Ezra, "the best of a poem is its lie," with which he represents the generation subsequent to Ibn Gabirol's of more derivative Hebrew poets.)

What results is a rebirth of a most direct relation to the natural powers and a symbolism that anticipates in many respects the French school of the last century. For instance, he admits naively that the light of the moon dominates his creativity as a thinker. His Endymionic rapture, the "lunacy" of the poet, is neither a learned allegory nor a fashionable classical gesture; it is a genuine phenomenon, reborn as the poet's reality and voiced with "pagan" innocence. For such domination of a natural power over a mind as great as his, felt and avowed, I have not found a parallelism in the Judeo-Christian mediaeval records. In a strangely genuine titanism, the poet, almost like Nietzsche's Zarathustra, associates himself with other natural powers as his friends and foes[11]. Although we are able to trace from pagan and gnostic sources the trend of Arab thought which leads

Notes 7—11

to this titanism in Ibn Gabirol's Hebrew, yet within the context of his genuine mood his poetry sounds fully convincing and not derivative. The poet speaks innocently but authentically of "Time" (Fate) and the "Daughters of the Days," pre-Islamic personifications like the "Fates" or the ancient Μοῖραι which are, even as a common Arabic figure of speech, alien to his monotheistic heritage[12]. This spontaneous soul, comparable to that of Hölderlin, infused these inherited names and motives with individual emotion. However, just as the Greek gods, for all that they were experienced as *numina* by Hölderlin, did not interpose themselves between him and his Christianity, these sometimes genuinely encountered powers, as well as his neo-Platonic panentheism, could not make Ibn Gabirol, with his Renaissance mind, consciously heterodox. The other Hebrew poets used Arabic conceits of this kind as well, although obviously merely as a *façon de parler;* and if he had worked within this fashion Ibn Gabirol would have escaped the inadequate vigilance of his Jewish contemporaries. Yet his true immediacy and his specific and obvious enthusiasm apparently scandalized some of his contemporaries to the point of their calling him a "Greek" or "Hellenist[13]." In fact he remained, with his secular poetry and also with his philosophy, an outsider.

Ibn Gabirol does not seem to be aware of being heterodox. It depends, of course, upon the contemporary *communis opinio* who deserves this epithet. As to philosophers, neither Philo nor Ibn Gabirol had, within their inner circle (and with their subjective piety), a reason to feel heterodox any more than, in the Christian sphere, e. g. Joachim of Flora received this stigma officially in his time. How an important personality rates himself in comparison with predecessors and "authorities" of his time is a pathetic chapter of history which has never received, as far as I know, a worthy discussion. Ibn Gabirol's place in the history of western thought, within which he is much more than a living encyclopedia of his era, will have to be reconsidered.

If we compare Hölderlin's literary impact upon the Germans with that of Schiller, we have *mutatis mutandis* an analogy of Ibn Gabirol's appreciation by his co-religionists (as far as they were interested in Hebrew poetry) as compared with that of Jehuda Halevi. Indeed, the latter's musical splendor, and the virtuosity of Moses ibn Ezra, overshadowed the greatness of the generation preceding them. The passage by the still later Hebrew poet al-Ḥarīzī, who appointed himself the great poetical literary arbiter somewhat in the fashion of Wolfram von Eschenbach, assigning to the major members of Hebrew school their ranks and marks, praised Ibn Gabirol's poetry highly but also complained that his poems (like those of Samuel han-Nāghīdh) were too sublime and difficult to understand[14].

(2) "THE LAND OF POETRY" – ARABIC AND HEBREW MYTHOPOETRY

The Arabic school had discovered a certain pseudo-mythology and its possibilities in the realm of the metaphor. We discover that the very process of expressing such Arabic conceits in the diction of Biblical Hebrew did, in the case of Ibn Gabirol, in no way demythologize them; his employment of these quasi-real *causae secundae* rather enhanced their "reality" with a new oscillating sentiment for them. This is to say, we shall observe that our Hebrew poet employs the pseudo-mythological language of the pre-Islamic period which was revived and in vogue among his Arab contemporaries along with pseudo-pagan personifications such as hostile "Time," or "the Daughters of the Days," the Night, Thunder, Lightning[15]. Although the Hebrew poets would avoid references to beings like the *jinn*, who belong to the "serious" Muslim mythology which they reject, and mythological beings found in the Bible, such as Belial, Azazel or, even more within the frame of reference to chance and mischance, to the ancient god Gad, if such a connection belonged to his ken, they, as did their Arab contemporaries, saw no more in such pseudo-pagan references than mere harmless diction and allegory. In this respect they resembled those Christian Renaissance poets who could innocently employ the names of Greek and Roman deities. This "palingenesis of mythical thought without mythological consciousness," and the acknowledgment of an artistic "sphere of the imaginary" in Persian poetry is discussed by Hellmut Ritter in his *Über die Bildersprache Niẓāmīs*, where he quotes from al-Jurjānī's *Asrār al-balāgha*'[16] "There is no love like that to the first beloved." In other words, such a return to old mythology due to a never-dying desire of the still burning "first love" remains little more than a "platonic" relationship, and no longer offends a moral code of theological behavior. Ritter observes excellently that the metaphor is allowed to become a fictitious source of causation, and individual metaphors are linked to a minor concatenation of *quasi-causantes*. For instance, clouds are compared with the sails of a ship; and, linked with this simile, thunder is explained as the warning signals blown by the sailors on watch among the sails of such a boat (in Ibn Gabirol's *'Abhey sheḥāqīm*, pp. 743f.).

This phenomenon, which deserves explanation as well as observation, has its precedent and counterpart in the arts of Byzantium. There the suppression of a naturalistic artistic expression gave birth to a thaumatopoetic urge, which worked with surrealization, animation, dematerialization and distortion towards an impression of, so to speak, Solomonic magic. Islamic monotheism had created the same conditions among this already highly imaginative people. A belief in Fate, however, is somewhat more

Notes 15—16

genuine than the figure of a Wind lustful for rain, and weeping Clouds, and belongs to a certain heathen underground below the monotheistic layer, not deemed to conflict too overtly with dogma. Yet the moon is no metaphor, no *juxta id* becoming *propter id* but a most immediate *factor causans*.

We may now turn to the poem itself, which begins *Anī hā-īsh*. It shows the poet at work, revealing this expansive mind in its most intimate hour. In the attempt to interpret the poet and his poem in detail we may be guided by Goethe's advice that "to understand the poet you must enter the poet's land," and "to understand the poetical art you must enter poetry's land." It may be said that poems often convey themselves, their ambiente, and their meaning better than any account or introduction. However, being today so far from this ambiente, we shall after reading the poem need to discuss again what the poet's "land" and poetical school and tradition were. Here is the poem in a metrical translation made in collaboration with Werner Heider:[17]

Moonlit Night — The Great Nature Poem

Anī hā-īsh — *Bialik-R.* I, p. 6ff.

⌣ - - - ⌣ - - - ⌣ - - (*Wāfir*) — Schirmann: *Shīrāh*, pp. 186ff.

Schirmann: *Nibḥḥ.*, pp. 1ff.

Rhyme: *-rō (-r-ō)*

I am that man who bound his belt; its tightening — Job XXXVIII. 3; I Ki. XVIII. 46
shall suffer, till my pledge redeemed, no lightening, — (Num. XXX. 6ff.)

The one whose heart is frightened by his heartbeat,
whose soul rejects its in-the-flesh-abiding.

Since boyhood wisdom choosing, Time would choose him — Is. XLVIII. 10
for sevenfold affliction's furnace-testing.

Fell Time uprooted, hewed all his plantations, — (Ps. LXXXIX. 41) Mi. II. 13
and breached his walled enclosure, razed his building.

Behold, my friend, were he not scorched by hardship, — Lam. III. 5
a captive of the Hours', Days' Daughters', offspring,

Note 17

(Jer. XXXI. 37) He would have climbed the pinnacles of virtue
and wisdom, bared the highest stores of knowing.

Be sure, unless a man has worn his flesh, consumed it,
he never shall unveil the secrets' shrouding.

But yesterday I bought a mite of knowledge,
yet Time rose early, asked full price, unheeding.

It may today refuse its mule to saddle,
yet all my days for knowledge I ride seeking.

This heart will ne'er be weaker than its portion,
fulfills its vow, protects its pledge from crumbling.

Job III. 25 I feared, my friend, what things might come upon me.
Is not the very thing man fears ensuing?

(Job XXXVI. 32; 'Twas night time and the firmament clean-handed,
Ps. XXIV. 4) (I Ki. XVIII. 44) therein the moon, a pure heart, splendor casting.

And Moon led me on passages of knowledge,
Is. LIX. 13 and taught me thought-begetting, guiding-faring.

In fear of mischance then I pitied moonlight,
Mal. III. 17 much like a father for his firstborn feeling.

(I Ki. XX. 38; Job XXXVI. 29) Then Wind sent forth against him sails of cloud-cloth,
upon Moon's face a mask of ashes spreading.

As if he were impelled by lust for a down-pour
the Wind pressed hard the clouds and set them weeping.

The sky was filled with blackness and the Moon was
as one in death, the clouds his shrouds and tombing.

Gen. XXXVI. 32; Num. XXII. 5f. As once the Arameans wept for Balaam,
thus for the Moon the sky clouds fell to crying.

The Night put on her armor, darkness, pierced by
the javelin which the Thunder hurled: swift Lightning.

As Lightning whirred through space it seemed as if he
about the stricken Night made mock in dancing,

The Sky then turning bat-like, wings unfurling,
has routed heaven's ravens by her glancing.

And Lightning barred my quest for God: heart's pleasure
he tied like wine-hose, top and bottom bottling;

My heart he fettered with a rope of darkness,
bestirred himself, a knight his castle leaving. Ps. CXVIII. 27; LX. 11

I'll wait no more, my friend, and hope for Moon that Job XXX. 26; XLI. 1
I saw into the heart of darkness turning. (Prov. XX. 20)

Because the Clouds bear grudge against my soul, they
deny to me, I think, Sky Lantern's shining.

When Moon unveiled his face I gazed, exulting,
as does a servant at his lord's addressing. Ps. CXXIII. 2

As one embattled, with his spear drawn, who then
in rushing throws and senses he is stumbling,

Behold, thus fares a man beset by mischance
although his shrine he raise in Hesper's dwelling.

The poem follows the tradition of the Arabic kasida[18]. The meter, called *wāfir*, is the most frequent in Ibn Gabirol.

(3) THE TWO THEMES

In an analysis of our poem by Ibn Gabirol we find two themes. The first, which forms an "envelope" or frame, joining beginning and end, is an expression of strong sentiment, a lament over his ineluctable misfortune, imposed strangely upon the traditional Arabic topic of "self-praise." The second theme, that of a storm-ravaged night, belongs to the category of "description" (of nature), a topic of wide range among Arabic poets. Paradoxically, the personal part (the first theme) is written in the third person, while the descriptive section, related more loosely to the poet himself, often employs the first person. Such a change of person as well

Note 18

as a change of topic is a traditional Arabic stylistic usage frequently found in the Koran and in secular Arabic poetry. According to the technical terms of Arabic stylistics, the appearance of a second theme in our poem could be classified as *iltifāt* or *istiṭrād*, 'digression', or as *i'tiraḍ*, 'insertion', and the completion of the frame could be termed *rujū'*, 'return' (to the previous theme). Such return could also be connected with the stylistic category termed self-correction of previous statements[19].

This technique, however, as employed in our poem, serves a novel artistic purpose, that of contrasting inner and outer happenings within the poet's *Umwelt.* Yet the two themes emerge as a unit, both of them equally illustrating the poet's plight and despondence. To repeat: of the two motifs, self-praise *(fakhr)* is the framing topic, and the night is the subject of a more freely developed *recitativo* inserted in this frame. To interpret the opening line:

Dist. 1: *Anī hā-īsh asher shinneṡ ezōr-ō*
we-lō yereph 'adhey yāqīm eṡōr-ō

I am the man who bound his belt, its tightening
shall suffer, till my pledge redeemed, no lightening.

(a) First Part: Self-Praise

This self-predication, although quite old in its *genus*, was most likely inspired by the famous line of al-Mutanābbī beginning:

Anā 'l-ladhī naẓara 'l-a'mā ilā adab-ī

paraphrased by R. A. Nicholson:

My deep poetic art the blind have eyes to see
My verses ring in ears however deaf they be[20].

Or as in our literal and metrically faithful version:

It's I and, matchless, my art which blind have eyes to behold:
nay, ears I pierce which are deaf, my prosodies to instill ...

and later in the same kasida:

The saddled horse and the night, the desert likewise I know,
also the sword and the spear, the parchment leaf and the quill ...

Notes 19—20

The self-predication of the first line seems to have two different, though most likely not unconnected, origins: its form is found in very old epigraphs, as for instance, on royal tombs[21], and in the bard's or mystic's exalted proclamation of his rank or rapture.

Western readers may be familiar with this eastern motif of self-praise through Goethe's lines:[22]

Selbstlob! Nur dem Neide stinkt's
Wohlgeruch Freunden
Und eignem Schmack

or through Friedrich Rückert's "Dichters Selbstlob," both of them imitations of the Arab bard's *fakhr*[23]. As another example, contemporary with Ibn Gabirol, Ibn Ḥazm calls himself "the sun that shines from the sky of sciences" and who boasts:

Where I dismount, there it (my poetry)
will dismount as well and in my tomb it will be buried[24].

This favorite theme of the Arab poet, *fakhr*, has an origin as much in the character and position of the Arab bard as in ancient Near Eastern, Hellenistic, and Roman poetical tradition. An innocuous type of self-aggrandizement could have grown out of rhetorical exercises. For instance, the rhetorical exercises of the sophist tradition carried on in the schools of the Hellenistic towns contributed to this practice, in that they consist in belittling the opponent and praising one's own virtues or those of the defended "cause," man, city, custom, flower, etc. These *genera* lived on in Greek literature under categories named ζήτημα, σύγκρισις, and κακοζηλία[25], and the Arabs inherited them soon after their conquest of Byzantine territory. But we also observe an element of sacrilege rooted in (and to be termed) titanism.

Excursus: Titanism

The titanism of our poem is, of course, the superlative of self-praise. The romantic feeling of lifting one's crown into the clouds already found expression in mankind's early literature: to speak with Thorkild Jakobsen:[26] "Man endeavors to drench every part of his body in immunity by such identification with gods and sacred emblems." Jakobsen quotes a Babylonian text which reads:

Notes 21—26

Enlil is my head, my face is the day;
Urash, the peerless god, is the protecting spirit leading my way.
My neck is the necklace of the goddess Ninlil,
My two arms are the sickle of the western moon,
My fingers tamarisk, bone of the gods of heaven;
They ward off the embrace of sorcery from my body;
The gods Lugal-edinna and Latarak are my breast and knees;
Muhra my ever-wandering feet.

Such supplicant protestations and, for instance, the Pharaohs' official cultic self-identification with the sun, are matched in the sidereal worship and flattery of the Roman emperor[27].

Laeta bis octonis accedit purpura fastis
Caesaris insignemque aperit Germanicus annum
Atque oritur cum sole novo, cum grandibus astris
Clarius ipse nitens et primo maior Eoo.

Statius, *Silvae*, IV, 1, 1–4

In Sauter's exposition: "The emperor opens the New Year with the new sun. He rises, his own planet beside the others. He exceeds them in brightness and majesty." What is for the emperor tradition and cultic prerogative develops a ring of blasphemy in the mouth of the poet. I refer to Ovid's well known lines of hybris:

Jamque opus exegi, quod nec Jovis ira nec ignes,
Nec poterit ferrum, nec edax abolere vetustas.

and to Horace's:

Exegi monumentum aere perennius....

Ancient Near Eastern motifs live on in the mystery religions and in gnosticism. The spheres of the cosmos have to be conquered by the soul of the initiated and the hostile *archontes* in them, blocking his ascent to the heavenly sanctuary, defeated. By such deeds the gnostic hero can, so to speak, defatalize himself. According to Zosimos, mankind is divided into those beneath, and those above the εἱμαρμένη[28]. "The Mithraic votary, when their wrathful and tremendous faces break in upon his vision, answers them unterrified: ἐγώ εἰμι σύμπλανος ὑμῖν ἀστήρ, "I am your fellow wanderer, a star[29]." The Orphic carried to the grave on his golden

Notes 27–29

scroll the same boast: "... I am the child of Earth and of the starry heaven." H. Jonas reminds in his passage on "The Ascent of the Soul" of the afterlife of gnostic ideas in Omar Khayyām's Rubā'ī 31 which reads in Fitzgerald's translation:

Up from the earth's center through the seventh gate
I rose, and on the throne of Saturn sate,
And many a knot unravel'd by the road;
But not the master-knot of human fate.

A *gesteigertes Selbstbewusstsein* or rather ecstatic self-experience recurs as a typical ingredient of Islamic mysticism where it is, just as in our poem, the other pole to the feeling of the mystic *fanā'*, the 'fading away'. This is amply exemplified by Ritter[30]. The mystic Bayazid Bisṭāmī, who died in 874, pronounces *Subḥānī wa-mā a'ẓama sha'nī (Erhaben bin ich und wie gewaltig bin ich!)* [31]

The work of Farīd ad-dīn 'Aṭṭār (died 1221 or 1234) abounds with the mystic's titanism[32]. The classic case of sacrilegious titanism was al-Ḥallāj who was executed in 922 for statements like *anā 'l-ḥaqq*[33]. The same phenomenon is discussed widely in R. A. Nicholson[34] after whom I quote from *Jalāl ad-dīn Rūmī's Diwāni Shamsi Tabrīzī*' "I am both cloud and rain, I have rained in the meadows," and Firdausī:

If I could spend a night at your bosom
I would stretch my proud head to the sky

I should break the writing reed in the hand of Mercury
and robbed the diadem from the head of the moon.

I surpassed in value the ninth sphere of heaven
I rubbed the pate of the sphere with my heel.

Ibn Gabirol's secular poetry abounds with lines of titanism, in complete contrast to his religious poetry, where he clings to normative conceptions of humility. I quote his claim, which has a gnostic ring, in '*Aṭeh hōdh* (dist. 59): [35]

Their soul is nipped off from earth ... (Job. XXXIII. 6)
our soul is pearly stuff ...

which belongs to the tradition of the gnostic "Hymn of the Pearl," telling of the fall and lost state of the heavenly soul in the confusion and danger

Notes 30—35

of the world[36]. We find similarly, but in more contrite vein, in Ibn Gabirol's *Kingdom's Crown* that whereas our body is a "pinch of clay" our soul is of divine origin: "of flames of intellectual fire hast Thou wrought its form ..." "because the Lord descended on him in fire[37]." This is the monotheistic transformation of the ancient belief that the souls are "an ἀπόῤῥοια τῶν ἄστρων[38]."

Less philosophical and closer to Arabic poets' "self-praise" sound his lines in Neṭōsh lū:[39]

I am indeed a heavenly sphere
whose constellations are Man's abode.

and in *Ke-shemesh merōm-īm:*[40]

The dome of the skies is enshrined in my heart
while the world is enshrined in the dome of the skies.

Ibn Gabirol's titanism has its roots, as it appears clearly, in an old tradition of royal, gnostic, and poetical self-assertion and self-predication, a specific gnostic self-experience, and finally the inherited integration of these elements in the Arabic tradition of self-praise, be it truly titanic or merely the verbal bravado of the knightly bard. Finally, in terms of Arab stylistics, *fakhr*, 'self-praise', lends itself naturally to *mubālagha*, 'exaggeration', one of its categories[40a]. The Hebrew poets of this time, among them Ibn Gabirol, use different variations of exactly these ideas.

(α) The Loins Girded

To return to the first line, self-praise in the beginning of a poem of this time might serve a twofold purpose: it is, as it were, the rattling of arms before the tournament to attract the attention of the spectators, a prelude or overture anticipating the coming triumphs of the oeuvre; but it might also serve a second purpose — to invoke the poet's own poetical inspiration; in other words, is it the poet's "Ανδρα μοι ἔννεπε, Μοῦσα ? The image "bound his belt," i. e., girded his loins, and similar expressions mean, of course, "to make oneself strong and bold[41]."

As usual, Arabic poetry has a counterpart to this, for instance, in dist. 54 of the *mu'allaqa* (prize poem) by 'Amr ibn Kulthūm:[42]

We hasten to the attack with our loins girt *(ghāratan mutalabbib-īna)*.

Notes 36—42

But in this wording we also find, as I think, an echo of God's address to Job in XXXVIII. 3 and XL. 7, "Gird up thy loins a man ..." and with this language taken from Job, which pervades the entire poem, we discover a complete transvaluation. Compared with naive Arabic self-praise, that of Ibn Gabirol has undergone a change into almost its contrary, into despair, until we understand his tragic level: he reaches at such a stage an acceptance of his fate which is, as one might say, an *amor fati pugnans*.

:. 2 (7): A split separates his soul (or heart) from his innermost soul. The poet's pride in his own determination, the despairing courage of his heart, frightens him in his more physical 'heart'. Yet his ecstatic soul chooses the consumption of his flesh rather than give up an iota of his quest. His soul — thus he persuades himself — hungry for more than secular illusions, despises its abode in the flesh (as Plotinus did and the mystics and gnostics, craving authenticity of initiation).

(β) Consuming the Flesh for Knowledge

The poet's soul hates to dwell further in the body. This mood must not be equated with Job's suicidal wishes, which were the direct result of unbearable torment. Our poet's desire to escape his flesh is motivated by a most un-Hebrew, gnostic urge to unite the soul with the stuff of its origin and to initiate her into the mysteries of genuine being in her true heavenly abode. The topic reappears in the seventh distich. A very similar line in another poem reads:[43]

Do not marvel at a man whose flesh pines away Ps. LXIII. 2
that he may attain wisdom's heights and who succeeds ...[44]

(γ) Body vs. Soul (The Inner Split).

The negative idea of the body being a grave for the soul is known from the ancient Orphic formula σῶμα-σῆμα. Among the Arabs of Ibn Gabirol's period the melancholy al-Maʿarrī is the typical spokesman for the disharmony of body and soul:

wa-kaunu 'n-nafsi fī 'l-jasadi 'l-khabīth(i).
The stay (being) of the soul is in the vile flesh.

The affirmative Platonic idea that the "I" (and all its subjectivity) is an impediment to insight and must be overcome so that we may intuit, underlies many sayings of the Muslim mystics[45] and motivates the ascetic's hatred of the flesh; yet the eleventh century in Spain (and its precedent

Notes 43—45

in many respects, the ninth century in Baghdad) was not universally ascetic. As a variation to this idea, a poet might very well waste away in excessive yearning of secular love. This motive appears in Ibn Gabirol's love songs and, for instance, in the lines of prelude on the topic of PASTURING THE STARS, quoted in the Excursus on Lions and Oxen in Part II, which are otherwise akin to our poem:[46]

Yeghōn ḥesheq *Bialik-R.* I, pp. 127ff.

⏑- - - ⏑- - - ⏑- - *(Wāfir)* Rhyme: *-r-īm*

Grief of longing passion and boyhood love
abandoned me disheartened in anxiety,

My eyes kept open, not finding sleep
for the gates of love which were barred ...

Griefs pressed and constrained me,
yea, put me sevenfold to a smelting test in crucibles . . .

The source of the poet's suffering in our Nature Poem is not love. He attributes his suffering to Time or Fate, to a more consummate causation.

In the heroic vein of an individualist, al-ʿAbbās ibn al-Aḥnaf, the famous Baghdad troubadour who flourished at the ʿAbbāsid court under Harūn ar-Rashīd and died about 808, had boasted:[47]

ṣirtu ka-annī dhubālatun nuṣibat
tuḍīʿu li-n-nāsi wa-hya taḥtariqu

I have become a wick [of a lamp] which has been placed
to give light to the people while it is being consumed[48].

The "wasting away" of the lover, related to our topic, is the content of a chapter in Ibn Ḥazm's *The Dove's Neck-ring*[49], which must have influenced Ibn Gabirol's pining love poems.

Dist. 3: Our poet who oscillated between the philosopher's reason, his contempt for the flesh, and the eleventh-century affirmation of the senses had to strengthen his soul to accept such early 'consumption' (even if this were merely a "rationale" for his early bodily wasting), just as Shakespeare did in his 146th Sonnet. He suffers for knowledge, yet not from it; whereas skeptic thinkers discovered with despair that, contrary to expecta-

Notes 46—49

tion, their acquired knowledge does not deliver them from death and anxiety, but leads to increased frustration. The ancient Egyptian "Song of the Harper" illustrates this[50] and so does the formula of Ecclesiastes that "whosoever accumulates wisdom accumulates grief." (Eccl. I: 18). That the tragedy of knowledge (paired with that of mortality) exceeds in bitterness the frustration of ignorance, is borne out by the Biblical Paradise story. The Greek μαθήματα-παθήματα warns us about knowledge, since its acquisition entails suffering — yet it is only through suffering that we learn[51]. On the other hand, praises of ignorance are alien to Ibn Gabirol. Rather would the Germanic myth of Wotan, who voluntarily sacrificed one eye and hanged himself on the "world ash tree" for wisdom, reflect the mood of our poem.

Dist. 3ff.: He derives his pride from his quest for metaphysical knowledge, which he upholds in spite of — and maybe for the very reason of — challenging Time or Destiny which lets him pass through the fiery furnace of a last ("seventh") purification and destroys time and again his constructions. This language is taken from Job and occurs again in the last line of the poem.

If the first verses were a passionate *quand-même*, the next two verses of self-praise sound meeker, appearing in the subjunctive and describing with exaggeration what could have been achieved, if Time had been propitious and obstacles had not impeded the poet.

A specific self-praise, his boast of being hated by Fate itself and the claim of being hardened by this, may very well be inspired by other very famous lines in al-Mutanabbī:[52]

Time smote me with so many afflictions,
 that my very heart became hid in a cover of arrows;

So that when more arrows struck me,
 their heads broke against one another.

Similarly, Ibn Ḥazm, in his *Ṭauq al-ḥamāma*, set, as I think, this urbane tone of resignation (and others) for Ibn Gabirol:[53]

I have made hopelessness my fortress and my coat of mail,
 I did not don the garment of one wronged . . .

jaʿaltu ʾl-yaʾsa lī ḥiṣnan wa-darʿan
 fa-lam albas thiyāba ʾl-mustaḍām

Notes 50—53

The common self-assertion of the Arab knight boasting of his prowess indeed underlies Ibn Gabirol's language, but, in a manner which has its precedent in al-Mutanabbī's lines quoted above, such a boast has a tragic-heroic note. If al-Mutanabbī, however, takes pride in his warrior's-and-poet's hardship, Ibn Gabirol is tragically consumed by his "philosopher's neurosis." He interprets his inescapable quest in a gnostic mood as the urge of his soul, imprisoned in his flesh, to liberate itself from these fetters, but he also admits that his innermost soul trembles when it considers his determination to pay for his "mite of knowledge" with an early sacrifice of his life. Yet it is only this risk that assures his human rank. In his "Song of Complaint" we hear the poet speak similarly (dist. 50):

> I exert my flesh for knowledge and shall understand
> to the extent my flesh and my strength expires.

Dist. 5: There appears here and there (dist. 5; 7; 11; 24) an address to some person who understands, a "Thou" who is adjured to witness Fate's doing and undoing. Although such an apostrophe belongs to an Arabic literary tradition, often, as in *yā khalīlay-ya* ("O, my friends"), a mere *façon de parler*, we have the support of the verses of the "Song of Complaint" (dist. 5f.) where such an apostrophe has a fuller sound:[54]

> Whom shall I address, to whom confess
> and call to witness for my grieving?

> Were there a compassionate consoler
> for me, my right hand holding ...

We might, therefore, assume that "I" and "Thou" are the selfsame soul, to speak with Stefan George.

(δ) Poet vs. Witness (The Inner Split, resumed)

For this reason, someone could deny almost any *Wirklichkeitswert* by arguing that the occasional addresses to a witness are mere Arabic cliché *(iltifāt)*. Certain Hebrew poems, the manuscripts of which lack vowels, do not even allow a decision whether the plural or singular, "O friend" or "O friends," was the poet's wording, e. g., in our dist. 24. Our poem, however, uses addresses in the singular like *gāsh* ("come hither;" "look here") in dist. 5 and *da'* ("be sure") in dist. 7. It could be argued that such

Note 54

addresses might have been inserted by the poet in order to fulfill the stylistic demands of the "intent" of the Arabic kasida. The inner dialogue, however, between the poet and his soul is so much the very core motivation of our poem that it outgrows, as far as I see, this Arabic stylistic cliché. In fact, the poet's address to himself or to his heart is another commonplace throughout Arabic poetry. Here we observe a genuine dialogue between Ibn Gabirol's genius and his faltering morale, which he experiences as his second ego. Even if expressed in contemporary commonplaces, these dialogues between himself and his soul or genius, his bewilderment by his own innermost heartbeat, are the poet's realities, however quixotic they be. His splits are indeed quixotically real, and his steps are dizzy. What was said above about Arab playful personifications hardly applies to Ibn Gabirol's inner dialogues.

Dist. 2: The experience of an inner split in a human person originates, of course, in the most basic conflicts between the various human urges. Its specific accentuation and verbalization was afforded when man developed the conceptions of a soul, a mind, a heart, spirit, etc. and is found in both pagan and Biblical vocabulary.

The classic dramatization of such a split is a person like Samson whose own strength, manifest in his warrior's deeds as well as in superhuman passions, kills him, in a way illustrated also in Andromache's words to Hector:

δαιμόνιε, φθίσει σε τὸ σὸν μένος . . .

(*Iliad* VI, line 407)

This has its roots in strong mythopoesis and hypostatizing, as also found in the Homeric τέτλαθι δὴ κραδίη (Od. XX. 18) with which the hero addresses himself or his θυμός. Similarly, the poet invokes his Muse[55].

The line from Canticles V. 2, "I am asleep but my heart is awake", bespeaks such an inner split between the body and the true self, 'heart', or 'soul'. This is most familiar to us from the popular Scottish song, "My heart's in the Highlands, my heart is not here . . .," but is found so much earlier in the palm tree poem by 'Abd ar-Raḥmān I, quoted on p. 231), and in Ibn Gabirol (as well as in Jehuda Halevi's famous Song of Zion). Ibn Gabirol would not have been a good son of his time had he not fallen in with its convention. All mediaeval poetry is, to some degree, conventional and is conceptual; our directness would have been barbarian in those centuries. Our modern situation is illustrated by Ezra Pound: "Six centuries of derivative convention and loose usage have obscured the exact significances of such phrases as: 'The death of the heart', and 'The departure of the soul'."

Note 55

The saying "the bottom of my heart" (as e. g., in Psalm XXXVI. 2) seems to be the closest parallel to dist. 2 of our poem, which reads literally translated: "the heart frightened (dizzied) by its heart." The concept of a split between two 'spirits' or between a man and 'himself', as for instance in Plato's "he was better than himself" κρείττων ἑαυτοῦ.

Dist. 2: From another point of view of style, Ibn Gabirol's speaking of his "heart, being confused by its heart" is akin to the type of Arabic oxymora afforded by using the same word once in its material and once in its ideal sense as opposites within the same phrase; e. g., "I kissed the wall but not the wall." Such form of speech in another line by our poet induced an editor to regard the text as wrong. The line means that the poet would not "allow his heart (mind) to put its heart (mind) to a certain fact."

(ε) *Despondency and the Defiance of Fate*

Dist. 6: If in the first five couplets — written in the third person — the poet describes his virtues and at the same time his clearly realized but unbearable Fate that refuses him the mount (literally "donkey") to help him ascend the summit of accomplishment, then we understand that with this appeal — "*Viel Feind, viel Ehr*" — he invokes the defiance of his soul. For if Fate in person honors the poet with its envy, his soul must be worthy of this and also determined enough to brave Fate and to fulfill "his vow" (dist. 10), his dizzying endeavors. Yet in the depths of his mind lingers the fear that Fate might not be the true danger, but rather that his own soul had become too tired to spread its wings and now stumbles between stony pride and reluctant melancholy. The danger of such defeatism is described in an address to his soul *māh 'l-lākh, yeḥīdhāh*.[56]

> What aileth thee, soul, that thou art cowering
> mute, like a captive king?
>
> The wings of hymns thou furlest
> and draggest thine own sorrow's wing ...

In the light of all this, the introductory part of our poem is, although it is not addressed to his soul, in fact the poet's "Ἄνδρα μοι ἔννεπε, Μοῦσα?

Biblical allusions chime through the frame of the poem and give the poet's lament — tuned to sound as if it were self-praise — its weight: Lamentations III.1: "I am the man ... that has seen affliction ..." Isaiah XLVIII. 10, "I have chosen thee in the furnace of affliction," and Lamentations III. 5, "He has ... encompassed me with gall and travail,"

Note 56

whereas the inserted part on the topic of a 'nocturnal rainstorm' uses less direct Hebrew and rather immediate Arabic imagery. The poet's lament, however, is urbanely subdued: he bewails "mischance" or "travails." Using the third person, he accuses "Time" or "Fate," a *causa secunda*, instead of accusing God, as he might have, or, as he did in his earlier "Song of Complaint," his hostile countrymen, hurling at them names such as "fools," "crooks," and "crickets[57]." In this stage, his pride made him accept the challenge of greater foes, the allies of hostile Fate, among them the cosmic powers like Clouds and Wind, Lightning and Rain. He knows that hardly a second mortal stands on his titanic stage and is honored with their enmity, and that even if he succumbs, only his was the heroism to accept that challenge. To discover the difference between Ibn Gabirol's sentiment and the piety of a Muslim, we may compare al-Maʿarrī who invokes God against Fate, trusting that God "directs the darts of fate":[58]

... *ajiddu ka-mā jaddū wa-alhū ka-mā lahū*

wa-ashhadu annī bi-qaḍā'i ḥalaltu-hā
wa-arhalu ʿanhā khā'ifan ata'alla-hu

... I am toiling just as they ⟨the others⟩ toiled and I delight just as they delighted;

And I testify that I inhabit it ⟨the lower seculum⟩ by [Fate's] Decree
And that I shall move out of it praying to God [for help] in fear.

The poet's other, even closer relative is again al-Mutanabbī who links his tribulations to 'Time' i. e. 'Fate', against which he wages his lonely war, and not directly to God (although he speaks of Him in other connections quite often) in the lines quoted above:

Time smote me with so many afflictions ...

We also find in Ibn Gabirol the typical apostrophes to Fate, like that in "What ails you, Time," following a usage found, for instance, in Ibn al-Muʿtazz:[59] *Yā dahru yā dahru yā 'bā 'l-ʿajab* (O Time, o Time, o father of astonishment).

Samuel's archenemy, Ibn ʿAbbās, vizier of Almeria, bragged that Fate would never be permitted to destroy him, and was poetically fated to doom by such daring of Fate in his poetry (as the contemporary world must have felt).

Notes 57—59

Ibn Gabirol, in a similar mood and to be excused because his intent was to flatter, boasted in his very youthful poem:[60]

I incite to anger the Daughters of the Days and laugh in their faces
because they shout, "Who is he that he subdues us?

Did you thrust us in whom there is no power,
or is the hand of Yeqūthīel upon our necks[61]."

This is to say that the poet who claims a victory over adverse Fate owes this victory to his protector Yeqūthīel[62].

In this case, if the poet is not simply taking over an Arab usage, we would observe an origin

(a) in common popular fatalism which survived from pagan days, but was later developed by the theologians and by the promotion of astrology into a specific Muslim determinism. The popular fatalism was shared, no doubt, by wide circles of contemporary Jewry, and its learned circles discussed theological determinism and related theoretical astrology. It should be remembered that Ibn Gabirol shared the mediaeval belief in astrology; his great meditation "The Kingdom's Crown" bears out that, to a great degree, divine power is delegated to and transmitted through the stars. A more general outline of the phases of a conception of and belief in Fate in the monotheistic orbit of Judaism, Christianity, and Islam would exceed our frame[63]. Yet we must not forget the belief of the Essenes and/or other Jewish sects of the intertestamental period in the εἱμαρμένη, as attested by Flavius Josephus, Philo, and the Dead Sea Scrolls. A cult of *Tyche* was still carried on under the first Christian emperors in Byzantium and pervades much later, mainly secular, Christian writing, formulae for oaths, laws, etc.[64].

(b) in a poetical tradition. Hellenistic novels, linking their adventures with Fate, set the tone for poetical speech for a long time. Akin to this is, no doubt, the Arabic poet's playful engaging in mythopoesis, in his make- or fake-believe in general. Fate in the monotheistic system is, of course, or should be at least, a pseudo-causality. However, one would think that the common belief of that period in Fate was more than poetical speech (living on in Iberian songs to this very day), but was rather a truly felt power, something stronger than Ibn Gabirol's other pseudo-mythological personifications or animations which we encounter in our poem. The reference to Fate lacks the spiderweb frailty of the 'as-if'-personifications underlying the metaphorical mythopoesis of the Islamic school. In general, to derive Ibn Gabirol's harangue about Fate exclusively from the usage in his environment, for all that he employs the typical tropes and similia of his period, would be unduly simple. The poet's lament, therefore, has a genuinely renascent ring of the tragic.

(c) in an urbane aversion to using the name of God, in keeping with Jewish tradition, e. g., based upon the Ten Commandments and in the Rabbinic usage of *hash-shem* or *ham-māqōm* for God and in the New Testament expression: "Kingdom of Heaven" for "Kingdom of God," observable, as I think, more in the poems of the older Ibn Gabirol than in his earlier ones.

(d) in philosophical ideas by which the deity has acquired a transcendent character and the natural laws and secular ideas have been stressed, as in the theory of "necessity" promoted by the Muʿtazila philosophy which flourished under the early ʿAbbāsids in Baghdad[65]. Such ideas are in many ways related to a gnostic tradition. Ibn Gabirol's gnostic streak, which we have observed before, could in its expression be derived from al-Mutanabbī, with whose lines I compared distich 7 of our poem or, much more so, from his posthumous follower, Abū 'l-ʿAlā' al-Maʿarrī and this blind poet's renunciation of the world. I shall discuss this framework of gnosticism, to be felt even in Ibn Gabirol's love poetry, later.

Henri Pérès detects the source of the specific conception of Fate in the eleventh century in the skepticism of this period[66]. Since Ibn Gabirol is a liberal but far from skepticism, I would rather also link his reference to Fate with the newly begotten delight in the foreground, the world of the visual and factual and with the ensuing playful disinterest in true causes, all for the sake of a poetical "artistry." This attitude is borne out exemplarily in the anecdote referring to Ibn Ḥazm which has been mentioned in my Introduction.

The misery of his life no longer deserves to be mentioned in his song; the fatal powers have been "accepted," as aforesaid, with *amor fati* as — foes[67]. His own greatness, as he wishes to believe, attracted these enemies, and they in turn challenge his will to greater strides.

(ζ) The Greed and Envy of Fate (Time)

Dist. 8: Fate and its allies cannot deny him access to the secrets of the universe, although shamelessly greedy Fate demands in the morning the price for any mite of blissful inspiration enjoyed the day before. There is a very similar line in Ibn Ḥazm:[68]

Notes 65—68

> This mortal world whose gifts to man
> are loans demanded back again . . .

We find the theme resumed in distich 25.

Dist. 9f.: Even if his life or his 'flesh' is the price for what he experiences he does not bargain. We are reminded by this stance of Goethe's:

> Wie auch die Welt ihm das Gefühl verteure,
> Ergriffen, fühlt er tief das Ungeheure.
>
> (*Faust* II, Act I, "Finstere Galerie")

Having discussed the paradoxical phenomenon of fatalism in a Jewish poet like Ibn Gabirol, we observe the wording in distich 5 where the poet speaks of 'Time' and also of the 'Daughters of the Days'. So much ancient mythology, we find, is alive and we are reminded of Kronos or the *Parcae* or *Horae*, but the language is borrowed from the Arabic: the *banāt ad-dahr* ('Daughters of Fate'), a typical Arabic conceit appearing in Ibn Gabirol's *Nĕṭōsh lū* ("Reject 'If'")[69] or *Zemān bōghedh* ("Treacherous Time")[70]. In Pre-Islamic poetry, *zamān* ('Time') stands for 'Fate', and death, for example, is called 'the trouble of Time'. Sometimes the word *dahr* is an equivalent for *zamān* and in other cases for death, e. g., "Fate — its downpour reaps whatever it sows" *(wa-d-dahru yaḥṣadu raibu-hu mā yazraʿu)*, an image closely related to our distich 4[71]. Man is mostly called upon to persevere patiently against Fate's vicissitudes. Such an attitude persisted, although Muḥammad inveighs against a belief in Fate in Sur. XLV. 23. Also a *ḥadīth* ascribed to Muḥammad reads:[72] "Revile ye not Fate *(dahr)*, since the (true Efficient of) Fate is God." In many cases — for instance, in that of al-Maʿarrī — Fate stands for "the power of fickle or treacherous circumstances," for "life as it is by natural laws, without the interference of God." The Arabic poets speak of the Powers:[73]

> *wa-mā fasadat akhlāqu-hā bi-'khtiyāri-nā*
> *wa-lākin bi-amri ṣabbanat-hu 'l-maqādiru*

> Our natures have not become depraved by our (own) choice
> but rather by a decree issued by the "Powers."

(η) Portent and Event

Dist. 11: The poet is filled with forebodings of misfortune, and these come true. The fatalism and pessimism-in-anticipation are couched in the words of

Notes 69—73

Job (III. 25): "For the thing which I greatly feared is come upon me." A glancing allusion to Proverbs X. 24 may also be felt: "The fear of the wicked, it shall come upon him." Yet the poet's fatalism has not only its other source in older Arabic poetry, but possibly its very wording from the poet Aus ibn Ḥajar:[74]

> O soul, show yourself composed in grief
> for what you dreaded has come to pass!

In his very early eulogy of his father on his death, Ibn Gabirol said that what he had feared had materialized, that "his fears came upon him" (Proverbs X. 24):

> Enough, since my fear has come
> no longer will I see evil, and this is share enough[75].

He had been so crushed by this early loss of his father that no further evils seem to matter. An echo of this juvenile cry of the bereaved son seems to reverberate here, although it is reversed and has become the fear of a "father for his first-born" in dist. 14. He has become impervious to distress; hardened by pains, he lives with an heroic stoicism expecting nothing from the world, her evils no longer evils, only hindrances. Such hindrances he expects here.

The conception of the tragic is not known in Islam, since the Greek tragic creations are not part of its hellenistic heritage. Neither did normative Rabbinic Judaism preserve such a notion from the heroic age of the nation. biblical and Islamic pious pessimism, however, infused here, as we have observed, with the chivalrous 'bravura' of al-Mutanabbī and Arab gnostic titanism, comes rather close to a tragic conception — enough to be developed further by Ibn Gabirol. Like his elder contemporary, Ibn Ḥazm, who in imitation of al-Mutanabbī proclaims himself to be wrapped 'in distress as in a mail-coat', the young Ibn Gabirol professed to be protected by pessimism against evil[76]. But the poet is closer to al-Mutanabbī who, in the lines quoted above, beginning:[77]

> Time smote me with so many afflictions,

glories in the defiance of Fate than to Ibn Ḥazm, whose poetry in itself is quite derivative, having similar sources. I shall return to the discussion of the poet's fatalism, pessimism and titanism later on. At this part of the poem, his doom was forgotten for a brief interval of bliss. The poet is enchanted by a sky 'clean-handed' and by the moon, appearing upon it like a 'pure heart'. The wording is taken from Psalm XXIV. 4: "Who shall ascend

Dist. 12ff.: unto the hill of the Lord? He that hath clean hands and a pure heart ... He shall receive the blessing from the Lord." If the reader bears this context in mind, then the moonlit sky is 'the hill of the Lord'. The poet employs this wording, however, in a highly original way to allow for Arabic personification of nature.

Fate has allies, but the poet also has his great protector. It is, strangely enough, the Moon, whose light fills the poet with visionary bliss.

(b) Second Part: The Moonlit Night (Again, Hebrew Mythopoetry)

The second part of our poem pictures a moonlit night. Celestial happenings are not only the poet's fascination; they determine the poet's reality, that part of his life which is less physical than mystical, yet which is his sustaining reality: creativity. This he states himself and I believe that he had reached this stage for more than a fleeting moment. The poet describes an ecstatic rapture, his hour of creative enchantment by moon and night, which had replaced, for a short while, the extreme agony of despair. The dire realities of the night sky are, owing to the poet's mystical nature, either his bliss or doom.

This middle part could be entitled, like Longfellow's poem, "Ode to the Night," or even better, like Klopstock's poem, *Mond, Gedankenfreund*[78]. What he has to offer to his soul is a night kingdom to which he is transported by the moon, his ferryman. The space of the universe unveils its secrets on journeys of speculation. Wisdom has been his only goal from childhood (Dist. 3). Lunar inspiration determines his quest for God, his cosmological speculation, which may not be identical with his secular poetical genius. Neither is his lunar inspiration a trance; it has nothing in common either with the emotional cult or the inarticulate "purging" exercises of the "low" churches. It is also, so to speak, both Apollinian and Dionysian, or rather an enlightening and formative Platonic *mania*. Such derivation was not betrayed by his sober and even dry scholastic writings. We shall have to realize that what deceptively appears in his *Fons Vitae* as dry scholasticism is not the product of a purely logical and dogmatic bent at all. The two ways of expression in poetry and philosophical prose are segregated only in their expression; their origin is identical. Only here, however, in this ecstatic night does the interdependence of the various spheres within the poet become apparent.

(4) "THE POET'S LAND": HERITAGE AND TRANSFORMATION

The account of the ill-fated moonlit night is urbanely introduced as an example of his misfortune. "Description of nature" is the Arabic category

Note 78

under which the literary historian has to place this part of the poem, just as he places the first part under "self-praise," although that contained little actual praise and much more resignation and final acceptance of his tragic conditioning.

To understand the originality of this second part of the poem, I shall compare it with other typical Arabic "descriptions" of night, the main motifs of which are found in Ibn Gabirol's poetry as well. It is very often the lover whose passion deprives him of sleep so that he *pastures* the *stars*[79]. There are also the old images comparing the *sky* with a *garden*, the *stars* with *flowers* (named *nauriyya* in Arabic) and the *moon* with a *pond*, to be discussed later on[80].

The poet is able to draw upon centuries of Arabic artistic description of nature. The great masters of pictorial poetry are Ibn al-Muʿtazz, born in 861 as son of the ʿAbbāsid caliph al-Muʿtazz; al-Buḥturī, born in Manbīj in 820; and aṣ-Ṣanaubarī, born in Antiochia[81]. Ibn Ḥazm describes love's labor in the hackneyed conceits of the late crooning bard:[82]

I guard the stars as if I had been commissioned
to guard all the fixed stars and the planets

Also:

I converse at night with the full moon when my beloved is late and I see
in the moon's light, on account of its brightness, a lucky accident

And I spent the night bound by agreement, and sharing in affection
And rejoicing in union, while estrangement was on the run.

There is hardly a link between the lover's lament by night and that of the ecstatic *pensieroso*[83], for our poet feels initiated to hidden realms of knowledge. He admits naively that he lives in expectation of the Moon's
Dist. 26: mystic sight and call, "exulting, as does a servant at his lord's addressing." One of the seven prize poems allegedly chosen and "hung up," as the name was meant to imply, in Mecca around the time of the rise of Islam, the famous *muʿallaqa* of Imruʾ 'l-Qais (died in 540 A. D.) contains a vivid description of a thunderstorm. I cite from this, for the purpose of comparison with our poem, lines 72—74, which are strangely realistic, and more akin to Ibn Gabirol:[84]

O Friend — see the lightning there! it flickered and now is gone;
as though flashed a pair of hands in the pillar of a crownéd cloud.

Notes 79—84

Nay, was it its blaze, or the lamp of a hermit that dwells alone,
and pours o'er the twisted wicks the oil from his slender cruse?

We sat there, my fellows and I, 'twixt Dārij and al-ʿUdhaib,
and gazed as the distance gloomed, and waited its on-coming.

But there is another link with Arabic night poetry, that with titanism for the poet's misery, inflicted by nothing less than hostile and envious Times — these pseudo-pagan personifications — is, whatever it may do to him, a hero's lot. His alliance with the Moon, even if it is an alliance of vicissitudes, is the poet's titanic pride. Many Arabic poets chose a titanic tone, a baroque grandiloquence to go with the euphuism of this time. Abū Muḥammad ibn Sufyān addressed his patron, princeling of Morviedro Abū ʿĪsā ibn Labbūn:[85]

Abū ʿĪsā, does this remind you of the moment when we
halted to camp on the summit of the stars?

We pressed below our horses the flowers of the Pleiades
and we watered them from the Milky Way when they were thirsty.

We descended upon the Forehead of the Lion, intruding communication
when the full moon passed by like a hunted animal ...

We went, covered by the night, towards the canopy of the Virgin,
and we entered there to surprise her in all security;

When the Twins sang us a song, we stretched forth
our right hand to untie their cincture;

When the palm of the Pleiades was extended to us,
we snatched the bracelets and the rings from them;

When Canopus for our frolic burst with jealousy of Sirius,
you would have believed he was seized with folly;

We passed from al-ʿAbūr [α of Sirius] to al-Ghumaiṣa [α of Procion]
without feeling fright in the face of Hydra coming clearly into view.

The titanesque verbosity of Ibn Sufyān appears to be painfully learned. Its cosmic travelogue fails to convince, but evokes gnostic memories,

Note 85

Valentinian trips through the spheres mixed with echoes of ancient astral myths. A certain rapture may still be echoed; but there is a manneristic playfulness, and cosmic awe has yielded to rather sober astronomic knowledge and the cosmic journey to a boastful exhibition of verbosity[86].

It is with apologies to our poet, from whose progress of thought and feeling I have hitherto tried not to veer, that I insert, as an excursus, an analysis of the word *ṡahar*, employed in his Great Nature Poem for 'moon'.

Excursus: Full Moon or Sickle Moon?

Ṡahar has often been associated with the theme *ṡ-ḥ-r* meaning 'to travel around'. This topic of 'the moon as traveling guide' occurs in distich 13, which I discuss later. *Ṡahar* appears in the distich of a *nauriyya* by Ibn Gabirol which also contains the standard comparison of the *moon* with a *pond* in a garden:[87]

Ha-lō thir'eh — *Bialik-R.*, I, p. 155

⌣--- ⌣--- *(Hazaj)* — *Brody-Albrecht*, p. 39

Rhyme: *-gan*

Behold, my friend,
 the sky is like a garden bed

With the stars like roses
 and the moon like a pool[88].

The Hebrew *aggān* for 'bowl' or 'basin' in the last line is the word interpreted by 'goblet' in Canticles VII. 3 quoted above. It appears with the same meaning in Ibn Gabirol's wine songs[89]. The two words in our distich taken from Canticles VII. 3, *ṡahar* and *aggān*, indicate that the poet interpreted the Bible verse as "Thy navel is a full moonshaped round bowl." 'Bowl' or 'basin' could hardly be imagined as crescent-like; also, the cognate Arabic *ijjāna* 'trough', 'tub', 'amphora' has a semantic influence here. I shall return to the Canticles line.

In another poem (a fragment describing the late hours of a night) the moon is compared in one of the sporadic hellenistic metaphors — surviving e. g. from Sappho's third Ode which compares the moon with a mistress and her servant girls[90] — with a bride and her maids and a hind[91].

Notes 86—91

We-ālīn wa-anī nibhhāl *Bialik-R.*, I, 154; IV (VII), p. 3

⏑ - - - ⏑ - - - ⏑ - - *(Wāfir)* Rhyme: *-rāh*

Camping at night I am astir, as if
the sleep of my eyes had been detained [by force] from my eyes,

While the sky is like a tent with its hosts
around which the night is wrapped.

The moon looks among her Hyades
like a bride radiating upon her maidens,

Like a hind which gazelles surround
toward whom [threatening] the Night is a lioness.

The Pleiades, among the stars a cluster, are
like lamps placed upon the [seven-armed] candelabrum.

(Is. LVIII. 5) The head of the Night is bent by its grey age (lining)
like one sixty and twenty and ten,

The stars of the sky run towards me
like runners demanding to take a message[92].

The word used for moon in distich 3 was *lebhānāh*, which definitely stands for the full moon. The question is still open whether *ṡahar*, as it is used in our nature poem, can also stand for full moon. *Ṡahar*, in the sense of 'month', occurs in post-biblical Hebrew, mostly in poetical texts. (See Ben Jehuda's *Thesaurus*.) In the line I mentioned, Canticles VII. 3, the word *ṡahar* appears as a ἅπαξ λεγόμενον and is therefore hard to define. It is translated in the King James Version "Thy navel is like a round goblet," the word 'round' standing for *ṡahar*. The cognate words *ṡōhar*, translated 'roundness', 'stockade', and *saharōn* (in Judges VIII. 21), translated 'ornaments', or 'little moon-amulets', both refer to things of a curved shape, yet not exclusively circular[93]. The meaning of the Arabic cognate word (which, no doubt, determines the Hebrew of our poem) *shuhr* is 'moon', 'new moon', and 'month'. The Arabic stem also refers to round things. Nothing in our investigation so far has either cogently supported or strongly contradicted the assumption that the poet was speaking in our nature poem of the full moon.

In this third poem, *ṡahar* is compared with the Hebrew letter *yōdh* which may remind us of a very full sickle yet not of a circle.

Notes 92—93

The Moon as a Letter

Demūth śahar — *Bialik-R.*, I, p. 205

⏑--- ⏑--- ⏑-- (*Wāfir*) — Rhyme: *-shāh*

The moon that carves the heights of the welkin looks (Is. XL. 22; Job XXII. 14)
like a carbuncle upon an engraved amethyst;[94] (Exod. XXVIII. 19; 11)

And there is a star taking shelter in its shade
and [thus] it looks like an accented Iota;

It causes the hair of the men of [mystic] insight to stand up, (Job IV. 15)
reminding [them] of the three letters following the one.

The moon is, of course, the celestial *yōdh* (Iota), and the star sheltered in its curvature looks like the Hebrew emphasis point. The lonely letter *yōdh* inspires the poet to associate with it three more letters which, together with the *yōdh*, form the tetragrammaton. The verse, with its reference to the sky's *tremendum*, is reminiscent, as Bialik pointed out, of Ps. VIII. 4: "When I look at the heavens, the work of thy fingers the moon and the stars which thou hast established, what is man that thou are mindful of him? . . ."

Only the 'dotted', 'punctuated' *yōdh* was visible; the three following letters are mystically inspired for the "men of insight" by the one, 'the accented'.

Also in a fourth instance Ibn Gabirol, using *śahar*, clearly refers to the crescent. *Śahar be-mōlādh-ō*, literally translated, is the moon in her *status* (or *locus*) *nascendi* in the following verse:

The diadem upon her head is like a moon newly born[95].

The four moon poems quoted here compare *śahar* with (1) a bowl, (2) a bride, (3) a hind (reminding one of the poem by Ibn Sufyān quoted in the section entitled *The Land of Poetry*), (4) a carbuncle, and (5) the letter *yōdh*. In other words, whereas the first four comparisons for *śahar* seem to inspire associations of a full shining body, the last simile cannot stand for the full moon, since the *yōdh* indicates a partial (yet nevertheless diamond-like brilliant) crescent luminary in which the star can find shelter. It,

Notes 94—95

therefore, appears that *śahar* may stand for both full and partial moon. In our nature poem, I am convinced, it is the full moon.

Dist. 13: The moon leads the poet "on passages of knowledge" and teaches him "thought-begetting, guiding-faring," i. e., 'to ride and to meditate', 'to procreate and to teach'. The two words in the Hebrew each contain a twofold connotation and are thus translated into four. They are borrowed from the veiled language of Isaiah LIX. 13: "In transgressing ... conceiving and uttering from the heart ..." The etymology of *śahar* to which I referred before as "traveler," is made clear through the connection of the two related verbal themes.

(a) The Moon's Influence

(α) As the Intellectual Guide

The learned Hebrew reader recognizes in the wording *nāhōgh we-hōrō* an allusion to Is. LIX. 13 with a similar cognate reading, *hōrō we-hōghō,* for which there is no common satisfactory exegesis. The King James Version and the Revised Standard Version have "... conceiving and uttering from the heart words of falsehood" ("lying words"). We must examine the two infinitives *hōrō* and *hōghō* separately, although *hōghō* in Isaiah is replaced in our poem by the related infinitive *nāhōgh.*

NĀHŌGH means 'to travel', 'to drive'; *hāghō (hōghō)* means 'to utter', as in Psalm XXXVII. 30, according to the *R. S. V.* ("The mouth of the righteous utters ...;" *K. J. V.* renders 'speaketh' or, as in Isaiah LIX. 3, 'mutters' or 'hath muttered', whereas in Isaiah LIX. 13 *hōghō* is translated 'to pronounce', in other words 'to meditate aloud'. Ibn Gabirol's slight modification of the accepted Isaiah text may imply his own exegesis of the Isaiah passage in the sense of 'drive', 'remove'; and by using the root *n-h-g* in the previous line 13 a he identifies the two roots and accomplishes an oscillation of meaning which, in its complexity, comprises the idea of "the wandering of the poet's thought." The idea that the moon, the traveler, is also a guide who finds and directs at the same time is ancient and common. A primitive riddle poem by Ibrāhīm ibn Muḥammad al-Murādī, quoted by an-Nuwairī in the *Nihāyat al-'arab*[96], employs the Arabic root *n-h-y* in connection with the moon in the line:

Leave that; speak to people: Who is the nightly wayfarer
that comes to you openly without fright?

He has no spirit *(rūḥ)*, although
he rides the back of the dark piebald [horse].

Note 96

An old man who still saw Adam in his epoch
 and until now he retains a clean cheek,

He has measured out the jail together with his people,
 he is not wearied by his narrow path.

The same poem, by the way, speaks of the moon's "clean cheek" *(khadd naqīy)* which may remind us of our dist. 12 and also compares the moon to a skiff (see below).

A literal translation of distich 13 is: "he taught me with [his] light to fare (or 'to meditate or 'to prosodize') and to teach (or 'to guide' or 'to conceive')." With this, Ibn Gabirol retains mankind's ancient associations with the moon, compressing these into his two phonemata 'traveling-guiding': addressing the moon as wayfarer and as guide of soul and intellect.

Before tracing, briefly, the ancestry of these ideas of the moon's influence upon the earth's creatures I must stress once more that, whereas ancient and contemporary beliefs ascribe to the moon a general biological influence upon the elements and spirits, the influence of the moon which our poet experiences is neither astrological nor, in the typical sense, literary-aesthetical. The idea of the moon as an (intellectual) guide is found in the lore of many nations. Plutarch, in *De Iside et Osiride*[97], observed that the effect of the moon is similar to those of reason and wisdom. The Greeks gave Selene the epithet πάνσοφος and to the related Artemis ἀριστοβούλη. A Babylonian prayer to the Moon God contains:

O Sin, O Nannar, glorified one ...,
Sin, unique one, who makes bright ...,
Who furnishes light for the people ...,
To guide the dark-headed people aright ...
When the great gods inquire of thee thou dost give counsel ...
In truth and justice be favorable to me; may my road
 be propitious; may my path be straight[98].

The moon finding unfailingly her "narrow path" is praised in Enoch and so are "the daily moons" ... "one more resplendent than the other" which proceed "from a receptacle ... on their rich, unchangeable" progress, "disunited and undiminished" ... in their "observance of a mutual fidelity by a stable oath" and in their "proceeding forth before the sun and their adherence to the path allotted to them, in obedience to the command of the Lord of the spirits." The course of the moon's path to the righteous

Notes 97—98

is light, but to the sinners darkness. The hapless Arab caliph-poet, Ibn al-Muʿtazz, following the ancient tradition, compares the moon with a skiff[99].

The moon's power in directing the human soul carries with it, of course, its fatal aspect: the Moon may carry away our soul, we may become moonstruck, σεληνιαζόμενοι, lunatics. Hermes who was also a moon-god was believed to be the guide of souls, chiefly of the souls of the dead[100].

In Ariosto's *Orlando Furioso*[101] Astolfo has to fetch back from the moon the senses of Orlando. The intoxicating power of the moonlight is borne out by the *Rig Veda's* calling the moon a drop of Soma[102]. The moon is regarded as the source of trance and lunacy and of the poet's inspiration during his vigils.

HŌRŌ could be derived from the root *h-r-h*, meaning "to conceive and to become or be pregnant" or from the root *y-r-h* in the *hiphʿīl*, meaning 'to guide' or 'to teach'. This identification or eisegesis into Isaiah accomplishes the Greek equation of γίγνεσθαι and γιγνώσκειν. In the Dead Sea Scrolls, however, our root is related to the root *'-o-r* 'to illuminate', 'to enlighten', so that the word 'Teacher' (of Righteousness) combines the meaning of *mōreh* (ṣedheq) 'teacher' and 'the one who brings people to see the light' and makes them "sons of light[103]." According to Ibn Sīnā, Ibn Gabirol's contemporary, and the later Ibn Rushd *(De substantia orbis)* the moon is the lowest of the pure separated Intelligences, or Active Intellect, and as such dispensing divine wisdom to man[104].

(β) The Physical Influence of the Moon

The poet speaks of the intellectual influence of the moon upon him. We know that he also believed, astrologically, in a physical influence of the moon upon the earth and its beings[105]. He puts these customary views into words in his great meditation, *The Kingdom's Crown.* Although Ibn Gabirol declares that the moon is nothing but a reflector of the sun's light and that its eclipses, like those of the sun, are instituted as a memento to discourage men from unduly ascribing independent and divine powers to this luminary[106], we read in his *Kingdom's Crown:*

> . . . (the moon) eventuates with every month's renewal
> the changes in the world and new events,
> its good and evil accidents.

Although the poet's "conceiving" refers to his intellectual creation, he regards the moon as the source of fertility and increase inspired by the

Notes 99—106

tradition of the ancient conception of "cosmic sympathy." The moon was deemed to be the source of cosmic growth and, therefore, planting and sowing were carried out during its waxing[107]. A specific testimony to the moon's rule must have been the nature of women, which seemed to follow the lunar cycle. A trace of the Hebrew's belief in the fertilizing influence of the moon is preserved in Moses' blessing (in *K. J. V.*) in Deut. XXXIII. 14, where Joseph is promised "Precious things put forth by the moon," (or, with the *R. S. V.*), "the rich yield of the months." With regard to similar beliefs and a pagan cult among his compatriots, Jeremiah castigated them (in VII. 18 and XLIV. 17) for baking "cakes for the Queen of Heaven," and "pouring out divine offerings to other gods." Plutarch credits the Egyptians with the belief that the moon with its procreating and fertilizing light is favorable to the procreation of animals and plants[108].

Like the minstrel who brought "the hand of the Lord" upon Elisha (II Kings III. 15), here the Moon, as long as "he" is visible, inspires the poet in his need for enchantment.

Dist. 14: The abyss of the moonlit night is magically unisonant with the depth of his thought. The feeling of being "led" by the Moon "on passages of knowledge" (dist. 13), in his "quest for God" (dist. 22), may be inspired by the crescent which, like a lonely skiff on the ocean of the sky, unfailingly finds its path. Or is it the full moon? This current image, however, had to remain implied. The power of the moon is a personal one: the poet experiences the siderial I-thou call of the planet rather than only its abstract astrological I-it influence, and his creative disposition responds. The moon is reality; this power ruling his soul belongs to a genuinely reborn "pagan" *Naturgefühl.*

Eastern literature abounded with documents of the poetical "lunacy" of moon-dominated poets and poetesses. In ancient days the devotees to the chaste cult of the moon were rewarded by a vaticinary gift. I shall come back to the implications of this relationship of the poet to a cosmic power later. A Persian story is told: a young poetess praised as her true and only love the Moon. After she had defeated the prince of her province in a poetical contest he offered her his hand in marriage, but she declined. Shortly afterwards her body was found in a pond where she had sought death, uniting her body with the picture and splendor of her lover. The moon of those latitudes is powerful: "*Cuando hay luna en Toledo, no se encienden las luces,*" says a Spanish proverb.

There is also told a story of a mystic:[109]

> It is related that one night Shaykh Bayazid went outside the city and found everything wrapped in deep silence, free from the clamor

of men. The moon was shedding her radiance upon the world and by her light made night as brilliant as the day. Stars innumerable shone like jewels in the heavens above, each pursuing its appointed task. For a long time the Skaykh made his way across the open country and found no movement therein, nor saw a single soul. Deeply moved by this he cried: "O Lord, my heart is stirred within me by this Thy court displayed in all its splendour and sublimity, yet none are found here to give Thee the adoring worship which is Thy due. Why should this be, O Lord?" Then the hidden voice of God spoke to him: "O thou who art bewildered in the Way, know that the King does not grant admission to every passer-by. So exalted is the Majesty of His Court that not every beggar can be admitted thereto. When the Splendour of My Glory sheds abroad its radiance from My sanctuary, the heedless and those who are wrapped in the sleep of indolence are repelled thereby. Those who are worthy of admittance to this Court wait for long years, until one in a thousand of them wins entrance thereto.

Dist. 15: At this moment the wind, a familiar power, sends her 'spreadings of cloud thickets' (as may be the literal translation of this ἅπαξ λεγόμενον found in Job XXXVI. 29 which may be also translated 'swayings' of the clouds, whereas in Job XXXVII. 16 we find the corresponding form 'the balancings of the clouds'). The poet loves ἅπαξ λεγόμενα like this for their indistinctiveness or wide realm of allusion, but the context elucidates the poet's exegesis of the passage through the simile of the mask of ashes, mentioned in the story of I Kings XX. 38: "So the prophet departed and waited for the king (Ahab) by the way and disguised himself with ashes upon his face."

The strict parallelism, like that of biblical poetry, of these two lines (which was — like other biblical heritages — overcome by this generation of Hebrew poets) introduces an emphatic note of hopeless finality. Thus far, to speak in Arab terms, the poet encountered accidents and now their full fatality is not far off.

(b) The Wind, again

Dist. 16: With heightened personification, Wind, feminine as before, is filled with the desire for the 'streaming of rains'. The word *zerem*, 'flood', 'downpour', may recall the powerful ring of Habakkuk III. 10: "... the overflowing of the water passed by: the Deep uttered his voice, and lifted up his hands on high." We discover that a biblical personification, 'the Deep', was the precedent for Ibn Gabirol's, similar to others appearing in the Psalms and in Job, but he owes more to his Arabic masters.

The conceit of a Wind which Desires the Downpour of the Clouds is found in the Ṭā'ijite aṭ-Ṭirimmāḥ:[110]

> The east wind lures it [the cloud] as the shepherd [lures] a she-camel for milking,
> and he brushes her teats, the wide channels of which let flow ample milk.

Although possibly new in Hebrew, the simile is a cliché of Arabic nature poets like Ibn Khafāja. We shall encounter personified clouds, mostly as nurses of the thirsty Earth or vegetation, in Ibn Gabirol's other spring messages. A classic antithesis is afforded by the Weeping Clouds and the Laughing Earth or Flowers;[111] but an even more current contrast is that of the Laughing Lightning and the Weeping Clouds which follows.

(c) Cloud and Moon
The Clouds as the Moon's Grave

By now the sky is entirely blackened and what was a small cloud mask is now deep cloud thickets which will become the moon's grave. With this somber topic of the grave, the poet combines the topic of wailing in distich 18. If these are clichés in Arabic poetry, Hebrew, recently adapted to express such topics, is a more chaste and, by its Biblical echoes, a more sonorous medium. At this point the poet transgresses, still within the artistic medium of the Arabo-Persian school, the sphere of the isolated simile; the funeral of the moon is now the "as if" causation for the rain "explained" as the weeping of the clouds. The color of mourning is black among the Jews, whereas it is mostly white among the Arabs. The Arab poet al-Munfatil ("The Convert") refers to the black garments of mourning[112].

Ibn Gabirol's personifications owe their origin, of course, to the Arab pseudo-"dynamism" (to use H. Frankfort's term) or pseudo-paganism[113]. The first personifications in our poem, appearing after that of the Moon, are the Wind with his lust and the weeping Clouds.

Notes 110—113

(d) Clouds Personified

The Weeping Clouds

An Arabic precedent for the very frequent metaphor of "weeping clouds" is a poem by Ibn al-Muʿtazz, quoted by al-Jurjānī:[114]

Which nocturnal Cloud, untiringly weeping,
whose tear flows upon the cheeks of the Earth,

While it is still night, she pierces the morning
with a lightning like an unsheathed Indian sword . . .

Mourning throngs, as a simile for rain-clouds, are an Arabic conceit. The image of a celestial body bewailed by the rain-clouds appears, for example, in a fragment by Abū Isḥāq ibn Khaira aṣ-Ṣabbāgh. Here it is The Sun Bewailed by the Rain.

fa-l-ghaithu yabkī faqdaha
wa-l-barqu yaḍḥaqu mithlu shāmitī(n)

The Rain weeps for having lost her,
whereas the Lightning laughs like a malicious mocker.

The clouds in Arabic poetry were often compared with armies, as they are in a poem of praise for al-Muʿtaṣim, King of Almeria, by Abū 'l-Qāsim ibn Billīṭa:[115]

One would say that the darknesses were an army of Negroes,
for the routing of which the dawn sends out the Copts.

Ibn Gabirol compares the clouds with the nation of the Arameans bewailing *Ben Beor*, (literally translated "As once Aram wept for his Ben Beor," Aram standing for the nation). The reader has to know that this is Balaam Ben Beor, who had come from the territory of the Arameans (Numbers XXIII. 7) and was slain by the Children of Israel (Numbers XXXI. 8). A desired veiledness of diction is achieved partly by the learned abbreviation, *Ben Beʿōr-ō*. This comparison of the clouds with the nation of Aram, developed almost to the point of a *midrash* to the Biblical story, seems to be invited somewhat by the rhyme word (Balaam) *Ben Beʿōrō*, but this name is laden with allusion.

Since this imagery has no biblical precedent, the key for it may be found in the customary equation of Aram and Edom, who belonged,

Notes 114—115

according to Numbers XXIV. 18, to the same ancestry — for this reason, the editors of our poem could rightly choose to read Edom instead of Aram. The Hebrew letters of the two names look almost identical. Balaam has been identified occasionally with Jesus[116]. I therefore think that this simile for an atmospheric wailing procession stands for a Good Friday ceremony of which the poet must have been a witness.

We probably need not go so far as to think that the poet refers indeed to the *midrash* according to which Balaam, when pursued by the Hebrews, covered himself magically with clouds, and the Danite Zaliah, using a sword lent to him by Phineas and employing a counter-spell, killed him. The connection with clouds could, however, establish such a link[117].

The poem continues:

Dist. 19: The Night put on her armor, darkness, pierced by
the javelin which the Thunder hurled: swift Lightning.

(e) Night Personified

THE NIGHT PIERCED BY LIGHTNING; LIGHTNING — A WEAPON

This image has beside remote Greek precedents that of the lines by Ibn al-Muʿtazz, quoted above:

There is a cloud which pierces the morning ...
with a lightning like an unsheathed Indian sword.

LIGHTNING — A SWORD

The simile of a sword for lightning appears for instance in a line by as-Salāmī, a contemporary of al-Mutanabbī:

... a lightning like the sparkling of an unsheathed sword.

This is an inverted simile: normally a sword is compared with a lightning-flash (as 'flame' is the regular word for the 'blade' of a sword, e. g. Gen. III. 24); here the lightning is compared with a sword. Compare Ibn Gabirol's poem beginning: "Is this lightning or the lightning of a polished sword" *(Ha-bārāq ...)*.

ARMOR OF THE NIGHT

This imagery is found in a line by Abū 'l-Qāsim ibn ʿAbd al-Ghafūr:[118]

Softly, Full Moon, for I see that the white camel cows are emaciated,
now that the stars are moving out.

The skin of the dawn was shredded into stars
and that among them the patched armor of the night was left.

Our poem continues:

Dist. 20: As Lightning whirred through space, it seemed as if he
about the stricken Night made mock in dancing.

After dist. 18, in which "the sky clouds fell to crying," we might expect to find the current antithesis of the wind laughing; but instead it is the lightning that laughs. This idea appears indeed early in Ibn Muṭayyir when speaking of a rainstorm:[119]

Its clouds have fringes hanging with sparkling droplets.
Before they burst there is a fine rain continuous, persistent.

Its lightning resembles a conflagration in which the wind
has fanned the wood of *ʿarfaj* and of the *alā*.

It seems that in its beginning, before it was piled up,
it was sky's downpour, a torrential whirl.

Bursting with laughter in its lightnings, rain sheds a flood of tears
which leave pupils which no dust caused to weep.

Without pain and without joy
his laughter is joined with tears.

The Hebrew verb for 'laughing' also entails the wild dancing and mocking gestures of the 'motoric' man of southern latitudes. The twitching of the lightning in Ibn Gabirol's comparison is therefore no less pictorial. The image of the Mocking Lightning appeared in Ibn Khaira aṣ-Ṣabbāgh. However, the direct source for both Ibn Khaira aṣ-Ṣabbāgh, quoted above, and Ibn Gabirol seems to be a distich of Ibn al-Muʿtazz with which the two have almost a full line in common, although here it is the morning which smiles:[120]

wa-ṣ-ṣubḥu qad kashafa ʿan anyābih(i)
ka-annahu yaḍḥaqu min dhabābih(i).

Notes 119—120

The Morning shows his teeth as if
laughing at her (the Night's) running away.

Another line by the same poet reads:

The cloud is weeping while, within, the Thunder laughs.

The antagonists on this cosmic stage are the Wind that collects the clouds and makes them weep under his pressure and, even more so, the Lightning. Defiantly jubilant, Thunder, and later Lightning, pierces the Night dressed, because of her fear, in her armor of clouds, and he dances in his glee around the slain one. He is the true titan like Gilgamesh or the indomitable superman of the pre-Islamic bards, 'Antar, or the god Mithra, or any killer of the mythological age, as described more clearly further on in distich 23. The idea of the night bringing sorrow permeates Arabic poetry. Our poem has led through depression, forebodings, elation to deeper depression[121].

The heavenly drama which Ibn Gabirol describes and in which he is the passive "actor" ends in an ominous sight and the poet goes on:

Dist. 21: ... then turning bat-like, wings unfurling.

The Wings of the Night, an Arabic conceit, already found in the Koran, is also found in a poem by Ibn Gabirol which begins *Ha-phāras laylāh:*[122]

Does night spread his wing over the day.

These wings now grow into a bat-like cloud formation. Although the bat[123] is at this moment no more than a comparison, evoked by the masses of cumuli covering the skies, the same bat, this mere "quasi-reality," this *juxta id*, becomes in the next line a *propter id*, making a fictitious link which is — to repeat — according to Ernst Cassirer (quoted by H. Ritter) characteristic of mythical thought[124]. For now this bat is able to flush with its terrifying glance 'the ravens' of the sky, which could be, either like the bat, another metaphor, namely for the tempest-tousled shreds of clouds, or genuine birds of dawn:

... has routed heaven's ravens by her glancing[125].

Such a practice on the part of these poets should remind us of Rosenstock-Huessy's warning never to speak of a "mere metaphor," for it is the metaphor which relates the transitory, the ephemeral, with the higher realm of the eternal concepts.

(f) Symbols of the Dawn

THE RAVEN OF THE NIGHT FLUSHED BY (THE FALCON OF) THE DAWN

The flushing of ravens in general is a portent of misfortune. ʿAlqama, a pre-Islamic poet, has the line:[126]

> Whoever flushes the ravens frivolously
> although he be happy, will certainly fall into misery.

Old Arabian poetry also speaks specifically of "the raven of separation" *(ghurāb al-bain)* without necessarily thinking of ravens disturbed, like ʿUrwa ibn Ḥizām:[127]

> O you two ravens of the (dung-) traces of her abode, intimate me:
> is it about the separation from ʿAfra that you (two) are wailing?

Similarly Qais ibn Dharīḥ:

> O raven of separation, woe unto you, foretell me,
> with your knowledge, of Lubnā, since you are omniscient.

Also al-Mutanabbī:[128]

> The raven of separation croaks among us.

More urbane and derivative, the enlightened Baghdadi poet-prince, Ibn al-Muʿtazz, employed this accepted image without the inherent portent of separation which the *alba* brings for the lovers, but merely for the crack of dawn as such. He composed the following lines:[129]

> When the light of the morning incited the darkness of night to hurry,
> it was as if we flushed a raven with white wing tips.

This favorite simile finds a most detailed discussion in al-Jurjānī's *Mysteries:*

> The poet compares the night's darkness at that moment when the dawn appears therein, with the figure of a raven, with the supposition

Notes 126—129

> that its anterior sarcels are white. This, because there appear around the rims of given parts of the nightly sky, beside the dawn proper and its column-shaped zodiacal light, stripes of light which call forth to the eye of fantasy the form of white sarcels. The perfect exactness and the charm of this comparison, however, consists of something different, namely in that the poet causes the dawn — on account of the vigor with which it appears and dispells the darkness of night — to chase away darkness, as it were, to hurry it on and to allow it no retarded motion.

The Hispano-Arabic poet inherited this metaphor. Thus Ibn as-Sīd al-Baṭalyausī:[130]

> The night, blushing (or encircled) flushes her raven
> and the Morning pursues him with a blond (or grey) falcon.

In our case, Ibn Gabirol does not speak of the ravens he flushed, but the ominous sight evokes the most acute ill-bodings and the immediately following separation from the intellectual enchantment afforded by the night, all this in a symbolic *chiffre*. This line is, in every respect, a *fermata*. We were prepared to a degree, to repeat, for the discovery that all the events in the night sky were sentimentally connected with the poet's moods. For natural powers were felt to be in league against the poet and were the antagonists on this cosmic stage: the Wind that collected the clouds to shroud the moon and, even more so, the Lightning.

But only now do we realize fully that the poet's emotional development from enchantment and ecstasy through ill forebodings to despair were, so to speak, projected into the sky. If there is any doubt as to such a two-level stage, the lines following this *fermata* (the ravens of the sky stirred up) bluntly shift the scene to the true stage — the inner one; and thus it proves that all the time inner events were mirrored by the outer realm in a complete "projection."

We should expect, at this point, either an end of the poem or a continued description of dawn. Nothing of this sort. Without any explanation of this shift of stage the poet continues:

Dist. 22 f.:

> And Lightning barred my quest for God: heart's pleasure
> he tied like wine-hose, top and bottom bottling;

> My heart he fettered with a rope of darkness ...

Note 130

Lightning puts the poet's inner beauties in fetters of darkness and destroys the enchantment of his visionary meditations upon God.

Although the poet had forebodings before, in his premonition that the bliss of the moonlight night, magically consonant with the depths of his thought, might not last long, now, after the succumbing of the moon to the darkening clouds and an immediate first signal of dawn has appeared, the despair of the poet reaches its climax. Ibn Gabirol inherited these motifs from the Arabic tradition, although he recoins them according to a different inner and outer situation to which these motifs belong. The lover in many Arabic morning poems dreads and attempts to ignore the coming of the morning, which deprives him of the "union" with his beloved[130a]. Our poet is dejected when cast out of his "union" with the moon-inspired philosophical ecstasy.

At this point, the poet, rightly confident of having the reader in the grip of his emotion and turning from the outer scene to the inner one of his dejection, accomplishes a dynamic element denied to Arabic and Persian poetry in general and in particular to their artistic detachment from nature. According to Ritter, to repeat his characterization[131]. "The feeling of nature is ... oriented toward the decorative ... Almost in every verse [of their description of nature] a connection of space, or time, or physiology has been transcribed into a fantastic connection, mostly taken from a sphere of human actions and relations."

In other words, isolated details of events or scenes are in Arabic poetry mere substrate to carry an incrustation with inserted stylistic jewels whereby the individual link in a chain of metaphors is quite isolated. But Ibn Gabirol has reached, at this point, a dramatic pitch and his immediate return to the frame topic, his dejection and struggle against Fate, is most likely expected by the reader. But the note of dejection is re-introduced by this, the poet's darkest line:

Dist. 21: ... has routed heaven's ravens by her glancing.

The poet's ecstatic inspiration is suspended; Fate (ever watchful, greedy) has finally struck him and he feels exiled from his realm of creativity. Lightning has blocked "his heart's pleasure," the rapture of meditation:

Dist. 22: ... like wine-hose, top and bottom bottling.

This image can be traced in later Persian poetry, where it is related to the world. Niẓāmī (1135-1203) has the line:

The world became for man as narrow as a bottle ... [132]

The line, in Arabic, at the end of Ibn Gabirol's "Song of Complaint" refers to the world in the same terms,

... my desire in it is being choked.

(g) Lightning Personified
Lightning — the Knight

Lightning, mentioned again, and described as a violent doer of deeds, victorious and inflamed with force who

Dist. 23: bestirred himself, a knight his castle leaving,[132a]

was the poet's opponent who killed his beloved Night and was his true opposite. The imagery seems to be taken from Islamic poetry which speaks, for instance, of the 'castle of the sun' (somewhat reminiscent of Psalm XIX. 5). Because, in spite of our poet's boast, it is not he who is the successful hero; in contrast to Lightning, this victorious shining hero, the poet with his lot of defeat and banishment (inflicted by Lightning) can only sound a flat, though heroic, note.

At this point, we feel that what could hitherto be interpreted as mere juvenile grandiloquence (with which he had bragged to be "the sphere in which man dwells" and to "walk with his mind across the clouds") is here an authentic dimension of the poet's soul[133]. What was in his early poems boastful language borrowed from the gnostic "journeys of the soul" and passed on to him through the diluting valves of Persian and Arabic poetry, is authenticated here by a true and tragic egomania, an illusion, momentary and quixotic, but nevertheless spell-binding. A heedless modern psychologist might pigeon-hole this as the poet's mechanism of escape from an unbearable life. But the poet does not feel that he merely protects himself and withdraws into unreality; he wrestles most passionately to maintain his creativity. What holds true of such a diagnosis is, indeed, the element of 'despair', which goads him to persevere. Let us, however, not forget that between the poet's experience and his expression lies the filter of art; but even this medium is, like his theological metaphysics, more of the poet's reality than any other.

Our poet's 'description' of nature and 'self-praise' is no longer imitative and naive but highly dynamic and symbolistic. What was a *Bildungserlebnis* (literary encounter), owed to his "school" and its tradition (the artistic imagery adopted from the Arabic school) becomes *Ur-erlebnis* (the original expression of a most real experience encountered by the poet). I have been unable to find an Islamic counterpart for such symbolism created by the parallelism between an outer and an inner event. We must turn for examples to the French Symbolist school of the last century whose technique of 'projection' Ibn Gabirol would most strikingly seem to anticipate. We may quote Stefan George's "Advice for the Creative" as the typical doctrine of this Symbolist school[134]. He assures the poets that they will be understood when projecting their "untamed desires into a stormy night." In the same manner Ibn Gabirol transfers his dejection into the lunar drama. The mingling of two or more elements or topics and, beyond this, their parallelization, is characteristic of the contracted nature of his late style. Sometimes he compresses into a few lines the material for long odes of the old style. Here the very incompatibility of two topics introduces, in itself, a dramatic element, and presses for a solution. The poem's twisted thread, which keeps the reader in suspense, is in itself a parallel of the dramatic knot in the poet's heart. We may be sure that the conclusion of the poem will retain its hypsos.

(5) COMPLETION OF THE FRAME

The poet is thrown back upon himself, and he resumes his existential complaint as soon as the shudder of his soul allows him to resume his language after the *fermata* of distich 21. Yet for the poet's "acceptance" of Fate, he avoids a graceless lament or a barbarous outcry. The same urbanity prevails to the end of the poem; he resumes his address to the witness, and speaks in general terms of his desperate decisions.

Dist. 24: Completing the frame, he returns to the third person of the introduction and remains within his imagery and subdued tone; without any pathos he declares he will nol onger wait for moonlight. 'Waiting' has all the pathos of the Psalmist and of Job's waiting for deliverance.

Dist. 25: The poet's complaint is mitigated by playful repetition and a subdued modulation of the topic "the greed of Fate." Thus the seeming arrogance of the introduction, and the desperate self-praise which we observed, no longer prevail. The poet had, even before, avoided elevating his plight to that of a Job, by accusing Lightning instead of God as his antagonist. Now, at the end, his new accusation of hostile clouds, typical agents of Fate, is so sublimated in art that pathos seems to be dissolved in music.

Note 134

(a) Greed and Envy of Fate (Time) continued

The lines entail more than the quasi-animistic "causations" in Arabic poetry, but these inspired the language. Al-Jurjānī quotes aṣ-Ṣūlī:[135]

The Wind begrudges you to me — I had not deemed him hostile;
as I offered a little kiss, he blew back the veil over the face.

The poet, having affirmed that he was luckless, now takes courage from the very dimensions of his plight and his enmities. We find this idea in the tenth-century prince Qābūs ibn Washmgīr:[136]

Does Time fight except against men of eminence ...

and in a paraphrase of these lines by Ibn-i-Yamīn:[137]

It is the sun and the moon alone that suffer eclipse ...

Dist. 27: The poet knows his predicament and realizes that he is succumbing more and more to his despair. As before, the spheres of personal prowess in art and knowledge, of self-praise and of exultation in nature, the lonely philosophical kingdom of his night, remain linked with secular references; they do not allow an invocation of God. The secular and the religious are different hemispheres of his expression. In rigid denunciation he teaches his soul not to bewail what Fate and the insubordinate World deny him. His journeys of thought under the spell of the Moon leave enough comfort and confirmation of his status. As a final picture of his resignation, he chooses the image of a spear-thrower who stumbles while aiming. This ancient image, familiar to us, though not to Ibn Gabirol, from Pindar, indicates the same tragic transformation of the element of self-praise which we find in the introduction[138].

Dist. 28: It is difficult to decide whether there is a glimmer of hope in these last lines. The poet upholds the shrine where his inspiration dwells. In some way this is a proud assertion similar to that in Ibn Gabirol's *Qūm haz-zemān*, where we find at the end the words *lī khōkhebhey shaḥaq hamōn-ekhā* or *me'ōn-ekhā'*:[139]

To me belong the sky's stars, your abode,

which formula has the proud ring of "we two are star dwellers!" In our poem, however, it is not the abode, but more modestly the shrine in the

Notes 135—139

sky which is aspired to as the poet's intellectual domicile, where his inspiration dwells, yet from which greedy Fate has cut him off.

Thus the poet ceases to bewail his fate and, ending upon a subdued note, reminiscent of Milton's "Sonnet on His Blindness," he proclaims that he will no longer "stand and wait." But even this very note sounds determined, entails a self-hardening, and concentration upon his dignity and art. The poet no longer expects favors. He resigns himself to the poet's fate on earth so well described in Baudelaire's *L'Albatros,* that bird who is master of the heavens and who is destitute on the earth:[140]

Qui hante la tempête et se rit de l'archer;
Exilé sur le sol au milieu des huées,
Ses ailes de géant l'empêchent de marcher.

The progress of ideas in our poem is involved: the description of the night is not entirely spontaneous but from memory and placed in a meditative soliloquy. The poet's resignation in distich 24, vowing that henceforth he will not wait for the moon, precedes distich 26 in which he professes his dependence upon it, "as a servant," and the exultation he felt when the moon "unveiled his face." But within the frame of the meditative progress the poet recants all the professions of steadfastness and defiance of Fate in the first distichs.

(b) Hesper — the Abode in the Spheres

The poet chooses as a *pars pro toto* for the heavenly abode of his illumination where "his shrine is established," the planet Venus or Hesper *(noghah)* replacing with this the moon, the other night planet, mentioned before. This word *noghah* has the basic meaning of 'splendor' or 'radiation of light' and appears in the Bible, in connection with the moon, in Isaiah LX. 19, as "The 'splendor' of the moon." A translation of our line as "although he raise his shrine in the house of splendor" is, therefore, no less correct. I am sure, however, that *noghah* refers here specifically to the planet. Our poet speaks, in his previously mentioned meditation "The Kingdom's Crown," of the planet Venus as *noghah* and quotes Proverbs IV. 18, usually translated "the path of the righteous is like the light of Venus *(noghah)*" or by others 'light of splendor' or 'splendid light'. The reference to a "house of *noghah,*" however, recalls a star 'mansion' or constellation in which a planet takes up his abode. The word *debhīr* seems to be akin to Hebrew *heykhāl* (in Arabic *haikal*) which is used as 'palace'

Note 140

of a star. *Debhīr*, which I translated, as 'shrine', is found for instance in Psalm XXVIII. 2, with reference to the Hebrew sanctuary's "inner sanctum." In his early poem 'Aṭeh hōdh, the poet spoke of himself in a similar astral frame of reference, "the sphere in which man finds his abode," but he is here, as mentioned above, more modest or avowedly dejected[141].

Such a claim of being housed in a star constellation is involved in the name of the palace, "the Pleiades," built by the 'Abbāsid caliph Mu'taḍid, which gave the 'Abbāsid prince and poet Ibn al-Mu'tazz the opportunity of writing the above-quoted lines[142].

> You are abiding in the Pleiades, the best home and house —
> may it never cease to be inhabited, a blessed palace!

On the other hand, the ruined palace of the Sāsānian king, Kosro (Khosro), is mentioned by the 'Abbāsids' house poet al-Buḥturī with a line alluding to an unpropitious star:

> Jupiter dwells in it — a star of ill-boding.

Somehow, in an inverted way, the meaning of Proverbs IV. 18 makes 'Hesper' or 'Venus' the star of the righteous, a pleasant *pars pro toto.* Our poet's beliefs in the physical impact of the planet Venus are expounded thus in his "Kingdom's Crown":[143]

> ... thou hast encompassed the second sphere with a third sphere
> And therein ... brightness ⟨Venus⟩ like a queen amid her hosts,
> And her garments adorned like a bride's ...
> And she reneweth in the world, by the will of her Creator,
> Peace and prosperity, dancing and delight,
> And songs and shouts of joy ...
> And the love-cries of bride and bridegroom from their canopies.
> And it is she that conspireth the ripening of fruit and
> Other vegetation ...

But at this mature stage, the poet's inner relationship to the star is, as it were, neo-platonically felt, just as is his relationship to the moon, rather than being astrological and, as such, mechanistic. Mediaeval thought entailed the idea that everything in the mundane sphere beneath the moon is transitory and changing, whereas above the moon everything is eternal and immutable[144].

Notes 141—144

The last words of resignation are reminiscent once more of Nietzsche, who comments in a letter to his friend, Overbeck, that he lives in the fashion of a *quand-même* against despair of illness and he feels that he is "no longer waiting for external help, only for internal resources to be mobilized."

(6) CONCLUSION AND COMPARISON

I have singled out this specimen of secular Hebrew poetry which belongs to the Cordovan Arabic school. It employs the entire apparatus of the Arabic playful descriptions of nature; yet by relating his topics to his own mood of a poetical enchantment and its disruption, the poet achieves a great emotional congruity, unknown to the Arabic school.

Ibn Gabirol went further by his universality, Platonism, and "visuality" towards the Italian Renaissance than anyone else in this generation of Arabs and Jews. To summarize some details, no theological prohibition prevents him from admitting his factual and tragic dependence of his creativity upon an inspiring natural power: the moonlight. We are witnessing the first appearance of a typical Renaissance phenomenon, anticipating what was to take place much later elsewhere, and reflected in later European literature. The poem shows an artistic unity, and this according to modern aesthetics, through an organic counterpoint (which goes beyond the mere outward element of unity in Arabic poetry: the monorhyme). Whereas the Arabic poet, working with his *disjecta themata* of nature and plastic art and philosophical maxims, disdains, in his conception of pure urbane artistry, the impression of a dominant mood, Ibn Gabirol, in some instances, though by far not all, reaches an all-pervading pathos. It is hard to decide whether the Hebrew poet derived this change of aesthetic values merely from his own literary upbringing and the associations of his Hebrew medium or whether Ibn Gabirol's conscious association with the great Hebrew archetypes, the Patriarchs, a Saul, a David, a Ruth, and Job, set him off against his entire milieu. If the philosopher Jaspers is right in calling the Old Testament the most western of books, then we realize that even this caused our poet to transcend his eastern ambience. Yet it remains hard to decide whether the poet strove consciously himself for liberation from the motif, the contrived stylistic flourishes, to a higher unity and a Western melos or whether this was achieved by the dynamics of the poet's distress and the greatness of his ecstatic soul bent on fulfilling his poetic purpose.

The poet is not aware of having outdone his masters and the models of the Arabic school. And, to repeat, measured by the standards of Arabic poetic, such symbolistic unity of tone and topic, and in particular such sentimental introduction of the poet's ultimate realities, might have been regarded as unartistic, bombastic, unwitty, unduly self-revealing[145]. Ibn Gabirol's distress and his vehement inner struggle, together with his innate chastity and discretion, have formed in this poem a unique language which, so far as can be determined, is unknown elsewhere in this period. Yet, at the same time, the poet anticipates astonishingly much of the accomplishments of nineteenth century symbolism. If, according to Friedrich Schiller, the naive poet is nature whereas the sentimental poet seeks nature, then Ibn Gabirol most certainly is the sentimental — no less in the moments when he seems to have found nature as a most personal revelation.

Indeed, the rebirth of man's modern relation to nature took place also within the Christian orb in a very few, who were enlightened towards a new visual "dimension" by a Platonic spark, kindling suddenly from Neo-Platonic philosophy. These seem to be the same souls that felt secular love to be their share of the universe's Love which "moves the spheres," and who therefore sanctified and emancipated it. Book and blood, to repeat, unfetter mediaeval man, his eye and his heart. His love and his vision are still deeply ecstatic, transcendental. Yet lucubration yields here to a fusion between the sphere of outer nature and the sphere of his abstract mind.

It could be said that the Christian West, though denying itself naive enjoyment and contemplation of nature as an end in itself, allows the human eye a religious edification by the representative arts, whereas, as A. Mez rightfully stresses[146], in Islam, "poetry had to assume also the other role, that of plastic art." Even if some naive joy derived from nature is expressed in the mediaeval *volgare* poetry and very occasionally in Latin lines, official mediaeval Christianity wished to look through and behind nature at the Creator only; nature served merely as a looking glass for "speculation." This attitude is well presented by Curtius[147] in a paragraph entitled "Das Buch der Natur," in which he quotes the most representative lines by Alan of Lille of the twelfth century:

Omnis mundi creatura
Quasi liber et pictura
Nobis est et speculum.

To demonstrate the complete heterogeneity of our poem from contemporary epigonic Latin '*versiculi*', with the same topic, I refer to Walahfrid Strabo's moon poem:[148]

Notes 145—148

Cum splendor lunae fulgescat ab aethere purae
(Cf. Horace, *Carm.*, ii: 3. 23) Tu sta sub divo cernens speculamine miro,
Qualiter ex luna splendescat lampade pura
Et splendore suo caros amplectitur uno
Corpore divisos, sed mentis amore ligatos,
Si facies faciem spectare nequivit amantem,
Hoc saltem nobis lumen sit pignus amoris.
(Cf. Virgil, *Aen.* vii. 291) Hos tibi versiculis fidus transmisit amicus;
Si de parte tua fidei stat fixa catena,
Nunc precor, ut valeas felix per saecula cuncta.

In English translation:

When from the firmament cloudless the splendor of moon is reflected,
Stand in the open beneath enjoying the heavenly vision;
See how outside the moon shines forth: an immaculate lantern,
Keeps in the one embrace of his light the dearest companions,
Only in body divided but bound by the love of the spirit.
Though one affectionate face be barred from seeing the other,
May at least then the light provide a pledge of affection.
Take these lines of a friend as a token of loving devotion.
If you too will keep the bond of fidelity sacred,
Then I'll pray for your welfare, both now and in ages eternal.

A passage from the Merlin Epic by Galfrid (Geoffrey) of Monmouth written about 1155 and describing the hero's prophetic inspiration afforded by nocturnal nature, shows even greater enthusiasm, very close to our topic and unique: [149]

Nox erat, et nitidae rediabant cornua lunae
Cunctaque convexi splendebant lumina caeli,
Purior aer erat solito, nam frigidus atrox
Expulerat nubes boreas caelumque serenum
Reddiderat sicco detergens nubila flatu.
Virg. *Aen.* III. 515 Sidereum cursum vates spectabat ab alto
Monte, loquens tacite sub divo . . .

It was night, the horns of radiant Luna were glinting;
All luminaries of the sky's shell shone clearly;
Purer also the air than was wont, for grim and chilly
Boreas had driven out the clouds and left the heaven

Note 149

Serene, blotting away with dry breath the mist.
The seer watched the stars in their courses from a mountain's
Height, silently speaking beneath the firmament.

At another instance, the hero decries winter and praises the standard *locus amoenus* and the warm seasons quite sentimentally:[150]

O utinam non esset hiems aut cana pruina; Ov. Ep. 5. 16; Verg. Georg. II. 376
Ver foret aut aetas, cuculusque canendo rediret
Et philomena, pio quae tristia pectora cantu
Mitigat, et turtur conservans foedera casta,
Frondibus inque novis concordi voce volucres Verg. Cul. 146
Cantarent aliae quae me modulando foverent,
Dum nova flore novo tellus spiraret odorem ... Ov. Met. 13. 394
Gramine sub viridi, levi quoque murmure fontes
Diffluerent juxtaque daret sub fronde columba
Somniferos gemitus irritaretque soporem!

O were it not winter and bleak the hoar-frost,
That it were spring or summer when the cuckoo returns
Calling and the nightingale soothing saddened breasts with
Pious song, and the turtle-dove that keeps chaste vows; that,
Among new leaves, other winged ones sang in unison,
To comfort me with their melodies' variations,
While with new bloom a new earth breathes fragrance!
And that beneath lush lawns with tender murmur
Welled the springs and nearby the dove under leaves
Offered moaning lullabies inviting slumber!

The twelfth-century poet divulges that this intercourse with nature, paired with the hero's divinitory inspiration, is an aspect of his ascetic life close to nature. The intellectual situation of the Welsh poet, writing in a language not the common, is similar to that of the Hebrew poets in Spain whose common language was Arabic (and/or Spanish). Vulgate Latin was the sacred language of the former, but he was also familiar with the rather different vocabulary of Ovid and Virgil whom he imitated. The latter knew Arabic poetry most intimately, yet they imitated this in their sacred language. Hebrew had to be revived for such a secular poetical usage, but this was done as a part of a Solomonic renascence and emancipation which included many other activities of the circle of Cordova (and the same in Granada). The main difference between Ibn Gabirol's relationship to nature and that professed in Galfrid's epic is, therefore, the unfettered admission of the poet's own dependence upon the moon and his fight against Fate and its allies, the other animated natural powers; all this, however, for an artistic end.

In analyzing another of Ibn Gabirol's poems, I have tried to demonstrate his genuinely Platonic passion for his idealized disciple. In this very poem, outer visions and a domination by the unfolding view seem to demonstrate man's re-awakening to the world of the visible. A comparison with any other mediaeval document of nature observation will show the fundamental difference between descriptive allegorism there and emotional symbolism here. Ibn Gabirol's relation to nature was a rare merger of contemporary neo-Platonism (otherwise mostly the possession of Sufis and scholars of an inward orientation rather than of the aristocratic and all-too-artistic poets) with the eye of the Andalusian descriptive poets (such as Ibn Khafāja, thirty-six years younger than Ibn Gabirol). This merger could take place in a man who embodied, in addition to the heritage of these two groups, the nature, depth and refinement of the elite of the old nation, and who, by his personal ingenuity and an inner and outer independence, overcame his conditioning 'backgrounds'. Hebrew millennial asceticism and withdrawal from the sphere of the aesthetic seem to be suspended for a moment. All this is due to the enthralment exerted by Cordovan humanism, even after its downfall, over a very few receptive minds. Yet, if we ask what conditioned this individual poem, we may have to add to the above constitutive elements the urbanism of the eleventh century, the associations and lucidity of revived Hebrew and, causing all this to merge, the poet's genius.

Notes to Part III B

B. Ibn Gabirol's Great Nature Poem

1. See S. T. Coleridge, *Complete Poetical Works* (Oxford, 1912), I, p. 362, and Thomas Percy, *Reliques of Ancient English Poetry*, London, 1794, I, p. 80. *Varia lectio:*

    Late, late yestreen I saw the new Moon,
    With the old Moon in her arms;
    And I fear, I fear, my dear Master
    That we will come to harm.

    The similarity of motives with that of Ibn Gabirol's line (Dist. 14):

    In fear of mischance then I pitied moonlight etc.,

    was observed by my learned colleague, Professor Rhodes Dunlap.
2. See the present writer's "Ibn Gabirol's Poem beginning Ahavtikha ..." in *Review of Religion*, 1950, and "Die Bedeutung des Weltalls für Gott nach Ibn Gabirols philosophischem Gedicht," in *Zeitschrift für Religions- und Geistesgeschichte*, VI, 1954, pp. 18ff.; See also R. Klibansky, *The Continuity of the Platonic Tradition during the Middle Ages*, London, 1939, pp. 36, 42, and 45—47, presenting Marsilio Ficino's letter of 1489 to his friend Martin Prenninger, in which he enumerates these "transmitters," and among them "*Avicebron, De Fonte Vitae* ..."
3. See, among more recent literature, John Goheen, *The Problem of Matter and Form in the De Ente et Essentia of Thomas Aquinas*, Cambridge, Mass., 1940; James Collins, *The Thomistic Philosophy of the Angels*, Washington, D. C., 1947; E. Gilson, "Pourquoi S. Thomas a critiqué S. Augustin?," in *Arch. d'hist. doctr. et litt. du moyen-âge*, I, 1926—27, pp. 5—128, *passim* after p. 25.
4. See H. Pflaum, *Die Idee der Liebe, Leone Ebreo*, Tübingen, 1926, pp. 95; 100—101 and 134.
5. See C. H. Becker, *Islamstudien*, Leipzig, 1924, p. 37: "The 'I' symbolizing individualism is an occidental discovery."
6. Abraham ibn Dā'ūd, *Ṡepher hā-emūnāh hā-rāmāh*, "*Das Buch 'Der Erhabene Glaube'* ... *verfasst in Toledo* 1160," Berlin, 1919.
7. Moses ibn Ezra (born in Granada about 1060; *vide E. J.*) criticized Ibn Gabirol's bold Hebrew innovations in his *kitāb al-muḥāḍara wa-l-mudhākara.* See J. and H. Derenbourg, *Opuscules et traités de Abou 'l-Walid Merwan Ibn Djanah*, Paris, 1880, pp. XVIIf. (quoted as Derenbourg, *Opuscules*); and D. Yellin, *Tōrath hash-shīrāh haś-Ṡephāradhīth*, Jerusalem, 5700, 1940, p. 81; p. 305 (quoted as *Yellin*). Compare in *Bialik-R.*, III (V): *Shīrey ḥōl*, p. 33, No. 58, a poetical example of Ibn Gabirol's bold reply to criticism.
8. The problem of the documentary value of descriptive poems by this school (a related phenomenon) is discussed in Part II of this book. Ibn Gabirol inherits, of course, together with the Arabic metaphors, their deliberate "pathetic fallacies," to use a term of English literary criticism, and the playful pseudo-causality of the Arabic poets, discussed above and below; but the

poems, chiefly, in which his own experience is directly related, and skies, gardens, and castles are described, partake of the veracity of a new Arabic school of poetry and its forerunners to which, in particular, the old Arab bard ʿAlqama belonged.

9. Abū 'l-ʿAlā' al-Maʿarrī (born in 973 C. E. near Aleppo, *vide G. A. L.*, S. I, p. 449) stressed particularly the veracity of his poetry and has strongly influenced the Cordovan circles of Ibn Ḥazm (born in 993 in Cordova; *G. A. L.*, I, p. 400; S. I, p. 692; *E. I.*, II, pp. 384f.) as well as Samuel han-Nāghīdh. Ibn Gabirol is ostensibly dependent upon al-Maʿarrī's pessimistic world view and "tone." A poem like *we-lebh nābhūbh* in *Bialik-R.*, I, p. 146, is unthinkable without al-Maʿarrī. Al-Maʿarrī's statement about his new veracity is found in Nicholson, *Studies*, p. 50, n. 2.
10. As-Suyūṭī was born in Cairo in 1445 (*G. A. L.*, S. II, pp. 143ff.). His statement is found in the same footnote by Nicholson.
11. For instance in "Vor Sonnenaufgang" in his *Zarathustra*.
12. See below the passages "DESPONDENCY AND DEFIANCE" and "THE GREED AND ENVY OF FATE."
13. *Bialik-R.*, I, pp. 4f., distich 26, "Song of Complaint," beginning *Niḥar*.
14. I discuss the employment of the Arab *ars poetica* in the subsequent interpretation of poems. As for Hebrew Poetry I refer to I. Goldziher, "Bemerkungen zur Neuhebräischen Poesie," in *Jewish Quarterly Review*, XIV, pp. 719–736 (quoted as *Goldziher*); for Arabic poetry to G. E. v. Grunebaum, "The Nature of the Arabic Literary Effort," in *Journal of Near Eastern Studies*, III, 1948, 116ff. I quote from Nicholson, *Studies*, p. 53: "... Even in the case of the best poets ... the tyranny of the rhyme exacts a crushing toll of repetition, monotony, banality, obscurity, and affectation ... No doubt al-Maʿarrī appears occasionally weighed down by his chains, but often he can move in them with such dexterity and ease that they impress rather as an ornament than a hindrance." Many particular elements of Arabic (and Hebrew) poetics could be pointed out in this poem; but, even if we know that, for example, the twofold use of the verb *b-ḥ-r*, meaning both 'to choose' and 'to purify' or 'refine' (in dist. 3a and b), is an example of *tajnīs (double entendre)*, or that the amplification and anaphora of dist. 7–8, "Fate wrought destruction, hewed ... broke open ... razed" is a technique of style emphasized by the Arabic school, little has been gained. The technical means do not carry this poem, the poem carries them. On the metrical merits of this poem see *Yellin*, pp. 60, 64. For plays upon roots, repetitions, etc. also see E. Bräunlich, "Literaturgeschichtliche Betrachtungsweise altarabischer Poesien," in *Der Islam*, XXIV, 1937, pp. 235f. (quoted as Bräunlich, *Poesien*).
15. Hellmut Ritter, *Über die Bildersprache Niẓāmīs*, Berlin, 1927 (quoted as [Ritter,] *Niẓāmī*). Ritter quotes for such an artistic turn the formula of the Arab stylist al-Jurjānī (died 1079), answering the question why an abstract thought should be illustrated by a visual simile.
16. The author of the *Asrār al-balāgha*, pp. 69f., al-Jurjānī. Lived in the Persian region (*G. A. L.*, I, pp. 28f.).
17. My readings in the text of "The Great Nature Poem" as they appear in the text below are discussed in the *Variae lectiones* later on:

אֲנִי הָאִישׁ אֲשֶׁר שִׁנֵּס אֱזוֹרוֹ / וְלֹא יֶרֶף עֲדֵי יָקוּם אֱסָרוֹ,
אֲשֶׁר נִבְהַל לְבָבוֹ מִלְּבָבוֹ / וְנַפְשׁוֹ מָאֲסָה לִשְׁכֹּן בְּשָׂרוֹ,
וּבָחַר בַּתְּבוּנָה מִנְּעוּרָיו, / וְאִם כּוּר הַזְּמָן שֶׁבַע בְּחָרוֹ
וַיַּהֲרֹס כָּל אֲשֶׁר יִבְנֶה, וְיִתֹּשׁ / אֲשֶׁר יִטַּע, וְיִפְרֹץ אֶת גְּדֵרוֹ·

וָגֹשׁ-לוּלֵי אֲשֶׁר הַקֵּף תְּלָאָה / וְיֶלֶד מִבְּנוֹת יָמִים סְגָרוֹ-
לְקַצְּוֵי מַעֲלוֹת חָכְמָה וּמוּסָר / וּמוֹסַד אוֹצְרוֹת שֵׂכֶל-חֲקָרוֹ.
וְדַע כִּי לֹא יְגַלֶּה עַד יְכַלֶּה / צְפוּנֵי תַעֲלוּמוֹת אִישׁ שְׁאֵרוֹ,
וְקָנִיתִי תְמוֹל שֶׁמֶץ תְּבוּנָה / וְהִשְׁכִּים הַזְּמָן לִדְרֹשׁ מְחִירוֹ.
וְעוֹדִי, אֶרְכְּבָה לִדְרֹשׁ תְּבוּנָה, / וְאִם לֹא יַחֲבֹשׁ הַיּוֹם חֲמוֹרוֹ,
וְלֹא יֶחְלַשׁ לְבָבִי מִזְּמַנִּי / אֲבָל יָקִים אֱסָרוֹ, בַּל הֲפֵרוֹ.
וְיָגֹרְתִּי, מְיֻדָּעַי, אֲשֶׁר בָּא- / וְלֹא יָבוֹא לְאִישׁ כִּי אִם מְגוֹרוֹ.
בְּעֵת לוּנִי, וְהַשַּׁחַק נְקִי-כַף, / וְהַסַּהַר טְהָר-לֵבָב וּבָרוֹ,
נְהָגַנִי עֲלֵי אָרְחֵי תְבוּנוֹת / וְהוֹרַנִי בְּאוֹר נָהֹג וְהֹרוֹ,
וְחָמַלְתִּי, בְּפַחְדִּי מִתְּלָאוֹת, / עֲלֵי אוֹרוֹ כְּאָב עַל בֶּן-בְּכוֹרוֹ.
וְרוּחַ שִׁלְּחָה בוֹ מִפְלְשֵׂי עָב / וּפָרַשׂ עַל פְּנֵי סַהַר אֲפֵרוֹ,
כְּאִלּוּ אוֹתָהּ זֶרֶם גְּשָׁמִים / וְתִשָּׁעֵן לְעָב עַד כִּי תְקֵרוֹ.
וְשַׁחַק הֶעֱטָה קַדְרוּת, וְסַהַר / כְּאִלּוּ מֵת, וְהֶעָנָן קְבָרוֹ,
וּבָכוּ אַחֲרָיו עָבֵי שְׁחָקִים / בְּכוֹת, כִּבְכוֹת אֲרָם עַל בֶּן-בְּעוֹרוֹ.
וְלָבַשׁ לַיְלָה שִׁרְיוֹן אֲפֵלָה / וְרַעַם בַּחֲנִית בָּרָק דְּקָרוֹ,
וְהַבָּרָק עֲלֵי שַׁחַק מְעוֹפֵף / כְּאִלּוּ הוּא מְשַׂחֵק עַל דְּבָרוֹ,
אֲשֶׁר פָּרַשׂ כְּנָפָיו כַּעֲטַלֵּף / וְעָפוּ עוֹרְבֵי חֹשֶׁךְ בְּשׁוּרוֹ.
וְסָגַר מַחֲשַׁבְתִּי אֵל, וְחֵפֶץ / לְבָבִי מִשְּׁנֵי פָנִים אֲסָרוֹ,
וְאָסַר בַּעֲבוֹת חֹשֶׁךְ לְבָבִי / וְהִתְעוֹרֵר כְּגִבּוֹר מִמְּצוּרוֹ.
וּבַל אוֹחִיל, יְדִידַי, וַאֲקַוֶּה / לְאוֹר סַהַר, אֱשׁוּן חֹשֶׁךְ הֱמִירוֹ,
כְּאִלּוּ קִנְאוּ עָבִים לְנַפְשִׁי, / וְעַל כֵּן מָנְעוּ מֶנִּי מְאוֹרוֹ.
וְאַשְׁקִיף עֵת יְגַל פָּנָיו, וְאָגִיל / כְּגִיל עֶבֶד אֲשֶׁר אָדוֹן זְכָרוֹ.
בְּהִלָּחֵם אֱנוֹשׁ יִפְתַּח חֲנִיתוֹ, / וְעֵת יָרוּץ אֲזַי יִמְעַד אֲשׁוּרוֹ-
וְכֵן אִישׁ יַדְבְּקוּ אוֹתוֹ תְלָאוֹת, / וְלוּ יָשִׂים בְּבֵית נֹגַהּ דְּבִירוֹ!

A German translation of this poem by Karl Wolfskehl and this writer appeared in *Schocken Almanach auf das Jahr 5698*, Berlin, 1937, pp. 51f. The English translation made by my friend Werner Heider after my raw translation is based upon Bialik-Ravnitzki's text. The poem is also found in Schirmann's anthology. Whereas Bialik-Ravnitzki, who did the pioneer work in collecting and restituting Ibn Gabirol's poetry, indicate the *variae lectiones* of the manuscripts and *corruptelae* of the text in a proper *apparatus criticus*, Schirmann, who had the advantage of having access to the unique Manuscript 37 of the Schocken Genizah in Jerusalem and to Brody's amendments of Bialik's text (which he fails to mention), omits to state which text he found in his *Vorlage*. Therefore, and also because of a lack of poetical understanding, his editions of the text remain dubious. The key to the container of this manuscript, Schocken 37, was in Tel Aviv when this writer was in Jerusalem to see it; written requests for photo copies of pages of MS 37 (Schocken), issued by University of Iowa officials, were answered in a similarly evasive fashion.

Notes to the Text and to the Translation

Dist. 1: This selfpraise is discussed in *Yellin*, p. 64.

Dist. 5: Schirmann reads *asher tīyqadh telā'āh* instead of Bialik-R.'s *asher huqqaph telā'ōth*. With this change the allusion to Lamentations III. 5 is lost ("... enveloped me ... with tribulations," in the *Revised Standard Version*); the singular *telā'āh* is, of course, acceptable, if it has manuscript support. The next line, literally translated, reads: "a child from the Daughters of the Days."

Dist. 6: Schirmann's variant *u-mōśadh ōṣer-ōth*, if found in a manuscript, would be supported by Jer. XXXI. 37 (which he fails to quote).

Dist. 9: The variant *hay-yōm* adopted by Schirmann instead of *haz-zemān* seems to be preferable for metrical reasons and, as a counterpart to *themōl* in dist. 8, *haz-zemān*, mentioned in dist. 8, remains, in any case, the subject; a second *haz-zemān* would be repetitious.

Dist. 11: Schirmann's *biltī* seems inferior to Bialik-R.'s *kī im*, only to be excused if a manuscript supports this.

Dist. 12: As Bialik-R. observed beautifully, *neqī khāph* may allude to I Kings XVIII. 44 where the size of a cloud is compared with a hand (palm). *Neqī khāph*, in connection with a cloud, may therefore also suggest the interpretation: "clean (even) of a hand [-sized cloud]." The reading *be-ʿeth layil* was Bialik-R.'s conjecture on the basis of *be-ʿeth l-y-m* found in previous texts. Schirmann (or Brody?) may be correct when reading *be-ʿeth lūnī*. The usage of the verb *lūn* in the sense of 'spending the night time awake' is accounted for in *Bialik-R.*, I, p. 154, *we-ālīn wa-anī nibhhāl* referring to a vigil rather than to sleep.

Dist. 13: The poet employs, instead of the Masoretic text of Is. LIX. 13 *hōrō we-hōghō*, the wording *nāhōgh we-hōrō*. In other words, he related the two roots *n-h-g* and *h-g-h* and this to gain new shades of meaning for the exegesis of the Isaiah passage and for this own usage. The line will be discussed later in detail.

Dist. 15: I prefer, instead of *miphresey ʿābh*, *miphlesey ʿābh*, with the Masoretic text of Job XXXVII. 16 to which the poet refers; *miphlesey ʿābh* is there a ἅπαξ λεγόμενον; yet it is also accounted for in some Bible manuscripts in Job XXXVI. 29 ('The balancing of clouds', in the *Revised Standard Version*). The change is of a minor nature and can be defended by Ibn Gabirol's penchant for ἅπαξ λεγόμενα; also the root *pāras* is found in the next line 30 and *miphrās* might, therefore, appear somewhat redundant (in spite of the Semitic predilection for the *figura etymologica*).

Dist. 16: The poet's wish to revive ἅπαξ λεγόμενα is borne out in his *teqer-ō* after Jer. VI. 7 ("... as a fountain casteth out waters ..." in the *King James Version*). This interest in rare verbal roots grew out of discussions within the poet's circle, such as those between the grammarians and linguists born in Cordova around 990 like Ibn Janāḥ, Ḥayyūj, and Shemū'el han-Nāghīdh, who constituted the two fronts of heated literary battles. See the introduction to Derenbourg, *Opuscules*. Compare a very similar couplet in a poem by Samuel han-Nāghīdh in Habermann, *Diwan*, II, p. 135, 1. 14. Did one plagiarize the other?

Dist. 19: Typical *ṣila* construction. *Vide* also dist. 28.

Dist. 20: Schirmann adopted in his *Shīr-īm Nibhḥār-īm* the reading *azay shaḥaq* 'then Sky', but abandoned this later in his *Shīrāh* in favor of Bialik-R.'s previous *ʿaley shaḥaq*, which is supported of course by Gen. I. 20 *yeʿōpheph ʿal hā-āreṣ*.

Dist. 21: Schirmann reads *ʿōrebhey hōṣhekh* instead of Bialik-R.'s *ʿōrebhey shaḥaq*, which is acceptable if it has manuscript support. The ambiguity of *be-shūr-ō* borrowed from an uncertain line in Psalm XCII. 12, to which it alludes, enhances the poetical climate of the line. However, its employment here also reflects (as ever) upon the poet's interpretation of the Biblical passage. Various readings have been suggested for the doubtful word *be-shūr-ī* in the Psalm: (1) with the current *Qere*, *sōrer-āy* or *shōrer-āy* to mean "in my glancing my eye has looked at my adversaries;" or (2) (with the *Revised Standard Version*) "My eyes have seen the downfall of my enemies" (reading *be-shōḇ?*). Ibn Gabirol's own interpretation seems to employ the meaning of the verb *shūr* as in the Song of Solomon IV. 8 'to look down', which would render the Psalm verse "My eye glanced upon my adversaries in my looking down."

Dist. 22: Bialik-R.'s variant *maḥashabht-ī el* seems to be far superior to Schirmann's *maḥshebh-ōth-ay el.* In the former text the two words form a construct in which *el* is the *nismākh*, meaning "my meditation of God." In the latter case *el* becomes the subject of the sentence, which is unthinkable; it is not God who fetters the poet's meditation but Lightning, (still the subject) about whom the poet complains, who fetters the poet's mind. The interposition of the personal suffix (of *maḥashabht-ī*) in a construct is, of course, the usage found in Arabic poetry and otherwise in this Hebrew school of poetry. Cf. W. Wright, *A Grammar of the Arabic Language*, Cambridge, 1951, II, pp. 222ff. A concept similar to *maḥashbabht-ī el* is *daʿath elōh-īm* in Ibn Gabirol's *Niḥar be-qor'-ī gherōn-ī*, *Bialik-R.*, I, p. 5, 1. 34. For the suffixes in constructs of names like Ben-ō Labrāṭ, *Bialik-R.*, I, p. 65, 1. 1.

Dist. 23: *Mim-meṣūr-ō* in *Bialik-R.'s* text seems to be better than *mim-meṣōr-ō* of Schirmann. Cf. Ezekiel IV. 8 and any dictionary.

Dist. 24: See footnote to this line.

Dist. 25: I read *qinne'-ū* with the normal Piʿel reduplication; it does not seem likely that Ibn Gabirol would have adhered to an occasional Masoretic inconsistency as in *qine'-ū-nū* in Deut. XXXII. 21 (contrary to many regular *Piʿel* forms of this verb in the Masoretic text).

Dist. 27: *Yukkath*, adopted by Schirmann instead of Bialik-R.'s *yiphtaḥ*, fails to satisfy the demands of gender and meaning in the passage. The various attempts made to heal this obvious *corruptela* are remarkable. Duke's text after "Edelmann's copies," quoted in Geiger, pp. 124f., reads *y-p-t*; upon this Geiger based his sensible conjecture *yiphtaḥ*, which was subsequently adopted by Bialik-R. H. Brody suggested various other healings, among them active forms of the root *k-t-t* (or *p-t-t* in Lev. II. 6) 'to forge (iron)'. The poet, however, describes in this distich how a well-equipped warrior throws a spear and how he is frustrated in missing his aim by stumbling. The battle is, of course, no longer the moment to forge a weapon (which point of view also justifies the removal of Bialik-R.'s *we-ʿeṣ yaḥaṣ* in the next line by Brody and Schirmann). I propose to read, with Psalm XXXV. 3, *yārīq* (which was most likely the word misread as *y-p-t*). The passive masculine *yukkath*, suggested by Schirmann, is quite absurd. Brody's (and Schirmann's) amendment of *ʿeṣ yaḥaṣ* into *ʿeth yārūṣ* is also justified. It also has the support of Moses ibn Ezra as quoted by *Yellin*, p. 67.

18. According to accepted Arabic norms, our poem would be classified as a kasida. For instance, the variety of topics and the return to a previous topic are typical for a kasida. "The modulated connection of the motives serves the poet as a means to carry a personal note into the kasida;" see Bräunlich, *Poesien*, pp. 229f. The theory of the kasida is discussed with authority by Ibn Qutaiba, *Muqaddimat kitāb ash-shiʿr wa-sh-shuʿarā'*, edited and translated by Gaudefroy-Demombynes, Paris, 1947, pp. 13ff. (quoted as Qotaiba, Demombynes). The translator also quotes the opinions of later *literati* in his footnote 50. The word *qaṣīda* was often interpreted as "poem of intent," e. g. praise of a prince and/or application for support. Other poems by Ibn

Gabirol, *Bialik-R.*, I, pp. 106f., begin with a description of nature and end with invective "intent." The topic of self-praise, often observed in the *maqāma*, will hardly warrant ascribing this poem to that category; although this point, as von Grunebaum justly pointed out in a letter to me, could, at least, be argued.

Von Grunebaum discusses the *maqāma* in his "Islam, Essays in the Nature and Growth of a Cultural Tradition," in *American Anthropological Association Memoir*, LXXI, 1955, pp.105–109. See also *G. A. L.* I, pp.94f. The definition and topic given for the *maqāma* there is "caucus of learned men for the purpose of a discussion of literary and other topics connected with the vagabondage."

19. Grunebaum, *al-Bāqillānī*, pp. 42, 45.
20. Quoted from Nicholson, *History*, p. 307, from *Al-Mutanabbī, Diwan*, ed. Dieterici, Berlin, 1858ff., pp. 481ff.
21. Such self-predications, as found for instance in the inscription on the tomb of Cyrus, recorded by the Greek historians, are discussed by Eduard Norden, the famous founder of form criticism, in his *Agnostos Theos*, Darmstadt, 1956, p. 177, with various examples all beginning: "I am ..." The mystic's responses to his call in archetypes like "I am the word," or "I am I, the son of the mild ones," quoted in H. Jonas, *The Gnostic Religion*, Boston, 1958, pp. 80–83 (quoted as *Jonas*), are also related to our following topic of titanism and will be discussed there.
22. In Goethe, *West-Östlicher Divan*, "Suleika Nameh," a poem beginning: *Die schön geschriebenen ...*
23. For selfpraise see, for instance, G. W. Freytag, *Darstellung der arabischen Verskunst*, Bonn, 1830, p.392. About Hebrew selfpraise, see *Yellin*, pp.36–38; 267–269; also an article by Habermann in *Tarbīṣ*, XIX, p. 187, quoted after Baron, *History*, VII, p. 292.
24. M. Asín Palacios, *Abenmasarra y su escuela*, Madrid, 1914, p. 237, after *al-Maqqarī*. For the Arabic text see *Yāqūt*, *Irshād al-arīb*, ed. D. S. Margoliouth, Leyden, 1911, V, pp. 95f.
25. The rhetorical contest for supremacy, called by the Greeks σύγκρισις, by the Arabs *munāẓara*, appears in Ibn Gabirol's Alhambra poem. A discussion of this is found in G. E. von Grunebaum, "Greek Form Elements in the Arabian Nights" in *J. A. O. S.*, LXII, 1942, pp. 277ff. (quoted as Grunebaum, *Elements*). Von Grunebaum on p. 287 n. 107 rejects H. Ethé's belief in an independent Persian origin of the *munāẓara*, appearing in Ethé, "Über persische Tenzonen," in *Verhandlg. d. Fünften Int. Orientalisten-Congresses*, 1881, Erste Hälfte, p. 52 and 52 n. 1. Grunebaum also quotes Reitzenstein, *Poimandres*, 1904, p. 165, and (p. 280 in footnote 261) Poebel, *Das appos. best. Pronomen d. ersten Person Sing. d. west-sem. Inschriften und im Alt. Test.*, 1932. See e. g. E. R. Dodds, *The Greeks and the Irrational*, Berkeley, 1951, p. 148 (quoted as *Dodds*).
26. In H. and H. A. Frankfort, *et al.*, *Before Philosophy*, 1949, p. 145; American edition, *The Intellectual Adventure of Ancient Man*, Chicago, 1946, p. 133.
27. See Franz Sauter: *Der Römische Kaiserkult bei Martial und Statius*, Stuttgart, 1934, pp. 138ff.
28. *Jonas*, p. 96.
29. Quoted by Gilbert Murray, *Five Stages of Greek Religion*, London, 1943, p. 148.
30. H. Ritter, *Das Meer der Seele*, Leiden, 1955; specifically pp. 622ff. (quoted as *Ritter*).
31. *Ritter*, p. 630.
32. *Ritter*, pp. 157; 260; 588ff.; 601.

33. *Ritter*, pp. 629 f.
34. R. A. Nicholson, *The Idea of Personality in Sufism*, Cambridge, 1921, p. 52.
35. *Bialik-R.*, I, p. 99.
36. *Jonas*, p. 125 (112 ff.).
37. *Davidson-Z.*, p. 105.
38. Murray, *op. cit.*, p. 147.
39. *Bialik-R.*, I, p. 27.
40. Ibidem., I, pp. 185 ff. (187), dist. 31.
40a. For exaggeration, *mubālagha*, see Grunebaum, *al-Bāqillānī*, pp. 29 f., 40, 102.
41. The term appears also in a religious poem by our poet, *Bialik-R.*, II, No. 7, p. 9 (Distich 4):

 Thou wilt strengthen *Yinnōn* and gird his loins.

 where the same Hebrew word *shinneś* is used. Yinnon is the name of a (or the) Messiah.
42. F. E. Johnson, *The Seven Poems* etc., Bombay, 1893, p. 147.
43. *Bialik-R.*, I, p. 164, distich 1.
44. Also related are distich 39 and 48 ff. of the poet's Song of Complaint.
45. See *Ritter*, pp. 585 ff.
46. *Bialik-R.*, I, pp. 127 f. Quoted with slight variations in the "Excursus on Lions and Oxen" in Part II. Dist. 2 reminds us of Walther's *Mir ist verspart der saelden tor (Walther von der Vogelweide*, ed. H. Paul, Halle, 1882, p. 97).
47. *Vide E. I.*, II, p. 360, and *G. A. L.*, S. I, p. 114.
48. Quoted in J. Hell's article "Al-ʿAbbās ibn al-Aḥnaf ...," in *Islamica*, II, 1925, p. 275.
49. In Ibn Ḥazm, *Neck-Ring*, pp. 148 ff., or in Ibn Ḥazm, *Ring*, pp. 197 ff.; Petrof's edition of the Arabic text (1914) pp. 96 f.
50. J. B. Pritchard, *Ancient Near Eastern Texts*, Princeton, 1950, p. 467.
51. For LEARNING-SUFFERING, alluded to in Ecclesiastes I. 18 and e. g. in *The Aristeas Letter*, ed. Moses Hadas, New York, 1954, p. 181.
52. Quoted after *Daudpota*, p. 106.
53. Ibn Ḥazm, *Neck-Ring*, p. 221; Arabic text, p. 153.
54. *Bialik-R.*, I, 4, dist. 5.
55. An excellent summary of these Greek conceptions is found in *Dodds*, p. 8, 16. He quotes the above Greek phrases and continues: "... for Homeric man the *thumos* tends not to be felt as part of the self; it commonly appears as an independent inner voice ... This habit of ... objectifying emotional drives, treating them as not-self, must have opened the door wide to the religious idea of psychic intervention ..."
56. *Bialik-R.*, I, 14, translated in this book. Similar addresses to his soul are found in many religious poems by Ibn Gabirol beginning similarly to his *Mah 'l-lākh, Yeḥīdhāh, Bialik-R.*, I, 14, "What aileth thee, soul ... ?" an entire poem addressed to his soul. Such apostrophes are discussed in Grunebaum, *al-Bāqillānī*, p. 40.
57. *Bialik-R.*, I, pp. 4 ff., dist. 20, 25, 31.
58. A. von Kremer, "Philosophische Gedichte des Abū 'l-ʿAlāʾ al-Maʿarrī," in *ZDMG*, XXX, 1877, pp. 40—52; XXXI, 1878, pp. 471—483; XXXVIII, 1885, pp. 499—528; also a foreword to this, "Ein Freidenker des Islam," XXIX, 1876, pp. 304—312 (quoted as *Kremer*); the following line is found in XXIX, p. 45:

 The darts of your fate never fail their targets:
 they must not err because they follow the command of God.

Similarly, the Talmudic rabbis teach that repentance and prayer can avert even preordained events; the parallel ideas in Islamic theology are discussed in *Ritter*, pp. 61, 64, 68 and *passim* (see Index).

59. Ibn al-Muʿtazz, *Dīwān*, ed. B. Lewin, Istanbul, 1945, IV, p. 191.
60. Pérès, *Poésie*, p. 144.
61. *Halper*, p. 194.
62. *Bialik-R.*, I, p. 44, distich 9f.
63. This is found e. g. in Hastings' *Encyclopaedia of Religion and Ethics*, V, pp. 793f. For the Hellenistic conceptions of *tyche* see E. Rohde, *Der Griechische Roman*, Leipzig, 1900, pp. 506 and 508; for gnosticism see H. Jonas, *Gnosis und spätantiker Geist*, Göttingen, 1934, pp. 156ff.
64. See O. Treitinger, *Die oströmische Kaiser- und Reichsidee . . .*, Jena, 1938, pp. 120f.
65. See I. Goldziher, *Vorlesungen über den Islam*, Heidelberg, 1910, p. 104.
66. See Pérès, *Poésie*, p. 458; also 328f. and 460.
67. I owe to the kindness of Mr. J. B. Trapp of the Warburg Institute the reference to the following counterpart to our *amor antagonans Fati* (which may be rather only an *acceptio Fati*) in Andrew Marvell's poem, "The Definition of Love":

XXIV

Fate I come, as dark, as sad,
As thy Malice could desire;
Yet bring with me all the Fire
That Love in his Torches had.

ed. H. M. Margoliouth, Oxford, 1952, p. 36.

68. *Ibn Ḥazm-Arberry*, p. 271.
69. *Neṭōsh lū*, *Bialik-R.*, I, p. 27. *Zemān bōghedh* ("Treacherous Time") in *Bialik-R.*, I, p. 134, dist. 1 (see *Yellin*, p. 64), is translated in this book.
70. "The Time" or "the Daughters of Days" are found in many other lines of our poet, e. g. *Bialik-R.*, I, p. 123, line 1; these are the *banāt ad-dahr;* see *Goldziher*, p. 721; the "arrows of Time," also appear in *Bialik-R.*, I, p. 95. "The Daughters of Time" or "of the Days" are, in ancient tradition, the hours. See R. Reitzenstein, *Das Iranische Erlösungs-Mysterium*, Bonn, 1921, p.157.
71. Cf. W. Caskel, *Das Schicksal in der altarabischen Poesie*, Leipzig, 1925, pp. 48—50; Helmer Ringgren, *Studies in Arabian Fatalism*, Uppsala/Wiesbaden, 1955, p. 77.
72. Quoted in Lane, *Arab. Dictionary*, III, p. 923, column 3. It is interesting for the recurrence of pagan ideas that another *ḥadīth*, related to ʿĀ'isha, saying "God will protect you against (ruining) social obligations" *(nawā'ib al-ḥaqq)* was quoted by al-Maqrīzi with *nawā'ib ad-dahr* ("vicissitudes of Fate"). See M. J. Kister, "God will not Disgrace Thee," in *JAOS*, 1965, pp. 27ff.
73. "The Powers," a line quoted by Alfred von Kremer, in *Sitzungsberichte der Kais. Akademie der Wissenschaften, Phil.-Hist. Klasse*, Wien, 1888, CXVII, 95 and 106, line 1.
74. For this poet see T. H. Nöldeke, *Beiträge zur Kenntnis der Poesie der Alten Araber*, Hannover, 1864, p. 11 (quoted as "Nöldeke, *Poesie*"); also see Nicholson, *History*, p. 131; see for this line Qotaiba, *Demombynes*, p. 6.
75. *Bialik-R.*, I, 91, Dist. 14.
76. *Bialik-R.*, I, pp. 90f. last distich.
77. *Daupota*, p. 106.
78. See footnote 1.
79. For "*Pasturing of the stars*" see Grunebaum, *Response*, p. 139, quoting Nabīgha. Nicholson: *History*, p. 131; Nöldeke, *Poesie*, pp. 11; 43. Verses referring to

such nightly vigils by Ibn Ḥazm are quoted in Nykl, *H.-A. Poetry*, pp. 82f. This motif appears in Ibn Gabirol's *Rebhībhey dhimʿa-khā*, *Bialik-R.*, I, p. 31, dist. 15ff.

80. See the excursus on *Full Moon or Sickle Moon?* below.
81. For the three poets Ibn al-Muʿtazz (see *G. A. L.*, I, pp. 79f.; S. I, pp. 128–130, 940), al-Buḥturī (see *G. A. L.*, I, p. 80), and aṣ-Ṣanaubarī (see *G. A. L.*, S. I, p. 145). For the ancient Arabic poetry see in particular Sir Charles J. Lyall, "The Pictorial Aspect of Ancient Arabic Poetry," in *JRAS*, 1912, p. 149, and his *Translations of Ancient Arabian Poetry*, New York, 1930, p. 103.
82. Ibn Ḥazm, *Ring*, p. 39, 119; Ibn Ḥazm, *Neck-Ring*, pp. 20, 87.
83. The typical Hispano-arabic poems describing the night are collected in Pérès, *Poésie*, pp. 219–227.
84. F. E. Johnson, *The Seven Poems*, etc., Bombay, 1893, pp. 26f.; A. J. Arberry, *The Seven Odes*, London/New York, 1957, pp. 55f.
85. Pérès, *Poésie*, p. 222, after al-Fatḥ ibn Khāqān, *Qalāʾid al-ʿiqyān* (born near Granada, died 1134 or 1140; *vide G. A. L.*, I, p. 339; S. I, pp. 579, 758).
86. Henri Pérès points out the close relationship of such cosmic journeys to the contemporary *Risālat al-ghufrān* by Abū 'l-ʿAlāʾ al-Maʿarrī (died in 1057); and with this we are not far from the *Scala di Mahoma* quoted as one of the Islamic ancestors of Dante's *Commedia.* See Pérès, *Poésie*, p. 222 (36).

    For earlier representations of such cosmic exaggeration of praise for a patron, one might quote al-Buḥturī's kasida for a Maecenas who was the governor of Rayy (ca. 862–866) (quoted after Grunebaum, *al-Bāqillānī*, p. 103):

    Muḥammad ibn ʿAlī ranks so high
    that he sees the Gemini only from above.
    His is a cloud whose showers, did they not pour
    on us continuously, would rain on us every eve unstintingly ...

    A lyrical poem by the great Persian poet Firdausī voices such poetical titanism, before Ibn Gabirol's time. This is quoted in Ethé, "Firdausi als Lyriker," in *SB. d. Bayer. Akad.*, 1872, p. 297. (The standard image of a cloud for the generosity of a Maecenas is found in the Alhambra poem, distich 41.)
87. *Bialik-R.*, I, 155, no. 81 *(Ha-lō thirʾeh)*.
88. A comparison of stars with flowers is developed as a literary genre, named *nauriyya*. See Pérès, *Poésie*, p. 166, with a longer discussion of the *poème floral*, and Ritter, *Niẓāmī*, p. 24, for the typical comparison of the sky with a meadow and the moon with a sickle or the moon with a boat on a pond. See Ibn al-Muʿtazz in *Daudpota*, pp. 127f.
89. For a drinking goblet, compare Ibn Gabirol's wine song in Schirmann, *Shīrāh*, I, 217, dist. 14.
90. See Grunebaum, *Elements*, p. 285.
91. *Bialik-R.*, I, 154, No. 179 a fragment, in a fuller form also in *Bialik-R.*, IV (VII), p. 3.

Dist. 1: 92. According to *Bialik-R.'s* notes, the ms. does not indicate clearly the first *ʿeynay* 'my eyes', so that this may also be read *laylāh* 'night' instead:

    "as if the sleep of my night were under a ban imposed upon my eyes,"

    or as *Bialik-R.* interpret, "as if sleep were forbidden to my eyes."
    This is the sense for the governance of the verb *'-s-r* by *ʿal* (cf. Nu. XXX. 3). See Samuel han-Nāghīdh, *Mī lō yeshallaḥ*, in *Diwan*, III, p. 75, dist. 36. Since 'night' (which is implicit in the Hebrew *ālīn* meaning 'to spend the night')

has not been mentioned in the first line (although we had to translate this explicitly), it seems to me most likely that, indeed, *laylāh* should be read instead of the first *ʿeynay*. The translation, however, is affected only slightly by the variant.

Dist. 2: The Arabic idiom 'to wrap' or 'to take on darkness like a cloak' underlies the imagery of the last line of the second couplet (cf. the second line of the *Shīrāh Yethōmāh*, 'The Matchless Song', by Joseph ibn Ḥaśday) and means 'to venture into the night', 'to expose oneself to the night'. It may be that here *qeshūrāh*, which appears to be at a first glance the normal passive particle, is the singular (coined by Ibn Gabirol) *qishshūr-im* (or rather *qeshūr-im*) in Is. III. 20, 'girdles of a bride'. This may be far-fetched; yet the idea of a bride is on the poet's mind, as this appears in the next line. *Laylah* is (in this line and in the fourth couplet) used in the feminine gender, which poetical licence is inspired by the Arabic conceit of a personified feminine Night (whereas *laylāh* in Hebrew is commonly masculine). Therefore, Bialik's text of dist. 6 must be amended to read *kāphūph* 'bent' instead of *kāphaph*, 'he bent'.

Dist. 5: The seven-armed candelabrum appears to be a symbol of the Seven Sisters, the Pleiades. There is an article by Enrique Perpiña, entitled "Las Pléyades y la poesía árabe," in *Al-Andalus*, XVIII, 1953, p. 439ff. The Septuagint translates *kīmāh* by 'Pleiades' (Job XXXVIII. 20).

Dist. 6: The subject to which the masculine *seybh-ō* refers is of course *rōsh*, standing in the construct with *laylāh*. The grey, developed by an aging Night towards dawn, is a well known Arabic conceit which is blended here with Is. LVIII. 5 *(R. S. V.)*: "... is it to bow down his head as a bull-rush ...?"

Dist. 7: Instead of "towards me" one ms. could be read, according to Bialik-R., "towards it;" but the titanism of the poet makes this unlikely.

93. For *saharōn* see Ibn Gabirol's "Song of Complaint" *Bialik-R.*, I, 5, dist. 30; and his "Song of Justification," *Bialik-R.*, I, p. 166, dist. 1. In Ibn Gabirol's *Mī z-zōth kemō* (*Bialik-R.*, I, p. 61, dist. 5) he describes in an encomium for Samuel han-Nāghīdh the crown of the appearing Muse adorned with a crescent moon symbol, most fitting in connection with the Muse as the intellectual wayfarer. Such a head adornment can be seen in the paintings of Quṣair ʿAmra (as published by Musil in *Kuṣejr ʿAmra*, Vienna, 1907, Plate XXVI).

94. The comparison of the moon with a carbuncle or similar precious stones reminds one of the Arab poet's typical comparisons of the stars with "pearls upon a sky of agate" by Yazīd ibn Muʿāwiya, quoted after Grunebaum, *Response*, p. 150, n. 110. The second distich reminds us of the comparison of the crescent — a starved, waning Ramadhan sickle moon — snapping at the planet Venus. See Pérès, *Poésie*, p. 221, referring to Mughīra ibn Ḥazm:

> When I watched the crescent moon, leaning against the dawn's
> white face, enter conjunction with Venus,
>
> I compared him — and my eyes can testify to it —
> with a crooked staff about to strike a ball.

The union of star and crescent is an object of pagan worship. In adoration scenes on Assyrian and Babylonian seals star and crescent symbolize Ishtar and Sin. The symbol is also common in Aramaic, Phoenician, Ammonite, and Moabite seals. Cf. A. Reifenberg, *Ancient Hebrew Seals*, London, 1950, fig. 31, 35, 38, 42. Quoted after N. Avigad in "A Seal of 'Manasseh Son of the King'," in *IEJ*, XIII, p. 133.

95. Ibn Gabirol's *Mī z-zōth kemō*, *Bialik-R.*, I, pp. 60f., dist. 5.

96. An-Nuwairī, *Nihāyat al-arab*, Cairo, 1923, I, pp. 54f. (died 1332, cf. Nicholson, *History*, p. 455).
97. Plutarch, *De Iside et Osiride*, ed. G. Parthey, Berlin, 1850, chapter 41, p. 73.
98. J. B. Pritchard, *Ancient Near Eastern Texts*, Princeton, N. J., 1950, p. 386.
99. Fr. Dieterici, *Mutanabbī und Saif ad-daula*, Leipzig, 1847, p. 198.
100. Quoted after Oskar Rühle, *Sonne und Mond im Primitiven Mythos*, Tübingen, 1925, p. 31 (quoted there: E. Seeke, *Hermes der Mondgott*, 1908).
101. Quoted after Knut Tallquist, *Manen I myt och dikt* ..., Stockholm, 1948.
102. See S. H. Langdon, in *Mythology of all Races*, Boston, 1931, V, p. 48. According to Hindu law, the moon, a lucky and inspiring force, is called Čandra, the left eye of Nārāyana, whereas the sun is the right eye (quoted after al-Birūnī, *Ta'riḫ al-Hind*, in *Alberuni's India*, ed. E. C. Sachau, London, 1914, p. 216).
103. Th. Gaster, "The Sons of Light," in *Commentary*, September, 1956, p. 233. (Also for the root *hāghō* compare the book *Hagu* or *Hagi* of the *Qumran* sources.)
104. See Munk, *Mélanges*, p. 332.
105. *The Physical Influence of the Moon.*

A scholar as late as Francis Bacon classifies the influence of the moon in his posthumous *Sylva Sylvarum or a Naturell History*, London, 1631, pp. 228ff. in the following fashion:

> The influence of the Moone, (most observed are Foure:) The Drawing forth of Heat: The Inducing of Putrification: The Increase of Moisture: The Exciting of the Motions of Spirits.
> As for the Exciting of the Motions of the Spirits, you must note that the Growth of Hedges, Herbs, Haire, etc. is caused from the Moone, by Exciting of the Spirits, as well by Increase of the Moisture. But for Spirits in particular, the great Instance is in Lunacies. There may be other Secret Effects of the Influence of the Moone, which are not yet brought into observation.

Besides its influence upon the human and other spirits, the moon was considered as the source of fertility and growth in keeping with the ancient conception of sympathetic magic.

Again, Plutarch, op. cit., chapter 43, describes Isis as the principle of growth.

The moon's influence upon growth in nature is described by Francis Bacon (l. c.).

> It may be, that if it so fall out, that the Wind by North, or North-East, in the Full of the Moon, it increaseth Cold; and if South, or South-West, it disposeth the Aire, for a good while, to Warmth, and Raine; Which would be observed.
> It may be, that Children, and Young Catell, that are brought forth in the Full of the Moone, are stronger and larger, than those that are brought forth in the Wane: And those also which are begotten in the Full of Moone: so that it might be good Husbandry, to put Rams, and Bulls to their Female, somewhat before the Full of the Moone. It may be also, that the Eggs lay'd in the Full of the Moone, breed better Bird: And a Number of the like Effects, which he brought into Observation: *Quaere* also, whether great Thunders, and Earth-Quakes, be not most in the Full of the Moone?

Much of this information was supplied by the obliging and learned member of the Warburg Institute in London, Mr. J. B. Trapp. The poet W. B. Yeats distinguishes two principles of the moon's influence by ascribing to the moon in his dial-like system the phases 1 and 15 which represent cultural ascendency (I owe this information to the helpful and well-informed Mr. Anthony Friedson).

106. *Bialik-R.*, II, p. 65, lines 82ff. The same argument for the disavowal of astral worship displayed cosmically can be found in the encyclopedia of the Brethern of Purity of the 10th century. Cf. F. H. Dieterici, *Die Lehre von der Weltseele bei den Arabern* ... Leipzig, 1872, p. 157. For Ibn Gabirol, however, the moon not only announces the new tidings with its changes but brings them about.
107. See Tallquist, op. cit., pp. 309f. on sympathetic growth.
108. *Tallquist*, p. 72.
109. Margaret Smith: *Readings from the Mystics of Islam*, London, 1950, pp. 26f.
110. Quoted from Bräunlich, *Poesien*, p. 236.
111. We find a large number of poems devoted to the topic "the sky and the atmospheric phenomena" in Pérès, *Poésie*, pp. 219ff. The topos of the LAUGHING EARTH is found in Ibn Gabirol's spring poem (*Bialik-R.*, I, p. 106, dist. 4) beginning:

    Raintime fulfills his vow, upholds
        his pledge to the lily of Valleys;

    and in his second message of spring in which the WEEPING (and lowing) CLOUDS appear (*Bialik-R.*, I, p. 153, dist. 8; see pp. 341f., 347f.), beginning:

    The Sky's clouds lowed like oxen,
        for Winter was grim and his countenance evil.

    See Pérès, *Poésie*, pp. 228ff. with many examples; also al-Maʿarrī's line quoted in Nicholson, *Studies in Islamic Poetry*, p. 72 (218):

    Seest not the cloud, when 'twas moved to laugh, how hoarsely it
        wailed?'

    For weeping clouds and the laughing earth see Elías Terés, "Préstamos Poéticos en Al-Andalus," in *Al-Andalus*, XXI, 1956, pp. 419ff. More examples for this pseudo-personification or animation are found in Bräunlich, *Poesien*, pp. 235ff. where a specimen of the conceit THE CLOUDS' INABILITY TO WITHHOLD THEIR RAIN is quoted on p. 235. (See for another example p. 328 below).
112. I am preparing a translation of the passage dealing with Ibn al-Munfatil in the *k. adh-dhakhīra* by Ibn Bassām. See Pérès, *Poésie*, pp. 269 ff.; 300f.; 316f.
113. For the personification of the night as in our poem see Pérès, *Poésie*, pp. 220–225.
114. The lines by Ibn al-Muʿtazz are quoted in H. Ritter, *Wortkunst*, p. 225. The poem by Abū Isḥāq ibn Khaira aṣ-Ṣabbāgh found in al-Maqqarī, *Analectes*, Leyden, 1855ff., II, p. 326; translated in Pérès, *Poésie*, p. 229. Other instances are quoted in Grunebaum, *Response*, p. 151, footnote 114, e. g. the storm clouds are likened by Labīd to Abyssinians and also to wailing women.
115. In Pérès, *Poésie*, p. 225; I cite this poem by Abū 'l-Qāsim al-Asʿad ibn Billīṭa (died 1048), found in al-Maqqarī, *Analectes*, II, p. 490, etc., in Professor Arberry's translation.

    ... Darkness' Ethiop soldiery
    Are routed now and flee:
    Dawn has loosed his Coptic horde
    To put them to the sword.

    Arberry, *Moorish Poetry*, pp. 76f.

116. For Balaam see J. Klausner, *Jesus von Nazareth*, London, 1947. Also L. Baeck, *Aus drei Jahrtausenden*, Tübingen, 1958, p. 177.
117. Cf. L. Ginzberg, *Legends of the Jews*, III, p. 410f.; the following two Arabic counterparts to the similes of PIERCING OF THE NIGHT and LIGHTNING — A SWORD are quoted in Ritter, *Wortkunst*, pp. 225f.
118. The poem is found in *al-Maqqarī*, II, p. 373, translated in Pérès, *Poésie*, p. 226. A similar image is found in Firdausī's *Shāhnāmah*, ed. Vullers, Leiden, 1877—84, p. 185, verse 16, translated in Grunebaum, *Response*, p. 150, note 113:

    In the early morn when the sun drew the dagger and the
    dark night became invisible from fear.

    In Greek mythology the goddess Night (Nyx) wields clusters of stars as her weapon. The northern fries of the Berlin Pergamon altar shows her while killing a serpent-legged dweller of the earth. See Simon, *Mysterienvilla*, pp. 137f.
119. Quoted in Qotaiba, *Demombynes*, p. 26; 75 (notes).
120. LIGHTNING, THUNDER, OR MORNING — LAUGHING: This line by Ibn al-Muʿtazz is often quoted: e. g., in Ritter, *Nizāmī*, p. 9, note 1; "the cloud is weeping while within it the thunder laughs," quoted by Grunebaum, *Response*, p. 141, footnote 24.
121. The topos THE NIGHT BRINGS SORROW in Arabic literature is discussed in Grunebaum, *Response*, p. 139, n. 7.
122. *Bialik-R.*, I, 16.
123. For the bat as a demonic being, see W. Stammler, *Frau Welt*, Freiburg, Switzerland, 1959, p. 63. The other ominous winged being is the raven, appearing in the same distich. We find the image of a bat for the night in Tennyson's *Maud*, section 22, stanza 1 (line 850):

    Come into the garden, Maud,
    For the black bat night has flown.

124. See the discussion in the introduction to this chapter.
125. The motif of the *alba*, the morning dawn, which shortens the lovers' nocturnal happiness, is an ancient Arabic topic. We find it in the Diwan of Abū Firās. (See *G. A. L.*, S. I, p. 143, and also before this, in the poetry of ʿUmar.) Compare the discussion in Heger, *Ḫarǧas*, pp. 25, 28.
126. Quoted by J. Wellhausen, *Reste arabischen Heidentums*, Berlin, 1897, p. 203, (also pp. 200 and 209). The pre-Islamic poet ʿAlqama of the tribe Tamīm flourished around 600 in Arabia (*G. A. L.*, I, p. 24; *S.* I., p. 48).
127. Compare *Goldziher*, p. 721. I am greatly indebted to my well-informed assistant, Miss Coralie Noltenius, for being referred to the following quotations concerning the bird which invokes upon the lovers the grief of parting, found in Th. Nöldeke, *Delectus veterum carminum Arabicorum*, Berlin, 1890, pp. 7 and 9.
128. See Helmer Ringgren, *Studies in Arabian Fatalism*, Uppsala/Wiesbaden, 1955, pp. 69, 77.
129. Quoted in Ritter, *Nizāmī*, p. 24, and Grunebaum, *Response*, p. 149. The subsequent passage from al-Jurjānī is quoted after Ritter, *Wortkunst*, p. 198.
130. This verse by Ibn as-Sīd al-Baṭalyausī, who was born in 1052 in Badajoz (*G. A. L.*, I, p. 427; *S.* I, p. 758) is found in *Analectes*, II, p. 469, and, with a slight change, in I, p. 428, and quoted in a French translation in Pérès, *Poésie*, p. 225 (349):

    wa-l-laylu munkhafirun yuṭīru ghurābahu
    wa-ṣ-ṣubḥu yatruduhu bi-bāzin ashhab(a)

130a. As for the spread of the theme of the *alba* (the Provençal word for 'dawn'), an equivalent for Juliet's wish to pretend that the lark's call was the nightingale's can be seen in the Indian miniature with the same topic of the *alba* on which a lover, lying in bed with his sleeping beloved, aims his arrow against a perching rooster who is about to disturb her slumber by proclaiming the morning. In our poem it is a moment of utter darkness preceding the crack of dawn which the poet decries as ominous.

131. See Ritter, *Niẓāmī*, p. 7.

132. Ritter, *Niẓāmī*, p. 23.

132a. The Sun or the Lightning launching himself from his Castle. A specimen of this is found in Niẓāmī's *Khosrau and Shirin*, in Panĕa, Bombay, 1265, p. 15, quoted by Ritter, *Niẓāmī*, p. 23, and Grunebaum, *Response*, p. 151, n. 113:

> When the sun [coming forth] from an azure fortress pitched
> camp upon a yellow wall (i. e., of the early light).

133. *Bialik-R.*, I, p. 27, dist. 8f. and ib., I, p. 187, *Ke-shemesh merōm-īm*, dist. 31.

134. Stefan George, *Tage und Taten*, Berlin, 1925, p. 84.

135. Ritter, *Wortkunst*, p. 301.

136. Quoted after *Daudpota*, pp. 105f.

137. The poem by Ibn-i-Yamīn is found in Browne, *Persian Literature*, III, pp. 221f.

138. In Pindar's first Pythian Ode, v. 44 (lines 82ff.).

139. *Bialik-R.*, I, p. 70, variant to dist. 57 (line 110).

140. Baudelaire, *Oeuvres*, *Les Fleurs Du Mal*, "L'Albatros," Paris (Pléiade), n. d., p. 22.

141. *'Aṭeh hōdh*, dist. 12, *Bialik-R.*, I, p. 96. A line very similar to the one from *Qūm haz-zemān* quoted before. In a related reference, Ibn Gabirol praises, in a long rose poem, his patron, the donor of the roses:

> Thus they witness that your hand elated on high
> with the sky's stars stores pledges.

142. G. E. Grunebaum, "Aspects of Arabic Urban Literature . . .," in *Al-Andalus*, XX, 1955, p. 267, where on p. 268, the subsequent quotation from al-Buḥturī is found. Ibn Gabirol's Alhambra poem preserves an echo of such a conception; I quote in the subsequent part a description of the palaces of Seville from the pen of their builder.

143. *Davidson-Z.*, p. 92.

144. We find in the commentary of Macrobius on the *Somnium Ciceronis*, I, XVII. 4 (a quotation from Cicero): *Infra autem eam (lunam) nihil est nisi mortale et caducum praeter animos munere deorum hominum generi datos. Supra lunam sunt aeterna omnia.*" Quoted after W. Deinert, *Ritter und Kosmos in Parzival*, Munich, 1960, p. 7 n. 2.

145. Verlaine's poem *Art Poétique* seems to have remained valid as the poetics of modern symbolism; in this he advises the avoidance of the all too manifest and obvious:

> . . . *Fuis du plus loin la Pointe assassine*
> *L'Esprit cruel et le Rire impur*
> *Qui font pleurer les yeux de l'Azur* . . .

To Stefan George must be attributed the symbolistic formula: "*Die Landschaft ist die Seele.*" (See above.)

146. A. Mez, *Die Renaissance des Islams*, Heidelberg, 1922, p. 248 (henceforth quoted as Mez, *Renaissance*).

147. E. R. Curtius, *Europäische Literatur und lateinisches Mittelalter*, Bern, 1948, p. 322.
148. *Monumenta Germ. Hist.: Poetae Latini aevi Carolini*, II, p. 403. A German translation is found in W. Ganzenmüller, *Das Naturgefühl im Mittelalter*, Berlin, 1914, p. 79.
149. The Merlin Epic, *Vita Merlini*, by Geoffrey of Monmouth, written about 1155, ed. E. Faral, in *La légende arthurienne*, III, Paris, 1929, p. 319; also ed. J. J. Parry, *The Vita Merlini*, *University of Illinois Studies*, X, Urbana, 1925, p. 54, lines 424ff., quoted after Wolfram v. d. Steinen, "Natur und Geist im Zwölften Jahrhundert," in *Die Welt als Geschichte*, 1954, pp. 79ff.
150. Parry's text, p. 38, lines 155ff.

C. Ibn Gabirol's Garden and Spring Poems

(1) SPRING I: THE GARDEN BED RESURRECTED AND THE SUN

'Eth niṣṣebh-ū — *Bialik-R.* III, p. 25, No. 35

- - ⏑ - - - ⏑ - - - *(Sarī‘)* — Schirmann: *Nibhḥ.*, pp. 58f.

Rhyme: *-ṡe-hā; -sē(y)-hā*

Ex. XV. 8; Ps. XXXIII. 7; CXLVII. 18
When its dewdrops, chilled, stand up as in a heap
Ex. XV. 2; Am. IX. 13
God sends forth His word that melts it,

So that they drip upon the vine incessantly
until its musts drop upon me.

The garden bed! — it puts forth its blossom, wherein
every narcissus opens its clasps for us;

It wafts incense of myrrh into our countenances,
while we proceed to meet its myrtles,

And when you walk, it offers you every petal-wing;
(Jer. XLVIII. 9)
yea, it gives you a wing, lest you tread upon it.

The sun's frame looks like a bride's
whose beauty makes her sun-diadems shine;

Time after time the sun flies upon the sphere's flame platform,
although no pursuer puts her to flight,

So that we take her for a king's chariot,
(Nahum III. 2)
which is swaying with its horses;

When she passes [at noon] by the garden bed, you see
Is. XLV. 9; Prov. XXVI. 23
a silver covering upon its sun-potsherds;

Yet when the day is turning into evening, it spreads out
green-yellow sun-gold all over its boundaries. Ps. LXVIII. 14

So you might think when the sun goes a-bowing in, that
she prostrates herself to the ground before her maker;

And when she speeds to enter [like a bride], it would appear Ps. XIX. 5
as if God covered her with purple.

Ibn Gabirol's garden and spring poems show a very advanced stage of the poet's integration of Arab nature poetry with a thoroughly Hebrew diction. Arabic poets, when they were exposed for the first time, in countries colder than their homeland, to ice and snow, were greatly fascinated by these natural phenomena and never ceased, even in Spain, to describe them in their works. As a parallel to Ibn Gabirol's Spring Poem I, I quote lines by Ibn Khafāja, although this poet could have influenced Ibn Gabirol only in his later years[1]. The reader is invited to observe the fantastic "causation" in Ibn Khafāja's poem.

Often heavy drops congeal, and from those the hail descends
from heaven to adorn therewith the neck of the Earth.

This congealed water stones the valleys,
but the Earth is only touched by a dissolving chastisement.

The Sun laughs, showing forth necklaces of stars
which are distributed now that the frowning Sky knits his eyebrows.

You would say that the Earth has committed adultery,
wherefore a stoning Cloud was so outraged as to throw stones.

Dist. 1-2: Ibn Gabirol's first Winter Rain poem does not speak of falling hail, but rather of dew drops congealing — while appearing on plants like the vine. The wording of the first distich, "God sends forth His word," which dissolves the icy drops, is a literal take-over from a Psalm line (Ps. CXLVII. 18), "He sendeth out His word and melteth them" (the ice morsels). One could rightly say that the poem is a bold variation of this Psalm, in particular if one spells God's 'word' with a capital W. The second distich, speaking of the melting water as it drips and finally produces the effusion of must from the grapes, seems to draw more from viticultural knowledge than spontaneous observation, but affords a beautiful antithesis.

Note 1

Dist. 3: The word 'clasps' (*qereš*, 'hook' or 'loop'), appears in the Bible in connection with the Tent of Meeting. The action of the flowers *(ḥabhaṣṣeleth)*, 'crocuses', unbuckling the hooks 'for us' personifies these and establishes a relationship of favor on their part with the sentimental visitor. We are reminded of the line in Samuel's poem on Yehōseph's garden construction, translated in our Alhambra section, when he speaks of the companions "with pathways to their hearts." We should think that the word *ḥabhaṣeleth* stands for the crocus or the jonquil, a very early spring flower emerging from the snow, which also has a powerful fragrance very much like the narcissus[2].

Dist. 4: The source of the 'fragrance' is not clearly stated; it could be the 'myrrh-like' aroma emanating from the myrtles, of which the Arabic poet says "Its fragrance, diffusing, breathes tranquility and joyfulness into the soul, letting you believe that they were cut in paradise[3]." The poet turns from the garden bed to 'the Sun'.

Dist. 6: The simile of the bride for the sun is quite common. We quote as another instance for a sunset-lit garden al-As'ad ibn Billīṭa (died 1048—49)[4]:

Had you seen us this afternoon when the cloud wept over us
with the eyes of a man shedding abundant tears,

And when the sun prolonged the clarity of its rays upon the earth,
at the moment when it seemed to slope toward its setting,

You would have believed that the fine rain was silver filings
which one sifted upon a carpet of gilded copper.

For the sun emerging from rain clouds, Ibn Ḥazm has an image of a young virgin or a slave girl[5], which is also found in Ibn 'Ammār[6].

As a parallel we cite, from the Arabic poet Ibn ar-Rūmī (born 836 in Baghdad), the picture of a sunset in which the setting sun is called ailing under the approaching wing of the night ('wing of night', an image found in Sura XIII, v. 4). In a subsequent simile the sun is compared with the 'sinking' of an eye behind the eyelid of a tired person[7].

Dist. 7: The reference to the sun's rotating sphere, with its etymological allusion to *riṣpāh*, 'glowing stone' (Isa. VI. 6), is probably not immediately descriptive but full of resonance. The reference to the various times of the day, which see the sun circling, again belong less to visual observation than to a learned indirect category. We observe the same treatment of the daily cycle of light, more abstract than visual, in the improvised fishing party poem of Abū 'l-Faḍl ibn Ḥasdāy.

Notes 2—7

Dist. 8: The image of a royal chariot for the sun, replacing the image of a bride observed elsewhere, is, for a mediaeval Hebrew poet, astonishing, though the image is found, for instance, in Firdausī, and should be traceable in Arabic poetry as well. Yet in the light of II Kings XXIII. 11, "And he (Josiah) took away the horses that the kings of Judah had given to the sun at the entering in of the House of the Lord . . . and burned the chariots of the sun with fire . . .," we expect to find the poet inhibited and avoiding mythological imagery, rare as such specimens in Arabic poetry may be. In the last part of the poem we discover an even more dangerous blend of religious and secular conceptions[8].

The poet, however, in no way refers to these ignominiously destroyed idols. He may have seen representations of the sun god of Persian origin, and the apocryphal *Odes of Solomon*, which Ibn Gabirol hardly knew, say: "I ascended to the light as if on the chariot of truth," even as gnostic texts speak freely of the horses and chariot of the sun[9]. The chariot of the sun belongs, of course, to learned imagery as well.

Dist. 9: The phrase 'potsherd covered with silver' is a quotation from Proverbs. In addition to this take-off, the poet plays with the two words *ḥereś* (sun, which remains unmentioned) and *ḥeres* 'clay', 'potsherd'. In spite of all the burden of learning, the ambiguous text quoted from Proverbs is brought to visual life.

Dist. 10: A play on the same root is maintained, this time with *ḥarūṣ* (translated 'sun-gold'), which describes the pale greenish golden evening light on the garden bed; the wording 'sun-gold in greenish' *(ḥārūṣ bi-y(e)raqraq)*, appearing in Ps. LXVIII. 14, is a real *trouvaille* for the poet, who shares the Arab taste for pale greens, as Ibn Gabirol shows in his Rose Poem and Ibn Ḥazm does in the *Dove's Necklace*. But this brief reference to such a hue is too derivative to convince us of the poet's sense of color when we come to the Rose Poem just mentioned.

Dist. 11: At this point the poet, as only on rare occasions, mixes the realms of the secular and the spiritual. The allusion to the sun as a bride, which had appeared before in distich 6, now receives full development. A feminine conception of the sun belongs to Arabic poetry (in Ps. XIX. 5, the sun is a bridegroom). The sun as God's bride or servant is a topic which may demonstrate the nearness and possible overlapping of the areas of nature poetry with its pseudo-pagan neo-mythology and that of the mystical personification of the deity. This motif of a faithful servant appears in several versions in Ibn Gabirol's religious poems; for instance in *The Kingdom's Crown*[10], "Every day he prostrates himself before his King and halts at the place of the path." And also:[11]

Notes 8—11

For by the greatness of slaves the greatness of their masters is known
to those who can know,
And in the slave is revealed the might and glory of the lord . . .

As in the prelude prayer *(reshūth)*, presented further on, the sun appears as a bridegroom and also as a servant: *Shemesh ke-ḥāthān*, 'The sun like a bridegroom'[12].

There are numerous other Rain-end and Spring poems. Some of them, akin to the Alhambra poem, have the jubilant note of an announcement of Spring's arrival.

Notes to the Text

Dist. 1: I prefer the variant *kī* 'when' to Bialik's *'eth* (also 'when'). A second *'eth* introducing the second part of Dist. 2 would be an unlikely duplication.

Dist. 2: If *'eth* 'when' in the first line is correct, we might expect here *'adh* 'until', confused with *'eth* quite often in our texts. The 'withheld' subject of the first distich, a feminine singular, appearing in 'her' drops (translated by me as 'its dew drops') could either be the vine of distich 2 — bearing the wintry dew drops *(resīs-īm)* and the autumnal 'musts' *('asīs-īm)* which stand in antithesis and rhyme with each other — or else the garden bed of distich 3, personified to some degree in Arabic poetry and in Ibn Gabirol.

Dist. 3: The word *tāṣīṣ*, standing with emphasis in the beginning and translated 'in blossom is', could also mean 'she looks out'. It would thus intensify the personification.

The word *ḥabhaṣṣeleth*, occurring in Canticles II, 1, and mostly translated as 'rose', or as 'narcissus' appearing in the ligature 'Rose of Sharon', is also alluded to in the Alhambra poem (dist. 7) in the mere abbreviation 'Sharons', but translated by me as 'roses'; it also appears with a wide range of allusion in *Qūm haz-zemān*, distich 54.

Dist. 7: *Me-'eth le-'eth*, 'time after time', as Bialik-R. point out in their notes to this poem, means most likely every twenty-four hours. Their paradigms are taken from Talm. *Niddāh*. Cf. *Bialik-R.*, II, p. 49, No. 48, Dist. 5.

Riṣaphath, as the metre demands, from *riṣpāh*, which has been interpreted as '(tesselated) pavement' (e. g. Ez. XL. 17), and also 'a baking stone' (Is. VI. 6), has been connected with two Arabic roots, *r-ṣ-f* 'to join together' and *r-ḍ-f*, 'to roast' or 'to cauterize'; I therefore translate 'flame-platform'. The poet is definitely aware of employing assonances of etymological depth with all sophistication.

Dist. 9: The poem contains plays upon words, some referring to the sun as in distich 6 with *shebhīs-īm*, 'sun-diadems' found in Is. III. 18, 'a small sun', and part of the bridal outfit (cf. *Qūm haz-zemān* by Ibn Gabirol, distich 1). The metaphor, sun as a bride, receives support from this.

Ḥeres (ḥarāse(y)-hā), 'its sun-potsherds', found in Prov. XXVI. 23, "like a glaze covering an earthen vessel" *(R. S. V.)*, or "potsherds covered with silver drops" *(K. J. V.)*, entails a play upon *ḥārūṣ* in dist. 10. Our line is a take-off on this Proverbs line and also on Job XLI. 22 (30), "His underparts are like sharp potsherds; he spreads himself like a threshing sledge on the mire" *(R. S. V.)*, or "Sharp stones are under him: he spreadeth sharp pointed things upon the mire" *(K. J. V.)*. In this line from Job *ḥeres* and *ḥārūṣ* appear in a parallel form which the translations do not imitate. *Ḥārūṣ yeraqraq* in dist. 10 is

Note 12

taken from Ps. LXVIII. 14 (13); *bi-y(e)raqraq ḥārūṣ* "(the wings of a dove covered with silver, its pinions) with green gold" *(R. S. V.)* and "yellow gold" *(K. J. V.)*. We translate 'green-yellow sun-gold' to remind the reader of the 'sun's potsherds' and of the poet's consciousness of etymological kinships. For *ḥereṣ* cf. *Bialik-R.*, I, p. 71, dist. 23, stanza 12, Ibn Gabirol's encomium on Samuel han-Nāghīdh, beginning *Tehillath ha-ḥokhmāh:*

In vigorous race
The heavens race in precision
To uphold the mound of the earth:
"cast solidly of dusts." Job XXXVIII. 38

Dist. 11: I translate the word *ḥereṣ* by 'precision'.
'Ose(y)-hā, 'her maker' (literally 'her makers'), is something like a plural-singular, as in Job XXXV. 10; *ereṣ* is a virtual accusative standing for *arṣāh* as it does in the Masoretic Bible.

As a counterpart to the twelfth distich of "The Garden Bed Resurrected," I insert a religious poem, a "Prelude."

Excursus: Sunset — a Reshūth

Shemesh ke-ḥāthān — *Bialik.*, II, p. 41, No. 34

- - ⏑ -   - - ⏑ -   - - *(Sarī')* — Schirmann, *Shīrāh*, I, p. 252

Schirmann, *Nibhḥ.*, p. 88

Davidson-Z., p. 16

Brody-Albrecht, p. 41

Rhyme: *-dhār (-dār)*

The Sun, like a bridegroom, dons a garment of light, Ps. CIV. 2 Ps. XIX. 5
emanated from Your splendor which yet is never lacking.

He learned to circle towards the seam of the West,
bowing down before Your throne, cloaked in glory.

From the day of his serving You, he is a prince; for a servant
who glorifies the face of his master will thus be glorified.

He, day by day, prostrates himself before You, while
You wrap upon him a robe of glory.

This poem has been translated many times and into various languages – into German, for example, by Karl Wolfskehl (*Collected Works*, II, p. 163).

The first distich describes the evening sun in words taken from Psalm XIX. 5: "... the sun which comes forth like a bridegroom leaving his chamber," and declares that its light is an emanation of God's own splendor, in words taken from Psalm CIV. 2 which addresses God "who coverest thyself with light as with a garment." The poet's religious poetry is tinged here by his Plotinism, which teaches that the light is by its character an eternal outflow from an ever undiminished source.

The sun appears before God every evening like a servant who, after having performed his duties, pays his master a call of respect, in the words of Ibn Gabirol's *The Kingdom's Crown* (in Bernard Lewis's translation):[13]

Every day he prostrates himself before his King and halts at
the place of the paths,

And at dawn he lifts up his head, and bows it at evening to
the West — ...

Through him may be known something of the ways of his Creator,
and a particle of His mighty deeds, of His Power
and His wonders.

For by the greatness of slaves the greatness of their master
is known to those who can know,

And on the slave is revealed the might and glory of the lord –
'for all the goods of his master are in his hand'.

As we know from the poet's general neo-Platonism it is the *appetitus et amor* (*Fons Vitae*, V. 32) towards formation active in all matter which makes all the planets move in the same direction towards God's throne which, as we read in Talm. *Baba Bathra*, must be thought of as situated in the west[14]. The thought that serving a noble lord ennobles a servant is Talmudic. "The servant of a king is like a king[15]." Thus it is God's glory which bestows rulership on God's foremost servant. The inspiration of the poet through nature – the purple clouds which are the garment of honor of the setting sun – informs this sunset poem.

Another sunset poem which is one of the poet's elegies for his patron Yeqūthīel interprets the nocturnal darkness of the sky as its mourning for the beloved Maecenas. It is translated in my German book on Ibn Gabirol.

Notes 13–15

Notes to the Text

Dist. 1: Davidson lists a variant *me-hōdh-khā* 'from your majesty' instead of *me-ōr-khā* 'from your light'.

Dist. 3: Davidson replaced the *yeḥradh* 'he will fear (tremble)' in the previous editions by *yehdar* 'he will glorify'.

(2) SPRING II: RAIN — THE CALLIGRAPHER

Kāthabh śethāw — - - ⏑ - - - ⏑ - - ⏑ - - - (*Sarī'*)

Bialik-R. III, p. 27, No. 39
Schirmann: *Nibhḥ.*, p. 59
Millás, p. 30

Rhyme: *-bh-āw*

Winter rain wrote in the ink of his showers and his drenchings,
with the pen of his lightning flashes, and with the hand of his clouds I Ki. XVIII. 44

An epistle upon the garden in shades of blue and purple,
as they were not composed by the most artful artist. Ex. XXXI. 2-4

Thus, when the Earth delighted in the face of the Sky,
she embroidered the canvas of her garden beds with his stars.

This second *Winter* Rain poem is also a garden poem. Whereas in the first, only the flower beds were granted personified action, we have here a chain of more vivid metaphors, the main actors being the Rain and the Clouds.

a. Rain is compared with ink,
b. Lightning with a pen in the hand of the clouds,
c. The garden with an epistle,
d. The surface of the earth with a garment,
e. The garden bed with the sky,
f. Flowers with stars (merely alluded to).

Winter Rain, Sky and Earth are personified; the Rain is the devising artist; the clouds are only the executors, very much as in the poem beginning *Yeshallem haś-śethāw* (following later)[16].

The hackneyed Arabic comparison of a patron's hand with a cloud shedding a benevolent rain, encountered previously in the Alhambra poem and discussed there, is varied here. According to I Kings XVIII. 44

Note 16

("... Behold, a little cloud like a man's hand is rising out of the sea. And he said, Go up, say to Aḥab, 'prepare your chariot and go down, lest the rain stop you' "). A cloud, no larger than a hand, brings rain; but here Winter Rain itself bestows fructuous moisture and inscribes the earth. In the second line it rather directs the lightning, which is compared in turn with the pen; so that an elaborate level of pseudo-reality or pseudo-causality is achieved. This lightning pen (velocity, however, is not stressed) draws in blue and purple (and here we again encounter the poet's love for colors) a calligraphic letter, for which the garden is the recipient parchment. Such is the artistic calligraphy of this letter that it remains unmatched even by the master artist, who is, without his name being mentioned, Bezalel, the son of Hur (Ex. XXXV. 30).

In the last distich the causality is changed. It is the earth herself, in love with and in imitation of the beloved beautiful sky, who embroiders for herself the flower beds of her garment with starry flowers to please and honor the sky. This comparison of flowers with stars connects the poem with the Arabic genre of *nauriyya*. The typical comparison of white flowers with stars appears in the lines of Abū Firās, a prince of the Ḥamdānid Dynasty (died 968):[17]

> The Sky wept upon them the drizzling of its tears
> whereupon she [the meadow] began to smile showing stars of the sky ⟨*i. e.* flowers, like a mouth showing teeth⟩.

Ibn Gabirol's poem *Yeshallem haś-śethāw*, which follows, shows the earth giving birth to green sprouts, but the beds themselves don tunics, which the clouds had plaited or flattened. The image of garden beds forming a letter was alluded to in Samuel's garden poem, where the beds formed the columns of the scroll.

Note to the Text

Lā-khen 'thus' of the third distich may introduce the new causality referred to, but since it is so closely related to Arabic *lākin*, one might also think the poet had in his mind the meaning of 'however'.

(3) SPRING III: RAIN RESTORING NATURE AND THE POET AGONIZED BY LOVE

Bārāq asher ʿeyn-ō — *Bialik-R.*, I, p. 155; III, p. 23

- - ⏑ - - - ⏑ - - - - (*Kāmil*) — Schirmann: *Shīrāh*, I, pp. 218f.

Rhyme: *-eqeth*

Note 17

O Lightning—whose eyeflash resembles the flashing beryl's brilliance—
send down to the myrtle garden a nursing [cloud-lass]! Ex. XXVIII. 16

Visit the Bed of balsam plants and rein in Josh. IV. 18
the Rain-cloud lest she draw herself away. Ps. LXV. 10

O Lightning, lighten towards the Myrtle, for she is sinking Ps. CXLIV. 6
and she stands before you, knocking [in despair]; Cant. V. 2

But the Cloud herself refused to pass by until she had refreshed Is. XXIX. 8 Ps. LXV. 10
the soul of the Bed which was parched. Is. XXXIV.

My heart saw the miracles of the Almighty, beholding
the Cloud crying while the Bed rejoiced.

She sprinkles her drops with a diligent hand, like Prov. X. 4
the hand of Aaron sprinkling his altar; Lev. XXI. 16

She fashions stippled writing with her blossoms Lev. XIX. 28
and embosses into the patterns byssus and crimson. II Chron. II. 13

The Balsam-field fumes forth a perfume of myrrh incense towards
a helm-cloud which bursts open and races to pour.

Seeing its plants they said: "Shingled are they with pale green,
yet not with shingles of pallor, and no inflammation." Lev. XIII. 12

O that you friends of my soul could see her, your bondmaid,
amidst the shade of every fruit tree, a-groaning:

If I succumb from the turmoil of sorrows before you, Lam. III. 47
shingle my bones with the wood of the red vine! — Gen. XLIX. 11

"Do not shake out your bosom against those who chastise you Neh. V. 13
when your soul is enmeshed in loves.

Rather, behold, like a scourge of light the charming hind is standing
against you; and if she spoke up a [certain] neck would break." — I Sam. IV. 1

O do not mention nor stir up love; Cant. II. 7
for youthful love is as fire flaming! Cant. III.5

Dist. 1: The poet, avoiding lifeless description, commences with an apostrophe of lightning. Since *bārāq* is also appellative in Judges IV and V, and since he ascribes to this *bārāq* an eye, the personification, after a moment of planned confusion on the part of the reader, is perfect. Lightning is asked to hurry a wet-nurse to the thirsty myrtle garden.

Dist. 2: This distich discloses to us that the nurse is a cloud, as in the metaphorical language of the previous poems. The 'visitor' of the earth who brings rain in Ps. LXV. 10ff. is God.

Dist. 3: In an even more daring transposition, a Biblical line (Ps. CXLIV. 6: "Flash forth the lightning-flash, and scatter them!"), an appeal to God, is directed to Lightning with the same etymological play (after the first line had contained another play between *bārāq* and *bāreqeth*). With Bialik I interpret the word 'knocking' to mean both 'tousled' by the wind and also 'hustled' (as it does in Gen. XXXIII. 13, where it refers to flocks which were 'overdriven' or 'hustled') and as well the knocking of a desperate importuning supplicant. To make Lightning the god of the myrtle bed, before whom she stands in prayer, is as charming as the adaptation to and the appropriation of the biblical text is daring.

Dist. 4: Without any slight transition, the poet describes how the cloud answered herself to the need of the parched flower bed. The play upon words between *iwwethāh*, 'she desired', and *riwwthāh* (thus according to the meter), 'she slaked', could only vaguely be imitated (cf. The "Great Nature Poem," dist. 16).

Dist. 5: The image of the crying cloud and the smiling earth is not too well integrated and is even weakened further by the observed parallel of a divine miracle, which is merely humdrum. A similar observation of God's power in nature, in a dangerously playful manner, appears in the two *aperçu* distichs with the topic of a sunrise — a counterpart to the sunset.

Excursus: The Rising Sun

Yaḥshōbh lebhābh-ī — *Bialik-R.* I, p. 154

- - ᴗ - - - ᴗ - - - *(Sari')* — *Brody-Albrecht*, p. 39, No. 37

Rhyme: *-bhōn*

My heart thinks when the sun is rising
that in subtle transaction His actions are carried out:

When the earth demands its light,
He holds the Cups of the Bear as a pawn.

Dist. 6:   In a rather far-fetched but definitely original Hebrew metaphor, a sprinkling cloud is compared with the hand of the high priest, sprinkling blood upon the altar, alluding to Lev. XXI. 16.

Dist. 7:   Varying the image of the cloud as weaver-calligrapher, encountered in the other rain poems, the poet makes her here more an embosser of the bed's surface, possibly to be interpreted rather as an artist of a stippled kind of tattoo, fashioning multicolored flourishes. As an Arabic counterpart I quote lines by ʿAlī ibn M. ibn Jaʿfar:

> Environments — as if their meadows were
>   clad with embroidered borders.

Similar but more pictorial is the metaphor in *Kāthabh ṡethāw*, quoted before in full [18].

> When the Earth delighted in the face of the Sky,
>   she embroidered the canvas of her garden beds with his stars.

It remains astonishing, time and again, to what degree the revival of Hebrew nature poetry invited our poet to use the vocabulary of Psalms for those *nugae* (Ps. LXV, CXLIV).

Dist. 8:   The paronomasia, 'fuming forth of myrrh perfume', is a complete commonplace, but this image gains originality by making the thurification before the helm-cloud a 'nature rite', possibly as thanksgiving or supplication for rain.

Dist. 9:   The complicated play of two "self-corrections" of the poet, among which the first is a seeming self-contradiction, reminiscent of an oxymoron, was hard to render into English. The root *k-ṡ-h* has the meaning 'to cover', very often connected with an illness, like a rash; or, as for instance in Lev. XVII. 13: "its blood, and covers it with dust," 'to conceal' or 'to clothe', which nuances seem to be involved here. It seems to entail a meaning like 'they were clothed' or 'covered', but not 'concealed'. Or if we thought of a derivation from *k-ṡ-ṡ*, used once in Ex. XII. 4, yet not in the Puʿal, it could mean 'covered', but not 'divided' or 'numbered'.

    The two words *yerāqōn* and *dalleqeth*, mostly translated 'green consumption' and 'inflammation', appear in the sense of a real sickness. Thus the words are used in a poem beginning *ʿAley gizʿ-āh* [19]. Strangely enough, green, a favorite color of the Arabs, is used in a positive way as, according to English taste, an olive complexion is to the advantage of a human face. Compare the lines by Ibn al Muʿtazz: [20]

How should his cheeks not be green,
being slaked by the waters of beauty?

For the "morbid ideal" entailed in the 'sickly looking green' see the Rose poem:[21] "... every tawny green like that of an ailing woman ..." For the reference to illness attached to both *k-ś-h* (or *k-ś-ś*) and the two names for illnesses, and in particular for the return of *k-ś-h* (or *k-ś-ś*) in distich 11, in which the poet declares he wishes to be 'covered' with vines, I introduced the neutral word, 'shingled', with its glancing reference to illness 'covering' the human skin with red spots.

Dist. 10: In a way somewhat more passionate than customary the poet addresses the (mostly purely literary, make-believe) friends as "lovers of my soul." The Arabic poetical device of 'address of friends', in a 'wish' sentence, which is here in the subjunctive of irreality, appears in: "If you could only see my soul who is your bondmaid a-groaning even within this paradisical environment!" The poet had complained before that his soul was enslaved to the friends; for instance in his *We-ahbhāth-ī we-sibhr-ī*, he had explained:

I am the earth-ground for my intimates, my confidants, my allies,
and the dust-soil for their feet.

With this distich 10 the poet not only turns to his friends, but also to a second theme, which is his love.

Dist. 11: The poet, however, does not seem to demand that his confession of love be taken too seriously — distich 11 ends surprisingly in the frivolous vein of some Persian and Arabic love songs which echo Dionysian ideas. He wishes, when dead, to be covered with vines — which must mean to be eternally united with the source of happy intoxication. (The word for 'covered' is translated 'shingled' to imitate the play upon the word translated 'shingles', referring to a skin ailment.) If this is not merely a frivolity as among libertine Muslim poets, for whom wine should be taboo, then a high-pitched poetic emphasis is achieved by such blasphemy. Isolated as this outcry is, it seems to bespeak an intoxication — is it with love? Or is this a revolutionary wallowing in forbidden realms of feeling?

To mention briefly the connection: the so-called vat-like sarcophagi (ληναῖοι), found in the Mediterranean countries, having the form of a vat and mostly two lion heads inserted into them to look like spouts, seem to find their explanation in the mystery cults which promise the initiate that his death will be no less than a fermenting, strengthening process for the soul, so that it conquers the gates to the blest abodes.

Note 21

Dist. 12: The next two distichs seem to be reproachful replies by the friends in a fashion known from Ibn Gabirol's Wine-Love Song *Meḥāṣa-nī*[22]. The wording is based upon the Nehemiah passage, generally translated "I shook my lap, and said: So God shake out every man from his house, and from his labor, that performeth not this promise; even thus be he shaken out and emptied." The friends seem to decline the responsibility and reprove the poet for his predicament of love which is — as we hear in the next line, *ya'alath ḥen* — for a charming hind or a young girl. They call themselves 'your reproachers' and demand to be heard by the poet without being bothered with the confessions of his love plight or complaints. I assume that the line is related to the symbolism of the magnificent *We-ra'yāth-ī mehullālāh*[23], which ends with the poet's confession of being just as much in love as he is unable to consummate this love.

Dist. 13: The friends seem to chide the poet for stubbornly clinging to his professed gloom, instead of allowing himself to be brightened or frightened into a confession of love by the 'scourge of light', the impatient girl.

The word scourge entails a second allusion to chastisement, and indeed she is as infuriated by the poet's seeming indifference as was the lady of *We-ra'yā-th-ī* (dist. 4ff.):

... She contends with me when I flow with tears
and send forth waters down my cheeks.

I answered her, "How shall I delight, exult?
How can I lift my heart to joyful shouts

When there is no wine, no must in the vats,
no grain, no wheat in the storing bins?

or the lady, most likely the same, in *Ḥaqor we-'habh* [sic] introduced (in dist. 3) with: [24]

Who said: "How long will your love
be hidden, not seen, not revealed?

The harvest — they harvest with a scythe,
putting in a sickle, 'the blade to the crop'."

The almost Freudian or Baudelairian symbolism or metaphors, even reminiscent of Boccaccio, referring to unconsummated love and, as in the first poem, to the poet's inability to consummate this, have remained

Notes 22—24

hitherto undiscovered in the commentaries of the editing anthologist and will be discussed in a subsequent study.

The line, "and if she spoke up, a neck would break," Schirmann takes to mean that the poet would break his own neck in his apprehension, like Eli in I Sam. IV. 18. But I think he would do so figuratively, under the reproaches of the enraged girl.

Dist. 14: Very faint are the last words of the poem, although they are a further confession of being consumed by burning 'love of youth' (couched in the words of Canticles) — the poet's plea for clemency poorly hides his begging off and his falling back into helpless crooning. Is all this to be excused by the wine motif with its absurd interlude? The poet was no longer a very young man when this poem was composed.

Notes to the Text

Dist. 9: For the quasi-oxymoron of *we-lō kass-ū*, I read *khuṡṡ-ū we-lō kuṡṡ-ū* as in the poem *Yeshallem haṡ-ṡethāw*, distich 5, which line seems to elucidate this distich. If the text is correct, such self-correction of the poet is not isolated. One might compare a similar quasi-oxymoron in the first line of *Yedhaʿtī-khā we-lōʿal hay-yedhīʿāh*, "I knew you, yet not on the basis of so-called knowledge or acquaintance," *Bialik-R.*, III, p. 12. Or in the poem *ʿAbhey sheḥāq-īm*, distich 7, *ṡōdh-ōth yedhāʿ-ām īsh we-lō nōdhāʿ-ū*, "like secrets which a man knows yet which can never be regarded as known," *Bialik-R.*, I, p. 153. One might also compare *Hinney bhen-ōth ʿāghūr* in almost the same connection, where the second part of the first distich reads: *shār-ōth ʿaley phō'r-ōth we-lō lummedh-ū*, "sing in the crowning foliage (songs) unlearned (without being taught)." On these grounds I think that the consonant text is correct, and I discussed the linguistic question in my notes to the text. Schirmann takes over Bialik's *khoṡṡ-ū we-lō khāṡṡ-ū*. This seems to be the pronunciation to follow from their punctuation although this destroys the true *tajnīs*, which the poet seems to have aimed at. They also neglect the *raphē* reading of the *k* after *āmer-ū*, to be read at least *khoṡṡ-ū*, a Puʿal form appearing in Ps. LXXX. 11, "the mountains were covered with its shade . . .," to be translated 'to be covered', 'to be clothed'. I read *khuṡṡ-ū we-lō kuṡṡ-ū*, to keep the *tajnis* as pure as possible, as the text editions read this form in the parallel distich (5) of the poem *Yeshallem haṡ-ṡethaw*, which follows. Brody, quoted by Bialik, wishes to read *khiṡṡ-ū we-lō khiṡṡ-ū*, 'they covered and did not cover', a version which is not convincing, for there is no object to refer to. The same would be the case if they derived this word from *k-ṡ-ṡ*, 'to clip'. Neither does Brody's reading *be-yerāqōn u-bhe-dhalleqeth* (see below) make any more sense than the destruction of the two-fold oxymoron in similar grammatical patterns.

The implied subject of 'they said' is even more fictitious than the friends addressed in the next line. The play between *yerāqōn we-lō dalleqeth*, 'green-ishness yet not with burning fever', based on Deut. XXVIII. 22: "The Lord will smite you with consumption and with fever, inflammation, and fiery heat . . . and with (green) mildew . . .," where the rhyme word *dalleqeth* appears as well, is a second self-contradiction of the poet, paralleling that of *khuṡṡ-ū we-lō kuṡṡ-ū* and supporting the correctness of the previous words. *Yerāqōn* seems to stand for 'a green look', or 'a greenishness', not to be interpreted as 'green consumption' or 'chlorosis'.

Dist. 12: I read *lim-yaṡṡere(y)-khā* [sic], following Brody, in the plural, 'to your chastisers', for the poet's address to many friends in distich 10.

Dist. 13: The text of this line is not easily understood. *Ya'alath ha-ḥen* 'the charming hind', taken from Proverbs V. 19, where it refers to a 'wife of your youth', is well integrated with the next line, speaking of love of youth. Also the root *y-ś-r*, 'to chastise', in distich 12 is related to *khe-shoṭ ūr*, 'like a scourge of fire', (as I read differently from Schirmann and Bialik-R., who read *bhe-shuṭ ōr*). *ūr*, 'fire', is a better reading than *ōr*, 'light', read by Bialik and Schirmann; this although a 'scourge of fire' seems to be without biblical precedent. If this should be a pun upon (or a misreading of) *keśūth-ōr*, 'a garment of light' (from that root *k-ś-h* dealt with previously), we would have to understand that the friends chide the poet for wishing a 'covering of vines' in his grave instead of accepting, while alive, a 'covering of fire', which is the girl. This interpretation, however, is not very plausible.

(4) SPRING IV: ANNOUNCEMENT OF SPRING

Yeshallem haś-śethāw — *Bialik-R.* I, 106f.

- - - ⌣ - - - ⌣ - - *(Wāfir)* — *Brody-Wiener*, p. 107

Geiger, p. 128

Jews' College Jubilee Vol., 1906, p. 192

Rhyme: *-q-īm*

Raintime fulfills his vow, upholds
his pledge to the Narcissus of Valleys. Cant. II. 1

A Summer's Day peers forth at Winter's side: I Sam. IV. 13
will the harbinger of the green buds come —

Buds the Earth will bear without a pang, Ovid, *Fasti* IV. 330 (April)
children the Clouds shall nurse. Gen. III. 16

Observe the smiling World, her cheeks
now smooth which of late were hard.

The Parterres are clothed in linen tunics Ps. LXV. 14; Esth. I. 6
which the Clouds have crisscrossed with crimson;

Their appearance is the appearance of goldleaf work Ezek. I. 16ff.
and their crests are the crests of emeralds.

Jer. VIII. 7 — The turtledove, the warbler, the wheeling swallow rose,
(Judges VII. 2) — preening themselves above the doves of brooks;

(Cant. II. 8) — And when they point their heads to leap,
one would think they were mincing in shackles,

But when sun's radiance reflects on them,
necklaces cover their napes ...

Respond: can you cover the light?
Are you fit to abase the skies?

What need to make your heart a cliff
Is. VII. 19 — toward me — that you fissure it with clefts?

Judges XIV. 4 — Why do you seek provocation against me?
Provoking words are shallow and hollow.

Why do you throw your spears at me,
Job XLI. 7 (15) — are not the shields of our youth imperforate?

Amos VI. 12; Nah. I. 3 — Our horses run across the cliffs
and cover the skies with dust.

Lev. XXII. 24 — Must you despise the small, preferring size?
Your own sacrifice to your God — it is crippled.

The years loom out of months,
the days loom out of minutes.

If you wish to lead men of heart,
Prov. XX. 5 — draw deep waters from the heart of man.

Dist. 1: In spite of rabbinic injunctions against a literal interpretation of Canticles, Ibn Gabirol, in the same way as in his Alhambra poem, uses the second chapter of Canticles, which is an announcement of Spring, for a Spring poem. The Hebrew word *śethāw*, mostly interpreted as Winter or Autumn, is used here with its Arabic cognate *shitā'* for a personified Time of Rain in the manner of the great *ʿAbbāsid* poets like Ibn al-Muʿtazz. The personified Winter is faithfully keeping his promise to restore the sleeping bulbs to wakeful life and bloom.

Dist. 2: Also Summer is not far off, for he is personified as looking out – as the old Eli did when he waited for his sons to return with the Ark from the battle "who was sitting upon his seat by the road, watching" (I Sam. IV. 13) – beside Winter, waiting for the first green sprouts. A daring and charmingly ingenious variation!

Dist. 3: Most unexpectedly, the Latin commonplace from Ovid's *Fasti*, *Herbae, quas tellus nullo sollicitante dabat*, appears in a Hebrew garment, transmitted most likely through Arabic precedents and authenticated most aptly by the biblical "in pain you shall bring forth children," (Gen. III. 16), the curse of which, the poet feels, has been revoked here in a renewed Paradise. The earth gives birth and, in an image we have encountered many times, the clouds are the nurses of the flowers in the garden beds.

Dist. 4: Since the surface of the water was compared by Ibn Khafāja in his "How many flower chalices . . . ?" cited above, with the cheek of a laughing person, and similarly in his "Drink from small cups . . .," distich 7: "the evening came to gild the cheeks (the garden's)," we can be sure of having an Arabic metaphor of the smiling cheeks of Lady World which had been chafed, but are now smooth. The cheeks 'which were hard' are to be understood not solely in terms of their physical roughness but also of their severe expression, in the way of "Winter" whose countenance is 'evil' in the poem following hereafter. There are numerous lines by Hispano-Arabic poets mentioning hills which have smiling mouths with most beautiful teeth:[25]

The skies weep above the hills, while in these
mouths are smiling with most beautiful pearls.

And similarly by the ʿAbbāsid Ibn al-Muʿtazz earlier:

On the one side the heavens weep;
on the other Spring is smiling.

Dist. 5: The metaphor of parterres donning colorful tunics has occurred in Arabic poems quoted above. Hebrew poetry anticipated this in Ps. LXV. 13: "the meadows clothe themselves with flocks, the valleys deck themselves with grain . . ." We discover in the Bible that the Psalmist employs, most decidedly, metaphorical animation, but Ibn Gabirol's anthropomorphism is reinfused by the Arabic school (perpetuating, in this case, Ovidian pagan tradition).

Dist. 6: Quite stunning is the employment of Ezekiel's imagery (I. 13, 14, *R. S. V.*): "As for the appearance of the wheels and their construction:

Note 25

their appearance was like the gleaming of a chrysolite; and the four had the same likeness, their construction being as it were a wheel within a wheel. When they went, they went in any of their four directions without turning as they went. The four wheels had crests and they had spokes; and their crests were full of eyes round about." (I translate the word rendered there 'crests' as 'rims'.) This imagery is strangely heightened by Arabic influences, as it appears, and visualized by the Arabic sense of contour. The above quoted poem by Ibn Nufail continues, following Seco de Lucena's translation:[26]

> While (Spring) weeps, the backs (hills) of the Earth laugh,
> showing flowers of dazzling whiteness.

Dist. 7: The turtle doves of Solomon's Song, and two kinds of birds, hard to identify, carry on the *munāẓara (tenzone)*, a contest for supremacy, "preening themselves above the doves of brooks," reminding us of the Alhambra Poem, distich 29, where, however, vice versa, the doves declare: "We rank above the turtle doves."

Dist. 8: Vainly so, because the doves are the most beautiful of creatures according to the taste of the time, because of their tripping steps, like those of a refined city girl, described in Ibn Gabirol's *Mī z-zōth asher*, "Who is the one who ...[27]," whose 6th distich describes the poet's inspiring Muse:

> ... For she appeared to me from a distance that I deemed her
> a dove which skips across the field; this although she flew.

Dist. 9: And jewel of all jewels, in the taste of this time, is the dove's necklace, also alluded to in the Alhambra poem, dist. 30. Here, however, the poet is quite specific, mentioning the rainbow effect of the sun's reflection upon the neck feathers. Thus, distich 9 sounds out like a finale, with a strong accent on beauty.

Dist. 10: With this the poet turns to address a competitor, following the habit of Arabic poetry of using the theme of Spring as an introduction to an encomium of a patron, as Ibn Gabirol did in his Alhambra poem.

Dist. 11: But the poet rather chides an addressee, reproaching him for having become an unfriendly critic. Hence this part of the poem is presented to this critic as a challenge. He asks him, rhetorically, whether he can darken light and lower the skies, using the vainglorious language shared with Ibn at-Tāqāna in the poet's Saragossan days. He accuses the addressee not only of having made his heart a rock toward him but also having filled this with 'clefts', in other words of being both callous and cagey (as in

Notes 26—27

Isa. VII. 19). In the same terms, the poet speaks in *Ke-ayin nishshe'-ū*[28], "Well nigh they were deluded ..." (dist. 8):

Who, if he placed, on a hot day, the soles [of his feet]
against a cliff — then this would open its clefts.

Dist. 12: The word 'pretext' is reminiscent of the Samson story where it says: "... for he (the Lord) was seeking an occasion ('provocation') against the Philistines," (Judges XIV. 4). This allusion is very telling. One may deduce from this that the addressee had attacked Ibn Gabirol. A poem of chiding by Samuel beginning *Shema' has-sār*[29], "Harken, Patesi" (or "Prince"), most likely a censure on Ibn Gabirol who had termed himself "prince of poesy" may cause one to think of a possible connection. There Samuel employs the same word in its distich 4 in, as it were, a retort (2ff.):

When your epistle came I fancied
it might be fraught with grief and with obstinacy,

And that it contained but retribution
for vast offence and complaint.

(Lo, who plows provocation will reap
soon — as he was provoking.)

Dist. 13: The boast of being protected by the shields of youth has a Greek origin. Anacreon speaks of "beauty being equal to all shields": Κάλλος ἀντ' ἀσπίδων ἁπασῶν[30]. Most important for the spirit of this time and the acceptance of new knightly (chivalrous) values of the Arabs by the Hebrew and its later transmission to the Provençal poets is the appearance of the word 'youth'. The Arabic word *futuwwa*, meaning literally 'young manhood', is a key word for chivalry. The equivalent in Provençal poetry is *jovens* (and as such is the subject of an excellent study by Father Denomy)[30a].

The word *aphīq-īm*, 'strong shields', employed, appears in this meaning in Job XLI. 7 in a unique way: "His (Leviathan's) back is made of rows of shields ..."

Dist. 14: In parallelism to the shields, the proud image of horses running across cliffs has a threatening note, for the heart of the addressee was compared in distich 11 with a cliff in which there were clefts. The wording contains the implicit boast of trampling over the stony heart of the Maecenas. The language is taken from Amos VI. 12, "Do horses run upon rocks?" where it is a rhetorical question; but the young Ibn Gabirol boastingly asserts

Notes 28—30a

that he can accomplish the impossible, and in pursuance of this proud image he claims that his horses cover the skies with dust. The poet speaks similarly in a poem of praise for Samuel, beginning *Tehillath el.*[31].

A line referring to God (Nahum I. 3), "And the clouds are the dusts of his feet" is employed more than merely verbally by the poet, who equates himself implicitly with God.

Dist. 15: The poet accuses the addressee of rejecting the small and of favoring the merely impressive; the reader has to guess that the Maecenas expected and demanded from Ibn Gabirol long kasidas of praise and remained indifferent to our poet's most artful, polished gems. (I translate a few brief encomia by Ibn Gabirol in my German book.) In a blunt counter-jab he blames the Maecenas: "You sacrifice on the altar of your God (or even 'your gods') the crippled." This can only refer to the Maecenas' own intellectual production, most likely his poetry. The wording "your God" sounds almost cynical. The imagery of the crippled is taken from Leviticus XXII. 24: "... any animal ... torn or cut, you shall not offer to the Lord ... since there is a blemish in them ... they will not be accepted."

Dist. 16: What the poet meant by "the small" appears in this line: every unit can have equal importance, like years constituted of distinct small entities and like days, consisting of their moments. These lines are painfully reminiscent of Ibn at-Taqāna's repetitious style, for which reason I date this letter in the Saragossan period.

Dist. 17: The last distich, conditioned though it is in a sentence with 'if', contains some flattery and at the same time an admonition to strive for the deep and truly human. The wording reminds one of Pindar who speaks of drawing from the human heart, and of Proverbs XX. 5: "The purpose in a man's mind is like deep water, but a man of understanding will draw it out."

Geiger's assumption that this poem was written to a man who preens himself on his long poems and who rejected Ibn Gabirol's brief but choice compositions might again lead to the conclusion that the poem was addressed to Samuel han-Nāghīdh whose rank as intellectual leader appears to be acknowledged with great reserve. I may point out that length was indeed Samuel's forte. The great victory thanksgiving which Ibn Gabirol derided in a poem that begins "Dead was, Samuel!, Ibn Labrāṭ" contained no less than a hundred forty-nine distichs[32]. Later on Ibn Gabirol addressed Samuel, at the time when he was his patron, in long kasidas indeed. Did he have to show that he was able to fulfill such a task as a commission?

Notes 31—32

NOTES TO THE TEXT

Dist. 1: *Ḥabhaṣṣeleth ʿamāq-īm*. From "rose of Sharon, lily of the valleys" (Cant. II. I) the poet crossbreeds "rose of the valleys," perhaps " the poet's narcissus."

Dist. 5: Instead of *kothn-ōth ḥūr* ('fine linen tunics'), Brody reads *kothn-ōth 'ōr*, 'tunics of light'. A. Geiger has reconstructed the text of this poem to an astonishing degree from the faulty manuscripts at his disposal.

Dist. 6: Brody has an inverted order, in literal translation:

> Their crests are like crests of fine gold jewelry
> and their appearance is the appearance of emeralds.

I translate *berāq-īm* which, as Bialik recognized, is not 'lightnings' but the plural of *bareqeth*, 'the lightning stone', as 'emeralds'; but the Ezekiel context to which the poem alludes contains a play upon the word 'lightning'. The poet expresses himself similarly in his *Ulay demāʿ-ōth*, *Bialik-R.*, I, pp. 10ff., distich 26. Speaking of stars, the poet compares them to buds blooming during the raintime, which equal, with their crests, emeralds and fine gold.

Dist. 8: Instead of *le-qappeṣ*, which is Geiger's reading, Brody reads *le-qannen*, 'to make a nest', which, as I think, is inferior.

Dist. 10: I prefer *itt-ākh le-*, 'it is in your power to', to *attāh le-*, 'you are able to', as Brody wishes to read.

Dist. 12: A reading of *dall-īm* instead of *daqq-īm* would destroy the homoioteleuton.

Dist. 13: This line is quoted by Ibn Ezra in *Halper*, p. 166.

Dist. 15: *Tibhḥar*, 'you choose', a reading which Bialik would consider instead of *tibhzeh*, 'you despise', destroys the connection with the next line: if the addressee would indeed show preference to the small components, more precious than something all too comprehensive, then he would have to praise the addressee for understanding how entities like a day and a year are composed of small particles.

(5) SPRING V: NOCTURNAL WINTER'S END RAIN AND SPRING

ʿ*Abh-ey sheḥāq-īm* — *Bialik-R.* I, p. 153

- - ⏑ - - - ⏑ - - - ⏑ - *(Rajaz)* — *Brody-Wiener*, pp. 107f.

Geiger, p. 124 (39)

Rhyme: -*āʿ-ū*

The Sky's Clouds lowed like oxen, Ecc. VII. 3; Gen. XL. 6
for Winter was grim and his countenance evil.

They are like masts which the storm puts to flight,
wherein commanders, as it were, blow rams' horns.

The Sky's Children stagger in the mist,
even morning's stars were lost, astray,

Which the Sun carried away on his trains across
Is. LVIII. 8; Job XXVI. 8 — the earth, and when these dispel, those are dispelled.

Ex. XXXIX. 3 — The sheets of the Rain — the gale hammers them thin and the thick cloud
is shredded into ropes reaching to the Netherworld.

Ps. LXV. 11 — He watered, softened her clods and also
Ps. LXV. 10 — prepared her furrows so they may be sown.

Job XXVIII. 2; Prov. XXVII. 25 — He unveiled the mountains' herbage, hidden hitherto,
like secrets known to man and yet unknown.

All winter wept his clouds till the trees of the field
revived which had been in death throes.

The portrait of a nocturnal rainstorm is a close counterpart to the "Great Nature Poem" and it shows, since it belongs to an entirely different mood and different frame of reference, how versatile our poet is.

Dist. 1: This powerful piece is a striking example of the typical "fallacious" mythology. It would hardly be worthwhile to differentiate here between simile and metaphor; the personification beloved of this period, appearing everywhere, builds up a large cast of make-believe actors; and if a reader were entirely naive, he might ascribe certain lines to Theocritus or Ovid.

The rolling thunder, not thunder claps, so that we might think of a Winter too advanced and tired for more vigorous representations of his power, is compared with the lowing of oxen. This is confirmed by describing Winter as angry and of an 'evil' countenance.

Dist. 2: In distich 2 we encounter a model of linked metaphors forming a level of pseudo-causality characteristic of this highly developed poetry discussed previously. The masts, most likely to be imagined as bearing sails, and a *pars pro toto* for a marine vessel, are hurled along by a storm; and what was before a mere image for the clouds now becomes the pseudo-"causality" for the thunder. Mounted upon the first metaphor, surrealizing it is a second: thunder, still muffled, yet frightening, is "explained" in terms of quasi-physics, as the warning horn signals, most likely distress calls, sounded by the commanders of the ship (Pl. 26). The Arabic critic al-Jurjānī gives a discussion of such a technique in many details[33].

Dist. 3: The description of the storm and of violent uncontrolled motion is carried on, but the actors are now the 'children of the sky', which are, as the second line indicates, the stars and which 'stagger' (like the drunken priest and prophet staggering under the wine in Is. XXVIII. 7). A

Note 33; Plate 26

related line by Ibn Shuhaid reads in J. Dickie's translation:

Why are the stars perplexed tonight?
Have they missed their direction or are out of orbit?[33a]

Dist. 4: The dizziness which the poet feels when watching the disappearing and reappearing stars is projected into the dramatics of the sky.

At daybreak the 'trains of the sun', an Arab image as bold as that of the 'chariot of the sun', which are of course long veils of mists or, possibly, cirrus belts within clouds, seem to carry away the stars across the earth. The second line of this distich, using the same word in two different meanings, is difficult to imitate in English. Its meaning is: 'when the clouds are caved in and dispelled on becoming thin, then also the star constellations have been dispelled'.

Dist. 5: The image of the clouds becoming 'thinned', *nibhqa'*, is carried on by the use of a very similar word, *riqqe'-ām* (this poem has a great many allusions to sound): The Wind, the great "hammerer," beating the clouds into sheets, alludes to the artist Bezalel, working on the Tent of Meeting. (Ex. XXXIX. 3). A cloud may burst and vanish by losing its water or be torn by the gales. A cloud in which "He binds the water — is not rent" under its load is mentioned in Job XXVI. 8, the language of which is used here.

It is most likely the Wind who cuts the cloud thicket into rope-like strips which reach to the Netherworld. (One might think that the entrance to the Netherworld is by the horizon, where the black shreds seem to be anchored.) The reader is reminded of Ḥōnī, "the circle drawer" or "eisorcist," mentioned in the Talmud, *Ta'anith* 23*a*, who spoke to God: "I requested a strong rain sufficient for the cisterns, underground ditches, and for the heights."

Dist. 6 f.: Since the subject is withheld, the reader is forced to supply this almost from the beginning of the poem, and it is 'Winter Rain'. The poet, with a switch to the idyllic, following closely Ps. LXV. 11, leads the reader from the crack of dawn and from storm to daylight and the breakthrough of Spring, and describes the soothing effect of a mild rain, softening the surface of the earth and making its furrows ready for the seed. Without reference to God, it is Spring who uncovers the mountains' hitherto hidden fertility; but with a chaste turn towards the mysterious, alluding to Proverbs XXVII. 25, the poet compares this revealing of the verdure with the secrets which man knows and fails to know at the same time, an oxymoron I shall discuss in connection with the Rose Poem.

Dist. 8: The last line, which personifies the Clouds, attributes to them the feeling of mourning: they wept as long as the trees were in the throes of death.

Note 33a

NOTES YO YHE TEXT

The poem contains a large number of masculine plural forms, which together with the rhyme syllable *-āʿ-ū* and also other words containing an *ʿayin*, which frequently occur, affords a sonorous symphony by itself.

Dist. 2: The text, offering an assonance between *therān-īm* [sic] 'masts' and *śarney* (not *śerān-īm*, 'tyrants', 'superiors'), was reconstructed by Bialik and Schirmann, and a parallel to this from Jehuda Halevi, which proves the correctness of this text, is quoted in Bialik's notes.

Bialik's *u-bhney* [sic] *shehāq-īm*, 'Children of the Skies', is preferable to *u-phney* [sic] *shehāq-īm*, 'the face of the skies', since a face or 'surface' can hardly be lost, and it stands in parallelism with 'morning stars'. Arabic poets have similar expressions like "the Sky's Children," and "Daughters of the Water;" *cf.* Pérès, *Poésie*, pp. 216 f. The image of a bursting cloud is found with the similar wording *nibhqaʿ* in the Spring poem beginning "O Lightning – whose eyeflash." *Nibhqaʿ*, in its connection with the cloud, may have the connotation of 'bursting', as in I Kings I. 40. In the other connection with the stars the verb may stand for 'to be broken in two', 'to be conquered', as it does in II Kings XXV. 4.

Dist. 4: For *nibhqāʿ-ū* see *Yellin*, p. 27.

In order to enable the reader himself to establish whether Ibn Gabirol merely used Hebrew material to produce a poetry which is entirely Arab in character or whether the spirit of his Hebrew heritage transformed the contemporary poetic mode, it may be worthwhile to list the specific material which the poet adopted for his purpose.

a. Ex. XXXIX. 2: "And gold leaf was hammered out and cut into threads, to work into the blue and purple and the scarlet stuff and into the fine twined linen, in skilled design."
b. Ps. LXV. 11: "Thou crownest the year with thy bounty; the tracks of thy chariot drip with fatness."
c. Prov. XXVII. 25: "When the grass is gone, and the new growth appears, and the herbage of the mountains is gathered ..."
d. Job. XXVI. 8: "He binds up the waters in his thick clouds, and the cloud is not rent under them."

As for Arabic counterparts, I cite again the lines by Abū Isḥāq ibn Khaira aṣ-Ṣabbāgh, quoted in connection with Ibn Gabirol's Great Nature Poem in the section "Weeping Clouds":[34]

... Rain weeps because he lost the sun
 and Lightning laughs like a mocker.

Thunder sermonizes with great eloquence,
 while the sad atmosphere remains silent.

The garden is watered by the Rain
 while the Flowers look perplexed. –

Note 34

Drink and be happy in a garden,
be merry because life is fleeing.

Other counterparts, referring to weeping skies and smiling landscapes showing their radiant flora, were quoted above[35].

(6) SPRING VI: INVITATION TO A BANQUET

Hinney bhen-ōth 'āghūr *Bialik-R.*, III, p. 26, No. 38

- - ⏑ - - - ⏑ - - ⏑ - *(Sarī')* Rhyme: *-dh-ū*

Behold, the warbler lasses in assembly Is. XXXVIII. 14
sing in the foliage what no one taught them. Ezek. XXXI. 8

How can you hear their voice in the walnut grove, Cant. VI. 11
swelling, and not drink and rejoice, [my friends]? (Job III. 6; Ex. XIX. 9)

What of the branches' beauty which the young season
rejuvenated, and the blossoms begotten in the garden?

When the Wind sweeps over them, the box shrubs,
like chatterboxes, bow down to each other.

The present writer once found in a musical score by an Israeli composer the words "*Molto Vivaldi.*" In the same way, I should like to preface this poem with "*Molto Khafāja.*" It comes closest to the Arab taste, in particular with the banquet motif at the end.

The language of Solomon's Song, e. g., II. 11 f.: "For lo, the winter is past, the rain is over and gone; the flowers appear on the earth; the time of the singing of birds is come, and the voice of the turtle is heard in our land" is used by Ibn Gabirol in three different connections: (1) in religious poems in which the maiden of the Canticle is Israel and the lover the Davidic Messiah; (2) in nature poems and love poetry with the language of the Canticles used in its literal meaning; (3) in a third group of poems as, e. g., the Alhambra poem and possibly here, we encounter two levels, a literal one of praise of natural beauty (found in gardens or the open country) and a messianic tone for certain hearers who see in such poems

Note 35

the description of a messianic Spring with Israel's redemption — very specifically, the forthcoming redemption through the Naghrāllas. This poem belongs, most likely, to the second group.

Dist. 4: Twigs or flowers moving like human beings in love or conversation is a motif very much like a common Arabic conceit which appeared in many of the above cited poems by Ibn Khafāja.

Notes to the Text

Bialik did remarkably well in reconstructing the text. Furthermore, Arabic models contribute greatly to its understanding.

Dist. 1: The connotation of *ʿāghūr* is dubious. It appears in Isa. VIII. 7 and XXXVIII. 14. It must be a singing bird, and I use 'warbler' as having both a specific and a general connotation.

In order to assess further Ibn Gabirol's special merits as exhibited in his Great Nature Poem, we have to put ourselves at a distance from it. We must realize that the Hebrew language seems not to have been used to describe the sentimental secular plight of an individual since early post-Biblical days. In order to ascertain whether Ibn Gabirol (as I think) achieved a new level of poetry, which is sentimental and in which he transcended the merely descriptive or the exclusively subjective type of previous Hebrew poetry in a new synthesis, I present a night poem by Samuel han-Nāghīdh which was most likely composed earlier than that of Ibn Gabirol.

Excursus: Samuel han-Nāghīdh: Nocturnal Rainstorm

Aṣappeh eley shaḥaq — Abramson: *Ben Qōheleth*, pp. 11 f.

⏑ - - ⏑ - - - ⏑ - - - *(Ṭawīl)* [36] — Habermann: *Dīwān*, II, pp. 30 ff.

Sassoon, p. 259, No. 23; p. 35, No. 53

Rhyme: *-se(y)-hā; -ṡe(y)-hā*

I look out to the sky and its stars
    and on the earth scan its creeping throngs,

And understand in my heart that creating them
    was creation in skillful craftsmanship.

Behold, the height of the skies is like a canopy,
    its clasps interlocked with loops, Ex. XXVI. 6

The moon with its stars like a shepherdess
    who sends out her sheep into a meadow; Gen. XLI. 2

Note 36

5 It is the crescent between the cloudy mists Ps. CXXXV. 7
like a ship passing, its pennons flying,

8 The dwellers like a regiment stretched out (II Sam. XXIII. 13) Job XXXIX. 9;
for night rest — their dwellings the granaries, Jer. L. 26

* While the men on earth are a-warring, the food
for their mouths keeps them running like horses. —

6 And the cloud as a young maid who walks over
a garden and waters its myrtles,

7 The mist of dew like unto a lass shaking Is. XVIII. 4
from her hair drops upon the Earth Is. LII. 2

** Which now turns drunkardess — the torrents Ho. IV. 18;
are her drinks, their floods her new-wines; Ps. LXXVIII. 16

9 And all flee before the terror of death Mekhilta, Be-shallah, 82
like a dove which a falcon puts to flight.

10 At the end she comes to resemble a bowl
whose sherds are crushed to smoothness.

Samuel was in no way a nature poet, but his mastery of the Hebrew language enables him to compose conventional verse at the level of competent applied art. We may be unfair to his genius if we say allowances should certainly be made for his *vita activa*, because it is on the one hand a miracle to find a statesman and great scholar writing poetry as prolifically as he did; but on the other hand it is obvious that he did not have the time to polish and finish his poems. We have to judge on the basis of the objective final product. A piece like his "Nocturnal Rainstorm" has its counterpart in Ibn Gabirol's "Great Nature Poem" and a comparison of the two gives us the means of assessing the value of Samuel's. His strength is indeed description which reaches the level of true virtuosity in his battle poems and his no less dramatic poetical reports of "The Whale" and "The Rabbis" ("Graceless Performance"). There he reaches, intermittently, the grim immediacy of the Arabic models, of the *ayyām al-ʿArab* tradition and the bragging humor of Abū Nuwās. He concentrates upon the relation of facts and his technique consists in the artful accumulation of hyperbolic metaphors, gleaned from the entire bulk of Arabic poetry. His art is entirely different from that of Ibn Gabirol who called Samuel's poetry "icy," a word which implies, among Arab literary critics, that it was contrived and lacking in an appeal to higher feelings. Samuel, though he was hurt by this reproof, was nevertheless willing, at certain moments, to subordinate his talent to that of the other. The modern reader may feel that this was justified, yet also be willing to give Samuel credit for a certain modesty and restraint: it would have been unbecoming for a warlord and shrewd statesman to indulge in artificially heightened sentiments. Yet, whenever such sentiments are expressed by Samuel, they carry conviction and we cannot overlook the beauty of such restraint when it compels him to express his fear almost parenthetically, in a mere comparison such as "the sun, like my heart, was blackened."

Though these poets may have been able to improvise (like Samuel when reciting his poem on Yehōseph's garden) they certainly worked as well with rhyme dictionaries and first composed individual distichs to be connected with each other later in a final effort — and this possibly not in an absolutely logical order but, after the style of an ancient bard, rather with certain deliberate *hystera protera*. We cannot then expect an all-pervading mood or an uninterrupted action. In a smaller piece like the "Nocturnal Rainstorm," which may have to be regarded as a *parergon*, we find no silver thread of sentiment or a convincing mood, and when we compare it with a poem by Ibn Gabirol — who had the advantage of belonging to a generation further in the direction toward an Ibn Khafāja — we are bound to find it inferior.

Dist. 1: The poet turns to the sky and from there to the earth with "its creeping throngs," which is an image which would be pictorial only if one looked down from the sky. The poet is inspired by very general religious feelings for the great craftsmanship of the Creator. If the poet's inspiration was of an immediate mystical nature he certainly does not voice this, but he may feel able to rely upon the reader's supplementation. He is reminded, in the conventional Talmudic tradition, of the biblical Tent of Meeting, the construction of which, as described in Exodus XXVI, consisted of "ten curtains of fine-twined linen and blue and purple and scarlet stuff: with cherubim skillfully worked." According to Talm. *Shabbath* 99a, the 'clasps' in the 'loops' of the Tent of Meeting looked like stars in the firmament.

Dist. 4: From here on the poet uses Arabic similes which are no less commonplace. The moon is compared with a shepherdess whose sheep are the stars, reminiscent of Hoffmann von Fallersleben's "*Wer hat die schönsten Schäfchen? Das ist der goldne Mond.*" The sentimental adjectives in "*most beautiful* sheep" and "the *golden* moon," warm, child-world personifications, have no counterpart here. Samuel's poetry suffers from an all too artistic distance from its similes.

Dist. 5: A second simile for the moon, entirely unrelated and actually destroying the reality of the first 'shepherdess' simile, that of a sailboat between clouds, whereby the clouds are supposed to be the sails of the moon-skiff, is entirely unpictorial for reasons of size and coordination. I compare Ibn Gabirol's lines in "Spring V":

The sky's clouds lowed like oxen . . .

They are like masts which the storm puts to flight,
wherein commanders, as it were, blow rams' horns.

The sky's children stagger in the mist,
even morning's stars were lost, astray,

Which the sun carried away on his trains across
the earth, and when these dispel, those are dispelled.

Ibn Gabirol's different technique allows his description to spread out over various distichs, breathing an all-pervading *stimmung*. The vagueness of Ibn Gabirol's diction, exemplified by "masts which the storm puts to flight," evokes only indirectly, in the way of a hint, the image of sails.

I have discussed the ancient motif of the moon boat in connection with Ibn Gabirol's "Great Nature Poem" in my commentary to distich 13.

Dist. 8: I insert here a distich which is in the printed editions the eighth within the poem. It belongs, as I shall show, to the celestial scene and contrasts with its wording "the dwellers . . ." with "the men on earth . ." of the (now) subsequent distich. It may fit even better, describing a calm scene, after distich 3, since with distich 4 (in the present order) the celestial scene begins to move. My free handling of the distich order finds its justification in the unfinished character of the piece and in variations and changes in its various transmissions. As to relating this distich to the description of the sky, the comparison of the stars with an army sleeping at night is current in this school of poetry; compare (with Abramson) Samuel's poem beginning *Yedhīdh-ī, qūm* ("My friend, arise"):[37]

. . . The earth in our eyes is like a maid
playing, and the world a dancer;

The sky like an army asleep at night,
every man placing before his tent a pyre.

Note 37

If Samuel's image of the nocturnal army camp refers to the sky then it is quite poetical, reminiscent of the *mishmār-ōth* of the 'wards'or 'hierarchies' of the angels. This, however, is not at all clear. The poet seems, in a way parallel to distich 1, to cast a second glance to the sky, and then in the next line to shift back to the earth.

Dist. *ff.: In contrast to the sky which seems to be static like a calm army bivouac, the earth seems to be in a turmoil (as in dist. 1) which is now motivated by a fight for survival. But the nocturnal character is absent from the description of the earth henceforth, which must destroy the reader's illusion. After this (mooted) shift to the terrestrial scene, there seems to be in the resumed description of the sky a possible progress from night to dawn, suggested by mentioning dew, and with this the poet returns, for the entire remaining part, to the earth. But the new topic is rain which, as we would assume from the simile of a girl watering myrtles, falls in some abundance; while in the subsequent distich, the poet narrows his focus and merely speaks of drops which a lass shakes out of her hair. All this is quite idyllic and, with the good will of the reader, the illusion of a nightscape is maintained. The first idyllic simile of the young maid is ill-integrated anyway with the 'lass' of the next distich, and the 'mist of dew' *('ābh ṭal)* in distich 7 is less ethereal than the cloud *'ānān* in distich 6. But since we are not sure of the order the poet intended for the distichs, one might try out other variations and — arrive at other incongruities. Distich 7, however, seems to be assured in its place within the poem because earth, appearing at its end, forms the subject of the next distichs.

Dist. **: I discussed in Samuel's victory poem the Arab tradition of neglecting the logical order of a longer kasida and of a seeming predilection for the *hysteron proteron* which can be observed there. We may as well assume that the poet never polished the piece to the maximum. The rain is now intensified and we are confronted with torrents and floods, the result of heavy downpours. The personified Earth, however, compared with a wine-bibbing woman, avidly imbibes torrents and floods. This imagery appears in the Arabic flower portraits by Ibn Alī abū 'l-Ḥasan in which the jonquil is compared with a woman in the company of topers, and in lines by Ibn Baṭṭāl al-Mutalammis, with similar comparisons.

Dist. 9: The poet turns abruptly from the idyllic to the terrifying sight of men fleeing before the flood, although the reason for this panic is again to be inferred only. The comparison of a dove fleeing before a falcon, though Arabic in derivation, has a counterpart in Talmudic literature: it is found, according to Abramson, in *Mekhilta*, *Be-Shallaḥ*' "At the same hour Israel resembled a dove fleeing before a falcon."

Dist. 10: Returning to a reconciliation of the terrifying with a more idyllic theme, the last stanza describes the earth as a broken bowl, the sherds of which form a level surface, which consists of smooth and brittle particles. It is reminiscent of Ibn Gabirol's poem "Spring" V, distich 6:

> He watered, softened her clods ...

The reader may feel that the poem is incomplete in that there is no return to the topic of night, which appears in the introductory distich. He might have expected a mention of the coming dawn, or of the phenomena of the sky with which the poem began. Not only is there no overall emotional theme, to be compared with Ibn Gabirol's feelings of fear of losing the moon and premonitions that his hour of inspiration is doomed to vanish, as in his "Great Nature Poem," but there is not even a unity of motifs: the gardening girl and the hair-shaking lass appear only fleetingly. There is no unity of tone and no musicality. It must, however, be borne in mind that this poem is, for Samuel, a mere *parergon*.

Notes to the Text

I attributed to the distichs of the poem the numbers which they have in the printed editions. The additional lines are marked by asterisks.

This piece is found in two of the three books which together form Samuel's *dīwān;* in *Ben Qoheleth*, 'The Modern Ecclesiastes', where the distichs 10 and 7 (in my order) do not appear, and in *Ben Tehill-īm*, 'The Modern Psalms', where these appear after distich 8 (in my order). Also, in the latter book the piece is inserted into a frame consisting of two introductory lines beginning *'Aley-khem, beney Thōrāh we-thōphse(y)-hā* [sic]. I indicate the variant sequence of the poem by marginal figures in parentheses.

> It is upon you, sons of the Torah and her embracers,
> it is upon you to uncover her stored treasures
>
> For the sons of man are in dark places
> on earth, while you are like her suns,

and ending with sixteen lines completing the frame with the topic of praise for an unknown Rabbi David. The opening lines of the transition to the new topic read:

> It is as if the earth's territory in the eventide Ecc. VI. 4;
> were, like a negress, covered with a black Shihor covering, (Jer. II. 18)
>
> Whereas the sight of Rabbi David upon his place
> is like a sun which lights up her [the earth's] limits ... Ps. LXXVII. 19

This poem was also interwoven, with slight changes, into the *Ṣaḥ-ōth* of Abraham ibn Ezra, according to the notes to this poem in *Abramson*, p. 179. The topic of Samuel's night poetry is discussed in a Hebrew article "The Star-gazer and Observer of Clouds," by M. A. Jack, in *Meozenayim*, 1945, pp. 215ff.; 375f. with many fine observations.

The additional distichs quoted above: The poet speaks of utter darkness as "a negress, covered with a black Shihor covering;" Shīḥōr is most likely the name of an eastern branch of the River Nile, reminding one by assonance of *shāḥōr* 'black' and, geographically, of something generally outlandish. *Gebhūl* 'territory', being the only masculine noun, the verb should be read *yekhuššeh* 'will be covered' instead of Habermann's *yekhaššeh* 'will cover'. If *kūshīth* 'negress' were the subject the verb should read *tekhuššeh* (*kešūth* 'cover' would demand *tekhaṣṣeh* 'will cover'); since the comparative *ke*, 'like', appears twice before in *ke-illū* 'it is as if', and in *ke-khūshīth* 'like a negress' the interpretation of *kešūth* as *ke-šūth* 'like a vesture' is excluded; otherwise this would provide the needed masculine subject.

Dist. 2: Compare Ibn Gabirol, *Bialik-R.*, I, p. 154, No. 80.

Dist. 3: Addressed with "behold" are many. For 'the loops of the spheres interlocked like those of a tent', see, e. g., Ibn Gabirol's *Kether Mal(e)khūth*, in *Bialik-R.*, II, p. 64, *uit.*

Dist. 4: There is a variant to *be-thōkh āḥū* 'in the midst of a meadow', reading *be-yadh āḥū*, wherein *yadh* stands, as in Dt. XXIII. 13, for 'place'. Both readings can be defended and do not affect the translation.

Dist. 5: 'Pennons' or 'sails', cf.Ibn Gabirol's poem beginning *ʿAbhey sheḥāq-īm* ("Spring V") first distichs, presented above.

Dist. 6: This distich referring, as I think, to the sky and the stars, is found in *Sassoon*, p. 259 and in Abramson, *Ben Qōheleth*, p. 12 as distich 8, and in *Sassoon*, p. 35; also in *Habermann* (as a part of *Ben Tehill-īm* with two additional lines in the beginning, quoted above, and with the two distichs, appearing as 10 and 7 in my order) as distichs 12f. I place the distich numbers of the arrangement in the poet's diwan in parenthesis. *Ḥayyāh*, in the meaning of 'army', 'regiment' occurs in II Samuel XXIII. 13 and it is, as Abramson notes, replaced in the same context occurring in I Chronicles XI. 15, by a synonymous *maḥaneh* 'camp'. *Ebhūš*, generally translated 'crib' stands here, as Abramson thinks, for 'granary', as in Jer. L. 26. *We-ḥaṣe(y)r-ōth-ām*, 'their dwellings', in *Sassoon* is, for metrical reasons, corrected by Habermann and Abramson to read, with the same meaning, *we-ḥaṣr-ōth-ām*.

Dist. 9: The pun *naʿarāh tenaʿer* 'the lass shakes' could not be imitated in English.

Dist. 10: *We-haythāh* [sic] 'she became' or 'turned' is Yellin's good emendation for *hāyāh* in *Sassoon*, 'he' or 'it was'.

Dist. 11: The fine pun *han-neṣ yenīše-hā*, 'the falcon puts her to flight', could be rendered into English only by a vague assonance. Sassoon's *meḥathah* [sic] p. 35 is emended on p. 259 and in *Habermann* and *Abramson* to read, metrically correctly, *me-ḥathath*.

Dist. 12: For this imagery see Samuel's *Mezimm-ōth-ay* 'My plans', Habermann, *Dīwān*, III, p. 124. I prefer to read *shubber-ū* 'they were broken' to Abramson's *shibber-ū*, 'they broke'; as 'sherds' is most likely the subject, an unknown subject, 'they' in 'they broke' seems to be harder to understand.

Samuel's Night Poem recalls Yeats' "Byzantium," (in *Collected Poems*, New York, 1954, p. 243):

> The unpurged images of day recede;
> The Emperor's drunken soldiery are abed ...

D. Arabic Flower Portraits

The Arabic poets of Spain continue the tradition of the flower portraits, and may replace what they lack in a broad vision and sense of a mood of nature by their devotion to detail. Ibn 'Alī abū 'l-Ḥasan[38] praises a jonquil (a masculine word in Arabic):

He has a golden cup, narrow at the bottom,
but widening toward the top, which he shows to be admired.

He is a bouquet of flowers when you inhale his fragrance
and also a bowl for good sodality when cups are desired.

When he inclines the neck, drunk with delight which he harbors,
he imitates the swaying of a drunk man craving sport,

Or a slender woman who in a garment of green silk
leans over the topers with a golden cup in her hand.

We observe the following comparisons and metaphors:

a. A flower chalice filled with dew is transposed into a banquet cup.
b. And then, in a two-fold extension of the imagery, it is attributed to the jonquil flower the animation of a drunk man who also is a passionate gambler.
c. Finally the entire jonquil plant, and in particular its green leaves, are rather compared in the well known manner of the 'correction' or 'retouch' with a woman dressed in green, leaning over the gay company of celebrants and their cups.

It does not seem likely that the good company is an image for insects intoxicated by the dew (as in the following poem, the plant itself is drunk). The reader rather associates with this wording various jonquils, all of them waving their cups. The flower, thus personified, shows pride and wishes to please with its fragrance, feels human well-being in fellowship and displays a humorous mood. The comparisons constitute a whole canopy of an "as-if" reality. Abū Ayyūb ibn Baṭṭāl al-Mutalammis, famous for his garden pieces, equally personifies the plants of a garden:[39]

The earth shows herself very proud to our gaze
  for the splendor of her garments;

Her flowers are like cups which
  the fingers of the drinkers push forward.

The branches are like arms, seeking
  to touch one another.

The flowers call forth so much admiration from the insects
  that they trill in ecstasy.

When they embrace each other under the spell of the south wind,
  you might call them young girls exchanging kisses.

The blossom crowns filled with dew are like
  eyes that weep at the separation of friends.

This poem contains hardly a new image. The last distich presents a bold new version of the old conceits: the chalices of the flowers are compared with cups, although this comparison is merely implied after it had occurred in the second distich, but in the final line the comparison is shifted to eyes weeping for the separation of friends — the dew being the tears. Such a sentimentality is in no way motivated, not even by a make-believe mood of preciously described scenery.

A sentimental discription of carnations at night, containing the motifs of 'promise and expectation', found in Ibn Shuhaid's eulogy for al-Mahdī (killed by the Slavs in 1010), reads in Dickie's translation (op. cit. p. 258):

The gilly-flowers of spring amongst the blossoms
  under the night rise like a watcher

Who fervently hopes his love
  will visit him according to his promise

And stays awake all night in expectation ...

There exists one flower portrait by Ibn Gabirol with as much detail as can be found elsewhere only in his self-tormenting description of his skin disease. The style is so advanced in its combination of various distichs into longer units, that one might assign this to a later period in his life; but the skin disease was, most likely, a juvenile affliction.

E. Ibn Gabirol: The Present of Roses

Qerā' haṣ-ṣīr — *Bialik-R.* I, pp. 116ff.; III, pp. 21f

⏑ - - - ⏑ - - - ⏑ - - *(Wāfir)* — Schirmann: *Sīrāh,* I, 221ff.

Rhyme: *-m-ōth*

Arabic prefatory remark by the compiler of Ibn Gabirol's Diwan, according to *Bialik-R.*: [40] "His is also a poem for one who praised him (?)," or according to Schirmann, "Among the poems in which he attained specific elegance *(ṣaḥūth)* in expression and artfulness of presentation, ranks (this) poem, addressed to one of his friends who had sent him a bowl with 'rose-sūsans'."

Messenger, hail with "Peace, peace!" my brother
to whom there is no equal in the lands,

Whose magnificent gifts my heart will remember
and not forget as long as it lives.

For he sent me a bowl filled with fragrances
(may God fill his hand with amenities!) Ps. XVI. 11

In which there was every tawny green, the kind Ps. LXVIII. 14
of an ailing woman, her tunic torn away.

Also ruddy maidens! of whom a human eye catches
what otherwise his heart catches from dreams.

I liken their bodies chaliced within their dresses
to some spot nestling between a moat and walls Is. XXVI. 1; II Sam. XX. 15

Or to a froward son whom his father expelled
and on whose cheek shame and fears are gathered.

Note 40

There are those whom a male has known and others
Gen. IV. 1 — unknown by man and still being barred,

Some who cover their faces with ivorine veils,
Nah. III. 11 — like women who are in hiding from men

Yet who will appear when removing the veil
Is. XLVII. 3 — before a man in wrath, prone to take vengeance,

With countenances as if they were guilty before him;
and, although not guilty, they are filled with disgrace.

Is. XVIII. 4 — There appears from their faces a light as is the sun's light
Mi. I. 13; II Kings XXIII. 1 — when the "chariots of the days" are still harnessed.

Job XXXVII. 16 — And they show, though themselves not wise,
to one beholding them, mysteries of (divine) wisdom and sapience.

The eye of a man beholding their glory would look like
the heart of a ruler encompassed by intrigues

Or be like the heart of a man frightened by a dream
or like fallen ones craving to find uplifting;

Or even like a bird of prey panicking in a trap
or like a student puzzled by the Levirate Treatise.

I, regarding their splendid image, may know them well
yet find no expression in words or images,

Ps. XLIX. 9 — Like people whom I have known by appearance,
yet who were not spelt out to me by name.

Time has shaped their frame greenish,
yet fashioned their tunics red,

So that there arises a flame as if
they were woven with scarlet and purple.

Ex. XXXII. 20 — Also Time devoured their skin till worn thin
and consumed from off their flesh the bones;

(Their flesh being chastened for no reason,
like a soul that was chastened from sinfulness)

And caused a wind of perfumes to hover about them, Gen. I. 2; Deut. XXXII. 11
and upon them the Summer Cloud has woven patterns.

They blush under the eye of one languishing for them Ps. LXIX. 4
and they sway with the breath of sighing souls;

A man's spirit delights in their scent, no less
than the heart of a sage finding out secrets.

Indeed, were they laid upon the face of one
abandoned by sleep, he would cease to care for slumber; Job VII. 4

If given to one dead, he might take them
and enjoy them in his coffin, however dead he be.

And came they into the House of Hegai, for the splendor Esth. II 3
of their looks they could not be distinguished from the maids.

Cut, as they were, from the garden bed, they came
and had no feet, and their legs were withered. Gen. XLI. 23

Yet as the Prince sent them to be presented to me,
I deemed them a king's epistle sealed.

As they were broken loose as a bunch in a fist,
they were intertwined like sheaves therein; Hos. VII. 8

As if they had a zealous strife with one another
and presented before me their arguments. Is. XLI. 21

Paragons of glory and beauty, lacking
not a jot and, like your own deeds, perfect! Ezek. XXVII. 3

Sterling ones, as your own heart sterling
and chaste, without wickedness and fraud; Ps. XVIII. 3

Thus they witness that your hand, uplifted on high Lev. V. 21
with the sky's stars, hoards pledges.

Your sublime virtues smite the cheeks of the Fates,
Is. XLVII. 9 making them blood-flushed, as stained.

May God fulfill with you His graces,
Prov. XXIV. 7; Ezek. XXVII. 16 Iob XXVIII. 18 and may He increase with you pearl and coral,

And may He destroy the enemies before you
I Sam. XVII. 17 and elevate your rank above all ranks.

A Maecenas has presented the poet with a bowl filled with roses of strong fragrance. Ibn Gabirol reciprocates with a poem entirely in the taste of the Arabic flower portraits. (It is, as mentioned, related to the horrifying description of his skin disease, translated in my German book, but is gracefully different from it.) The poet reaches here a very modern and, as I think, in Hebrew hitherto unattained, art of flower portraiture: the apparatus and the sophistication of metaphors employed for hyperbolic homage to his patron is astounding. The last traces of biblical parallelism of members are discarded. Here for the first time, we discover the poet's particularly refined sense of color in addition to his sense of light, shape, and smell.

Dist. 4: The green color is compared with that of "an ailing woman, her tunic torn away," reminding us descriptively of the rough rose stem, disappointing to the eye, or the petals at the point where they emerge from their wrapping of covering leaves. To illustrate the Arabic models of such pieces I quote a few typical metaphors from those: "The rose whose mantle is pierced shows red tunics," or "She is dressed in tunics with purple gems, one whose buttons break through the collars;" "She has come to say goodby in great haste, dressed in green veils and red tunics;" "She has veiled her face with a *burquʿ* and she stepped forward seductively towards us like a bashful young girl who veils herself lest one see her beautiful, precious face[41]." Al-Maqqarī quotes a poem in which a rose is described by Abū 'l-ʿAlā' Saʿīd:

They brought you a rose, Abū ʿĀmir, whose fragrance reminds one of musk;
she resembles a virgin whom a curious one eyes and who hides her head with her cloak.

'Every tawny green', *yeraqreqeth* 'greenishness' or 'greenish gold color', is taken from the biblical line in Ps. LXVIII. 14, which was discussed before as a felicitous find to express the poet's admiration of the "dove's

Note 41

necklace," the rainbow effect on the neck feathers admired during this period: "the wings of a dove covered with silver, its pinions with green gold," a line we quoted before. The hues of shimmering green were observed by Arabic poets. Von Grunebaum quotes various passages by Abū Tammām, Ibn al-Mu'tazz, al-Buḥturī, and others, where green appears in the description of a man's skin or of the night.

Dist. 5: Moreover, the flowers, just emerging from their sheathing bud petals, are compared with the girls, unveiled and partly bared, of our dreams.

Dist. 6: In typical heaping-up of metaphors — a means to express the poet's enthusiasm — a bare spot of the flowers, slit-like, is also compared to the strip of dry ground appearing at the foot of the castle walls beside the water-filled moat.

Dist. 7: In the following distichs, the flowers are metaphorically animated: out of human emotions their coloring is motivated. First it is the blushing cheek of a rejected (or a returning lost) son, and in distichs 8f. the reference is to women put to shame in various ways. Some roses (or lilies) are compared to fully blooming wives and others to well-sheathed virgins: white from being sheltered and kept in "purdah." The slight red flush of the flower faces whose immaculate innocence is so impressive is explained, by the use of the pathetic fallacy, as the result of unjust reproaches at the hands of a brutally jealous man before whom they are forced to withdraw their veils. This pseudo-causation goes together with a sophisticated diction and contradiction in keeping with the Arabic techniques of style.

Dist. 12: The image of the chariot is here connected with the days, reminding one of the chariots of the sun, more fully developed in the poem "The Garden Bed Resurrected" and the Sun poem (cf. Micah I. 13; II Kings XXIII. 1):

> Time after time the sun flies upon the sphere's flame platform,
> although no pursuer puts her to flight;
>
> So that we take her for a king's chariot
> which is swaying with its horses.

The gnostic or other Eastern sources are allowed to contribute to the emancipated poet's stock of metaphors, this in contrast with the subsequent pious thirteenth distich.

Dist. 13: The craftsmanship of the divine Creator is praised, as in Ibn Gabirol's descriptions of the stars and moon, and as in the poem (referring, if I am not mistaken, to Yehōseph ibn Naghrālla) in which he compares the "divinely" shaped lip of the child with Solomon's Brazen Sea. For the poet's own visual bewilderment by the roses he finds various somewhat stereotyped similes in the following distichs.

Dist. 14-18: The similes stand for the shock of the ruler on discovering a conspiracy against him, or that of a man upset by dreams, or finally that of one fallen to the ground, unable to lift himself up. A charming, deliberately witty, deflation of his *hypsos* is distich 16, with the reference to *Maššekheth Yebhām-ōth*, an intricate Rabbinic treatise on the levirate. The poet was visibly lured into this by the opportunity provided by the rhyme.

The oxymoron of knowing, and at the same time, not knowing, being at a loss to understand the origin of such a miraculous beauty, appeared as well in the "Spring Poem V" of Ibn Gabirol beginning:

> The clouds of the skies like unto oxen lowed

with a line, alluding to the vegetation, mysteriously sprouting up after the rain (dist. 7):

> Like secrets of which man knows though never made known to him.

Dist. 19: In a surprisingly heathen and naive fashion the poet makes Time or Fate the creator of the flowers. The laudable aim of the poet to keep the mundane and the religious neatly apart must be, together with the First Commandment, his vindication.

Dist. 21: Here the poet returns to the topic of his enchantment by the greenish color combined with the red, which he compares with a flame, and he immediately goes on to the other color of the mode, the pallor of sickness, as it were *vert mourant*, and not only *verdâtre*. In discussion of the theme of Time being the devourer, I refer elsewhere to the "eternal change of day and night which wastes away man" in the poem by A bū 'l-'Alā' al-Ma'arrī, which anticipates Michelangelo's epitaph for Lorenzotdi Medici. Also we remember the motif of wearing out the flesh from the inroduction of Ibn Gabirol's "Great Nature Poem," where the poet wastes his body in his quest for knowledge, which was thwarted by Fate or Time.

Dist. 23: Roses cannot be fully described without mentioning their fragrance; the poet's olfactory sense seemed, in other poems, to be as keen as the visual. In a modulation of the Genesis line: "... the Spirit of God was hovering over the face of the waters," we again find Time, instead of God, causing the fragrance to 'hover' around the flowers. This is so, provided that the grammatical subject is still Time, governing from the lines before. The vague diction, an element of Arabic poetical taste, could, however, also be interpreted "the wind caused fragrances to hover about them."

Dist. 24: The topic of blushing appears in a new and slightly repetitive variation. The red of the rose being by shame is an Arabic commonplace[42]. (One

Note 42

might almost wish to assign this line a place after distich 7 or 11.) Their swaying is interpreted by their empathy for souls languishing for them. The twofold causation for blushing and swaying is artfully integrated.

Dist. 25: In lines of humorous and partly exaggerated imagery — flattering to the wit of the addressee — the poet expresses his enchantment with the flowers in every renewed motif. The following lines remind us of the ecstatic exclamations in praise of the central hall with its rotating dome in the Alhambra poem (distichs 15ff.):

In which rejoices the heart of the poor and burdened
and the perishing forget poverty and distress.

I saw this and forgot my burden
and my heart was comforted from sorrows;

Yea, my body was almost lifted up
in my joy as upon eagle's pinions.

We notice with no great regret that the pathos, so typical of the young Ibn Gabirol, is absent here.

Dist. 28: Only one other line after distich 16 seems to be unduly knowledge-laden with the pedantry appearing in his wine song for Yiṣḥāq, translated in my German book[43]. The house of Hegai assembled the flower of Persian maidens, from whom one would be chosen as the royal wife of King Ahasuerus.

Dist. 29: This distich reminds us of the shocking descrtipion of the poet's skin disease, his boils or pox. These look (in distich 14):

... like roses whose pluckers carried them,
even cut their thigh at their market.

Dist. 33: Here the poet's praise for the flowers is directed to the true addressee, and the patron is addressed in the second person ... "like your own deeds perfect."

Dist. 35: The last line of Ibn Gabirol's "Great Nature Poem" referred to his abode erected by Hesper's dwelling. Very similarly the hand of the Maecenas containing pledges is lifted so high that they are as safe as the stars.

Dist. 36: The idea of being able to "smite the cheeks of the Fates" belongs to the self-aggrandizement of a man daring Fate's power, like that of Samuel han-Nāghīdh's arch enemy, Ibn ʿAbbās, who exclaimed, not long before his downfall:

Note 43

The eyes of (bad) Events are asleep for me;
to overthrow me is forbidden the Fates[44].

Literally, 'the Daughters of the Days', i. e., the personified 'Events' or 'Hours'[45].

Dist. 37: 'Pearl and coral' are to be understood on the basis of Job XXVIII. 15—18 in a passage about wisdom: "Wisdom cannot be gotten for gold . . . no mention will be made of coral or of pearls: for the price of wisdom is above rubies."

Dist. 38: The blessing of the patron at the conclusion is graced with an unusual diction, boasting rare words like *ra'm-ōth* (explained as 'corals and seashells') and *ʿār-īm* (explained as 'jealous ones'). This type of toastlike ending appears in various poems like *Qūm haz-zemān* and *Nesī umm-ō.*

Notes to the Text

In the Hebrew translation of the prefatory remark Schirmann quotes the vague Arabic term, used in the original, *ward sūsān*, 'rose lily', which leaves the question open, whether the poet refers to a rose or a lily. The editor of Ibn Gabirol's *dīwān* himself may by using the two words betray his own puzzlement and the poem itself does not offer sufficient clues. The Hebrew word *shōshannāh* commonly denotes 'rose', but being the cognate of the Arabic *sūsān*, 'lily', we may doubt, in the case of the Andalusian poet, to what he referred. The addition of *ward*, 'bloom', or 'rose bloom', may stress that roses are meant, but in principle it could also stand for 'rose lilies'. The limited and often oscillating vocabulary, only then activated for secular poetry, may have denied the poet precision. Names of birds like *śūś*, *ʿāghūr*, are equally equivocal. For this type of poetry, compare Pérès, *Poésie*, p. 166.

Dist. 2: *ʿāṣūm* 'magnificent' seems to be tinged by the Arabic cognate *ʿaẓīm* 'mighty'.

Dist. 3: *Kaph*, either 'palm of hand', referring to the hand of a messenger and corresponding with *yādh-ō* 'his hand' of the following line; or with 'vessel like the hollow of the hand', a 'hand cup', or 'bowl'.

Dist. 5: This is a typical Arabic *mā min* construction; literally 'red ones', (feminine plural): "it is being retained from them (masculine plural) by the eye of a man what is retained by his heart from his dreams." *Adhumm-ōth* 'ruddy ones' (feminine), introduces another hidden subject, which must be flowers. These, originally introduced as a mere metaphor for 'girls', later become more and more elaborately the main topic. The slight inconsistency of *me-hem* instead of *me-hen* after *adhumm-ōth* can be a copyist's slip or pardonable license. Masculine and feminine pronouns are sometimes used *promiscue* as we find in line 6 in *gewiyyāth-ān* 'their bodies', referring to the same ruddy ones (maidens) as well as *lebhūsh-ān* and, also in line 11 after *appe(y)-hen* 'their faces' still referring to the maidens and immediately afterwards, *we-hem* 'although they' (masculine). The modern editors might at least have remarked on this.

Dist. 7: *Ne'śaph* is equally free use of grammar; one expects *ne'śph-ū.*

Dist. 9: Schirmann reads *naʿalām-ōth*, to be explained either as 'with obscured senses', or 'swooning', as in the context of Nahum III. 11 *(R. S. V.)*: "You also will be drunken, you will be dazed" or as 'concealed', as in Ps. XXVI. 4: "Those who concealed themselves" or "their thoughts," i. e., as dissemblers. Much more plausible seems to be the reading *neʿelām-ōth* 'concealed', in this connection with *me-anāsh-īm*, which can only mean 'hidden from men', and hardly 'swooners' or 'dissemblers away from me'.

Dist. 12: *Bialik-R.* observed in their notes that *ṣaḥ* stands for 'day' and 'sun', similar to Isa. XVIII. 4, where *ṣaḥ* stands, together with *ḥom*, for 'clear heat' and, with *ʿale(y) ōr*, is translated 'in sunshine'. Parallels are found in *Bialik-R.*, I, p. 23, line 23 (see Bialik's notes to this). The image of the 'chariot of the sun' also appears in the "Garden Bed Poem," *Bialik-R.*, III, p. 25, dist. 7f.

Dist. 18: This line reminds one of Ibn Gabirol's poem beginning *Yedhaʿ-tī-khā* (*Bialik-R.*, III, p. 12).

Dist. 21: Schirmann's *ʿadh daq* is taken from Exodus XXXII. 20, where the form *ʿadh asher dāq* is mostly interpreted as a Qal perfect, "and he thinned out;" but I am inclined to read *ʿadh dōq*, and to interpret *dōq*, not as 'curtain' but as an infinitive of *d-ū-q*, a stem whose existence can be established on the basis of Ezekiel IV. 2 to mean 'until thinned', and to be understood in parallel to *ʿadh bōsh* 'until being ashamed' (an infinitive construction in Judges III. 25). Regardless of grammar, the meaning of the word *daq* or *doq* is based upon Exodus XXXII. 20: "And he took the calf which they had made, and burnt it with fire, and ground it to powder (literally 'until thinned')." Powder is possibly implicit, as it is explicit in Is. XXIX. 5: *ābhāq daq* 'fine powder'.

Dist.23: Instead of Schirmann's *baʿadh-āh*, the form *baʿadh-ān* seems to be preferable. The poet or the copyist uses the personal suffixes of the masculine plural *promiscue* (cf. *we-yar'-ū* in dist. 12) with the feminine plural, but all these references are to a plural, and there is no singular feminine noun to which *baʿadh-āh* could logically refer. Compare the note above to Distich 5. Bialik reads *baʿadh-ām.*

Dist. 36: *Kethūm-ōth* 'stained', or *ke-thumm-ōth* 'like perfect ones' (with Is. XLVII. 9), can have various implications for the imaginative reader for whom this is a tidbit. The genre of the riddle is cultivated by all these poets, but darkness as such is not regarded as a poet's virtue. *Kethūm-ōth* is most likely derived from the theme *k-t-m* 'to be stained', which would have, though, an ominous connotation. It could also be derived from *kethem* 'fine gold', to mean 'gilded', indicating that the Maecenas, while smiting the Fates, metamorphosed them into precious gold and/or gave them a surface of this. It is still less likely that with the Isaiah passage, where *ke-* is a preposition and *thumm-ām* belongs to the theme *t-m-(m)*, one should exegete 'as in their perfection', referring to two punishments which will come. Finally it could be derived from *thom.*

The cycle of the studies is, however, not yet consummated. I intend to publish a sequel concerning the Umayyads and their throne ideology which, though not accessible from any single written document, can be reconstructed from certain literary sources and from the inferences to be drawn from their court ceremonial and the actions of themselves and their courtiers. It will be necessary to complete the picture of Samuel han-Nāghīdh on the basis of his poetry, of which I have translated the great victory and battle poems, the white whale poem, and numerous others which seem to refer to his relationship with Ibn Gabirol. This relationship must be investigated anew in relation to all that might possibly refer to it.

The importance of Jewish participation in love poetry — in those countries where the Jews were close to those Arabs who practiced this art — deserves our attention and all the love poetry of Ibn Gabirol must be presented and discussed. Finally, Ibn Gabirol's neo-Platonism, which is even more apparent in his secular poetry than in his philosophical work, deserves elucidation. The blend, so hard to understand, between his philosophy and cosmology, his astrology and mysticism, and his orthodoxy must be examined.

This is the task I propose to undertake in a future volume. Just as the painter El Greco was for centuries excluded from the pantheon of Spanish art as represented by the names chiselled on the walls of the Prado Museum in Madrid, so Ibn Gabirol, also a "foreigner," has never found due honor and understanding in Spain or the rest of Europe. It demanded a conscious and repeated effort on the part of Julius Meier-Graefe to bring about the revelation that El Greco was one of the greatest painters of the modern age. A revolutionary readjustment of the optical sense was necessary. The same revolutionary reappraisal is necessary for Ibn Gabirol, who may justly be called one of the great emancipators of the human spirit. Not only was he, as was long ago observed, a decisive influence in the intellectual development of Spinoza, but also one of the great transmitters, as Marsilio Ficino himself allowed, of the Platonic heritage to a revivified West. His own nation is not yet aware of his true importance, in spite of the fact that every Hebrew schoolboy is familiar with some of his poems. Heine, in almost visionary fashion, recognized his solitary stature and inspiration in 'that Gothic night'.

Only when Ibn Gabirol and the Naghrāllas are fully understood can we form a just picture of the eleventh-century Hebrew Renaissance in Granada, of which the Alhambra is the noble architectural expression.

Notes to Part III C, D, E

C. Ibn Gabirol's Garden and Spring Poems
D. Arabic Flower Portraits
E. Ibn Gabirol: The Present of Roses

1. Pérès, *Poésie*, p. 231. There are similar poems on snow e. g. by the twelfth-century Egyptian versemaker, Ibn Mammātī, composed in Aleppo, which I translated.
2. Pérès, *Poésie*, pp. 172ff.
3. *Ibid.*, p. 168.
4. Pérès, *Poésie*, p. 229; Nykl, *Poetry*, p. 196.
5. Arberry, *Ring of the Dove*, p. 192; Nykl, *Neck-Ring*, p. 144.
6. Pérès, *Poésie*, p. 229.
7. Grunebaum: *Response*, p. 147; *Kritik und Dichtkunst*, p. 46.
8. For Jewish representations of the sun god in his chariot, see E. R. Goodenough, *Jewish Symbols in the Greco-Roman Period* (n. d.), I, 248f.; II, 257f.; III, figure 640.
9. "Such winged horses appear in every branch of Sāsānian art," R. W. Hamilton, *Khirbat al-Mafjar*, Oxford, 1959, p. 239, Plate LIV, 1 and 2.
10. Bernard Lewis, *The Kingly Crown*, London, 1961, p. 38; *Bialik-R.*, II, p. 66, line 120; *Davidson-Z.*, p. 93, line 180.
11. Lewis, *op. cit.*, pp. 39f.; *Bialik-R.*, II, p. 67, line 120ff.; *Davidson-Z.*, pp. 94f., line 199f.
12. *Bialik-R.*, II, p. 41.
13. B. Lewis, *The Kingly Crown*, London, 1961, pp. 38ff.
14. A tenet ascribed to R. Abbahu in Baba Bathra 25a; Sanhedrin 91b:"... she sinks down to the west to bid 'Peace' to her owner." See *Davidson-Z.*, p. 146.
15. "The servant of a king is like a king," is found in Shebuot 47b.
16. *Bialik-R.*, I, pp. 106f., lines 6—10; lacking another way of identification, I somewhat reluctantly capitalize the personified Beings as before.
17. Ritter, *Wortkunst*, pp. 227f.
18. The Arabic lines are quoted in Ritter, *Wortkunst*, p. 226; the following Hebrew lines in *Bialik-R.*, III, p. 37, No. 39.
19. *Bialik-R.*, I, p. 168, dist. 3.
20. Quoted in *Daudpota*, p. 153.
21. Schirmann, *Shīrāh*, p. 221.
22. *Bialik-R.*, III, p. 30, No. 5.
23. Schirmann, *Shīrāh*, I, p. 214.
24. *Ibid.*, p. 213, No. 2.
25. 'Abd al-Malik ibn Nufail, quoted by Luis Seco de Lucena, in *Al-Andalus*, XXI, p. 419.
26. *Loc. cit.* after Abū 'l-Walīd al-Ḥimyarī, *Badī'*, p. 13.
27. *Bialik-R.*, I, pp. 60ff.
28. *Ibid.*, p. 84, distich 8.

29. Habermann, *Diwan*, I, 2, p. 70.
30. In Εἰς γυναῖκας, in T. S. Stanley and A. H. Bullen, *Anacreon*, London, 1893, p. 4.
30a. "Jovens, The Notion of Youth among the Troubadours, its Meaning and Source," in *Toronto Mediaeval Studies*, XI, 1949, p. 9.
31. *Bialik-R.*, I, pp. 74ff., lines 183, written when Ibn Gabirol was 16 years old.
32. *Bialik-R.*, I, p. 65.
33. Ritter, *Wortkunst*, pp. 278ff.; 291; 299ff.
33a. See Dickie, *Shubayd*, p. 302. The metaphor of the "commanders" who "blow rams' horns" recalls a Ravenna mosaic showing a horn-blowing sailor. (Pl. 26).
34. Pérès, *Poésie*, p. 229.
35. For other examples of 'weeping clouds' 'laughing spring', or 'laughing flowers' see Eliás Terés, "Préstamos Poéticos ...," in *Al-Andalus*, XXI, 1956, pp. 415ff. (419f.).
36. D. Yellin defines this meter, not found in classical Arabic poetry, as a form of *ṭawil* (Schirmann, *Shīrāh*, III, p. 727).
37. Habermann, *Diwan*, III, p. 138, distich 5f.
38. Pérès, *Poésie*, pp. 172f.
39. Pérès, *Poésie*, p. 163.
40. Found in *Bialik-R.*, III, notes, pp. 22f.; Schirmann, *Shīrāh*, p. 221.
41. Pérès, *Poésie*, p. 179; Maqqarī, *Analectes*, I, p. LXVIII.
42. See Ritter, *Wortkunst*, p. 307.
43. See Schirmann, *Shīrāh*, I, pp. 216f.
44. Nykl, *Poetry*, p. 182.
45. Cf. *Bialik-R.*, I, p. 6, dist. 5. See commentary to this.

Plate 26

Abbreviations

Abramson	Sh. Abramson, ed., R. Shemū'el han Nāghīdh, *Ben Mishley*, Tel Aviv, 1948
Analectes	see Maqqarī, *Analectes*
Baron, *History*	S. W. Baron, *A Social and Religious History of the Jews*
Beylié	Beylié, Général Louis de, *La Kalaa des Beni-Hammad, une capitale berbère de* l'Afrique du Nord ... Paris, 1909
Bialik-R.	H. N. Bialik and Y. H. Ravnitzki, *Shīrey Shelōmōh ben Yehūdhāh ibn Gabirol* ..., Tel Aviv, 1925–32
Bräunlich, *Poesien*	E. Bräunlich, "Literaturgeschichtliche Betrachtungsweise altarabischer Poesien," in *Der Islam*, XXIV, 1937, pp. 235 ff.
Daudpota	U. M. Daudpota, *The Influence of Arabic Poetry on the Development of Persian Poetry*, Bombay, 1934
Davidson-Z.	I. Zwangwill and I. Davidson, *Selected Religious Poems of Solomon Ibn Gabirol*, Philadelphia, 1923
Derenbourg, *Appendix*	J. Derenbourg, Appendix to F. Girault de Prangey, *Essai sur l'architecture des arabes ... en Espagne*, Paris, 1841
Derenbourg, *Opuscules*	J. and H. Derenbourg, *Opuscules et traités d'Abou'l-Walid Merwan Ibn Djanah* ..., Paris, 1880
Dickie, (*Ibn*) *Shuhayd*	James Dickie "Ibn Šuhayd, a Biographical and Critical Study," in *Al-Andalus*, XXIX, 1964, pp. 243 ff.
Dodds	E. R. Dodds, *The Greeks and the Irrational*, Berkeley, 1951
Dozy, *Ibn 'Idhārī*	R. Dozy, *Ibn-Adhari de Maroc' Al-Bayano 'l-Mogrib*, Leyden, 1848–51
Dozy, *Islam*	R. Dozy, *Spanish Islam*, London, 1913
Dozy, *Recherches*	R. Dozy, *Recherches sur l'histoire et la littérature de l'Espagne*, Paris/Leiden, 1881
D.-Provençal, *Histoire*	R. Dozy, *Histoire des musulmans d'Espagne*, ed. E. Lévi-Provençal, Leiden, 1932
Dreyer	K. Dreyer, *Die religiöse Gedankenwelt des Salomo ibn Gabirol*, Leipzig, 1930
Dubnow	S. Dubnow, *Weltgeschichte des jüdischen Volkes*, Berlin, 1925–29
Dunlop, *Khazars*	D. M. Dunlop, *The History of the Jewish Khazars*, Princeton, 1954
García Gómez, *Poetas*	E. García Gómez, *Cinco poetas musulmanes*, Madrid, 1944
Geiger	A. Geiger, *Salomo Gabirol und seine Dichtungen*, Leipzig, 1877
Glück-Diez, *Islam*	H. Glück and E. Diez, *Arte del Islam* in *Historia del Arte Labor*, V, Barcelona, 1932
Goldziher	I. Goldziher, "Bemerkungen zur Neuhebräischen Poesie," in *Jewish Quarterly Review*, XIV, 1902, pp. 719–736
Gómez-Moreno, *Ars Hispaniae*, III	M. Gómez-Moreno, *El arte árabe español hasta los Almohades* (*Ars Hispaniae*, III), Madrid, 1951

M. E. Gómez-Moreno, *Mil Joyas*	Maria E. Gómez-Moreno, *Mil Joyas del Arte Español*, Barcelona, n. d.
Gothein, *Gartenkunst*	Marie-Luise Gothein, *Geschichte der Gartenkunst*, Jena, 1926
Graetz, *Geschichte*	H. Graetz, *Geschichte der Juden* ..., Leipzig, 1865–90
Graetz, *History*	H. Graetz, *History of the Jews*, Philadelphia, 1956
Grunebaum, *al-Bāqillānī*	G. E. von Grunebaum, *A Tenth-century Document of Arabic Literary Theory and Criticism ... al-Bāqillānī's I'jāz al-Qur'ān*, Chicago, 1960
Grunebaum, *Elements*	G. E. von Grunebaum, "Greek Form Elements in the Arabian Nights," in *Journal of the American Oriental Society*, LXII, 1942, pp. 277 ff.
Grunebaum, *Response*	G. E. von Grunebaum, "The Response to Nature in Arabic Poetry," in *Journal of Near Eastern Studies*, IV, 1945, pp. 137–151
Habermann, *Diwan*	A. M. Habermann, *Kol shīrey R. Shemū'el han-Nāghīdh*, Dīwān, Tel Aviv, 1947
Halper	*Ṡepher Shīrath Yisrā'el, kitāb al-muḥādhara wa-l-mudhākara le-R. Mōsheh ben Ya'qōbh ibn 'Ezra*, transl. into Hebrew ... by Ben-Zion Halper, Leipzig, 1924
Heger, *Ḫarǧas*	K. Heger, *Die bisher veröffentlichten Ḫarǧas und ihre Deutungen*, Tübingen, 1960
Ibn Ḥazm, *Neck-Ring*	A. R. Nykl, trans., *The Dove's Neck-Ring ... by ... Ibn Ḥazm*, Paris, 1931
Ibn Ḥazm, *Ring*	A. J. Arberry, trans., Ibn Ḥazm, *The Ring of the Dove*, London, 1953
Jonas	H. Jonas, *The Gnostic Religion*, Boston, 1958
Kaempf	S. I. Kaempf, *Nichtandalusische Poesie andalusischer Dichter*, Prag, 1858
Kremer	A. von Kremer, "Philosophische Gedichte des Abū 'l-'Alā' al-Ma'arrī," in *Zeitschrift der Deutschen Morgenländischen Gesellschaft*, XXX, 1877, pp. 40–52; XXXI, pp. 471–483; XXXVIII, 1885, pp. 499–528; and foreword, "Ein Freidenker des Islam," XXIX, 1876, pp. 304–312
Klausner	J. Klausner, *The Messianic Idea in Israel*, New York, 1955
Lafuente, *Inscripciones*	Emilio Lafuente y Alcántara, *Inscripciones Árabes de Granada*, Madrid, 1859
Lagarde	P. de Lagarde, *Iudae Harizii Macamae*, Hannover, 1924
Maqqarī, *Analectes*	R. Dozy et al., *Analectes sur l'histoire et la littérature des arabes d'Espagne*, Leyden, 1855–61
Maqqarī, *Dynasties*	Pascal de Gayangos, *The History of the Mohammedan Dynasties in Spain*, London, 1840–43
Marçais, *Architecture*	Georges Marçais, *L'architecture musulmane d'occident*, Paris, 1954
Mémoires	E. Lévi-Provençal, "Les 'mémoires' de 'Abd Allāh, dernier roi Zīride de Granade," in *Al-Andalus*, III, 1935, pp. 232–244; IV, 1936–39, pp. 29–145; VI, 1941, pp. 1–63
Mez, *Renaissance*	A. Mez, *Die Renaissance des Islams*, Heidelberg, 1922
Mowinckel	Sigmund Mowinckel, *He That Cometh*, tr. G. W. Anderson, New York, 1956
Munk, *Mélanges*	S. Munk, *Mélanges de philosophie juive et arabe*, Paris, 1859

Munk, *Notice*	S. Munk, "Notice sur Abou 'l-Walid Merwan ibn Djana'h ..." part II, in *Journal Asiatique*, XVI, 1850, pp. 201 ff.
Nicholson, *History*	R. A. Nicholson, *A Literary History of the Arabs*, Cambridge, 1941
Nöldeke, *Poesie*	Th. Nöldeke, *Beiträge zur Kenntniss der Poesie der Alten Araber*, Hannover, 1864
Nykl, *H.-A. Poetry*	A. R. Nykl, *Hispano-Arabic Poetry*, Baltimore, 1946
Nykl, *Inscripciones*	A. R. Nykl, "Inscripciones árabes de la Alhambra y del Generalife," in *Al-Andalus*, IV, 1936–39, pp. 174–194
Pérès, *Poésie*	H. Pérès, *La poésie andalouse en arabe classique au XIme siècle*, Paris, 1937
Perlmann, *Eleventh Century*	M. Perlmann, "Eleventh-Century Authors on the Jews of Granada," in *Proceedings of the American Academy for Jewish Research*, XVIII, 1949, pp. 269 ff.
Provençal, *Espagne*	E. Lévi-Provençal, *Histoire de l'Espagne musulmane*, Leiden, 1950–53
Qotaiba, *Demombynes*	Ibn Qutaiba, *Muqaddimat kitāb ash-shiʿr wa-sh-shuʿarā'*, ed. and transl. by M. Gaudefroy-Demombynes, Paris, 1947
Ringbom, *Graltempel*	Lars-Ivar Ringbom, *Graltempel und Paradies*, Stockholm, 1951
Ritter	H. Ritter, *Das Meer der Seele*, Leiden, 1955
Ritter, *Niẓāmī*	H. Ritter, *Über die Bildersprache Niẓamī's*, Berlin, 1927
Ritter, *Wortkunst*	ʿAbd al-Qāhir al-Jurjānī, *Die Geheimnisse der Wortkunst*, ed. H. Ritter, Wiesbaden, 1959
Sassoon	D. S. Sassoon, *The Diwan of Shemuel Hannaghid*, London, 1934
Schiaparelli	C. Schiaparelli, *Il Canzoniere del Poeta ... Ibn Ḥamdīs, il Siciliano*, Roma, 1897
Schirmann, *Diwan*	J. Schirmann, "Le Diwan de Šemū'el Hannāgīd considéré comme source pour l'histoire espagnole," in *Hespéris*, Rabat, XXXV, 1948, pp. 163–188
Schirmann, *Fils*	J. Schirmann, "Jehosef, fils du nagid," in *Hespéris*, Rabat, XXXV, pp. 164 ff.
Schirmann, *Samuel*	J. Schirmann, "Samuel Hannagid, the Man, the Soldier, the Politician," in *Jewish Social Studies*, IV, 1951, pp. 99–126
Schirmann, *Shīrāh*	H. Schirmann, *Hash-Shīrāh hā-ʿibhrīth bi-Ŝephāradh u-bhe-Provence*, Jerusalem, 1959–60
Schirmann, *Yehōŝeph*	H. Schirmann, "Yehōŝeph han-Nāghīdh," in *Me'oznayim*, Tel Aviv, VIII, 1938, pp. 49–58
Schissel, *Garten*	Otmar Schissel, "Der Byzantinische Garten," in *Sitzungsberichte der Akademie der Wissenschaften in Wien*, Phil.-hist. Kl., 221,2, Vienna, 1942
Simon, *Mysterienvilla*	E. Simon, "Zum Fries der Mysterienvilla bei Pompeji," in *Jahrb. d. D. Archäol. Inst.*, LXXVI, 1961, pp. 137f.
Terrasse, *L'art*	H. Terrasse, *L'art hispano-mauresque des origines au XIIIme siècle*, Paris, 1932
Toporobhski	Y. Toporobhski, *Taḥkemōnī*, Tel Aviv, 1952
Torres Balbás, *Alhambra antes*	L. Torres Balbás, "La Alhambra de Granada antes del siglo XIII," in Cronica Arqueológica de la España musulmana," VI, in *Al-Andalus*, V, 1940, pp. 159 ff.

Torres Balbás, *Ars Hispaniae*, IV	L. Torres Balbás, *Arte almohade, arte nazarí, arte mudéjar* (*Ars Hispaniae*, IV), Madrid, 1949
Torres Balbás, *Almorávides*	L. Torres Balbás, "Nuevas perspectivas sobre el arte de Al-Andalus bajo el dominio almorávide," in *Al-Andalus*, XVII, 1952, pp. 402–433
Wünsche. *Thron*	E. Wünsche, *Salomos Thron und Hippodrom*, Leipzig, 1906
Yellin	D. Yellin, *Tōrath hash-shīrāh haš-Šephāradhīth*, Jerusalem, 5700 (1940)

Index A:

Proper Names (including dynasties, nations, religions, sects)

Index B:
Subjects of Fine Arts

Index C:

Literary Subjects (including Metaphors)

Compare lists of metaphors or pages 251—255 — Metaphors are set off by hyphens

Index D:
Geographic Names

Index E:

Book Titles*

*See also list of abbreviations; *k.* standing for *kitāb* 'book' in Arabic book titles is mostly omitted.

Index F:

Poems listed by their Beginning Words

Index G:
Foreign Words

LIST OF ILLUSTRATIONS

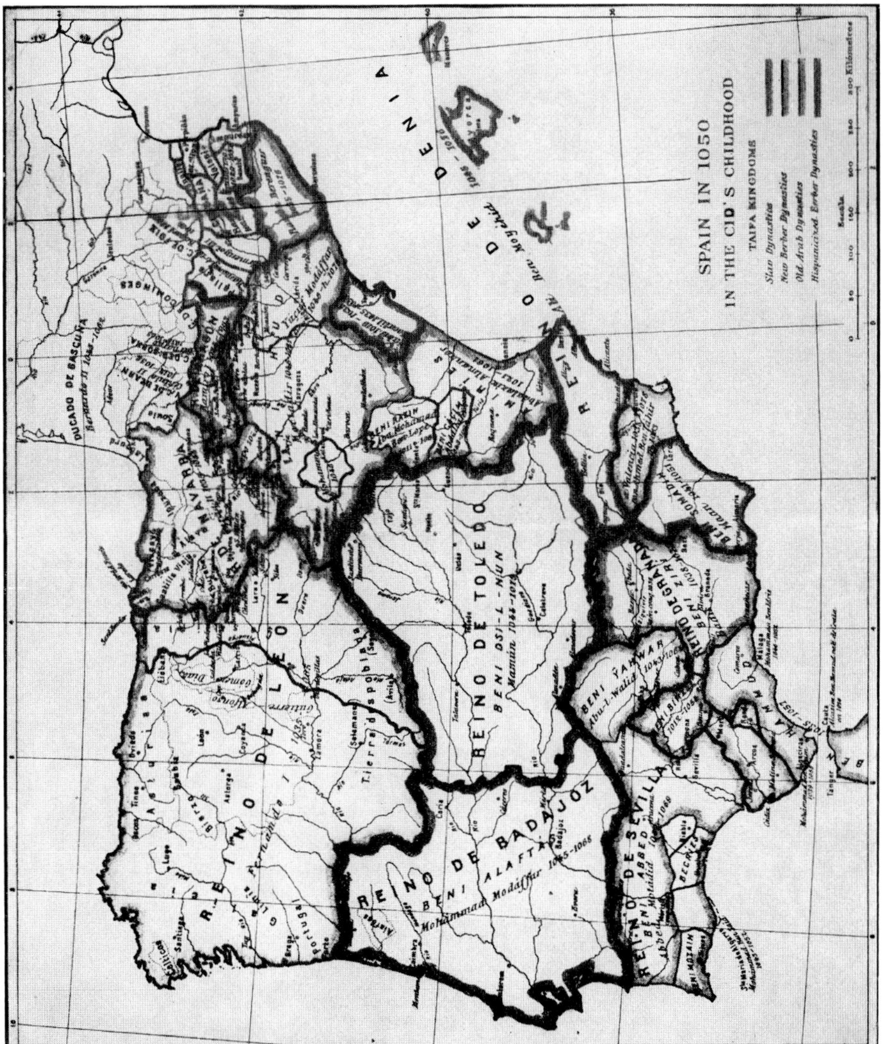

Plate 1 (p. 89): Map of Spain in 1050 (Courtesy Hispano-American Society, New York)

Plate 2 (pp. 2, 101): Court of Lions with Fountain

Plate 3 (p. 105): Example of "Striped" Zīrid Masonry in "La Puerta delVino" of the Alhambra (as in Diocletians's Palace in Spalato)

Plate 4 (p. 105): "Striped" Zīrid Masonry in the Towers of the Alhambra Fortress (Courtesy Foto MAS, Barcelona)

Plate 5 (p. 114): Fischer von Erlach's Reconstruction of Solomon's "Brazen Sea"

Plate 5a (pp. 6, 151): Small Iranian Basin with Lion Protomes

Plate 6 (p. 117): Detail of Lion with Bared Teeth, supporting the Alhambra Basin (Courtesy Foto MAS, Barcelona)

Plate 7 (p. 123): Dodecagonal Basin, most likely the Original, Supported by the Lions, now in the Abencerages Hall (Courtesy Bildarchiv, Marburg)

Plate 8 (p. 105): "Striped" Zirid Masonry in the Fortress of Malaga (Courtesy Foto MAS, Barcelona)

Plate 9 (pp. 118, 123): Miss Eliason's Sketch of a Reconstructed Original Arrangement of the Alhambra Fountain

Plate 9a (pp. 150, 210): Deities on Pedestals of Animals from Hittite Maltaya Rock Relief

Plate 10 (p. 151): Temple Basin of Carchemish with Lion Reliefs

Plate 10a (p. 151): Fragment of Tripod from Olympia, supported by Human Figures Standing upon Lions

Plate 11 (pp. 173, 215): Stone Elephant from Caliphal Aqueduct near Madinat as-Zahrā’ (Courtesy Foto Cortes, Cordova)

Plate 12 (p. 153): Statue of Caliph upon Pedestal of Lions from Khirbat al-Mafjar (Courtesy Palestine Museum, Jerusalem)

Plate 13 (pp . 153, 155–156): The Two Spouting Lions of the Partal Basin of the Alhambra

Plate 14 (p. 157): Pila of Ḥabbūs, Berber King of Granada (Courtesy MAS, Barcelona)

Plate 15 (p. 165): Crocodile, originally Spouting Water, in the Villa of Hadrian in Tivoli

Plate 16 (p. 177): Indian Miniature (about 1556—1605) of the Cincinnati Art Museum, showing a Water Wheel (Courtesy Cincinnati Art Museum)

Plate 17 (p. 178): View of the Court of Lions, with the Four Channels

Plate 17a (p. 178): Central Basin of Court Excavated in Lashkarī Bazār by Professor D. Schlumberger (Courtesy Professor D. Schlumberger)

Plate 18 (p. 178): Fount of Lions with Water Channel (Detail)

Plate 19 (p. 178): Garden Rug, Showing a Cross of Water Channels (Courtesy Metropolitan Museum, New York. James T. Ballard Collection)

Plate 20 (p. 179): ʿAbbāsid Fountain from Sāmarrā, now in ʿAbbāsid Palace in Bagdad

Plate 21 (p. 189): Dome of Embajadores Hall with Inlaid Work: Stars in Tiers (Courtesy Foto MAS, Barcelona)

Plate 22 (pp. 187–188): Dome of Abencerages Hall, showing the Light Effects, slightly Spoiled by Missing Shutters (Courtesy Bildarchiv Marburg)

Plate 23 (pp. 124, 188): View from Dos Hermanas Hall upon Fount of Lions, in its Old State (Courtesy Foto MAS, Barcelona)

Plate 24 (p. 194): Elvira Gate of Granada (Courtesy Foto MAS, Barcelona)

Plate 25 (p. 143): Islamic Bronze Brazier, decorated with Birds, Museum Dahlem (Stiftung Preussischer Kulturbesitz)

Plate 26 (pp. 350, 374): Mosaic showing Ship with Sailor Blowing Signal Horn (XIII cent. Mosaic, Basilica di S. Giovanni Evang., Ravenna)

FRANZ ALTHEIM und RUTH STIEHL

Die Araber in der alten Welt

Fünf Bände
Groß-Oktav. Ganzleinen

Band I

Bis zum Beginn der Kaiserzeit

Mit Beiträgen von ARISTIDE CALDERINI, JAN BURIAN, PIETER LAMBRECHTS, EBERHARD MERKEL, JUTTA MUTH, ERIKA TRAUTMANN-NEHRING und HUBERT VAN DE WEERD

XII, 747 Seiten. 13 Abbildungen. 1964. DM 170,–

Band II

Bis zur Reichstrennung

Mit Beiträgen von ROCH KNAPOWSKI, RAIMUND KÖBERT S. J., EUGEN LOZOVAN, RUDOLF MACUCH, JOACHIM REHORK, ERIKA TRAUTMANN-NEHRING und JÓZEF WOLSKI

X, 631 Seiten. 19 Abbildungen. 1965. DM 150,–

Band III

Anfänge der Dichtung. – Der Sonnengott. – Buchreligionen

Mit Beiträgen von HÉCTOR HERRERA CAJAS, DIONYS KÖVENDI, GERHARD RADKE, EBERHARD RESCHKE und ERIKA TRAUTMANN-NEHRING

X, 536 Seiten. 26 Kunstdrucktafeln. 1966. DM 150,–

Band IV

Neue Funde

Mit Beiträgen von JOHANNES IRMSCHER, RAIMUND KÖBERT S. J., DIONYS KÖVENDI, HARTMUT LAUTERBACH, RUDOLF MACUCH, GERHARD RADKE, WILHELM RÖLLIG, OSWALD SZEMERÉNYI, ERIKA TRAUTMANN-NEHRING und HANS WEHR

X, 738 Seiten. 80 Abbildungen, 1 Frontispiz. 1967. DM 200,–

Band V (Erster Teil)

Weitere Neufunde – Nordafrika bis zur Einwanderung der Wandalen Dū Nuwās

Mit Beiträgen von JAN BURIAN, JÜRGEN DUMMER, ROCH KNAPOWSKI, DIONYS KÖVENDI, RUDOLF MACUCH, GONZAGUE RYCKMANS, GOTTHARD STROHMAIER und ERIKA TRAUTMANN-NEHRING

X, 537 Seiten. Mit 64 Abbildungen auf Kunstdruck. 1968. DM 180,–

Band V (Zweiter Teil)

Nachträge. Das christliche Aksūm

Mit Beiträgen von JOSÉ MARIA BLÁZQUEZ, L. I. GUMILEW, W. E. JAMES, EUGEN LOZOVAN, FRIEDER MELLINGHOFF, HEINRICH MERTENS, PETER NAGEL, ERIKA TRAUTMANN-NEHRING, HANS WEHR

In Vorbereitung
